CALIFORNIA BEACHES

ALAN BISBORT & PARKE PUTERBAUGH

MAP CONTENTS

Crescent City

OREGON

Northern California

Arcata

Eureka

NEVADA

Fort Bragg

Mendocino

Bodega Bay

SACRAMENTO

Pt Reyes

SAN FRANCISCO

Half Moon Bay

Central California

Santa Cruz

Salinas

Monterey

Big Sur

Morro Bay

San Luis Obispo

Pismo Beach

Santa Barbara

Ventura

Malibu

LOS ANGELES

Southern California

Long Beach

Laguna Beach

Oceanside

SAN DIEGO

USA

PACIFIC

OCEAN

MEXICO

200 mi
200 km

© AVALON TRAVEL

Contents

How to Use This Book

Moon California Beaches reads from south to north, meticulously combing 13 coastal regions.

Each chapter begins with an introduction to the region and a list of its best beaches. The chapter also includes a map of the area it covers. Beaches are identified with numbers, which correspond to the numbers on the maps.

Write-ups of each community or locale open with a general essay describing its physical look and layout, attractions and activities, history and sociology, and anything else that might enhance a useful overview. We've also supplied contact information for local chambers of commerce, convention and visitors bureaus, and tourist development councils.

Additional information follows under the following headings: Beaches, Recreation and Attractions, Accommodations, Coastal Cuisine, and Nightlife.

BEACHES

We offer the lowdown on what you can expect to see and do at every publicly accessible beach. This includes a description of a beach's natural features and any other relevant observations. Each beach also has its own "beach profile": a listing of practical information, including directions, activities, parking and day-use fees, hours, facilities, and contact number. A **BEST** symbol also accompanies the profiles of best beaches.

Each beach profile also includes symbols for certain activities beyond the beach basics of swimming and sunbathing. Since one can go fishing on virtually any beach, we haven't included a special fishing symbol. However, our jetty and pier symbols indicate when those particular angling opportunities are available. The activity symbols are as follows:

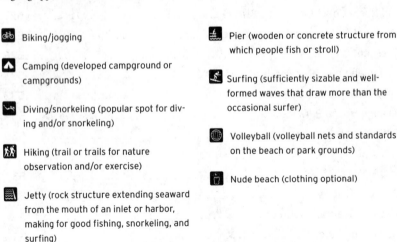

Biking/jogging

Camping (developed campground or campgrounds)

Diving/snorkeling (popular spot for diving and/or snorkeling)

Hiking (trail or trails for nature observation and/or exercise)

Jetty (rock structure extending seaward from the mouth of an inlet or harbor, making for good fishing, snorkeling, and surfing)

Pier (wooden or concrete structure from which people fish or stroll)

Surfing (sufficiently sizable and well-formed waves that draw more than the occasional surfer)

Volleyball (volleyball nets and standards on the beach or park grounds)

Nude beach (clothing optional)

We've also included information on facilities available at each beach:

- Concession (food and drink available at or near beach)
- Lifeguards (year-round, unless identified as "seasonal")
- Picnic area
- Restrooms
- Showers
- Visitors center (staffed facility with information and exhibits)

RECREATION AND ATTRACTIONS

This selective listing of up to 12 attractions and recreational services is a kind of quick-and-dirty Yellow Pages that we've compiled for selected communities.

- Bike/Skate Rentals (bicycles, in-line skates, and other fun stuff)
- Boat Cruise (sightseeing trips on the water)
- Dive Shop (diving equipment and/or dive trips)
- Ecotourism (canoe/kayak outfitter or site for ecotourist outing)
- Fishing Charters (guided fishing trips)
- Horseback Riding
- Lighthouse
- Marina (boat dockage)
- Pier
- Rainy Day Attraction (something to do indoors when the weather is inclement)
- Shopping/Browsing (shopping district, center, or mall of note)
- Sportfishing
- Surf Report (surf forecast)
- Surf Shop (surfboards and surf gear)
- Vacation Rentals (beach houses and/or condos for short-term rental)

ACCOMMODATIONS

We offer a general overview of lodging options in a given community, as well as brief descriptions of selected hotels, motels, and resorts we'd recommend when planning a beach vacation. Our write-ups are based on actual stays and site visits. Because room rates fluctuate, we provide general guidelines of price range. Our $–$$$$ symbols are offered as general indicators of the nightly charge in season for a standard room with two beds.

$ = inexpensive (under $80 per night)

$$ = moderate ($80–129)

$$$ = moderately expensive ($130–179)

$$$$ = expensive ($180 and up)

COASTAL CUISINE

We offer a general overview of the dining scene in each locale, as well as descriptive write-ups of restaurants specializing in seafood and/or regional cuisine that are located on or near the beach. We cast a favorable eye upon places that have been around a while and have maintained a reputation for consistency and quality. Our $–$$$$ symbols are general indicators that reflect the median cost of an à la carte dinner entrée.

$ = inexpensive ($10 and under)
$$ = moderate ($11–17)
$$$ = moderately expensive ($18–24)
$$$$ = expensive ($25 and up)

NIGHTLIFE

Our concept of nightlife is people gathering to relax or blow off steam after the sun sets. Our listings run the gamut from tiki bars and coffeehouses to clubs with live music or deejays—in other words, anywhere you can kick back and have fun during and after sunset. We've made the rounds, looking for the liveliest good times. And we let you know when you're better off not wasting your time.

MAP SYMBOLS

▨▨▨▨	Expressway	(80)	Interstate Freeway	✕	Airfield
————	Primary Road	(101)	U.S. Highway	✈	Airport
————	Secondary Road	(21)	State Highway	○	City/Town
▫▫▫▫	Unpaved Road	[66]	County Highway	▲	Mountain
··········	Ferry	◍	Lake	♠	Park
—··—··—	National Border	◌	Dry Lake	⟨ʃ	Pass
—··—··—	State Border	◍	Seasonal Lake	◉	State Capital

INTRODUCTION
A Note from the Authors

We have spent a fair portion of our adult lives dodging gainful employment in order to visit and write about beaches. We have written four books on beaches, and this is the fourth edition of one of them. Why do we do it? We love California—the beaches, the outdoors, the cool people, the coastal climate. It never fails to put smiles on our faces.

Moon California Beaches is aimed at all who want to visit, revisit, or read about the greatest and most varied coastline in America. One simple statistic says it all: California claims 1,264 miles of beautiful and changeable coastline.

Beaches have insinuated themselves into the psyche of Californians like nowhere else. Much of the state's population is pressed against the coast, and they live or play at the beach with great frequency. Others cross mountains and valleys to get to them on a more occasional basis. Many cross state lines and even international borders to spend time on the Golden State's beaches.

Whether you're planning a trip to the coast or simply want to do some armchair beachcombing, you can visit every publicly accessible beach in the state—more than 400 of them herein. We intend *Moon California Beaches* to be both a useful tool and an entertaining read—a hybrid travel guide and travelogue, in other words.

It is a travel guide in that we've provided plenty of useful information, such as directions, phone numbers, entrance fees, hours of operation, and beach ratings. It is a travelogue in that you can wander up the coast as you read, finding continuity in the journey and a spirit of close cultural observation in the writing.

© DREAMSTIME.COM

We've also liberally spiked the book with brief boxed essays. They have been placed outside the narrative to break up a very long trip with the reader's equivalent of rest stops. Some offer practical information, others anecdotal accounts of various and sundry encounters.

Our methodology is simple. We travel up the coast, looking for and at beaches, striking scenery, coastal geology, local color, beach activities, and great places to sleep, eat, and have fun after the sun sets. We work hard, play hard, do lots of research, and take plenty of notes. We mull over our experiences and then tell the truth as we see it. People spend a lot of money on trips and vacations, so they deserve a candid and informed opinion before ransoming their time and money.

In *Moon California Beaches,* we've covered the California coast from San Diego to Smith River, including every beach that can be reached by foot, car, or ferry.

Climb in and take the trip with us!

— Alan Bisbort and Parke Puterbaugh

Best Beaches

Here are our picks for the best beaches, arranged in alphabetical order within each list.

◖ TOP BEACHES IN SOUTHERN CALIFORNIA

Black's Beach, page 62. Nature in the raw, and naturists in the raw, too. How can so much deserted beach lie so close to San Diego?

Doheny State Beach, page 103. When the Beach Boys sang about surfing "down Doheny way," this is what they meant. It's a classic Southern California beach and beach scene.

Hermosa City Beach, page 168. This relaxed, well-heeled town boasts a two-mile beach, a paved beachside recreation trail, a quarter-mile pier, and the South Bay's most superlative dining scene.

Huntington City Beach, page 134. You've heard of "Surf City"? Huntington Beach is it. Big pier, wide and lengthy beach, scads of surfers, squeaky-clean city.

La Jolla Cove, page 56. Hard to pick just one beach in La Jolla, but the water in this splendidly scenic cove is warm, by West Coast standards, surpassing 70 degrees in late summer.

Leo Carrillo State Park, page 207. Here you'll find a slice of Malibu without hype or celebrities but with plenty of drama in the interplay between mountains and ocean.

Los Trancos, page 120. This sylvan Orange County treasure stretches from the beach up into the San Joaquin Hills and also incorporates an offshore underwater preserve.

Main Beach, page 114. Tony Laguna Beach has dozens of tiny, hidden coves and this large, accessible one. It's made for people-watching, so stroll the boardwalk or hang out in the park.

Newport Beach Municipal Beach, page 125. One of Southern California's most unpretentious and sociable beaches, Newport Beach unfurls along the Ocean Front promenade. Grab a bike and a beach towel, and go for it.

Pacific Beach, page 44. Can you say P-A-R-T-Y? This high-energy beach town is action central for surfers, students, and party animals.

Zuma County Beach, page 204. The biggest beach in Malibu is a Southern California classic, from its stupendous natural setting to the big, bruising waves that roll ashore.

◖ TOP BEACHES IN CENTRAL CALIFORNIA

Asilomar State Beach, page 329. Pacific Grove has all of the scenery and none of the pretension of neighboring Pebble Beach, and Asilomar State Beach is its gorgeous natural centerpiece.

Bonny Doon Beach, page 377. Of all the oversized, otherworldly beaches in north Santa Cruz County, Bonny Doon gets our vote since it's slightly more accessible than the others.

East Beach, page 247. Santa Barbara might just be America's most perfect city, and East Beach is its sandy welcome mat and playground.

McGrath State Beach, page 216. Huge dunes, a wide beach, and a shaded coastal campground make McGrath a sweet surprise between Malibu and Ventura.

Moonstone Beach, page 289. Scenic Moonstone Beach is a great place to escape. Stroll the blufftop paths, surf the waves, or serenely watch it all from your room.

New Brighton State Beach, page 357. This south-facing beach is one of the Santa Cruz area's most inviting. Its flat sandy beach is backed by grassy dunes and steep cliffs.

Pfeiffer Beach, page 310. This is a rare accessible beach in rugged Big Sur. Watch waves slap rock formations silly and marvel at nature's fury and beauty commingled.

Pismo Beach, page 271. This the home of the Pismo clam, massive dune fields, a sturdy old pier, and a beach you can drive cars on.

Seabright Beach, page 371. This locals-favorite spot is a choice alternative to the boardwalk hubbub of Main Beach. Good surf, a mile-long beach, volleyball nets, a jetty, and lighthouse make this a great place to hang.

Seacliff State Beach, page 356. This multiuse park offers camping, picnicking, and the novelty of fishing from an old WWI supply boat. Great beach hiking in these parts—head down to (or up from) busy Rio Del Mar Beach.

◖ TOP BEACHES IN NORTHERN CALIFORNIA

Agate Beach, page 518. The lovely Trinidad area reaches a sandy crescendo at Agate Beach, reached via a lengthy staircase and running a good distance.

Black Sands Beach, page 497. You can hike for two dozen miles along this beach, whose color and name reflects its volcanic origins. It's a wild place, with the King Range rising behind it.

Dead Man's Beach, page 496. You want out of the way? Try this beach, which starts at the south end of remote Shelter Cove. The scenery is mesmerizing, but be sure to carry tide tables.

Enderts Beach, page 528. This quarter-mile crescent, a wilderness beach falling within Redwoods National Park, requires a bit of effort to reach but is worth every step.

Gold Bluffs Beach, page 522. There may be no prettier beach on the California coast than this one, with its gold-flecked sand and towering bluffs.

High Bluff Beach, page 523. Small but stunning, this secluded jewel is as magnificent as it is remote. Not easily reached but well worth seeking out.

Kehoe Beach, page 433. The elements are almost overwhelming on Kehoe Beach. Everything out here seems more daunting, impressive, and beautiful.

Limantour Beach, page 433. This is the best swimming beach on Point Reyes and a good spot for whale-watching. And you'll pass through lovely Inverness en route.

MacKerricher State Park, page 484. This eight-mile beach in Mendocino County is among the North Coast's best. Saddle up a horse and take an unforgettable ride on its shoreline equestrian trail.

Stinson Beach, page 421. A bonafide beach town in the middle of Marin County? Bring a beach towel and spread out on this wide, white sandy beach, backed by breathtaking cliffs and headlands.

SAN DIEGO COAST

The United States could not have rolled out a more inviting welcome mat on its southwest border than the beaches of San Diego County. They extend for 76 miles, from the wide-open party towns of Ocean Beach, Mission Beach, and Pacific Beach to the upscale, uphill village of La Jolla, and from the rugged setting of Torrey Pines State Beach to the discreet charms of north county communities like Del Mar and Carlsbad. Admittedly, it all ends with a thud at the military city of Oceanside and the nuclear reactors at San Onofre. But the many miles of this state-sized county cover a broad range of settings: lengthy stretches of soft sand; thin, silvery strands of hard-packed sand; cobble-covered beaches that have lost their sand; and rocky coves, sea caves, and sandstone cliffs. There are also bays, lagoons, estuaries, and underwater reserves.

There is beach erosion as well—a recurring problem that has necessitated large-scale "beach renourishment" projects along various thinning parts of the coast. The future of such costly interventions is seriously in doubt, and some coastal scientists believe the best policy is strategic retreat. What we have witnessed over the past quarter century in all parts of San Diego County resembles the ordeal of Sisyphus: the beach erodes, the beach is widened, the beach erodes again, and the cycle repeats ad infinitum. From one end of San Diego County to the other, on beach after beach, studies conducted in this decade all come to the same conclusion: "Ongoing beach and seacliff erosion threatens public and private development, as well as public safety." These drumbeats calling for continual renourishment have become as repetitive as a mantra. And continuing to throw money at vanishing sand has become increasingly hard to rationalize for those who are not kept busy by such projects.

San Diego's varied coastal locales play host

SAN DIEGO COAST

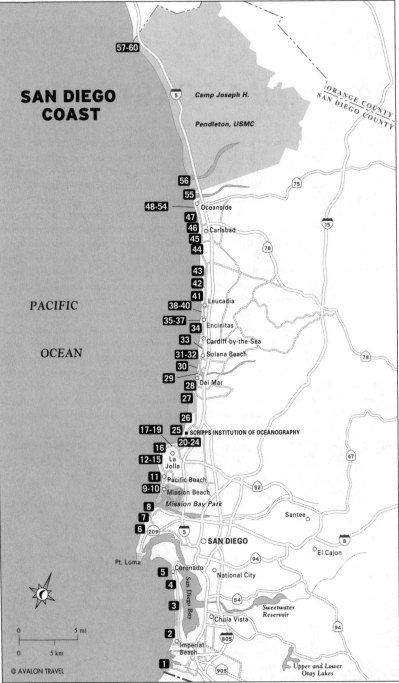

57-60

5

Camp Joseph H.

Pendleton, USMC

75

SAN DIEGO COAST

56

55

48-54 Oceanside

47

46 Carlsbad

45

44

15

78

43

42

41 Leucadia

PACIFIC

38-40

35-37 Encinitas

34

33 Cardiff-by-the-Sea

OCEAN

31-32 Solana Beach

30

29 Del Mar

28

27

78

26

17-19 25 ■ SCRIPPS INSTITUTION OF OCEANOGRAPHY

20-24

16

12-15 La Jolla

67

11 Pacific Beach

9-10 Mission Beach

52

8 *Mission Bay Park*

7

6 209 5 **SAN DIEGO** Santee

8

Pt. Loma El Cajon

5 Coronado 94

4 National City

San Diego Bay

3 54 *Sweetwater Reservoir*

94

2 805 Chula Vista

Imperial Beach

905

Upper and Lower Otay Lakes

0   5 mi

0   5 km

1

ORANGE COUNTY
SAN DIEGO COUNTY

© AVALON TRAVEL

BEST BEACHES

◖ **Pacific Beach, page 44**   ◖ **Black's Beach, page 62**

◖ **La Jolla Cove, page 56**

to every manner of activity that beach lovers live to indulge in: surfing, swimming, sailing, sunbathing, biking, fishing, camping, volleyball, and ogling one another. Then there are the post-sundown activities in these mostly revved-up beach towns: beer drinking, taco scarfing, partying, flirting, hanging out…you get the idea. In short, San Diego County is the apotheosis of the beach life. Its communities offer the quintessential Southern California beach experience.

This was brought home to us on a recent Fourth of July. At midnight, on some inexplicable impulse, we found ourselves wandering out to Windansea Beach in La Jolla. The surfers were off partying at their favorite dive bars and overcrowded apartments, but the waves continued to roar. We sat on a stony ledge, inhaling huge drafts of salt-sprayed air while staring at the dark, endlessly churning sea. It could have been the setting for everything from *The Endless Summer* to more '60s flicks than you could shake a beach blanket at. Whoosh, splash, boom, roar. This short detour to Windansea Beach invigorated us for days thereafter, like a contact high with a vast oceanic fountain of youth.

Border Field State Park

We tend to spill more words on Border Field than this godforsaken place merits because it's where California begins and is therefore where our coastal treks begin as well. It is a fascinating place for a variety of reasons, none

of which has much to do with beaches. So if you want to skip this epistle about a crumbling state park in the middle of nowhere, you won't hurt our feelings. But if you are into the symbolism of starting points, then Border Field must be visited. Just be careful if you come out here.

Border Field sits on the California-Mexico border and serves as a favorite point of entry for illegal aliens. They either scale the rusty 10-foot fence that separates the United States from Mexico—at least until the more impregnable wall that's under construction is completed—or brazenly wade out at low tide

© PARKE PUTERBAUGH

Border Field State Park

ON THE BORDER

All the issues that plague California have been compressed onto the beaches near the Mexican border. You name it, they've got it: illegal immigration, sewage disposal, farm runoff, ocean contamination, shoddy development, flooding, erosion, vandalism, overpopulation, litter.

We learned this on our first visit to Border Field State Park and the Tijuana River Estuary back in 1988. The trip started out promisingly, with green, irrigated sod fields bordering Dairy Mart and Monument Roads and rugged, dry hills in the distance. It did not take long for things to turn nasty.

Hand-lettered signs sprang up on the side of Monument Road as we headed toward the ocean. One announced: Environmentalists Destroy Human Lives. Another trumpeted: Welcome to No Man's Land. Environmentalists. Illegal Aliens. Smuggling. Flooding. Sewage. Garbage. A series of signs blamed environmentalists for hurting the economy, for "desperate animals caught in the mud," and for the drownings of 24 illegals. At the bottom of one such sign were spray-painted the ominous words: Remember Waco, Texas.

On the Mexican side, shoddily built villas could be seen dotting the dry brown hillsides, some clinging precariously to their high perches, which are now illuminated at night by powerful mobile floodlights. Border Patrol minivans could also be seen, secreted behind clumps of dry weeds and dirt. Like enormous metal insects, the feds' paddy wagons lie in wait for fence-hoppers who might try their luck inland from the more popular Border Field State Park. This entire end of the U.S.-Mexico boundary is the most sieve-like in the country, accounting for nearly one-third of all illegal alien arrests. As many as 80,000 arrests have been made in the peak months of April and May, when seasonal employment lures migrant workers.

Things did not improve at the beach. The state park ranger who took our fare was as beat as the scene around him. "Do you ever get busy at the park?" we asked, cheerful naïfs that we are.

"We used to," he said, ever so slowly, "but not no more."

Then he sighed and, as if cutting off further questions, said, "It's a long story.... It has nothing to do with the park."

Indeed, the parkland seemed a splendid setting. Then we pulled into a parking lot filled with vehicles sporting Mexican license plates or no plates at all. One group of Mexicans in cowboy hats had disassembled a car, leaving engine parts strewn about the asphalt. They seemed in no hurry to reassemble it.

Mexican radio stations blared from every direction like a musical EKG. Families ate food from plastic bags, bickered and laughed, and fell asleep on the grass and walls. Screaming kids were running everywhere. None, curiously, ventured down to the ocean, where the waves seemed much more enticing than the hot asphalt.

and walk around it into the United States, as if beachcombing.

For those who visit Border Field legally, this makes for an intriguing sociological study but a bummer of a beach trip. Some might argue that only sadists would go out of their way to visit Border Field State Park. Think of us what you will, but we've made a perverse ritual out of beginning every trip up the California coast

here at Border Field. On our visit for the previous edition, torrential rains had nearly washed out the final leg of the rutted dirt road that leads to the parking area on the bluff above the beach. We could see the cement monument that marks the international boundary and the bullfight ring of Tijuana just beyond it, but we could not get up to them. Wary of miring a rental car in this muddy impasse, we

Pregnant women fanned themselves with the lids of take-out fried-chicken buckets. One young couple groped passionately in the grass while an infant lay napping beside their intertwined bodies.

We asked one of the friendly tykes why he wasn't playing in the ocean.

"I used to but not no more."

"Why? Too cold?" No answer. "Smell bad?"

Big smile and a nod.

The ocean waters for several miles north of the border smell bad most of the time. The Mexican sewage treatment plants can't keep up with the load from the burgeoning population, and when the system breaks down, raw sewage flows into the surrounding Tijuana River Estuary and, ultimately, into the ocean. This creates what the Mexicans call *aguas negras* (black waters) – as many as 20 million gallons of it in a single day, which necessitates the closing of beaches as far as 50 miles away by San Diego health officials.

The sewage issue is one for which the United States has been no less culpable than Mexico. In 1999, a much-needed treatment facility – the International Wastewater Treatment Plant – began pumping partially treated sewage from Tijuana into the ocean via an outfall off Imperial Beach. On the American side, a new complex – the South Bay Water Reclamation Project – was up and running in 2002. Fully online now, it treats up to 15 million gallons of sewage a day from the communities of San Ysidro, Chula Vista, and Imperial Beach. Nonetheless, in May 2008, as the summer season was starting, the beaches of Imperial Beach were closed to swimming due to sewage spills. Likewise, it goes without saying that Border Field State Park had barred swimming. The most frequent signs seen on beaches of southernmost San Diego County read: Keep Out. Sewage Contaminated Water. Exposure May Cause Illness.

As if tempting the fecal finger of fate further, "planned communities" are being built right up to the Mexican border. On the Mexican side, a "bi-national" border sewage treatment plant – the Bajagua project, to be built in Tijuana – has been batted around for years and, as of this writing, is still being debated.

On a less gloomy note, we noticed that the ominous hand-painted signs along Monument Road are now gone, and a Border Patrol guard informed us that illegal border crossings had been declining. He also cogently observed, "We don't have any room to talk about Mexico when you look at the way we treat our own beaches and oceans."

Even so, the latest issue for the beleaguered area is that the federal government has proposed building a "security barrier" that would encroach 150 feet into Border Field State Park. As one local environmental group put it, "The magnitude of the cut and fill proposed for the fence is totally unacceptable. We are concerned that the alteration of natural landscapes, slope stability, and sediment production will create untenable problems in the Border Highlands, the Tijuana River Valley and its estuary."

stopped, took some photographs, and turned back. Still, even in what some might term a hellhole, we admired the hard blue sky and small, puffy white clouds rimmed with silver linings, and the extensive marsh grasses of the estuary—among the last significant coastal wetlands in California.

While readying this edition, we discovered that the state has simply closed the park completely on weekdays, except for those entering either on foot or on horses. So Border Field is open for "normal" use only on weekends and some holidays. So what can you do here? Well, one time we saw a group of men disassembling a car.

The area is not without historic and environmental interest, however. The border with Mexico, which runs east from Border Field for

1,952 miles, was established on October 10, 1849. That was the date on which California was officially whisked away from Mexico to become a part of the United States. A cement monument makes note of this event, and informative placards recount both nations' histories and prehistories. Other signs contain tidbits about the ancient geological uplift that created this ruggedly beautiful beach and the wildlife that presumably still roams it.

Unfortunately, the words on most of the markers have been worn away by sun, sand, and surf. The spray-painted Spanish graffiti on the walls is more legible. More overwhelming than anything nature might devise is the sprawl of Tijuana, which comes right up to the fence. Tijuana is a city twice the size of San Diego that continues to grow at an alarming rate. It is the land of last hope for rural Mexicans who come looking for work or wait until dark to make the illegal stroll north. A sobering statistic: 400 people a year die while trying to cross illegally from Mexico to the United States. (Listen to the Bruce Springsteen song "Matamoras Banks" for a chilling account of one such casualty.) That number is greater than were ever killed trying to scale the Berlin Wall. And now the United States is constructing a veritable Berlin Wall along the border with Mexico with much the same purpose: to make sure that those on one side cannot enter the other.

One of the few pleasant pastimes that can be enjoyed at Border Field is riding horses. They can be rented in the area and ridden on designated trails in the adjoining Tijuana River National Estuarine Reserve.

For more information, contact Border Field State Park, 619/575-3613, www.parks.ca.gov.

BEACHES

A visit to Border Field offers up stark dichotomies: the lulling sound of crashing waves suddenly interrupted by the screech of an Immigration Service paddy wagon lurching from behind a clump of dried grass to snag another undocumented alien. Another contrast:

a gorgeous stretch of wild, windswept sand surrounded by wildflowers, marshlands, and jagged geological formations—dotted with signs warning that swimming is prohibited due to raw sewage spills washing northward from Tijuana. Even when the water is sewage-free, the rip currents and in-shore holes can be nasty, and there's no lifeguard on duty. As a sign at the park entrance starkly puts it, Swimming and Wading Unsafe. Yes, Border Field State Park is a real party pooper.

❶ BORDER FIELD STATE PARK

Location: From I-5 near the Mexican border, take Dairy Mart Road exit and turn right. Follow Dairy Mart Road for 1.5 miles, then turn right on Monument Road and follow into park.
Parking/Fees: $5 entrance fee per vehicle on weekends; free for pedestrians and equestrians at all times
Hours: 9:30 A.M.-5 P.M. Pedestrians and equestrians are allowed on weekdays. Vehicles are allowed into the park only on weekends. Flooding may sometimes close the park even on weekends.
Facilities: restrooms, picnic tables, and fire pits
Contact: Tijuana Estuary Visitor Center, 619/575-3613

Imperial Beach

Depending on your perspective, Southern California—as a way of life and a state of mind—begins or ends at Imperial Beach (population 27,000). It is the southernmost beach town in California. Here you'll find the state's southernmost strip malls, trailer parks, libraries, baseball fields, and skateboard ramps—not to mention the southernmost McDonald's and Taco Bells. (Speaking of Taco Bell, we should point out that no one's running *for* the border in these parts; they're running *from* it.) You'll also find a modest-sized community of mostly middle-class citizens trying hard to ignore the looming presence of Tijuana, so close by that on smog-free days the bullring is visible from the beach.

Folks here make a concerted effort to sell the town as a placid resort, billing it as the "South Coast Hideaway." Still, the bottom line in Imperial Beach, as stated by a city booster in 2008, is this: "People don't stay here because we don't have the accoutrements that they want." On the positive side, Imperial Beach has a 2.5-mile beach, abundant year-round sunshine, and pleasant natural backdrops to the east (distant hills and mesas) and south (Tijuana Slough National Wildlife Refuge). Yes, Imperial Beach has a lot going for it. So why the hangdog expressions? Well, this is the beach town that has been most impacted by the sins of Tijuana. The issue of raw sewage and ocean contamination has been a hot one for decades. So has beach erosion, necessitating periodic sand-renourishment projects (though federal money for these Band-Aid solutions tends to dry up when the economy is stressed).

Two main drags, Palm and Coronado Avenues, lead through town to the ocean. These parallel routes are Imperial Beach's commercial corridors, lined with a random hodgepodge of liquor stores, taco huts, decrepit bars, pool halls, and countless car-related enterprises: dealers, repair shops, tire stores, and places to wash your ride. Imperial Beach has been endeavoring to replace its blighted neighborhoods (read: trailer parks) with new condos and apartment buildings. In its futile attempts at gentrification, Imperial Beach recalls Ashbury Beach, New Jersey. In both places, the more things change, the more they stay the same. Meantime, the latest twist is that Imperial Beach has turned to ecotourism to spur interest. Indeed, the **Tijuana River National Estuarine Research Reserve** (301 Caspian Way, 619/575-3613, visitors center 10 A.M.–5 P.M. Wed.–Sun.) is that rarity in California: a coastal wetland that hasn't been destroyed. Trail-riding can be done daily from a half-hour before sunrise to a half-hour after sunset.

Imperial Beach

© PARKE PUTERBAUGH

For more information, contact the Imperial Beach Chamber of Commerce, 702 Seacoast Drive, Imperial Beach, CA 91932, 619/424-3151, www.ib-chamber.biz.

BEACHES

Imperial Beach runs for 2.5 miles. This municipal beach's assets include the sturdy 1,500-foot Imperial Beach Pier, healthy surf and an army of healthy surfers, and the town's renovated Pier Plaza. This pier-side park complex includes picnic pavilions, shops, a play area, and a sculptural tribute to the sport of wave-riding called *Surfhenge*. (It looks like multicolored McDonald's arches.) Cleverly, Pier Plaza even provides surfboard-shaped benches to sit on. Posted snippets detail Imperial Beach's early history as a wave-rider's mecca. Every summer Imperial Beach celebrates Sandcastle Days, which culminates with the **U.S. Open Sandcastle Competition.** Held the last weekend in July, it is the world's longest-running sand-sculpting contest.

The surf at Imperial Beach is among the most challenging in San Diego County. In

TOUGH TIMES ON THE TIJUANA RIVER ESTUARY

As you watch any of the 340 bird species that have been spotted in the Tijuana River Valley, you'd never know that a raging controversy runs through the beautiful estuary. The Tijuana River Estuary is an integral part of California's remaining coastal wetlands, 90 percent of which have been lost to dredging, development, and pollution. Located between Border Field State Park and Imperial Beach, they are among the last wetlands in San Diego County.

Most of the Tijuana River runs through Mexico, draining 1,700 square miles. The five-mile tail end of the river cuts across the U.S. border and snakes through San Diego County, where it meets the ocean. Those five miles and the 3,000 acres of federal and private land drained by it have been battled over as intensely as any five miles of the western front in World War I. They are owned by private parties, the city of San Diego, the county of San Diego, the state of California, and the federal government, which administers the majority of it (2,531 acres). Each has an idea about how best to save the estuary from the many slings and arrows constantly hurled at it.

The best way to see the estuary is on foot. A free walker's guide to the Tijuana River Estuary is available from the Southwest Wetlands Interpretive Association (P.O. Box 575, Imperial Beach, CA 92032, 619/575-0550). This useful tool reveals the lay of the land – from footpaths and horse trails to hitching posts and overlooks. We recommend a look-see at this wonderful, threatened spot to anyone concerned about coastal ecology.

The **Tijuana River National Estuarine Research Reserve** – which also encompasses the Tijuana Slough National Wildlife Refuge – has a visitors center (301 Caspian Way, Imperial Beach, 619/575-3613). From here, one can access the estuary's trails. The visitors center is open Wednesday to Sunday, 10 A.M.-6 P.M. in summer, and to 5 P.M. in winter.

There is no better learning lab than the Tijuana River Estuary, where you can discover the difference between mudflats, tidal sloughs, uplands, riverbeds, and low, middle, and high marshes. Then there are the hundreds of species of plants and animals that live here. One of the tips in the walker's guide should be mandatory etiquette at every beach in the world: "Feel free to pick up as much litter as you like!"

---

fact, it was the first real big-wave surfing spot on the Southern California surfing scene, dating back to the 1940s. (Before Imperial Beach's incorporation in 1956, surfers called this sacred area "Tijuana Sloughs.") Today, surfers of all ages vie for space near the pier, which provides an excellent vantage point from which spectators can view their prodigious skills. After watching one particularly nice run by a blond surfer—during which he executed several 360-degree spin moves to keep abreast of his chosen wave—the grandfatherly chap next to us shouted down to him, "Good show!" The surfer shrugged and said, "No, I blew it!"

But he was obviously pleased that someone had noticed.

The downside is the danger that these powerful waves pose to the uninitiated. Each year the vigilant lifeguard squad in Imperial Beach makes upward of 600 rescues. In addition to strong surf, rip currents—some extending outward for three-quarters of a mile—are capable of pulling even the strongest swimmer under. (Be sure to check the daily advisories posted at the lifeguard stands.) This air of danger only adds to the edgy appeal of Imperial Beach for surfers and lifeguards alike. Incidentally, there are fewer restrictions on where you can surf in

Imperial Beach than on the more urbanized beaches elsewhere in Southern California. As one lifeguard said, "We are one of the last truly open beaches. You can surf anywhere."

Massive infusions of sand dredged from San Diego Bay have restored the Imperial Beach's width on several occasions, but it always seems to vanish during winter storms. On a recent visit, at the residential south end of Seacoast Drive, the beach was essentially nonexistent, the raging Pacific held back by riprap and prayers.

The newest sand-renourishment project, proposed in 2007, has aroused the ire of local surfers, who have complained that it might wreck the surfing at the legendary Tijuana Sloughs. They also worry about the quality of sand used, which would have practical and aesthetic impacts as well. The surfers have reason to worry. Dredge spoil dumped on local beaches in 2002 and 2005 turned the water murky and surfboards black. The fact that more sand is already needed testifies to the pointlessness and squandered expense of sand renourishment. And how's this for a no-win scenario? Their choice of sand is either a north county source, filled with cobblestones, or from the mouth of the Tijuana River, which is entrained with toxic pollutants.

This latest boondoggle is called the Silver Strand Shoreline Renourishment Project, and it's projected to last for 50 years, with sand infusions every decade. It is the largest such project on tap along the entire West Coast. Once again, the work is being done by the U.S. Army Corps of Engineers, the organization that's made a habit of fighting Mother Nature and losing. Actually, we the taxpayers wind up being the real losers, since we're footing the bill for their follies. The surfers are trying to introduce some sense into the debate by involving themselves as interested and informed parties. Without question they're capable of making better decisions than the hapless Corps. At present, the Corps is still looking for $60 million to fund their latest sandy crap shoot.

② IMPERIAL BEACH

Location: Seacoast Drive between Palm and Encanto Avenues in Imperial Beach
Parking/Fees: metered street and lot parking
Hours: 24 hours
Facilities: lifeguards, restrooms, and showers
Contact: Imperial Beach Lifeguard Service, 619/628-1419; surf report, 619/595-3954

ACCOMMODATIONS

The **Seacoast Inn** (800 Seacoast Drive, 619/424-5183, $$), centerpiece of Imperial Beach's oceanfront, is currently undergoing renovation. Located just north of the pier, the landmark promises to be a bit more of a beacon on Imperial Beach's oceanfront. When completed, it will have 78 oceanview rooms and a renourished beach. But, take notice: Redevelopment had not even begun when this book went to press. In the meantime, you can bunk down at **Hawaiian Gardens Suite Hotel** (1031 Imperial Beach Blvd., 619/429-5303, $$).

COASTAL CUISINE

The most scenic dining spot in Imperial Beach is the **Tin Fish,** at the end of the Imperial Beach Pier (910 Seacoast Drive, 619/628-4214, $). Fried platters are the favorite, but you can opt for something healthier like grilled halibut or grilled calamari. And you can take in all the surfing and angling going on all around you. A good bet for seafood and breakfast is **IB Seafood and Breakfast** (809 Seacoast Drive, 619/429-1129, $$). Ask about fresh-fish specials at dinnertime. As for breakfast, what else but an IB High Surf Omelet (bacon, sausage, cheese, and onion)? Not that you'll have the stomach to surf after downing that leviathan. Also near the ocean is the **Beach Club Grille** (710 Seacoast Drive, 619/628-0777, $). Adjacent to Dunes Park playground, it's a good place to hit for deli fare or a gyro.

You won't have to wander far in this border town to find tolerable taco huts. Here are three of them: **Mi Ranchito Taco Shop** (805 Sea-coast Drive, 619/424-8260, $), **Tacos Corita** (757 Seacoast Drive, 619/429-6565, $), and **El Tapatio's** (260 Palm Avenue, 619/423-3443, $). Over the years we've scarfed Mexican grub at all three establishments, leaving happily with full stomachs and the knowledge that we ate well for next to nothing.

NIGHTLIFE

Beer joints and pool halls line Palm and Coronado Avenues. **Ye Olde Plank Inn** (24 Palm Avenue, 619/423-5976) is the most popular of this lot. That is not exactly a ringing endorsement, as most of the guys we saw sported biker garb. One visitor here described the Plank as a cesspool of the dregs of the military and transplanted Midwesterners. (We'll bet he didn't say that to their faces.) The most appealing beachfront tavern is the **IB Forum** (1079 Seacoast Drive, 619/429-7507), which accurately bills itself as "the most southwesterly bar and grill in the U.S." You can grill your own steaks here.

San Diego

A thousand years ago, the land on which San Diego now stands was a paradise inhabited by the Kumeyaay. They thrived along the bountiful waters of this big bay, one of the largest natural harbors in the world. With Point Loma to the west, fish- and wildlife-rich marshlands to the south, and protective mountains to the east, they no doubt thanked the gods profusely for their good fortune.

Of course, fortunes like this don't remain secret for long. In the 16th century, Portuguese explorer Juan Rodríguez Cabrillo stumbled upon the Kumeyaays' bay. The last of the conquistadors, Cabrillo came in search of gold. Instead he sailed into this perfect harbor on September 28, 1542. He named it San Miguel and claimed it for his royal patrons. Then he sailed away. This one quick visit earned Cabrillo the distinction of having "discovered" the

West Coast. Cabrillo brought his knowledge of the Kumeyaays' paradise back to Europe with him. Sixty years later, explorer Sebastian Vizcaino sailed into San Miguel and renamed it San Diego de Alcalá.

On July 2, 1769, the Catholic mystic-priest Father Junípero Serra established the first Spanish mission in California on Presidio Hill in San Diego de Alcalá. More a charismatic visionary than a humble padre, Serra inaugurated an ambitious plan for his town, combining a military battalion with a Catholic parish into a philosophy of conquest that would become known as the "mission system." His mission was clear enough (to convert the heathen natives), and his system eventually spanned 21 settlements, a network that subjugated the native populations of California.

Serra's recruitment method was known as "the cross or the sword." By the time the Spanish overlords were finished, the Kumeyaay had been left either dead by the sword or dependent on the mercy of the cross. Old Town San Diego stands in testament to his legacy. Today it's mostly a shopping mall set among period buildings. Yet Old Town is home to Serra's original mission and chapel, where mass is still held every Sunday.

California remained loyal to Spain and then Mexico, after the latter won its independence in 1821. California was admitted to the United States and San Diego was incorporated in September 1850. San Diego County became the first county in California. In 1867, a fast-talking Easterner named Alonzo Horton purchased San Diego's entire waterfront and laid out a grid of streets upon which the business district was built. Even today, Horton's "new town" looks new, dominated by nondescript skyscrapers. A plaza stands in tribute to Horton—another upscale shopping and hotel area.

In 1884, the transcontinental railroad reached San Diego. In 1917, the U.S. Navy landed here, building shipyards and installations on every available scrap of land and creating a gray military presence that dominated San Diego until recent times. Because of the harbor, San Diego soon became the permanent base for the nation's largest West Coast fleet, numbering well over 100,000 personnel. This, of course, attracted military contractors, which subsisted on the government tab for years. However, the military downsizing of the early '90s hit San Diego particularly hard. The city rebounded with the nation's tech-driven economic upturn during the Clinton years. And while the war on terrorism may keep San Diego's naval installations and defense contractors occupied, the steady economic downturn of the Bush years, combined with problems peculiar to California, has had a sobering effect on San Diego's fortunes and self-image in the new millennium.

In some ways, San Diego is still a navy town, but it's been looking elsewhere for its identity. As the 17th-largest metropolitan area in the country, with a bayfront that is the envy of the world, it certainly has ample resources to draw upon. In fact, the area has swelled like a dry sponge dropped in a tidepool. Many people are retiring here, while others sail in as part of the leisure-boat crowd. The San Diego metro area's population is inching up on 3 million. That figure, it should be noted, includes not just the city of San Diego proper but surrounding communities that fall under its municipal umbrella, including Ocean Beach, Mission Beach, Pacific Beach, and La Jolla. Annually, the city receives 30,000 new residents and boasts about 15 million overnight visitors.

There is a reason for this prodigious immigration. The weather in San Diego is ideal for anyone who doesn't crave variety. Temperatures year-round rarely stray from the 70s. It seldom rains in the summer, and when it does, according to a local resident, people stare at the heavens as if witnessing a solar eclipse. Within easy reach are beautiful mountains and unique desert communities (including one with the intriguing name of Plaster City). There are zoos, museums, theme parks, and theaters galore. And, of course, there are 70 miles of ocean beaches in the county.

Over the years, self-promoting San Diego has adopted all of the following nicknames: Sports Town USA, Golf Land USA, America's Finest City, California's Oldest City, The Place Where California Began, California's Plymouth Rock. Even areas of dubious history or merit are trumped up into Disney-esque attractions, carrying touristy names such as Seaport Village and Gaslamp Quarter. Then there are genuinely worthwhile attractions such as Balboa Park, SeaWorld, and roughly 90 museums. Of course, negotiating spread-out San Diego requires a maze of superhighways. Interstates intertwine across the scorched brown terrain like seaweed, giving a novice driver headaches, twinges of anxiety, and watery eyes. You may hear otherwise, but there is smog in San Diego.

The pace of life here is deceptive. Though leisurely on the surface, the city throbs with an undercurrent of manic activity. Cars are in constant motion, glittering like metallic bugs in the dry heat as they scurry along the freeways. Bicycles, in-line skates, skateboards, Segways, unicycles, and even pogo sticks hound the heels of sedate pedestrians. Joggers saunter along the harborfront. Sailboats and yachts cut through the bay like stilettos. The race is on all the time, even if you can't figure out where the finish line is or what you get if you win. Perhaps an eternal round of golf.

There's been some real trouble in paradise of late. The city manager and city auditor were forced to quit in 2004 over a pension-fund scandal. The city's sitting mayor was a casualty of the brouhaha as well. He was replaced by an acting mayor who himself was quickly found guilty of taking bribes from a strip-club owner and imprisoned. Beyond the taint of political scandal, San Diego has suffered severely from the collapse of California's overheated real estate market in this decade. No surprise here: The median price of a home in San Diego has been running three times the national average. Foreclosures are soaring in a market hit especially hard by the sub-prime mortgage lending crisis. It didn't take a crystal ball to anticipate this as the inevitable outcome of bad planning by those in real estate, construction, investment banking, and mortgage lending, where greed routinely trumps common sense.

Even in tough times, the lure of San Diego is obvious. It starts at the water, with its vast and appealing harbor. Because our yacht was repossessed in a previous lifetime, we generally spend less time on the bay—except for a meal, a stroll along the Embarcadero's Marina Park, and a visit to Balboa Park—and head straight to the beaches of San Diego. That is where we encourage our readers to start and finish their experiences of this remarkable city. Each of the beach communities within reach of downtown San Diego—Coronado, Point Loma, Ocean Beach, Mission Beach, Pacific Beach—is covered in the following pages. Each has its own unique flavor and appeal.

For more information, contact the San Diego Convention and Visitors Bureau, 2215 India Street, San Diego, CA 92101, 619/236-1212, www.sandiego.org; Greater San Diego Chamber of Commerce, 402 West Broadway, San Diego, CA 92101, 619/544-1300, www.sdchamber.org; San Diego Visitor Information Center, 2688 East Mission Bay Drive, San Diego, CA 92109, 619/276-8200 or 800/422-4749, www.infosandiego.com.

RECREATION AND ATTRACTIONS

- **Bike/Skate Rentals:** Cheap Rentals, 3698 Mission Boulevard, Mission Beach, 858/488-9070; Hamel's, 708 Ventura Place, Mission Beach, 858/488-5050
- **Boat Cruise:** San Diego Harbor Excursion, 1050 North Harbor Drive, San Diego, 619/234-4111
- **Dive Shop:** Blue Escape Dive, 1617 Quivara Road #B, San Diego, 619/223-3483
- **Ecotourism:** H&M Landing, 2803 Emerson Street, San Diego, 619/224-1134 (whale-watching); Seal Tours, Seaport Village, 619/298-8687; La Jolla Kayak & Company, 2199 Avenida de la Playa, La Jolla, 619/459-1114

- **Fishing Charters:** Islandia Sportfishing, 1551 West Mission Bay Drive, San Diego, 619/222-1164
- **Marina:** Commercial Basin, Shelter Island, 619/291-3900; Sheraton, Harbor Island, San Diego, 619/291-2900
- **Piers:** Crystal Pier, Mission Boulevard at Garnet Avenue, Pacific Beach; Imperial Beach Pier, Seacoast Drive, Imperial Beach
- **Rainy Day Attraction:** Birch Aquarium, Scripps Institute, 2300 Expedition Way, La Jolla (I-5 at La Jolla Village Drive exit), 858/534-3474
- **Shopping/Browsing:** Gaslamp Quarter Downtown Historical District, Third and Fourth Avenues, San Diego
- **Surf Report:** 619/221-8884
- **Surf Shop:** South Coast Surf Shop, 5023 Newport Avenue, Ocean Beach, 619/223-7017; Bob's Mission Surf, 4320 Mission Boulevard, Mission Beach, 858/483-8837
- **Vacation Rentals:** Penny Realty, 4444 Mission Boulevard, San Diego, 858/272-3900 or 800/748-6704

Coronado

Coronado gleams with a gilded, moneyed loveliness that stands in stark contrast to the border-town blues of nearby Imperial Beach. Driving north from Imperial Beach along Silver Strand Boulevard, you pass from a land of no money to a land of new money. First you notice the yachts that fill the Glorietta Bay Marina, their long masts standing as tall and straight as a fistful of pencils jammed in a cup. Then you realize that the price of gas has jumped by 10 percent in the space of 10 miles. Finally, turning onto Orange Avenue, which leads into downtown Coronado, you roll by a historic old resort hotel and rows of opulent private homes fronted by lawns that are better tended than country-club putting greens.

The rich have perched alongside the naval air base on this spit of land enfolding San

Diego Bay. They have erected high-rise condos, private estates, and tropical gardens where flowers of flaming crimson, deep purple, and passion pink add a splash of color to what would be, in its natural state, an arid landscape. Coronado (population 22,850) is a verdant garden by the sea, an oasis made possible by sprinkler systems, cheap immigrant labor, and big money.

The story of Coronado's founding is emblematic of how it went in the glory days of California's birth: Some wealthy guy would get an idea, and all of a sudden a desert would magically become a Technicolor resort in year-round bloom. Coronado's past is linked with some of the wealthiest figures in California's history, and their presence sets a standard of luxurious living that endures to this day. The founding fathers of Coronado are railroad tycoon Elisha Babcock Jr. and piano magnate H. L. Story. The two spent time hunting on the wild, majestic Coronado peninsula, enjoying the place so much that they eventually switched their quarry from rabbits and quail to tourist dollars. The pair formed a syndicate, the Coronado Beach Company, and bought the entire peninsula for $110,000 in 1885.

Ground was broken on the Hotel del Coronado in January 1887. It was envisioned as a wondrous resort that would become the "talk of the Western world." Barely a year later, "the Del," as it is informally known, was open for business. Babcock and Story were later joined in their venture by John D. Spreckels, a wealthy San Francisco–reared heir to a sugar fortune who sailed his yacht down to San Diego in 1887, dropped anchor, and essentially brought the city to life. He built the first wharves in San Diego's natural harbor and linked the city to the outside world with the construction of the San Diego, Arizona, and Eastern Railway. He also bought newspapers, installed streetcars, and founded a bank. To his credit, he ensured that the development of San Diego proceeded along pleasingly aesthetic lines, seeing to it that the city was generously laid out with parks and that the parks were planted with his favorite flowers: geraniums. His financial stake in the Del grew to the point that he bought out the other partners by the turn of the century. There have been only four owners since Spreckels, and in the new millennium the Hotel del Coronado projects a casual splendor, much as it did a century ago.

If you can afford it, Coronado is the ideal vacation town, as tourism is the only industry in what is otherwise an upscale bedroom and retirement community. There's evidence of money everywhere. Even the sand on Coronado's beaches is speckled with what looks like gold dust, glittering every time it's washed over by a wandering wave. The feel-good feeling radiates outward from the Hotel del Coronado to the downtown area, where a graceful S curve carries motorists through a squeaky-clean shopping district of modestly upscale shops and restaurants along Orange Avenue. Coronado's cafés and stores service the needs of locals and tourists alike. Everyone casually strolls, bikes, or in-line skates along the sun-dappled streets in search of swimwear, surfboards, frozen yogurt, and real estate.

Continue away from the beach along Fourth Avenue and soon you'll be headed out of town via the narrow San Diego–Coronado Bridge, a breathtaking engineering marvel that arches like a roller coaster and makes a 90-degree turn at mid-span. It's high enough that navy destroyers can pass beneath it. It also attracts would-be jumpers, judging from signs lining the bridge that offer a phone number for suicide counseling. Incidentally, in 2002 they stopped charging a toll to cross the San Diego–Coronado Bridge.

The naval presence is everywhere. The Naval Air Station North Island claims to be the birthplace of naval aviation, based on the fact that a navy lieutenant transferred here to receive flight instruction in 1910. More history was made in 1927, when Charles Lindbergh took off from here for New York and then embarked upon his famous first transatlantic flight. The Naval Air Station North Island is the hub of Naval Base Coronado (NBC). These seven affiliated naval installations collectively occupy 57,000 acres and employ 36,000 personnel. It is the largest command in the Southwest United States. In addition to the Naval Air Station, whose constantly incoming and outgoing flights might keep you awake, amphibious units are trained at Naval Amphibious Base (NAB) Coronado, located along Silver Strand between San Diego Bay and the ocean. Interestingly, a six-building complex at NAB Coronado was inadvertently constructed in the shape of a swastika. Oops.

For more information, contact the Coronado Visitors Bureau, 1100 Orange Avenue, Coronado, CA 92118-3418, 619/437-8788 or 800/622-8300, www.coronado.ca.us; or the Coronado Chamber of Commerce, 875 Orange Avenue, Suite 102, Coronado, CA 92118, 619/435-9260, www.coronadochamber.com.

BEACHES

Heading north from Imperial Beach along Silver Strand Boulevard, you begin to see the pipe rooftops of Coronado Cays, clustered together so tightly that the development looks like one continuous orange roof. Along the south side of the bay is the South Bay Marine Biological Study Area, a wildlife refuge that affords visitors a close look at a wetland environment. A nature trail leads into the study area, where bird-watching is excellent. On the ocean side of the highway, **Silver Strand State Beach,** a long beach occupying a skinny splinter of land no more than two football fields wide, connects Imperial Beach with Coronado. In season, RVs are jammed together as close as possible while still allowing their occupants to open the doors. The 2.5-mile beach can take on all comers, with parking for more than 1,000 vehicles. Being so far south, the waters here are as swimmable as any in California from the standpoint of temperature, topping off at around 70 degrees by late summer.

Coronado Shores Beach fills the breach between Silver Strand State Beach and Coronado City Beach. It's accessible via the Coronado Shores condo development—a ghastly, humongous array of seaside towers—and is widely used by surfers, swimmers, shell collectors, and anglers.

Coronado City Beach (a.k.a. Central Beach) runs for 1.5 miles, from the Hotel del Coronado up to the airstrip at the Naval Air Station North Island. The beach is wide and flat, dimpled with half-formed dunes. The north end of the beach is locally known as Dog Beach, for obvious reasons. There's even some tidepooling to be done. To our inquiring eyes on a recent visit, the early-summer waves were tame, and the beachgoers were similarly benign.

A wall of boulders stands where the beach meets Ocean Boulevard, which has plentiful on-street parking. In Coronado, parking doesn't seem to be as horrific a problem as it does elsewhere in Southern California beach towns. On a gorgeous Saturday over a Fourth of July weekend, we found metered, on-street parking both available and reasonably priced at a quarter an hour—a good omen. Away from the beachfront, between Sixth and Ninth Streets along Orange Avenue, free street parking borders a lovely green park.

Beaches, in fact, abound on both the bay and the ocean—28 miles of them in all. Along the bayfront is the city-owned Glorietta Bay Beach, which is a park with a small calm-water beach. Renting a bike is a good way to check them out; 15 miles of bike paths wind their way around Coronado and down toward Silver Strand State Beach. Bikes and 'blades can be rented at **Bikes and Beyond** (1201 First Avenue, 619/435-7180) and **Little Sam's Island and Beach Fun** (1343 Orange Avenue, 619/435-4068).

◱ SILVER STRAND STATE BEACH

Location: 4.5 miles south of Coronado, at 5000 Silver Strand Boulevard/Highway 75
Parking/Fees: $8 entrance fee per vehicle;

camping fees $25-30 per night beachfront, $20-25 per night inland, plus $7.50 reservation fee
Hours: summer 8 A.M.-8 P.M.; winter 8 A.M.-7 P.M.
Facilities: lifeguards, restrooms, showers, picnic area, and fire pits
Contact: Silver Strand State Beach, 619/435-5184

4 CORONADO SHORES BEACH

Location: at the south end of Coronado, at the Coronado Shores condo complex, on Silver Strand Boulevard/Highway 75
Parking/Fees: free parking lot
Hours: 6 A.M.-11 P.M.
Facilities: none
Contact: Coronado Recreation Services, 619/522-7342

5 CORONADO CITY BEACH

Location: in Coronado at Ocean Boulevard and F Avenue
Parking/Fees: metered street parking
Hours: 6 A.M.-11 P.M.
Facilities: lifeguards, restrooms, picnic area, and fire rings
Contact: Coronado Recreation Services, 619/522-7342

ACCOMMODATIONS

On the outdoor deck of the **Hotel del Coronado** (1500 Orange Avenue, 619/435-6611, www.hoteldel.com, $$$$), we heard a quintet playing a mix of blues and jazz. An elderly black man was singing, "I got the blues." He must have been the only one within earshot who did, as the crowd—a well-heeled lot who were either reclining on chaise lounges amid a sea of red-and-white umbrellas, playing tennis, or swimming in the Olympic pool—were having the time of their lives. A food kiosk offered "super burgers," "yummy hot dogs," and "healthy chicken breasts." It was quite a sight: a herd of happy people renting a small piece of paradise, basking in the midday sun. On another deck Frank Sinatra could be heard belting out the words "I'm king of the hill, top of the heap, A number-one!" His lyrics were reaching the right audience, bathing the upscale resort crowd in positive reinforcement.

The centerpiece of Coronado, the Del is a vast, capacious resort that's far more inviting than your typically stuffy corporate high-rise hotel. The grounds are impeccably well maintained, with walkways that meander among tropical greenery and such exotica as the rare "dragon tree" (imported from China in the 1920s). The Del lives up to its reputation by sweating the details so that pampered guests can take their ease. Most of them seem to realize that lying out on a breezy deck in a chaise lounge, with an icy drink and a gaggle of musicians tooting jazz on a small bandstand, is what a vacation is all about.

The Del claims to be the largest full-service beachfront resort on the Pacific Coast. We've certainly seen nothing in our travels to dispute that. The resort encompasses 689 rooms, and every one is different. Built in 11 months according to plans that were improvised day by day, the hotel is one of the architectural wonders of the Western world. At the time of its construction, it was the largest electrically lighted structure outside New York City. Four hundred rooms are originals, dating from 1888; the rest are in a wing constructed in the 1960s. Try to stay in the main part of the hotel. This four-story marvel rambles around in a rectangle that surrounds a green courtyard filled with palm trees and brightly colored flowers. The on-premises amenities include two giant outdoor pools, six tennis courts, volleyball nets, and a croquet green. Just be advised that you will pay dearly for all this privileged access, as oceanfront rooms start at around $480 per night. However, they were offering a "third night free" as a recent promotion, so perhaps business isn't booming.

More impressive than the statistics is the feeling of informal elegance that fills the place. Rambling around the Del is like exploring a rich old relative's mansion. If you come here, you may be living above your station (as we most definitely were), but you'll be made to feel right at home. "You've stayed with us before?" asks a bellhop as you arrive, as if assuming you've returned to renew an old friendship. The hotel's brick-red turrets and gleaming white Victorian exterior make it look less like a hotel than a castle. Indeed, it is a national landmark that has played host to 11 U.S. presidents. Hollywood seems to like the place, too. *Some Like It Hot,* starring Marilyn Monroe, was filmed here, and the Emerald City in *The Wizard of Oz* was patterned after the Hotel del Coronado's castle-like design.

Across the street is the mission-style **El Cordova** (1351 Orange Avenue, 619/435-4131, www.elcordovahotel.com, $$$), whose 40 rooms are like small apartments, tucked into stairwells around a brick courtyard of ground-level shops and restaurants. Originally a private mansion built in 1902, when the area was still relatively rural, El Cordova opened as a hotel in 1930 and is currently maintained as one of the most homey and nicely appointed suite-style hotels we've encountered in our coastal travels.

Over on the bay, the former mansion of sugar baron John D. Spreckels is the centerpiece of the **Glorietta Bay Inn** (1630 Glorietta Boulevard, 619/435-3101, $$$), a relaxed but regal inn. Many rooms overlook the bay, while others face out on gardens. The setting is quiet, yet downtown Coronado is just a few walkable blocks away. And rooms start at $185, which offers some relief from the other venues hereabouts. The staff is unusually friendly and attentive. We're forever in their debt for finding and forwarding a pricey computer accessory we left behind on one visit.

COASTAL CUISINE

The best and most neighborly place to start the day is **Coronado Bakery** (1206 Ocean Avenue, 619/435-9272, $), which is a locals' favorite, and one of ours, too. You've got to try the "glazed rings" (doughnuts) or muffins (e.g., pumpkin raisin walnut bran) and watch the world jog by as you ingest delicious calories from a streetside table.

We had our first encounter with healthy, low-fat Mexican cuisine (no, that's not necessarily an oxymoron) in Coronado, courtesy of a fast-food chain called **La Salsa!** (1360 Orange Avenue, 619/435-7778, $). The legend printed on the beverage cups relates the chain's culinary philosophy: "No can openers. No microwaves. No freezers. No lard. Skinless chicken. Lean steak." We ordered vegetable tacos and watched the cook carefully slice onions and tomatoes, grill and place them on a soft taco, slather on black beans, and top it all off with shredded cheese, lettuce, avocado wedges, and fresh cilantro. Customers can ladle on salsa from a salsa bar, choosing from four grades of heat. Although the California Burrito has 18 grams of fat (it's the avocado's fault), by Mexican food standards even this is lean cuisine. La Salsa! has franchises all over Southern California, including locations in La Jolla, Pacific Beach, and Newport Beach. Coastal travelers craving a Mexican meal that won't send them down the road to a coronary bypass should keep this name handy.

Good-quality Mexican food in a sit-down environment is served at **Miguel's Cocina** (1351 Orange Avenue, 619/437-5237, $$), in the courtyard of El Cordova. It's known for fish tacos, which we can unhesitatingly recommend. Also very good are calamari (sauteed squid steak) and chicken (charbroiled free-range chicken) served on a *torta* roll with avocado, tomato, lettuce, and sauces.

Another reasonably priced and down-to-earth Coronado eatery is the **Fish Company** (1007 C Avenue, 619/435-3945, $$), a fresh-fish market and outdoor café with catch-of-the-day specials and a sushi bar.

On the bayside is the locally popular **Bay Beach Cafe** (1201 First Street, 619/435-4900, $$). Set among a dockside bazaar called Ferry Landing Marketplace, it looks out on the San Diego skyline. It's especially good at dinner, when seafood specials turn up on the menu. Incidentally, the San Diego Bay Ferry shuttles commuters between San Diego's B Street Pier, Coronado's Ferry Landing Marketplace, and the Naval Air Station North Island.

At the upper end of the scale is the posh and expensive **Azzura Point** (4000 Coronado Bay Road, 619/424-4477, $$$$), at Loews Coronado Bay Resort. You'll pay $25–60 per person for its culinary innovation and world-class views. Though Azzura Point lost an executive chef to the newly opened Nine-Ten in La Jolla, it remains one of the choicest "big occasion" restaurants in the San Diego area. Try the salmon in black truffle sauce or 10-spice ahi tuna. **Chez Loma French Bistro** (1132 Loma Avenue, 619/435-0661, $$$) puts a French twist on fresh California ingredients in a romantic setting. It has the added advantage of history, occupying a landmark building dating from 1889.

Over at the Hotel del Coronado, the **Crown-Coronet Room** (1500 Orange Avenue, 619/435-6611, $$$$) has served kings, presidents, movie stars, sheiks, and tycoons from all over the world. It is the largest of six restaurants on the premises. The room is as long as a football field, and the ceiling is 33 feet high, making it one of the largest freestanding wood structures in North America. At ground level, the menu tends toward "progressive continental" preparations, and the panoramic view is as delectable as the food. The most formal dining room at the Del is the **Prince of Wales Room** (1500 Orange Avenue, 619/435-6611, $$$$). We were advised of the dress code by our bellhop: "California formal—which means coat and tie and shoes."

Finally, a popular afternoon or after-dinner stop is **MooTime Creamery** (1025 Orange Avenue, 619/435-2422, $), a retro dessert diner with a life-size Elvis Presley sculpture out front. It also has a smaller unit inside the Hotel del Coronado.

NIGHTLIFE

Don't come to Coronado expecting nightlife. In fact, you can expect to be largely free of it. (Sometimes this is a blessing.) Your choices on the Coronado side of the San Diego–Coronado Bridge are pretty much limited to a handful of Irish pubs along Orange Avenue. The busiest of these is **McP's Irish Pub & Grill** (1107 Orange Avenue, 619/435-5280), which has been around since 1982 (it was founded by a former Navy SEAL) and bills itself as "Coronado's hottest night spot." By the standards of low-key Coronado, McP's does get fairly raucous.

For some serious whoopee head over the bridge to San Diego, which deposits you on Harbor Drive. Then proceed north to Fifth Avenue, which leads into downtown San Diego and its bustling Gaslamp Quarter district. There you'll find an abundance of restaurants and nightclubs.

Point Loma

Heading out to Point Loma from Ocean Beach, the land rises—first gently, then steeply—until you're high above the beaches and the bay. From this promontory the ocean glitters like a diamond choker and the cliffs take on a deep red hue at dusk. The area of Point Loma that enjoys these views, roughly between Ocean Beach and the Naval Ocean System Center, looks to be one of the choicest places to live in San Diego.

For a free glimpse of some of the most dramatic scenery on the peninsula, drive along Sunset Cliffs Boulevard from Point Loma Avenue to Ladera Street. This area is known as Sunset Cliffs Park; rather than an actual picnic-and-Frisbee green space, it is a series of parking areas and dirt trails that run along cliffs, allowing you to scuttle down like a crab to the edge of a heart-stopping drop-off. Some determined surfers and divers make their way down the steep paths to the sandy and rocky coves below. Be cautious, however; cliffs here are succumbing to wave-driven erosion at an alarming rate. Several parking turnouts have been closed, and signs at other turnouts warn visitors to keep a safe distance.

To continue out Point Loma, turn off Sunset Cliffs Boulevard onto Hill Street—an aptly named vertical grade—and then hang a right onto Catalina Boulevard/Highway 209. This becomes Cabrillo Memorial Drive and leads out to Cabrillo National Monument at the tip of the peninsula. The landform narrows as you pass through the gates of the Naval Ocean System Center and past a large military cemetery filled with small white crosses. This is **Fort Rosecrans National Cemetery,** and it spreads along the rolling contours of the peninsula—as tranquil a resting place as Arlington National Cemetery.

At **Cabrillo National Monument,** a fee of $5 per car will give you access to a stone statue of the Spanish conquistador and explorer Juan Rodríguez Cabrillo; views over San Diego Bay and Coronado; and the **Old Point Loma Lighthouse,** a harbor light and coastal beacon that illuminated the coast from 1855 to 1891. A skylit visitors center houses exhibits on Cabrillo's voyage and a well-stocked bookstore and gift shop.

For hiking and nature study, there's a one-mile (one-way) trail on the bay side and tidepools on the ocean side. Also on the bay side, inside the crook formed where Point Loma bends south, are two islands created in the 1960s from dredge spoil. ("Dredge spoil" is the nasty stuff sucked off the bay or ocean floor to deepen a channel for boat traffic.) The resulting sandbanks were christened **Shelter Island** and **Harbor Island,** and developers poured millions into building high-rise resorts, restaurants, and yacht basins. Familiar hotel and motel chains (Sheraton, Best Western, Holiday Inn) have perched upon these artificial paradises. Both are slanted to boaters and

convention crowds, though Shelter Island has the decided advantage of a sandy beach.

For more information, contact the San Diego Peninsula Chamber of Commerce, P.O. Box 6015, San Diego, CA 92166, www .peninsulachamber.com.

Ocean Beach

In the medical profession it's a maxim that a patient's condition either improves or worsens over time, which is another way of saying that nothing remains the same for very long. The same bit of wisdom holds true for beach towns. Having taken the pulse of the California coast at regular intervals over the past quarter century, we've discovered that it's possible to come back to a community after several years' absence and sense immediately whether it's gone up or down. Ocean Beach, happily, has gone up. During our earliest visits we found it to be a low-rent slum by the sea. In an earlier book, we bluntly described it as "a sub-Coney Island maze of dirty streets, litter-strewn parking lots, sun-faded storefronts, and rough-looking bars." That no longer is true. Ocean Beach— or "O.B." for short—has gotten a much-needed makeover. And while no one will mistake it for La Jolla just yet, it's a comfortably funky beach town with just enough upscale refurbishing to inspire visitors to stick around rather than hurry away. It's possibly the hippest community in San Diego.

That is to say, Ocean Beach (population 28,000) has improved in much-needed ways, but not to the point that it has become unrecognizable. The community is a mix of the raunchy, the respectable, and the alternative. On one side of a street you'll see a decrepit bungalow occupied by ragtag post-hippies drinking in the yard. On the other side will sit a well-tended house with a neatly clipped lawn and a new coat of paint. The two opposing sensibilities—upscale and downtrodden—are literally staring each other down, though apparently coexisting.

The heart of Ocean Beach is along Newport Avenue from Sunset Cliffs Boulevard till it ends at the beach. What used to be an ugly array of failing liquor stores and five-and-dimes now runs the gamut from decent, lively burger joints for the surfer crowd to trendy restaurants with neon-scripted names. Most of the merchants are local; franchises are frowned upon. The sidewalks are clean and litter-free. Where once was a liquor store is now a fitness center. Even the local tattoo parlor seems vaguely respectable, offering custom tattooing "in the San Diego tradition." Aqua-colored tiles have been glued in a line along the curb with the names of local businesses inscribed on them.

For more information, contact the San Diego Peninsula Chamber of Commerce, P.O. Box 6015, San Diego, CA 92166, www .peninsulachamber.com.

BEACHES

Ocean Beach has gone to the dogs. We mean that literally and, oddly enough, positively. Where Voltaire Street runs out at the beach is **Ocean Beach Park.** At the north end is Dog Beach, a stretch of sand given over to the frolics of our canine friends. The sign reads: "Welcome to Dog Beach. This is a dog 'free' beach. Leashes are not required." Dogs do indeed have the run of the place. Their owners stand off to the side like helpless chaperones at a party gone haywire. The canine revelers scamper and yap; dig holes as if tunneling to China; sniff one another, fore and aft; relieve themselves indiscriminately; and run in and out of the water with tails wagging. In other words, they generally behave no differently than humans at the beach. We saw no fights, no snarling territorial disputes—just a happy pack of mutts and purebreds alike set free by their owners to romp to their hearts content. We should all get along so well. A postscript on water quality, however: It's awful off Dog Beach, so leave the scampering in the surf to the dogs.

Just up from Ocean Beach Park is **Ocean Beach City Beach,** a mile-long strand of mu-

nicipal beach with the pier as its heart and soul. The ocean itself is unquestionably dangerous, due to both rough surf and polluted water. According to the head of lifeguard operations for San Diego County, "My impression is that Imperial Beach and Ocean Beach and the south end of Black's Beach are the most treacherous in San Diego. They have the strongest rip currents that are consistently pulling."

Surfers congregate around the sturdy, T-shaped concrete pier. At 1,971 feet, it's the longest on the West Coast. Midway out is a café serving hot coffee and good, hearty food. We walked out on the pier and watched a group of surfers waiting for the right wave. To us, watching surfers in action is nearly as much fun as surfing itself. They bob up and down on the swells in their wet suits, making small talk until…look out, here comes a monster! Just before it starts to curl, they steer into it, emerging astride their boards in a shower of flying foam while negotiating the sloping face of the spilling wave with perfect body English. Before it breaks on the beach, the surfers U-turn out of it and resume a belly-down position on the board, paddling back out to wait on another ride.

For the adventurous, the south end of Ocean Beach, along treacherous Sunset Cliffs Boulevard, offers numerous breathtaking views of the rocky coastline. A dirt parking lot at the end of Cornish Drive and a stairwell at the end of Ladera Street lead to a small rocky beach. The area is known as **Sunset Cliffs Park.** Various esoteric and locally known surfing spots, bearing such colorful names as "North Garbage" and "Bird Shit," can be found along the length of Sunset Cliffs Boulevard between Point Loma Avenue and Ladera Street.

6 SUNSET CLIFFS PARK

Location: Sunset Cliffs Boulevard between Ladera Street and Point Loma Avenue in Ocean Beach

Ocean Beach

Parking/Fees: free parking lot at Cornish Drive and Ladera Street
Hours: 24 hours
Facilities: restrooms
Contact: San Diego Coastline Parks, 619/221-8901; surf report, 619/221-8884

◼️7 OCEAN BEACH CITY BEACH

Location: 1950 Abbott Street in Ocean Beach
Parking/Fees: metered public lots and street parking
Hours: 4 A.M.-2 A.M.
Facilities: restrooms and lifeguards
Contact: Ocean Beach Recreation Center, 619/531-1527; surf report, 619/221-8884

◼️8 OCEAN BEACH PARK

Location: in Ocean Beach at the end of Voltaire Street
Parking/Fees: metered parking lot

Hours: 4 A.M.-2 A.M.
Facilities: lifeguards, restrooms, showers, and picnic area
Contact: San Diego Regional Parks, 619/235-1169; surf report, 619/221-8884

ACCOMMODATIONS
The choices are limited and, cool as Ocean Beach may be for a day trip, you probably are better off staying elsewhere in San Diego. Still, the **Ocean Beach Hotel** (5080 Newport Avenue, 619/223-7191, www.obhotel.com, $) is a surfer's dream: plain, utilitarian, and cheap. The **Ocean Villa Motel** (5142 West Point Loma Boulevard, 619/224-3481, $$) is a bit nicer and takes pains to enforce a "no pets/no parties" policy. Rooms start at $170.

COASTAL CUISINE
Set in a typical bungalow that is the architectural trademark of Ocean Beach, **The Bungalow** (4996 West Point Loma Boulevard, 619/224-2884, $$) offers French/Continental cuisine at moderate prices. The house specialty is duck, but fish and chicken dishes are good as well.

At the other end of the scale, **Hodads** (5010 Newport Avenue, 619/224-4623, $) claims to serve the world's best burgers, proudly hanging a McDonald's-dissing sign that reads: "Under 99 billion sold." Another sign conveys the hang-loose atmosphere of the place: "No shirt, no shoes, no problem." The burgers are great messy slabs of beef stuck between a big bun and served in a basket. One table was fashioned from the sawed-off front of a VW bus. A buzzing hive of surfers chomps away at all hours, making a racket while gnawing on burgers the size of boogie boards.

NIGHTLIFE

Across the street from Hodads, the **South Beach Bar and Grill** (5059 Newport Avenue, 619/226-4577) is a great place to eat and/or down a few. We downed a few, eyeing the action on the pier from barstools pulled up to the picture window. The brew of choice is Hale's Pale Ale (say that three times fast), poured frosty cold from the tap. The restaurant serves fresh grilled thresher shark tacos, Baja fish tacos, and ceviche cocktail, among a full menu of other tasty seafood appetizers and entrées. While we were there, Bob Marley was playing on the sound system, while the San Diego Padres were on the boob tube. At a stool adjacent to ours, a prototypical beach girl with sun-damaged hair and reddened face reverently remarked to her male consort, "The ocean—what an amazing thing." We toasted this truism with raised mugs as the last rays of the day glinted off the distant waves.

Two spots for live music in Ocean Beach are **Winston's Beach Club** (1921 Bacon Street, 619/222-6822) and **Dream Street** (2228 Bacon Street, 619/222-8131). You might hear rock, reggae, punk, or cover bands with names like Downpour and Fortress.

Mission Beach

Mission Beach and Pacific Beach—neighboring communities welded together by paved,

three-mile Ocean Front Walk—complement one another. This stretch of San Diego's shoreline epitomizes what a trip to a Southern California beach ought to be. Mission Beach, with a population of around 6,000, is the smaller of the two fraternal beach towns. Each is a "Community of San Diego," which is to say, they're not technically autonomous, though in reality they seem quite disconnected from San Diego proper.

It is not until you've made your way to the Mission Beach/Pacific Beach strand that you actually feel as if you're entering the pumping aorta of a true California beach town. You know, the kind you've always heard about: skateboards, roller skates, and in-line skates, volleyball on the beach, surfboards, surf shops, surf bars, surf bums, surf bunnies, and more bronzed flesh than you'll see on any 10 MTV Spring Break specials. Mission Beach is a great, relaxed party town where college students from UC San Diego and other nearby schools live the beach life to its fullest, majoring in sun, surf, sand, suds, and good times, in addition to whatever it is they're purportedly studying up the hill in La Jolla. Our observation is that surfers and other twenty-somethings are happily non-materialistic, living in the outdoors beside the ocean with a few pairs of cutoff jeans and a diet of cheap tacos and beer. Who needs more?

Mission Beach, though limited in area as a peninsula, is wall-to-wall real estate. In that sense, it is indistinguishable from Pacific Beach. Added to the eclectic mix of types who come here—from families and preppies to punks and the homeless—is a veneer of understated civility and good, clean fun that wasn't always evident before. This renaissance was symbolically ushered in by the 1990 reopening of **Belmont Park,** an antique amusement park and shopping area with a mountainous red, white, and blue roller coaster (the 77-year-old, 73-foot-high Giant Dipper) that defines the revived spirits of the town. More moms, pops, and kids are coming to Mission Beach, yet it still retains a tolerant attitude toward fun in the sun. This is important, as no less an authority than Sir Kenneth Clark proclaimed tolerance to be the key element of all civilizations.

Perhaps the scene around here takes its relaxed cue from the beat cops. They wear shorts, ride bikes, mingle, laugh, and eat ice cream cones like everyone else. They don't needlessly provoke confrontations; in fact, they spend a good deal of time defusing them. Even the homeless have found a haven of sorts in Mission Bay Park, a nice swath of green across from Belmont Park where they loll on the grass next to their shopping carts. Tanned redder than rare roast beef, they chat, drink from bags, and pass out without fanfare. Again, tolerance is the key.

Two different waterfronts are available to visitors here: the ocean and the bay. They offer opposing but equally appealing beach styles. The oceanfront was, is, and always will be *Animal House* and *American Graffiti* rolled into one. Mission Beach is not unlike Mardi Gras, except that it goes on for months instead of days. The human parade provides endless hours of spectator sport available only in Southern California. Strolling Ocean Front Walk, the paved oceanfront promenade that runs along Mission and Pacific Beaches, on any summer day is like walking along fraternity row during Rush Week. Shirtless guys clutch tall beers and lean off balconies of their rented apartments, passing judgment on the human parade below or squirting one another with water guns, while bikini-clad beauties casually lean back in chaise lounges and toy with mixed drinks and sunscreen, lathering their lithe bodies while the guys leer and yelp and yahoo. We saw a pet pig on someone's patio, strutting and wagging its tail like a dog. Meanwhile, one sun-bronzed fellow calmly stood atop his skateboard while two leashed, panting dogs gamely pulled him down the boardwalk like miniature huskies.

The scene on Mission Bay is more middle-class than back-of-the-class. Executive types and their families play badminton on putting-green-type grass along the water. Barbecue grills are on display, as are American flags. Catamarans are lashed to the dock or pulled onto the sand. Another three-mile paved track, Bay Side Walk, runs along the water, but the pace back here is more leisurely, less chaotic. It is most popular with joggers, who no doubt appreciate the safety factor. The houses and villas are a pleasant and eclectic blend of architectural styles, and they're fun to study while strolling beside the bay.

Our advice to novice visitors is to leave the car at the motel and rent bikes at one of the outfitters on Ocean Front Walk. Mission Beach has devoted only a limited amount of its precious open space to parking. If you do drive in Mission Beach, try to park on the bayfront, at Mission Bay Aquatic Center. To get there from Mission Boulevard (the main drag), turn east toward the bay on Santa Clara Place and follow it into the lot. It is within walking distance of the beach as well as a host of great bars and restaurants.

For more information, contact the San Diego Visitor Information Center, 2688 East Mission Bay Drive, San Diego, CA 92109, 858/276-8200 or 800/422-4749, www.info sandiego.com.

BEACHES

South Mission Beach begins at the channel that leads into San Diego Bay. The beach is especially wide and suitable for volleyball here. In fact, this is a very recreation oriented beach, with basketball courts and permissible areas to play "Over the Line." The central axis in **Mission Beach** is at the foot of Ventura Street, by Belmont Park, the main lifeguard stand, and a cluster of shops and restaurants. Mission Beach has designated areas for board surfing, bodysurfing, and swimming. Water conditions are updated on a board outside the lifeguard station (e.g., "Lots of rip currents and deep holes on the inside of the surf zone. Ask us where to swim."). Mission Beach runs up to, and into, Pacific Beach. It's neither clear nor important where one ends and the other begins, as it is all one happy, boardwalked, two-mile strand, from Mission Bay Channel to Crystal Pier.

On Ocean Front Walk, a human comedy that would have amused the French writer Honoré de Balzac glides past on bikes, in-line skates, shopping carts, and anything else to which wheels can be affixed. Somehow they don't collide, even though all are traveling at different speeds. In the midst of all this sauntered an old crone with a Hefty sack full of returnable cans and bottles, riffling through the trash cans for more. A gang of sun- and booze-battered longhairs of late-1960s vintage came riding around the corner on low-to-the-ground banana bikes that looked like something our sisters played on when they were six. It is all in the spirit of Mission Beach, a town where the laugh track runs continuously.

One summer day, we waded along the ocean's edge for a good distance. The water, at first cold to our feet, felt good and warmed quickly. Mission Beach, incidentally, appears friendly to surfers of all skill levels. The surf is more forgiving to beginners than La Jolla's storied beaches, but under the right swell conditions, Mission Beach also presents challenges for experts.

9 SOUTH MISSION BEACH

Location: south end of Mission Boulevard, from Avalon Place down to Mission Bay Channel in Mission Beach
Parking/Fees: free parking lot
Hours: 4 A.M.-2 A.M.
Facilities: lifeguards, restrooms, and showers
Contact: San Diego Coastline Parks, 619/221-8901; San Diego Regional Parks, 619/531-1527; surf report, 619/221-8884

10 MISSION BEACH

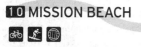

Location: Ventura Place at Mission Boulevard in Mission Beach

Parking/Fees: free parking lots
Hours: 4 A.M.-2 A.M.
Facilities: lifeguards and restrooms
Contact: San Diego Coastline Parks, 619/221-8901; San Diego Regional Parks, 619/531-1527; surf report, 619/221-8884

ACCOMMODATIONS

The rents on the bayfront are higher than those on the oceanfront, but the noise factor has to be considered. You do want to go to sleep eventually, right? We saw a cozy little cottage on the bay side that rented for $750 a month, but next door was a chic *Architectural Digest* centerfold that was going for closer to $750 a week. The scuttlebutt is that all the good, affordable ones are booked months, if not years, in advance, usually by people who faithfully return each summer. We can't blame them. For rentals in the area, contact **Discover Pacific Beach** (1503 Garnet Avenue, Suite 113, Pacific Beach, 858/273-3303).

This leaves motels, of which there aren't many in Mission Beach. The largest and best option is the **Catamaran Resort Hotel** (3999 Mission Boulevard, 858/488-1081, www.catamaranresort.com, $$$), with 313 units, many with bay views. There's a safe bay beach at the back, where you can rent sailboats and get windsurfing lessons, and there's a tropical pool on the premises. Things occasionally get hopping at the on-premises lounge, tastefully named the Cannibal Bar, if you're looking for a little après sail.

COASTAL CUISINE

As if to reinforce the twin themes of fun and nourishment, the best places to eat in Mission Beach are often the best places to drink, too. Our favorite is **Guava Beach Bar and Grill** (3714 Mission Boulevard, 858/488-6688, $$). With doelike innocence, the friendly waitresses at Guava Beach Bar hustle about, making small talk and refilling drinks within seconds of last sips. Most of the staples on the menu have a Mexican flavor, and all items are reasonably priced and perfectly unfancy.

Guava Beach offers "Baja Bargains" every day, happy-hour specials like the Cabo quesadilla with sour cream, spicy Rosarito fish taco, and brie and calypso salsa quesadilla.

The best antidote for the inevitable hangovers you will suffer in Mission Beach is **The Mission Café** (3795 Mission Boulevard, 858/488-9060, $), which is by general consensus the best breakfast place in the area.

NIGHTLIFE

There are two camps in Mission Beach's nightlife: those who are preparing to party and those who are already partying heartily. The prelude to a party animal's evening in Mission Beach is to watch the sunset from one of several Ocean Front Walk bars. The hottest one during our expedition was **'Canes** (3105 Ocean Front Walk, 858/488-1780). If you can find the roller coaster, you can find 'Canes, which practically sits in its shadow. Formerly one of the legendary Red Onion clubs and then a popular place called Chillers (we've imbibed at both incarnations), 'Canes carries on the tradition with live rock and roll. The club regularly brings in great national acts, too. We kicked ourselves for missing, by one day, an appearance by NOFX and Rancid, two of the more intelligent punk bands rattling the cage. 'Canes gets some serious competition for "party central" honors with **Wavehouse** (3125 Ocean Walk, 858/228-9283), which, in addition to wall-to-wall beach revelers, boasts a simulated wave called the Flowrider. Believe it.

The **Open Bar** (4302 Mission Boulevard, 858/270-3221) is one block off the beach, but equally popular with locals for preludes to serious partying. Ditto for the **Pennant** (2893 Mission Boulevard, 858/488-2223), at the south end of the peninsula. It is a sloppy hut with a wooden bar and booths, plastic cups of draft beer, and boisterous and sometimes slurred conversations.

Finally, we present one of our new favorites in all of Southern California: the **Liars' Club** (3844 Mission Boulevard, 858/488-2340). Its jukebox and draft beer selections have attracted a loyal local following. Most Mission Beachers who don't hunker down for the duration at one of these spots end up heading to the even more boisterous bars in Pacific Beach.

Mission Bay

Tucked behind the peninsula of Mission Beach, Mission Bay is a world unto itself and a beach haven that, though popular, remains nicely out of the way. The beaches here are on the bay, of course, and many visitors come to sail out on the water, not splash about the calm shoreline. This 4,600-acre aquatic park—the largest on the West Coast—can be accessed via numerous ramps, landings, and marinas to the north and west and on Fiesta Isle, the largest of the two fabricated islands in the bay itself. Watery activities pursued here include fishing, sailing, windsurfing, water-skiing, and swimming, and the sight of people doing all of these things at once gives the scenic and unpolluted bay a sort of relaxed elegance, not unlike a Seurat painting of a scene along the Seine.

Mission Bay is also a living lesson in democracy. Everyone comes here, from wealthy bon vivants, relaxing on deck in sailor suits and caps, to camping anglers, bunking in tents and RVs at the two campgrounds on the north shore. The bay is, in fact, appealing in so many ways that it's almost a shame it has to "compete" with the ocean beaches just a Frisbee toss to the west. But that only means there's plenty for everyone in San Diego.

From a tourist's standpoint, the centerpiece of Mission Bay Park is **SeaWorld** (500 Sea World Drive, 619/226-3901, www.seaworld .com). This 150-acre marine zoo stars Shamu (a two-ton killer whale), dolphins, otters, walruses, sharks, eels, and stingrays. There are also shark and penguin encounters, Dolphin Discovery, and Cirque de la Mer (Circus of the Sea). SeaWorld isn't cheap ($51 for kids 3–9, $71 for everyone else), but it's open

9 A.M.–11 P.M. in the summer (9 A.M.–dusk the rest of the year). If you hang out long enough you might get your money's worth.

For more information, contact the San Diego Visitor Information Center, 2688 East Mission Bay Drive, San Diego, CA 92109, 619/276-8200 or 800/422-4749, www.info sandiego.com.

BEACHES

They're not ocean beaches, but there's a bevy of sandy bay beaches to be found on **Vacation** and **Fiesta Islands,** as well as Mission Bay's mainland shoreline. Probably the best among half a dozen of them is to be found at **De Anza Cove,** on the bay's northeast flank. Here you'll find a well-equipped public park, as well as private campgrounds for tents and trailers.

ACCOMMODATIONS

Two excellent and affiliated RV campgrounds are available. Along Mission Bay, **De Anza Harbor Resort** (2727 De Anza Road, 858/581-4281, $), off North Mission Bay Drive, has 250 spaces for RVs ($39–45 per night, 858/273-3211). The much larger and more scenic **Campland on the Bay** (2211 Pacific Beach Drive, 858/581-4200, $) is a "premium RV resort" boasting 750 spaces for both tents ($40) and RVs ($67 per night). SeaWorld is right across the bay.

If you want more in the way of creature comforts, try the **San Diego Paradise Point Resort** (1404 West Vacation Road, 858/274-4630, www.paradisepoint.com, $$$) on Vacation Island in Mission Bay. It's stocked to the gills with everything you could possibly desire, including five pools, a golf course, and a bayside beach. Formerly the San Diego Princess Resort, the property has undergone several phases of renovation in recent years. The goal is to recapture its original charm, back when it was a "vacation village" conceived by a Hollywood producer turned resort developer back in 1962. Rates run $185 and up for a standard guest room.

COASTAL CUISINE

For dinner we ventured over to the San Diego Paradise Point Resort, on the smaller of two man-made isles in the heart of Mission Bay. In a setting of tropical gardens, **Baleen** (1404 West Vacation Road, 858/490-6363, $$$$) serves superb seafood-oriented cuisine, offering a dining experience that's tough to top in San Diego. Every table in the spacious and casually elegant dining room has a postcard-perfect view of the bay. Wood-roasted fish such as mahimahi and salmon are highly recommended. Just be forewarned that everything is à la carte, and you'll pay $30–35 per entrée, plus $6.50 for vegetable side dishes and $7 for desserts, accruing a very pricey tab on your culinary pleasure cruise.

Pacific Beach

Any beach town that names itself after the world's largest ocean better have the waves to back it up. Happily, Pacific Beach (or "P.B." as it is known to locals) has waves upon waves of great surf, great beaches, great weather, great bars, and great cheap eateries. In short, Pacific Beach (population 40,000) is the quintessential Southern California beach town and is among our favorites on either coast. Despite the occasional encounter with a shirtless drunk sporting a bad attitude, P.B. is still the place to go if you want to have serious fun in San Diego.

There is an unstated rivalry between Pacific Beach and La Jolla, the jewel on the hill four miles north. Natives have bemoaned the gentrification that has trickled down from their wealthier neighbor. They've mockingly dubbed themselves "Baja La Jolla" for all the rich preppies who come here to party. And, indeed, some overly trendy boutiques have muscled onto the scene in Pacific Beach. Still, it seems unlikely that any business that charges $32 for designer T-shirts is going to last long.

The irony about this give-and-take between the two towns is that P.B. itself, beyond the

BAD VIBES IN PACIFIC BEACH AFTER DARK

Southern Californians are unabashedly sensual. They are children of the sun, as Jim Morrison dubbed them, physically fit and mentally uncomplicated. The state of profligate fun that colors their every waking activity is played to an unending soundtrack of laughter and rock and roll, and they never seem to tire of each other's presence. This is never more evident than at night when they come out to play after a hard day of hanging out in the ever-shining sun.

On the surface the nocturnal rites of Southern California unfold in a relaxed and thoroughly appealing state of anarchy that somehow manages to stay within the bounds of civilized behavior most of the time. Perhaps this is simply due to the fact that every day is nearly perfect here, at least from the perspective of weather-beaten East Coasters like ourselves. Since tomorrow is a clean slate, it's no big deal if things don't work out today.

Southern Californians owe this sunny outlook to the fact that they are always engaged in some physical activity and therefore don't have time to develop the pathologies that haunt sedentary folks in other places. Of course, all this fun in the sun also leaves little time to develop the mind, beyond periodic dabbling in the latest New Age manifesto. Hey, if there's an awesome happy hour going on somewhere, who's got time to get serious? And, more important, who needs to?

If it all seems too good to be true, it is. The pressure of paradise produces its own pathologies. We saw this dark side rear its head one night in Pacific Beach. Actually, it was the Fourth of July, of all symbolic days, and the festivities had come to a begrudging end around 2 A.M., at which point a hungry contingent of beach bums descended on one of several Mexican fast-food outlets that stay open all night in P.B. We did likewise.

At the first taco hut we visited, a sad-comic scene ensued. While we studied the hand-lettered menu, a grocery cart entered from stage right, listing like a rusty galleon with a tall load of empty cans and Hefty bags. The cart was pushed by a sun-pulverized woman of indeterminate age, perhaps 35, perhaps 70. She was wearing a grease-stained miniskirt, fluorescent orange fanny pack, dirty knee socks, and torn, untied sneakers that were too small for her swollen feet. From out of the shadows staggered her consort: a shirtless, shoeless man with tattoos covering his bare, distended belly.

commercial corridors of Garnet Avenue and Mission Boulevard, is a well-tended, suburban, and relatively pricey place in which to live. That left us wondering where all the wasted Marky Mark look-alikes go at the end of the night. There must be a whole lotta house sharin' goin' on. We know for a fact there's a whole lotta shakin' goin' on in those shared houses, as a stroll down any Pacific Beach side street after dark will reveal. One night, while setting out for a round of Garnet Avenue pub-crawling, we parked in front of a house where beer, music, and conversation were flowing loudly from a second-story balcony. A young woman, oblivious to the fact that she was broadcasting her monologue to an entire city block, shamelessly recounted the previous night's drunken revelry to her male consorts.

You've gotta love the carefree mindset of the P.B. surfer dude. Late one afternoon, we popped into a drugstore for notebooks and drinks. The tanned surfer clerk at the front register didn't just point us to the proper aisle. This genial, sunny dude gave us a guided tour of the entire store! We learned more about his life in five minutes than a team of therapists would have gotten out of either of us in a week. He even complimented us on our choice of

He answered to "Bear," the name shouted by the woman as he stumbled across the street. She loudly begged Bear for a dollar, the modest sum needed to buy an order of rolled tacos. Bear growled and extended a paw, proffering a moist, wadded bill extracted from the unfathomable folds of his soiled jeans. While she approached the window to order, he proceeded to gruffly panhandle the other people in line. We left at that point, having witnessed more human pathos than we could stomach after a night of prowling among the Barbies and Kens of San Diego.

The second Mexican restaurant we visited provided a scene of actual mayhem that had only been hinted at by the first. After ordering quesadillas, we retreated to a corner booth, feeling bad for the man behind the counter. Before taking our order he had been verbally abused by a Surfer Joe-type who accused him, in mock Mexican dialect, of withholding the sour cream from his burrito. The place was as loud as the bar we'd just left; the revelry never seems to end in Pacific Beach.

We tried to enjoy our food, though the helpings were so large that they seemed to multiply like protoplasm with each bite. As we were finishing, an odd series of events took place. Like a row of dominos stood back to back, it only took one jolt to send them all tumbling down. The jolt was provided by a skateboarding local and his companion, a woman in overalls. Her mate took offense at something he heard in line. This ignited a bizarre scene that ended with an athletic man who was not even involved in the original dispute punching the woman wearing overalls so hard that her head hit the front window of the restaurant with a sickening thud. A college kid ran outside to break up the fight, during which a heavy trash can got overturned.

The collegian ended up getting pummeled, as did the skateboarder who'd set things off. After leaving the parking lot strewn with four prone, moaning bodies, the assailant took off down Garnet Avenue. The cops arrived at that point, trying to sort out something that had no rationale. The final grace note was provided by one of the original disputants, an oblivious guy in line whose chance remark had touched off the fracas. Exiting the restaurant with his takeout order, he surveyed the parking lot and exclaimed, "I started all this, and I didn't even get punched!"

The quesadillas weighed heavy on our stomachs as we rehashed this turn of events. In a way, we felt like we'd lost some of our innocence about Southern California. For all its paradisiacal trappings – and the day at the beach that was now ending had been one of the most perfect we've encountered – we detected an underlying dissatisfaction, the ennui of the pampered American psyche that wants more of everything: sex, money, power, sun, surf, and good times.

thirst-slaking beverages, proudly informing us that he had risen at 7 A.M. to stock that very drink refrigerator himself. As he was ringing us up, he sincerely offered us his best wishes. And we sincerely bade him the same.

On the way out, we passed a man entering the store. He was dressed in a toga, with a band of ivy tied around his head. He was not in a costume drama, as far as we could tell. Out in the parking lot, we came upon a classic Mutt-and-Jeff duo, P.B.-style: a short, shirtless, tattooed construction worker and a tall, gangly, long-haired dude on crutches. The guy with crutches was toting a 12-pack of Bud-

weiser, lightened by the brewskis the pair had already knocked back. They spied a woman coming out of the drugstore and stopped to admire her pulchritude. (There's nothing subtle about P.B. dudes with beer in them.) The woman, blond and surgically improved but no more attractive than 90 percent of the gals in P.B., climbed into her shiny black, vanity-plated SUV. Hobbling toward her, the dude on crutches urgently shouted, "Miss! Miss!" The woman rolled her window partway down, perhaps thinking there was something wrong with one of her tires. "You're sexy!" the guy on crutches blurted with a crooked grin. "There, I

SAN DIEGO COAST

said it!" Then he hobbled away, giggling with his drinking buddy.

Two blocks away, on the boardwalk near Crystal Pier, two athletic California beauties were jogging side by side. After they passed a gaggle of guys, one gasped to the other, "Did you check out those dudes, dude?"

So it goes in P.B., dude, a party town without equal.

For more information, contact Discover Pacific Beach, 1503 Garnet Avenue, Pacific Beach, CA 92109, 858/273-3303, www .pacificbeach.org.

BEACHES

The main beach at Pacific Beach is part of a two-mile strand that extends south from Crystal Pier down to Mission Bay Channel. It is, quite simply, the most popular beach in San Diego and is jam-packed all summer long. Surfers in particular like **Pacific Beach,** rising with the sun to catch the early-morning waves. Areas for swimmers and surfers are marked off, to avoid confusion and collision. A cement walkway for strollers, runners, inline skaters, skateboarders, pets and owners, plus those who simply like to ogle the passing parade, links Pacific Beach and Mission Beach. A crew of San Diego city lifeguards surveys the scene at both beaches.

On the north side of Crystal Pier is **North Pacific Beach,** which runs for a mile up to Tourmaline Surfing Park in La Jolla. North Pacific Beach is a little narrower and rawer than the main beach strand—the cliffs begin to rise en route to La Jolla's curvaceous coves—and a bit less crowded as a result.

11 PACIFIC BEACH

  BEST (

Location: from Crystal Pier (Garnet Avenue and Mission Boulevard in Pacific Beach) south to Mission Beach
Parking/Fees: metered street parking
Hours: 4 A.M.-2 A.M.

Facilities: concessions, lifeguards, restrooms, showers
Contact: San Diego Coastline Parks, 619/221-8901; San Diego Regional Parks, 619/531-1527; surf report, 619/221-8884

12 NORTH PACIFIC BEACH

Location: from Crystal Pier (Garnet Avenue and Mission Boulevard) in Pacific Beach) north to Tourmaline Street in La Jolla
Parking/Fees: limited street parking
Hours: 4 A.M.-2 A.M.
Facilities: concessions, lifeguards, restrooms, showers
Contact: San Diego Coastline Parks, 619/221-8901; San Diego Regional Parks, 619/531-1527; surf report, 619/221-8884

ACCOMMODATIONS

The **Pacific Terrace Hotel** (610 Diamond Street, 858/581-3500, www.pacificterrace .com, $$$$) is the best place to stay in the area. The three-story pink and brown hotel blends as unobtrusively with the sand as a 73-room inn possibly can, and the location, just north of the Crystal Pier on the beach, is unsurpassable. Built on the site of what used to be a transient flophouse, the Pacific Terrace is a modern luxury hotel, comfortable and clean without being stuffy. Many of the rooms have balconies overlooking the ocean and the large heated pool. Purchased in 1989 by a large property management corporation, the Pacific Terrace has embraced some La Jollan affectations in recent years (valets in safari outfits), but no other place on the beach in San Diego can match it. However, with rooms starting at $260 a night in the summer, it is not for beach bums on a budget.

In contrast to the Pacific Terrace, the **Crystal Pier Motel** (4500 Ocean Boulevard, 858/483-6983, $) is more affordably priced. The name does not lie. It sits directly on the short, historic Crystal Pier (dating from 1927).

© PARKE PUTERBAUGH

Pacific Beach

The rooms are actually separate cottages affixed to both sides of the weather-beaten pier. Each cottage has a different sea creature carved into the cute blue shutters (in case you forget your room number, just remember "Sea Horse"), as well as an enviable pier-side private patio. The Crystal Pier Motel is popular with fishing families, members of which drop their lines into the water from their patios. It's not luxurious, but it is clean and unique.

COASTAL CUISINE

Restaurant-wise, P.B. is a battle royal between burgers, burritos, and fish 'n' chips, with no clear winner. Too many franchises have muscled their way onto the scene in recent years, but there is an alternative: buy the same fare from the locals. For example, the best burgers in town are served at **Cass Street Bar and Grill** (4612 Cass Street, 858/270-1320, $), which is also a great watering hole for locals, many of whom eat here so often it might as well be an extension of their refrigerators.

Close by, for seafood, try **The Fishery** (5040 Cass Street, 858/272-9985, $$$), where you can sit down beneath mounted fish and

dig into California swordfish piccata or cast-iron-blackened ahi. Mosey over to Thomas Avenue, where you'll find the **Green Flash** (701 Thomas Avenue, 858/270-7715, $$) and **Nick's at the Beach** (809 Thomas Avenue, 858/270-1730, $$). Beyond that, we've never seen a town so thick with taco shops, burger stands, bars, and other spots to duck into for quick, cheap bites.

NIGHTLIFE

In the immortal words of a local P.B. party animal, "For me there's living at the beach. Then there's middle age. And then there's death." Perhaps this deep philosophical musing best captures the transcendent wildness of the nightlife here. On our numerous visits to P.B., we've hung out at enough places to fill a scorecard and once even managed to get pulled over by the cops. We looked at it as a rite of passage.

The old reliables—**Cass Street Bar and Grill** (4612 Cass Street, 858/270-1320) and **Kahuna's Surf Bar** (873 Turquoise Street, 858/488-6201)—are still around. The latter is perhaps the ultimate unrefined surf bar on the

Southern California coast. As with the pipeline of a wave, only dauntless surfers venture inside. Surf music plays on the jukebox, longboards hang from the ceiling, surfing footage plays continuously on video monitors, and the place is packed with rowdies, especially on the "rage nights" of Friday and Saturday. When we last visited, the place was run by a scary-looking guy with a gray beard and baggy, soiled shorts. Throughout the evening he taunted and regaled the crowd over a microphone, offering free shots of tequila to any woman who'd bare her breasts for him, leaping over the bar to referee a fistfight that he helped instigate, and leading cheers of "Kahuna! Kahuna! Kahuna!" as he paced behind the bar like a trapped panther.

Moondoggies (832 Garnet Avenue, 858/483-6550) is a tamer, trendier chain sports/surf bar that caters more to surfer wannabes. It's got comedy nights, deejay nights (one devoted to "industrial" music), and drink specials (like "Surfers on Acid"), and it's definitely not our style.

Two other old reliables on the P.B. scene are **Hennessey's Tavern** (4650 Mission Boulevard, 858/483-8847) and **Pacific Beach Bar and Grill** (860 Garnet Avenue, 858/272-4745). The former, though part of a chain, has been adopted by locals mainly because it occupies the site of a late, lamented Mexican cantina. The latter has an excellent jukebox, an outdoor patio, and a line out the door all night long. Year after year, it remains the most popular spot in town. There are generally more people waiting outside to get in here than there are partying inside at most other bars, so come early and grab a meal from the surprisingly voluminous and tasty menu. Try a Longboarder: corn tortillas stuffed with mahimahi, salsa fresca, and white sauce. The main dining room has long wooden tables with cheap plastic deck chairs at which you sit unabashedly with others, as if on a big indoor picnic, which makes for good and downright unavoidable mingling. On a recent visit, we were joined by six garrulous UCSD students who might've been even louder had they not been stuffing their faces so frantically.

The place with the longest lines and loudest crowds on our last cakewalk up Garnet Avenue was the **Typhoon Saloon** (1165 Garnet Avenue, 858/373-3444). Security personnel in yellow slickers self-importantly communicate with one another via walkie-talkie, and this "bad-ass" joint teems with noise and bodies on the move and on the make.

If dance music is your thing, try **Club Tremors** (860 Garnet Avenue, 858/272-7278), which shares an address and is associated with the infinitely more preferable Pacific Beach Bar and Grill. Like luscious lemmings who come to honor a monument to their own narcissism, guys and dolls crowd into Tremors on hot summer nights, primped and preened and mirror-conscious. Formerly the trendy Club Diego's, it's a massive multimedia complex. You must pay a cover to hear taped hip-hop music played at a volume that could scare off the gulls circling nearby. It certainly sent us fleeing. Similar deejay fare is offered at the tonier **Plan B** (945 Garnet Avenue, 858/483-9921), which nonetheless seems to attract a slightly seedier clientele.

If you're as averse to electronic dance music as we are, there are plenty of alternatives in Pacific Beach. Two of our favorites are **Plum Crazy Saloon** (1060 Garnet Avenue, 858/270-1212) and **Cafe Crema** (1001 Garnet Avenue, 858/273-3558). The former is an extremely friendly place, with good music, countless drink specials (68 beers on tap!), pool tables, and delirious locals, typified by a blond woman who pantomimed every song played, replete with pelvis and lip twitches and tabletop leg kicks. Cafe Crema is part of the coffeehouse craze, which has overtaken even beery Pacific Beach. Open 22 hours a day, Cafe Crema bakes its own pastries and offers an excellent array of rich coffees, plus treats like "Latte of the Month" and "Creme de la Crema" (44 ounces of espresso, ice cream, whipped cream, chocolate, and banana), as well as healthy soups and salads, and alcoholic beverages. Books and magazines are strewn about, card and chess games are in progress, and folk music is earnestly strummed. Last time we dropped in, a professorial duo delivered an earnest, academic seminar on acoustic blues. Most of the inattentive clientele was absorbed in novels, textbooks, and alternative newspapers. It was a Friday night, and all hell was breaking loose on the streets and in the darkened saloons of Pacific Beach. The well-lit Cafe Crema, by contrast, offered a civilized, if woozy, alternative to the alcohol-fueled festivities outside the picture windows.

Speaking of which, **Blind Melons** (710 Garnet Avenue, 858/483-7844) rocks P.B. with live music at the foot of Crystal Pier. Blues-rock seems to be the genre of choice at this corner bar, where we heard a Janis Joplin sound-alike going for broke one balmy weekend afternoon.

La Jolla

On May 3, 1987, the town of La Jolla celebrated its centennial. In its coverage of the event, the *La Jolla Light* recounted the glorious spring afternoon in 1887 when La Jolla came

into being. The first line of the story said it all: "It could not have been a better day for selling real estate." It was boom time in California, and settlers scurried westward to join in the land grab. One historical account claims they were sold a false bill of goods: "The plots were touted as having water mains and convenient telephone and rail service, none of which was true." It didn't matter. The setting was so much like paradise, perched high above the ocean on tawny, pine-covered bluffs, that no one was to quibble over phone lines.

La Jolla (pronounced la-HOY-a) means "the jewel" in Spanish. Indeed, La Jolla does look like a jewel—maybe the prize bauble on the marble-topped vanity of coastal California. Wealth is palpable, both in the natural bounty of a marvelous setting and the material prosperity evident in the cars residents drive, clothes they wear, houses they live in, and the shops that cater to their every caviar-like whim. They make their money hawking real estate and trading stocks, occupations that allow them to bask in a perfect environment, squired away in upscale, uphill semi-exclusivity. The tone is set by signs that welcome

© PARKE PUTERBAUGH

La Jolla Cove

TOP TEN THINGS TO DO
ON THE FOURTH OF JULY

On our nation's birthday, this was listed on the blackboard by the lifeguard shack at La Jolla Cove:

10. Watch fireworks.
9. Drink a beer.
8. Look for a parking space.
7. Eat veggie burgers and tofu dogs.
6. Drink another beer.
5. Yell at the guy who "stole" your parking space.
4. Swim at the Cove.
3. Drink another beer.
2. Ask the lifeguard a question.
1. Feel very patriotic.

visitors with the warning, "No shouting within city limits."

Technically, La Jolla (population 42,800) is a "Community of San Diego," but in every imaginable way it is a world removed. The freeway cacophony of downtown San Diego is miles away. La Jolla is distanced by attitude and altitude from rabble-rousing Pacific Beach and Mission Beach. Every attempt is made to cultivate a village atmosphere. La Jollans boast of having a "significantly high standard of living." It is a community whose residents lead a life of sensory indulgence. They are impeccably attired. They appreciate good food, wine, and art. They are masters at landscaping. Their hair is perfect. And, like all busy people pursuing wealth and privilege in the new millennium, they often appear to be harried as they bustle around their little seaside sanctuary.

The corporate heart of La Jolla is the intersection of Prospect and Fay Streets, which looks like a bonsai version of Wall Street. Outside the offices of Paine Webber and Merrill Lynch are arrayed gleaming rows of Mercedes and BMWs—foreign-made cars for patriotic free-enterprise capitalists. The working women, who tend toward the real-estate professions, likewise fix their steely gazes on the pot of gold at the end of the corporate rainbow. We actu-

ally overheard a couple of them at a seaside café discussing, over lunch, the origin and meaning of the company name "Re/Max."

The men all look to be some indeterminate, forever-young age, resembling those perfectly coifed leading men on daytime-TV melodramas. They include gray-haired bon vivants driving racy red convertibles, consorting with blonde gold-diggers half their ages. We spied one younger, upwardly mobile professional, whose dirty-blond long hair was heavily moussed and neatly swept back, pecking furiously at a calculator while nursing a grande latte at the local Starbucks. We could imagine him, like a surfing Superman, changing out of his Clark Kent office attire into baggies and sandals, grabbing his board and making for the waves at Windansea when 5 P.M. rolled around.

The ocean exerts a near-mystical pull upon all who live in La Jolla. At day's end they gravitate to the ocean's edge, gazing over the broad expanse at the setting sun like Bedouins engaged in prayer rituals. They watch from porches and balconies. They pull up to curbs in cars and vans with surfboards jammed in back or tethered on top. They jog along Coast Boulevard. Some bring picnic baskets, crawling onto sandstone shelves to toast the rosy sun as it slides into the crystal goblet of the Pacific.

SURFER GIRLS

Surf Diva Surf School, in La Jolla Shores, was founded in 1996 by Isabelle ("Izzy") Tihanyi, a legendary surfer who has competed in professional tournaments, and her twin sister Coco. Among the things that the Tihanyis and their instructors teach are how to read waves; how to "pop up" (go from a horizontal to a vertical position, like a human jack-in-the-box); how to maintain proper knees-bent, arms-out standing position; how to paddle against the prodigious West Coast waves; how to maintain balance on the board; and, of course, how to safely take a spill.

Surf Diva is not for wimps. Surfing is strenuous exercise. As Tihanyi told one magazine, "An hour of surfing is equivalent to 200 push-ups, and if you catch fifty waves, it's like doing sprints all day long." Tihanyi also suggests that students be competent swimmers (able to swim 200 yards) and "be comfortable in the ocean."

Surf Diva charges $165 for a two-day weekend surfing clinic and $390.50 for a five-day clinic. They also have summer camps for kids (boys and girls). The school provides equipment (boards, wet suits, lines, etc.), but women should bring all other items they'd normally bring to the beach (sunscreen, swimsuit, towels, sunglasses, hat, bottled water, food). Preregistration is required.

For more information, contact Surf Diva, 2160 Avenida de la Playa, La Jolla, CA 92037, 858/454-8273, www.surfdiva.com.

The scene at sundown is emblematic of the Southern California experience. On one especially lovely late afternoon in midsummer, we set up camp at Windansea to watch the unfolding parade. Vans lined the street, their doors slid open to reveal fur-covered seats, carpeted floors, and knee-high card tables at which guys in cutoffs sat cross-legged, cracking jokes and sipping beer. A trio of divers with yellow tanks strapped to their backs waded into the water, caucusing briefly before disappearing beneath the surface. An apple-cheeked beauty with shiny blond hair jogged by wearing a turquoise sweatshirt and coral sweatpants. A surfer in a wet suit came sprinting down a side street, board tucked under one arm, anxiously scanning the waves. People assumed the lotus position on rock ledges, hands shielding eyes from the harsh glare of the dimming sun as they gazed seaward. A girl in a bulky sweater, guitar slung over a shoulder, sang, strummed, and strolled out onto the rocks as if serenading the sea. On the water a surfer caught an amazing ride, tunneling through the foam and down a sloping wave until he was shoot-ing the curl. Moment by moment, the setting sun slowly turned the buff-colored sandstone to honey.

Despite its lofty perch, cracks in La Jolla's facade have periodically emerged, depending on the temper of the rocky markets. Prospect Street has seen a gradual incursion of less tony shops. In the midst of all the jewelers, perfumeries, and art galleries displaying Miró lithographs have come low-rent T-shirt stores and bargain rug merchants. Even McDonald's—designated a "McSnack" and mercifully lacking in golden arches—has stiff-armed its way onto a prime block of Prospect Street. We've seen panhandlers wandering the streets, a further blight to La Jolla's formerly unalloyed brilliance. One evening we followed the incongruous sound of banjo-picking to a downtown street corner, where a faux hillbilly whose hat lay upturned at his feet played bluegrass for the well-to-do Californians who strolled around him. On the street, a woman offered Tarot readings and on-the-spot counseling to those wandering by. She gazed deeply into the eyes of a customer, holding her hand while consulting

"DID YOU GIGGLE TOGETHER?"

The high-pressure lifestyle of making and spending money in volatile economic times is bound to take a toll that no amount of tennis or scuba diving can adequately soothe. This perhaps explains why La Jolla, a town of 40,000, lists 200 psychologists and psychiatrists in its Yellow Pages, not to mention the usual array of psychic problem-solvers (mediums, astrologers, fortune-tellers). Stress remains a hot topic of conversation. Signs of trouble in paradise are evident and even audible, as we discovered one afternoon. While strolling past a gorgeous estate in La Jolla, we heard its occupants screaming so loudly at each other that we thought the stucco was going to crack.

Relationships are casually psychoanalyzed down to the most intimate details. At dinner one night, we were seated near a medical professional and his date (whose occupation went undivulged). Both were in their early 40s, recently divorced, and talkative to the point of indiscretion. We certainly heard every word.

The male interrogated his partner with highly personal questions whose premises were profoundly silly. "Did you ever get to the point where you dug each other on a soul level, or was it all fantasy?" he earnestly queried. "Did you giggle together?" he asked with deep concern. By this time we were giggling together, heads buried in our plates so as not to draw attention. The conversation proceeded to a lengthy recounting of a humiliating tongue-lashing he'd received from a psychic nutritionist with whom he'd consulted. Despite his wounded ego, he generously interpreted her insults as "a loving gesture."

This recalls another true story, related to us by a former New Englander now living in suburban San Diego. He attempted to organize a reading circle. He explained the concept to his well-tanned but apparently poorly read neighbors, one of whom looked perplexed.

"You mean we read books and then sit around and talk about them?" he asked.

"Yes, that's the idea."

"Indoors?!"

the cards. We tried to read her lips; it looked like she was saying, "I can feel your pain."

Despite occasional signs of slippage along the fault line dividing haves and have-nots, La Jolla remains Southern California's premier ocean-resort community, possessing a setting as splendid as any on the coast.

For more information, contact the La Jolla Chamber of Commerce, 8602 La Jolla Shores Drive, La Jolla, CA 92037, 858/454-1444, www.lajolla.com.

BEACHES

The ruddy sandstone cliffs and caves of La Jolla are a perpetual work-in-progress. The humans who scamper along the sandy, erodable rocks overlooking the sea are unwittingly contributing as much to its sculpted form as the force of the waves that batter it from below. The beaches of La Jolla are among the most varied and striking on the Southern California coast. A new discovery waits around every turn in La Jolla, be it a blufftop vista, a stairwell leading to a small, sandy cove beach, or a rocky tidepooling zone. In their geological undulations and scenic variety, La Jolla's beaches are comparable with up-coast Laguna Beach. Both are among our favorite stretches of coastline in all of California.

La Jolla's sandy procession starts from the south with **Tourmaline Surfing Park,** at the west end of Tourmaline Street along the border between Pacific Beach and La Jolla. Tourmaline Surfing Park is off-limits to swimmers but is nirvana to surfers. Waves here are notoriously large and break a good distance from shore. There are no sand beaches to speak of between Tourmaline Surfing Park and Windansea Park, but there is public access to the shoreline—and excellent opportunities for tidepooling—at **Bird Rock Beach.** This residential area features some of the most palatial homes and desirable real estate in La Jolla. Stairs leading to the rocky beach can be found at the foot of Bird Rock Avenue and at North Bird Rock Vista Point (on Camino de la Costa between Cresta and Corta Avenues).

La Jolla's beach bounty—and the more public parts of its coast—begin at Winamar Avenue and continue up to La Jolla Cove. A paved path at the end of Winamar Avenue leads to a small, sandy beach. This is the start of an impressive trio of beaches—**La Jolla Strand Park, Windansea Beach,** and **Marine Street Beach**—that collectively occupy about a mile of prime La Jolla coastline. The beaches are flatter, sandier, more expansive, and less dramatic than the ones up along Coast Boulevard. These in-town favorites draw sizable numbers of surfers, anglers, swimmers, and divers. As the fabled locale of Tom Wolfe's *Pump House Gang,* Windansea is legendary among Southern California's surf elite. The famous "pump house" itself is located at Gravilla Street and Neptune Place. The waves are equally impressive at La Jolla Strand Park and Marine Street Beach, offshore of which lie Big Rock and Horseshoe Reefs.

Along Coast Boulevard, from its southern intersection with Prospect Street up to Ellen Scripps Park and La Jolla Cove, are arrayed small beaches and inviting green spaces for swimming, sunning, surfing, and picnicking. The linear park along Coast Boulevard is equipped with benches and huts that people use for barbecues or as places to erect an easel and paint the coastal scenery. The seaside path along this stretch of coast is pure delight; we can scarcely imagine a better way to greet the morning or end the day. Our strategy is to park on Coast Boulevard (free street parking) and walk its length, resting on benches or lolling on grassy knolls every few hundred feet.

The coast vistas are among the finest in the world. Beach accesses along this enchanted strip commence with Nicholson Point Park, between the 100 and 200 blocks of Coast Boulevard, where a hard-to-find stairwell leads to a small, sandy cove. Next up are two small beaches known mainly to locals—**Whispering Sands Beach,** at the end of Bishop's Lane, and **Wipeout Beach,** south of Ellen Scripps Park on Coast Boulevard.

The crème de la crème of La Jolla's beaches is **Children's Pool Beach,** where Coast Boulevard meets Jenner Street. A breakwater curves out and around, protecting the beach's inner flank from waves and creating an ideal place to swim or sun. At least that's what the local harbor seals and sea lions think. They've appropriated Children's Pool Beach, while humans discreetly watch them doing nothing from the breakwater or bluff top. Waves slam the base of the breakwater, which has a walkway with a handrail from which one can survey the seals' and sea lions' laid-back version of beach blanket bingo. Sea spray from crashing waves sometimes soaks those standing on the breakwater, which can be refreshing on a hot day or a shivery nuisance on a cool one.

One summer afternoon we counted 44 sea mammals sunning themselves on Children's Pool Beach. Arrayed in the sand like fat sausages, they bark, cuddle, roll over, and occasionally shuffle and flop into the water for a cooling lap. Typically, they "haul out" of the water to relax and sun themselves for seven hours a day. They seem perfectly content to be around humans and their point-and-shoot cameras. Don't let your kids get too close, though. They are marine animals, capable of inflicting injury, no matter how "cute" they may appear. Nonetheless, it's a strikingly pleasant scene here all the way around.

Just north of Children's Pool Beach is **Ellen Scripps Park,** a bluff-top green that's perfect for picnicking, Frisbee tossing, or simply lying on your back and looking up at the sky. One Fourth of July, we saw people doing all those things and more. Vendors sell inexpensive, often

THE WORLD ACCORDING TO SURFER JEFF

We had just finished swimming laps and lifting weights at our hotel, thereby maintaining the Olympic stamina that allows us to keep pace with the tireless Southern California hordes after the sun goes down. Heading for the hot tub, we spotted a blond-haired lad. He turned out to be a surf bum in his mid-20s named Jeff. He hailed us as we approached, congratulating us for keeping in shape while handing over a couple of beers – lukewarm Bud Lights plucked from a 12-pack that was already more than half demolished. He was not a registered guest at the hotel, just a local who'd wandered onto the property to dangle his feet in the hot tub and knock back some brews.

His worldview was a mixture of hedonism and pathos, an outlook common to those who outwardly have it all yet inwardly feel a spiritual void. It is the subject behind just about every song the Eagles ever wrote, including "Hotel California," the ultimate hand-wringing anthem for conflicted hedonists. They talk like this only to make themselves feel less guilty for having so much fun. We refer to it as "sunny angst."

Surfer Jeff was the peroxide-blond embodiment of sunny angst. After handing us our beers, he struck up a friendly conversation. He wasted no time informing us, a pair of total strangers, that "it's time for me to get my life together." He paused, then confessed, "I'm getting old. I'm almost 25." He'd like to get out of La Jolla, he said. It's a town where "your life is everyone else's business," where people stab you in the back. He admitted to having family problems; his folks were less than thrilled that their high-school-dropout son was still perfecting his form on the waves but had no career prospects. In addition, he intimated that among the townsfolk he was widely regarded as a wastrel who'd worn out his welcome.

"I've got a bad reputation around here," he confessed. "I don't know why, but I do."

Outwardly, he was an exemplary specimen of young California manhood, neatly massaged to a lean, muscular turn by sun, wind, and waves. His skin had been bur-

environmentally themed T-shirts. Windswept trees form a canopy over the sidewalk, sculpted so that their limbs grow horizontally. A broad, brown band of kelp floats offshore. Those who are so inclined can stroll out onto a staircase of sandstone ledges and watch the sunset.

At the south end of Ellen Scripps Park, stairs lead to **Shell Beach,** a steep, sloping beach tucked into a small cove, whose coarse brown sand is evidence of a rough, high-energy surf zone. Shell Beach gets packed with sunbathers, but few venture beyond the point where the waves break. Just below Point La Jolla, at the west end of La Jolla Cove, is **Boomer Beach,** a popular spot for bodysurfing. Surfboards are forbidden because of dangerous rip currents.

The beach at **La Jolla Cove** is the most popular in the vicinity, and it's invariably choked with a thick tide of beach blankets and bodies at the height of summer. It is staffed by lifeguards who post jargon-filled daily swimming and diving conditions on a blackboard; e.g., "Surf: Picking up slightly 1–2' west with a southern component that is spuratically (sic) trying." During one of our visits in early July, the water temperature hit 69.2 degrees and the locals were exultant. To them this was bathwater, very close to the yearly high of 71 degrees, reached in August and September. Further cause for celebration was this note, posted on an information board near the lifeguard stand: "Ocean water testing at the cove and shore will be suspended until October. Results have shown that water off the cove is generally excellent during the summer and early fall months." In other words, you don't nished to a ruddy brown, while his windblown hair bore the color of Midwestern hay. He positively glowed with the boisterous virility of a life lived outdoors. But now he found himself an unwilling adult with no career and no life beyond that of hanging ten and then guzzling at least that number once he'd climbed out of the water.

"I've got no tools," he lamented, holding up his hands as if to display his lack of real-world skills.

He possessed nothing beyond an ability to ride the waves and to party all night long. That may be all you need to get by while in the throes of a reckless California youth, but it won't pay the bills or feed a family. Not that he's got (or wants) a family or material goods, however forcefully they're urged on him by a culture that won't take no for an answer. In Surfer Jeff's world, who really needs anything more than a warm day, a nice southern swell, and a tall, cool brew?

We figured out that he's basically contented with his life, uttering remorseful monologues from time to time to convince others that he's "serious" about the future. In reality, his philosophy is like that of Henry Miller, who opened the novel *Tropic of Cancer* with these lines: "I have no money, no resources, no hopes. I am the happiest man alive."

Surfer Jeff recast that sentiment in his own words: "I've tried to get away, but the beach keeps calling me back. There's just something about it. It's so much fun that there's no real incentive to think of doing anything else. Just when you get bored with the whole scene, there's always somebody new who will wander down the beach with a cooler full of beer. It's like, 'Where's the next pool? Where's the next party? Where are we going now?'"

At this point a friend who waited tables in the hotel restaurant wandered into the pool area for a smoke. Surfer Jeff instantly switched out of his introspective mode and loudly greeted his buddy with a series of birdlike squawking noises. They slapped a mighty high-five, and the new arrival accepted the beer shoved at him, even though he was still on duty in a tuxedo. They talked about plans for later that evening. "If you come up with something to do," pleaded Surfer Jeff, "please drag my sorry ass along with you, man."

have to worry about swimming in a soup of fecal coliform bacteria, as you might elsewhere in Southern California.

La Jolla Cove and Underwater Marine Reserve stretches in a broad, tongue-shaped curve from Ellen Scripps Park up to Scripps Pier, at which point the coast resumes its northwesterly course. The area has been designated an ecological reserve in which boats, spears, floats, dogs (between 9 A.M. and 6 P.M.), and glass are prohibited. The public beach at the west end of La Jolla Cove (by Ellen Scripps Park) is protected and calm, and therefore gets quite crowded. The cove itself fills with scuba divers, snorkelers, and long-distance swimmers, some of whom are well over 60. They make the chilly swim across the cove, emerging like amphibians at La Jolla Shores.

Then they shake themselves off until presentably drip-dried and hitchhike back to La Jolla, wearing only their Speedos. The locals know them on sight, so rides come easily.

Incidentally, another local attraction is the **Coast Walk,** a cliff-hugging and footbridge-crossing dirt path for the hale and hardy that begins above **La Jolla Caves** and proceeds about halfway toward La Jolla Shores. The caves lie 144 steps below the Coast Walk; both sights are worth the trouble.

The focal point of La Jolla Shores, a suburb northeast of La Jolla, is **La Jolla Shores Beach–Kellogg Park.** The mile-long beach is flat and the summer waves often gentle enough to make this a good family beach. Kellogg Park is a grassy picnic and play area behind the beach. Our first impression of La Jolla Shores

Beach–Kellogg Park, on one slamming summer day, was that it looked like a refugee camp. The sand was as thick as a bamboo jungle with people. Packs of children threw blacksand mudballs at one another and screamed as they braved the surf on the broad beach. La Jolla Shores Beach–Kellogg Park belongs to the people, and the people do indeed turn out to frolic on it. We've rarely seen a beach as crowded as this one, though it's calmer on weekdays and at other times of the year, as we've verified on subsequent visits.

One memorable year we ended a daylong Fourth of July ramble around town at Windansea. We wound up wandering out to the beach after demurring on a party to which some surfers had invited us. It had sounded promising: the waiter/surfer/college student who told us to come described life at his apartment complex, a few short strides from Windansea, as a nonstop episode of *Melrose Place*. Apparently, we came too late. By the time we arrived, it looked more like an episode of *Sanford and Son*. Trash cans full of empty beer cans and pizza boxes were already being dragged to the curb, and except for a rap record blaring in the apartment and a girl skating in the driveway, the party was over. We kept walking down Bonair Street till it ended at Windansea. Then we perched on a sandstone ledge, listening to the soothing sounds of the sea in the aftermath of the holiday fireworks. We've said it before and we'll say it again: California can be a paradise to rival any on earth.

13 TOURMALINE SURFING PARK

Location: west end of Tourmaline Street, at Chelsea Street and Crystal Drive, in La Jolla
Parking/Fees: free parking lot
Hours: 4 A.M.-2 A.M.
Facilities: lifeguards, restrooms, showers, and picnic area
Contact: San Diego Coastline Parks, 619/221-8901; surf report, 619/221-8884

14 BIRD ROCK BEACH

Location: in La Jolla at the end of Bird Rock Avenue
Parking/Fees: free street parking
Hours: 4 A.M.-2 A.M.
Facilities: none
Contact: San Diego Coastline Parks, 619/221-8901; surf report, 619/221-8884

15 LA JOLLA STRAND PARK

Location: in La Jolla at Neptune Place and Palomar Avenue
Parking/Fees: free street parking
Hours: 4 A.M.-2 A.M.
Facilities: none
Contact: San Diego Coastline Parks, 619/221-8901; surf report, 619/221-8884

16 WINDANSEA BEACH

Location: in La Jolla at Neptune Place and Bonair Street
Parking/Fees: free street parking
Hours: 4 A.M.-2 A.M.
Facilities: none
Contact: San Diego Coastline Parks, 619/221-8901; surf report, 619/221-8884

17 MARINE STREET BEACH

Location: in La Jolla at the end of Marine Street
Parking/Fees: free street parking
Hours: 4 A.M.-2 A.M.
Facilities: none
Contact: San Diego Coastline Parks, 619/221-8901; surf report, 619/221-8884

18 WHISPERING SANDS BEACH

Location: in La Jolla at the end of Bishop's Lane
Parking/Fees: free street parking
Hours: 4 A.M.–2 A.M.
Facilities: none
Contact: San Diego Coastline Parks,
619/221-8901; surf report, 619/221-8884

19 WIPEOUT BEACH

Location: in La Jolla on Coast Boulevard
Parking/Fees: free street parking
Hours: 4 A.M.–2 A.M.
Facilities: none
Contact: San Diego Coastline Parks,
619/221-8901; surf report, 619/221-8884

20 CHILDREN'S POOL BEACH

Location: in La Jolla at Coast Boulevard and
Jenner Street
Parking/Fees: free and metered street
parking
Hours: 4 A.M.–2 A.M.
Facilities: lifeguards
Contact: San Diego Coastline Parks,
619/221-8901; surf report, 619/221-8884

21 SHELL BEACH

Location: base of stairwell at south end of
Ellen Scripps Park (Coast Boulevard at Girard
Avenue) in La Jolla
Parking/Fees: free and metered street
parking
Hours: 4 A.M.–2 A.M.
Facilities: lifeguards and restrooms
Contact: San Diego Coastline Parks,
619/221-8901; surf report, 619/221-8884

22 BOOMER BEACH

Location: south end of La Jolla Cove,
reachable from Ellen Scripps Park (Coast
Boulevard at Girard Avenue) in La Jolla
Parking/Fees: free and metered street parking
Hours: 4 A.M.–2 A.M.
Facilities: lifeguards and restrooms
Contact: San Diego Coastline Parks,
619/221-8901; surf report, 619/221-8884

© PARKE PUTERBAUGH

Children's Pool Beach

23 LA JOLLA COVE

BEST (

Location: in La Jolla at Coast Boulevard and Girard Avenue

Parking/Fees: free and metered street parking

Hours: 4 A.M.-2 A.M.

Facilities: lifeguards and restrooms

Contact: San Diego Coastline Parks, 619/221-8901; surf report, 619/221-8884

24 LA JOLLA SHORES BEACH-KELLOGG PARK

Location: in La Jolla Shores at Camino Del Oro and Calle Frescota

Parking/Fees: metered parking lots

Hours: 4 A.M.-2 A.M.

Facilities: lifeguards, restrooms, showers, picnic tables, and fire pits

Contact: San Diego Coastline Parks, 619/221-8901; surf report, 619/221-8884

ACCOMMODATIONS

The inns and hotels of La Jolla tend to be on the sumptuous (read: expensive) side, so don't come here looking for budget Best Westerns. The nicest are the European-style hotels downtown and overlooking the cove. Our pick of the litter is the **Grande Colonial Hotel** (910 Prospect Street, 858/454-2181, www.thegrandecolonial.com, $$$$), a well-appointed hostelry that dates from 1913. Rooms are plush, and amenities include a heated pool in a gorgeous courtyard and free valet parking. You'll pay anywhere from $225 for a standard village view room to $365 for a deluxe ocean view. Then there's the lavishly appointed **La Valencia** (1132 Prospect Street, 858/454-0771, www.lavalencia.com, $$$$), a salmon-colored stucco wonder that looks and feels like "old California," if not the Old World. This "luxury destination resort" charges some mad money here: $275 for a "petite room," $350 for an ocean view, $525 for a King deluxe, with

suites going to up to $1,050 and the La Valencia Suite going for $3,500—per night. You could buy a decent surfboard for one night's stay here! In any case, the beaches of La Jolla are just steps away out the back doors of the Colonial Inn and La Valencia.

Even closer is **La Jolla Cove Suites** (1155 Coast Boulevard, 858/459-2621, www.lajolla cove.com, $$$), a four-story modern structure that trades what it lacks in architectural distinction for a prime location directly overlooking La Jolla Cove and a few steps away from Ellen Scripps Park. Oceanfront balconies, heated pool, and proximity to La Jolla's downtown shopping district are added pluses. Rooms run $170–250; suites are more expensive.

Another of the fancy in-town hotels, the **Empress Hotel of La Jolla** (7766 Fay Avenue, 858/454-3001, www.empress-hotel .com, $$$), swaddles its guests with old-world elegance and contemporary luxury. Large, comfortable rooms are appointed with marble-tiled baths, well-stocked minibars, and terrycloth robes that hang inside mirrored closet doors. Mauve cloth napkins are placed next to a gilt-edged ice bucket. (You get the idea.) On the lobby level is a gourmet Italian restaurant called **Manhattan;** in the basement, an exercise room, spa, sauna, and showers. Rooms are surprisingly affordable; in the summer of 2008, a room for two was going for $199–225—a bargain by La Jolla standards.

Being partial to beachside locations, we've found the **La Jolla Shores Hotel** (8110 Camino Del Oro, 858/459-8271, www.ljshores hotel.com, $$$$) to be the best combination of location and comfort in the area. Formerly the Sea Lodge, its 128 rooms surround a tropical-plant-filled terra-cotta courtyard. All rooms have balconies or lanais, and La Jolla Shores Beach–Kellogg Park is literally steps away. The feeling out here is more outdoorsy, rustic, and recreational than it is in La Jolla's business district. With its arched, wood-plank ceilings, it feels more like a ski lodge than a sea lodge—until you sniff the salt air blowing off the ocean. Recreational facilities include a heated outdoor pool and tennis courts; the hotel also will provide guests with beach equipment, such as chairs, umbrellas, and volleyball equipment. It's highly recommended—and very expensive ($350 and up, in season). To help defray some of the travel expense, the hotel is offering gas cards and "free parking for hybrid vehicles," though we'd just prefer they drop the room rates and not charge for parking.

The **Hotel La Jolla at the Shores** (7955 La Jolla Shores Drive, 858/459-0541, www .hotellajolla.com, $$$) is a modern, 11-story high-rise four blocks from La Jolla Shores Beach–Kellogg Park. In addition to panoramic ocean views from the recently renovated rooms, the Hotel La Jolla boasts a world-class restaurant, **Crescent Shores Grill** (858/459-0541, $$$), on its top floor. The menu is oriented toward California/American cuisine: steak, seafood, pasta, and good wines. In-season rates at the hotel run $169 and up.

Finally, for corporate chain partisans, the 400-room **Hilton La Jolla Torrey Pines** (10950 North Torrey Pines Road, 858/558-1500, $$$$) overlooks the ocean and sits next to a golf course. A perfectly adequate and reasonably priced **Radisson Hotel** (3299 Holiday Court, 858/453-5500, $$) reposes in the hills west of town center, where I-5 meets La Jolla Village Drive.

COASTAL CUISINE

La Jolla's restaurant scene is dominated by **George's at the Cove** (1250 Prospect Street, 858/454-4244, $$$), a three-story restaurant that offers diners the option of semiformal indoor dining downstairs or a more casual setting on an outdoor deck that overlooks La Jolla Cove. On a midsummer evening, we took the latter option, enjoying the extensive view out to sea and up the coast. We dined on grilled marinated swordfish and a mixed grill of three fish, both of which were absolutely delicious. The third-level deck looks out on the ocean as if from the bow of a ship. Plexiglas panes keep the wind at bay, and heat lamps provide a note of warmth to counter the chill. Yes, we were

dining on the beach in Southern California in July and heat lamps were needed. There's a pronounced fall-like tang in the air even in midsummer along the California coast, thanks to the ocean's giant cooling engine.

Downstairs, the more formal dining room at George's specializes in creative seafood preparations done with a California flair—e.g., apple-smoked salmon served with fennel, miso, and Hawaiian pesto; and halibut in chicken fumet with poached leeks, garlic, and shallots. George himself can be seen bustling around the premises, impeccably attired and super-competent, yet possessing a dry, seen-it-all wit reminiscent of John Cleese. George's at the Cove is a La Jolla landmark and a must-try for visitors.

On the Mexican side you'll find decent sit-down Spanish and Mexican restaurants along Prospect Street, such as **Jose's Court Room** (1037 Prospect Street, 858/454-7655).

Overlooking the water near La Jolla Cove is **Brockton Villa** (1235 Coast Boulevard, 858/454-7393, $$$). This historic, restored "red rooster" beach cottage gained a second lease on life as a popular breakfast and lunch spot. (It also serves dinner now.) A favorite dish is chicken curry with jasmine rice. We dug into a delicious Moroccan halibut salad and pulled pork quesadilla after a long hike around La Jolla's curvy, majestic shoreline on as perfect a day as you could ever hope to find.

La Jolla's dining scene is rich and varied enough to reward serendipitous browsing. We had an excellent late lunch at **Bollicine** (8008 Girard Avenue, 858/454-2222, $$$). It's a great multilevel Italian restaurant and martini bar just up the hill from La Jolla Cove. Bubbling water tanks are shaped like martini glasses. The restaurant's main emphasis is salmon, prepared in all sorts of ways. Try the riso salmon entree (chunks of fish in riso pasta with a side of penne—simple but good) or a salmon sandwich on focaccia. Have a salmon lunch or dinner with a martini to wash it down and you'll be thanking us for the tip.

Tapanade (7612 Fay Avenue, 858/551-7500, $$$) is a relatively recent arrival (1998).

A nice but not too fancy place, Tapanade has an excellent, unpretentious menu inspired by the Provence region of France. Be sure to try the wild mushroom ravioli.

Pannikin Coffee (7458 Girard Avenue, 858/454-6365, $) has been around since 1968. It's great to sip coffee or Mexican hot chocolate on the patio.

NIGHTLIFE

La Jolla has steadily been losing some of its stuffy air, which has helped liven up its formerly stultifying nightlife. Today the multilevel mini-malls of Prospect Street contain the likes of a **Hard Rock Cafe** (909 Prospect Street, 858/454-5101) and **Moondoggies** (909 Prospect Street, 858/454-9664), one of a small but growing chain of spacious, upscale surf bars (find the oxymoron). However, in our judgment **Jose's Court Room** (1037 Prospect Street, 858/454-7655) is the place to go. A combination Mexican restaurant and bar, it was by far the liveliest joint we encountered in La Jolla. A loud CD jukebox sprayed its decibels upon a throbbing, three-deep crowd of beautiful people surrounding the oval island of the bar. The Mexican grub is good, but folks (especially singles) really crowd in for the company. So call out for an ice-cold Pacifico and join in the brew-ha-ha.

It's always a good idea to check what's on at the **La Jolla Playhouse** (2910 Village Drive, 858/550-1070), which was founded over 50 years ago by Gregory Peck, Dorothy McGuire, and Mel Ferrer.

Scripps Beach

A few miles north of La Jolla lies Scripps Beach. It belongs to the University of California at San Diego Scripps Institution of Oceanography (SIO), which maintains research facilities here. People generally come to Scripps to tour the Birch Aquarium, which is the most public of its facilities.

For more information, contact Scripps Institution of Oceanography, 9500 Gilman Drive, La Jolla, CA 92093, 858/534-3624, www.sio.ucsd.edu.

BEACHES

At **Scripps Beach** you'll find a research pier; offshore is a rocky reef and submarine canyon. While the beach here is sandy, it's not really appropriate as a place to come with the typical beach pursuits in mind. Therefore, if you're looking for a beach to frolic on, you're better off heading down to La Jolla Shores or up to Black's Beach/Torrey Pines State Beach.

25 SCRIPPS BEACH

Location: 0.6 miles north of Scripps Institution of Oceanography. From La Jolla Shores, proceed north on La Jolla Shores Drive for one mile. Turn left on El Paseo Grande and right on Discovery Way.
Parking/Fees: metered parking lots after 5 P.M. weekdays, holidays, and weekends; very limited street parking before 5 P.M. weekdays
Hours: 4 A.M.-2 A.M.
Facilities: none
Contact: Scripps Institution of Oceanography, 858/534-3624

Black's Beach and Torrey Pines State Beach

Before we hit the beach, let's spend a moment looking down on it from **Torrey Pines State Reserve.** One of the gems of the state park

THE SCRIPPS INSTITUTION OF OCEANOGRAPHY

The Scripps Institution of Oceanography is one of the oldest centers for marine research in the world. It was founded as an independent research lab in 1903 by a UC Berkeley biology professor and christened the Scripps Institution for Biological Research in 1912 for its benefactors, Ellen Browning Scripps and E. W. Scripps. Over time it focused its research efforts on the sea – an evolution that was recognized in 1925 when it was renamed the Scripps Institution of Oceanography.

The institution's assets include a fleet of four oceanographic vessels and two research platforms, classrooms and laboratories, shoreline and underwater reserves, seismological observatory and satellite oceanography facility, pier and aquarium/bookstore, major marine sciences library, and faculty and staff numbering more than 1,000. At any given time there may be 250 research programs underway, ranging from beach erosion to the physiology of invertebrates. If studying oceanography, marine biology, or earth science interests you, Scripps is the place to go for graduate training.

Even if doctoral studies in the geomorphology of ocean basins or manganese-nodule formation is not in your future, Scripps still has something to offer: the **Birch Aquarium at Scripps,** which is open to the public 9 A.M.–5 P.M. daily. Admission is $11 for adults and $7.50 for children ages 3-17. The Birch Aquarium and Ellen Browning Scripps Memorial Pier are in La Jolla Shores, just up from La Jolla Shores Beach-Kellogg Park.

The aquarium's glass tanks might contain everything from a spiny lobster to a gray grouper. Highlights include rainbow-colored exotics from Micronesia and the frozen-in-glass coelacanth, a nearly extinct relic from an ancient biological regime that looks like a battered piece of luggage. As a museum attached to a university-funded research facility, it's not quite as oriented to public visitation as the Monterey Bay Aquarium. But Scripps does offer a squid's-eye view of everything from kelp beds to coral reefs to the "Wonders of Water," plus a sense of the important research being conducted at the institution.

On that last note we'd like to lob this bit of wisdom at our readers, copied years ago from one of the exhibits, as we've seen evidence of its truth on every coast we've traveled: "Man has interfered with nature's supply of sand to our beaches, thus compounding the erosion problem, and we are now seeing the results of this intervention. Putting it bluntly, we are losing our beaches."

Scripps, however, is not losing its beach. In fact, Scripps Beach and the surrounding tidepools offer a wonderful way to learn about coastal ecosystems. It's all part of the Scripps Shoreline Underwater Reserve.

For more information, contact the Scripps Institution of Oceanography, 9500 Gilman Drive, La Jolla, CA 92037, 858/534-3624; or the Stephen Birch Aquarium Museum, 2300 Expedition Way, La Jolla, CA 92037, 858/534-3474, www.aqua.ucsd.edu.

Torrey Pines State Beach

© PARKE PUTERBAUGH

system, the reserve occupies a setting so peaceful you'll easily forget it brushes against a city of over a million. Trails lead into stands of the rare, long-needled Torrey pine, which grows only in this park and on Santa Rosa Island, 175 miles to the northwest. A 1.6-mile hike leads out to **Razor Point,** a breathtaking overlook from atop a 300-foot bluff. On a clear day, you can view the swell-dappled surface of the Pacific Ocean to the distant horizon. An old lodge, dating from 1902, serves as a visitors center. Some 436 plant and animal species are native to the park, including 144 birds, 110 invertebrates, 85 plants, 39 mammals, 28 reptiles, 23 fish, and seven amphibians.

In addition to its flora, fauna, and spectacular geology, the reserve is rich in fossils, and is close to where archeologists discovered the bones of Del Mar Man, believed to be the oldest human remains yet discovered in North America. The tranquility of the park is interrupted only by rustling breezes and the occasional sight of a gopher breaking open a Hottentot fig. The park offers a truly all-natural remedy for urban stress: an oasis of calm set beneath an awesome canopy of *Pinus torreyana.* On weekends, ranger-led walks are conducted at 10:30 A.M. and 2 P.M. It's

a very peaceful place to commune with nature and one of the better spots for coastal hiking in Southern California.

For more information, contact Torrey Pines State Reserve and Torrey Pines State Beach, 858/755-2063, www. parks.ca.gov.

BEACHES

The shore below Torrey Pines is **Black's Beach,** probably the most infamous nude beach in the country, and **Torrey Pines State Beach.** This lengthy strand lies at the base of the tall bluffs between Scripps Pier and Los Penasquitos Lagoon, and is as controversial as it is hard to reach. It is so out of the way we wonder why anyone would bother to get uptight about people enjoying the sun, surf, and sand in the buff. Yet the dimensions of the feud have occasionally plunged Black's Beach into the national news. Nudity was banned on Black's Beach in 1977, when a voter referendum revoked the "clothing optional" status. However, nudity has been the unofficial norm since then at Black's Beach. It is now official to the extent that an area of the beach—roughly between the Glider Part to the south and Mussel Rocks to the north—has been parceled off for nudists and marked with signs to that effect. Since July 7, 1999, the city's anti-nudity municipal code has been enforced on the southernmost section of Black's Beach, from Scripps Pier north for about seven-tenths of a mile. The fine for nudity outside of the marked area is $135, and for lewd conduct it's much worse. In other words, no lewd conduct. Got that?

From our perspective, the concern over nudity is grossly overstated. On a sparkling June afternoon some years back—Mother's Day, as fate would have it—all we saw were half a dozen men wandering the beach wearing only white socks and tennis shoes. On a warm afternoon in mid-July several years ago, the sum total of bathers in the buff consisted of an overweight couple of AARP age and several bearded male loners. We saw scant public nudity on Black's Beach on a balmy May weekend. Though we hiked till our feet hurt, we saw nothing but the occasional solitary bare-assed male. We did see lots of families, some picnicking on blankets. This gave the lie to the general impression of Black's Beach as America's premier nude beach.

In case you're curious, we were finally able to decode the putative partitioning of who disrobes where along Black Beach's two-mile stretch, thanks to a gatekeeper at Torrey Pines. Here's the lowdown: the north end is for men, the middle part is coed, and the south end is for surfers. "It's our Hawaii," said the gatekeeper, whose attention had to be pried away from a pod of dolphins whose offshore movements he was monitoring with a pair of binoculars. A surfer himself, he added: "The waves are good all over the coast, but for some reason they're particularly big down there." That is because a near-shore submarine canyon amplifies the swell, creating waves twice the height of others in the area.

The walk down to and along Black's Beach from Torrey Pines State Beach is one of the great environmental beach hikes in America. It includes a perilous scuttle around a point of land, called Flatrock, into which the merest sliver of a foothold has been carved into the rock. It is impassable at high tide. The geology

of Torrey Pines and Black's Beach is an awesome spectacle. The sandstone cliffs are fascinatingly textured and colored with bands of red, yellow, and orange. Boulders and mounds of talus occasionally lie at the base of the cliffs. You might see an environmental artist creating human figures from rocks. We watched one tireless soul, who had created several dozen such sculptures for passersby to enjoy. Obviously, he could not sell or take them home. He was simply motivated by a compulsion to create something from the formless mounds of rock. The little figures did seem to have lifelike qualities, as if he'd created a village of hobbits from the variously shaped stones he stacked and arrayed.

Getting to Black's Beach is actually easier from above. A stairway descends from the Glider Port (off Scenic Torrey Pines Road). Steeply etched into the cliffs, this point of entry comes with a warning: Stairway and Cliffs Unsafe and Unstable. The warning goes unheeded, and the foot of the staircase roughly demarcates the surfer's zone from the coed nudists' encampment. The safest way down, however, is via the service road that begins where Blackgold and La Jolla Farms Roads meet. You can't drive a car down to it, but your own two feet will deposit you on the beach in 10 minutes or so. Free on-street parking is available, and there are a sufficient number of spaces (with two-hour limits) to handle demand most of the time, summer weekends and holidays excepted. The road to the beach drops steeply in a series of switchbacks, passing warning signs (Danger: Hazardous Cliffs Subject to Landslide) and irreverent graffiti (Do Not Eat or Feed Nudists) before depositing walkers onto the south end of Black's Beach, with Scripps Pier in plain view.

For our money, though, we prefer the longer, ground-level hike south from Torrey Pines State Beach, which offers a Kodak carousel's worth of dramatic slide-worthy scenery: enormous toppled boulders, giant talus piles at the base of the towering cliffs, and huge sheets of blackboard-smooth rock. The whole landscape has a wild, otherworldly appearance, which no painter can capture and no photograph does

© PARKE PUTERBAUGH

Black's Beach

justice. You simply must see it for yourself. Hikers should keep a watchful eye on incoming tides, which could potentially strand the unwary in a cove.

The less adventurous or ambulatory may prefer to stay put near the parking lots at Torrey Pines State Beach, a day-use beach. An ample parking area abuts Los Penasquitos Lagoon. Arrive early if you want a parking spot on a good beach day. Just be aware that the cobble-filled beach is inferior to the sandy, scenic, and less crowded expanses of Black's Beach. Our advice: Take a hike!

26 BLACK'S BEACH (A.K.A. TORREY PINES CITY BEACH)

BEST

Location: Hike down to the beach via the steep, gated, paved path that begins at the junction of La Jolla Farms Road and Blackgold Road in La Jolla. Or walk north along the beach from Scripps Pier or south from Torrey Pines State Beach.

Parking/Fees: limited free street parking on La Jolla Farms Road; $8 entrance fee at Torrey Pines State Beach

Hours: 4 A.M.-2 A.M.

Facilities: none

Contact: San Diego Coastline Parks, 619/221-8901; surf report, 619/221-8884

27 TORREY PINES STATE BEACH

Location: in Torrey Pines. Take the Carmel Valley Road exit off I-5, five miles north of La Jolla. Turn onto McGonigle Road and follow it to the beach.

Parking/Fees: $8 entrance fee per vehicle, or free along U.S. 101 6 A.M.-11 P.M.

Hours: 8 A.M.-sunset; visitors center, 6 A.M.-6 P.M.

Facilities: lifeguards, restrooms, and picnic tables

Contact: Torrey Pines State Beach, 858/755-2063

Del Mar

The never-ending boutiquing of Southern California reaches a modest crescendo in Del Mar (population 4,400). Del Mar is a trendy, buzzing little hive in town and a jazzed-up mall-o-drama out by its famous racetrack. The pace of traffic has picked up, giving Camino Del Mar a taste of the fumy, bumper-to-bumper backup that congests Laguna Beach. That's not to say the place has lost its charm, just that it's experiencing growing pains. But this is par for the coast; there's scarcely an available acre within sight of water in Southern California that hasn't been built up or targeted for development.

All the same, Del Mar is the closest you will come to finding a true village atmosphere in coastal San Diego County. Thanks to the vigilant attempts of the populace to keep development under control, coupled with the relaxed atmosphere of the beach and racetrack, Del Mar has the air of a less harried time in California's past. To a great extent, it has geography to thank. Del Mar is on a hill between two lagoons, with a canyon to the east and ocean to the west. If you're entering town from the east, a heart-stopping plunge down Del Mar Heights Road lets you know you're nearing the water. During our travels for this edition, Del Mar is where we began our coastal trek. When we came over the crest of the hill and saw the Pacific Ocean laid out before us, sighs of contentment at this auspicious sight simultaneously issued from our lips.

The land thins to precipitous strips at the lagoons: Los Penasquitos to the south (at Torrey Pines State Reserve) and San Dieguito behind and around the river mouth at the north end of town. There's only so much you can build out here that hasn't already been constructed or attempted. In the mid-1980s environmental prerogatives saved the San Dieguito Lagoon from plans to construct a cluster of hotels, shops, and freeway access ramps.

In town the only major project that's survived the legal gauntlet has been **L'Auberge Del Mar,** a $45 million luxury hotel and spa built on the site of the old Del Mar Hotel (which was demolished in 1967). Even so, it took the developer, a Del Mar resident, more than a decade to gain approval of the plan. The heart of the village, along Camino Del Mar from about Sixth to 15th Streets, is a cavalcade of small shops catering to a consumer's every whim. Folks mosey from cafés to shops, grazing and browsing, as traffic moves in fits and starts along Camino Del Mar while drivers scour the streets for parking spaces. The modest town center is a tasteful smattering of New Age shops (Earth Song Books), classy cantinas (El Fuego), and restaurants of long standing (Bully's North). Away from the main drag, Del Mar's blocks are filled with small but smartly designed trophy homes with amazingly landscaped lots on which every square foot is maximized.

The town is best known for the thoroughbred racing season at the **Del Mar Thoroughbred Club.** The brief, 43-day season runs from late July to early September, packing the town with racing buffs. The racetrack was built in the 1930s as the brainchild of local celebrities Bing Crosby, Jimmy Durante, and Pat O'Brien. Their cosponsor in the venture was the Works Progress Administration, which pulled out midway through construction. The celebs were left holding the bag, having to borrow funds to bring the track to completion. Crosby wrote and recorded a song to commemorate the track's opening in 1937. "Where the Surf Meets the Turf" is still played before the first race with all the dewy-eyed sentimentality of "My Old Kentucky Home" at Churchill Downs. The track lies inside a triangle formed by Via de la Valle, Camino Del Mar, and Jimmy Durante Way. The grounds are also the site of the annual **Del Mar Fair,** a June/July to-do that draws three-quarters of a million San Diegans. The rest of the year is given over to horse shows, trade shows, and concerts.

Before the first ". . . and they're off!" echoed around the track, Del Mar was already trotting along on an initially shaky but eventually well-heeled course. In 1883 developer Jacob Taylor Shell bought the strip of coastline upon which Del Mar sits today. He built a seaside spa on his 338 acres that included the Casa Del Mar Hotel, a dance pavilion, a bathhouse and pool, and a railroad depot. It briefly thrived before succumbing to bankruptcy, flood, and fire (in that order) by 1890. The town received a facelift during the roaring '20s: a renovated hotel, rebuilt pier, and new roads into town. The fairgrounds came in 1936, the racetrack a year later. Del Mar has grown slowly but steadily ever since, trying its best to remain—as a *Newsweek* article described it nearly 30 years ago—"a sleepy little seacoast town."

For more information, contact Del Mar Regional Chamber of Commerce, 1104 Camino Del Mar, Del Mar, CA 92014, 858/755-4844, www.delmarchamber.org.

BEACHES

Del Mar City Beach was a sunbather's paradise, quickly filling to capacity on summer days until 1998's winter storms nearly washed it away. It has since been "renourished" as part of an ongoing and expensive beach restoration project in northern San Diego County. Short concrete seawalls offer scant protection to homes that have been built too close to the water's edge. The high tide line, marked by seaweed and scalloped wave lines, runs up to the very base of the seawalls, which does not bode well for the future.

Even so, there is much to commend the beach at Del Mar, which widens as one nears the bridge over San Dieguito Lagoon. The main beach area has been subdivided into areas for different activities, with arrows delineating "Surfing and Beach Games" from "No Surfing and Beach Games." The south end of the beach has gone to the dogs, with leashed and unleashed canines chasing tennis balls into the water and romping around the sand. Many folks come here with their animal companions, so this might not be the best stretch of sand for sunbathing

unless you're really into wet noses and sandy pawprints.

Finding a spot to lie out on the beach is less of a problem than finding a place to park close by. There's on-street metered parking along Coast Boulevard and a few pay lots. The early bird gets the parking spot while the loser cruises; parking in the summer months is pure hell. The beach itself is great for swimming and bodysurfing.

A grassy play area, **Seagrove Park,** sits on the short bluffs overlooking the beach from the south end. Del Mar's green bluff-top park is reminiscent of the village greens that are a mainstay of New England towns. On a sunny weekend afternoon—and few of them aren't sunny—students from UCSD, picnicking families, joggers, bicyclists, and walkers pack the park and its walkways.

Del Mar Bluffs City Park is just north of Del Mar City Beach, across the mouth of the San Dieguito River, where the land begins to rise again. A small sand beach here is popular with fishers. A steep wooden staircase laden with sand leads to a spectacular overlook from the top of the bluff. The panorama encompasses the ocean, racetrack, and town. Straddling Del Mar and neighboring Solana Beach is **Del Mar Shores,** a sandy stretch reachable from a tiny municipal parking lot at Del Mar Shores Terrace. These beaches are popular with locals and tourists alike, not the least reason being that in season you might catch trainers working their horses on the beach. Skin diving and surf casting are also popular here.

28 DEL MAR CITY BEACH

Location: in Del Mar at the west end of Camino Del Mar and 15th Street
Parking/Fees: metered parking lot
Hours: 24 hours
Facilities: lifeguards, restrooms, and showers
Contact: Del Mar Community Services, 858/755-1524

29 DEL MAR SHORES

Location: Del Mar Shores Terrace at South Sierra Avenue in Solana Beach
Parking/Fees: free street parking and free parking lots
Hours: 6 A.M.-10 P.M.
Facilities: lifeguards (seasonal)
Contact: Solana Beach Department of Marine Safety, 858/755-1569

ACCOMMODATIONS

Some things never change. **Del Mar Motel on the Beach** (1702 Coast Boulevard, 858/755-1534, www.delmarmotelonthebeach.com, $$) is where it's always been: smack dab on the beach. A charmingly unpretentious place that's been around since 1946, it's the only place in the area that can make that claim. The rates are much friendlier off-season ($139–179) than in the summer ($259–279).

Such homey motels are more the exception than the rule, as Del Mar and other North Coast communities are more typically represented these days by places like **L'Auberge Del Mar** (1540 Camino Del Mar, 858/259-1515, www.laubergedelmar.com, $$$$). You'll pay through the nose to be pampered at this resort spa. Visitors can select seaweed body packs, aromatherapy, reflexology, Shiatsu massage, and the ever-popular Balneo Therapy Revitalizing Bath from a menu of spa services more extensive than the list of ice cream flavors at Ben & Jerry's. It's a splendid resort, to be sure, with beautiful interiors, inviting pool area, multilevel decks, and walkways that meander among walled-in gardens that suggest a place far removed from the reality of a busy street corner. Large and well-landscaped grounds confer that all-important sense of splendid isolation that justifies room rates that run $200–385 in season (and around $700–800 a night for suites).

We are partial to the **Best Western Stratford Inn of Del Mar** (710 Camino Del Mar, 858/755-1501 or 888/478-7829, $$),

within walking distance of town but burrowed into a hillside in a real neighborhood. Constructed of gray, weathered wood, the Stratford Inn blends nicely into its environment. The grounds are invitingly quiet, featuring two heated pools.

COASTAL CUISINE

Down by Del Mar City Beach, a pair of restaurants with picture-window views of the ocean do a brisk business. **Jake's Del Mar** (1660 Coast Boulevard, 858/755-2002, $$$) and the **Poseidon Restaurant** (1670 Coast Boulevard, 858/755-9345, $$$) are the places to go if you want to dine by the water. Jake's offers a more imaginative menu of seafood prepared with a creative, Pacific Rim–style orientation, such as sesame-seared ahi with dark soy honey glaze. The Pacific seafood chowder (with fish, clams, and diced veggies) is rated among the best on the coast. The Poseidon sticks more closely to baked or broiled seafood basics. Both restaurants are overpriced—the cheapest entrée at Jake's, for instance, is $16, and the general range is $18–23—but you're paying not only for food but location, ambience, and a bit of history. The Poseidon has an especially inviting modern interior of varnished pine walls, tile floors, and big panoramic windows facing the ocean. It is a "view" restaurant offering breakfast, lunch, and a seafood-themed dinner menu.

The toast of the waterfront these days is **Pacifica Del Mar** (1555 Camino del Mar, 858/792-0476, $$$$). It is the best restaurant in town. You can't go wrong with choices like barbecued sugar-spiced salmon, which is the signature dish on a Pacific Rim–themed menu.

The **Fish Market** (640 Via De La Valle, 858/755-2277, $$) is an unpretentious, bustling sure bet for fresh seafood. If you're in a quandary about what to order, walk up to the fresh-fish counter, decide what looks good to you, and order it back at your table. The market smokes its own fish—the salmon/albacore combo is a must-try appetizer. Fresh fish entrées range from Utah rainbow trout to local thresher shark, plus skewers of scallops, oysters, ahi, and more. The Fish Market is close to the racetrack.

A good choice in town is **Carlos & Annie's Cafe** (1454 Camino Del Mar, 858/755-4601, $$), a Southwestern-themed restaurant that regularly wins "best breakfast" awards on the strength of such offerings as Carlos' Omelet (chicken, salsa, avocado, cheese, and Spanish sauce). On the other side of the street, **Cafe Del Mar** (1247 Camino Del Mar, 858/481-1133, $$) serves brick-oven pizza and creative pasta dishes, such as sautéed salmon with dill vodka sauce over penne, all priced very reasonably.

NIGHTLIFE

Generally, the night moves made in Del Mar are the sort of stretching and yawning calisthenics performed immediately before crawling into bed. As in most professedly quiet towns, there's not much to do beyond eating well, strolling a few blocks through the village after dinner, or maybe downing a highball at L'Auberge Del Mar to the polite accompaniment of a tinkling piano. You might find a little action in the bar at **Bully's North** (1404 Camino Del Mar, 858/755-1660), a prime-rib palace with an outdoor patio that's open till midnight. Otherwise, if you want nightlife you'll just have to roll up to Solana Beach, which has plenty of it.

Solana Beach

Solana Beach's claim to fame has been as party headquarters for north San Diego County. The townsfolk, whose per capita income of $65,000 per year is said to be even greater than that of Del Mar, haven't exactly been thrilled that their community has been the one to play Pied Piper to a hip-hopping party crowd. They've been working to change their image with tighter permitting and more vigilant law enforcement. As a result the nightlife has gradually become more evenly spread around this end of the county, spilling into Cardiff

and up into Carlsbad. Ultimately, northern San Diego County is one big seaside overflow valve for the city of San Diego, 25 miles to the south.

Solana Beach (population 13,000) calls itself "the best spot under the sun." It's got two miles of beach, a number of decent restaurants and delis, and the Belly Up Tavern, one of the best live-music clubs in the country. In the past decade, Solana Beach has become a trendier spot, with splashy architectural and landscaping statements being made by hip entrepreneurs who've gravitated here. The San Diego Freeway (I-5) splits the town into east and west halves. U.S. 101 is the coast road in these parts, and this is where the town lets its hair down.

On an odd note, Solana Beach was the home base of the Heaven's Gate religious cult, whose members committed group suicide in March 1997. Economically, they fit the profile of the area. Mostly young, they designed websites for a living. They wore Nike tennis shoes ("just do it") the night 39 of them made their attempted afterlife rendezvous with a comet.

For more information, contact the Solana Beach Chamber of Commerce, 210 West Plaza Street, Solana Beach, CA 92075, 858/755-4775, www.solanabeachchamber.com; or San Diego North Convention & Visitors Bureau, 360 North Escondido Boulevard, Escondido, CA 92025, 760/745-4741 or 800/848-3336, www.sandiegonorth.com.

BEACHES

Access to Solana Beach's beaches is blocked, to a great degree, by residential housing. However, you can get through at **Seascape Surf Park,** accessible from the 500 block of South Sierra Avenue. A half mile north, Sierra Avenue meets Lomas Santa Fe Boulevard, dumping traffic into a large free parking lot at Fletcher Cove.

The coastal park in Solana Beach—we hesitate to call it a beach—is **Fletcher Cove Park.** It's an attractive natural setting, especially from the bluff-top vista point, which looks out over the pretty but fragile cliffs to the churning ocean below. The cove was blasted into being by early settlers, who dynamited the cliff bases. Obviously, environmental regulations would prohibit such a knuckleheaded move now.

Not surprisingly, there is no longer a beach at Fletcher Cove Park. It was devastated by a series of El Niño's (especially in 1998), and they trucked in sand from Yuma, Arizona, to raise the beach by six feet. That washed away, too, so now there's just the newly built park, complete with artificial turf. The beach is gone and the grass is fake, so you can draw your own conclusions. Ours aren't so favorable.

A half mile farther north is **Tide Beach Park.** At the base of a bluff reachable by a stairway, it's good for tidepooling, spear fishing, surf casting, and scuba diving. Nearly all of Tide Beach Park was lost in the winter of 1998, and subsequent renourishment projects have replaced sand with pebbles, making barefooting nearly impossible. The reef here is known as Table Tops. It makes for striking scenery but a bummer of a swimming beach.

30 SEASCAPE SURF PARK

Location: stairwell at 500 block of South Sierra Avenue in Solana Beach
Parking/Fees: free parking lot and street parking
Hours: 6 A.M.-10 P.M.
Facilities: lifeguards (seasonal) and showers
Contact: Solana Beach Department of Marine Safety, 858/755-1569

31 FLETCHER COVE PARK

Location: 111 South Sierra Avenue in Solana Beach
Parking/Fees: free parking lot
Hours: 6 A.M.-10 P.M.

Facilities: lifeguards, restrooms, showers, and picnic tables
Contact: Solana Beach Department of Marine Safety, 858/755-1569

32 TIDE BEACH PARK

Location: Pacific Avenue and Solana Vista Drive in Solana Beach
Parking/Fees: free street parking
Hours: 6 A.M.-10 P.M.
Facilities: lifeguards (seasonal) and showers
Contact: Solana Beach Department of Marine Safety, 858/755-1569

ACCOMMODATIONS

Solana Beach isn't exactly geared toward the tourist trade. The best choices are franchises: the **Courtyard by Marriott Solana Beach** (717 South U.S. 101, 858/792-8200, $$) and **Holiday Inn Express** (621 South U.S. 101, 858/350-0111, $$). Both are clean, attractive hotels within walking distance of the beach.

COASTAL CUISINE

A hip hangout on the relatively starved Solana Beach dining scene is **Pacific Coast Grill** (437 South U.S. 101, 858/794-4632, $$$). Diners can bring their dogs and sit on the garden patio (thereby obviating the need for a doggie bag). A good spread of Mexican food can be had at **Fidel's** (749 Genevieve Street, 858/755-5292, $$), a crowded cantina with an unpretentious atmosphere.

NIGHTLIFE

The **Belly Up Tavern** (143 South Cedros Avenue, 858/481-9022) enjoys a national reputation and is beloved by musicians and music fans alike. A roomy club, it is typical of other well-run, similarly sized nightclubs around the country that provide a living to musicians who might otherwise be applying for unemployment benefits. These include ghosts of the 1960s who have gone from stardom to cult status, as well as current up-and-comers. One night we caught a droll, low-key set by Dan Hicks, the San Francisco scene pioneer and gypsy jazz-pop stylist whose justifiably cynical disenchantment with the music business made for entertaining between-song patter.

Roots-oriented journeymen like Dave Alvin and Jorma Kaukonen and bluesy jam bands like the Radiators, along with a hefty number of reggae and R&B acts, fill the calendar at the Belly Up. The acoustics are great throughout, and the whole operation is first-class. Note that you must be 21 or older to come here. Some years back the club added a bistro-style restaurant next door, the **Wild Note Cafe** (143 South Cedros Avenue, 858/720-9000). The food is affordable, healthy, and hearty, while the music tends toward singer/songwriters and light jazz and funk. One duo name we'll never forget: Bongo and John. Check the Belly Up Tavern's website (www.bellyup.com) for concert schedules.

Cardiff-by-the-Sea

Cardiff-by-the-Sea takes its name from the Welsh seaport city. It is the most unassuming of the north San Diego County beach towns. The only industry that Cardiff (population 11,800) ever had dates back to 1912—a kelp-processing operation that closed three years later. Its chief attractions are the quiet residential neighborhoods east of U.S. 101 and two state beaches located opposite lagoons one at each end of town. Most of Cardiff lies uphill and east of the beach and railroad tracks. Given the condition of the beaches, these residents are no doubt glad they don't own beachfront property. Technically, Cardiff-by-the-Sea is part of the City of Encinitas, having participated in a four-in-one municipal conjoining back in 1986. In reality, the town has its own identity crisis. The identity is low-key, and the crisis is ruined beaches.

For more information, contact the Cardiff-by-the-Sea Chamber of Commerce, 2013 San Elijo Avenue, Cardiff-by-the-Sea, CA 92007, 760/436-0431, www.cardiffbythesea.org; or San Diego North Convention & Visitors Bureau, 360 North Escondido Boulevard, Escondido, CA 92025, 760/745-4741 or 800/848-3336, www.sandiegonorth.com.

BEACHES
Cardiff State Beach lies west of San Elijo Lagoon, separated from it by Old U.S. 101. The beach was once great for swimming, windsurfing, board surfing, and surf casting, but nearly all of the beach and the sidewalk and fencing behind it are gone, victims of a succession of El Niño years and winter storms. Cardiff is among the most severely impacted beaches in California. It is hard to describe the devastation, except to say that the scene is one of cataclysm. The parking lots are rutted and narrowed, the collection kiosks abandoned. The chain-link fences are listing, having absorbed repeated poundings from an ocean that has sent the beach into retreat—except there's no place to retreat, because of the seaside parking lots, restaurants, and highway. It is a disaster area, pure and simple, with gouged chunks of concrete and rusted metal skeletons littering the landscape in mute testimony to the ocean's might.

San Elijo State Beach is best known for camping, being the southernmost developed campground in the state system. Set high atop a jagged cliff, San Elijo's 171 sites fill up quickly. Reserve early, especially for the summer months. The campground is nicely laid out, with scraggly hedges providing some shade and privacy. The sites closest to the cliff's edge are the best. From these spots you can hear the waves crashing at night. You're also closer to the wooden stairs that lead to the beach. It is a long, lifeguarded beach and a good place to savor a gorgeous California sunset. The ongoing problem is that the narrowing campground has been pinned between a rock (U.S. 101) and a sandy place (the eroding beach). There's been talk of rerouting the channel connecting the lagoon and ocean so that it doesn't run on a beach-paralleling north-south route, which wreaks havoc on the bluffs and beach at Cardiff-by-the-Sea. A countervailing argument might go that the natural erosion of bluffs provides the very sand that replenishes these beaches, so it's probably the highway that ought to be moved.

To the east is the **San Elijo Lagoon Ecological Reserve,** a 1,000-acre wildlife haven that is one of the last wetlands of this size and purity in Southern California. Thanks to local activists, not only are the wetlands saved from developers, but the lagoon is accessible to hikers and bird-watchers.

33 CARDIFF STATE BEACH

Location: one mile south of Cardiff-by-the-Sea along Old U.S. 101 at San Elijo Lagoon
Parking/Fees: $8 entrance fee per vehicle
Hours: dawn to dusk
Facilities: none
Contact: San Elijo State Beach, 760/753-5091

34 SAN ELIJO STATE BEACH

Location: Cardiff-by-the-Sea along Old U.S. 101 at Chesterfield Drive
Parking/Fees: $8 entrance fee per vehicle; camping fees for sites on the ocean $39-44 per night with hookups, $30-35 per night without hookups, plus $7.50 reservation fee; inland campsites $10 less per night
Hours: dawn to dusk
Facilities: lifeguards, restrooms, showers, and picnic tables
Contact: San Elijo State Beach, 760/753-5091

ACCOMMODATIONS

If camping in the sand at San Elijo State Beach is too rustic for your taste, try the **Countryside Inn** (1661 Villa Cardiff Drive, 760/944-0427, $$). It's a 102-room Colonial-style hotel, once independent but now part of the Comfort Inn chain, with bed-and-

breakfast amenities. One of the more striking constructions along this stretch of coast is **Cardiff by the Sea Lodge** (142 Chesterfield Drive, 760/944-6474, $$$). With its themed rooms, circular architecture, and rooftop fire pit for sunset savoring, this 17-room lodge makes a cozy romantic hideaway for couples.

COASTAL CUISINE

Cardiff has its own beachside "restaurant row" along Old U.S. 101. The place to dine is the **Beach House** (2530 South U.S. 101, 760/753-1321, $$$), a pricey, glitzy seafood restaurant so close to the beach the fish could practically swim from the ocean to the broiler. A rock revetment is all that stands between restaurant and waves. The parking lot attests to its popularity, as an army of young valets in tennis shorts and monogrammed pullovers take turns running the 40-yard dash, car keys jangling, to park or retrieve vehicles. The ocean views are fantastic, so try to come at sunset.

Next door, **Charlie's by the Sea** (2526 South U.S. 101, 760/942-1300, $$$) forthrightly advertises "any closer and you'd be wet." In truth, any closer and it'll be closed, as Charlie's by the Sea looks more like Charlie's *in* the Sea. The stylistically varied menu offers such entrées as macadamia-dusted scallops, sesame-seared salmon, and sea bass stuffed with smoked lobster and crab. Again, the picture windows look out on the vast churning ocean and the boulders that protect the restaurant from its fury.

Another neighbor on Cardiff's restaurant row is the **Chart House** (2588 South U.S. 101, 760/436-3751, $$$). It's part of a chain that serves excellent and inventive seafood dishes (sesame-crusted salmon, grilled tuna with mango relish) from choice ocean-view locations. If you miss it here, there are Chart Houses in Coronado, La Jolla, Oceanside, and Malibu, all of which have unsurpassable ocean views. Try to wrangle a window table, because the sights are as good as the edibles. Avoid the valet fee at the Chart House and Beach House by parking alongside U.S. 101 for free.

NIGHTLIFE

The **Kraken Bar & Restaurant** (2531 South U.S. 101, 760/436-6483) bills itself as "the bar by the beach...where the locals still and probably always will party." It has pool tables, pinball machines, and six color TVs. Summer happy hour runs 4 P.M.–7 P.M.

Encinitas and Leucadia

In 1986, Encinitas became a municipality made up of four formerly autonomous towns: Encinitas, Leucadia, Cardiff-by-the-Sea, and Olivenhain. Their conjoining is mainly a governmental matter. Olivenhain is rural and inland, while Cardiff stands apart from the others by virtue of geography. Encinitas and Leucadia, however, do seem joined at the hip—with the emphasis on hip, for these are two of San Diego County's most swinging coastal communities.

Encinitas is bounded at the south and north by the San Elijo and Batiquitos lagoons. The town is subdivided into "Historic Encinitas"— the area along U.S. 101, near the beaches—and "New Encinitas," along El Camino Real. The town's main problem is beach erosion. For years it's been fighting to save its beaches and ocean-front real estate. At one time there were Sixth and Fifth Streets in Encinitas. They do not exist now, having been annexed (so to speak) by the Pacific Ocean. A local geologist, using old surveys and maps, has determined that 800 feet of Encinitas's shoreline has disappeared in the last hundred years. The cliffs are made of sandstone, shale, and siltstone. Constant assault by waves opens cracks and fissures that eventually cause the cliff tops to pitch forward. Some coastal access points have washed out, and their precipitous stairwells are off-limits.

This is not to say Encinitas's beachfront does not have appeal. Despite the obstacles, the beaches are popular, primarily with teenagers (many from inland communities). Occasionally they exhibit threatening behavior and upset residents who have been coming here for years. The biggest story in town during one visit concerned "drunken abuse" taking place along the stairwell to Stone Steps Beach, where beer-drinking slackers were trying to intimidate families into leaving "their" beach, forcing them to join the crowds down at Moonlight Beach.

One of our favorite places in downtown Encinitas is **La Paloma Theater** (471 South U.S. 101, 760/436-5774). A slice of Southern California's socio-cultural past, this funky old single-screen movie palace dates from 1927. Today, it hosts everything from rock bands to first-run films to independent flicks. Spirit, one of California's greatest rock groups—led by the late, lamented Randy California— recorded a live album here. It's the sort of place where the latest surfing documentary is accorded the same fanfare that a new James Bond flick receives in Los Angeles. If you can believe it, they still show *The Rocky Horror Picture Show* on Fridays at midnight.

Another must-see attraction in Encinitas is **Quail Botanical Gardens** (230 Quail Gardens Drive, 619/436-3036, www.qbgardens .org). It's a 30-acre collection of plants and trees native to California, as well as exotic tropicals, palms, and bamboos. Visitors can take a self-guided tour of the premises, which includes a chaparral grove, a bird sanctuary, and more than 5,000 species of botanical life. Several of the many exotic environments include Africa, New Zealand, and the Canary Islands. Admission is $10 for adults and $5 for children 3–12, and it's open 9 A.M.–5 P.M. daily year-round. Interestingly, in the hills surrounding Encinitas, a thriving nursery and greenhouse industry grows most of the carnations dyed and sold on city streets around the world.

Leucadia is welded to Encinitas at a point where the latter's strip malls give way to un-moored (that is, un-malled) businesses, some of which look one season away from bank-

SAN DIEGO COAST

SELF-REALIZATION FELLOWSHIP HERMITAGE AND MEDITATION GARDENS

The most intriguing spot in Encinitas is a place of worship. The 17-acre grounds of the Self-Realization Fellowship Hermitage and Meditation Gardens (215 K Street, Encinitas, 760/753-2888) cling to the cliffs at the southern end of town. The nearby **Self-Realization Fellowship Temple** (939 Second Street, Encinitas, 760/436-7220) is visually dominated by three towers that loom above U.S. 101 like an exotic hallucination. The lotus towers were designed by Paramahansa Yogananda (1893-1952), the spiritual leader who founded the center in 1937 and built the temple in 1938. At the time, it was the largest building on the Southern California coast.

Yogananda dedicated his life to uniting East and West through the ancient art of meditation. He lived in the hermitage for several years and helped design the cliffside meditation gardens. He planted the ancient ming tree on the site of his favorite pond, which was drained when the cliffs collapsed in 1941. Yogananda made a name for himself internationally with his *Autobiography of a Yogi*, which he completed here in 1946. It is now considered a classic of spiritual literature. The lively, detailed text traces the spiritual awakening of this gentle man, whose teachings profoundly affected the lives of many Westerners, including Greta Garbo, Leopold Stokowski, and Christopher Isherwood.

The best indication of Yogananda's spiritual openness is that his retreat and gardens have always been open to visitors. You are free to stroll and meditate to your heart's content, with no attempts at proselytizing. The meditation gardens are open for visitation Tuesday-Saturday 9 A.M.-5 P.M. and Sunday 11 A.M.-5 P.M. The nearby temple is open daily (except Monday) for meditation and prayer noon-4 P.M. Incidentally, the gardens are just steps away from a great beach (Swami's) and an eatery called **Swami's Cafe** (1163 South Highway 101, 760/944-0612, $$), specializing in smoothies and "whole foods."

ruptcy. Founded by English spiritualists in 1888, Leucadia lies along a congenial, tree-lined, and slightly run-down stretch of U.S. 101 that parallels the crumbling sea cliffs. Leucadia retains a bit more of an alternative flavor than Encinitas. It's the kind of place where New Age vegans, old-guard hippies, and dying VW bugs go to roost. The town that time forgot, Leucadia seems happily stuck in a tie-dyed mindset that feels more like the 1960s than the new millennium.

We like it here, as they've managed to keep heavy-handed developmental imperatives at bay. Instead you'll find small, nonfranchised businesses from taco shops to smoothie stands, from psychics to espresso bars, from greenhouses to New Agey places with names like The Energy Within. Eucalyptus trees line the

road, and a homey, naturalistic ambience is exuded. A huge hill separates the road and town from the beach. Turn west off the highway onto any side street and you'll climb up and then dipsy-doodle down toward the beach.

Leucadia means "Isle of Paradise" in Greek, and the streets here are named for Greek deities (Daphne, Diana, Phoebe, Glaucus). But as in the Elysian Fields, not much goes on here. The number-one industry appears to be the selling of used merchandise, with a disproportionate number of businesses along U.S. 101 involved in the secondhand trade (thrift shops, consignments, used clothing, etc.). Our favorite was a yellow U-Haul on whose sides was inscribed an offer to buy used blue jeans 10 A.M.-3 P.M. on Sundays. A roadside motel called the Ocean Inn is not on the ocean at all,

SURF WRITERS

Because of their good surf, hidden coves, and relative affordability, Encinitas and Leucadia are popular with surfers, especially older ones with the means to live on the coast. Among the best known is Chris Ahrens, the publisher of the now-defunct *Longboarder* magazine and author of a book of true surf stories called *Good Things Love Water*. It's a sympathetic, if somewhat sentimental, collection of tall tales and profiles. One surfer described it as "someone standing around a fire ring talking with other surfers."

Longboarder magazine, back issues of which are fetching collectors' prices on the Internet, shared space on the magazine rack with *The Surfer's Journal, Longboard Magazine* (both based in San Clemente), *Surfer*, and others. Ahrens on the surfer's raison d'être: "Once you're out in the water, the rules of the land are left behind. A whole new government takes place. It's a kind of peaceful anarchy." (Or maybe not so peaceful: Plenty of bloodshed over territory and waves rights occur on California's choicest wave-riding beaches.)

Other surf writers of distinction include Greg Noll, whose *Da Bull: Life Over the Edge* is this legend's oral history, generally regarded as the best book about surfing in existence. Mike Doyle, a surfing legend in his own right, has published a memoir called *Morning Glass*, which captures the halcyon days of surfing. The diary-like entries are written chronologically and make a good historical reference tool.

We can't resist commenting on *The Pump House Gang*, Tom Wolfe's 1966 attempt to capture the manners and mores of a group of surf bums who made their home on the beaches of La Jolla. His sneering portrait is universally reviled by surfers. Here is an excerpt: "Their backs look like some kind of salmon-colored porcelain shells. They were staring out to sea like Phrygian sacristans looking for a sign.... I foresaw the day when the California coastline would be littered with the bodies of aged and abandoned Surferkinder, like so many beached whales."

Here is a hand-picked selection of books on the subject of surfers and surfing:

- *All for a Few Perfect Waves: The Audacious Life and Legend of Rebel Surfer Miki Dora*, by David Rensin. Gripping bio of legendary surfer/con man and self-proclaimed "King of Malibu."

- *Book of Waves*, by Drew Kampion.

- *California Coastal Access Guide* (Berkeley: University of California Press, 6th edition, 2003). This resource guide provides definitive information, in written and tabular form, on every publicly accessible beach. Changes from one edition to another are so minor that, unlike this book, each new edition is really more like a reprinting.

- *California Surfriders*, by John Heath "Doc" Ball. First published in 1946 and now reprinted, this pictorial record of "thrills, spills, personalities, and places of California surfing" was lovingly put together by Doc Ball, the first professional surf photographer.

- *Caught Inside: A Surfer's Year on the California Coast*, by Daniel Duane. An episodic, readable account of a guy who spent a year chasing waves. He doesn't sugarcoat the surfing life — some of the characters he befriends are deplorable — which makes the book all the more authentic.

- *Complete Guide to Surfing*, by Peter L. Dixon. Part history but mostly how-to, it's a good, contemporary (published in 2001) addition to the surf-book shelf.

- *Cowabunga!: A History of Surfing,* by Lee Wardlaw. Although not as definitive as *Surfing: The Ultimate Pleasure,* it has its charms.

- *Girl in the Curl: A Century of Women in Surfing,* by Andrea Gabbard. The fairer sex takes its turn in the lineup.

- *Hawaiian Surfriders 1935,* by Tom Blake. This is the first book ever written on the history of the sport. The author is the inventor of the paddle board, and a surfing legend in his own right.

- *Learning Hawaiian Surfing: A Royal Sport at Waikiki Beach, Honolulu, 1907,* by Jack London. Yes, this is *the* Jack London, who learned the sport in the summer of 1907 from the great George Freeth.

- *Let's Go, Let's Go! The Biography of Lorrin "Whitey" Harrison: California's Legendary Surf Pioneer,* by Rosie Harrison Clark.

- *Photo/Stoner,* by Matt Warshaw and Jeff Divine. The chronicle of Ron Stoner, who in the mid-1960s was generally regarded as the best surfing photographer. His images, in fact, helped define the sport in the mind's eye of young Americans, an innocent idyll before condominiums aesthetically ruined America's coastlines. At the peak of his fame and talent, Stoner disappeared, lost to drugs and madness. This book sympathetically captures his lost art and his precipitous fall.

- *Stoked: A History of Surf Culture,* by Drew Kampion.

- *Surf Rage: A Surfer's Guide to Turning Negatives into Positives.* The author, Nat Young, wrote this book after being assaulted while trying to surf his home break. He is to be commended for bringing the darker side of surfing to light. We hope it does some good.

- *Surf Science: An Introduction to Waves for Surfing,* by Tony Butt. Surfing meets physics and oceanography, and the attentive wave-rider is the winner.

- *Surfer's Start-Up: A Beginner's Guide to Surfing,* by Doug Werner. An easy-to-read and best-selling how-to guide. Warner also wrote *Longboarder's Start-up: A Guide to Longboard Surfing.*

- *Surfing California,* by Bank Wright. An older guide to the best surfing beaches, written in inimitable surf-speak by one of the legends.

- *Surfing San Onofre to Point Dume, 1936–1942,* by Don James.

- *Surfing: The Sport of Hawaiian Kings,* by Ben R. Finney and James D. Houston.

- *Surfing: The Ultimate Pleasure,* by Leonard Lucernos. By general consensus, this is the best history of the sport.

- *The Big Drop! Classic Big Wave Surfing Stories,* by John Long and Hai Van Sponholz (eds.).

- *The Encyclopedia of Surfing,* by Matt Warshaw. Includes 1,500 entries on surfing, arranged encyclopedia-style by a noted surf writer who has authored three other books on the sport.

- *The Surfin'ary,* by Trevor Cralle. There are 3,000 entries in this surfer's dictionary.

- *Waikiki Beach Boys,* by Grady Timmons. A chronicle of the original Hawaiians who gave the world the sport of surfing.

The **California Surf Museum** (223 North Coast Highway, Oceanside, 760/721-6876) is a good place to begin your hunt for many of these titles. Some are out of print, but you might luck out at used bookstores and eBay!

being situated at the foot of a hill blocks from the Pacific. A generic trailer park bears the misleadingly pastoral name Mobile Village—Valley of Dreams.

Still, folks in Leucadia live and let live, work construction jobs when available, eat tacos and brown rice, use environmentally safe products, and stare unconcerned when cars pass through town. They simply don't need vacationers in Leucadia, which is just as well, because the beaches aren't big enough to attract them and the cliffs are eroding. The sign at one washed-out beach access had this spray-painted addendum: No tourists. Go home. It might as well have read: No beach. Go home. In a funny way, being so removed from the breakneck world of the 21st century, it's the sort of place we don't just like visiting but could see ourselves calling home.

For more information, contact the Encinitas Chamber of Commerce, 859 Second Street, Encinitas, CA 92024, 760/753-6041, www.encinitaschamber.com; or the San Diego North Convention & Visitors Bureau, 360 North Escondido Boulevard, Escondido, CA 92025, 760/745-4741 or 800/848-3336, www.sandiegonorth.com.

BEACHES

The beaches of Encinitas generally look a lot healthier in this decade than they did the previous one, thanks to a major sand renourishment project. Still, you can renourish the beaches all you want, but you're only buying time and wasting money. A wise investor would not want to own oceanfront property in Encinitas, no matter how splendid the view. Signs warn, Unstable Cliffs and Frequent Bluff Failure, and the sandstone along this stretch of coast is especially prone to erosion. At least in the short term, the beaches of Encinitas are more fun to play on than they've been in a while.

Starting from the south, **Swami's Surf Beach** is below Seacliff Roadside Park (free parking, day-use only), a bluff-top city park at the south end of the Self-Realization Fellowship Retreat, Gardens, and Hermitage.

During the winter, this is surfer heaven, and in the summer it still offers plenty of rough fun for surf riders. A long stairwell topped by white wooden crests leads along the cliff face to a fabled small beach. Surfers bob a good distance from shore while lifeguards look on. The cliff face has been reinforced with plantings, and the stretch of bluff from here north to D Street has been designated a Marine Life Refuge. Swami's Cafe is across from the Moonie temple and the beach.

Just above Swami's, and accessible only on foot, is **Boneyard Beach.** At low tide, small, protective coves afford romantics, nudists, and surfers privacy for their various activities. Just don't get caught by a rising tide with your drawers down.

D Street Viewpoint is accessible at the end of D Street in Encinitas. Steps lead down to a rock-backed city-run beach not unlike Swami's, with a lifeguard. Speaking of views, we caught a dandy one at the D Street beach overlook. Stairs descend along the cliff face, with gorgeous plantings on either side. At the top of the stairs, we admired both the beach vista and a nearly perfect specimen of California pulchritude hanging out with her surfer pals. This is, we decided, what is meant by California dreaming.

At the foot of Encinitas Boulevard is **Moonlight Beach,** the centerpiece of the coast in these parts. There's a free municipal parking lot, plenty of facilities, volleyball nets, pumped-in sand, and a pack of happy sunbathers. If you're not partaking of the party on the sand—and Moonlight Beach is one of the most accessible and popular beaches in north San Diego County—then you should at least drop by to gaze down on the action from the bluff-top parking lot. What a view! Just one troubling thing: Water quality has historically been a cloudy issue at Moonlight Beach, owing to its proximity to a sewage treatment plant.

The access to **Stone Steps Beach** is on Neptune Avenue. Park for free in the quiet neighborhood along Neptune's curbs and climb down the steep and plentiful (97 by our count) stone steps, paying homage to the mural of a mermaid on the half-shell. A lifeguard stand, marked with surf and tide advisories, is at the bottom of the stairwell. The beach attracts scores of surfers. If you walk north from Stone Steps Beach, you'll reach the **Encinitas Beach.** There is no other direct access to it from shore, which makes it secluded enough to please space-seeking swimmers, surfers, and solitary sorts.

Formerly Leucadia State Beach but now a city-managed area, **Beacon's Beach** lies at the foot of a yellow sandstone cliff and can be reached by hiking down a treacherous trail of sandbags, stairs, and switchbacks. You can park for free at the Beacon's Beach access and scuttle down to the beach, where the copious kelp that washes ashore gets entangled with the equally abundant litter. You can look up and down the coast from the base of the cliffs at Beacon's Beach and see the same things: steep, eroding cliffs and packs of surfers competing for waves. From "Kenzie of Leucadia," a Beacon's booster: "Locals love to boast that the only place more crowded than our line-up is I-5 at rush hour after a heavy rainstorm."

Above the beach in the lot, a roving surfing instructor (his van read "Kahuna Bob's Surf School") was giving preliminary lessons to a group of youngsters who looked so eager to hit the water that they were positively shivering with excitement. (Call **Kahuna Bob's Surf School,** 760/721-7700.) Beyond them, another Leucadia resident, also a surfer, stared wistfully at Beacon's rugged waves. He'd suffered a shoulder injury in a nasty spill some weeks earlier and found himself beached until it healed. In the meantime he pedaled a bike to stay in shape, but it just wasn't the same. Leucadia was his alternative to Pacific Beach, where he'd been living until he was squeezed out by mounting crowds and rents. Pacific Beach had, in turn, been his alternative to Ocean Beach, which had been his alternative to Imperial Beach. Gradually, he said, he will make his way north to the magic land of Santa Barbara. "I want to live at the beach forever," he announced with no solicitation. For now Leucadia is home; relaxed, uncrowded, and nontrendy, it is his isle of paradise. Besides, he knows someone with private access to the beach.

At the north end of Neptune Avenue is **Grandview,** another city-run beach access. It's nicely landscaped, with palm trees running down the hill beside the stairwell. It's a grand spot from which to wistfully gaze at the horizon, especially at sunset.

35 SWAMI'S SURF BEACH

Location: 1298 First Street, below Seacliff Roadside Park in Encinitas
Parking/Fees: free parking lot
Hours: 5 A.M.-10 P.M.
Facilities: lifeguards, restrooms, and picnic area
Contact: Encinitas Parks and Recreation, 760/633-2740

36 BONEYARD BEACH

Location: in Encinitas north of Swami's, between E and J Streets
Parking/Fees: free street parking
Hours: 5 A.M.-10 P.M.
Facilities: none
Contact: Encinitas Parks and Recreation, 760/633-2740

37 D STREET VIEWPOINT

Location: in Encinitas at 450 D Street
Parking/Fees: free parking lot
Hours: 5 A.M.-10 P.M.
Facilities: lifeguards
Contact: Encinitas Parks and Recreation, 760/633-2740

SAN DIEGO COAST

© PARKE PUTERBAUGH

Swami's Surf Beach

38 MOONLIGHT BEACH

Location: in Encinitas at Fourth and B Streets
Parking/Fees: free parking lot
Hours: 5 A.M.-10 P.M.
Facilities: lifeguards, restrooms, showers, picnic tables, and fire rings
Contact: Encinitas Parks and Recreation, 760/633-2740

39 STONE STEPS BEACH

Location: in Encinitas at Neptune Avenue and El Portal Street
Parking/Fees: free street parking
Hours: 5 A.M.-10 P.M.
Facilities: lifeguards
Contact: Encinitas Parks and Recreation, 760/633-2740

40 ENCINITAS BEACH

Location: in Encinitas north of Stone Steps Beach
Parking/Fees: free street parking at Stone Steps Beach
Hours: 5 A.M.-10 P.M.
Facilities: none
Contact: Encinitas Parks and Recreation, 760/633-2740

41 BEACON'S BEACH

Location: in Leucadia at 948 Neptune Avenue
Parking/Fees: free street parking
Hours: 5 A.M.-10 P.M.
Facilities: lifeguards
Contact: Encinitas Parks and Recreation, 760/633-2740

42 GRANDVIEW

Location: in Leucadia at the north end of Neptune Avenue

Parking/Fees: free parking lot

Hours: 5 A.M.-10 P.M.

Facilities: none

Contact: Encinitas Parks and Recreation, 760/633-2740

RECREATION AND ATTRACTIONS

• **Bike/Skate Rentals:** B & L Bike, 211 North Coast Highway, Solana Beach, 858/481-4148; Nytro, 940 South Coast Highway, Encinitas, 800/697-8007

• **Ecotourism:** San Elijo Lagoon Ecological Reserve, Cardiff-by-the-Sea, 760/436-3944

• **Rainy Day Attraction:** Self-Realization Fellowship Retreat, Gardens, and Hermitage, 215 K Street, Encinitas, 760/753-2888

• **Shopping/Browsing:** Carlsbad Company Stores, Paseo del Norte, Carlsbad, 760/804-9000

• **Surf Shop:** Solana Beach Surf Shop, 363 U.S. 101, Solana Beach, 760/481-1354; Salty Sister, 2796 Carlsbad Boulevard, Carlsbad, 760/434-1122

• **Vacation Rentals:** A&N, 6986 El Camino Real, Suite H, Carlsbad, 760/438-6811

ACCOMMODATIONS

Beware of motels with "Ocean" or "Beach" in their names that are located on a highway bypass nowhere near a beach. In particular they should be avoided in Encinitas and Leucadia, where flyblown motels tout "sea breezes" and "views" when the only views they offer are of traffic and consignment shops. The only place that's actually on the beach in either town is the **Moonlight Beach Motel** (233 Second Street, 760/753-0623, $), a functional and affordable three-story place with balcony views of the town's biggest beach.

The **Pacific Surf Inn** (1076 North U.S. 101, 760/436-8763, $) in Leucadia has a clean, well-tended appearance. An offbeat alternative is **Leucadia Inn-by-the-Sea** (960 North Coast Highway, Leucadia, 760/942-1668, $$). Though it's not "by" the sea but three blocks away on a busy highway, its six "whimsical theme rooms" will amuse lovers of roadside oddities. They range from African Safari to Hollywood Nostalgia, and from Nantucket to Mexico, which is quite a geographic spread.

Other viable bunking options are the campground at San Elijo State Beach, straddling Cardiff-by-the-Sea and Encinitas, and a **Holiday Inn Express** (607 Leucadia Boulevard, 760/944-3800, $) in Leucadia.

COASTAL CUISINE

Along U.S. 101 to the south, Encinitas is top-heavy with Italian and Mexican cafés. Their shopping-plaza backdrops are good indicators of the predictable fare they offer. Keep driving up the road to **DB Hackers** (101 Old U.S. 101, 760/436-3162, $), which serves good, quick fixes of seafood. The entrées are mostly fried and the outdoor patio treats you to car noise and construction, but the staff is friendly and the food is relatively cheap. We were more than sufficiently rejuvenated by the fish tacos we ate and the Jimmy Cliff tunes that were playing.

For breakfast head to **George's Restaurant** (641 South U.S. 101, 760/942-9549, $), a legendary hangout that was the original home of the California Surf Museum (now in Oceanside). The specialty is Surf's Up, a no-nonsense protein-heavy feed with scrambled eggs, ham, and American cheese on an English muffin, served with hash browns.

NIGHTLIFE

The friendliest bar in town is the **Full Moon Saloon** (485 First Street, 760/436-7397), which offers live music and a game room. More live music can be found at **First Street Bar** (656 First Street, 760/944-0233), which is popular with locals and is regularly voted best neighborhood bar.

Encinitas and Leucadia have, over the years, attracted a sizable contingent of New Age groupies and ex-hippies, some of whom can be found knocking back soy-milk lattes at the **Naked Bean Coffee Co.** (1126 First Street, 760/634-1347). The Naked Bean also features live music on weekends.

Carlsbad

Carlsbad is an anomaly. Of all the towns that cling to the Southern California coast, it is the only one not founded by a Spaniard or profoundly shaped by Latin influences. Instead, Carlsbad was the brainstorm of Gerhard Schutte, a German who came west from Nebraska to found a town of "small farms and gracious homes." His dream was made possible in 1883, when the Arizona Eastern Railway was completed, linking Southern California with the rest of civilization. This line also opened the land between Los Angeles and San Diego to homesteaders. Schutte headed up the list and moved on out.

Spanish and Native American influences are not entirely absent from the historical record. For centuries prior to Schutte's arrival, the Luseino tribe lived on the land between the two lagoons that form the boundaries of Carlsbad. However, they were quickly run off or subjugated by the missions when, in 1769, conquistador Gaspar de Portolá arrived with his faith-filled sidekick, Father Juan Crespi. Even though the entire area was under Spanish rule, the only lingering trace of their influence today is Agua Hedionda, the name given to one of the local lagoons. It means "stinking waters."

By the time Schutte arrived, the mission system was destroyed and the land grab was on. Schutte and his followers purchased a chunk of real estate and began planting eucalyptus trees and squaring off lots for a town. In the process they discovered that the mineral water from their wells was identical to that found at the renowned Ninth Spa in Karlsbad, Bohemia (now Karlovy Vary, in the Czech Republic).

The town took its name and identity from that happenstance, becoming a bastion of Old Europe in the New World. When word got out about the water, settlers began arriving. Humble, hardworking, and mostly English, these folks built their town to reflect their no-nonsense values.

Surprisingly little of the town has changed to this day. Original buildings are restored, and the subsequent growth of the town adheres to an established code, allowing Carlsbad to call itself a "village by the sea" (albeit a very high-toned and expensive village). With its Victorian, Dutch, and Bohemian architecture, Carlsbad has retained an appealingly antiquarian personality. This is remarkable, considering that Carlsbad lies between the drab military metropolis of Oceanside and the teeming asphalt sprawl of metropolitan San Diego.

Some of the local buildings—such as Magee House, Twin Inns, and the Santa Fe Railway Station—have been designated National Historic Landmarks. The best place to orient yourself to town history is the Visitor Information Center, inside the **Santa Fe Railway Station** on Carlsbad Village Drive. Built in 1887, it's the oldest commercial structure in town.

Another must-see is the **Alt Karlsbad Haus,** on Carlsbad Boulevard. Built in 1964 on the site of the first mineral well, it's an exact replica of Antonín Dvořák's house in Prague. The great composer, whose patriotic *New World Symphony* had achieved national notoriety when the town was founded, is honored by a plaque on one wall. On another wall is a plaque that reads, "The formation of the Hanseatic League in the 13th century gave birth to modern civilization, and through commerce and trade lifted Europe out of the Dark Ages." This is not the sort of plaque one is accustomed to reading in Southern California. Incidentally, Dvořák was a Bohemian who, out of love for his adopted home, offered to write a new national anthem for America. His spirit is a fitting one to symbolize the village of Carlsbad, which has lifted itself above

ALL ABOARD THE COASTER!

The Coaster is a "beach train" that offers regular rail service at eight stops in San Diego, Solana Beach, Encinitas, Carlsbad, and Oceanside. The Coaster also serves Old Town and downtown San Diego and Sorrento Valley. Environmentally, it is a viable alternative, burning low-sulfur-content fuel with high efficiency, greatly reducing particulate emissions. When operating at full capacity, each Coaster car means 700 fewer cars from I-5.

The Coaster carried 700,000 passengers during 1995, its first year of operation. By 2004, it was carrying 1.4 million passengers annually. The train is also good for one's mental health, sparing you the stress of highway car travel. The Coaster is scenic, too, running on tracks that parallel the ocean for most of its route. It operates from early morning to early evening, Monday through Saturday. At each station, you are dropped off a few short paces from the beach. Northern San Diego County has also instituted **The Breeze,** a clean-running bus system, and **The Sprinter,** which uses the first Diesel Multiple Units in the country to propel light rail trains.

For more information, contact **North County Transit District,** 810 Mission Avenue, Oceanside, CA 92054, 760/966-6500, www.gonctd.com.

the Dark Ages of the early 21st century by holding fast to civilized values.

Today, Carlsbad (population 95,500) seems to have everything going for it. Its public school system is one of the best in the country. The unemployment rate is the lowest in San Diego County. The public library is larger than some college libraries. The average daily temperature ranges from 58 degrees in January to 73 degrees in July. The young people look healthy, happy, well-groomed, and tattoo-free. ("Hey, John," one Beaver Cleaver look-alike yelled out a car window to a pal, "your new haircut looks great!") The old folks who choose to live out their years here look contented, too. After a few hours, you begin to wonder if this isn't the town Norman Rockwell was painting all those years.

Yes, Carlsbad is not just a place to vacation. It's a place to settle down and attend the church of your choice. This is a town of churches: Lutheran rest homes stand hard by humble Hispanic Pentecostal churches. We passed one of the latter, a sort of Quonset hut with a steeple, on the way to dinner. The door was open to the street and we heard the congregation singing and banging drums and tambourines. Two hours later, on our return

stroll, they were still at it, exhorted by a shouting minister.

Of the 37 square miles that fall within the city limits, less than one half have been developed, and the residents are vigilant against creeping mall sprawl. According to a resident, "We're putting the screws on too much more growth." Of course there's always something nipping at those Utopian heels. Most recently, it's a children's theme park called Legoland ("your destination for real family fun!"), which was built on Carlsbad Ranch, east of town. California's first new theme park in 25 years, the 128-acre **Legoland California** (1 Lego Drive, 760/918-5346) opened in March 1999 with much fanfare. Legoland has nine play areas inside the park, including Explore Village, Dino Town, Fun Town, and Land of Adventure. There are more than 50 rides on property. World landmarks, animals, and what-have-you have been rendered in plastic Lego bricks by the millions. There's also a Sea Life U.S. aquarium, a recent addition, which costs extra.

We don't know what it all signifies, but this much we can tell you: Adults pay $60 per day ($75 for a two-day pass), while kids 16 and under and seniors 61 and over are charged $50 apiece ($65 for a two-day pass). In addition, you're hit with a $10 parking fee. A family of four will spend $230 for a day at Legoland California even before the kids whine for their first soda pop or souvenir trinket.

We're more inclined to head to **Carlsbad Mineral Water Spa** (2802 Carlsbad Boulevard, 760/434-1887) for a rejuvenating soak. It's been around since 1882 and is a California Historic Site. More to the point, the pure water that comes from a 1,700-foot aquifer is 9,500 years old and full of rejuvenating minerals. The spa offers body wraps, massages, mud facials, mineral baths, and more.

For more information, contact the Carlsbad Convention and Visitors Bureau, 400 Carlsbad Village Drive, Carlsbad, CA 92008, 760/434-6093 or 800/227-5722, www.visit carlsbad.com; the Carlsbad Chamber of Commerce, 5934 Priestly Drive, Carlsbad, CA 92008, 760/931-8400, www.carlsbad.org; or San Diego North Convention & Visitors Bureau, 360 North Escondido Boulevard, Escondido, CA 92025, 760/745-4741 or 800/848-3336, www.sandiegonorth.com.

BEACHES

A good deal of the beach in the Carlsbad area eroded since the construction of Oceanside Harbor to the north, and El Niño storms claimed more of the sand in the late 1990s. You never know what you'll find in any given year on the beaches of Carlsbad: a sandless, eroded plain of cobbles or a newly renourished beach that hasn't yet washed away.

Coming from the south, **Ponto Beach**—a unit of South Carlsbad State Beach—is up first. It's by Batiquitos Lagoon, between Carlsbad and Leucadia. The location is a bit distressed, with an ad hoc string of parking spaces along the west side of Carlsbad Boulevard (U.S. 101). A rusty chain-link fence keeps people away from the crumbling cliff edges. There's an abandoned parking lot and fences everywhere. The future is not promising, and the present at Ponto is fairly dismal. Though surfers still get their kicks here, it's

not the kind of place others would go out of their way to visit.

The main unit of **South Carlsbad State Beach** is in some disarray, too. At one time, this was a highly desirable 226-site state-park campground occupying an inspirational blufftop setting overlooking the beach. Now campers are shoehorned into a narrow strip between the eroding cliffs and the four-lane boulevard. South Carlsbad appears to be fighting a losing battle against the elements. In some forthcoming year, the campground will succumb and the road will be next. Already, you can see stretches of U.S. 101 (designated "Old Coast Road") that have been abandoned and relocated east.

South Carlsbad State Beach runs into **Carlsbad State Beach,** which runs for four miles. A portion of Carlsbad State Beach has been designated **Tamarack Surf Beach** (where Tamarack Avenue meets Carlsbad Boulevard). This is a busy place; we found the sizable parking lot at Tamarack full on a Monday afternoon around sunset. Carlsbad State Beach is popular with all sorts of recreating types: bodysurfers, boogie boarders, swimmers, divers, and surf casters. Incidentally, another in-town stretch of sand has been designated **Robert C. Frazee State Beach,** but it (like Tamarack Surf Beach) is part of Carlsbad State Beach. The city of Carlsbad is none too happy that the state of California has decided to charge $8 per car to park at formerly free Tamarack. In fact the city has sued the California Coastal Commission to prohibit the charge, and the case was going to court as we were going to press. (Speaking of lawsuits, in 2007 the city of Carlsbad agreed to pay $12.5 million to residents of a condo complex after a landslide, caused by city-pipe discharges, destroyed eight condos.)

Carlsbad is a great town for walking, especially along its beaches. Two jogging/biking paths—one that runs beside Carlsbad Boulevard and one below it by the seawall that protects the beach—draw a tireless troupe of

California aerobicizers. They jog, they bike, they racewalk, they skateboard, they huff and puff…anything to maintain those hourglass figures. We watched a pair of toned-up girls sprinting up and down the stairs that link Carlsbad's pathways while conversing breathlessly about clothes, dates, and office politics. Many bring along their dogs, who run with their owners or pull them on skateboards.

The north part of town has been generously seeded with street-end accesses, each of which has stairs that lead to the beach (but no facilities). As in south Oceanside, north Carlsbad is a largely middle-class residential neighborhood, and the main point of these accesses appears to be to allow local residents to get to the beach.

Believe it or not, the "stinking waters" at **Agua Hedionda Lagoon** (east of Carlsbad City Beach) are popular with swimmers and water-skiers. Boats and water-skis can be rented at **Snug Harbor Marina** (4215 Harrison Street, 760/434-3089). A nice hiking/biking trail runs along the shore of the lagoon.

43 PONTO BEACH

Location: between Leucadia and Carlsbad on Old U.S. 101. Take the La Costa Drive exit off I-5 and follow it until it ends at Old U.S. 101 (Carlsbad Avenue) at Batiquitos Lagoon.
Parking/Fees: free roadside parking
Hours: dawn-sunset
Facilities: restrooms, showers, picnic tables, and barbecue grills
Contact: South Carlsbad State Beach, 760/438-3143

44 SOUTH CARLSBAD STATE BEACH

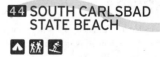

Location: three miles south of Carlsbad, along Carlsbad Boulevard

Parking/Fees: $8 entrance fee per vehicle; camping fees $20-25 per night inland, $30-35 per night beachfront, plus $7.50 reservation fee
Hours: dawn-sunset
Facilities: lifeguards, restrooms, showers, and picnic tables.
Contact: South Carlsbad State Beach, 760/438-3143

45 TAMARACK SURF BEACH

Location: Carlsbad Boulevard at Tamarack Avenue in Carlsbad
Parking/Fees: $8 entrance fee per vehicle
Hours: dawn-sunset
Facilities: lifeguards, restrooms, and picnic tables
Contact: South Carlsbad State Beach, 760/438-3143

46 ROBERT C. FRAZEE STATE BEACH

Location: in Carlsbad along Carlsbad Boulevard at Ocean Street
Parking/Fees: free street parking
Hours: dawn-sunset
Facilities: none
Contact: South Carlsbad State Beach, 760/438-3143

ACCOMMODATIONS

It's not cheap to stay in the "village by the sea." The village mentality can be a little tough on the wallet. **La Costa Resort & Spa** (2100 Costa del Mar Road, 760/438-9111, www.la costa.com, $$$$), a 500-room golf and tennis resort, attracts celebrities by the Lear-jet load and hosts golf and tennis tournaments. It's got two PGA courses and 21 tennis courts, plus a spa and "Chopra Center" (as in Deepak, the New Age guru), where you can "harness your creative genius, create perfect health, and access blissful, peaceful states of existence." With room rates that range $340–520 nightly (more for suites), you'll need all the bliss you can lay your hands on.

A few steps down in price and many steps closer to the beach is the **Carlsbad Inn Beach Resort** (3075 Carlsbad Boulevard, 760/434-7020 or 800/235-3939, www .carlsbadinn.com, $$$), an appealing beach and tennis complex built in the center of town under the community's watchful Old World architectural guidelines. A swimming pool, workout room, and kids' spa make this a winner. Another worthy beachfront choice is the **Tamarack Beach Resort** (3200 Carlsbad Boulevard, 760/729-3500, www.tamarackresort.com, $$$), which is more like a time-share condominium than a motel. Each suite has a washer and dryer, full kitchen, and stereo.

For a front and center location on the beach, you can't better the **Best Western Beach Terrace Inn** (2775 Ocean Street, 760/729-5951, www.beachterraceinn.com, $$$). Located in a quiet residential neighborhood, the Beach Terrace Inn has as sunny a disposition as you'll find at the beach. Plus, you can practically jump off the balcony into the ocean (though we'd advise against it). Nearly as appealing is the **Best Western Beach View Lodge** (3180 Carlsbad Boulevard, 760/729-1151, $$), which lies close to but not quite on the ocean and will earn you a significant break on rates relative to the other resorts and inns mentioned herein.

COASTAL CUISINE

If you like fried seafood, it can be ordered by the basket at **Harbor Fish South** (3179 Carlsbad Boulevard, 760/729-4161, $), an outdoor-patio joint beside the ocean and next to a surf shop. The clientele is young and not very discriminating about their diet. The Surfer's Special, for instance, is a cheeseburger and fries. But the view and ambience are perfectly beachy. Somewhat disappointingly, the

fish in the fish 'n' chips basket is not local but comes from Alaskan waters.

The best local seafood we found was at **Fish House Vera Cruz** (417 Carlsbad Village Drive, 760/434-6777, $$), a pleasant stroll over the railroad tracks just east of the town center. The name derives from a fishing boat that scours the Pacific coast from Baja to Alaska to nab the goodies they serve here. Everything is mesquite-grilled to perfection, and prices are moderate. The place even looks like the hold of a fishing vessel, with lots of nautical knickknacks.

Niemans (300 Carlsbad Village Drive, 760/729-4131, $$$) is worth visiting because it's housed in the oldest Victorian structure in town. If you're not inclined toward "proper attire," you can at least stroll the grounds and pretend to be studying the menu, which tends toward hearty fare (prime rib, filet mignon, leg of lamb) with a smattering of seafood items.

NIGHTLIFE

In a Norman Rockwell kind of town, you're lucky to find a place that serves even something as harmless as frozen yogurt after dark. Carlsbad, fortunately, does have a semblance of nightlife. The primary source of activity is **Sandbar Cafe** (3878 Carlsbad Boulevard, 760/729-3170), which sits across the street from the roaring ocean surf and is home to live rock and blues on many nights. Another hopping haunt is the local **Hennessey's Tavern** (2777 Roosevelt Street, 760/729-6951), which has live music on weekends. For more low-key good times, the **Kafana Coffee Shop** (3076 Carlsbad Boulevard, 760/720-0074) offers warbling folkies and good, stiff belts of caffeine.

Oceanside

For decades Oceanside has been a sprawling military/urban wasteland. Though the reputation hasn't changed much over the years, the city lately appears to be on the upswing. Yes, the past is behind Oceanside and the future's so bright you gotta wear shades. At least it's been sprucing itself up and putting its best foot forward, and we're pleased to report that Oceanside has been steadily improving since we first began visiting in the mid-1980s. Back then, it wore the sad-sack look of a military town that existed largely to serve the practical and prurient needs of thousands of U.S. Marines stationed at Camp Pendleton. Although we certainly wouldn't describe it as a destination mecca for those traveling the California coast, there's no reason to actively avoid it these days, either.

To fully understand Oceanside (population 170,000), it's necessary to do like the Marines and hit the beaches. You would expect a town with a name like Oceanside to be blessed in that department. From Buccaneer Beach to Oceanside Pier to Harbor Beach, this unpretentious place has been adopted by beachgoers from as far afield as Encinitas. They come to Oceanside because their own beaches are either crowded or disappearing, and because parking is easier, prices are cheaper, and attitudes are conducive to casual enjoyment.

Even given these enviable conditions, Oceanside has a tale of woe regarding the beach that sits on either side of the formidable Oceanside Pier (which, at 1,942 feet, is the second longest on the West Coast). According to the still-angry locals, the main culprit is the U.S. Army Corps of Engineers. In the 1960s, having conducted only minimal study of the impact on the surrounding coastline, the Corps created a harbor at Oceanside. This one is big, slick, and modern, with 950 slips for pleasure craft and yachts, a marina, restaurants, condominiums, and a shopping plaza designed to resemble a Cape Cod seaport village.

Before the architectural surgery, Oceanside had one of the widest, longest, and best-loved beaches on the southern coast. It was a Sahara of sand that was especially attractive to surfers. Imagine, if you will, a sea monster coming ashore and taking a five-acre bite out of the center of this beach, then spitting the sand back into the water several miles offshore.

This, essentially, is what has happened in Oceanside. According to a local historian who was in high school at the time, he and his classmates, as a science project, conducted a study of the proposed harbor project. They foresaw the damage that would be done to their beloved beach. They presented their study to the Corps and were basically told, "Beat it, kids, you don't know what you're talking about."

Alas, they did know. Photographs of Oceanside City Beach taken in 1946 show an uninterrupted swath of sand as wide and straight as any we've seen on either coast. The same beach today is certainly lovely to behold, but it's nowhere near the size of the beach back in the 1940s. The jetty that was meant to ward off rough waters from luxury vessels in the harbor was built at the wrong angle. The sand that normally flowed south with the longshore currents in years past now winds up at the bottom of an offshore canyon, lost forever. To make this tale even more shameful, the Army Corps of Engineers must dredge the harbor two or three times a year to keep it navigable. "It's amazing that Carlsbad doesn't sue the Corps," opined our local historian, referring to the devastating effects of the disrupted sand flow south of Oceanside. "It's a pretty big thing to lose your beach."

Thankfully, a sand-bypassing operation has been developed that has begun to replenish the shoreline. It involves shooting sand through six-inch tubes located around the harbor, where it can resume its natural southerly drift with the currents. In a sense, Oceanside has lost and found its beach. And it has been gearing up for bigger things. The 100 acres behind the pier—except for the California Surf Museum—have been slated for development. The Marriott hotel chain has already signed on, and four 10-story buildings are on the drawing board. But unlike the residents of most coastal towns, the natives aren't opposed to a massive facelift in Oceanside. We'd agree that, for once, it actually makes sense.

CALIFORNIA SURF MUSEUM

As everyone knows, surfing is more than a sport. In Southern California, perhaps more than anywhere else except Hawaii, it is a religion. Around these parts, the church of choice is the California Surf Museum, near the Oceanside Pier.

The museum's history is not unlike that of a wandering religious mystic. Founded in 1985 by Jane Schmauss and Stuart Resor, it was originally housed at George's Restaurant in Encinitas. It moved to Pacific Beach, then back to Encinitas's Moonlight Plaza. Finally it arrived at its Canaan – a former VFW hall and beach bar in the heart of surfer country.

The California Surf Museum is a delight for devotees of the sport and the merely curious. The history and lore of surfing are lovingly told with original relics, informative placards, vintage photographs, clothing, clippings, books, and shrines to dead surfers. Exhibits are changed regularly, and various events celebrate the sport's history, which is particularly rich in this locale. The most sacred moments and mementos are devoted to the pantheon of greats who've taken that one last ride to surfer heaven. Their stories read like the lives of saints. They include:

- George Freeth, the Hawaiian who introduced surfing to California and then became a lifeguard in Oceanside. Freeth died of pneumonia in 1910 after rescuing several people in the rough waters off Oceanside Pier.

- Leroy "Granny" Grannis and Doc Ball, two great surfers who were also the first surf photographers. They understood that no one can take pictures of surfers in action better than those who understand the sport from the inside.

- Duke Kahanamoku, the Polynesian who popularized surfing worldwide. He also reintroduced surfing to Hawaii after missionaries had forbidden it. He took his nickname from the Duke of Edinburgh and won three gold medals in swimming at the 1912 Olympics. One of the Duke's redwood longboards is on display at the museum.

- Bob Simmons, a daredevil whose only possessions were a 1937 Ford and a longboard. He developed the "spoon nose" (a lift at the front of the board that helps avoid nosedives) and was the first surfer to use rope hand grips. He was inexhaustible, surfing from sunup to sundown. On September 27, 1954, while surfing Windansea in La Jolla, Simmons caught a bigger wave than even he could handle. His board made it to shore, but he never did.

Anecdotes like these and the countless items for perusal and sale bring surfing alive, even for the uninitiated.

For more information, contact the California Surf Museum (223 North Coast Highway, Oceanside, CA 92054, 760/721-6876, www.surfmuseum.org). The museum is open daily from 10 A.M.-4 P.M. Admission is free, though donations are welcome.

"It won't be Cement City, like they did to Huntington Beach," a longtime local told us. "It will be more like a seaport village, made of wood, with an educational Sea Center. We want it." After all it's been through, the rough-and-tumble city of Oceanside deserves whatever upscaling it can wrangle.

The main reason for Oceanside's size and almost the sole reason for its existence is **Camp Pendleton.** Occupying 250,000 acres (200 square miles), it is the world's largest U.S. Marine base. Camp Pendleton is literally next door to Oceanside, its back gate opening onto Oceanside Harbor. Sixty thousand marine and civilian personnel work and train at the camp. Those who don't live on base reside in Oceanside with their families.

At first glimpse Oceanside doesn't look like the stereotypical military town. Great pains have been made to disguise this fact, especially on the water. Still, Oceanside is at its core a military town, and this makes for such incongruities as a champagne brunch at the Taste of Europe restaurant two blocks from the Paradise-by-the-Sea RV Park. It may not be a bona fide war zone, as many landlocked military towns are. But as you pull away from the upscale harbor you begin to notice more liquor stores than you might expect to see in a town of this size. Broken-bulb saloons, low-rent food stands, thrift shops, discount clothiers, and flat-roofed duplexes—all are signs of a military lifestyle that has remained largely unchanged since World War II. No slight intended, as one of us was an army brat who spent the happiest years of his childhood on and around military bases.

Incidentally, the **Buena Vista Lagoon Ecological Reserve** is south of town, between Oceanside and Carlsbad. This large natural wetland—one of the few remaining in Southern California—is a habitat for birds and vegetation (including rare species of both). A trail along the shoreline makes for pleasant sightings. The **Buena Vista Audubon Nature Center** (2202 South Coast Highway, 760/439-2473) provides exhibits, lectures,

and group tours; it's open 10 A.M.–2 P.M. Tuesday–Saturday.

Oh yes, extra credit is available for those willing to drive four miles inland on Highway 76 to see **Mission San Luis Rey de Francia** (4050 Mission Avenue, 760/757-3651). Founded in 1798 by Father Fermin de Lasuen, the "King of the Missions" was named for King Louis XI of France. The largest of the Franciscan-run missions, it was lavishly decorated to be something of a showpiece. Today, it houses an active order of Franciscan monks and a museum, which is open to the public for viewing and souvenir buying. A fiesta is held here every year during the third week of July. Of particular interest are the paintings by local Native Americans.

For more information, contact the Oceanside Chamber of Commerce, 928 North Coast Highway, Oceanside, CA 92054, 760/722-1534, www.oceansidechamber.com; or San Diego North Convention & Visitors Bureau, 360 N. Escondido Boulevard, Escondido, CA 92025, 760/745-4741 or 800/848-3336, www.sandiegonorth.com.

BEACHES
Palm-lined Pacific Street runs along Oceanside's beach from the south end of town up to Oceanside Pier. Hereabouts is a pleasant residential neighborhood of newish homes that betray a fondness for the New England architectural style rather than the Spanish vernacular of stucco and pipe roofs one generally finds in Southern California. Beach accesses are plentiful at street ends and parking on side streets is abundant. At the south end, however, a wall of riprap boulders protects homes from the ocean's incursions along a section of shoreline.

Oceanside's sandy bounty begins inauspiciously with **South Oceanside Beach** (on South Pacific Street). You park in the neighborhood along an enormous cement embankment and pass between condos onto hard-packed sand; not worth the trouble, as much better beaches lie ahead.

More easily accessed is **Buccaneer Beach,** which is in the same residential neighborhood.

The beach here is a tiny pocket of sand free of rocks and debris. It's nice, but nicer still is pondering what the beach would be like if it weren't hogged by all the houses built right on top of it. Across the street is **Buccaneer Park,** an inviting green space with play area, picnic tables, snack bar, restrooms, and showers. Also quite nice is **Loma Alta Marsh,** a small lagoon east of the beach. A trail passes beneath a railroad trestle, and birds can be heard chirping happily.

Several more beach accesses with lifeguard towers are strewn between Buccaneer Park and Oceanside Pier. Named for the streets that meet Pacific Street in their vicinity, they are (from south to north) **Oceanside Boulevard Beach, Wisconsin Street Beach,** and **Tyson Street Beach.** The last of these has a park with picnic tables and playground, much as at Buccaneer Park. It's hard not to like Oceanside from the perspective of these grassy seaside parks and broad, sandy beaches.

A one-way oceanfront street with benches and green space called The Strand flares off of Pacific Street south of the pier and rejoins it just north of the pier. It's great for family strolls or lonely naps in the grass. Down by **Oceanside Pier,** you'll find a wide, pleasant beach extending in both directions. A sand renourishment project undertaken in 2001 has for the most part remained in place along this popular stretch. (Of course, all that could change in a single stormy winter.) The area south of the pier is called **Pier View South.** It is a narrower strand than the beach between the pier and breakwater, which is designated **Pier View North.**

The beach just south of Oceanside Harbor is called **Breakwater Way,** and it is a quiet, safe, and relatively out-of-the-way family beach. The jetties up at this end of Oceanside protect the mouth of the San Luis Rey River. North of the river is Oceanside Harbor and **Harbor Beach.** Because it abuts the north jetty, which intercepts the ocean's attempted transport of sand across the river mouth, Harbor Beach is among the widest beaches in San Diego County. The beach and harbor area are

filled with amenities, from picnic tables and volleyball nets to deep-sea fishing trips and kayak rentals. Motels, shops, and restaurants, too! Oceanside Harbor even has its own fishing pier, making this a two-pier town.

The beaches in the vicinity of the pier can get crowded on summer weekends, but owing to the fact that Oceanside is a military town and not a tourist destination—or even a huge favorite with day-tripping inlanders—it is not as jammed as other in-town beaches in northern San Diego County (which is one more reason to come here). The Oceanside town planners have done their best to make the pier an inviting area, with stands of palm trees, green and cleanly kept park space, a pier-side amphitheater, and concessions (including, unfortunately, a McDonald's, which says volumes about the typical beach visitor). The sand is soft, light brown, and well patrolled by lifeguards; there are a dozen lifeguard stands along Oceanside's beaches. You can park near the pier along Pacific Street for $0.50 an hour—a bargain, by beach standards. (Not to digress, but just to give an idea of the flavor of life in Oceanside, here's a newsy tidbit from January 2002: "No leads have been developed in the theft of 10 parking meters last week from the downtown area, police said.")

The massive Oceanside Pier is a broad, dark-planked old affair with a devoted fishing clientele. No license is needed to fish off the pier, and a trolley runs to and from it. A community center is attached to the pier in the complex at its base; its gym is open to the public. Just behind the pier sits the **California Surf Museum** (223 North Coast Highway, 760/721-6876), a required stop for people who like people who like beaches.

47 SOUTH OCEANSIDE BEACH

Location: Cassidy and Pacific Streets in Oceanside

Parking/Fees: free street parking
Hours: 24 hours
Facilities: none
Contact: Oceanside Department of Harbors and Beaches, 760/966-4535

48 BUCCANEER BEACH

Location: 1506 South Pacific Street in Oceanside
Parking/Fees: free parking lot
Hours: 24 hours
Facilities: concession, lifeguards, picnic area, restrooms, and showers
Contact: Oceanside Department of Harbors and Beaches, 760/435-4005

49 OCEANSIDE BOULEVARD BEACH

Location: Oceanside Boulevard at Pacific Street in Oceanside
Parking/Fees: free street parking
Hours: 24 hours
Facilities: concession, lifeguards, picnic area, restrooms, and showers
Contact: Oceanside Department of Harbors and Beaches, 760/966-4535

50 WISCONSIN STREET BEACH

Location: Wisconsin Street at The Strand in Oceanside
Parking/Fees: pay parking lot and metered street parking
Hours: 24 hours
Facilities: lifeguards, restrooms, and showers
Contact: Oceanside Department of Harbors and Beaches, 760/435-4005

51 TYSON STREET BEACH

Location: Tyson Street at The Strand in Oceanside

Parking/Fees: metered street parking
Hours: 24 hours
Facilities: concession, lifeguards, picnic area, restrooms, and showers
Contact: Oceanside Department of Harbors and Beaches, 760/435-4005

52 PIER VIEW SOUTH

Location: in Oceanside along Pacific Street, between Witherby Street and the San Luis River
Parking/Fees: metered lot and street parking
Hours: 24 hours
Facilities: concession, lifeguards, restrooms, showers, and picnic tables
Contact: Oceanside Department of Harbors and Beaches, 760/435-4005

53 PIER VIEW NORTH

Location: in Oceanside along Pacific Street, between Witherby Street and the San Luis River
Parking/Fees: metered lot and street parking
Hours: 24 hours
Facilities: concession, lifeguards, restrooms, showers, and picnic tables
Contact: Oceanside Department of Harbors and Beaches, 760/435-4005

54 BREAKWATER WAY

Location: in Oceanside at the end of Harbor Drive, off Pacific Street
Parking/Fees: $5 entrance fee per vehicle
Hours: 24 hours
Facilities: lifeguards, restrooms, and picnic areas
Contact: Oceanside Department of Harbors and Beaches, 760/435-4005

55 HARBOR BEACH

⛺ 🎿

Location: in Oceanside at the end of Harbor Drive, off Pacific Street
Parking/Fees: $5 entrance fee per vehicle; RV camping fee $15 per night
Hours: 24 hours
Facilities: lifeguards, restrooms, and picnic areas
Contact: Oceanside Department of Harbors and Beaches, 760/435-4005

56 DEL MAR BEACH (CAMP PENDLETON)

🎿

Location: north of Oceanside Harbor, inside Camp Pendleton Military Base
Parking/Fees: free parking lot accessible only to military personnel and their guests
Hours: 8 A.M.-7 P.M. (until 4 P.M. in winter)
Facilities: concession, lifeguards, restrooms, showers, and picnic areas
Contact: Del Mar Lifeguard Station, 760/725-2703

RECREATION AND ATTRACTIONS

- **Bike/Skate Rentals:** El Camino Bike Shop, 121 North El Camino Real, Encinitas, 760/436-2340; Millennial Motors, 505 Mission Avenue, Oceanside, 760/722-2225

- **Boat Cruise:** Helgren's Oceanside Sportfishing, 315 Harbor Drive South, Oceanside, 760/722-2133, www.helgrensportfishing.com

- **Dive Shop:** Pyramid Divers, 282 Harbor Drive South, Oceanside, 760/433-6842

- **Ecotourism:** Buena Vista Audubon Society Nature Center, 2202 South Coast Highway, Oceanside, 760/439-2473

- **Fishing Charters:** Helgren's Oceanside Sportfishing, 315 Harbor Drive South, 760/722-2133

- **Marina:** Oceanside Harbor & Marina, 1540 Harbor Drive, 760/966-4580

- **Pier:** Oceanside Pier, Pacific Street and The Strand, Oceanside, 760/722-5853

- **Rainy Day Attraction:** Mission San Luis Rey, 4050 Mission Avenue, 760/757-3651

- **Shopping/Browsing:** Carlsbad Company Stores, Paseo del Norte, Carlsbad, 760/804-9000

- **Surf Shop:** Action Beach Board Shop, 310 Mission Avenue, Oceanside, 760/722-7101

ACCOMMODATIONS

Oceanside has been sorely lacking in lodgings as inviting as its beaches, but it's begun moving in the right direction. Finally, after years of talk and planning, a contemporary new construction has materialized beside the Oceanside Pier. It's the **Wyndham Oceanside Pier Resort** (333 N. Myers Street, 760/901-1200, $$$), and it opened in 2008. For a posh resort on the California coast, the prices aren't half bad—$118–177 per night for rooms ranging from studios to two-bedroom "condos."

Oceanside Marina Inn (2008 Harbor Drive North, 760/722-1561, www.omihotel.com, $$$) has kitchens and fireplaces to go with its location at Oceanside Harbor. If you're not staying on the harbor, then you're probably best off staying at the **Best Western Oceanside Inn** (1680 Oceanside Boulevard, 760/722-1821, $$), a well-appointed chain motel adjacent to I-5.

COASTAL CUISINE

Meals in Oceanside are grabbed on the run or casually eaten at picnic tables or beach blankets. The surfer theme is mined at the **Longboarder Cafe** (228 North Coast Highway, 760/721-6776, $) and the **Beach Break Cafe** (1902 South Coast Highway, 760/439-6355, $), which serve hearty staples (pancakes, omelets, salads, burgers, burritos) in bright, ocean-themed surroundings. We also like the look of the flash-fried, seafood-filled Baja

Buckets at **Rockin' Baja Coastal Cantina** (258 Harbor Drive South, 760/967-6199, $$), a party-themed bar/restaurant with a franchise on Oceanside Harbor (and only three others in California, so far).

A good, cheap, quick, south-of-the-border-style bite can be had at **Johnny Mañana's** (308 Mission Avenue, 760/721-9999, $). Heaping helpings of fresh, guilt-free Mexican fare are served at low prices in a pleasant, beachy atmosphere. The house special is a BLT burrito, served with guacamole and salsa. It's hard to spend more than five or six bucks here. You can make off with a plain cheese quesadilla and a cold Pacifico beer, served with complimentary salsa and chips, for under $6. The breakfast burrito has jump-started many a surfer's morning.

The oldest restaurant in Oceanside is **101 Cafe** (631 South Coast Highway, 760/722-5220, $), a 1950s-themed flashback to the world of *Happy Days* on Old U.S. 101. The restaurant's origins, in fact, go all the way back to 1928. Stick-to-the-ribs sandwiches, salads, and burgers rule the menu, and time seemingly stands still.

NIGHTLIFE

Oceanside's nightlife can be a bit raw. After a week of sweating in the hills of Camp Pendleton, a marine can work up a profound thirst. To quench it he or she heads into Oceanside, where bar signs offer greetings like "Welcoming Those Who Have Served and Those Serving." Here's a sampling of the cocktail lounges in Oceanside: **Bub's Whiskey Dive** (301 Pier View Way, 760/757-2827), **The Rusty Spur** (406 Pier View Way, 760/722-2216), and **One More That's It Pub** (431 Airport Road, 760/433-3781). Bottom's up!

San Onofre State Beach

The last stop in San Diego County, San Onofre State Beach butts up against the Orange County line. Several things about San Onofre might make some visitors uneasy. First, it sits in the shadow of the San Onofre Nuclear Generating Station, whose twin peaks are visible from the park. Second, San Onofre is surrounded by **Camp Pendleton,** the largest U.S. Marine base in the nation. In fact, the 3,000-acre coastal-canyon park lies on Marine Corps land that has been leased to the state. Camp Pendleton occupies a staggering 250,000 acres, and you never know what might whiz by this deceptively empty landscape. We were enjoying the view from a freeway vista point when an amphibious tank came roaring across the terrain, kicking up dust. We also heard a few jets break the sound barrier. Third, the area is full of rattlesnakes. This is the only venomous snake species found in California, but they sink their fangs into roughly 200 unlucky Southlanders a year. Other snakes native to San Onofre include red racer, gopher, and king. Even so, the most common animal-related injury is the sting of the stingray, which settles in the sand close to shore.

On the positive side, because it lies on a military reservation, San Onofre is gloriously undeveloped. This is what the California coast used to look like way back when—except, of course, for the nuclear power plant.

For more information, contact San Onofre State Park, 949/492-4872, www.parks.ca.gov.

BEACHES

The lengthy stretch of beach at the south end of San Onofre—often referred to as **Bluffs Beach** or simply **San Onofre State Beach**—can be accessed via six numbered trails that descend steeply to it. It is a lengthy beach, with three miles of campsites running along the abandoned stretch of coastal highway (San Onofre Beach Road) above it. At the north end of the campground is a day-use area with parking. There's nothing fancy about **San Onofre Bluffs Campground,** whose 176 sites offer little in the way of shade and can get noisy (thanks to their proximity to

I-5). **San Mateo Campground,** a more recent addition, has 157 sites with electrical and water hookups and lies a mile east of I-5. A mile-long trail leads from this campground to the famed Trestles surfing beach.

San Onofre State Beach is ideal for beginners—"the Waikiki of California," we've seen it called—and surf camps are held along its shores. Want to learn how to surf while camping at San Onofre? Contact Jason Senn at **Endless Summer Surf Camp** (949/498-7862, www.endlesssummersurfcamp.com). This surf expert offers five-day overnight surf camp packages that are often booked solid in the summer months.

Okay, things get a little confusing at this point, so follow closely. Proceeding north from the campground, you encounter San Onofre Nuclear Generating Station (SONGS, of all unlikely acronyms), Old Man's Beach (part of San Onofre State Beach), San Onofre Recreational Beach (which belongs to Camp Pendleton), and Trestles Beach (part of San Onofre State Beach).

Old Man's Beach is a popular spot for older surfers on longboards ("geezers," in surfing lingo). The vibe is mellower than at beaches where adrenalized young surf punks on shortboards carry out their version of *Fight Club* for wave-riding rights. Mexican-style thatched cabanas and volleyball nets add to the festive air.

Next up is **San Onofre Recreational Beach** (a.k.a. Churches Beach), one of two lifeguarded beaches for Camp Pendleton military personnel only. (The other is **Del Mar Beach,** just above Oceanside.)

Rounding out the lineup at San Onofre is **Trestles Beach** ("Trestles," for short, a reference to railroad trestles). Located at San Mateo Point, Trestles offers the best break in San Diego County and one of the best in the continental United States. Trestles is a big reason why so many world-class surfers make their home in nearby San Clemente—and why so many surfers go to the trouble of trotting a half-mile down a pathway with surfboards on their heads to get there.

Trestles Beach

57 BLUFFS BEACH

Location: three miles south of San Clemente via Basilone Road exit off I-5; six bluff-top trails lead to the beach from San Onofre Bluffs Campground
Parking/Fees: $10 entrance fee per vehicle; camping fees are $20–25 per night, plus $7.50 reservation fee
Hours: 6 A.M.–sunset
Facilities: lifeguards, restrooms, showers, and picnic tables
Contact: San Onofre State Beach, 949/492-4872

58 OLD MAN'S BEACH

Location: south of San Clemente via Basilone Road exit off I-5; bluff-top trail leads to beach from north of San Onofre Nuclear Generating Station
Parking/Fees: $10 entrance fee per vehicle
Hours: 6 A.M.–sunset
Facilities: none
Contact: San Onofre State Beach, 949/492-4872

59 SAN ONOFRE RECREATIONAL BEACH (CAMP PENDLETON)

Location: north end of Camp Pendleton, at San Onofre State Beach
Parking/Fees: free parking lot; the lot and beach are accessible only to military personnel and their guests
Hours: 8 A.M.-7 P.M. (until 4 P.M. in winter)
Facilities: concession, lifeguards, restrooms, showers, and picnic areas
Contact: San Onofre Lifeguard Station, 760/725-7935

60 TRESTLES BEACH

Location: accessible by a one-mile hike along path accessed at Christianos Road near I-5 in San Clemente
Parking/Fees: camping fee at San Mateo Campground $29–34 per night with hookup, $20–25 per night without hookup, plus $7.50 reservation fee
Hours: 6 A.M.–sunset
Facilities: none
Contact: San Onofre State Beach, 949/492-4872

ORANGE COUNTY

Although the oranges are mostly gone and the county embodies the worst aspects of America's addiction to cars, shopping malls, suburban sprawl, right-wing politics, environmental despoliation, corporate wheeling-dealing, and youth-culture narcissism, the glorious beaches of Orange County are here (we hope and pray) forever. They start with pleasant understatement at San Clemente, an almost quaint community that's lifted into the present tense mainly by its world-class surfing scene. And they work their way up to Seal Beach, a charming town sandwiched between the hulking Goliaths of Huntington Beach and Long Beach.

Most of Orange County's oceanfront was similarly low-key only decades ago. Many beaches singled out by name in the Beach Boys' 1963 classic "Surfin' USA" are in Orange County. But in the years since they celebrated Southern California in song, a major real-

estate land rush has effectively walled off much of the prime beachfront in Orange County for the private enjoyment of...God knows who. Nobody we consort with, that's for sure! The worst sins were committed at Dana Point and Huntington Beach—great surfing spots where those who most love the shore (and who have the least impact upon it) are now persona non grata. They're the ones with living memories of how these places used to be.

Orange County's mid-1990s fiscal meltdown, the entire state's turn-of-the-millennium dot-com collapse, the stock market slide and corporate accounting scandals of 2002, the subprime mortgage meltdown and recession of 2008 have all revealed the viciously destructive end results of the greed agenda. Perhaps these revelations will pave the way for a more environmentally and socially responsible mind-set that will spare Orange County's lovely shoreline further developmental

© PARKE PUTERBAUGH

ORANGE COUNTY

desecration. Granted, it's a far-fetched theory, but we're not above grasping at straws. In reality, we know full well that in a place where money and its materialistic flaunting function as a surrogate religion, any changes to the status quo will be slow in coming and staunchly resisted.

The legendary reputation of Orange County as a bastion of starchy conservatism is well deserved. In this decade, the progeny of all these filthy rich Republican Party donors have become the subjects of several highly successful fictional and "reality"-based TV shows: *The O.C., Laguna Beach,* and *The Hills.* The last of these, which tracks the lives of a few mindless skirts and their party pals, is enough to dissuade a thinking person from ever even visiting Orange County. Here are brief synopses of a few episodes: "Lauren receives flowers and another phone call from Jason." "Heidi gets her big chance to work in the nightclub scene." "Heidi finds out the results of her pregnancy test while Lauren and Whitney are asked to cover a major fashion show."

Orange County's world of political conservatism, social vapidity, and gas-guzzling consumerism has also given rise to its attitudinal opposite: a subculture of punk-rock and hardcore bands who loathe all forms of authority, stupidity, and conspicuous consumption. It's quite a mix of sensibilities going on here in "O.C.," once you start scratching beneath the surface. But we're beach writers first and sociologists second, so we'd simply advise ignoring this mindless cacophony and heading to the shimmering sand beaches of Orange County. Many of its beaches are succulent treasures that will lift the spirit and body like fresh oranges plucked right off the tree. Two of its beach towns—Laguna Beach and Newport Beach—are among our all-time favorites.

San Clemente

Nestled in the hilly contours of the California coast halfway between San Diego and Los

ORANGE COUNTY

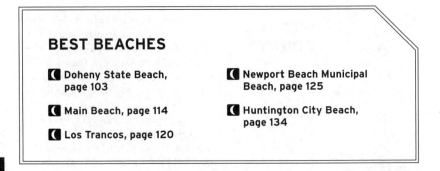

BEST BEACHES

((**Doheny State Beach,**
page 103

((**Main Beach, page 114**

((**Los Trancos, page 120**

((**Newport Beach Municipal**
Beach, page 125

((**Huntington City Beach,**
page 134

Angeles, San Clemente (population 62,000) is fully removed from the sprawl that slithers toward it from all directions. It has little in common with the harried metropolitan world that bears down upon it. Rather, San Clemente is an entity unto itself, rather like a small-scale Santa Barbara.

Promoting this sense of cozy self-containment is the layout of city streets, which take their cue from the area's geography. San Clemente's roads meander in awkward semicircles, following topographical contours. This confuses one's sense of direction and forces visitors to pay closer attention to their surroundings than they would if driving some boring old grid. And pay attention you do: to beautiful houses, verdant shrubs and gorgeous flowers, and surrounding hills that plunge dramatically to the sea.

The town is built above some striking beaches, with weathered bluffs and scantily vegetated hills rising behind it. Avenida del Mar links El Camino Real (the main drag, which parallels I-5) with the municipal pier and beach. It passes through the heart of town, a shopping and business district that could pass for Anytown, USA. For every cutesy boutique there's a plain old mom-and-pop store serving some basic community need for things like prescription drugs, camera equipment, stationery, and "notions." (When was the last time you heard that word used?) You can sip a civilized cup of coffee at an outdoor café and watch folks amble by, evincing none of the stressful hysteria that sends the rest of us to shrinks, doctors, and an early grave.

Perhaps it is this restful calm that inspired a sitting U.S. president to acquire a second home in San Clemente. The late Richard Nixon put this small town on the map in 1969 by turning Casa Pacifica—a Spanish-style, red-roofed estate at the south end of town—into the Western White House. Built in 1927 by one Hamilton Cotton, Casa Pacifica served as Nixon's home away from the White House during the tumultuous era of Vietnam and Watergate. Coincidentally, the estate faced one of the best surfing spots in all of California (Cotton Point, informally known as "Cotton's"), and surfer lore is filled with tales of trying to outfox the Secret Service in an effort to get to it. Though the way to the waves is more easily negotiated these days, it's still no picnic. Surfers face a half-mile hike down paths of scalding sand and asphalt with boards atop their heads. There's nothing to suggest the Prez attempted the feat himself, but maybe he was actually hipper than anyone knew. During a tape-recorded tour of the Nixon Library (40 miles from San Clemente, in Yorba Linda), the late president allows that "if there had been a good rap group around in those days, I might have chosen a career in music instead of politics." Would he have called the act Tricky Dick and DJ Watergate?

The return to pre-presidential calm after Nixon left office suited San Clemente just fine. It's a lovely, unassuming town that looks much as it did when it was advertised to prospective buyers in 1925 as "a village done in the fashion of Old Spain." Named in 1602 by the

THE ORANGE COUNTY THEME SONG

(sung to the tune of "Green Acres")

male voice:
Orange County is the place to be
Golf and tennis is the life for me
Fairways spreading out so far and wide
Suburban sprawl
To hell with the countryside!

female voice:
Newport is where I come to play
I try on clothes and shoes all day
Shopping binges are what I adore
Darling, I love you
But give me Fashion Island's stores.

he:
Golf balls!

she:
Huge malls!

he:
Corvettes!

she:
Credit debt!

both:
We are alike
We love our moneyed life!
Orange County
We are there!

ORANGE COUNTY

explorer Sebastian Vizcaino in honor of Saint Clement—whose feast day coincided with the date of discovery—San Clemente was one of California's first planned communities. The founder was Ole Hanson, a former mayor of Seattle. In 1925 Hanson and three partners purchased and designed a 2,000-acre parcel in the classic Spanish style, hoping to attract folks who'd grown tired of big-city living to "San Clemente by the Sea." More of an aesthetic visionary than today's barf-it-up developers, Hanson rhapsodized, "San Clemente is just a painting five miles long and over a mile wide...its foreground the sea, its background the hills. We use for our pigments flowers and shrubs and trees and red tile and white plaster." Some 75 years later, the painting remains sufficiently impressive to make an art lover out of any visitor.

For more information, contact the San Clemente Chamber of Commerce, 1100 North El Camino Real, San Clemente, CA 92672, 949/492-1131, www.scchamber.com.

BEACHES

San Clemente is a town so full of civic pride that it has its own city song, "On the Beach of San Clemente." We can't warble that little

ditty, but we'll happily sing the praises of San Clemente's beaches. Avenida del Mar slams to an end at **San Clemente City Beach,** where a historic 1,200-foot pier dates from the 1920s. There's a municipal parking lot, restrooms and showers, and all the usual amenities of a well-tended city beach. The beach is accessible from the west end of Avenida del Mar and numerous street ends and paths along the two-mile stretch from San Clemente State Beach to Ole Hanson Beach Club (a public pool and playground), with the city beach at the center.

A small, hut-like Amtrak station sits next to railroad tracks so close to the ocean they practically get licked by the waves at high tide. The surf is strong all along the coast around here, drawing an enthusiastic knot of surfing devotees. At high tide large breakers slam into the pier pilings, turning the frothing water a milky green. The soft, brown-sand beach draws a vibrant young crowd, with surfers congregating around the pier.

Seaside bed-and-breakfasts and outdoor cafés face the beach along Avenida Victoria, which runs beside the ocean for a short distance before looping up, up, and away. On a nice summer day—and all the ones we've ever

GETTING AROUND THE BIG ORANGE

As a "humor columnist" for a local real-estate publication put it, "Orange County is car culture...You can be sleepless in Seattle, but don't get caught being carless in Orange County. Other cities have mass transit; here it's auto transit en masse."

As his column unfolded, the less amusing reality of this maniacal fume-sucking freeway gridlock reared its ugly head. For example, the dimwitted writer confessed that "some of us spend more time driving than we do with our families. Cell phones keep us connected, but it's a poor substitute for actually being there." Ya think?

He went on to offer these knee-slapping tips about getting around Orange County: "Avoid the El Toro Y at all times." *[Ba-da-bump.]* "There is never a good time to drive the 22." *[Ba-da-bump.]* "Avoid the 55 north during daylight hours." *[Ba-da-bump.]* "And evenings, avoid every road to the beach in the summer." *[Ba-da-bump.]*

Oh, sorry, apparently he was being serious there.

We know from personal experience that driving in Orange County is no laughing matter. It is a waking nightmare. This reality was brought home to us when we attended an Angels vs. Orioles major-league baseball game in Anaheim one summer evening. It was only 18 miles from our motel in Newport Beach to Anaheim. No problem! Or so we thought. We wound up mired in unmoving traffic jams both before and after the game. At 11 P.M. on a weeknight, traffic was backed up even worse than before the game. We found ourselves stuck on the freeway for what seemed like an eternity. The delay wasn't due to wrecks or a departing game crowd (only 15,000 attended). It was due partly to road construction – the freeway widening and repairing never ends in Southern California – and partly to the traffic that never abates at any hour. As midnight approached, the delay became absurd. An hour and a half to go 18 miles?

Orange County continues subsidizing freeway building and widening projects with revenue from Measure M, a half-cent sales tax approved by voters in 1990 and re-approved by voters in 2006. The proceeds fund countywide transportation improvements, with 43 percent earmarked for freeways. The question is, do more and wider freeways represent real "improvement" or just more problems? Road building has reached such an unutterable state of lunacy in Orange County that the

spent in San Clemente have been ideal—the area in the vicinity of San Clemente City Beach has the charmingly upscale aura of a Mediterranean village, with climate to match. You couldn't ask for better weather: average highs of 68 degrees in June, 73 degrees in September (the hottest month), and 66 degrees in December. There are less than 10 inches of rain and 342 days of sunshine per year. In a word, it's perfect.

San Clemente State Beach offers some of the best coastal camping (153 sites, of which 72 have RV hookups) in the state. Whereas the municipal beach is wide and hospitable to swimmers and surfers, the state beach is narrow, prone to rip currents, and almost primevally wild. A campground overlooks the mile-long beach from atop 50-foot bluffs. Trees afford some protection from the summer sun, and the place vaguely recalls national parks of the Southwest—Bryce or Zion Canyon, for instance—in miniature. An asphalt trail leads down a steep, dramatically eroded ravine to the beach. Railroad tracks run extremely close to the water, protected by riprap. Near the water's edge, the sand slopes sharply. Breakers scurry up the beach face, and an occasional tongue of foam licks the dry sand above it. It's great for beach hiking; the solitude and the scenic backdrop are stunning. Diving is popular but swimming is discouraged, and surfers choose to hotfoot

El Toro Y – the infamous bottleneck where the San Diego Freeway (I-405) and Santa Ana Freeway (I-5) meet – has been expanded to 26 lanes at its widest point. Moreover, they're proud of this "modern interchange," which is blithely referred to as "Orange County's Main Street."

Despite the terrible cost in wasted fossil fuel and lost time at home and on the job, Orange County has been slow to implement long-term transportation solutions. They've even nixed mass-transit projects. For instance, plans were drawn up for a light-rail system, the CenterLine, that would have connected some of the most densely populated and highly traveled population centers in O.C. The first phase in this long-overdue project was to be an 18-mile, 22-station line between Santa Ana and Irvine. However, after 12 years of planning and $68 million spent on studies, design, and lobbying, the Orange County Transportation Authority (OCTA) board of directors voted unanimously in April 2005 to indefinitely postpone the CenterLine light-rail project.

According to *Railway Age* magazine, "A primary reason for the board's action was lack of support for the 9.3-mile, $1 billion scheme among the county's mostly Republican congressional delegation, whose help would be vital to obtain $483 million in federal funding." The commentary just writes itself, doesn't it? One thing's for sure: Without decisive action, the Orange crush on the freeways will, if possible, only get worse. Future generations will curse those leaders who have been dragging their feet today.

For now, the most beach-friendly mode of conveyance is the excellent bus system run by the OCTA. Numerous routes operate from inland cities to such coastal locales as Huntington Beach, Seal Beach, Newport Beach, Laguna Beach, Dana Point, and San Clemente. The coast-hugging Bus Route 1 runs along Pacific Coast Highway from San Clemente to Long Beach. Yes, you can travel Orange County's entire coastline for a mere $1.25 fare! Moreover, any and all routes in the county can be ridden for $3 per day or $45 per month. We call that a bargain and a bright note amid all of Orange County's freeway madness.

For information, schedules, and fares, contact the **Orange County Transportation Authority,** 550 South Main Street, P.O. Box 14184, Orange, CA 92868, 714/636-7433, www.octa.net.

down to better waves at Cotton's and Trestles, which straddle the San Diego County line from opposite sides of San Mateo Point. If you happen to see a surfer or two studying the distant waves from a freeway off-ramp south of town, they're weighing whether it's worth the long walk to the water. And a long, sandy scramble it is, from the south end of El Camino Real near Carl's Jr. (which is where most people park) down to Trestles, which is part of San Onofre State Beach.

San Clemente is home to the **Surfrider Foundation** (120½ South El Camino Real #207, San Clemente, CA 92672, 949/492-8170, www.surfrider.org), the advocacy group that acts on behalf of coastal environmental matters and other issues of interest to surfers.

1 SAN CLEMENTE STATE BEACH

Location: Take the Avenida Calafia exit from I-5 in San Clemente and follow it west to park.

Parking/Fees: $10 entrance fee per vehicle; camping fees $29-34 per night with hookups, $20-25 per night without hookups, plus a $7.50 reservation fee

Hours: 6 A.M.-8 P.M. (to 10 P.M. during Daylight Savings Time)

Facilities: lifeguards, restrooms, showers, and picnic areas

Contact: San Clemente State Beach, 949/492-3156

ORANGE COUNTY

San Clemente

© PARKE PUTERBAUGH

2 SAN CLEMENTE CITY BEACH

Location: Avenida del Mar at Avenida Victoria in San Clemente
Parking/Fees: metered street parking
Hours: 4 A.M.-midnight
Facilities: concession, lifeguards, restrooms, showers, and picnic area
Contact: San Clemente Department of Marine Safety, 949/361-8219

RECREATION AND ATTRACTIONS

- **Bike/Skate Rentals:** San Clemente Cyclery and Sport, 2801 South El Camino Real, San Clemente, 949/492-8890

- **Ecotourism:** Orange County Marine Institute, 24200 Dana Point Harbor Drive, Dana Point, 949/496-2274

- **Marina:** Dana Point Marina, 34555 Casitas Place, Dana Point, 949/496-6137

- **Pier:** San Clemente Pier, 611 South Avenida Victoria, San Clemente, 949/492-8335

- **Rainy Day Attraction:** Mission San Juan Capistrano, 31414 Camino Capistrano, San Juan Capistrano, 949/234-1300

- **Shopping/Browsing:** Laguna Village, 577 South Coast Highway, Laguna Beach, 949/494-1956

- **Sportfishing:** Dana Point Sportfishing, 34675 Golden Lantern, Dana Point, 949/496-5794

- **Surf Report:** 949/492-1011

- **Surf Shops:** Rip Curl Surf Center, 3801 South El Camino Real, San Clemente, 949/498-4920; Costa Azul, 689 South Coast Highway, Laguna Beach, 949/4971423

- **Vacation Rentals:** Laguna Beach Oceanfront Rental, 900 Glenneyre Street, Laguna Beach, 949/494-8110

ACCOMMODATIONS

Across the street from San Clemente Municipal Pier is a charming block where a smattering of bed-and-breakfasts offer wonderful beach views at top-end prices. One is **Casa Tropicana** (610 Avenida Victoria, 949/492-1234, www.casatropicana.com, $$$), whose theme rooms (e.g., Out of Africa, Emerald

Forest, and South Pacific) overlook the pier at prices that will quickly bring you down to earth (up to $350 a night). Another is the **Villa del Mar Inn** (612 Avenida Victoria, 949/498-5080, www.seahorsesanclemente.com, $$$), whose condo-style suites offer beach-facing sundecks, big living rooms, and fully equipped kitchens. Rooms run $150–199 in the high season and drop by $70 a night the rest of the year. Since the weather barely changes from month to month, the off-season rates are a real bargain.

The **San Clemente Inn** (2600 Avenida del Presidente, 949/492-6103, www.san clementeinn.com, $$), which abuts San Clemente State Park, operates as a hotel condominium, offering apartment-style suites on grounds that include a pool and spa, shuffleboard courts, and gargantuan pineapple trees. In this largely unfancy town, the **Holiday Inn San Clemente Resort** (111 South Avenida del Estrella, 949/412-6126, $$), a white-stucco wonder convenient to the beach, has the chain-motel competition beat when it comes to amenities: heated pool, spa, fitness center, sundeck with a view, decent on-site restaurant.

COASTAL CUISINE

Look no further than the San Clemente Municipal Pier for dinner. You have two choices: the **Fisherman's Restaurant** (611 Avenida Victoria, 949/498-6390, $$$), on the left side of the pier, and **Fisherman's Bar** (611 Avenida Victoria, 949/498-6390, $$) on the right. They serve good, fresh, Pacific seafood at both places. The restaurant's dinner menu ranges from fish 'n' chips to whole Dungeness crab. If you're toting a huge appetite, ante up for an all-you-can-eat feast of clams, halibut, salmon, swordfish, or crab, served with salad, rice pilaf, sourdough bread, and Fisherman's chowder. The bar tends more toward heavy appetizers.

Across the street, the **Beach Garden Cafe** (685½ Avenida Victoria, 949/498-8145, $) is a cute, modern eatery serving omelets, sandwiches, pizzas, and entrées such as fish 'n' chips. On a more substantial note, the **Rib Trader** (911 South El Camino Real, 949/492-6665, $$$) serves ribs, steaks, and other hearty surf-and-turf fare. It also has a bar area set off from the main dining room that's a favorite place for the surfing cult to congregate and quaff a few after the sun's gone down.

Finally, in deference to the surfing community, we feel obliged to mention **Surfin' Donuts Coffee House** (1822 South El Camino Real, 949/492-1249, and 1110 South El Camino Real, 949/361-2120, $). After all, some of the best surfing spots, surfboard makers, and surfing magazines are headquartered here in unassuming San Clemente. In a town geared to surfers, it stands to reason that you can get some of the best "surfin' donuts" in all creation, too.

NIGHTLIFE

After sunset, best watched from the pier, San Clemente gets quieter than an orange grove. Laguna Beach and San Juan Capistrano are the nearest outposts of serious nightlife. A cocktail waitress at the San Clemente Pier tipped us off to a particularly lively club up the coast where it was reggae night. "Have you ever heard of reggae music?" she asked, as if she were an elementary school teacher introducing a new vowel sound. We didn't feel like letting our dreadlocks down that night and remained happily glued to our perches at **Fisherman's Bar** (611 Avenida Victoria, 949/498-6390), enjoying the pier's relative tranquility.

Capistrano Beach

Enfolding the coastline between Dana Point and San Clemente, the Capistrano Beach area has been rather overoptimistically marketed as "California's Riviera." In actuality, Capistrano Beach is a small and relatively uncrowded seaside sanctuary. That quality, a virtual novelty in overbuilt Southern California, sets Capistrano Beach apart from its neighbors. For instance, San Juan Capistrano—a larger town that has scared away its famous swallows

WHERE HAVE ALL THE SWALLOWS GONE?

The story of the swallows of San Juan Capistrano is a major chapter in California's legend and lore. Each year the swallows, ever-reliable in the constancy of their re-appearance, make the 6,000-mile trip from Goya, Argentina, to **Mission San Juan Capistrano.** They arrive on March 19, build nests and hatch their chicks, then depart for the winter on October 23. You can set your calendar by them.

The date of their spring arrival is known as St. Joseph's Day (a.k.a. Swallow Day). Large numbers of tourists turn out to greet the swallows, a ritual highlighted for years by the 8 A.M. ringing of the mission bells. Everybody oohs and ahs over the return of the little five-inch gliding birds. It's a great day for birds and bird-watchers alike.

In recent decades, however, the truth of the matter has become a little harder to, uh, swallow. On March 19, 1992, a reporter brought an ornithologist to San Juan Capistrano, and not a single swallow was spotted. In 1993, an estimated 25,000 tourists doubled the town's population over the weekend. Thousands turned out in the early morning to witness the flapping of four startled birds who were roused from the mission eaves by the aged bell-ringer. The swallows of Capistrano were outnumbered, according to published accounts, by pigeons. Nonetheless, a celebratory parade of 4,000 people, many on horseback, took place in the afternoon. That's a human-to-bird ratio of 1,000 to 1. Does something seem cuckoo about all this? Driven away by renovations at Mission San Juan Capistrano, among other things, they apparently went elsewhere. In 1997, they set up camp at the Tillman Water Reclamation Plant, in the San Fernando Valley. In 2000, six birds were counted.

In order to entice birds to the mission, it was reported that "mission officials tried to entice swallows by scattering ladybugs on the rose bushes, making mud puddles to be used for nest building, and even building fake ceramic nests to con the birds into thinking there were friends nearby." Do they take the swallows for birdbrains?

The reduction of insects in the area, due to development, has also contributed to the swallows' need to nest elsewhere. And so they no longer darken the skies of San Juan Capistrano, as they once did, though that doesn't stop the community from celebrating their arrival anyway. March 29, 2008, marked the 50th anniversary of the Swallow Day Parade in San Juan Capistrano.

by razing orange groves and constructing shopping malls and boxy stucco homes on every available square inch—offers what more cliché-minded travel writers would refer to as "fabulous shopping opportunities." To us it's just another infernal gash in the landscape drawn to bleed the unconscious consumer. Much of Orange County, particularly its interior sprawl, has come to resemble a Hieronymus Bosch vision of hell, with groaning condominiums and howling land speculators for harpies.

Stick to the beach; it's pleasant out here, and there's plenty to go around. Capistrano Beach has got a nice, unhurried way about it.

Whether you're looking out to sea from the beach or the palisades above, it's a pianissimo passage in the Wagnerian symphony of overdevelopment that characterizes much of the coast from San Diego to Los Angeles.

For more information, contact the Dana Point Chamber of Commerce & Visitor Center, Clocktower Building, La Plaza Center, Dana Point, CA 92524, 949/496-1555, www.danapoint-chamber.com; or the San Juan Capistrano Chamber of Commerce, 31781 Camino Capistrano, San Juan Capistrano, CA 92675, 949/493-4700 or 800/290-DANA, www.sanjuanchamber.com.

BEACHES

Capistrano Beach Park and Doheny State Beach (described later in this chapter) are the main access points in an unbroken stretch that runs along Capistrano Bight up to Dana Point. On a nice day the beaches here look almost too good to be true: a mirage of white sand and emerald water gleaming beneath a bright blue sky. Down on the shoreline, Capistrano Beach boasts a wide, unblemished public beach. A road called the Palisades drops down from steep residential hills to meet Pacific Coast Highway near the entrance to Capistrano Beach. A large parking lot with inexpensive metered parking faces the ocean, and pedestrian overpasses cross the highway at several points. The beach is popular but seldom overrun. At 7 A.M. one drizzly May morning, a group of teenage girls enthusiastically engaged in a little pre-school volleyball practice. Meanwhile, cars idled along the lip of the lot, their drivers lost in meditative contemplation before heading off to a hard day of hammering nails or making deals.

The parking lot runs beside the beach for a good distance, and people aerobicize along it in jogging shoes and in-line skates. By mid-morning a furious full-court basketball game was in progress. In the distance surfers congregated off Doheny Point. Just another day in the life of a prime Southern California beach. At the south end of Capistrano Beach, where Camino Capistrano runs out at Pacific Coast Highway, a pedestrian underpass leads to **Poche Beach,** a sandy surfing beach just above the landslide that closed a stretch of PCH in 1993. Incidentally, *Surfer* magazine is published in Capistrano Beach, and surfboards are manufactured here.

3 POCHE BEACH

Location: Camino Capistrano at Pacific Coast Highway in Capistrano Beach
Parking/Fees: free street parking

Hours: 6 A.M.-10 P.M.
Facilities: none
Contact: South Beaches Operation Office of Orange County Harbors, Beaches, and Parks, 714/834-2400

4 CAPISTRANO BEACH PARK

Location: El Camino Real at Palisade Drive in Capistrano Beach
Parking/Fees: pay parking lots ($1 per hour)
Hours: 6 A.M.-10 P.M.
Facilities: concession, lifeguards, restrooms, showers, and picnic tables
Contact: South Beaches Operation Office of Orange County Harbors, Beaches, and Parks, 714/834-2400

ACCOMMODATIONS

On the landward side of Pacific Coast Highway is **Capistrano Surfside Inn** (34680 Pacific Coast Highway, 949/240-7681, www .capistranosurfsideinn.com, $$$), a time-share condo complex that also operates like a hotel. Commodious one- and two-bedroom suites come with full kitchens and outdoor balconies stocked with furniture and gas grills. Rooms start at $275. A schedule of optional activities for guests includes day trips to beaches on Mexico's Baja Peninsula. Close by is **Holiday Inn Express** (34744 Pacific Coast Highway, 949/240-0150, $$$). Formerly the Capistrano Edgewater Inn, it offers comparable prices, views, and amenities.

COASTAL CUISINE

A famous Mexican restaurant called **Olamendi's** (34660 Pacific Coast Highway, 949/661-1005, $$) does a big business in burritos across from the beach. Its popularity is easy to gauge from the frequently full parking lot. Inside, moderately priced Mexican food of good quality is served at padded, semicircular booths. Tacos, burritos, and enchiladas are presented every conceivable way (stuffed with shredded beef, steak, chicken, fish, pork, and cheese). The menu carries a one-word endorsement from the late Richard Nixon: "Excellent." Up by the cash register hangs a picture of El Presidente, nervously posed with the kitchen staff. If you're hankering for something more high-end, head to nearby Dana Point or San Juan Capistrano.

NIGHTLIFE

The after-hours options in Capistrano Beach are as weak as the glow from a child's nightlight, but you stand a good chance of catching some great music at the **Coach House** (33157 Camino Capistrano, 949/496-8930) in nearby San Juan Capistrano. This 480-seat hall books singer/songwriters, alternative rockers, roots-oriented musicians, reunited New Wave groups, and recherche hair-metal bands. You might see anyone from the Blasters to L.A. Guns, Eve 6, and A Flock of Seagulls on the marquee when you're passing through. Unfortunately, in an age when the live-music scene is struggling, you might also see such god-awful dreck as a Chippendale's male revue. Coach House serves an appetizer-heavy dinner menu.

Incidentally, "San Juan Cap" (as it's known to locals) is a formerly quaint, mission-style community now beset with endless malls whose acreage rivals that of a cattle ranch. The train station is the hub of weekend nightlife. Everyone from wandering minstrels on down performs for the assembled masses, some of whom ride the rails down from Los Angeles just to be part of the crowd.

Dana Point

A nine-foot bronze statue of seaman and writer Richard Henry Dana Jr. looks out over the harbor that's named after him. Dana came here in the 1830s aboard the square rigger *Pilgrim*. He recorded his experiences as a naïf on the high seas in the autobiographical narrative *Two Years Before the Mast*, a California liter-

ary classic. He also described the cliff-backed cove at Dana Point as "the only romantic spot in California." We beg to differ with the estimable writer on this point. Number one, there are plenty of romantic spots in California. Number two, Dana Point is no longer one of them.

Of course Dana himself had nothing to do with the artificial facelift that turned the rugged environment he knew and loved into a sanitized playground for the wealthy, so we won't hold him accountable on this last point. Instead, we'll direct our venom toward those dissemblers of public-relations jive who use his words to promote the arid development that calmed the waves and transformed the landscape. The refashioning of Dana Point (population 35,700) into a 2,500-slip yacht harbor—which began in 1969, when the Orange County Board of Supervisors approved construction of a jetty, harbor, and harborside community—is the sort of tale that would have inspired a salty young sailor like Dana to mutiny. Indeed, were Dana around to see the area today, he would scarcely comprehend the changes that have taken place since his time. The man-made Dana Harbor has stilled the waves for yuppie yachts, while Mariner's Village developers have erected a faux New England fishing village that is a mockery of the real thing.

The brotherhood of surfers is still steamed about what the 1.5-mile jetty did to the surf at Doheny State Beach. "The mellow lines of Doheny are all but gone, replaced by the calm water of Dana Point Harbor," lamented surfing historian and chronicler Allan "Bank" Wright. In an essay entitled "The Boutiquing of the California Coast," lifelong surfer, beach aficionado, and journalist John McKinney writes how he nearly aborted a planned hike on the California coast because he grew so disgusted with the barricading of Dana Point. Stranded outside a gated residential community, McKinney wrote, "As I stand with Dana's memorial…the sun, which I cannot see, drops toward the ocean, which I cannot see, showering golden light on sandstone cliffs, where I cannot legally walk." Of the yacht basin, he wrote, "I walk across the acres of hot asphalt comprising the Dana Harbor parking lot. The sight of the huge antiseptic marina takes the wind out of my sails. A favorite surfing spot of my adolescence has been totally destroyed."

It's not only the squeaky clean fake seaport experience that rankles. Pacific Coast Highway has become clogged with strip malls on both sides through the Dana Point/South Laguna corridor. The buildup along the traffic-choked highway has been torrential since the mid-1980s, with very little unviolated "outdoors" visible anymore. Despite efforts to promote and trade on that very quality, it has all but vanished. Nonetheless, gaily colored ceremonial nylon flags fly from shops and subdevelopments alike. Those flags have lately taken on a patriotic air, being splashed with the red, white, and blue. But this seems as fraudulent as a flag decal on a gas-guzzling SUV. What is so all-American about tampering with what once was one of America's finest chain of beaches? It is, in fact, tantamount to treason.

For more information, contact the Dana Point Chamber of Commerce & Visitor Center, Clocktower Building, La Plaza Center, Dana Point, CA 92524, 949/496-1555, www.danapoint-chamber.com.

BEACHES

Two great Orange County beaches flank Dana Point. **Doheny State Beach** is enfolded by the long arm of the south jetty that protects Dana Harbor. Although the surf has been tamed, it's a great beginner's beach for surfers and still gets some decent peelers on a south swell. Swimmers, meanwhile, enjoy the relative calm of Doheny's wide, white beach, which runs for three-quarters of a mile. An early-morning arrival on summer days is recommended. An interpretive center offers a touch tank and five aquariums. A wooded 120-site campground, grassy picnic area, and bike path make this 62-acre park an exceptional unit in the state-park system.

North of Dana Point, **Salt Creek County Beach** preserves a mile-long stretch of beach, extending from the point up toward South Laguna. It's a historic spot, since it represents one of the earliest volleys fired in the battle for public beach access—especially in Orange County, where Salt Creek became a cause célèbre from the mid-1970s to the mid-1990s. As usual, it pitted public beach advocates against privatization schemers. For the most part, the public won. Situated on the bluffs above and behind the beach is **Bluff Park,** a section of county beach that has everything you could ask for: trails, picnic tables, restrooms, outdoor showers, grills and fire rings, basketball courts, and views of Catalina Island. It is also a good spot for whale-watching during the peak months of February and early March.

Mentioned only for the sake of completeness, there is a small calm-water beach at **Dana Point Harbor** among the shops and boat slips.

⑤ DOHENY STATE BEACH

 BEST

Location: Dana Point Harbor Drive off Pacific Coast Highway in Dana Point
Parking/Fees: $10 entrance fee per vehicle; camping fees $30-35 per night with hookup, $20-25 per night without hookup, plus a $7.50 reservation fee
Hours: 6 A.M.-8 P.M. (to 10 P.M. during Daylight Savings Time)
Facilities: concession, lifeguards, restrooms, showers, and picnic areas
Contact: Doheny State Beach, 949/496-6172

⑥ SALT CREEK COUNTY BEACH

Location: Pacific Coast Highway at Ritz-Carlton Drive between Dana Point and South Laguna

GOLF COURSE LIVING – OR, SELLING ORANGE COUNTY BY THE HOOK AND SLICE

Orange County is California's cradle of Republican values. Beyond its beautiful beaches, the county has all the lingering warmth and charm of a bank lobby. Every swath of green that doesn't have an ostentatious hacienda plopped onto it, with requisite backyard pool, is devoted to the preternaturally lush contours of a golf course. They even devised a euphemism for their lifestyle: "golf course living."

Orange County's cultural touchstones are Mickey Mouse and John Wayne. The political icon is Richard Nixon, whose library and grave are in Yorba Linda. The irony of all this staunch conservatism is that not so many years ago Orange County was a sleepy rural retreat from Los Angeles. Cities such as Anaheim were where little old ladies dreamed of going to get away from Los Angeles. Most of the land was either grazed by livestock or planted in orange groves.

But the little old ladies passed away. In their place came a determined battalion of mall designers, commercial developers, construction contractors, highway builders and entrepreneurial barracudas of all stripes. All put pressure on pliable government officials, most of whom shared the same party affiliation (read: Republican) to do their bidding. It's the American way, right?

No, it was the will of the Irvine Company, which basically orchestrated the whole scheme. The Irvine Company is the mysterious realty octopus that owns most of the undeveloped land in Orange County. It has built its empire on a real-estate plan whereby it leases land in 99-year increments, thereby ensuring that no one but the company ultimately owns it. Originally, most of Orange County was a land grant called Irvine Ranch. Five times the size of Manhattan, it is the largest private real estate holding in a major U.S. metropolitan area.

Just the name "Irvine Ranch" evokes the "Father Knows Best" patriarchy that governs every square foot of Orange County. Instead of cows, Irvine Ranch is grazed by golfers. Instead of orange trees, palm trees have been geometrically arranged around climate-controlled corporate campuses. To the east, the faceless, interchangeable towns that orbit them have been erected. For example, 134,300 people live in a city

---

Parking/Fees: pay parking lot ($1 per hour)
Hours: 5 A.M.-midnight
Facilities: concession, lifeguards, restrooms, showers, and picnic tables
Contact: South Beaches Operation Office of Orange County Harbors, Beaches, and Parks, 714/834-2400

ACCOMMODATIONS

Posh and pricey are the bywords in Dana Point. The **Ritz-Carlton Laguna Niguel** (1 Ritz-Carlton Drive, 949/240-2000, $$$$) swaddles guests in five-star luxury. It is probably the premier resort on the Southern California coast. We are hard-pressed to think of one more imposing in its roll call

of amenities: four tennis courts, three restaurants, two heated pools, and an 18-hole golf course—everything but the proverbial partridge in a pear tree. And the view, from a bluff 150 feet above the ocean, is exceptional. As they put it, "We overlook nothing but the Pacific." Well, they also overlook the average wage earner's ability to afford a night at a place like this.

Marriott's Laguna Cliffs Resort (25135 Park Lantern Drive, 949/661-5000, www.lagunacliffs.com, $$$$) is another opulent, sprawling pleasure dome whose 12 acres include biking and jogging trails. All 350 rooms have ocean views. In addition to health clubs, tennis courts, a basketball court (where one of called Orange. Ever heard of Orange? Does it evoke any tangible associations – natural, historical, cultural? Orange's claim to fame, so far as we could tell, is that it's home to "Southern California's largest entertainment and retail center" (in other words, a mall of monstrous proportions).

Another 202,000 people live in Irvine, a "planned community" that is livable and safe but antiseptic as Listerine. Ditto Costa Mesa, clocking in with 110,000. Another 340,000 live in Santa Ana, 345,000 in Anaheim, and 143,500 in Pasadena. It is a sprawl that never ceases. One morning we saw the following headline in a local newspaper, reported without irony or alarm: "Coto de Caza set to open five new neighborhoods." Coto de Caza is a guard-gated private community with a population of 16,000. In Orange County the old catchphrase "There goes the neighborhood" has been replaced with a new one: "Here comes the neighborhood."

The inevitable toppling of this house of cards came in 2008 with the sub-prime lending crisis, the collapse of venerable financial institutions, and the bottoming out of the Southern California real-estate market. Knowing that fortunes have been lost makes the quiet, upscale neighborhoods of Orange County appear all the more surreal these days. The real-estate crash caused housing prices in Orange County to fall by 20 percent. The housing market is expected to remain soft for a couple of years. Here are some recent headlines in the *Orange County Register* as we were going to press: "How Low Will Mortgage Meltdown Drag O.C.'s Economy?" and "Foreclosures Hit Even High-End Beach Cities." We sure didn't have to look far for bad news.

Okay, enough of all this. To us the beaches are the only parts of Orange County that retain any links to the county's historical, geological, and cultural past. Despite the fact that the moneyed minions have succeeded in snuffing out the Old California feel of Dana Point and Huntington Beach, parts of San Clemente, Laguna Beach, Newport Beach, and Seal Beach retain elements of their original charm.

Huntington Beach and Dana Point lost their battles because they were meccas for surfers – relative non-spenders who are run off the land whenever big money bullies its way into town. Still, some very important lessons about coastal development can be learned from Orange County. As we see it, Orange County represents an endpoint of greed and despoliation against which the rest of America's coastal communities ought to be on guard.

---

us trounced the other in a game of horse), and spas, it has one of the finest gourmet restaurants in the state, **Watercolors.**

The latest entry in the froufrou market is **St. Regis Monarch Beach Resort and Spa** (One Monarch Beach Drive, 949/234-3400 or 866/716-8116, www.stregismb.com, $$$$). Room rates on summer weekends start at $440. (Yikes!) The 400-room, Tuscan-style resort sits on the east side of Highway 1, peering down at the far Pacific. Yes, it is not ocean side but ocean *view.* It's a beach resort without a beach and a fitting symbol for all that's gone wrong at Dana Point.

For budget accommodations, drive a few miles up the coast to South Laguna, where unfancy beachside motels are strewn along Pacific Coast Highway.

COASTAL CUISINE

We've stated our biases against the exclusivity and landscape-shattering development at Dana Point. That doesn't mean we don't find things to admire about a few properties, particularly the Ritz-Carlton Laguna Niguel and Marriott's Laguna Cliffs. Both are first-class resorts that live up to every expectation. **Watercolors,** the restaurant at **Marriott's Laguna Cliffs Resort** (25135 Park Lantern Drive, 949/661-5000, $$$), went way beyond our expectations. The meal commenced with a pair of appetizers—tuna tartare and spring rolls filled with slices of grilled duck—so artistically rendered that we almost didn't dare disturb them. They proved as delicious to eat as they were to look at. Entrée preparations were similarly sumptuous. The room is light and airy, done in peach tones and brass accents, and the prevailing style is contemporary American cuisine: healthy, creative, and appealing to the eye and palate.

NIGHTLIFE

The lounges at the hotel resorts—particularly the Ritz-Carlton, which has an on-premises nightclub—are your primary options. After a day of tennis, golf, or sailing, and a good meal, you might not feel like much more than a civilized nightcap in any case. If you do, however, there's an old reliable **Hennessey's Tavern** (34111 La Plaza, 949/488-0121) in Dana Point.

Laguna Beach and South Laguna

When people hear the name Laguna Beach these days, they tend to think of Lauren Conrad and her crew from *The Hills* and from its predecessor, *Laguna Beach: The Real Orange County*. Well, these hugely successful MTV reality shows in fact document the *surreal* Orange County, as far as we're concerned. When we think of Laguna Beach, we're reminded of faraway places: the French Riviera, the Greek Isles, the coast of Italy. The town is something of a Southern California anomaly: a cultured seaside village that attracts its share of free spirits. It serves as a kind of Arts and Entertainment channel to the rest of Orange County's *Jackass*-style MTV charades.

Compared to the county's soulless suburban sprawl and fiercely unforgiving arch-conservatism, Laguna Beach is an island, set apart from the rest of Orange County by geography—hills and canyons on three sides, ocean to the west—and the disposition of its inhabitants, which is more creative than mercenary. This outlook was stated in a local publication by a resident who may have revealed more than she intended when she wrote: "Whatever you do, the waves will take your troubles far out to sea, leaving you mindless."

Above all else, Laguna Beach is an artists' colony. There are more than 90 art galleries in Laguna Beach, the lion's share arrayed along Pacific Coast Highway. Whereas other beach towns in Southern California host surfing competitions, lifeguard races, and volleyball tournaments, Laguna Beach (population 24,000) sponsors three art festivals every summer, among them the nationally renowned event Pageant of the Masters (see the *Laguna Beach's Art Affairs* sidebar). Easels are as abundant as surfboards, especially around sunset, when artists strive to capture the gold fire that illuminates the town's myriad coves and beaches.

South Laguna begins around Salt Creek County Beach and runs north to about Ocean Vista Drive (just below Victoria Beach). The differences between South Laguna and Laguna Beach are strictly jurisdictional and nomenclatural. In the words of a longtime resident, "It's all Laguna Beach to me." Indeed, they blend so thoroughly that only a mapmaker can tell them apart.

People who call Laguna Beach home love everything about it except for one thing: traffic. They revere the intellectual camaraderie that encourages self-expression and tolerates eccentricity; the cool, even climate; the striking beauty of cliffs that plunge to a dramatic shoreline (sometimes taking homes with them); and the quasi-European orientation of the community, with its emphasis on high culture and old money. There's even room for surfers, skateboarders, and all the less intellectual flotsam that washes ashore. Their presence helps keep the community from becoming swamped by its own pretensions.

That's not to say that there's never been trouble in paradise. An October 1993 fire in Laguna Beach destroyed hundreds of millions of dollars' worth of homes, with most of the damage confined to the canyons and

LAGUNA BEACH'S ART AFFAIRS

If you come to Laguna Beach in the summer, chances are you'll spend as much time looking at paintings of the ocean as you will at the actual thing. These three art festivals keep things hopping all summer long in Laguna Beach.

Art-A-Fair (777 Laguna Canyon Road, 949/494-4514) and the **Sawdust Festival** (935 Laguna Canyon Road, 949/494-3030) run from July 1 through August 29. Art-A-Fair is a juried art show that also features demonstrations and workshops. The Sawdust Festival is more of the same, plus food and entertainment, such as a juggler of fiery batons who wouldn't be out of place on Venice Beach.

The venerable **Festival of Arts** (650 Laguna Canyon Road, 949/494-1145) and its highlight, the **Pageant of the Masters,** runs from the first week of July through the end of August; general admission costs $7 for adults and $4 for seniors and students. It has been an annual feature of Laguna Beach life for more than 60 years. The Pageant of the Masters brings to life pieces of classic art using live, human subjects. Actors and locals three-dimensionally re-create paintings by the likes of Matisse, Van Gogh, Magritte, and Seurat for staged, 90-second sittings that take hours (if not months) to prepare. The evening culminates in a grand tableaux vivant setting of Da Vinci's *Last Supper.* The effect is both lifelike and eerily two-dimensional, thanks to creative lighting techniques.

The art scene is strong all year-round, as well. The first Thursday of every month is devoted to the **Artwalk.** Tours are led through the local galleries and the artists leave their studio doors open to all comers and goers.

The quality of the art varies widely. We saw eye-catching expressionist paintings and inventive takes on what would normally be clichéd coastal landscape paintings, as well as exceptional nature photography. But we also saw paintings, in high-end galleries no less, that were little better than paint-by-numbers in quality and others that would not be out of place on a sappy greeting card (e.g., portraits of waifish girls licking ice-cream cones, sailboats resting in harbor at sunset), not to mention cutesy sculptures of frolicking children and frisky dolphins.

Overall, though, the diversity of the galleries and their distribution throughout the nooks and crannies of this rare jewel of a town – a work of art in itself – make them well worth perusing.

houses ill-advisedly built in them. The AIDS epidemic has claimed a lot of local residents in this gay-friendly community.

Laguna Beach has always marched to the beat of a different drummer. Unlike much of California, which was parceled out in the form of land grants by the rulers of Spain and Mexico to friends of the throne, Laguna was homesteaded by tree-planting pioneers following the region's annexation by the United States. It was initially called Lagonas, from the Shoshone word for lakes, because of the freshwater lagoons situated behind the beaches where creeks pour into the ocean. The first arrivals were Mormons, who were followed by Methodists. Laguna's first hostelry opened in 1886 and has been operating ever since as Hotel Laguna.

Artists began forming an enclave here in the early 1900s, around which time the name was changed to Laguna Beach. Gradually, a style known as California impressionism began to evolve after an artist named Lewis Botts painted his famous *Girl of the Golden West* in 1914. Much in the style of Monet's French impressionist school, they painted the natural surroundings with rapid brush strokes and an eye for how sunlight bathed the landscape. The Laguna Beach Art Association was founded in 1918, and thereafter art galleries began popping

HANGING OUT WITH THE SURF ADDICTS

The nightlife of Laguna Beach is compacted into the midtown area near Main Beach. One can walk from bar to bar without having to get into a car. That seems a logical enough arrangement, but rarely are clubs laid out so conveniently. Some years ago, we were roaming around Laguna Beach after dinner when we heard live music wafting from this vicinity. Seduced by the siren call of electric guitars, we followed the noise to its source. Imagine our surprise to find three rock bands playing at open-door bars in close proximity.

After sampling all three, we decided to throw our lot in with the Surf Addicts, a local surf-punk trio who were blasting away at Hennessey's Tavern. Their music sounded like the most fun to our ears. The story and sound of this now-defunct band are fairly typical of the Southern California experience. They wrote witty, high-energy songs about the SoCal surfer/party-dude lifestyle.

"I want to live on the edge without falling over," explained the group's singer/guitarist, a live wire named Drew, in a post-show conversation over a table full of beer mugs. For him surfing was an activity as automatic as breathing. He'd found his own slice of wave-filled heaven, a cove beach in South Laguna that few others know about.

His idea of a perfect day in Laguna began with a bout of surfing in the A.M., followed by lunch at Papa's Tacos (a beloved Mexican food joint), and a gig with the Surf Addicts at night. At one time he wanted to join a reggae band. Then one day it occurred to him to write, sing, and play what he knew. In his case he knew about surfing and partying in Laguna Beach.

"We always partied with tourist girls," he told us, "so I wrote a song called 'Tourist Girls.' I grew up partying in Laguna, so I wrote a song called 'Party in Laguna.' I've always imagined what it would be like to surf Hawaii. I thought it would be kind of scary facing waves of that size, so I wrote a song around the line 'Don't hair out' – meaning don't chicken out – 'in Waianea.'"

The Surf Addicts encapsulated the Laguna lifestyle in an entertaining, infectious way that had a damn sight more to do with "reality" than the antics of Lauren and Heidi on The Hills. They sounded like the Police, Beach Boys, and Clash all riding the same surfboard. Their tapes were sold in surf shops and local record stores. Having witnessed their bracing, breakneck live show, we still find them hard to forget. They took the fun of riding a wave or chugging a beer and turned it into music that made you want to do both. One thing's for sure: They made two road-weary beach bums glad to be wide awake and rocking at the beach at two in the morning.

up all over. Today, small galleries hang signs in their front windows that read: "We buy Old Laguna and Old European paintings."

The artistic imperative meanders all the way down Laguna Canyon Road to the water. At Main Beach, an art deco chess table fashioned in a colorful mosaic of ceramic tiles sits in the grassy picnic area for all to admire or use. Don't be surprised to see eye-catching professional models posing and preening on the beach. A lot of fashion models and film-industry types live in Laguna Beach. The former estate of Bette Davis is a local landmark. From

its earliest days, the town has been a gathering place for the jet set. Celebrity residents have included Charlie Chaplin, Judy Garland, Rudolph Valentino, and Gregory Peck.

The main artery through Laguna Beach is Pacific Coast Highway, which unfortunately snakes right through the center of town. The steady stream of traffic mars the town's otherwise genteel village atmosphere. There is simply no other way to get from Dana Point to Newport Beach. A proposed freeway bypass a few miles inland was nixed years ago. All the whizzing traffic makes hazardous sport of getting in and out of a parked car. If traffic were rerouted away from town, Laguna Beach would be a far more pleasant place. As it is, the constant thunder of traffic, much of it aggressively hurrying through town on the only coastal artery, seriously blemishes the Laguna Beach experience.

Beyond the vehicular onslaught, Laguna has atmosphere, culture, scenic beauty, and fantastic beaches. The town at one time even had an unofficial greeter, Eiler Larson by name. This friendly, shaggy mountain man from Denmark would stand at the city limits, hollering "How are you?" to those coming and "Leaving so soon?" to those going for eight hours a day. After he died, numerous tributary wood likenesses began appearing on the town's sidewalks.

The community has its own activist beautification council, which successfully battled outside business interests that wanted to refashion Laguna Beach into a convention center during the 1970s. The would-be developers were sent packing and the threatened town center instead became the landscaped, open-air Main Beach Park. Along the coastline such happy endings are all too rare. This one deserves a standing ovation.

Laguna Beach still holds fast to its "walking village atmosphere." Though some grumble about the "mansionization of Laguna" that's taken place on the hillsides—bringing with it the moneyed morons who populate the aforementioned reality shows—the town has by and large maintained its architectural charm. That is largely because Laguna Beach has retained its activist edge. "There is a vocal design and review process in the community," an involved local told us. "People have a say here in what goes on." And what really goes on here is way more interesting than anything you'll ever see on *The Hills*.

For more information, contact the Laguna Beach Visitor Information Center, 252 Broadway, Laguna Beach, CA 92651, 949/497-9229 or 800/877-1115; or the Laguna Beach Chamber of Commerce, 357 Glenneyre Street,

Laguna Beach, CA 92651, 949/494-1018, www.lagunabeachinfo.org.

BEACHES

Laguna Beach comes stocked with beaches— more than 20 named ones tucked into coves along a hilly, undulating coastline. To give you an idea of its ruggedness, this small town's elevation ranges from sea level to 1,039 feet. **Main Beach** (a.k.a. Laguna Beach Municipal Park) is just that: the main place to congregate and recreate in Laguna. In a town of tiny coves and pocket beaches, this is the big enchilada. Balls are bounced and batted during daylight hours. With its volleyball and basketball courts, picnicking green, and long, sandy beach bordered by a winding boardwalk, Main Beach is a buzzing hive of activity and a great spot for sitting on a bench and surveying the very eclectic scene.

Beyond Main Beach, smaller beaches can be found in both directions along Pacific Coast Highway. It seems that every side street ends at the cliffs, with a stairway leading to a fan-shaped cove. We'll survey the more noteworthy ones, starting from the south with **1,000 Steps Beach.** It's where Ninth Avenue meets Pacific Coast Highway in South Laguna. You'll have to park a few blocks away on the highway's asphalt shoulder, since all the curbs are red in the immediate vicinity, but the walk from your car to the top of the stairs will warm up your calf muscles for the trek down the lengthy cement staircase to the beach. At the bottom of the stairs is a small beach pinned against steep cliffs. Gibraltar-sized rocks frame the cove, and huge waves run up on the beach with great force. Houses cling precariously to the eroding cliffs, each with its own set of ladder-like stairs. Climbing out of this grotto is the real acid test—and that's an apt choice of words, since Timothy Leary and his LSD-imbibing gang frequented this beach in the 1960s. The ascent actually numbers 219 steps, and you can amuse yourself on the return trip by reading the graffiti scrawled onto the vertical face of each step.

West Street Beach is one of the better bodysurfing spots in a town renowned for its waves. Shoehorned into a small cove at the base of a stairwell at the end of West Street, about 10 blocks north of 1,000 Steps Beach, it has a volleyball court and is seasonally popular with locals.

Aliso Creek County Beach lies along the heart of the motel/taco stand/gas station corridor of South Laguna. Ample metered parking draws the summertime masses, as does the fine board- and bodysurfing. The beach slopes steeply down to the breaking waves, which makes for hazardous swimming. All the same, it's packed with families. You'll also find a playground, fire rings, benches, restrooms, and a short pier with snack bar. When pushed along by the powerful south swell, the waves appear taller than the people playing in them. They break with a mighty crack, sending foam cascading up the brown, sandy beach. We saw happy packs of kids building communal sand castles and getting knocked over by the waves.

The lagoon formed where Aliso Creek empties into the ocean is a popular birdbath, which contributes to its poor water quality. The creek becomes steep-sided on its southern bank as it approaches the ocean. Don't climb into the creek, as its near-constant contamination is an issue that plagues Laguna Beach. Nonpoint source pollution from developments up the canyon fouls the creek, necessitating warning signs. But what to do? Officials haven't figured that out yet, despite much head-scratching, finger-pointing, and public debate. Parents, keep an eye on your young ones here. If the creek is contaminated, it stands to reason that the ocean into which it empties is polluted, too, in the immediate vicinity. The twin threats of water quality and water safety make this a less than ideal family beach, when all is said and done.

The prettiest beach in Laguna, **Victoria Beach** (a.k.a. Vic Beach), is one of the hardest to find. Given the lack of signs, it would appear the locals want to keep it that way. The beach can be entered at several points along Victoria Drive, a street off Pacific Coast Highway that's lined with homes pressed together as close as any block of Victorians in San Francisco. Residents have traded space for easy access to a common, sandy front yard along the ocean. Hiking down from the walkway and stairs at the north end of Victoria Beach, you pass private homes behind a yellow cinder-block wall. A final curve deposits you on one of the nicest beaches in Southern California—one that's especially popular with bodysurfers. It is broad and uncrowded, known mostly by locals, and an inviting spot to drop a beach towel.

Moving north from Vic Beach, **Woods Cove** is a small beach bounded by rocks (there's an especially large one at the north end) popular with locals and largely unknown to others. Diving and tidepooling are the big draws here, but watch out for hazardous surf. Nearby **Pearl Street Beach** (a.k.a. Agate Beach) is another small, locally popular cove beach bounded by rocky reefs. **Bluebird Beach** is right in front of the Surf & Sand Resort, and it's a smooth, sandy beach that's good for bodysurfing, boogie boarding, or just soaking up rays on a beach chair.

As you move more into central Laguna Beach, the distances between the rocky points that bound the cove beaches increase. **Mountain Road Beach** has a wide sand beach, but the surf is strewn with hazards—rip currents, submerged rocks, and offshore reefs—so proceed with caution. At the end of Brooks Street, facing Halfway Rock, is **Brooks Beach,** a rocky beach that surfing authority Bank Wright says serves up "the cleanest, best-shaped big wave in Laguna Beach." Have it your way.... Would you like some southern swell on that wave? Maybe a garland of kelp? A shark-fin appetizer? Brooks Beach is strictly for surfers. Everyone has his or her own favorite hidden cove in Laguna Beach, so there are potentially as many beaches as there are street ends. Don't expect locals to divulge their secrets to a stranger, but feel free to poke around—you might stumble on a deserted cove if you're lucky.

Bring the Frisbee to **Oak Street Beach,** which runs for a block or so on either side of Oak Street. A series of offshore reefs makes this a hot surfing spot, as are adjoining **Thalia Street Beach** and **St. Ann's Beach,** though neither is recommended for swimming because of their rocky reef bottoms. Moreover, St. Ann's has the worst rip current in Laguna Beach. All that changes in the matter of a block or so at **Sleepy Hollow Beach,** whose sandy-bottomed beach makes it fine for swimming and bodysurfing (not so hot for surfing). Sleepy Hollow Beach is popular with guests of Vacation Village Hotel, which overlooks it. At this point you are just south of Main Beach, about which we've already commented.

Jumping north of Main Beach, lovely **Heisler Park** serves as a point of entry to **Rockpile Beach** and **Picnic Beach.** Up at this north end of Laguna Beach, the erodable sandstone coast gives way to sturdier volcanic rocks that form points, with bays cut into the softer shales. The foremost feature at Heisler Park is the walkway that lines the coastal bluffs for about a mile. At dusk it's a magical sight. As fog settles in, the town's twinkling lights come on, rendering a real-life canvas as fanciful as any impressionist's pointillistic study. Rockpile and Picnic Beaches are accessible from Heisler Park via a stairway and ramp, respectively. Rockpile is a rocky, surfers-only spot in front of the Laguna Art Museum, where Jasmine Street meets Cliff Drive. At high tide, the beach disappears altogether. Picnic tables are nestled among the trees of Heisler Park, giving Picnic Beach its name. Down below, the beach is a diver's paradise but no picnic for swimmers.

Along the 600 block of Cliff Drive, at the north end of Heisler Park, is **Diver's Cove,** a family-friendly, football-field-sized beach that draws scuba divers and wading kiddies. Adjoining it to the north is **Boat Canyon Beach,** another rocky-bottomed diver's special that's a no-go for swimmers. A few blocks up, picturesque **Shaw's Cove**—yet another diver's dream (anglers, too)—has the bonus of tidepools at its south end.

The procession of public beaches ends at **Crescent Bay Point Park,** a bluff-top green with views of Seal Rock and Laguna Beach and a beach whose big, tubular waves make for great—and sometimes scary—bodysurfing. Anglers cast from the surf or the rocks, and ocean frolickers brave the somewhat risky (beware rip currents) surf. Because it is one of the longer beaches, running for a quarter mile, it is also one of the more popular in the area, so expect to find weekend crowds.

There are two pieces of good news on Laguna's beachfront. The first is the arrival of a trio of cove beach accesses adjacent to a luxury enclave completed in 2002. To get the permits to build this project, the developers were required to deed a third of the land back to the town of Laguna Beach. As a result, three adjacent coves—**Treasure Island, Goff's Cove,** and **Christmas Cove**—are now accessible to the public. They are the southernmost in a string of 20 city beaches overseen by the indomitable Laguna Beach lifeguards.

The second bit of good news is the **Beach Tram**—a town-run free shuttle bus that services the whole of Laguna Beach, from Aliso Creek to Crescent Bay Point Park. The shuttle also services two parking lots in the canyons. This has not only cut down on traffic and parking woes, but it's a sensible way to curb emissions from vehicles that would normally be stuck in never-ending, nerve-jangling Highway 1 gridlock.

7 1,000 STEPS BEACH

Location: Ninth Avenue at Pacific Coast Highway in South Laguna
Parking/Fees: metered street parking
Hours: 6 A.M.-9 P.M.
Facilities: lifeguards
Contact: South Beaches Operation Office of Orange County Harbors, Beaches, and Parks, 714/834-2400

8 WEST STREET BEACH

Location: West Street at Pacific Coast Highway in South Laguna
Parking/Fees: metered street parking
Hours: 6 A.M.-10 P.M.
Facilities: none
Contact: South Beaches Operation Office of Orange County Harbors, Beaches, and Parks, 714/834-2400

9 ALISO CREEK COUNTY BEACH

Location: 31,000 block of Pacific Coast Highway in South Laguna
Parking/Fees: pay parking lot ($1 per hour)
Hours: 6 A.M.-10 P.M.
Facilities: concessions, lifeguards, restrooms, showers, and picnic tables
Contact: South Beaches Operation Office of Orange County Harbors, Beaches, and Parks, 949/923-2280

10 TREASURE ISLAND

Location: just north of Aliso Creek County Beach on Pacific Coast Highway via a ramp at Montage Resort in Laguna Beach
Parking/Fees: metered street parking
Hours: 6 A.M.-10 P.M.
Facilities: none
Contact: Laguna Beach Department of Marine Safety, 949/494-6571

11 GOFF'S COVE

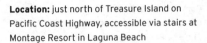

Location: just north of Treasure Island on Pacific Coast Highway, accessible via stairs at Montage Resort in Laguna Beach

Parking/Fees: metered street parking
Hours: 6 A.M.-10 P.M.
Facilities: none
Contact: Laguna Beach Department of Marine Safety, 949/494-6571

12 CHRISTMAS COVE

Location: just north of Goff Cove on Pacific Coast Highway, accessible via stairs at Montage Resort in Laguna Beach
Parking/Fees: metered street parking
Hours: 6 A.M.-10 P.M.
Facilities: none
Contact: Laguna Beach Department of Marine Safety, 949/494-6571

13 VICTORIA BEACH

Location: Victoria Street off Pacific Coast Highway in Laguna Beach, accessed by stairs
Parking/Fees: metered street parking
Hours: 6 A.M.-10 P.M.
Facilities: none
Contact: Laguna Beach Department of Marine Safety, 949/494-6571

14 WOODS COVE

Location: Diamond Street off Pacific Coast Highway in Laguna Beach
Parking/Fees: metered street parking
Hours: 6 A.M.-midnight
Facilities: none
Contact: Laguna Beach Department of Marine Safety, 949/494-6571

© PARKE PUTERBAUGH

Victoria Beach

ORANGE COUNTY

15 PEARL STREET BEACH

Location: Pearl Street off Pacific Coast Highway in Laguna Beach
Parking/Fees: metered street parking
Hours: 6 A.M.-midnight
Facilities: none
Contact: Laguna Beach Department of Marine Safety, 949/494-6571

16 BLUEBIRD BEACH

Location: Bluebird Canyon Road off Pacific Coast Highway in Laguna Beach
Parking/Fees: metered street parking
Hours: 6 A.M.-midnight
Facilities: none
Contact: Laguna Beach Department of Marine Safety, 949/494-6571

17 MOUNTAIN ROAD BEACH

Location: Mountain Road off Pacific Coast Highway in Laguna Beach
Parking/Fees: metered street parking

Hours: 6 A.M.-midnight
Facilities: none
Contact: Laguna Beach Department of Marine Safety, 949/494-6571

18 BROOKS BEACH

Location: Brooks Street off Pacific Coast Highway in Laguna Beach
Parking/Fees: metered street parking
Hours: 6 A.M.-midnight
Facilities: none
Contact: Laguna Beach Department of Marine Safety, 949/494-6571

19 OAK STREET BEACH

Location: Oak Street off Pacific Coast Highway in Laguna Beach
Parking/Fees: metered street parking
Hours: 6 A.M.-midnight
Facilities: none
Contact: Laguna Beach Department of Marine Safety, 949/494-6571

ORANGE COUNTY

20 THALIA STREET BEACH

Location: Thalia Street off Pacific Coast Highway in Laguna Beach
Parking/Fees: metered street parking
Hours: 6 A.M.-midnight
Facilities: none
Contact: Laguna Beach Department of Marine Safety, 949/494-6571

21 ST. ANN'S BEACH

Location: St. Ann's Drive off Pacific Coast Highway in Laguna Beach
Parking/Fees: metered street parking
Hours: 6 A.M.-midnight
Facilities: none
Contact: Laguna Beach Department of Marine Safety, 949/494-6571

22 SLEEPY HOLLOW BEACH

Location: Sleepy Hollow Lane off Pacific Coast Highway in Laguna Beach
Parking/Fees: metered street parking
Hours: 6 A.M.-midnight
Facilities: none
Contact: Laguna Beach Department of Marine Safety, 949/494-6571

23 MAIN BEACH

 BEST

Location: between Broadway and Ocean Avenues at Pacific Coast Highway in Laguna Beach
Parking/Fees: metered street parking
Hours: 6 A.M.-midnight
Facilities: lifeguards, restrooms, showers, and picnic tables
Contact: Laguna Beach Department of Marine Safety, 949/494-6571

24 ROCKPILE BEACH

Location: Cliff Drive at Jasmine Street, below Heisler Park, in Laguna Beach
Parking/Fees: metered street parking
Hours: 6 A.M.-midnight
Facilities: none
Contact: Laguna Beach Department of Marine Safety, 949/494-6571

25 PICNIC BEACH

Location: Cliff Drive at Myrtle Street, below Heisler Park, in Laguna Beach
Parking/Fees: metered street parking
Hours: 6 A.M.-midnight
Facilities: lifeguards and picnic tables
Contact: Laguna Beach Department of Marine Safety, 949/494-6571

26 DIVER'S COVE

Location: 600 block of Cliff Drive in Laguna Beach
Parking/Fees: metered street parking
Hours: 6 A.M.-midnight
Facilities: none
Contact: Laguna Beach Department of Marine Safety, 949/494-6571

27 BOAT CANYON BEACH

Location: off Cliff Drive, west of Boat Canyon Park, via stairwell beside Diver's Cove Condominiums in Laguna Beach
Parking/Fees: metered street parking
Hours: 6 A.M.-midnight
Facilities: none
Contact: Laguna Beach Department of Marine Safety, 949/494-6571

28 SHAW'S COVE

Location: Cliff Drive at Fairview Street in
Laguna Beach
Parking/Fees: metered street parking
Hours: 6 A.M.-midnight
Facilities: none
Contact: Laguna Beach Department of Marine
Safety, 949/494-6571

29 CRESCENT BAY POINT PARK

Location: Crescent Bay Drive at Pacific Coast
Highway in Laguna Beach
Parking/Fees: free street parking
Hours: 6 A.M.-midnight
Facilities: lifeguards and restrooms
Contact: Laguna Beach Department of Marine
Safety, 949/494-6571

ACCOMMODATIONS

You can expect to pay $300 and up a night
for the finer European-inn-type lodgings in
Laguna Beach. The **Surf & Sand Resort**
(1555 South Pacific Coast Highway, 949/497-
4477, www.surfandsandresort.com, $$$$) is
the hostelry of first choice. For starters, it is
right on Bluebird Beach (named for Bluebird Canyon Road), one of the more pleasant
beaches in town. Rooms are pleasantly and
airily appointed, and the oceanfront ones are
so close to the water that the crashing, splashing symphony of waves lulls visitors into a
blissful California state of mind (and a good
night's sleep). The rooms are done in light
brown earth tones, and the beds are exceptionally comfortable. The pool deck is on the far
side of the Surf & Sand's excellent restaurant,
Splashes. You literally might wind up making
a splash of another sort if you walk through
the restaurant in a bathing suit at lunch hour.
Seaview rooms at the Surf & Sand run about
$395 nightly in summer.

Nearby, **Cap'n Laguna Inn on the Beach**
(1441 South Pacific Coast Highway, 949/494-
6533, $$$) offers the same paradisiacal setting
without the gourmet trimmings and manda-
tory valet parking.

The **Inn at Laguna Beach** (211 North
Pacific Coast Highway, 949/497-9722 or
800/544-9479, www.innatlagunabeach.com,
$$$$) also has an unbeatable location—just
above Main Beach on a bluff next to our favor-
ite restaurant in town, Las Brisas. Your biggest
problem will be deciding how to allocate time:
hanging out on Main Beach, sitting on a private
ocean-facing balcony, sunbathing on the roof-
top sundeck, or strolling Cliff Drive. Moreover,
the Inn at Laguna Beach has an amenity worth
its weight in gold: an on-site underground ga-
rage. Alternatively, if you're feeling sentimen-
tal for Old California, you can always stay at
the **Hotel Laguna** (425 South Pacific Coast
Highway, 949/494-1151, $$$$), a midtown
treasure whose beginnings date back to the very
founding of Laguna Beach. It's popular with
European visitors and is oh-so-civilized.

South Laguna is the site of **Aliso Creek
Inn** (31106 South Pacific Coast Highway,
949/499-2271, www.alisocreekinn.com, $$$).
Aliso Creek runs through the property, and
you can follow it to the beach of the same
name, which is only a thousand feet away via
a pedestrian underpass. Despite its proximity
to the ocean, the inn feels like another world.
With views up a canyon and out on mountains,
its grounds are woodsy and secluded—a rare
find in the midst of a beach town. All rooms
are spacious one- and two-bedroom townhouses. The grounds encompass a nine-hole golf
course, a large heated pool, and Ben Brown's
Restaurant, which serves continental fare. Deer
and raccoons, even bobcats and mountain
lions, have been spotted on rare occasions.

A string of park-at-your-door motels cut from
plainer cloth can be found in South Laguna. The
Laguna Reef Inn (30806 South Pacific Coast
Highway, 949/499-2227, www.lagunareefinn
.com, $$) is the nicest of these, offering clean
rooms and a heated pool for half the tariff in

Laguna Beach proper. Note: The Laguna Beach Visitor Information Center will assist with hotel and restaurant reservations; call 800/877-1115.

COASTAL CUISINE

The food scene in Laguna Beach is a sensual indulgence bordering on the obscene. After one magnificent meal following another over the years, we've come to understand why the Romans invented vomitoriums.

Stalwart favorites from Laguna Beach's prodigious list of top-flight eateries include **Five Feet** (328 Glenneyre, 949/497-4955, $$$$) and **230 Forest Avenue** (230 Forest Avenue, 949/494-2545, $$$$). At Five Feet, chef Michael Kang oversees the preparation of "contemporary Chinese cuisine," an atypically creative East-meets-West hybrid that results in such signature dishes as catfish with tomato-ginger citrus sauce and wok-fried veal medallions and scallops in Thai basil garlic chili sauce. Kang calls his entrées "whimsical creations"; you'll call them heaven on a plate. With its sleek, urbane atmosphere, 230 Forest Avenue is Laguna's most popular spot for people-watching and martini-downing. Menu choices range from affordable pasta bowls to boldly simple preparations like seared peppercorn ahi, hazelnut-crusted halibut, and macadamia-crusted mahimahi.

Head to **Splashes** (1555 South Coast Highway, 949/376-2779, $$$$) for a refined, cosmopolitan meal in the unparalleled setting of a small, square dining room overlooking the ocean. Located in the Surf & Sand Resort, 25 feet above breaking waves, Splashes occupies a casually elegant setting with an indoor dining room and an outdoor deck a mere wave's splash from the churning Pacific. Chef Christopher Blobaum favors organic ingredients and Mediterranean cuisine. Signature seafood dishes include Pacific swordfish with herb risotto and lemon sauce and sautéed halibut with clams, capers, and black olives. Expect to spend about $80–100 for two, and don't pass up such desserts as chocolate *fondant* with banana ice cream. A postprandial stroll around hilly Laguna Beach will help assuage any guilt pangs.

For fine and fun dining with a view, nothing in Laguna can top **Las Brisas** (361 Cliff Drive, 949/497-5434, $$$). The indoor dining room and outdoor patio overlook Main Beach and the ocean from the bluff-top at the south end of Heisler Park. The house specialty is seafood with a south-of-the-border flair—everything from fresh ceviche to Mexican lobster. The lunch *ensaladas* are too good to be true. Save room for dessert. The restaurant serves a breakfast buffet, lunch, and dinner, with a popular five-course weekend brunch.

The **Beach House Inn** (619 Sleepy Hollow Lane, 949/494-9707, $$$) is another fine-dining option. The glass-walled dining room faces the ocean, so book your reservation at sunset. The menu selections tend toward creative California nouvelle-style preparations of seafood. The broiled filet of sole, for example, is accompanied by bananas sautéed in butter and brown sugar, with chutney and grated coconut. In an old house that used to belong to actor Slim Summerville (one of the original Keystone Cops), the Beach House Inn has retained its original architecture, and a relaxed air pervades the dining room.

The **White House Restaurant** (340 South Pacific Coast Highway, 949/494-8088, $$) is a local institution with a schizophrenic personality. It's a romantic room at the dinner hour that turns into a popular nightspot afterward. The interior of this 1918 vintage restaurant, once patronized by the likes of Bing Crosby, is filled with Tiffany lamps and varnished wood tables. Specialties include fresh pastas and halibut. Later on, the house shakes to everything from reggae bands to local rockers.

After a late arrival in Laguna Beach one Sunday night, we were famished and therefore prepared to take whatever we could find open. Fortunately, we were directed to **Woody's at the Beach** (1305 South Coast Highway, 949/376-8809, $$$), which would be a pleasant surprise at any hour. The tangy Dungeness crab and corn bisque made a soup-erb starter. The miso-crusted mahimahi was masterfully presented, with the filet served atop brown rice with wedges of grilled eggplant arrayed around it and the entire plate swimming in a satay-style peanut sauce. The changeable menu might also include such items as tamarind-glazed rare ahi and roasted striped bass with artichoke ratatouille, saffron cream, and roasted pepper coulis. This is not the sort of inventive fare one would expect from a restaurant whose sign out front is fashioned from a surfboard, or where the background music tends toward softly throbbing disco.

Down in South Laguna, your best bets are Mexican. At least ours were. A surfer/rocker who grew up here turned us on to **Papa's Tacos** (31622 Pacific Coast Highway, 949/499-9822, $), and after feeding on the plate-filling fish tacos and blackened shrimp quesadillas, all we can do is add a hearty "come to Papa's." Another local favorite is the **Coyote Grill** (31621 Pacific Coast Highway, 949/499-4033, $$$), whose motto is "A Taste of Baja at the Beach." A message on the menu says, "When we open our doors, we open our hearts." When we opened their doors, we opened our mouths for things like lobster Puerto Nuevo (whole lobster grilled with all the fixings) and *pescados frescos.* That's "fresh fish" to all of you who don't *habla español,* and it changes daily according to what's available. Coyote Grill is a three-meal-a-day restaurant whose outdoor deck makes a pleasant spot to enjoy a late-afternoon drink.

More and better restaurants arrive with every season in Laguna Beach—certainly more than we can possibly chart. Among the best of the relatively new venues is **Vertical** (234 Forest Avenue, 949/494-0990, $$$). We window-shopped at the latter, a stylish, open-aired, sleekly appointed space. The chef-owner calls his cuisine "casual, bold, exciting, playful, visionary." You are invited to "design" your own meal and pair it with wine by the taste, glass, flight (hence the name *Vertical*), or bottle. Vertical offers "boutique wine" samplings on the second and fourth Thursdays of every month.

Incidentally, a good place to start the day in Laguna Beach is **The Koffee Klatch** (1440

South Coast Highway, 949/376-6867, $), a locals' hangout nestled among the art galleries.

NIGHTLIFE

As the dinner hour wanes, several of Laguna's more popular restaurants morph into nightspots. The **White House Restaurant** (340 South Pacific Coast Highway, 949/494-8088) is popular with locals. Bar bands on weekends and reggae during the week seem to be the rule. **Las Brisas** (361 Cliff Drive, 949/497-5434) also attracts a sizable crowd of folks who hang out at the bar to meet and mingle. The **Marine Room Tavern** (214 Ocean Avenue, 949/494-3027) draws a mixed bag of bands, anything from country-rock to alternative. Across the street, **Hennessey's Tavern** (213 Ocean Avenue, 949/494-2743) is the kind of place that does a good business no matter what. On one of our visits, the band that was playing finished a poor second, in terms of patron interest, to the daredevil boating video on the big-screen TV. It all depends on the band, the night, and the mood as to which club is packing 'em in. Closely quartered down by Main Beach, the Marine Room, Hennessey's, and the White House are the Big Three in Laguna Beach.

Crystal Cove State Park

This state park, between Laguna Beach and Corona del Mar, is a happy surprise on the Orange County coast. Stretching from the ocean into the wooded San Joaquin Hills, its 2,791 acres provide excellent hiking opportunities, three separate coastal accesses (Pelican Point, Los Trancos, and Reef Point), 3.5 miles of beautiful golden-sand beach, an "underwater park" (Irvine Coast Marine Life Refuge), and a 32-site walk-in environmental campground three miles inland. With this bounty, Crystal Cove State Park is known to swimmers, surfers, sunbathers, and divers.

As if that weren't enough, a county-run upland parcel of 2,000 acres known as **Laguna**

BEACH GAMES

The following are some of the most popular games we've witnessed on our beach journeys:

- **Frisbee:** What can we say? The equipment is cheap, and the only rule is not to throw it out to sea. Any game in which a dog can participate is one we feel well qualified to play. Moreover, there's always a chance that the little plastic saucer will get away from you and land near a babe.

- **Hacky-sack:** You generally see circles of shirtless guys (often Deadheads or jam-band fans) kicking the hacky-sack around. Basically, the object is to keep a leather beanbag in the air with the use of your feet. It requires dexterity, concentration, endurance, and a lack of anything better to do.

- **Over the Line (OTL):** This exciting combination of softball, volleyball, and cricket is played on the sand in bare feet. The only equipment needed is a bat, a softball, and gloves (optional for real OTL studs). The OTL field is paced off, 60 feet in width (or 22 paces), with no limit on length. Two teams of three players each compete. As in softball, teams alternate batting and fielding, with three outs per inning, but the game lasts only five innings. Two foul balls or one strike constitutes an out, as does a caught fly ball. Another switch: The pitcher throws to his or her own teammates, kneeling three feet away in the sand and lobbing the ball into an optimum swinging zone (not unlike setting up a spike in volleyball). A "hit" is required to land "over the line" (about 55 feet, or 20 paces, from the batter) and between foul lines. Three hits in an inning scores one run; every subsequent hit in the same inning counts as a run as well. (For more information on rules and tournaments, visit the Old Mission Bay Athletic Club's website at www.ombac.org.)

- **Paddleball:** A combination of tennis, handball, and ping-pong, this game is played

---

Coast Wilderness Park and the 11,500-acre **Irvine Ranch Land Reserve** combine with Crystal Cove State Park to provide a huge mountain-to-ocean tract of natural habitat within otherwise densely populated Orange County. The Irvine reserve is a permanent conservation easement deeded by the Irvine Company to the Nature Conservancy in 2001. On the environmental front, it is not all bad news in Orange County after all.

For more information, contact Crystal Cove State Beach, 8471 Pacific Coast Highway, Laguna Beach, CA, 949/494-3539, www.parks.ca.gov or www.crystalcovestatepark.com.

BEACHES

Reef Point is the southernmost access to Crystal Cove, with a stairway to a beach, hiking trail, bike path, and restrooms. **Los Trancos** has the largest parking lot, located on the east side of Pacific Coast Highway, with a tunnel leading under the highway to the beach. **Pelican Point** is the northernmost access, with a bluff-top trail leading to a steep beach access ramp. The beach itself is covered with silvery drift logs, rounded cobbles, and coarse, golden-brown sand. From it you gaze up onto ochre-colored bluffs and grassy, rolling hills beyond. People run, hike, or repose on the beach, whose quietude is a balm from all the automotive mania of the coast cities to the north and south. Modest day-use fees are charged.

One sour note to this pristine coastal glory is the Newport Coast development just north of Pelican Point. Bought by the obsessively acquisitive Disney Corporation, this private community is devoted to luxury time-share as singles or doubles on a miniature tennis court. The rules are the same as tennis, with the exception of the racket, which is a wobbly-centered thing that looks like an oversized ping-pong paddle. The paddle cuts down on the range of a struck ball and presumably its velocity (although it looked plenty fast to us). When the sport is played well – as it is on the courts in Venice Beach and Santa Monica – it can be as exciting as Centre Court at Wimbledon (well, close). In the limited space of a paddleball court, doubles requires a series of movements as intricate as kabuki dance. Check it out.

- **Volleyball:** If you don't already know the rules of volleyball, move to the back of the bus. What makes this game so "California" are the two-person teams that play on the beach. How, you find yourself wondering in awe, do two people in bare feet cover that much ground? Will that bikini top stay on? And most important, how can anyone ever hope to return one of those spikes, routinely clocked at over 100 miles per hour? (Answer: They rarely do, which is why these games move so swiftly.) On some beaches – Manhattan Beach and Santa Cruz, for instance – volleyball is not just a game but an obsession. It's also a professional sport, one that has been embraced by advertisers, fashion designers, and ESPN. In 2008, Kerri Walsh and Misty May-Treanor beat a Chinese duo to win the gold medal in women's beach volleyball at the Beijing Olympics. They also won the gold medal in 2004, making them the only team to repeat the feat and indisputably the greatest beach-volleyball duo of all time.

- **Whiffleball:** You can make any batter look foolish if you're tossing one of these plastic balls with the wacky waffle holes. The game is played like baseball, though no gloves are needed. The best setup we observed was at Mission Beach, where some guys had placed their beer-laden cooler near home plate and used the ocean as the outfield. If the batted ball went beyond where the waves broke, it was a home run. If it landed in the waves, it was a double. The object was to drink as much as possible from the cooler while at bat.

condominiums for the loophole-loving rich, who will write off the cost of these multi-million-dollar second homes on their taxes. Just across the street from this monolith is the Shake Shack, a 75-year-old smoothie stand that's much more in keeping with the true spirit of the beach life. Buy one of the healthy smoothies—orange-date and raspberry-peach sound good—and thumb your nose at Newport Coast while you're at it.

The long-range plan is to create a Historic District within the state park to preserve and protect a community of 46 small cottages that date from the 1930s. Meanwhile, down at Reef Point, the El Toro mobile home park, which is a bit of an eyesore, is being "converted" to a public campground, picnic area, and life-guarded beach. Although no one likes to see people displaced, this is ultimately a good

thing for the public and the long-term health of the natural habitat.

30 REEF POINT

Location: Pacific Coast Highway between Laguna Beach and Corona del Mar
Parking/Fees: $10 entrance fee per vehicle; camping fee at hike-in campground three miles inland $11-15 per night
Hours: 6 A.M.-sunset
Facilities: lifeguards, picnic tables, showers, restrooms, and visitors center (at El Moro Canyon)
Contact: Crystal Cove State Park, 949/494-3539

31 LOS TRANCOS

     BEST **(**

Location: Pacific Coast Highway between Laguna Beach and Corona del Mar
Parking/Fees: $10 entrance fee per vehicle
Hours: 6 A.M.-sunset
Facilities: lifeguards, picnic tables, showers, and restrooms
Contact: Crystal Cove State Park, 949/494-3539

32 PELICAN POINT

Location: Pacific Coast Highway between Laguna Beach and Corona del Mar
Parking/Fees: $10 entrance fee per vehicle
Hours: 6 A.M.-sunset
Facilities: lifeguards, picnic tables, showers, and restrooms
Contact: Crystal Cove State Park, 949/494-3539

ACCOMMODATIONS

The big news at Crystal Cove is the renovation of rustic coastal cottages in the Crystal Cove Historic District. The **Crystal Cove Beach Cottages** (Crystal Cove State Park, 949/494-3539, $$) opened in June 2006, making it possible for beachgoers to rent these studios and one- and two-bedroom homes, as well as hostel accommodations. It's a rare opportunity to stay in some nifty, out-of-the-way beach bungalows, 13 out of 46 of which are renovated and rentable. And though they date back only to the 1930s, this does indeed qualify as historic in Southern California. Rates are surprisingly reasonable—two people can share a room in a dorm-style cottage with five bedrooms for $63 per night, while $185 per night will net you a two-bedroom cottage all your own. Reservations must be made through ReserveAmerica (800/444-7275); you

can reserve up to seven months in advance. Do jump on this one!

COASTAL CUISINE

As if the good news about Crystal Cove Beach Cottages wasn't enough, they've opened the **Beachcomber Cafe** (15 Crystal Cove, 949/376-6900, $$), a restaurant serving three daily meals, in one of the restored cottages in the Crystal Cove Historic District.

Corona del Mar

Corona del Mar literally translates as "Crown of the Sea," but to us it simply means "the good life." When this book hits the best-seller lists (hope springs eternal!) or we win the lottery, Corona del Mar would be high on our list of places where we'd happily relocate. For one thing, this small, mostly residential, and fabulously wealthy "neighborhood" in Newport Beach is blessed with a sweeping vista of the ocean. The town's financial standing is evident in the Lamborghini car dealership and chic boutiques that do a buzzing business along the main drag. It's a shame there's nowhere viable to stay in Corona del Mar, because the beaches and the bluff-top parks overlooking them are as gorgeous as any in Orange County. For the most part, people tear through town on the grievously overburdened Pacific Coast Highway. It's well worth exploring the beaches off the beaten path along Ocean Boulevard. In fact, a whole other world lies off to the side of the highway clamor.

We took time to get to know Corona del Mar better on our latest trip; henceforth, it will become a required annual visit. The primarily residential oceanfront here is a visual feast, both seaward and landward. A fascinating mix of architectural styles gives the ritzy neighborhood a distinctively civilized air. We came upon a group of plein air landscape painters, mostly elderly women in sun bonnets, who gather regularly for seaside painting sessions. Although they may be deemed amateurs by critics, some of their work is at least as good as the stuff that gets peddled for inflated sums in the galleries of Laguna Beach.

For more information, contact the Corona del Mar Chamber of Commerce, 2855 East Pacific Coast Highway, Suite 101, Corona del Mar, CA 92625, 949/673-4050, www.cdchamber.com.

BEACHES

A linear park runs above Corona del Mar's beaches along Ocean Boulevard. At the south end, a steep road leads down to a wonderfully secluded cove, known as **Little Corona del Mar Beach.** As you're walking, be sure to ogle the estates that line the creekside canyon above the cove. Also notice the rock formations, including a perfect arch, in the water. Little Corona del Mar Beach is a miniature paradise for snorkeling, scuba diving, and tidepooling.

Corona del Mar State Beach (a.k.a. Main Beach)—which is reachable from the other end of Ocean Boulevard via a drive that drops down to it—is gorgeous, as are the people who go there. It is a gigantic triangular drape of sand studded with volleyball nets and beach blankets. More than once, we've been content just to sit and drink for a while in this real-life version of *Baywatch*. It's a state beach that's run by the city of Newport Beach. We don't exactly understand how or why.

Corona del Mar lies on the south side of Newport Harbor. Climbing the rocks at the north end of Corona del Mar Beach, in defiance of the Don't Climb the Rocks sign, will net you a nifty vantage point from which to view the harbor. If you scramble down from Ocean Boulevard to the sandy cove known as **Rocky Point** or Pirates Cove, you can watch boats come and go in relative solitude. Just up from Rocky Point is **China Cove Beach,**

accessible via a stairwell at Ocean Boulevard and Fernleaf Avenue. You can also hike up to Rocky Point and China Cove from Corona del Mar Beach.

Back up on Ocean Boulevard, overlooking China Cove, is **Lookout Point.** It's a wonderful spot from which to gaze out on the harbor jetties, Balboa Peninsula, and the setting sun. Concrete benches provide perches for savoring the magnificent view. The grass is greener here, and we mean that literally. Any of the houses in the vicinity could be featured on the Home and Garden Channel. Especially in the dimming light of day, these contemporary and Spanish-style marvels personify the upscale California lifestyle—an aesthete's dream, with the ocean as heavenly backdrop. By the way, in the unlikely event that anyone who lives along Ocean Boulevard or Poppy Avenue in Corona del Mar wants to invite us to a party, consider this an automatic RSVP. We're there!

ORANGE COUNTY

33 LITTLE CORONA DEL MAR BEACH

Location: Ocean Boulevard at Poppy Avenue in Corona del Mar
Parking/Fees: free street parking
Hours: 6 A.M.-10 P.M.
Facilities: none
Contact: Newport Beach Marine Department, 949/673-3047

34 CORONA DEL MAR STATE BEACH

Location: Ocean Boulevard at Iris Avenue in Corona del Mar
Parking/Fees: $8 entrance fee per vehicle
Hours: 8 A.M.-10 P.M. PDT (to 8 P.M. PST)

Facilities: concession, lifeguards, restrooms, showers, and picnic tables
Contact: Newport Beach Marine Department, 949/644-3151

35 ROCKY POINT

Location: Ocean Boulevard at Harbor Channel in Corona del Mar
Parking/Fees: free street parking
Hours: 6 A.M.-10 P.M.
Facilities: none
Contact: Newport Beach Marine Department, 949/673-3047

36 CHINA COVE BEACH

Location: Ocean Boulevard at Fernleaf Avenue in Corona del Mar
Parking/Fees: free street parking
Hours: 6 A.M.-10 P.M.
Facilities: none
Contact: Newport Beach Marine Department, 949/673-3047

COASTAL CUISINE

While it lacks lodging options, Corona del Mar has some of the glitziest restaurants in Orange County. Among the more notable ones are the posh, contemporary **Trees** (44 Heliotrope Avenue, 949/673-0910, $$$) and the British-themed, jacket-required **Five Crowns** (3801 East Pacific Coast Highway, 949/760-0331, $$$$). The latter is an elegant re-creation of England's oldest inn, Ye Old Bell, that's faithful in every detail, right down to the Elizabethan garb worn by the wait staff.

Our personal favorite is **Oysters** (2515 E. Coast Highway, 949/675-7411, $$$), an informal but elegant (read: no dress code or valet parking) place that has been working magic with Pacific Rim–style seafood preparations since 1989. A recent meal here was one of the finest, from start to finish, we've ever had in our beach travels. The oyster sampler contained four distinctive types: Fanny Bays, from British Columbia (firm, salted cucumber flavor); Hama Hamas, from Washington State (mild fruity flavor); Hog Islands, from Tomales Bay (plump, smoky flavored, indescribably delicious); and Sunset Beaches, from Puget Sound (crisp and fruity). The kung pao calamari, a popular appetizer, was sheer perfection, a peerless combination of texture and flavors, and the helping was large enough for a meal.

For entrées, the flat-iron seared Hawaiian ahi—a thick, moist slab of crimson as tender as filet mignon—was brilliantly complemented by jasmine-nori rice, spinach, and a soy-chile glaze. The misoyaki northern halibut was another masterpiece of blended flavors and textures, served with fresh soybeans, oyster mushrooms, and a potato-daikon puree. Oysters is commendably participating in a restaurant industry campaign to "Take a Pass on Chilean Sea Bass" by replacing that popular fish with halibut. Without restrictions on the fishing of this species, the Chilean sea bass has been on the verge of commercial extinction for years. Oddly enough, the one thing that may save it is not a positive thing: Chilean sea bass has been found to have extremely high levels of mercury, and consumers are advised that more than two helpings per month is dangerous. Let's all take a pass!

For dessert, the vanilla bean crème brûlée was transformed by a topping of fresh raspberries and a "blowtorch fired" sugar glaze. Our genial waiter, previously a veteran of 10 years in French restaurants, was sold on Oysters, telling us the chef stands so firmly for consistency that restaurant regulars claim to wake up fantasizing about what they will order here, knowing it will be as good as the last time. We will remember Oysters for our next visit. Until then, visions of kung pao squid dance in our heads.

Newport Beach and Balboa

Newport Beach has been mislabeled. The goods are in order, but the writing on the can is all wrong. Before our initial visit way back in the mid-1980s, we'd been led to believe that it was "Nouveau Beach," a land of conspicuous consumption that looked down on anyone in flip-flops and cutoffs. We came expecting manic wheeler-dealer entrepreneurs and bored women dripping with jewelry. After all, Newport Beach was modeled on and named after Newport, Rhode Island, an exclusive community for the old-money yachting set. Indeed, Newport Beach has a few of its eastern kin's amenities, most notably the second largest pleasure-craft harbor in the country (with 10,000 berths). But Newport Beach also has an unpretentious, accommodating side that just doesn't jibe with its designer reputation. After numerous happy visits here, we've come to realize that Newport Beach is, at heart, a fun and funky beach town.

First of all, with a population of 84,200, Newport Beach is not a small town, nor is most of it truly on the beach. Many Newport Beach residents drive expensive imported cars with vanity plates, but they tend to live in gated subdivisions on the mainland or on the exclusive islands in Balboa Bay. The heart and soul of the city is out on Balboa Peninsula, a thin finger of land that reaches into the Pacific, then bends inward to protect the beautiful harbor. Back bays and waterways have been sculpted into the peninsula, and two small inhabited islands, Balboa and Lido, sit close by. Newport Beach is almost always sunny, relaxed, and dominated by watery pastimes. Boats dock right up against the back doors of houses.

The fun begins when you turn off Pacific Coast Highway onto Newport Boulevard or West Balboa Boulevard. The latter runs the length of Newport Beach's peninsula. It's a six-mile stretch ending at the Wedge, by the north jetty at the harbor mouth. To oversimplify, the big money is on the harbor side and all the fun is on the ocean side. Most beachgoers assemble in the general vicinity of the peninsula's ocean piers, Newport Pier and Balboa Pier.

The most boisterous activity can be found at and around Newport Pier. The first pier on this site was built in 1888 by the McFadden brothers, who founded the town and for whom the pier was originally named. Local history lingers here in the form of the beloved Dory Fleet, a fishing contingent that has launched wooden dories from this spot since 1891. Each day, the Dory Fleet leaves before dawn and returns by 7:30 A.M. to sell their fresh catch at Newport Pier. Their motto: Our fish is the freshest fish on earth. A wooden sculpture pays tribute to these stout-hearted laborers, and their method of selling fish right on the beach creates an authentic California atmosphere. Nearby, you might see street performers addressing the crowd. We observed a balloon sculptor singing spirituals in an operatic tenor while a long-haired sea dog took Polaroids of passersby posing with his beautifully plumed parrots.

In the 1980s Newport's nouveau-riche elite—exhibiting the shortsightedness that brought them wealth but wound up bankrupting Orange County in 1994—wanted to do away with the Dory Fleet and give the Newport Pier area a sprucing up. They were quickly shot down, offering further proof that Newport Beach's ordinary townsfolk possess the sense and spirit that the more moneyed mullet-brains lack.

Balboa Pier lies two miles farther out along the peninsula. Here, things are a little less crazy. On the harbor side behind Balboa Pier is Balboa Pavilion, a Victorian landmark that dates from 1906. A renowned hot spot during

ORANGE COUNTY

BIKING THE BALBOA PENINSULA

People of all ages flock to the area around the Newport Beach Pier and jam the Balboa Peninsula with traffic. During peak season it's not unusual to find traffic slowed to a standstill on Balboa Boulevard all the way out to the Pacific Coast Highway. Traffic is a thorn in Newport Beach's side. It's partly the result of a decision made many years ago not to have I-5 built closer to the coast here. (Ironically, the decision was made in order to preserve the peace and quiet of the community.) The strategy worked for a while but backfired when Newport Beach exploded with growth in the 1980s.

It goes without saying that driving here can be as gnarly as swimming through a kelp bed. Parking tickets come with stiff fines, and parking at most meters costs $0.25 for 15 minutes, with a six-hour limit. Six hours costs six bucks, and who carries 24 quarters around with them? The city experimented with "smart" meters, which didn't require coins, but went back to the old way of doing business.

The best way to see the beach at Newport Beach is on bicycle, coasting along on the Ocean Front promenade. The peninsula is flat and the city is bicycle-friendly. Local bike-rental outfits carry an excellent map of trails, with detailed tips and rules of the road that are useful anywhere, as well as local points of interest, license information and fees, hazards, and bike lanes along highways. Bike trails run as far east as Irvine, traversing the Upper Newport Bay, a state-managed ecological reserve. So save yourself some hassles – not to mention gas and parking expenses – and have twice the fun with half the wheels.

Here are three places to rent bikes near Newport Pier, right in the heart of the action:

- **Let It Roll Bike Shop,** 3130 West Balboa Boulevard, 949/675-3136
- **Newport Beach Bike and Skate Rental,** 2200 West Oceanfront, 949/675-1065
- **Boardwalk Sports,** 100 McFadden Place, 949/673-1767

the Big Band era, the pavilion still hosts events. You can catch a harbor-cruise boat (see the former homes of John Wayne, King Gillette, and Ron Popeil, inventor of the "Pocket Fisherman"!), take a whale-watching trip, or board a passenger ferry to Catalina Island. A cute quarter-a-ride ferry runs continuously to Balboa Island. It is mostly residential, tightly packed with the homes of wealthy people whose cars chirp like crickets as they approach and exit with electronic keys. The island has a sprinkling of upscale boutiques and tourist shops, but its most appealing feature is the walkway around it, which offers views of the bay and harbor.

Newport Beach is a quintessential California beach town by day and a rock-and-roll party zone at night. Despite the nonstop crunch of humanity, the peninsula is a friendly place. The most violent blows result from the affectionate pounding of backs, and the loudest shouts are those of approval for some minuscule sashaying bikini. One local restaurant goes so far as to offer "free salad for girls in bikinis." The pedestrian's best friend in Newport Beach is Ocean Front promenade, an asphalt trail that runs along the ocean for nearly the full length of the peninsula. It is the primary route for bicyclists, joggers, and in-line skaters, and the human parade along this walkway is an intoxicating sight in and of itself.

For more information, contact Newport Beach Conference and Visitor Bureau, 1200 Newport Center Drive, Suite 120, Newport Beach, CA 92663, 949/722-1611 or 800/942-6278, www.visitnewportbeach.com.

BEACHES

There are more than six miles of ocean beach and two massive piers on Balboa Peninsula. Starting at the south end, in Balboa, **West Jetty View Park** (a.k.a. The Wedge) is El Dorado for bodysurfers. Extremely rough surf, with waves as high as 20 feet, make the Wedge unsafe for board surfing and suitable only for highly experienced bodysurfers. Just across the harbor from the Wedge is Corona del Mar State Beach. Do not try to swim across. It may look like a short distance, but the water is treacherous. Just watch the boats sailing in and out of the harbor.

The stretch of sand from the Wedge to Balboa Pier is **Balboa Beach.** The dune structure along here is exceptionally healthy. This is what the Orange County coast must've looked like in the predevelopment 1950s, when it was primarily an escape for L.A. day-trippers. Families congregate on Balboa Beach for relaxed sunbathing and swimming.

The main beach on the peninsula is **Newport Beach Municipal Beach,** which runs for two and a quarter miles from Newport Pier to the Santa Ana River Jetty. Along this golden strand surfers prefer the beaches at 52nd Street, North Jetty, and from 61st Street Beach to **Santa Ana River Jetties** (a.k.a. Santa Ana River County Beach), which flanks both sides of the river mouth, just south of Huntington Beach. All beaches on the Newport Beach peninsula are subject to a 10 P.M. curfew.

We're certainly not telling you anything you don't know when we say that traffic on Balboa Peninsula can get hellish on weekends and busy on summer weekdays. The only advice we can give is to bring lots of quarters for the meters—a roll or two if you want to stay all day.

37 WEST JETTY VIEW PARK

Location: end of Channel Road at tip of Balboa Peninsula, in Balboa

Parking/Fees: free parking lot
Hours: 6 A.M.-10 P.M.
Facilities: none
Contact: Newport Beach Marine Department, 949/673-3047

38 BALBOA BEACH

Location: Balboa Boulevard at Balboa Pier in Balboa
Parking/Fees: metered street parking
Hours: 6 A.M.-10 P.M.
Facilities: lifeguards, restrooms, showers, and picnic tables
Contact: Newport Beach Marine Department, 949/673-3047

39 NEWPORT BEACH MUNICIPAL BEACH

Location: Ocean Front at Newport Pier in Newport Beach
Parking/Fees: metered lot and street parking
Hours: 6 A.M.-10 P.M.
Facilities: lifeguards, restrooms, showers, and picnic tables
Contact: Newport Beach Marine Department, 949/673-3047

40 SANTA ANA RIVER JETTIES

Location: Seashore Drive between Summit and 61st Streets in Newport Beach
Parking/Fees: metered street parking
Hours: 6 A.M.-10 P.M.
Facilities: lifeguards
Contact: North Beaches Operation Office of Orange County Harbors, Beaches, and Parks, 949/723-4511

ORANGE COUNTY

ORANGE COUNTY

© PARKE PUTERBAUGH

Newport Beach

RECREATION AND ATTRACTIONS

- **Bike/Skate Rentals:** Newport Beach Bike Skate Rental, 2200 West Ocean Front, Newport Beach, 949/675-1065
- **Ecotourism:** Upper Newport Bay Ecological Reserve, Newport Beach, 949/640-6746
- **Marina:** Newport Dunes Resort and Marina, 1131 Back Bay Drive, Newport Beach, 949/729-3863
- **Piers:** Newport Pier, McFadden Square, 22nd Street at Newport Boulevard, Newport Beach; Balboa Pier, foot of Main Street, Balboa
- **Rainy Day Attraction:** Newport Harbor Nautical Museum, 151 East Coast Highway, Newport Beach, 949/673-7863
- **Shopping/Browsing:** Fashion Island, Newport Center Drive, Newport Beach, 949/721-2000
- **Sportfishing:** Bongos Sportfishing Charters, 2140 Newport Boulevard, Newport

Beach, 949/673-2810; Davey's Locker, 400 Main Street, 949/673-1434
- **Surf Report:** 949/673-3371
- **Surf Shop:** Green Room, 4525 Pacific Coast Highway, Newport Beach, 949/548-3688
- **Vacation Rentals:** Beach 'n Bay Rental Company, 1501 West Balboa Boulevard, Balboa, 949/673-9368

ACCOMMODATIONS

Nightly lodgings directly on the beach are scarcer than gulls' teeth. A particularly nice and fairly pricey one that's only a few bare feet from the surf is the **Newport Beachwalk Hotel** (2306 West Ocean Front, 949/673-7030, www.newportbeachwalkhotel.com, $$$). Formerly a surf shop, its 20 elegant rooms, ranging $175–275, will put you in mind of the Italian Riviera. Only a block from the beach and three blocks from the pier, **Bay Shores Peninsula Hotel** (1800 West Balboa Boulevard, 949/675-3463, $$$) is a salmon-colored, 21-room inn with homey, comfortable rooms.

The inn provides a decent continental breakfast, not to mention everything from beach towels to boogie boards just for the asking. Plus you get a parking space—no small perk in Newport Beach.

Just off Balboa Peninsula, the most reasonably priced ($99 in season) and beach accessible of the motels that line Pacific Coast Highway is the **Newport Channel Inn** (6030 West Pacific Coast Highway, 949/642-3030 or 800/255-8614, www.newportchannelinn .com, $). It isn't fancy but it is clean and serviceable. The motel is across the street—the "street" being Pacific Coast Highway—from the wide, sandy beach at the north end of Newport Beach.

The friendly tone of the town and easy proximity to the sand makes a weekly or monthly apartment rental an appealing prospect here. Two agencies that specialize in beachfront rentals are **Villa Rentals** (427 31st Street, 949/675-4912, www.villarentalsinc.com) and **Balboa Newport Realty** (428 Third Street, 949/723-4494, www.balboanewport.com). The rental units on Balboa Beach are more family oriented, with a casual, kid-friendly ambience. Rates range from $750 for a week to $2,500 for a month. People recline in chaise lounges on back patios, reading newspapers and drinking highballs or coffee, oblivious to the parade passing just feet away on the Ocean Front promenade. The wildest characters you'll run across are adolescents trying to act raunchy. One 12-year-old sported a T-shirt that read "Will Work For Sex." Very funny, junior.

On either side of Newport Pier and continuing to the north end of the peninsula, rentals are snapped up by college kids or groups of party-minded guys whose spartan pads are open to the scrutiny of passersby. Shirtless, tanned, smiling, and perpetually holding beers, they hang loose on every balcony and porch. We peered into one unkempt bungalow where a surfboard lay on a bed and a skateboard hung on the wall. Only in California . . .

COASTAL CUISINE

The **Crab Cooker** (2200 Newport Boulevard, 949/673-0100, $$), one of our favorite eateries in the universe, has been serving its patented smoked and grilled fish for almost 50 years in a building that was once a bank. "We're the only seafood joint that keeps its fish in a vault," jokes owner Bob Roubian, who is an expert on the subject of fish. He is, in fact, obsessed with them. He thinks about fish all day and dreams about fish at night. He sculpts, poeticizes, and writes songs about fish. A recording of a song he penned, "Who Hears the Fishes When They Cry," is sold at the restaurant. (He sounds like Tom Waits.) Music and fish have a lot in common, he says; both have scales. He encourages everyone to "Eat Lots A Fish." This is his motto, and it is emblazoned on the front of the building, along with such nuggets of wisdom as "Slam Some Salmon" and "The main thing is to keep the main thing the main thing."

Near Newport Pier, the Crab Cooker is a local institution for several reasons, not the least of which is that Roubian enforces strict standards on the fish he serves. He buys only fish that have been caught by the hook-and-line method and are eviscerated (bled and cleaned) within five minutes of being pulled from the water, thus assuring their freshness. Fresh fish never smells fishy, he insists; if anything, it smells a little sweet, like watermelon. His fish, shrimp, crab, and scallops are cooked on wooden skewers over a charcoal grill, because that's the way his mother did it. All dinners come with homemade bread, coleslaw, and Romano potatoes. You can actually make a filling meal from the Crab Cooker's incomparably good smoked albacore and smoked salmon appetizers. (Get the large versions, which are $4.25 and $6, respectively.) The food is served on paper plates, like a picnic, and it is beyond compare in quality and price.

This wonderfully ramshackle place is always packed, but don't try to call for reservations or pay with plastic. Just show up and wait your

ORANGE COUNTY

turn in line. To Roubian this is democracy at work, and he'll make no exceptions—not for a U.S. president, not for his grandmother, not even for himself. John Wayne, a longtime regular, always had to wait his turn, as did Richard Nixon. Sometimes the wait can be long, but just settle back on the wooden benches outside, have a cup of the Crab Cooker's famous seafood chowder, and write someone a postcard. (Roubian provides cards and postage, if mailed from the restaurant.) But by all means "eat lots a fish" here as often as possible.

The **Cannery** (3010 Lafayette Avenue, 949/566-0060, $$$) also serves some fine fare. The calamari appetizer is as tender a take on this staple as we've ever had, and the grilled swordfish tomatillo is a winning catch. The restaurant is in a converted cannery, with implements of the trade hung on the wall: wheels, pulleys, conveyer lines, boilers, and processing machines. You can eat inside or on a deck overlooking the water. After dinner, the Cannery morphs into one of the livelier nightspots in Newport Beach.

Even if you're not casting a line you can still land a fish on Newport Pier. At pier's end, **Newport Grill and Sushi Bar** (1 Newport Pier, 949/675-9771, $$$) serves grilled fish, sushi, and steaks from its second-floor dining room. It's easily the best view in town.

For a quick bite with a nice view, hit **Ruby's Diner** (1 Balboa Pier, 949/675-7829, $) at the end of Balboa Pier. The fare is mostly burgers and the atmosphere is faux-1950s diner, rimmed with neon. But the view is the second best in town and the grub is fine, as far as burgers and dogs go. Another local institution is the **Shore House Cafe** (801 East Balboa Boulevard, 949/673-7726, $$), on the main drag.

At the other extreme is **21 Oceanfront** (2100 West Ocean Front, 949/673-2100, $$$$), an elegant fine-dining restaurant that serves fish flown in from all over the world. Abalone is a specialty, and entrées run $25–55. In other words, 21 Oceanfront is high-priced and high-end.

NIGHTLIFE

Most of the action after dark takes place on and around the piers. At **Balboa Pier,** set the wayback machine to the 1950s and step into a world of flirtatious adolescents on parade. Around and around the Balboa Pavilion circles an army of Annettes and Frankies too young to drink but too blitzed out on raging hormones to sit still. Dressed to thrill, they wander about, creating human logjams broken up by friendly beat cops on patrol. They walk around the pavilion again and return to the same logjam—cruising without cars, as it were.

The crowd is older, noisier, and more unpredictable at **Newport Pier.** Motorcycles and muscle T-shirts replace high fashion, and voices get raised a bit louder. The same cops survey the scene, but in a somewhat less amicable manner. Mostly, though, the chaos has a certain California etiquette to it, with lots of backslaps, handshakes, and high fives.

Blackie's by the Sea (21st Street and Ocean Front) is the beer-bar equivalent of the Crab Cooker. It is a timeless, changeless throwback, directly on Ocean Front promenade. On the door is a sign that reads Sorry, We're Open, and on the walls are mounted hammerhead sharks, team pennants, three TVs (each tuned to a different station), pool tables, and a jukebox. It is a classic beer-drinker's oasis at any time of the day or night. We'd give you the phone number, but it's unlisted—part of its homey charm.

Just to the north is **Mutt Lynch's** (23rd Street and Ocean Front, 949/675-1556), a raucous corner joint serving passable pizza, sandwiches, and sports-bar munchies, plus geysers of beer.

Around the corner, off Ocean Front, is the **Stag Bar** (121 McFadden Place, 949/673-4470). It is not, however, a stag bar. That is to say, women are welcome here. Reflecting a cutting-edge collegiate atmosphere, the Stag Bar is a raucous, beer-guzzling, hellyessing kind of place, with a great jukebox, pool tables, and no pretensions. Draft beer is served in schooners the size of bazookas. On an otherwise slow Monday night in early spring when the rest of Newport Beach was dead, we watched from our bar-side perches as the Stag Bar slowly but surely filled to capacity. By midnight the place was thumping to the beat of pool cues, jukebox jive, and erupting laughter. It occurred to us that, for a so-called stag bar, there were sure a lot of women. In fact, they outnumbered the men, at least on this particular evening. Because you cannot legally smoke in any bar or restaurant in California, the sidewalk outside the Stag Bar gets crowded with barflies taking frequent cigarette breaks. The smoke drifts into the bar, virtually negating the anti-smoking law's directive. We watched three college coeds celebrate the rites of spring by playing pool and drinking beer. The noise level grew and the shots became less accurate with each swig, but no one seemed to notice—ah, the delightful incoherence of youth. Meanwhile, a discombobulated woman who had just panhandled us for a buck wandered outside, where she collapsed in a heap on the sidewalk. We reminisced with the bartender about various punk bands we'd seen over the years, while the jukebox pumped out tunes by Sublime, X, and Social Distortion. We programmed a few selections of our own, including, appropriately, "L.A. Woman," by the Doors. We also played "Whole Lotta Rosie" (the live version) by AC/DC.

Speaking of rosie, you can do a beer-fueled version of ring-around-the-rosie in the Newport Pier area without having to drive a car. Perambulate Ocean Front, McFadden Place, and Balboa Boulevard, angling into the Stag Bar, Mutt Lynch's, Blackie's, **Baja Sharkeez** (114 McFadden Place, 949/673-0292), **Hooters** (2406 Newport Boulevard, 949/723-5800), and **Woody's Wharf** (2318 Newport Boulevard, 949/675-0474). The last of these is another wild hangout with live music (mostly blues and boogie) that gets mobbed on weekends. The clientele seems a bit wanton. It has an outdoor patio and a

harborfront dining area, but the main part of the club is configured all wrong and we wound up being wedged against the bar like sardines. Still, it's a hopping place if you want to frolic with the locals, who have been doing so here for 30 years.

Huntington Beach

Huntington Beach is an essentially faceless city whose every move is plotted to best serve the interests of the Orange County business community. Everywhere, it looks and sounds and smells like a city under construction (or reconstruction). This is not necessarily all bad news, but it does mean that Huntington Beach lacks any sort of defining personality. Newport Beach is a funky, low-to-the-ground beach town, and Laguna Beach is cultured and rarefied. By comparison, Huntington Beach feels like a completely sterile asphalt-and-concrete sprawl zone. As if its utter lack of personality weren't bad enough, its beachfront is hemmed between the fuming stacks of a power plant and an active oil field. Inland, the numbing concrete corridor of Beach Boulevard is lined for miles with strip malls and franchises all the way out to I-405.

There's a brief but welcome eruption of bright, squeaky clean commerce by the Huntington Beach Pier along Pacific Coast Highway at Beach Boulevard. The pier and the surfing scene are easily the best things about Huntington Beach. To be sure, the development landward of the beach seems endless (e.g., "4 New Home Neighborhoods Open Soon!"), as Huntington Beach—with a population of 202,500, Orange County's 4th largest and state's 20th largest city—is completely at the mercy of the real-estate industry. It looks like utter madness to us.

Once upon a time Huntington Beach was just another cow town close to Los Angeles with a beautiful beach that was much beloved by the surfing cult. They knew it then as "Surf City," and it still gets called that now,

Huntington Beach

though more by businessmen looking for a marketing handle than by loyal surfers. In Huntington Beach, as Jan and Dean sang in their number-one hit from 1963, the surf was always up and there was the added incentive of "two girls for every boy." During the golden era of surfing in the 1950s and 1960s, the surfers pretty much had the place to themselves. As recently as the mid-1980s, Huntington Beach was a pretty sleepy-looking place along Pacific Coast Highway, lined with unpretentious food shacks (usually Mexican), surf shops, and one-story motor courts. The town would awaken only for the annual Labor Day surfing tournament and the de rigueur riot that often accompanied it.

All that began to change with the arrival of the Waterfront Hilton Beach Resort, a 12-story, 290-room hotel. It has been joined by the Pierside Pavilion and Promenade—clusters of retail stores, restaurants, theaters, and office space that chased a lot of funky old joints off the beach. Hyatt Ocean Grand, a $142 million resort colossus, opened in 2003. This is big news along a coastline where permits for new construction are rarely granted. There's

also a gargantuan "mixed use" complex, including a high-end terraced retail mall, that occupies 34 ocean-facing acres. After having remained sleepy for so many years, this flat, foursquare cow town is now an all-too-wide-awake insomniac.

With a bit of imagination, the eye can trace its way across the landscape and imagine what Huntington Beach must have looked like at some remote point in the pre-settlement past: fields of large, fully vegetated dunes extending to the east, backed by lagoons and wetlands. In the early years of this century, the town was actually named "Pacific City" by a developer who wanted to see it become the West Coast's answer to Atlantic City. Pacific City was sold to a group who renamed it Huntington Beach, hoping that by paying nominal tribute to railroad magnate H. E. Huntington he would extend his Pacific Electric Railroad to the young city. (He fell for the ploy.) In 1919 Standard Oil leased 500 acres from the Huntington Beach Company; a year later, a well came in with a roar heard for miles. Nine million gallons a year are pumped out of Huntington Beach. Oil derricks are everywhere (except tourist

LEGEND OF THE DUKE

There's another "Duke" besides John Wayne who left his mark on Orange County. He is **Duke Kahanamoku,** a Waikiki wave-rider who became a California legend. More than anyone else, he spread the word about Huntington Beach, turning a withering, would-be resort into a bustling beach town.

Duke was a Hawaiian native, Olympic swimmer, and a world-class surfer – one of the first, in fact, to make a living at these things. Way back at the turn of the 20th century he publicly promoted the sport, gracefully skiing the sloping surf on his favorite plank. His salary was paid by railroad mogul H. E. Huntington, who wanted to give the public new incentives to travel his freshly laid stretch of track from Los Angeles to Huntington Beach. Duke wowed the locals in the 1920s by surfing under the pier – a dangerous but impressive feat.

Following Duke's lead, a small but growing surfing cult pointed their longboards toward Huntington Beach. In the early 1960s surfing seized the national imagination. When the Beach Boys, Jan and Dean, and the Surfaris took the sport into the Top 40 with a string of catchy surfing anthems, the entire nation suddenly became desirous of coastal access. Surfers trekked the entire West Coast in search of the perfect wave, but it was Huntington Beach that became known as "Surf City," after Jan and Dean's chart-topping hit. The first major surfing competition, the Pacific Coast Surfboard Championships, was held here. Since the early 1970s, the U.S. Surfing Championships have drawn hundreds of thousands to the brown-sugar beach at Huntington.

For many years, a small bust of Duke Kahanamoku gazed seaward from the foot of the Huntington Beach Pier. It has since been moved inside the **Huntington Beach International Surfing Museum** (411 Olive Avenue, 714/960-3483). These days, the late Duke – he died in 1968 at the age of 78 – is recognized as the father of surfing. Remnants and relics of surfing's golden age fill the museum, which is one of the few things worth visiting in Huntington Beach besides the beach itself. Artifacts include wildly designed Hawaiian shirts to a 13-foot, 135-pound wooden longboard. There's also memorabilia from the Huntington Beach Surf Theater, a bygone 1960s-era film house that showed only surf movies.

Ah, yes, those were the days.

ORANGE COUNTY

brochures): by the highway, in backyards, on the beach, atop offshore platforms. A gigantic active field runs for miles from Goldenwest Street north to Sunset Beach. The pumping drills extend as far as the eye can see, like an aerobics class of metallic black magpies doing toe-touching exercises.

Despite all the changes, Huntington Beach remains a people's beach. Families, surfers, and everyday folks still crowd the city and state beaches that run for a great distance in either direction from the pier. But the retail scenery around these beaches has been drastically altered. At one extreme, there's the Waterfront Hilton, a towering monolith. At

the other extreme, fast-food chains now rule the waterfront where once humble but lovable nonfranchised burger and taco huts used to stand. The heart of the action is where Main Street meets Pacific Coast Highway at Huntington Beach Pier. This intersection is home to the Pierside Pavilion and Promenade, a two-story boutique mall aimed at those whose idea of a day at the beach is shopping close to it. Lest we sound too harsh, experience has shown that shops in these glitzy new malls generally have limited life spans, while they displace less trendy stores and restaurants that might have been around for decades. In the process, we've lost—and continue to lose—

many of the beachside stands that stood sentry throughout the years when *American Graffiti* was being lived in reality instead of marketed as nostalgia.

The old Huntington Beach—a motley but likable cluster of surf shops, dive bars, and food stands—has fallen to the wrecking ball. City officials referred to the forced uprooting and relocation of mobile-home-park-dwelling oceanside residents, in *1984*-style double-speak, as a "conversion procedure." We have no delusions: We are not lamenting the passing of great architectural landmarks or businesses that can compete in the latter-day market-place. It's just sad to witness the end of an era. A generation from now, will anyone remember what the beach life was really like?

Consider the squabbling that ensued when Dean Torrance, of Jan and Dean fame, suggested to the Huntington Beach City Council in 1991 that they consider copyrighting the name "Surf City" for promotional purposes. "People from Iowa want to come here to the beach," noted Torrance. "All the city has to do is grab onto the coattails of this idea." A great and legitimate hook for reeling in the tourists, no? Not in the eyes of one councilman, who whined, "We want people who will spend several hundred dollars a day in our hotels and restaurants. With inland California surfers, we're lucky if they spend $10 or $15 a day." This is how minds in Orange County work: with myopic eyes fixed on the bottom line at all times. And then, ironically, Huntington Beach got in a great big fight with Santa Cruz to brand itself...you guessed it...Surf City.

Whether you're spending $10 or $300 a day, the only part of Huntington Beach that matters is its coastal frontage. The town that sprawls behind it, arrayed along broad, strip-mall-lined arteries that link Pacific Coast Highway with I-405, offers the visitor little that can't be found on or close to the beach. Beach Boulevard is the Big Kahuna of commerce in the area, offering a lengthy corridor of gas stations, franchise food stands, ATM machines, and strip malls. You can venture

down this sun-beaten ribbon of concrete in search of drive-through grub, suntan lotion, film, flip-flops, or a more affordable motel, if you like, but there's not much to distinguish the interior of Huntington Beach from Fresno or Des Moines.

Incidentally, we tried to get a balky laptop PC repaired in Huntington Beach. We hauled it to a computer shop way out Goldenwest Street, farther inland than we care to venture on our beach-research trips. The dude behind the counter informed us of the inflated cost of working on a PC (minimum charge: $75). We lug nearly worthless old laptops on our beach junkets for obvious reasons (i.e., they might get stolen), but they do a perfectly fine job of word processing. When we seemed disinclined to leave the malfunctioning PC for servicing, the clerk suggested something we might try to get it to work. Lo and behold, we were able to revive it back in our hotel room. What sticks in our mind about this episode was the youthful clerk's disengagement and glassy-eyed expression. He looked like a character out of *Children of the Damned*. It was like communicating with a robot. His detached demeanor is not, we hope, what becomes of people who live in a community where shopping-mall sterility takes over their every remaining brain cell, rendering them numb and dumb.

Here's the best indication we've yet run across of the Orange County mind-set. It was reported that Huntington Beach struck a sponsorship deal with Coca-Cola, making Coke the city's "official beverage" and forbidding the sale of Pepsi everywhere but private businesses. It's bad enough that fast-food chains, sports arenas, schools, teams, and rock bands sign exclusivity contracts with the corporations that make these sweet, fizzy beverages. But a sponsorship deal with an entire *city*? Is there no bottom they won't plumb for money out here?

This Beaver Cleaver paradise of concrete and stucco has periodically been wracked with divisive issues. From battles over construction of the Waterfront to a debate over what to do with the Bolsa Chica wetlands (develop or preserve was the choice, and of course they developed), Huntington Beach found itself in the hot seat a lot in the 1990s. Even the old reliable surfers, source of the "Surf City" drawing card, have been a scourge on occasion. Back in 1987, the same year in which Huntington Beach was declared the safest city in the United States, a major riot erupted during the Labor Day surfing tournament, making national headlines. They subsequently moved the tournament to August (when crowds would be smaller), beefed up the police presence, and worked to keep alcohol off the beach. We've attended the U.S. Open of Surfing in Huntington Beach and had a blast. The world's best surfers in the water, live rock bands on the beach, a sea of tanned and gorgeous bodies—what was not to like?

This event dates back to 1959 and it's inextricably linked to Huntington Beach. These days it's under sponsorship from Honda. (Yes, it's now the Honda U.S. Open of Surfing.) So who won? It was reported that "Nathaniel Curran overcomes marginal waves and computer glitches to become the 2008 Honda U.S. Open of Surfing men's champion." Yay, Nathan!

Meanwhile, back in the truth-in-packaging department, they still tout Huntington Beach as one of America's safest cities. A little sleuthing on our part, however, turned up the statistic that among U.S. cities with populations between 100,000 and 250,000, Huntington recently placed 167th in terms of number of murders. Just so you know.

For more information, contact the Huntington Beach Conference and Visitor Bureau, 301 Main Street, Suite 208, Huntington Beach, CA 92648, 714/969-3492 or 800/729-6232, www.surfcityusa.com.

BEACHES

Santa Cruz and Huntington Beach have been squabbling for years over which community has earned the right to the title "Surf City," but based on all available evidence, it's not even worth debating. Huntington Beach

rules! Summer surfing championships have been held here since 1928, and it is widely known as the International Surf Capital of the World. In July and August, Huntington Beach hosts the U.S. Open of Surfing, and in June the OP Pro Surfing Championships takes place. There's always something going on here, surf-wise.

People flock to Huntington Beach from the surrounding valley towns, as well as from surf-deprived Long Beach, with boards strapped to the roofs of everything from boat-sized woodies to old VW bugs. The beach is so extensive, sandy, and clean, and the tumbling waves that roll ashore so well formed for surfing, that Huntington was voted the sixth best beach in the world in a poll conducted by (of all things) *Lifestyles of the Rich and Famous*. Surfers tend to get a far-off look in their eyes when they ponder the unobstructed south swells that spill forward in perfect curls of wave and foam (known as "rooster tails"), which can reach up to 12 feet in height.

The beaches of Huntington Beach offer an archetypal Southern California experience. They run for 8.5 miles, encompassing **Huntington State Beach, Huntington City Beach,** and **Bolsa Chica State Beach.** The offshore breezes are refreshing, and the strand is among the widest in Southern California—at least along the adjoining state and city beaches. It costs $10 to park at both Huntington State Beach and Huntington City Beach. There are an incredible 2,400 parking spaces at the city beach, which allows RV camping except during the most popular times of year (late spring through Labor Day).

Bring your running shoes or bicycle, because you can jog or pedal for five ocean-hugging miles (10 miles round-trip) along the **Huntington Beach Path** and **Bolsa Chica Bike Path.** We've taken many rejuvenating morning runs here. Up around Bolsa Chica, the beach starts narrowing. Fences have been put up to keep people back from unstable, crumbling cliffs. In places, the beach has narrowed so severely that it is usable only at low

ORANGE COUNTY

tide. RV camping is available at Bolsa Chica in an "en route" parking lot.

When you've had enough fun on the beach, make your way to the **Huntington Beach International Surfing Museum** (411 Olive Street, 714/960-3483) and the **Surfing Walk of Fame** (Main Street at Pacific Coast Highway). At the museum—opened in 1988, and the largest of a growing number of them—you learn that surfing was first documented in 1778, when Captain James Cook of the British Navy watched Hawaiian natives ride waves on crude longboards. The Walk of Fame starts at Jack's Surfboards and runs up Main Street. Stone monuments salute surfers inducted in such categories as Surf Pioneer, Surf Champion, and Woman of the Year.

41 HUNTINGTON STATE BEACH

Location: Pacific Coast Highway from Santa Ana River to Beach Boulevard in Huntington Beach
Parking/Fees: $10 entrance fee per vehicle
Hours: 6 A.M.-10 P.M.
Facilities: lifeguards, restrooms, showers, and picnic tables
Contact: Huntington State Beach, 714/536-1454

42 HUNTINGTON CITY BEACH

 BEST (

Location: Pacific Coast Highway from Beach Boulevard to Goldenwest Street in Huntington Beach
Parking/Fees: $10 entrance fee per vehicle; RV camping fee $60 per night; camping not permitted late spring-summer
Hours: 5 A.M.-10 P.M.
Facilities: lifeguards, restrooms, showers, and picnic tables
Contact: Huntington City Beach, 714/536-5281

43 BOLSA CHICA STATE BEACH

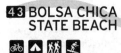

Location: Pacific Coast Highway at Warner Avenue in Huntington Beach
Parking/Fees: $10 entrance fee per vehicle; RV camping fee $39-44 per night oceanfront, $29-34 per night inland, plus $7.50 reservation fee
Hours: 6 A.M.-10 P.M.
Facilities: lifeguards, restrooms, showers, and picnic tables
Contact: Bolsa Chica State Beach, 714/846-3460

RECREATION AND ATTRACTIONS

- **Bike/Skate Rentals:** Dwight's Beach Concession, 201 Pacific Coast Highway, 714/536-8083
- **Ecotourism:** Bolsa Chica Ecological Reserve, Amigos de Bolsa Chica, 714/897-7003
- **Marina:** Huntington Harbor Marina, 4281 Warner Avenue, 714/840-5545
- **Pier:** Huntington Beach Pier, Main Street and Pacific Coast Highway, Huntington Beach, 714/536-5281
- **Rainy Day Attraction:** International Surfing Museum, 411 Olive Avenue, 714/960-3483
- **Shopping/Browsing:** Ocean Promenade, 101 Main Street
- **Surf Report:** 714/536-9303
- **Surf Shop:** Huntington Surf & Sport, 300 Pacific Coast Highway, 714/841-4000; 5th Street Surf Shop, 217 Fifth Street, 714/969-8930
- **Vacation Rentals:** Western Resorts Vacations, 8907 Warner Avenue, Suite 260, Huntington Beach, CA 92657, 714/596-2015

ACCOMMODATIONS

The posh, 12-story **Waterfront Hilton Beach Resort** (21100 Pacific Coast Highway, 714/960-7873, $$$$) claims to be the only oceanfront hotel between Laguna Beach and Redondo Beach. On Pacific Coast Highway between Main Street and Beach Boulevard, it's an attractive tower with rooms whose balconies look out onto Huntington Pier. No creature comfort is unmet. A large, shallow pool and hot tub occupy a landscaped courtyard teeming with greenery. The marble-filled lobby, with its enormous, arching walkways, is unusually opulent for a seaside hotel. The comforters are thick and heavy, making for blissful, mummified sleep. Every aspect of the Waterfront's design and landscaping envelops the visitor in an illusion of tropical delight.

The only sour note is the "Legend of the Surf Hero," a promotional motif. In this "legend," Huntington Beach's legitimate past as a surfer's mecca is turned into cheesy fiction. We quote: "The Surf Hero lived more than 200 years ago in a Native American village on what is now called Huntington Beach. His name was Mankota, and he was the greatest surfer of all time, in a region where surfing was a way of life. During one summer, the spirits became angry and threatened to make the ocean's waves cease forever unless the people offered a human sacrifice. To the surprise of the people, it was Mankota who volunteered. Later that night, Mankota paddled out to the waves for the last time. He caught a massive, churning wave, dropped into the curl and was never seen again...Today, on the beach where the Surf Hero took his final ride, the legend has been carefully preserved by the Waterfront Hilton Beach Resort."

C'mon now, give the surfers a break, not to mention some respect. The real legend of the local surfing scene is far more intriguing than this corporate tall tale. Duke Kahanamoku is no doubt rolling over in his grave. Moreover, the Waterfront can stand on its own without it.

The **Hyatt Regency Huntington Beach Resort & Spa** (21500 Pacific Coast Highway, 714/698-1234, $$$$) is next door to the Hilton. It is the latest dramatic surgery done on Huntington Beach's oceanfront since we began visiting in the early 1980s. On the other side of the Hilton is yet another gigantic, fenced-off lot. Behind it, earth movers have erected a new commercial/real estate complex. It never ends in Huntington Beach.

If you're after something a little more down to earth, try the modestly likable, single-story **Huntington Shores Motel** (21002 Pacific Coast Highway, 714/536-8861, $$). Likewise, the **Quality Inn** (800 Pacific Coast Highway, 714/536-7500, $$) has location (three blocks north of the Huntington Beach Pier, across from the beach), price (significantly less than the Waterfront), and condition (contemporary, clean) going for it. There's a string of small motels close to the beach between Beach Boulevard and Goldenwest Street on Pacific Coast Highway.

COASTAL CUISINE

The Huntington Beach dining scene is, like the town itself, rather undistinguished. One piece of good news is that down by the Huntington Beach Pier you have two upscale franchise options: **Duke's** (317 Pacific Coast Highway, 714/374-6446, $$$) and **Savannah Supper Club** (315 Pacific Coast Highway, 714/374-7273, $$$). "Duke's" refers to Duke Kahanamoku, the Hawaiian legend considered the father of surfing. The restaurant specializes in Hawaiian-style cuisine, such as *huli huli* chicken (grilled with soy, garlic, and ginger) and hibachi-style teriyaki ahi (grilled with lime salsa, papaya, ginger, and soy). Savannah Supper Club served contemporary American cuisine and has an extensive wine list.

Main Street, from the beach up to Olive Avenue, has some shops and restaurants that are fun to duck into. Not all of them are yuppiefied and/or nationally franchised, either. We hit **Wahoo's Fish Tacos** (120 Main Avenue, 714/536-2050, $) for a quick bite. We were first attracted by all the decals on the door and then by the casual, let-it-all-hang-out ambience

ORANGE COUNTY

of the place. You can get a combo plate with a tasty grilled fish taco (plain or Cajun-spiced) accompanied by black or white beans and rice. You could spend an entire afternoon watching surf videos or browsing the bric-a-brac on the walls at Wahoo's, which has a few other franchises in Southern California.

You can grab a decent breakfast or lunch at the **Sugar Shack** (213 Main Street, 714/536-0355, $). Surfers and local characters hang here, too, probably because it's one of the few old haunts that hasn't been given the bum's rush by developers with a myopic "vision" of Huntington Beach's future.

Out on PCH, **Tsunami Sushi Bar** (17218 Pacific Coast Highway, 562/592-5806, $$) draws twenty-something locals who jam the small place for drinks and raw fish. If there's a line, hang in there—it's worth the wait.

At the other extreme, you can always "run for the border." The local **Taco Bell** (818 Pacific Coast Highway, 714/536-1951, $) is crawling with surfers. They stand on the tiled floor, topless, shoeless, shirtless, and dripping wet, waiting for their orders to be called. This particular one, while outwardly no different than the 4,151 other Taco Bell franchises in the United States, is something of a landmark with the surfer crowd, and it was the first in the chain to serve Baja fish tacos. However, this fast-food rendition of the venerable fish taco is a pale imitation of more substantial fare to be found at countless authentic Mexican restaurants between Mission Beach and Malibu.

NIGHTLIFE

Surfers and party dudes with long memories still lament the passing of the Golden Bear, a great hangout that got nuked by the redevelopment prerogative. Most of the old bars in the vicinity of the beach, which we remember as being a little rough, have met a similar fate. In many cases, it was no great loss, but it doesn't appear that much of worth has come along to replace it beyond studied plastic re-creations of the 1950s surf-diner motif. And

so party-minded people in Huntington Beach head to **Hurricane Bar and Grill** (200 Main Street, 714/374-0500), which has live music seven days a week. Across the street is the **Huntington Beach Beer Co.** (201 Main Street, 714/960-5343), an excellent brew pub with live music on Saturdays.

Huntington Harbor, Sunset Beach, and Surfside

Huntington Harbor is a ritzy marina and residential development that split a significant wetland in two. Some of the remains of that wetland have been preserved as **Bolsa Chica Ecological Reserve,** southeast of Huntington Harbor, and as the **Seal Beach National Wildlife Refuge,** just inland from Sunset Beach and Seal Beach.

The saga of the Bolsa Chica wetlands reads like some sort of environmental soap opera. The story dates back to 1970—nearly 40 years ago—when Signal Landmark Inc. purchased 1,600 acres of coastal wetlands from the Bolsa Chica Gun Club, with the intention of building homes on them. This was just about the time that the environmental movement began gaining steam and people came to appreciate the ecological significance of wetlands. Thus began a three-decade tug of war over the Bolsa Chica wetlands. Part of the fun of tracking this story has been keeping up with all the name changes on the real estate side: Signal Landmark became Koll Real Estate Group, which became California Coastal Communities, which is now attempting to do business at Bolsa Chica as, rather absurdly, Hearthside Homes.

Seemingly every month, there's some new twist, lawsuit, filing, proposal, or decision, and yet everything and nothing changes. The initial plan, approved by the California Coastal Commission in 1985, was to build 5,700 homes and a 1,300-slip marina with

A SURFER LOOKS AT 50

One afternoon during lunch we overheard a fellow named Brian talking to a waitress at Woody's Diner, right on the Pacific Coast Highway in Sunset Beach. She was having a bad day, and he urged her to "fluff up her aura" and "receive some of our positive vibes, 'cause we're full of happiness." He was sitting with his 15-year-old son, plotting his future (surfing adventures on the Baja Peninsula) while leisurely downing a plateful of Super Spuds: hash browns fried in a skillet with mushrooms, onions, green peppers, and cheese. This stick-to-your-ribs concoction has been warming surfers' tummies at this location since the 1950s.

We engaged him in conversation, and he openly shared his life story and opinions on what's been happening along the California coast in recent decades. Of Huntington Beach, on whose sands he learned to surf, he said: "We're disgusted with it. We don't go to Main Street anymore."

As thick as the development of Huntington Beach's shoreline has grown since the arrival of the colossus known as The Waterfront, Brian revealed that plans were in the works to make it worse – plans that he, as an active member of the Surfrider Foundation and a concerned resident, has been diligently battling at the grassroots level. He is quick to point out that rules can be bent when influential Orange County businessmen want their bidding done. He rhetorically asks, "How did the Hilton Waterfront resort get around Proposition 13, which clearly forbids the further construction of high-rise fortresses along the ocean?"

Brian has been leading the good life while fighting the good fight, but for him the "Old California" of the 1950s and 1960s has become a fond, fading memory. He told of nights spent sleeping sitting up in a Jeep at Bolsa Chica (then known to locals as Tin Can Beach) in order to surf with the rising sun. A wearying day on the waves would be followed by a hearty plate of Super Spuds at a bait and donut shop on the site of what is now Woody's Diner. Today, here he is, decades later, still surfing waves and scarfing spuds on the same spot, but disenchanted with the takeover and makeover of his beloved California coast. He mourned the loss of Dana Point as a surfers' mecca since the man-made harbor eliminated one of the most challenging point breaks on the West Coast.

He's got his eyes pointed south, beyond California, where he'll stake his claim and surf out his days. Already, he shares a year-round lease on a shack at a beach on the Baja, well south of anything that could be described as Americanized. A paltry $900 gets it for the whole year. Divide that by six tenants, and you're talking next to nothing in living expenses. It's a sweet life. The locals like the gringos, and vice versa.

His smile was genuine and constant, the sense of pleasure he derives from his largely non-materialistic life an inspiration as he approaches his fiftieth birthday. Unlike those who fret over adjustable rate mortgages on their Huntington Beach condos, Brian is living free and easy, able to pull up anchor and move on at a whim.

"I've still got places to go and things to see and waves to ride," he concluded with a gleam in his eye.

ORANGE COUNTY

luxury hotels on a 2,000-acre wetland tract. It was met with opposition from grassroots environmental groups like Bolsa Chica Land Trust and Amigos de Bolsa Chica. In August 1994, the Orange County Planning Commission readied a proposal to rezone the Bolsa Chica wetlands from agricultural to residential use. However, the county's environmental impact statement was challenged by the city of Huntington Beach, which threatened to sue. By November the California State Coastal Conservancy, the cities of Huntington Beach and Seal Beach, the Sierra Club, and the League of Women Voters had all weighed in with preservation opinions. In addition to its inherent value as a wetland, it was pointed out that Bolsa Chica is a valuable archeological site. More "cogged stones"—used in Native American rituals between 6,000 and 3,500 B.C.—have been found here than anywhere else. "It is the mother of cogged-stone sites," said Pat Ware, president of the Pacific Coast Archeological Society.

Gradually, it dawned on people that, having destroyed 95 percent of its coastal wetlands, the state of California could ill afford to lose another acre. As regards Bolsa Chica, the state acquired 300 acres of its wetlands from what was then Signal in 1978. But the tide really turned in 1997 with the purchase by the state's Lands Commission of 880 acres of Bolsa Chica wetlands. Meanwhile, both before and after that sale, plans to develop Bolsa Chica kept shrinking in size. The dimensions of the proposals have gone down from 5,700 homes (1985) to 4,884 homes (1989) to 3,300 homes (1994) to 2,400 homes (1997) to 1,235 homes (1997) to 388 homes (2001). As it stands, Hearthside homes is building 356 homes on 105 acres of the upper mesa. The development is called Brightwater. The good news is, after all the wrangling, the Bolsa Chica wetlands are mostly preserved.

Shoreward of Bolsa Chica are the small communities of Sunset Beach and Surfside. The latter is a private beach colony accessible only to pedestrians and bicyclists through a gate. Sunset Beach is more in line with the old ways of Huntington Beach back when surfers had the run of this stretch of the coast. Remnants of that time are still evident in some of the funky restaurants and bars lining Pacific Coast Highway. Still, Sunset Beach is a confusing hodgepodge of upscale and downscale, old and new, fancy and decrepit. There seems to be no rhyme or reason to the retail landscape along Pacific Coast Highway, which grows more incoherent with each passing year.

BEACHES

Sunset Beach is the principal beach in this area of wetlands, man-made harbors, and private residential communities. While the developers make their move on Bolsa Chica, life goes on at Huntington Harbor and Sunset Beach. The first of these is a private marina that has some public docks and overnight slips for rental. The community of Sunset Beach, arrayed like a centipede along Pacific Coast Highway, has a linear park with restrooms, playground, and volleyball nets that runs between Warner Avenue and Anderson Street. This county park was acquired and constructed in the early 1970s to provide a public beach for those who couldn't gain access through the privatized beachfront of the Sunset Beach colony.

Surfside Beach is a small beach accessible at Anderson Avenue through the gates of the private Surfside community, just north of Sunset Beach. The beach at Surfside, though, is not worth the trouble it takes to get to it, as parking is virtually nonexistent. Most visitors to the area would do better to head down to the massive city and state beaches of Huntington Beach.

44 SUNSET BEACH

Location: Warner Street off Pacific Coast Highway in Sunset Beach
Parking/Fees: free parking lot
Hours: 6 A.M.-10 P.M.

Facilities: lifeguards, picnic tables, restrooms, and showers
Contact: North Beaches Operation Office of Orange County Harbors, Beaches, and Parks, 714/723-4511

45 SURFSIDE BEACH

Location: Anderson Avenue at Pacific Coast Highway in Surfside
Parking/Fees: no parking; accessible only via pedestrian gate
Hours: 6 A.M.-10 P.M.
Facilities: none
Contact: North Beaches Operation Office of Orange County Harbors, Beaches, and Parks, 714/723-4511

COASTAL CUISINE

Vestiges of the area's comfortably unglamorous past can be seen in places like **Harbor House Cafe** (16341 Pacific Coast Highway, 714/592-5404, $) and **Woody's Diner** (16731 Pacific Coast Highway, 714/592-2134, $). Harbor House has been around since 1939, and the site occupied by Woody's has a long and storied history as well. Both have menus heavy on omelets, seafood, and burger variations, offering something for everyone in pleasant surroundings.

Seal Beach

Seal Beach was named for the flappy sea mammal that was once so popular with the garment trade. By Orange County standards it's a modest town in the best sense of the word. It could just as easily have been named for its good fortune at having been "sealed" off from its neighbors. At the north end of Orange County and just across the San Gabriel River from Los Angeles County, Seal Beach is a seal among sprawling sea monsters.

Pacific Coast Highway swings wide of Seal Beach, sparing the town center the nonstop wall of traffic between Long Beach and Huntington Beach. One must vigilantly search for the turn-off at Seal Beach Boulevard or miss the town completely. Seal Beach (population 24,000) is a world unto itself, existing primarily for those who live here. It has a Main Street that looks like a Main Street should—shaded with trees, cobbled with bricks, and as civilized as one of Grandma's bedtime stories. It has a grassy park named for an American president, Dwight D. Eisenhower, whose memory is synonymous with a more reassuring past. There's a tiny historical museum housed in an antique railroad car, an art deco movie house with a Wurlitzer organ, an Irish pub, a couple of seafood restaurants, a municipal pier, and a city beach.

The main drag along the beach impresses with its lack of gratuitous commerce and its gosh-darn normalcy. The hottest ticket in town when we last visited was a Lion's Club fish fry. The community bulletin board was filled with solicitations for recipe-swapping and pen pals. Of course, we quickly signed up for the latter.

For more information, contact the Seal Beach Chamber of Commerce, 201 8th Street, Suite 120, Seal Beach, CA 90740, 562/799-0179, www.sealbeachchamber.com.

BEACHES

For all its small-town charm, **Seal Beach** is not completely undiscovered, as the surf here is middling popular. Many of the surfers who make the trek are too young to drive, so they ride the bus from Long Beach, boards tucked under their arms like briefcases. At 9:30 on a Monday morning, we counted 78 surfers on the north side of Seal Beach Pier. Looking like tropical fish in their fluorescent wet suits, they sat passively on their boards and stared west, bobbing up and down, not speaking to one another, just waiting for the perfect wave.

The wait can be a long one. The surf here approaches the beaches that run for half a mile on each side of the pier at a southerly angle. Sometimes this produces ideal waves, sometimes not. The surf's erratic quality

ORANGE COUNTY

SWINDLIN' USA

(sung to the tune of "Surfin' USA")

If every realtor had an ocean
Across the USA
There'd be a selling off the coastline
Like California
You see 'em building marinas
Time-sharing condos, too
Goofy goofy golf courses
Swindlin' USA
You'll catch 'em boutiquing Del Mar
Up to Orange County Line
Installing spas and Jacuzzis
And pouring vintage wine
All over the Southland
Like down Doheny way
Developmental frenzy
Swindlin' USA

They'll all be planning out a ruse
They'll pay some bribes real soon
They're shaking down their bankers
To fund a building boom
They'll be bulldozing all summer
Phase One by fall, hooray!
Tell the surfers they're comin'
Swindlin' USA
At Huntington and Newport
They always get their way
They're draining Bolsa Chica
Big homes and green fairways
All over the coastline
They're wrecking beach and bay
Developers gone crazy
Swindlin' USA

keeps the town from becoming another Huntington Beach. Even when the waves aren't cooperating, though, the currents and crosswinds are swift and potentially treacherous. Signs warn: Beware of Beach Hazards, Long Shore Currents, Rip Currents, Inshore Holes, Sand Bars, Underwater Objects, Pier Seawall, and Rock Structures.

The El Niño winter of 1997–1998 devastated Seal Beach. It's taken a lot of work to get the beach in working order. Nearby jetties and the cement base of the Seal Beach Pier, which acts as a kind of groin, conspire to impact natural sand-transporting mechanisms, to Seal Beach's detriment. The beach is narrower on the north side than on the south. Planners who constructed the jetty did not intend this to happen—instead, the jetty was meant to hold the sand equally on both sides.

Surfing is allowed on the shorter stretch of beach north of the pier and on Surfside Beach, below the south jetty (and belonging, in fact, to the small community of Surfside). The longest and widest stretch of beach, between the pier and the south jetty, is reserved for swimmers and sunbathers. The 1,885-foot pier was destroyed in January 1983 by the same storm that leveled Huntington Pier. The Seal Beach Pier was rebuilt the next year, with a placard to commemorate the town's industriousness and a cute bronze sculpture of a seal.

Oh, so you noticed the oil platforms offshore? Well, that's part of the scenery over which the town has no control. Occasionally, in fact, Seal Beach is the unwilling recipient of an oil spill that closes the beach until it's cleaned up. During one of our visits, Seal Beach was hit by a small but nasty spill from a leaky pipe on an offshore platform. While the oil-company execs ducked culpability, the town mobilized with bulldozers and volunteers to clean up the mess. As we were leaving, the beach had been reopened. Meanwhile, angry letters to the editor began to appear.

"The rigs not only besmirch the coastline," wrote one citizen, "they pose a constant threat to our beaches and sea life." Let's guess: Next came the press release from the oil company publicists reassuring the townsfolk how environmentally conscious they are. Then local officials reminded the citizens about the money and jobs the oil companies bring the local economy. Everyone forgets for a while, then another small but nasty spill occurs, and the cycle beings anew.

Anyway, here's to the good folks of Seal Beach. May your sand remain clean and may your beach stay in place for another year.

46 SEAL BEACH

🚴 ⚓ 🏄 🌐

Location: Main Street at Seal Beach Pier in Seal Beach
Parking/Fees: metered street parking
Hours: 4:30 A.M.-10 P.M.
Facilities: lifeguards, restrooms, and showers
Contact: Seal Beach Lifeguard Station, 562/430-2613

ACCOMMODATIONS

In this homey town, there's really only one large motel, the **Pacific Inn of Seal Beach** (600 Marina Drive, 562/493-7501, www.pacific inn-sb.com, $$). This former Radisson Inn is an easy walk from the beach, pier, and Main Street. Two small pools are on the premises.

You may opt for the 24-room **Seal**

Beach Inn and Gardens (212 Fifth Street, 562/493-2416, $$$), a restored 60-year-old inn with splendid gardens. It combines the best of bed-and-breakfast and hotel amenities under one roof.

COASTAL CUISINE

Walt's Wharf (201 Main Street, 562/598-4433, $$$) attracts the most devoted following. It's more upscale than most other restaurants in town, drawing a gregarious crowd in the late afternoon. There are nearly as many fish to choose from as there are imported beers on tap, and the seafood is as fresh as it comes.

NIGHTLIFE

Don't leave **Walt's Wharf** (201 Main Street, 562/598-4433) if you're looking for something to do after dinner. It's got a great bar with a kick-back-and-relax ambience and excellent appetizers to go with the brew. There's also a **Hennessey's Tavern** (140 Main Street, 562/598-4419) across the street. Hennessey's, a Southern California chain mining an Irish-pub theme, is an old reliable watering hole no matter the location.

LOS ANGELES COAST

We could have written a separate book about Los Angeles County's coastline, home to everything from the *Queen Mary* ocean liner in Long Beach to chainsaw jugglers in Venice Beach to the rich and famous who live in the secluded Malibu Colony. Just the familiar ring of the names of its beaches is enough to evoke images of endless summers, surfers, swimmers, and sun-worshippers. Who can resist the lure of Santa Catalina Island; Redondo, Hermosa, and Manhattan Beaches, down along the South Bay; Venice, Santa Monica, and Marina del Rey, all part of the pulse of daily life in Los Angeles? Even Malibu's 27-mile stretch is like a preview of the wilds one finds farther up the coast at Big Sur.

As beleaguered as this county can get during periods of fire, heat, storms, and mudslides, Los Angeles deserves an "A" for making its beaches safe and accessible to millions of residents and tourists each year. It is the nation's second largest metropolitan area, behind only New York City, so its beaches have got to serve about as many bodies as McDonald's serves hamburgers. We love the beaches of Los Angeles County, whose parks department could serve as a model of how to provide public access, service, and upkeep. In Los Angeles County, all the so-called state beaches are actually managed by the county under a lease arrangement. The only exception is Leo Carrillo State Park, up north along the Ventura County line.

It's just the rest of the so-called City of Angeles that drives us batty—from the gridlocked freeways and compulsive car culture to the loony celebrity culture to the fact that seemingly every single L.A. denizen has a cell phone glued to his or her ear or is pecking maniacally at a Blackberry, iPhone, or some other high-tech gadget, completely abstracted from the physical world they do their best to ignore. (End of sermon.)

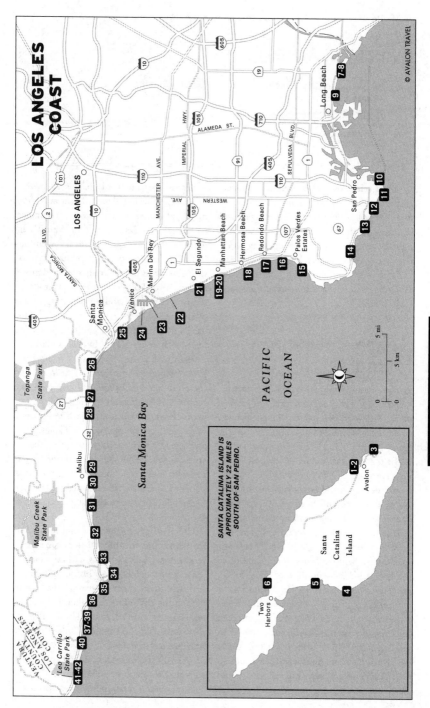

LOS ANGELES COAST

© AVALON TRAVEL

BEST BEACHES

❰ **Hermosa City Beach,**
page 168

❰ **Zuma County Beach,**
page 204

❰ **Leo Carrillo State Park,**
page 207

Los Angeles County has 74 miles of publicly accessible coastline, with many of the beaches more expansive than you might imagine and less crowded than you might think. So select a sandy oasis and let the maddening world that lies east of the ocean breezes go about its stressful scurrying while you fine-tune your tan and find out what California dreaming is really all about.

Santa Catalina Island

To visit Santa Catalina Island is to step back into the past. The prehistoric past, that is. Most of the island—86 percent of its 76 square miles, to be exact—is owned and protected by the Santa Catalina Island Conservancy, a nonprofit outfit that has maintained it as a wilderness preserve since 1972. Consequently, Catalina looks the way it did when sun-worshipping Native Americans inhabited it 4,000 years ago. Even the Spaniards, who arrived with Juan Rodríguez Cabrillo in 1542 and again with Sebastian Vizcaino in 1602, didn't leave any scuff marks behind. Today, only 3,500 or so live on the island—and most of them, by far, are concentrated in the town of Avalon.

Catalina is a rugged, rocky island 21 miles long and eight miles wide. Its jagged green hills rise out of the Pacific Ocean. Mount Oriaba, at 2,069 feet, is the highest peak. On days when the Santa Ana winds blow Southern California's smog away, Los Angelenos can clearly see the island.

Because the natural order has been allowed to prevail, Catalina Island is a different world from mainland California. The ecosystem is unique, with several species of plants and animals endemic to the island. The most celebrated flora is the Catalina ironwood, a tree that teeters on the brink of extinction; only two wild groves are left. A total of 395 species of plant life are native to Catalina, and a fascinating variety of animals make their home here. The island has its own subspecies of ground squirrel and fox, the latter a beautiful but elusive creature. Buffalo freely roam the island's interior. An herd of 14 buffalo was brought here in 1924 for the filming of *The Vanishing American;* now it numbers 400. Attempts to remove introduced herds of goats, sheep, and cattle have helped to restore indigenous vegetation. Wild pigs, goats, and deer also have the run of the place, though attempts to wipe out these feral intruders have met with less success. Some of the world's finest purebred Arabian horses are raised at El Rancho Escondido, a private ranch that is separate from the conservancy.

Unfortunately for humans (but fortunately for plants and wildlife), visitors can't easily reach many of the island's natural wonders, because exploration is fairly restricted. A permit is needed to travel anywhere more than a mile beyond the city limits of Avalon. Hiking and biking permits can be obtained by dropping by the **Santa Catalina Island Conservancy**'s headquarters in Avalon (125 Claressa Avenue, 310/510-1421), where you'll find trail maps, rules and regulations, and other information about the island. These permits can also be ob-

GETTING TO AND FROM CATALINA ISLAND

Although passenger ferries to Santa Catalina Island leave from several mainland points – including Long Beach, San Pedro, Dana Point, and Newport Beach – the logistics are about the same. The cost of parking on the mainland is not included in the fare, and generally costs $10–12 a day at the terminal. The extremely relaxing passage over to Catalina takes anywhere from an hour to two hours, one-way, depending on whether you take old-school ferries or express service. It costs an additional $5 to bring a bike or a surfboard.

- **Catalina Express:** Boats run year-round from San Pedro, Long Beach (from downtown and the *Queen Mary*), and Dana Point terminals to Avalon and Two Harbors. Round-trip fare is $66.50–68.50 for adults and $53 for kids 2–11. For more information, contact Catalina Express, Berth 95, San Pedro, CA 90731, 213/519-1212 or 800/481-3470, www.catalinaexpress.com.

- **Catalina Ferries:** Convenient for suburban Los Angelinos, this boat leaves from Marina del Rey (Fisherman's Village) and takes 90 minutes to Avalon and two hours to Two Harbors. Cost is $85 round-trip for adults and $66 for kids. (This includes a $10 fuel surcharge, added July 2008.) For more information, contact Catalina Ferries, 13737 Fiji Way, Marina del Rey, CA 90292, 310/305-7250, www.catalinaferries.com.

- **Catalina Flyer:** This triple-decker catamaran departs daily from Balboa Pavilion in Newport Beach. Round-trip fare is $68 for adults, $51 for kids 3–12. For more information, contact Catalina Flyer, Balboa Pavilion, 400 Main Street, Newport Beach, CA 92661, 949/673-5245 or 800/830-7744, www.catalinainfo.com.

- **Island Express:** This company flies helicopters from heliports at the San Pedro and Long Beach boat terminals to its pad near Avalon. Space is limited (only six passengers). Round-trip fare is $164, and the trip takes only 15 minutes. Hourly flights depart 8 A.M.–sunset. For more information, contact Island Express, 310/510-2525 or 800/228-2566, www.islandexpress.com.

LOS ANGELES COAST

tained at Two Harbors Visitor Services and Airport in the Sky. Hiking permits are free. Biking permits cost $50 per person and $75 per family and are good for a year (from May 1 through April 30). Hikers and bikers must return by dusk—unless, of course, they're camping and have the necessary permits for that.

Camping is a whole other matter. There are five campgrounds on the island: Two Harbors, Hermit Gulch, Little Harbor, Black Jack, and Parson's Landing. Camping reservations can be made at any of them by calling 310/510-8368. Alternatively, camping reservations can be made through the Santa Catalina Island Company by mail, fax, or online at www.catalina.com/camping. You can call the Santa Catalina Island Company at 310/510-2800

and ask that a camping brochure and request form be mailed to you. Finally, if you're on the island, you can book a campsite at three places in Avalon (Hotel Atwater, 125 Sumner Street, 310/510-1788; Pavilion Lodge, 150 Metropole Avenue, 310/510-2500; Discovery Tours, Crescent Avenue, across from Green Pleasure Pier, 310/510-2000), or at one place in Two Harbors (Two Harbors Visitor Services, at the foot of the main pier). Camping fees are $12 per adult and $6 per child ages 2–11. The season runs late March through the end of October; fees drop somewhat the rest of the year.

Here's a quick lowdown on the campgrounds. **Hermit Gulch Campground** is only 1.5 miles from Avalon, nestled in Avalon Canyon near the Wrigley Memorial and Botanical

PARADISE FOUND: CATALINA ISLAND'S LITTLE HARBOR BEACH

Though most of Santa Catalina Island's visitors confine their explorations to Avalon, there is an up-island sanctuary worth checking out. Little Harbor Beach is a crescent-shaped semitropical paradise midway down the windward, southwest-facing side of the island. Mountains rising to heights of more than 2,000 feet form a stunning backdrop to the wide, sandy cove. There are actually three beaches in one: There's Little Harbor proper, which has a beachside campground; a small, unnamed cove that's a Gauguin-in-Tahiti paradise; and Shark's Cove. These adjacent coves, separated by rocky protrusions, amount to about one-third of a mile of wild, gorgeous beach out of range of civilization.

Getting to this end of the island is half the fun, particularly if you enjoy a long hike. The cross-island hike to Little Harbor can be undertaken from Avalon or Two Harbors, the island's two population centers. The trek from Avalon is longer and more arduous, following a calf-bruising 17-mile trail that ascends spiny ridges and drops into canyons. The 6.8-mile walk from Two Harbors can be made either along the main road, which passes by Little Harbor en route to Avalon, or via the Banning House Road Trail. The latter is more interesting and invigorating, hugging the coastline and making significant elevation changes.

The 42-site campground at Little Harbor has outdoor showers, chemical toilets, and running water. Camping fees are $12 for adults and $6 for children, per person per day. Some visitors arrive via private boat, anchoring offshore. Anglers catch halibut and sun worshippers catch rays on the beach. Little Harbor is protected from the ocean by a small peninsula and offshore reef, making it excellent for snorkeling and scuba diving. Shark Harbor, which adjoins Little Harbor, gets wave action and is good for bodysurfing and boogie boarding. Have no fear of the name, however. Shark Harbor is named for a rock that looks like the dorsal fin of a great white.

Kayaks, diving gear, backpacking equipment, and more can be rented at Two Harbors. The Santa Catalina Island Company runs buses out to Little Harbor, arranges inter-island and cross-channel transportation, assists in travel planning, and issues camping and hiking permits.

For more information, contact the Santa Catalina Island Company, P.O. Box 737, Avalon, CA 90704, 310/510-2800, ext. 1412, www.visitcatalinaisland.com.

Garden. It's stocked with restrooms, showers, picnic tables, vending machines, grills, microwave, ice, and on-site ranger. **Two Harbors** is at a narrow isthmus about 20 miles up-island from Avalon, and there are primitive tent sites, less primitive tent cabins, and downright comfy "Catalina Cabins" with beds, refrigerator, heater, closet, and outdoor community kitchen. **Black Jack** is in the island's interior at the highest elevation. **Little Harbor** faces west onto two sandy beaches and is seven miles from Two Harbors; sites have picnic tables, fire rings, and barbecue grills, and the campground has chemical toilets, cold showers, and

potable water. **Parson's Landing** is the most remote campground, lying up at the north end of the island. You'll find chemical toilets but no fresh water and no showers. You're on your own, but you're on the beach. It's a shadeless beach, however.

All of these permits and prohibitions are sensible and laudable. They keep the island free of Jeep-driving bozos waving shotguns at the wild buffalo. The flip side to this, though, is that most visitors are off-loaded into the harborfront encampment of Avalon and see little more of the island. Avalon lies on the eastern side of Catalina, facing the mainland. Passenger ferries from San Pedro, Long Beach, and Newport Beach dock here, making the town something of a tourist side-pocket on the otherwise empty green billiard table of Catalina Island.

The first person we encountered at the end of the ferry gangplank at the Green Pleasure Pier in Avalon was a bearded son of a gun with a sailor's cap scrunched atop his gnarled web of red hair. With no encouragement from us—we were perfectly content to lug our bags—he pronounced himself "our man." This meant that for a modest fee he'd tote our bags to the hotel, which he warned was "all the way over on the other side of town." Avalon is all of one square mile, and many of its hotels are within easy walking distance of the harbor. Our man no doubt serves some useful purpose here. Just decide before being browbeaten by him or his like whether you can manage for yourself.

There are excellent ways to see other parts of the island without having to trek like a Sherpa. Several different bus tours depart the Avalon Harbor area regularly, and taxis can be hired for private trips. The most reasonable of the bus tours is the Skyline Drive ($39 for adults, $29 for kids), a two-hour trip that ventures 10 miles into the heart of the conservancy. The Inland Motor Tour ($79.50 for adults, $71.50 for kids) is a four-hour version of the trip. Glass-bottomed boat tours ($17.50 for adults, $13.25 for kids) operate out of Avalon Harbor, offering eyewitness proof of the prodigious underwater life teeming in the blue-green waters. Other boat tours sail around the southern tip of Catalina to the western side of the island, where the only other "town," Two Harbors, is located. Two Harbors is a jumping-off point for some of the best hiking trails on Catalina. There are snorkeling tours, too, and buffet cruises. For information on tours, call or drop by the **Catalina Island Visitor Bureau,** on the Green Pleasure Pier (310/510-1520), or **Two Harbors Visitor Services** (211 Catalina Avenue in Avalon and at the foot of the main pier in Two Harbors, 310/510-2800).

Many people travel to the island from the mainland on their own boats, at times turning the channel into a watery version of the Santa Ana Freeway. Some even swim over from Los Angeles. Each year an Ocean Marathon is held; the record time is 7.5 hours.

The salvation of our visit was a golf cart. Everyone on Catalina uses them, and they can be rented for $30–40 an hour, or around $100 for an entire day. After two hours of exhilarating travel into the arrow-marked hills above Avalon, we had seen everything we wanted to see. We also got a sufficiently uplifting feel for the natural riches of the island's interior to make us fantasize about a backpacking expedition at some later date.

Steer your golf cart south out of Avalon on Pebbly Beach Road. This state route hugs the shoreline, revealing placid waters with a rocky bottom—perfect for snorkeling and scuba diving, not so hot for swimming. Quite chilly, in fact. After two miles the road moves inland, up a steep and winding grade that peaks at Mount Ada and the Wrigley Mansion. Incredible as it may seem, Catalina Island used to belong to William Wrigley Jr., the chewing-gum magnate and owner of the Chicago Cubs. Upon his death he deeded the island to the organization that now maintains it as a nature conservancy. Along this route you'll pass the second oldest golf course in the country. It's a nine-holer that was wedged into a rugged canyon in 1892. The road also skirts the now-overgrown field where the Cubs held their spring training from 1921 to 1951 (with four years off for World War II).

The nicest Wrigley legacy is **William Wrigley Jr. Botanical Gardens.** The Wrigley Memorial, set at the top of the gardens, is an imposing structure (232 feet by 130 feet) that dwarfs the surrounding Avalon Canyon like a misplaced Lincoln Memorial. The memorial took a year to build, and plaques attest to its tonnage, craftsmanship, and sturdiness. The plaque at the courtyard entrance reads, "The building is dedicated to William Wrigley Jr., who in 1919 recognized the potential of Santa Catalina as a nature preserve."

The gardens next to the memorial are a

pleasure to stroll. Laid out in sections, they feature Catalina's indigenous plants, as well as oddities from around the world, like South Africa's red-hot poker. The most intriguing part of the garden is the separate wing devoted to cacti, some of which are the strangest and most Freudian we've ever seen.

One other noteworthy attraction is **The Casino,** a Mediterranean-style structure built by Wrigley on Avalon Harbor in 1929. It dominates the waterfront the way Wrigley's memorial overwhelms Avalon Canyon. At one time big bands blew hot and cool in the ballroom of this casino, which has also been used as a backdrop in many Hollywood films. Today, the Catalina Island Museum, featuring historic artifacts of human habitation on the island, is housed in its basement, and first-run movies play on the first floor.

For more information, contact the Catalina Island Chamber of Commerce and Visitors Bureau, 1 Green Pleasure Pier, P.O. Box 217, Avalon, CA 90704, 310/510-1520, www .catalinachamber.com.

BEACHES

First off, just know that you won't be coming to Catalina Island for the beaches—unless you take the trouble to visit the Little Harbor area on the island's backside. **Crescent Beach** (in Avalon) and **Pebbly Beach** (just south of Avalon) provide access to chilly, waveless harbor water. Crescent Beach has a bathhouse at 228 Crescent Avenue with lockers and a laundry. The beach itself is a tiny line of sand upon which you might place towels. A private beach, **Descanso Beach,** can be accessed via the beach club near the casino. Nonmembers must pay for access to this safe, sandy beach and its cabanas. Kayaks can be rented at **Descanso Beach Ocean Sports** (310/510-1226) or **Wet Spot Rentals** (310/510-2229).

Cove beaches can also be found farther up the north side of the island, above Avalon. (Gallagher Beach, Lava Wall Beach, and Starlight Beach are among the ones that have names.) This area is pocked with pebbly or sandy coves,

offering environmental camping on a first-come, first-served basis. **Little Fisherman's Cove** is the site of a campground right on the water close to Two Harbors, where you'll find a restaurant, bar, and dive shop.

The best pure ocean beaches are on the western side of the island, necessitating a long walk or a bus or boat ride from Two Harbors. **Little Harbor Beach** is a wide, sandy, protected beach—a real jewel for swimmers, snorkelers, divers, and campers. Four miles south is **Ben Weston Beach,** a nice sandy cove. Again, this beach requires some advance planning to gain access to it—not to mention an 11.5-mile trek from Two Harbors. For divers, the **Casino Point Underwater Park** sits just off Descanso Beach. Home to a sunken 70-foot schooner and all the squiggly marine life it attracts, the park can be explored via **Catalina Scuba Luv** (126 Catalina Avenue, Avalon, 310/510-2350) or **Catalina Divers Supply** (310/510-0330). For getting around under your own power, try **Catalina Kayak Adventures** and **Wet Spot Rentals** (120 Pebbly Beach Road, 310/510-2229).

■ DESCANSO BEACH

Location: at Descanso Beach Club, beside the Casino on Avalon Harbor
Parking/Fees: $2 per person entrance fee
Hours: 9 A.M.–sunset
Facilities: concession, restrooms, and showers
Contact: Descanso Beach Club, 310/510-7410

■ CRESCENT BEACH

Location: Crescent Avenue at Green Pleasure Pier in Avalon
Parking/Fees: no cars allowed
Hours: 24 hours
Facilities: concession, lifeguards, and restrooms
Contact: Santa Catalina Island Conservancy, 310/510-2595

3 PEBBLY BEACH

Location: on Santa Catalina Island along Pebbly Beach Road, one mile southeast of Avalon Harbor
Parking/Fees: no cars allowed
Hours: 24 hours
Facilities: none
Contact: Santa Catalina Island Conservancy, 310/510-2595

4 BEN WESTON BEACH

Location: on Santa Catalina Island at the end of Middle Canyon Trail, 11.5 miles south of Two Harbors
Parking/Fees: no cars allowed
Hours: sunrise-sunset
Facilities: picnic area
Contact: Santa Catalina Island Conservancy, 310/510-2595

5 LITTLE HARBOR BEACH

Location: seven miles south of Two Harbors on the western side of Santa Catalina Island
Parking/Fees: no cars allowed; camping fees $12 per adult, $6 per child per night
Hours: sunrise-sunset
Facilities: restrooms, showers, and picnic tables
Contact: Santa Catalina Island Conservancy, 310/510-2595

6 LITTLE FISHERMAN'S COVE

Location: Two Harbors, 12 miles northwest of Avalon, on Catalina Island
Parking/Fees: no cars allowed; camping fees $12 per adult, $6 per child
Hours: sunrise-sunset

Facilities: restrooms, showers, and picnic tables
Contact: Santa Catalina Island Conservancy, 310/510-2595

ACCOMMODATIONS

First, for bicyclists and hikers, the campgrounds on Catalina are among the most secluded in California. Permits are required for bicycles and hiking, and separate permits are required for camping. The best conduit to campground reservations and hiking trails is **Two Harbors Visitor Services** (888/570-2595). For bike permits, contact **Catalina Island Conservancy** (125 Claressa Avenue, Avalon, 310/510-2595). The **Hermit Gulch Campground** (310/510-8368), a mile outside Avalon, is privately run, but the only campground in the vicinity of Avalon ($12 adult, $6 child). Two county-run campgrounds within a reasonable hike of town—**Bird Park Campground** (75 sites) and **Black Jack Campground** (75 sites)—can be reserved through the County Parks and Recreation Department, but neither is anywhere near a beach.

Almost all of the lodgings on the island are in Avalon. In fact, Avalon seems like one large hotel. Our first night in town some years back reminded us of "Duncan," the Paul Simon song: "Couple in the next room bound to win a prize/They've been going at it all night long." We holed up in a Mediterranean-style "villa" that shall remain nameless, the brochure for which promised "a touch of Old World elegance and luxury." By "Old World," they apparently meant a windowless room with cots, tiny shower stall, a sliding glass door for an entrance, and the thinnest walls this side of an eggshell. Moral of the story: Book carefully on Catalina Island.

We have found sane and commodious sanctuary at the **Pavilion Lodge** (513 Crescent Avenue, 310/510-2500 or 800/851-0216, $$). The lodge spreads back from the harborfront street into a landscaped courtyard, replete with a two-ton piece of redwood that drifted from the mainland and was placed here with the aid of several trucks, tractors, and herniated laborers. The rooms are quiet and comfortable, too. Ah, golden slumbers.

The most venerable hotel in town is the **Glenmore Plaza Hotel** (120 Sumner Avenue, 310/510-0017, www.glenmorehotel .com, $$$$). This pastel-tinted beauty is over a century old and has hosted such eminences as Teddy Roosevelt (who hunted on the island) and Clark Gable. The wicker-filled rooms are airy and large, and the room rate includes wine and cheese in the courtyard each afternoon and a continental breakfast. All this starts at a reasonable $204. Avalon's poshest hotel is the **Hotel Metropole** (205 Crescent Avenue, 310/510-1884, www.hotel-metropole .com, $$$), a three-story beauty set in the Metropole Marketplace, overlooking Avalon Harbor. Rooms start at $200 in the summer and can cost $300 or more for even a partial ocean-view room.

Over at Two Harbors, lodging can be found at **Banning House Lodge** (Two Harbors, 310/510-2800, $$$), an 11-room bed-and-breakfast built in 1910 as a summer home for the Bannings, two island-owner siblings. This homey, unpretentious inn looks out over Two Harbors' Isthmus Cove from its hillside perch.

Crowds throng to Catalina Island in the summer, but the island is no less charming during its "undiscovered season," September–April, when the room rates run considerably lower. Oh, and there's nary a chain hotel or motel to be found.

COASTAL CUISINE

Around dinnertime one evening some years back we watched an elderly gentleman with hearing aids and a cane wheezing in front of a seafood restaurant on Crescent Avenue, Avalon's waterfront thoroughfare. Winded from his search for a suitable meal—a stroll that had covered three blocks and several posted menus—he turned on his wife when she sweetly suggested they eat at a place with

a "pot roast and potato pancake" special. "I'm not going to put that junk in my mouth!" he cried in frustration. Propped up by his cane, he turned and shuffled farther down the street, bound and determined to find something more to his liking.

Many visitors to Catalina Island find themselves in the same, ahem, boat. A hungry army, they wander the quaint Mediterranean streets of Avalon at sundown, studying one menu after another for some clue as to the cuisine. Much of the food here is necessarily brought over from the mainland. Even the little pier-side food hut serves a pretty generic paper boatload of fish 'n' chips. It also offers abalone burgers and buffalo burgers, which were described to us by a female buffalo-booster as being "leaner than beef."

The best bet for seafood is **Armstrong's Fish Market & Seafood Restaurant** (306 Crescent Avenue, 310/510-0113, $$$). Believe it or not, lobsters are local to these waters and are served in Catalina Island restaurants during a brief season that starts in late September. You can get local or Maine lobsters at Armstrong's or another popular restaurant, **El Galleon** (411 Crescent Avenue, 310/510-1188, $$$), which also serves prime rib and similar hearty fare. **Steve's Steakhouse** (417 Crescent Avenue, 310/510-0333, $$$) is another surf-and-turf-serving favorite overlooking Avalon Harbor and fairly priced, considering the island setting. Steaks and filet mignons run $25–33, and local swordfish is $27.

One night years ago during our first visit to the island, we settled on **Antonio's Pizzeria & Cabaret** (230 Crescent Avenue, 310/510-0008, $) because of the intriguing sign in the window: "This restaurant has been declared a genuine Catalina bomb shelter—come on in and bask in the ambience of the decaying 1950s while the world passes on." The place has moved from its original Sumner Street haunt to Crescent Avenue, into a building that is not bomb-proof, but where the spirit of the original lives on.

NIGHTLIFE

Unless you know someone at the members-only Catalina Yacht Club or the Tuna Club—the latter of which was founded in 1898 and has boasted Winston Churchill, Richard Nixon, King Olaf, and Hal Roach as members—your night moves will be as humble as the lonely buffalo. The best place is **J. L.'s Locker Room** (126 Sumner Street, 310/510-0258), a sports bar. Rams, Angels, and Dodgers photos adorn the walls, some inscribed to J. L. himself by players who have come all the way to Catalina to quaff a cold one at his pub.

Long Beach

This is a city whose fortunes tend to rise and fall with those of a famous British cruise ship. The *Queen Mary* is to Long Beach what London Bridge is to Lake Havasu City, Arizona: a grand relic of the crumbling British empire purchased and brought to America to confer a borrowed identity upon a place that has little of its own. In 1967, the ailing city of Long Beach welcomed the arrival of the *Queen Mary*. The world's largest ocean liner had itself fallen on hard times, as people had come to prefer the convenience of flying to making the time-consuming passage by water. The old boat was docked in the Port of Long Beach and refurbished into a combination hotel and tourist attraction. More important, perhaps, was the symbolism of the luxury liner. Laid to rest in Long Beach after 1,001 transatlantic crossings, the grande dame of the high seas became the city's beacon for a hopeful future.

It hasn't quite worked out that way. In terms of tourist revenue, the *Queen Mary* has had good years and bad years, and it's been as much of an albatross as a savior. The *Queen Mary*'s one-time companion in tourism—the *Spruce Goose*, a gargantuan wooden airplane that never flew, built by Howard Hughes before he began growing his fingernails—was sold off in 1992 and hauled off to Oregon. A 1993 editorial in the *Long Beach Press-Telegram*

wondered, "Who will save the Queen?" Citing maintenance problems, declining attendance, and the need for massive capital improvements at a time when no funding could be found, the editorial concluded: "The signal coming from the *Queen Mary* isn't all that clear, but it's beginning to sound like an S.O.S." The boat was re-christened on September 26, 1994, exactly 60 years after being launched on its maiden voyage in Clydebank, Scotland. The grandson of the vessel's namesake broke a bottle of champagne on its hull, but only a few hundred people showed up for the occasion.

In 2001, the *Queen Mary* laid off 175 employees. Four auctions of original *Queen Mary* furniture, fixtures, art, and tableware were conducted in 1996 and 1997. In 1997, Joe Prevratil—the *Queen Mary*'s president and CEO—was revealed to be hatching a secret plan to have the ship towed to Tokyo. Many complain of the exorbitant cost of touring the ship ($24.95 for adults, $12.95 for kids 5–15, and $15 for parking) or bunking down in one of the 365 staterooms ($159 and up per night).

During an overnight stay aboard the *Queen Mary,* we found the old ocean liner to be eerily deserted. Our fellow passengers included two elderly couples dancing to a jazz trio playing for an otherwise empty house at the Observation Bar; a smattering of foreigners as confused as we were about the layout of the boat; and a housekeeping staff who could not tell us how to get from one point to another. Admittedly, the *Queen Mary*—like the Long Beach Convention and Entertainment Center and all the surrounding hotels and restaurants that serve business travelers—does most of its business during the August–November "convention season." Even so, the historic vessel—a living museum that served both as a luxury liner "where the rich and famous took their ease" and as a World War II troop carrier—should be hauling aboard at least a moderate catch of tourist business during summer months.

The truth hurts, but Long Beach is simply not a prime vacation destination. Beyond

QUEEN MARY FACTS AND FIGURES

- **Number of workers involved in construction:** 300,000
- **Date work began:** December 1, 1930
- **Date launched:** September 26, 1934
- **Maiden voyage:** May 27, 1936
- **Date retired:** September 19, 1967
- **Number of transatlantic crossings:** 1,001
- **Period of wartime service:** 6.5 years (March 1940 to September 1946)
- **Number of troops transported in World War II:** 765,429
- **Number of miles sailed in World War II:** 569,429
- **Bounty placed on ship by Adolf Hitler:** $250,000
- **World War II nickname:** The Gray Ghost
- **Passenger capacity:** 1,957
- **Officers and crew:** 1,174
- **Number of decks:** 12
- **Number of lifeboats:** 24
- **Number of portholes:** 2,000
- **Number of rivets:** 10 million
- **Length of ship:** 1,020 feet

- **Weight of ship:** 90,985 tons
- **Height of ship (keel to top deck):** 92 feet
- **Cruising speed:** 34 mph
- **Fuel consumption:** 0.0025 miles per gallon (13 feet per gallon)
- **Fuel consumed per crossing (from Southampton, England, to New York City):** 1,267,600 gallons
- **Fresh meat consumed per crossing:** 77,000 pounds (38.5 tons)
- **Capacity of wine cellar:** 15,000 bottles
- **Record number of passengers carried at one time:** 16,683 (during World War II)
- **Record time, Atlantic crossing:** 4 days, 10 hours, 6 minutes (August 24-29, 1966)

The *Queen Mary* is open daily 10 A.M.-6 P.M. It is at the south end of I-710 (Long Beach Freeway). Self-guided tours cost $24.95 for adults and $12.95 for children ages 5-11.

For more information, contact the *Queen Mary*, 1126 Queens Highway, Long Beach, CA 90802, 562/435-3511, www.queenmary.com.

the *Queen Mary,* this is a town ruled by its harbor, which primarily exists to serve naval and shipping interests. Away from its harbor, Long Beach has big-city problems but lacks sufficient big-city compensations to make it very tolerable or interesting. Thus, local boosters and PR people are reduced to touting entertainment and recreational options that surround Long Beach—such as Disneyland, Catalina Island, and Knott's Berry Farm—rather than the city itself.

After the *Queen Mary*—which celebrated its 40th anniversary in Long Beach in 2007—has been talked up and talked out, antsy visitors may find themselves in figurative dry dock, their remaining options running to things like driving past the world's largest whale mural, which covers the Long Beach Arena. A local columnist, attempting a feel-good broadside on behalf of downtown Long Beach, wrote the following, which unintentionally confirmed our worst suspicions: "Anything can happen downtown. If it rains, you get wet. If it's hot out, you sweat. Panhandlers may ask you for money. A few people get mugged. Downtown is life."

Well, at least Long Beach—a city of 466,000 that is California's fifth largest and the nation's 36th largest—never stops trying to improve itself. The downtown intersection of Broadway and Pine Avenue has become the center of a gentrified urban island. The concentration of music clubs, restaurants, movie theaters, and coffeehouses is a strategy we saw repeated elsewhere in metropolitan Southern California (such as in Santa Monica). There's safety and strength in numbers, it seems, though sleazy sorts can still violate the permeable borders. The entire neighborhood throbs in hot pink and purple neon, implicitly buzzing the message "class and cool" but instead saying "trendy urban cliché." At least there is good food and music to be had in downtown Long Beach, and it feels reasonably secure.

Also well worth a visit is the **Museum of Latin American Art** (628 Alamitos Avenue, 562/437-1689). Located in the burgeoning East Village Arts District, this beautiful facility features contemporary works by Latin American artists. It is affiliated with **Viva** (644 Alamitos Street, 562/435-4048, $), a nearby restaurant that serves lunch only. The many dishes on the menu come from Cuba, Chile, Peru, Colombia, et al. It's a great way to travel abroad without leaving the table.

Hundreds of millions of dollars have been pumped into redeveloping Long Beach's shoreline and downtown. The **Long Beach Convention and Entertainment Center** (300 East Ocean Boulevard, 562/436-3636) boasts 224,000 square feet of meeting and exhibit space. The complex also includes the 13,500-seat Long Beach Arena (home of the Long Beach Ice Dogs professional hockey team) and the 3,050-seat **Terrace Theater,** a performing arts center. Since 1992, a major waterfront project—first called Disney Sea-Park, then Queensway Bay, next The Pike at Rainbow Harbor, and now simply The Pike Project—has been planned, presented, and battled over (and over). Ten years after Disney was sent packing, the bickering continues. Nevertheless, the **Pike Project** opened in

2003 and has been an unprecedented failure. Though hailed as the largest waterfront development in California history, the $130 million, 369,000-square-foot dining, entertainment, and retail complex essentially turned its back on the harbor and its blandness has not exactly won the hearts of the culturally diverse Long Beach.

Among the most notable arrivals over the last decade is the **Aquarium of the Pacific** (100 Aquarium Way, 562/590-3100). With more than 12,000 maritime creatures and 550 species, it is one of the nation's largest aquariums. Exhibits highlight underwater life in the three regions of the Pacific Ocean: Southern California/Baja Peninsula, the Tropical Pacific, and the Northern Pacific. (Be sure to check out the Shark Lagoon.) Admission is $18.75 for adults, $9.95 for children 3–11. The Aquarium of the Pacific adjoins Rainbow Harbor, a landscaped park with a 2,000-foot public esplanade, a fleet of commercial vessels, and the tall ships *California* and *American Pride.* Still, in typical Long Beach fashion, all is not well with the Aquarium of the Pacific. Attendance has been healthy but not sufficient to allow the aquarium to pay its own way, so Long Beach has had to help out with bond payments, inciting the usual rounds of editorials and citizen grousing in this financially strapped city.

Long Beach has been trying to rebound since taking a direct hit on June 23, 1995—a day referred to as "Black Friday"—when the Defense Base Closure and Realignment Commission announced the 1997 closing of the Long Beach Naval Shipyard. The city lost an estimated 3,000 military jobs and about $757 million a year in lost wages and spending. The announcement came a year after the Long Beach Naval Station and the Long Beach Naval Hospital closed their doors, taking a staggering 17,500 military and civilian jobs from the community.

Though most visitors never see it, there's more to Long Beach than the downtown waterfront. Miles and miles of poor, ethnic neighborhoods roll inland, interspersed with

SHOOTING HOOPS, DRINKING BEER, AND TALKING ABOUT ELVIS

We came to the **Acapulco Inn** (5283 East 2nd Street, 562/439-3517) in Long Beach looking for a Pop-a-Shot machine, a game that allows you to fire little basketballs at a miniature net six feet away. For two guys who'd spent their college years at the University of North Carolina, where basketball is king, an opportunity to shoot hoops was a welcome diversion – even at a scaled-down barroom game. Fortunately, or maybe not – we wasted tons of quarters – these stand-up shooting galleries are found in bars and pool halls all over Southern California.

With a mound of quarters in our pockets and frosty mugs in hand, we prepared to fritter away another five bucks or so feeding our basketball jones in the corner of the Acapulco Inn, a beer joint in Belmont Shore.

We were beaten by a millisecond to the hoops game by a pair of dudes named Greg and Kevin. The former was a construction foreman, the latter a construction worker and one-time marine. They'd just gotten their paychecks and were spending them on draft beer and miniature basketball. They asked us to join them, and we had a night-long round-robin, four-man basketball shootout that grew so noisy we would have been thrown out of any other bar but this one. Kevin wore a baseball cap, smoked fat cigars, made pitchers of beer disappear like magic, and had a wicked set shot. When he found his rhythm, he racked up the points.

A nonstop talker and self-promoter, he would lapse into a deadly accurate Dick Vitale impersonation after scoring a particularly high game. "Oh, bay-bee, he's shoot-ing out the lights tonight! Rock and roll!" He scored an evening-high 46, leaving the rest of us in the dust, and gloated to all within earshot that his score was unbeatable. That is, until one of us entered what is referred to as "a zone," swishing one after another and mounting up a final score of 54. It silenced Kevin for a little while. He gnawed on his cigar, looking annoyed. Then he tried to top it, feverishly popping quarters, game after game, until he bounced a ball so hard in frustration that it hit the ceiling. Then he declared he had finally had enough.

At this point he took a seat at the bar and shared his wisdom on any subject we cared to name. He knew everything about everything, challenging us to stump him. Elvis Presley, surfing, world geography, sports, the fairer sex, bar brawls – you name it. Likable almost in spite of himself, he embodied a good-natured self-centeredness that we'd seen across Southern California. This expressed itself in boundless brag-gadocio and a glaring lack of curiosity about anything outside his sphere of existence. He also made a blanket offer to drop whatever he was doing at any time to share with us his firsthand knowledge of the coast on behalf of our book. He'd be glad to take us around. In fact, we'd *better* call him, he said, jabbing a finger for emphasis.

As the beer flowed so did his rhetoric.

"You want to know about surfing? I've surfed up and down the coast since I was a kid. You name it: County Line. Oil Piers. Rincon. I finished sixth out of 12 in my first amateur competition. I'll take you anywhere you want to go. I can get you onto places you won't believe. I've got three boards. Used to have four. Sold one of them. Son-of-a-bitch still hasn't paid me for it."

"I don't like fighting, I'm a Christian person, but I won't walk away from a fight. I've been in 14 bar fights and never lost once. You want to try me? *[flexes biceps]* See that bartender? I've taken down guys bigger than him. No problem."

"What do you want to know about Elvis Presley? You wanna know Elvis? I know Elvis. I'm the biggest Elvis fan there is. I'm only 24 and I've got records, actual vinyl records, by Elvis. The Beatles? The Beach Boys? What do you want to know? I know it all."

block-long car washes, hangar-sized topless bars, huge rail yards, and horrific industrial plants that make you understand why British poet/visionary William Blake coined the term "dark satanic mills." One blighted ghetto bears the nickname "Dogtown." A hip-hop hotbed, Long Beach has produced such gangsta rappers as Snoop Dogg and Nate Dogg.

On a brighter note, Belmont Shore, a self-contained neighborhood along the water in south Long Beach, has excellent ocean- and bay-beach access and lively shopping and nightlife along Second Street. If you find yourself priced out of the high-rise hotels near the Long Beach Convention and Entertainment Center, Belmont Shore is a viable place to stay. We prefer it, in fact.

Long Beach, when all is said and done, is really more oriented to convention business than pleasure travelers. It is better described as a jumping-off point for attractions in the surrounding area than a bona fide destination in and of itself.

For more information, contact the Long Beach Area Convention and Visitor Bureau, One World Trade Center, Suite 300, Long Beach, CA 90831, 562/436-3645 or 800/452-7829, www.visitlongbeach.com.

BEACHES

Away from the downtown waterfront redevelopment zone, there are some fine neighborhoods along the water in Long Beach. Heading south along Ocean Boulevard from the Long Beach Freeway to its end at Alamitos Bay in Belmont Shore, you pass miles of beautifully landscaped, architecturally varied homes facing the green, linear Bluff Park that runs along the oceanfront. Long Beach has its own sandy, extensive city beach, but water quality can be poor and the offshore breakwater keeps the waves at bay, so to speak. Yes, the same breakwater that makes Long Beach's man-made harbor the busiest port on the West Coast cuts off the surf completely. The ocean is calmer than a farm pond. No waves roll ashore here, forcing natives to head

to points north and south to surf and swim. Over a Memorial Day weekend, the beach was all but empty. Those who could afford to had high-tailed it out of Long Beach for Santa Catalina Island or the Baja Peninsula. The rest simply threw surfboards and wet suits in the back and pointed their wheels to Huntington Beach.

Long Beach City Beach runs for four miles, between First Place and 72nd Place seaward of Ocean Avenue. It's a nice expanse of sand, but there are much better ocean beaches in the vicinity—for instance Seal Beach or the beaches of the South Bay Peninsula. The city beach is bisected by Belmont Pier, a 1,620-foot pier used by locals who appear not to be fishing for recreation but out of necessity, angling for their dinner. Looking across the rippled waters of Long Beach Harbor, one spies what appears to be a series of small resort islands with 10-story hotels built on them. They are, in fact, oil derricks, dressed up to be more appealing from the vantage point of the shoreline. These artificial islands received their designer look from the Disney organization. Named after dead astronauts (e.g., Island Grissom, Island Chaffee), the derricks are hidden behind high-rise camouflage and bathed in peach and green lighting; Long Beach's offshore oil industry is innovative—at least in its exterior design.

The best beach in Long Beach turns out to be on the bay—specifically, the inner flank of **Alamitos Bay Beach** in Belmont Shore. It's a calm-water strip of sand that runs along Bay Shore Drive between Ocean Avenue and Second Street. Locals refer to this bayside beach by the nickname Horny Corners. Old folks, young kids, hot babes from Cal State Long Beach, scarlet-skinned dudes with yellow hair—all are content to lie prone on a beach towel. Some fling Frisbees, others read or gawk at the flesh parade, and a few rent kayaks. Some even swim in the bay's glass-smooth waters. Bay Shore Drive is blocked off all summer, in deference to walkers, in-line skaters, parents with strollers, and so on.

LOS ANGELES COAST

Belmont Shore also has 15 blocks of ocean frontage along Ocean Boulevard.

7 ALAMITOS BAY BEACH

Location: Bayshore Drive at Second Street in Belmont Shore area of Long Beach
Parking/Fees: free street parking
Hours: 5 A.M.–10 P.M.
Facilities: lifeguards and restrooms
Contact: Long Beach Marine Services, 562/594-0951

8 BELMONT SHORE

Location: in the Belmont Shore area of Long Beach, along Ocean Boulevard between 39th and 54th Places
Parking/Fees: metered street parking
Hours: 5 A.M.–10 P.M.
Facilities: lifeguards and restrooms
Contact: Long Beach Marine Services, 562/594-0951

9 LONG BEACH CITY BEACH

Location: in Long Beach along Ocean Boulevard, from Belmont Pier to Alamitos Avenue
Parking/Fees: metered lot and street parking
Hours: 5 A.M.–10 P.M.
Facilities: concession, lifeguards, restrooms, and showers
Contact: Long Beach Marine Services, 562/594-0951

ACCOMMODATIONS

There are too many high-rise hotels and not enough bodies to fill them in Long Beach. The $80 million, 398-room, 15-story **Hilton Long Beach** (701 West Ocean Boulevard, 562/983-3400, $$$), which opened in 1991, contributed further to what was already a soft, saturated hotel market. Already plans

for further new hotel construction have fallen through. Take your pick of the brand names, all of them towering above the action in the area of the convention center, downtown, and waterfront. Other impressive contenders for your lodging dollar include the **Westin Long Beach** (333 East Ocean Boulevard, 562/436-3000, $$$), with rooms starting at $240, and the **Hyatt Regency Long Beach** (200 South Pine Avenue, 562/491-1234, $$$), with rooms starting at $200. If you've got a yen to stay on the beach at a budget price, the **Edgewater Beach Motel** (1724 East Ocean Boulevard, 562/437-3090, $) fits the bill, offering views of Catalina from its deck and five-minute proximity to the downtown hubbub.

Then there's the **Hotel Queen Mary** (1126 Queens Highway, 562/432-6964, www.queenmary.com, $$$). Her 365 staterooms are the largest ever built aboard a ship. Whereas they might have been a blast to stay in on a high-seas voyage four decades ago, today they are substantially less commodious than the rooms you'll find at one of the downtown high-rises (or even at a generic Travelodge). There's but a single porthole in each standard room that faces the water, providing a small, circular shaft of light onto the harbor. The rooms are dark and mildly claustrophobic, the bathrooms are small (and the plastic shower stalls scandalously cheap), yet the beds are comfortable and the unique experience of bunking down aboard a grand old ocean liner compensates for some of the drawbacks. The price is, for the novelty, right, with rooms starting at $159. The ship seems to be particularly popular with large wedding parties, with ceremonies conducted right on deck. To be perfectly honest, however, we'd recommend taking a daytime tour of the *Queen Mary* and laying your head elsewhere in Long Beach.

COASTAL CUISINE

The oldest seafood restaurant in town, **Fish Tale** (5506 East Britton Drive, 562/594-8771, $$), got larger new digs, but the old ambience (fish tales, antique artifacts) is still intact, as are the heaping helpings of fresh fish. There's also an oyster bar on the premises. Downtown, the **King's Fish House** (100 West Broadway, 562/432-7463, $$$) is a terrific choice for grilled or broiled fish served with light, creative, and tasty sauces, such as Chilean sea bass with dill chardonnay sauce (a house favorite) or blackened halibut with corn relish and red pepper coulis. The award-winning cioppino—a tomato-based fisherman's stew with clams, mussels, shrimp, crab, squid, and fish—is another excellent choice.

All manner of varied ethnic cuisine is available in Long Beach, but we were most surprised to find a place that served real Southern-style barbecue. The down-home fare at **Johnny Reb's Southern Smokehouse** (4663 Long Beach Boulevard, 562/423-7327, $$)—pit-cooked barbecue, crackling fried chicken, coleslaw, and hush puppies—sent this pair of erstwhile rebels home happier than hot hogs in cool mud.

We can't quit without mentioning **Joe Jost's** (2803 East Anaheim Avenue, 562/439-5446, $). It's the oldest continuously operating bar in California, and it has been run by three generations of Jost's. Papa Joe, God rest his soul, invented a deli sandwich that has become a local institution. Called Joe's Special, it consists of a hunk of Polish sausage surrounded by a slice of Swiss cheese with a pickle spear stuck into a V-shaped slit, all stuffed between mustard-slathered pieces of rye bread and wrapped in a waxed-paper handle. Joe Jost's serves hundreds of them every day, and just as many of the other house specialty: a basket of pretzels, peppers, and pickled eggs. As for what's on tap at Joe Jost's, they pump ice-cold Blitz beer, brewed in Oregon, in 20-ounce schooners.

NIGHTLIFE

The centerpiece of the Broadway/Pine Avenue downtown renaissance is a 16-screen AMC cineplex at **Pine Square** (245 Pine Avenue, 562/435-4262). Surrounding it is a neon galaxy of munchie parlors, coffeehouses, restaurants, and clubs. **System M** (213-A Pine Avenue, 562/435-2525) is the gathering place for Long Beach's new bohemians, with gentlemen on the outdoor patio affecting pince-nez, goatees, and Kramer-like explosions of hair while sucking contemplatively on cigarettes and watching the smoke curl against the fuchsia glow of the restaurant's neon. Food, drinks, coffee, and art are served within.

In the same vicinity, the **Blue Cafe** (210 Promenade, 562/983-7111) pays homage to the electric guitar along a largely undeveloped pedestrian promenade. Regionally popular blues, rock, and alternative musicians perform here for a modest cover charge. We paid $4 apiece on a Monday night to see a local band called Standard Fruit and had a fine time. Bathed in ubiquitous neon, it is, like every other business on this embryonic scene, an outpost of civility trying to stay afloat in a sea of economic uncertainty.

From there we felt like getting rowdy, so we proceeded down to Belmont Shore, a livelier and more organic community in south Long Beach. We've always had a good time rambling around the bars and taverns of Second Street. They are jam-packed with friendly and fun-loving college kids, neighborhood residents, and navy guys out for a brew. Take your pick and pull up a bar stool. There's **Legends** (5236 East Second Street, 562/433-5743), a sports bar that's always abuzz with folks ogling the action on the big screen; **Panama Joe's** (5100 East Second Street, 562/434-7417), an upscale "meet market" that gets good bands on weekends; and our personal favorite, the **Acapulco Inn** (5283 East Second Street, 562/439-3517). The latter is a collegiate dive bar that's wilder than any toga party John Belushi ever attended. At the "AI," students from nearby Cal State Long Beach cut loose in a party environment so out of control on big nights that it's almost a caricature of hell-raising. The jukebox leans heavily on 1960s party favorites, while an assortment of games—including a Pop-a-Shot concession that nearly cleaned out our wallets—gives

LOS ANGELES COAST

you something to do besides clutch a beer. If you can keep up with this crowd, you deserve whatever you wake up with the next morning: a hangover, a fellow party animal, or both.

San Pedro

Tucked behind the protective, ever-changing Palos Verdes Peninsula is San Pedro (population 86,000), the port town for the city of Los Angeles. In 1889, after heavy competition with other bay towns like Redondo Beach, it was chosen to house Los Angeles Harbor, thanks to the good offices of Senator Stephen M. White (after whom a main drag in town is named). Before it was enlarged to its present size, the harbor was so shallow that oceangoing vessels had to be anchored offshore and loaded and unloaded from there. Today it is known as "Worldport L.A." The harbor covers 7,000 acres and 28 miles of waterfront, making it one of the largest artificial ports in the world.

Overlooking San Pedro Harbor is formidable Fort MacArthur, once an integral part of our West Coast defense posture. San Pedro is home to 86,000 people, many of whom make their living on the docks. It was also the home of one of our favorite writers, the late Charles Bukowski. He came to live in San Pedro in 1978, leaving Los Angeles after 58 years of a squalid hand-to-mouth existence. According to biographer Neeli Cherkovski, Bukowski chose San Pedro because "unlike some of the other beach towns, the spirit of the 1960s hadn't settled on it." That much is true. The real lure of San Pedro for Bukowski was its proximity to the freeways, which afforded a quick escape from anonymous middle-class respectability to the racetracks at Hollywood Park and Santa Anita. Bukowski died here in 1993.

Despite the relative lack of beaches, elbowed out by the harbor, there's plenty of waterfront activity in San Pedro. The **Cabrillo Marine Aquarium** (3720 Stephen M. White Drive, 310/548-7562) has 38 aquariums with marine life native to Southern California, as well as a

multimedia show for kids, seasonal grunion tours, and whale-watching expeditions. It's only $5 per adult and $1 for children and seniors, and parking costs $1 per hour. Down on the docks is **Los Angeles Maritime Museum** (Berth 84, Sixth Street, 310/548-7618), which presents an assortment of maritime equipment, memorabilia, and historical photographs detailing the construction of the harbor and the old ferry days. Admission is $3 for adults and $1 for kids. In addition, you can take several tours out of San Pedro Harbor, including ferries to Santa Catalina Island and dinner and harbor cruises.

For more information, contact the San Pedro Peninsula Chamber of Commerce, 390 West Seventh Street, San Pedro, CA 90731, 310/832-7272, www.sanpedrochamber.com.

BEACHES

There are a few beaches in San Pedro worth seeking out if you're in the area. The main one—and the only sandy beach in San Pedro—is **Cabrillo City Beach,** east of Point Fermin on either side of the San Pedro Breakwater. The "harbor" side of the beach is protected and calm, with a boat-launching ramp. The "ocean" side, on the other side of the harbor fortification, receives the full force of the ocean—real waves for board surfing and windsurfing. The tidepools are rich in marine life, and in the summer the grunion hold some epic runs here. The Cabrillo Marine Museum elaborates on the local ecology. Attached to the breakwater at Cabrillo City Beach is a 1,000-foot municipal fishing pier. **Point Fermin Park** and lighthouse are on a bluff overlooking the ocean; steep trails lead to the rocky shore below.

West of Point Fermin, the parking lot below the cliffs at White Point is divided into **White Point County Park** (left) and **Royal Palms County Beach** (right). The former is a bluff-top park with playgrounds and overlooks, while the latter is a rugged, rocky shoreline popular with shell collectors and surf casters. Surfers like it, too, in winter.

The most remarkable feature of White Point/ Royal Palms, though, is the presence of mineral springs that lie offshore, which divers explore. When you tire of the beach, you can always wander the grounds of the old Royal Palms Hotel, which was washed away in a storm seven decades ago, though the royal palm trees remain. Tidepoolers and divers go to White Point, at the east end, while picnickers and sunbathers congregate at Royal Palms. The latter, incidentally, has received a $2.2 million sprucing up of its facilities and is really looking sharp.

10 CABRILLO CITY BEACH

Location: Stephen M. White Drive at 40th Street in San Pedro
Parking/Fees: $5 entrance fee per vehicle
Hours: 5 A.M.-10:30 P.M.
Facilities: concession, lifeguards, restrooms, showers, and picnic tables
Contact: Los Angeles County Lifeguard Service, Southern Section, 310/832-1179

11 POINT FERMIN PARK

Location: Gaffey Street at Paseo del Mar, near Point Fermin Lighthouse in San Pedro
Parking/Fees: free parking lot
Hours: 6 A.M.-sunset
Facilities: restrooms and picnic tables
Contact: Los Angeles County Lifeguard Service, Southern Section, 310/832-1179

12 WHITE POINT COUNTY PARK

Location: From Paseo del Mar in San Pedro, turn right on Kay Fiorentino Drive and follow it to the park. On the left side of the parking lot

is White Point County Park, on the right side is Royal Palms County Beach.
Parking/Fees: $2 entrance fee per vehicle on weekdays, $5-6 on weekends
Hours: 6 A.M.-sunset
Facilities: restrooms
Contact: Los Angeles County Lifeguard Service, Southern Section, 310/832-1179

13 ROYAL PALMS COUNTY BEACH

Location: From Paseo del Mar in San Pedro, turn right on Kay Fiorentino Drive and follow it to the park. On the left side of the parking lot is White Point County Park, on the right side is Royal Palms County Beach.
Parking/Fees: $5 entrance fee per vehicle
Hours: 6 A.M.-sunset
Facilities: lifeguards and restrooms
Contact: Los Angeles County Lifeguard Service, Southern Section, 310/832-1179

ACCOMMODATIONS

The **Sunrise Hotel** (525 South Harbor Boulevard, 310/548-1080, $$) happens to be the closest hotel in town to the harbor. Rooms look out on the harbor; amenities include deluxe continental breakfast, pool, and a hot tub. The best, most reliable of the chains in San Pedro is the **Holiday Inn San Pedro/Los Angeles Harbor** (111 South Gaffey Street, 310/514-1414 or 877/865-6578, $$).

COASTAL CUISINE

The **22nd Street Landing Seafood Grill & Bar** (141 West 22nd Street, 310/548-4400, $$$) serves more than a dozen types of fresh fish daily in a dining room that looks out on the harbor. For seafood it's the best choice for miles around. There are also a number of excellent Italian restaurants in the area. Tops among them is **Madeo Ristorante** (295 Whaler's Walk, 310/521-5333, $$$), adjacent to the Doubletree Hotel at Cabrillo Marina.

CROSSTOWN TRAFFIC:
DRIVING IN LOS ANGELES

It is nearly impossible to visit Los Angeles without spending a lot of time inside a car. In order to get around the spread-out city, you will have to drive and drive...and drive some more.

There are 200 bus lines in Los Angeles run by the Los Angeles County Metropolitan Transit Authority. They also operate three MetroRail light-rail lines, totaling 74 miles of track. The Metro Blue Line makes 22-mile runs from Los Angeles to Long Beach, with stops in San Pedro, Anaheim, and other communities. The Metro Green Line runs a 20-mile east-west route across southern Los Angeles County, including stops at Redondo Beach, LAX, Long Beach, and Norwalk. The Metro Gold Line travels from Los Angeles' Union Station to Pasadena.

The Metro Red Line, the city's first subway, opened in 1993. Today it runs from North Hollywood through Hollywood to Union Station, in downtown L.A. The Metro Purple Line runs from Union Station to stops along Wilshire Boulevard. There is a total of 17 miles of underground rail in Los Angeles.

For city bus, Metro Line, and MetroRail information, contact the **Los Angeles County Metropolitan Transit Authority,** 425 South Main Street, Los Angeles, CA 90013, 213/626-4455, www.metro.net.

Metrolink is a regional commuter rail system, established in 1991, that serves 56 stations across Southern California from its hub at Union Station. In terms of the coast, it goes as far south as San Clemente and as far north as Oxnard. They own about 256 route miles of track. Unfortunately, on September 12, 2008, Metrolink made national news when one of its trains collided with a Union Pacific freight train near Chatsworth, killing 25 and injuring 135 (40 of them critically). It was the deadliest U.S. rail accident in 15 years and the worst in Southern California in half a century.

For Metrolink commuter rail information, contact **Metrolink,** 700 South Flower Street, 26th floor, Los Angeles, CA 90017, 213/808-5465 or 800/371-5465, www.metrolinktrains.com.

If you are getting around Los Angeles by car, you will notice that the freeways loop into each other like asphalt pretzels. Perversely, the freeway carpool lanes in Los Angeles and Orange Counties are nearly always clear. The number of passengers constituting a High Occupancy Vehicle (HOV) has been dropped. Now you need only two passengers per car. And still the carpool lanes are empty. That is because nearly everyone in Southern California is a "Lindbergh" – a solo driver. So the roads stay jammed.

If you're in the area, it pays to learn the names and numbers of the freeways you'll be traveling:

Highway 2	=	Glendale Freeway
Highway 10	=	Santa Monica or San Bernardino Freeway
Highway 60	=	Pomona Freeway
Highway 90	=	Marina Freeway
Highway 91	=	Artesia Freeway
Highway 110	=	Pasadena Freeway
Highway 170	=	Hollywood Freeway
U.S. 101	=	Ventura, Hollywood, or Santa Ana Freeway
I-5	=	Golden State or Santa Ana Freeway
I-110	=	Harbor Freeway
I-405	=	San Diego Freeway
I-605	=	San Gabriel River Freeway
I-710	=	Long Beach Freeway

Keep track of traffic over the airwaves. Many radio stations offer traffic reports. The stations with the best coverage are KNX (1070 AM) and KFWB (980 AM).

KNX, an all-news radio station, gives traffic reports every six minutes, 24 hours a day. A typical traffic update sounds like this (imagine a fast-talking, mellifluous deejay voice): "It's stop-and-go all the way from Santa Monica to Pasadena, but the good news is there are no accidents blocking the road."

When an explanation for a traffic tie-up is warranted, the tone of the deejay's voice doesn't modulate and his update sounds like this: "There's a bus on top of a car near the Avalon exit on I-405. Ouch, that's gotta smart!"

Further coloring the experience of driving in Los Angeles is the haze of smog, plus vast wastelands of junkyards and salvage lots, oil refineries, and industrial complexes. But Los Angeles keeps on growing and, after each earthquake, roads are rebuilt before homes are, inviting more cars and creating more problems.

So what's the solution? In 2009, with the bottom falling out of the American economy and gas breaking the $5 per gallon barrier for the first time, it's certainly not "drill, baby, drill," as some would have it. In our opinion, the answer is smaller, more fuel-efficient hybrid vehicles, better mass-transit options (especially in sprawling L.A.), and the physical compacting of cities like Los Angeles in order to reduce commutation. One thing's for sure: The old way of driving by depending on cheap gas is history.

LOS ANGELES COAST

NIGHTLIFE

Most of the restaurants on the harbor have cocktail lounges. For a nonalcoholic alternative, duck into the **Sacred Grounds Coffee House & Art Gallery** (468 West Sixth Street, 310/514-0800), where art, live entertainment, and cappuccino are the house blend. Incidentally, if you really want to understand San Pedro, check out native Mike Watt's excellent 1997 CD, *Contemplating the Engine Room*.

Palos Verdes Peninsula

The enormous landmass known as the Palos Verdes Peninsula, in the southwest corner of Los Angeles County, is one that will (as Muhammad Ali used to say) "shock and amaze ya." As is the case in the northern part of the county—with the Santa Monica Mountains, the Malibu Peninsula, and the Hollywood Hills—the Palos Verdes Peninsula is an example of the incredible diversity of landforms found in and around the City of Angels.

This craggy, lunarlike peninsula is no party to the smog dish of the Los Angeles Basin. Even though its jagged, cliff-lined shore embraces 15 miles of Pacific coastline—from San Pedro to Torrance—the Pacific Coast Highway doesn't come near it. Instead, it moves inland, leaving the tough, shifting terrain of the peninsula to the hermitic wishes of the folks who live out here on the edge of the planet.

Driving around this wondrous peninsula entails following a series of small, winding back roads that pass through a quaking, unsettled landscape. Along this Jell-O-like terrain, a road sign warns, Constant Land Movement Next 8 Miles. What could this mean? we wondered. It means that sections of the road, particularly in the vicinity of Portuguese Bend, look like they've just been removed from a waffle iron and have more dips in them than an amusement-park roller coaster. The land here actually moves at a rate of one to six inches a month and has

been doing so since the mid-1950s, when highway blasting caused the top layer of rock to separate from and slip over the lower layer (a phenomenon known as "block-glide"). A prodigious chunk of the peninsula fell into the ocean in May 1999, taking with it a portion of a new golf-course development. (Talk about poetic justice!)

You will find yourself holding your breath for reasons other than fear, however, as one seductive panorama of sky, sea, and headlands follows another until you work your way off the peninsula at Torrance. Depending on how you approach it, the drive is either an unexpectedly nice side trip or the most unusual way to enter the back door of Los Angeles. At one time the entire peninsula was the rancho of the Sepulveda family, until they sold it in 1914 to a company with plans to develop it as a "millionaire's colony." To that end they called in the landscape firm of Olmstead and Olmstead (sons of Frederick Law Olmstead, designer of New York's Central Park). The Olmstead brothers planted trees on the barren lands and built houses among them, and the millionaires dug in for the long haul. They're still dug in out here, although the nerve-jangling land movement has driven many to abandon the sloping Portuguese Bend area. The houses that didn't slip into the drink have been sold off for a song to intrepid souls unafraid to live in them. Yet the neighborhoods behind the falling ridge remain some of the most exclusive properties in Los Angeles.

For more information, contact the Palos Verdes Peninsula Chamber of Commerce, 707 Silver Spur Road, Suite 110, Drive North, Rolling Hills Estates, CA 90274, 310/377-8111, www.palosverdeschamber.com.

BEACHES

The small, sandy coves on the Palos Verdes Peninsula are difficult to get to, but they are among the most prized in the county, due partly to their very inaccessibility. The most visited are Malaga Cove and Abalone Cove

Beach. **Malaga Cove**—also known as RAT (for Right After Torrance)—is the only true sand beach on the peninsula. It's popular with surfers and swimmers who climb down with their boards and towels from the paved access point at Via Arroyo, off Palos Verdes Drive West. There's a small, free parking lot. **Abalone Cove Beach,** which straddles the legendary Portuguese Bend off Palos Verdes Drive South, can be reached via a pay parking lot. Surfers' localism is at its worst on the peninsula, however, where the best surf spots are zealously (and sometimes violently) defended by local gangs. We were told you could avoid the parking fee by parking a block away on the roadside, which we noticed many people doing.

Even if you don't take the plunge to the beaches, the cliff-hugging route along the outer rim of Palos Verdes makes for an exciting afternoon drive. Particularly appealing is Paseo del Mar, a loop road that leaves Palos Verdes Drive and cuts through **Palos Verdes Estates Shoreline Preserve,** which runs for 4.5 miles and comprises 130 city-owned acres above a bluff top. Several precipitous paths leave the bluff top and zigzag down to cove beaches at Lunada Bay, Bluff Cove, and Malaga Cove. On the southwestern corner of the peninsula, the small **Point Vicente Park** offers free parking, restrooms, a whale-watching deck, and displays that interpret local history and ecology. At the park's pullout a dirt trail leads to **Point Vicente Fishing Access.** This magical fishing hole draws skin- and scuba divers as well as anglers. South of Point Vicente Park is the Point Vicente Lighthouse, which was built in 1926 and is now closed to the public.

The splendid architecture on the peninsula is worth checking out from a car window. It is something every developer should witness and learn from. Hidden among the trees and hills, the human habitations don't try to compete with the grandeur of the landscape. This philosophy of architectural noninterference reaches a zenith with the **Wayfarers Chapel**

(5755 Palos Verdes Drive South, 310/377-1650), on the mainland side of the road just beyond Portuguese Bend. Built in 1946 by Lloyd Wright (son of Frank), the predominantly glass edifice allows worshippers (devotees of the theologian Emanuel Swedenborg) to feel as if they're outdoors among the redwoods and gardens that surround the chapel. It is open to the public daily 11 A.M.–4 P.M. A small museum on the grounds has exhibits about "Swedenborgianism" and Helen Keller, a practitioner thereof.

One final note: It was on Palos Verdes that Marineland of the Pacific was built in 1954. Once the home and playpen for a small navy of Flippers, Orcas, and Jaws, the three-ring aquatic circus is long gone. The park's inaccessibility is the reason for its financial demise. The property was sold off, presumably to an eccentric millionaire with a penchant for large swimming pools.

14 ABALONE COVE BEACH

Location: Palos Verdes Drive at Narcissa Drive on the southwest corner of Palos Verdes Peninsula
Parking/Fees: $4 entrance fee per vehicle
Hours: 6 A.M.-sunset
Facilities: lifeguards, restrooms, and picnic area
Contact: Los Angeles County Lifeguard Service, Southern Section, 310/832-1179

15 MALAGA COVE

Location: Paseo del Mar at Via Arroyo on northwest corner of Palos Verdes Peninsula
Parking/Fees: free parking lot
Hours: 6 A.M.-sunset
Facilities: lifeguards, restrooms, and showers
Contact: Los Angeles County Lifeguard Service, Southern Section, 310/832-1179

Redondo Beach

Redondo Beach has fancied itself a vacation destination since the 1890s, when a trio of Spanish sisters sold the sand dunes they inherited to developers. Shipping was an important early industry, but after Redondo Beach unsuccessfully vied to have the Port of Los Angeles located here (San Pedro won), the town turned to tourism. A huge luxury hotel, along with tent cities for the fiscally challenged, drew vacationers to the pristine beach. The Hotel Redondo—which opened in 1890 and was stupidly torn down in 1926—actually was the sister establishment of the splendid Hotel del Coronado down the coast. During Redondo's heyday, folks would ride the fabled Pacific Electric "red cars" from downtown Los Angeles to the beach.

At one time Redondo Beach (population 67,100) had it all: big-band ballrooms, offshore gambling ships reached by water taxis, and a huge, heated indoor saltwater pool called "the Plunge." A Hawaiian native named George Freeth demonstrated the strange new sport of surfing to curious onlookers behind the Hotel Redondo. (Freeth was described biblically by developer Henry Huntington as "the man who could walk on water.") Redondo's glory days are documented in the **Redondo Beach Historical Museum** (320 Knob Hill Avenue, 310/543-3108), operated by the Redondo Beach Historical Commission.

Residents would no doubt like to see those golden days return, but that will take a long reprieve from the forces of nature and economics, and that is one tall order. Of the triumvirate of beach towns that are conjoined in the South Bay area of Los Angeles, Redondo Beach was spiked the hardest by economic recession and natural disaster. Whereas its sisters in sand and sun, Hermosa Beach and Manhattan Beach, are primarily residential communities and only secondarily tourist-oriented, Redondo Beach—at least that part of town seaward of the Pacific Coast Highway—seeks and depends on visitor dollars. The lineup of waterfront attractions in Redondo Beach includes the marinas at King Harbor (there are four of them), the International Boardwalk, the town's famous "horseshoe pier," and several resort hotels. You can gauge Redondo's dependence on visitors by the size of the parking decks. Whether you're berthing a yacht in one of the basins or wheeling a rented Escort into one of the garages, Redondo Beach is glad to have you and your pesos jingling around town. For this reason it is the most outsider-friendly of the South Bay communities.

Redondo is struggling gamely out of the hard times that have befallen it and rekindling some of the spirit that made it a beach-lover's mecca. Having persevered through repeated bouts of storm damage, plus a catastrophic pier fire, the collapse of a parking deck, and the impact of prolonged economic downturns in the early- to mid-1990s and in the present recession, Redondo Beach has a survivor's mentality.

Today, Redondo's waterfront complex is a catacomb of parking decks, food stalls along the concrete boardwalk, and a handful of pier-based restaurants. Still, we can't help but wonder what will happen the next time the Arctic or El Niño sends another unforgiving squall Redondo's way. How long this cycle of destruction and rebuilding can continue is anyone's guess.

On a cheerier note, one of the best-loved features of the waterfront, the **South Bay Bicycle Trail,** endures. A 26-mile paved path that extends from Torrance City Beach (just south of Redondo) to Will Rogers State Beach (in Malibu), it is a two-way concrete freeway for cyclists, in-line skaters, skateboarders, and joggers. Even the odd walker can be spotted, although mere strolling is a little too undemanding for this high-speed crowd. If you're not in shape, this isn't the place to reveal your unseemly bulges. The bike path is part aerobic runway, part fashion runway, and always crowded—the place to see and be seen.

Traveling south from Hermosa Beach, the trail swings onto the streets of Redondo for a few blocks before entering the innards of the

King Harbor-Pier Complex. Once past this maze, through which you're asked to walk your bike, the path resumes a straight and steady course south along Redondo State Beach, giving cyclists a superb view of the rugged bluffs of the Palos Verdes Peninsula. Cruising the South Bay is a popular pastime, and bikes can be rented at local shops, the best of which are in Hermosa Beach. The local climate almost mandates outdoor activity. The mercury rarely falls below 45 degrees in January or rises above 75 degrees in July. Los Angeles's chronic halo of smog doesn't choke the beaches of the South Bay. Cooling offshore breezes ensure that the air is generally clean and the skies blue.

And so Redondo Beach sits at the edge of the Pacific like a tarnished jewel in a splendid setting. It has been knocked around by Mother Nature and is still somewhat punch-drunk, yet its residents doggedly regroup, rebuild, and persevere.

BEACHES

The beach at Redondo Beach maintains a respectable width south of the pier, but it is narrow and eroded north of it. Erosion is the result of harborfront construction, including a breakwater that diverts sand into a submarine canyon just offshore. The same canyon causes wave crests to refract in a way that concentrates their energy onto the beaches north of the canyon, occasionally wrecking beaches and the houses built along them. In severe storms, the breakwater has been overtopped and damaged. Signs warn people away from what's left of the beach in the vicinity of the harbor, where the ocean angrily slaps walls of riprap that have been erected to protect the construction behind it.

The beach scene improves markedly on the south side of the pier along the strand encompassing **Redondo State Beach** and **Torrance City Beach.** Redondo State Beach runs for about 1.5 miles from the pier south to some restrooms, on the other side of which it becomes Torrance City Beach, continuing down to the Palos Verdes Peninsula for three-

quarters of a mile. It's the same beach—a flat swath of sand that widens between pier and peninsula, a nice place to come for a little more nature and a little less in the way of crowds than you'll find at Hermosa or Manhattan Beaches. To the delight of surfers, this stretch is serviced by the west swells of winter. Incidentally, though it's now called Redondo State Beach, this beach is lifeguarded and maintained by Los Angeles County. Similar city/county arrangements and nomenclature apply throughout the county.

For more information, contact the Redondo Beach Chamber of Commerce & Visitors Bureau, 200 North Pacific Coast Highway, Redondo Beach, CA 90277, 310/376-6911 or 800/282-0333, www.redondochamber.org.

16 TORRANCE CITY BEACH

Location: along Paseo de la Playa in Torrance
Parking/Fees: $4 entrance fee per vehicle
Hours: 6 A.M.-sunset
Facilities: lifeguards, restrooms, and showers
Contact: Los Angeles County Lifeguard Service, Southern Section, 310/832-1179

17 REDONDO STATE BEACH

Location: Torrance Boulevard at Esplanade in Redondo Beach
Parking/Fees: metered street and lot parking
Hours: 6 A.M.-sunset
Facilities: concessions, lifeguards, restrooms, and showers
Contact: Los Angeles County Lifeguard Service, Southern Section, 310/832-1179

ACCOMMODATIONS

To oversimplify, Redondo Beach has the hotels, Manhattan Beach has the restaurants, and Hermosa Beach has the nightlife. Numerous chain motels are located along and west of the Pacific

Coast Highway, only one-third mile from the beach. Down along the harbor are the two top choices: the **Portofino Hotel and Yacht Club** (260 Portofino Way, 310/379-8481, www.hotelportofino.com, $$$) and the **Crowne Plaza Redondo Beach Hotel** (300 North Harbor Drive, 310/318-8888, www .cpredondobeachhotel.com, $$$). The latter is an especially attractive property, an airy and spacious five-story resort hotel overlooking King Harbor from the dry side of Harbor Drive. Room rates are $180 a night and up in season. Private balconies, outdoor heated pool and sundeck, exercise facilities, sports bar, piano bar, on-premises restaurant, and more make this a prime place to lie in when visiting Redondo Beach.

Another option is the **Palos Verdes Inn** (1700 South Pacific Coast Highway, 310/316-4211 or 800/421-9241, www.palosverdesinn .com, $$$), only three blocks from the beach along a curve on the coastal highway, where it begins to skirt the uplands of the Palos Verdes Peninsula. The hotel is a self-contained city, with an excellent Continental restaurant (**Chez Mélange**, 310/542-1222, $$$), gourmet deli (**Chez Allez**, $), live-music venue (**Club Caprice**, 310/316-1700), and half-acre pool, spa, and gardens on the premises. Rooms are comfortably furnished, and many come with ocean-view balconies.

COASTAL CUISINE

In Redondo Beach, restaurants don't always go out of business due to bad reviews or word of mouth. Big waves wreck them. Several pier restaurants have been washed into the big drink over the years. Still, the harborside restaurant scene survives, particularly the **Blue Moon Saloon** (207 North Harbor Drive, 310/373-3411, $$$), a casual seafood eatery in the Redondo Beach Marina that has endured wind and wave to emerge as a long-lived institution on the waterfront. The International Boardwalk is home to **Quality Seafood** (130 South International Boardwalk, 310/374-2382, $$), a seafood market and snack bar that displays and

prepares all manner of fresh, colorful seafood: local crab and fish, plus Louisiana crawdads and New Zealand eel. Cooks will steam a crab for you on the spot, which you can take to a table and crack to your heart's content.

NIGHTLIFE

There's a **Hennessey's Tavern** (1710 South Catalina Avenue, 310/316-6658) in Riviera Village, a shopping area set back from the beach. Come to think of it, there's a Hennessey's in each of the three South Bay beach towns: Redondo, Hermosa, and Manhattan. You can also find a decent cocktail lounge at one of the seafood restaurants in King Harbor: the old reliable **Chart House** (231 Yacht Club Way, 310/372-3464) or the **Blue Moon Saloon** (207 North Harbor Drive, 310/373-3411). You might wander into a decent jam at **Papa Garo's** (1810 South Catalina Boulevard, 310/540-7272), a Mediterranean restaurant and music club where you'll find live blues music in a smoke-free environment, as incongruous as that might seem. What was formerly the Strand Supper Club is now **Club Caprice** (1700 South Pacific Coast Highway, 310/316-1700), the best music venue in town. On Pacific Coast Highway, a few blocks from the beach, **Coyote Cantina** (531 North Highway 1, 310/376-1066) leaves them howling with their 60-label tequila list.

Hermosa Beach

In Spanish *hermosa* means "beautiful," and it's an apt description of this unpretentious community, which seems light-years removed from the smoggy hubbub of Los Angeles, against which it brushes. The more things change around it, the more Hermosa Beach (population 19,400) remains the same. It is the most relaxed and laid-back of the South Bay communities, a town full of coffee bars and shops catering to the healthful prerogatives of a physically fit populace. Living beside

EAVESDROPPING IN HERMOSA BEACH: "I'M VERY THERE"

The following is a real-life play in one act. All conversation is reported verbatim. (Yes, we eavesdropped and took notes.)

Scene: The bright stucco interior of the Hermosa Beach Post Office on a summer afternoon.

He: A slouching, unshaven male who looks like he's just rolled out of bed. His face is stubbly, his hair unkempt. He is wearing soiled cutoffs, sandals, and a T-shirt that has grayed from one too many unsorted washings.

She: A former California beach queen now gone to seed in middle age. Her skin has been worn to alligator hide by the sun, her face is creased with age and worry lines, and her thighs sag with cellulite. Her hair is dirty blonde, and she wears Spandex bike shorts and a loose-fitting T-shirt. Her eyes are concealed by designer sunglasses.

[They meet at a counter in the front room of the post office, where he is addressing a package.]

He: You look great!

She: Thanks. I feel great. *[Pauses.]* But it just ain't enough. *[She cackles ruefully, then continues.]* People are so goddamned superficial out here. Everybody is chasing that big white cloud, and I don't know what it is.

He: Yeah, I know. I'm so busy, I'm just running around all the time. This is what my day looks like: I get up, go to work, look for a place to park, and work for eight hours. I don't even have time to eat. I'll call to have some food delivered then shove it down when I can grab a moment. Then it's off to classes. Then I get home and call for more takeout food while I'm doing my homework and whatever *work* work I've had to take home. I'm beat all the time. The harder I work, the more I fall behind. I just don't know what's wrong.

She: I know what you mean. I spent six years in therapy, and all I wanted to know was how to find peace. Now I've found it, but I'm in the minority.

He: I'm very there.

She: I just don't need it anymore.

He: Good for you!

She: I'm going to Costa Rica to look for work. I've had it with L.A. It's just too crowded for me. Everyone running around, getting in each other's way. You know what I mean? No one wants to admit it, but it's over. L.A. is over. I've had it.

He: Are you going to Costa Rica with your mate?

She: No. *[Thoughtful pause.]* We're taking a second look at where we're at right now. If it happens, it happens. We'll see.

He: I was talking to my mate about this. A relationship starts out with a certain amount of mass, and once that mass begins falling away, you're forced to interface with one another. *[Pauses to reflect.]* You know, I like that phrase.

She: That's so true. Well, gotta go. Gotta get back to work. We'll hook up sometime.

He: Bye.

She: Bye-bye.

[Both walk away.]

the ocean in an almost perfect climate tends to make people look after themselves. Even a place like the Rocky Cola Cafe, a 1950s-style burger-jukebox joint, offers a healthy menu, analyzing its food items in terms of fat grams and calories; the café leaves things like egg yolks out of its omelets and serves black beans and brown rice as side dishes.

Hermosa Beach has a solid sense of itself and has plotted its destiny well. In 1901 the beach was surveyed for a boardwalk, in 1904 the first pier was built, and in 1907 the town of Hermosa Beach was incorporated. At that time the city gained ownership over its two-mile oceanfront in a deed mandating that it be held in perpetuity as "beach playground, free from commerce, and for the benefit of not only residents of Hermosa, but also for the sea lovers of Southern California." Those ideals remain in force today. It is an aesthetically attractive town with a gleaming, well-maintained beach.

What's most magical about Hermosa Beach is the descent down Pier Avenue toward the ocean. Rounding a curve, the road yields a spectacular view of the ocean. The light sea breeze is constant, the air feels clean and continuously refreshed, and you just can't help but stroll around Hermosa Beach in a state of grateful rejuvenation. If you want to get out of the sun, you can always duck into Nations Travel Bookstore, a shop specializing in travel guides, maps, and videos.

While you're there, rent a bike or a pair of in-line skates at one of the shops down on the Strand, then take off for a spin along the bike path up to Malibu, down to Redondo—anything's possible. And the unfolding beach scenery is worth the legwork.

Parking remains the one big bugaboo in Hermosa Beach. There's barely enough of it for those who live here, much less for visitors. Street parking is hard to find and expensive, and parking-meter charges are enforced 24 hours a day. Hotel guests are covered, but day-trippers be advised: Come via rapid transit, on foot, or via bicycle, if possible. Otherwise you might find yourself incurring some degree of expense and/or hassle. To quote from a letter to the editor of the *Easy Reader,* a free local paper: "The nemesis of Hermosa Beach that there's just no getting around is parking." We can second that emotion. Still, we like everything else about Hermosa Beach and recommend it highly.

BEACHES

Hermosa City Beach stretches for two unblemished miles, part of the continuous strip of sand that runs along the Santa Monica Bay before slamming to a halt at the Palos Verdes Peninsula. The 1,328-foot-long Hermosa Pier is its centerpiece, offering year-round angling in the waters of Santa Monica Bay. At the foot of the pier is a statue of a surfer poised in mid-ride. Beneath the frozen surfrider's impassive gaze, swarms of people whiz by on the South Bay Bicycle Trail. Although everyone moves at different speeds and in different directions, this complex symphony of motion somehow plays through without a lot of serious spills or collisions.

In addition to all the hell-on-wheels aerobicizing along the South Bay Bicycle Trail, sand rats play volleyball and paddleball out here on the ample beach, which we have yet to see in a condition that could be described as overcrowded. One pastime that's not too big, oddly enough, is surfing. Apparently the breakwater that protects Redondo Beach's harbor knocks the waves here down to a size for which only novices and locals have much use.

For more information, contact the Hermosa Beach Chamber of Commerce, 1007 Hermosa Avenue, Hermosa Beach, CA 90254, 310/376-0951, www.hbchamber.net.

18 HERMOSA CITY BEACH

BEST (

Location: Pier Avenue at Hermosa Avenue in Hermosa Beach
Parking/Fees: metered street parking
Hours: 6 A.M.-sunset

Facilities: concessions, lifeguards, restrooms, and showers

Contact: Los Angeles County Lifeguard Service, Southern Section, 310/832-1179

ACCOMMODATIONS

The best place to stay in Hermosa Beach is the **Beach House** (1300 Strand, 310/374-3001, www.beach-house.com, $$$$). It's perched right on the beach, with 96 "loft suites" overlooking the ocean in the vicinity of the pier. It doesn't get any better (or better situated) than the Beach House, but $300–430 a night for a room is a bit rich for our blood, at least in funky Hermosa. We're also fond of a funky, down-to-earth place called the **Sea Sprite Motel** (1016 Strand, 310/376-6933, www.seaspritemotel.com, $$) that's perfect for a true beach lover. The Sea Sprite is an informal yet well-tended motel that rents rooms and apartment-style cottages. From the second-floor pool deck you can watch the world skate by on the bike path below or just enjoy the misty breezes rolling off the ocean. The hotel has even managed to shoehorn in a parking space for every room, a perk that's worth its weight in parking tickets. There's nothing fancy about the Sea Sprite, but when you're right on the ocean—and you couldn't be any closer except on a surfboard—who needs marble bathrooms and turn-down service?

Hotel Hermosa (2515 Pacific Coast Highway, 310/318-6000, www.hotelhermosa.com, $$), an attractively landscaped property five blocks away from the beach, has a more upscale feel. A recent arrival, it's a Spanish-style three-story hotel with a heated pool, Japanese garden, workout facilities, and comfortable rooms, many with ocean-facing balconies. We also got a nice room for a fair price at the **Quality Inn** (901 Aviation Boulevard, 310/374-2666, www.qualityinn.com, $$). A large room with two beds that was spacious, well appointed, and clean for only $125 at the height of summer qualifies as a deal in our book—and you're only a bracing, 10-minute walk from the beach.

COASTAL CUISINE

Restaurants are abundant in Hermosa Beach. Boasting the highest per capita income in the South Bay, the town is sufficiently cosmopolitan to support a high-quality, ethnically diverse restaurant scene. You can take your pick of Thai, Italian, Mexican, French, Peruvian, Greek, Japanese, Indian, Cajun, Middle Eastern, macrobiotic, and more in this village. The crowds really seem to gravitate to the Italian eateries, such as **Buena Vita** (439 Pier Avenue, 310/379-7626, $$), a popular restaurant serving a broad variety of creative pasta dishes befitting a restaurant whose name translates to mean "good life." Prices are very reasonable.

Sushi just might be the favorite food of all. There are more sushi bars in Hermosa Beach than you can shake a chopstick at. **Sushi Sei** (1040 Hermosa Avenue, 310/379-6900, $$) is the consensus choice of raw-fish fans in the South Bay, offering sushi and comedic sushi chefs. **California Beach Rock 'n' Sushi** (844 Hermosa Avenue, 310/374-7758, $$) is another good place to eat it raw. But just exactly what is the connection between rock and roll and sushi here? Beats us.

We had a hearty, healthy lunch at **Rocky Cola Cafe** (1025 Pacific Coast Highway, 310/798-3111, $), a combination 1950s-style diner and health-food restaurant. Amid the standard fare of burgers, floats, and onion rings is a "bodybuilder fitness menu," including such things as ahi tuna tacos (dolphin-safe, of course) and egg-white veggie omelets. Close by, we dropped into **El Pollo Inka** (1100 Pacific Coast Highway, 310/372-1433, $$) to sample the Peruvian-style grilled chicken. It's a good, inexpensive, rotisserie-style plate of chicken, served with salad and rice or French fries. If you're feeling a bit more adventurous, you can ante up for one of the seafood dishes, such as *saltado de camarones* (sautéed shrimp, onions, tomatoes, and red pepper). Excellent!

Coffeehouses are big in the South Bay (as they are all over California). At a place called **Java Man** (157 Pier Avenue, 310/379-7209, $), we sipped on big mugs of the coffee of the day (macadamia nut) and munched pastries with the other clientele, who were similarly absorbed in the *Los Angeles Times*. One serious and sensitive fellow, though, was drawing psychedelic swirls onto paper with colored pencils, attentively rendering paisley blobs in an abstract, Romper-Room-on-acid style. He accompanied these with poetic thoughts and lyric fragments. When he made a trip to the bathroom, we sauntered over to inspect his drawing pad. Sample verse: "I am looking for my vision/A sight to set me free." We returned to our java, muffins, and newspapers, burying our beaks in the latest revelations about Republican politicians' pasts.

NIGHTLIFE

We've rarely seen a row of bars and clubs as entrenched as the one in Hermosa Beach. It can be found on the south side of Pier Avenue before it ends at the Strand. Such constancy is almost unheard of at the beach. Like a stack of dominoes, four clubs are arrayed in a row. It might be you, however, that's falling over by the end of the evening. Your choices are **Hennessey's Tavern** (8 Pier Avenue, 310/372-5759), a franchised Irish-themed bar/restaurant; the **Lighthouse Cafe** (30 Pier Avenue, 310/376-9833), a once-legendary jazz club that traffics in contemporary sounds, though a change in ownership has returned jazz to the mix; **Patrick Molloy's** (50 Pier Avenue, 310/798-9762), yet another would-be Irish bar; and **Aloha Sharkeez** (52 Pier Avenue, 310/374-5668), a faux surf bar that is the most popular spot in town.

Around the corner from Pier Avenue's string of watering holes, facing the beach itself on the Strand, is the old reliable **Poop Deck** (1272 Strand, 310/376-3223), a well-worn and unfancy place where well-worn and unfancy types come to slake their thirsts on a daily basis. It's a good hangout for a celebratory brew at sundown.

Then there's the back-alley institution known as **Bestie's** (1332 Hermosa Avenue,

310/318-3818). Once owned by British soccer legend George Best, a player second only to Pele in the annals of the sport, Bestie's faithfully re-creates a friendly British pub atmosphere. The menu is filled with staples of British cuisine like lamb stew and bangers and mash. Bartenders will pull you a long, cool mug of inky Guinness draft, and you can play pool, toss darts, or watch sports on one of a dozen or so TVs strung up around the premises. On weekends a back room miraculously metamorphoses into BBC, a hip dance club. Though the address is on Hermosa Avenue, Bestie's is entered from an alley behind it. Because you must know what you're looking for, Bestie's/BBC is popular with locals and all but unknown to outsiders.

Manhattan Beach

The view of the sand in either direction from Manhattan Beach Pier is enough to convince anyone that living in Los Angeles is worth every hassle—meteorological, seismic, automotive—just to have access to such splendor. Volleyball nets are strung out to the south as far as the eye can see. Surfers bob in the water, waiting for the wave that will carry them shoreward. Hot, hard-bodied babes oil down and catch rays on the beach. Weather-beaten anglers stand poised against the pier railings, their poles and lines an excuse for sitting all day in the golden sun.

You could almost flip a coin when choosing among the three beach towns—Redondo, Hermosa, and Manhattan—strung out along the southern edge of Santa Monica Bay. The three have more similarities than differences. For starters, they're linked by the South Bay Bicycle Trail, which also serves as a boardwalk, and they all strive to cultivate as low-key a personality as possible, given their proximity to Los Angeles.

If there is any difference between Manhattan Beach and the others, it is evident away

THE ART OF SURFING

Charles Lynn "Chick" Bragg is obsessed with surfing. Ever since he walked away from the baseball diamond – where his Little League teammates included future major-leaguers Robin Yount, Pete LaCock, and Rick Dempsey – he has fallen head over heels for surfing. Now in his mid-50s, Bragg has surfed virtually every day of his life since he was 18. When he is not in Fiji, Java, or Hawaii searching for the perfect wave, he can be found hopping over the wall in front of his tiny Manhattan Beach studio and dashing toward the water.

"I'm not really a beach guy," says Chick. "I just surf. The beach just happens to be where the ocean is."

He is also abundantly blessed with artistic talent. The skill runs in the family. Chick's father is Charles Bragg, the painter, etcher, and sculptor best known for his satiric takes on the legal profession and America's right-wing pomposities. Chick Bragg has nurtured his own vision, which has gotten his artwork displayed all over the planet.

You've seen Chick Bragg's work without realizing it, on posters, prints, coffee mugs, and T-shirts in seaside gift shops from here to Timbuktu. You've even owned some of his work without knowing it. His paintings of undersea life – inspired by his secondary passions, scuba diving and underwater photography – were used by the U.S. Postal Service for a series of first-class stamps run off in "limited editions" of 255 million. He has also achieved the prominence of a rock star in Japan. His paintings are filled with the wonders of the water, a sort of Henri Rousseau meets Jacques-Yves Cousteau.

Bragg surfs right across from where he lives, in the El Porto section of Manhattan Beach, about a mile north of the town pier. He does not surf farther north, toward Playa del Rey, because the water is too polluted for his liking. A truly gentle spirit, he is a throwback to the civilized days of surfing. As such, he's disturbed by the combative nature of today's wave riders.

"That stereotype of the sweet-natured surfer boy is all wrong," he said. "There is nothing sweet or gentle about these younger guys. They'll fight you over a wave. I'll share a wave, but when it gets to be a hostile situation, I just get depressed and can't enjoy the rides. Young surfers have less respect for everything, and they're really impatient. I still have to compete with them, as much as I dislike it."

If you want to learn more about the point at which art and surfing intersect, point your browser to www.surfart.com. It is one of the more handsomely designed, useful, and fun sites to, uh, surf that we've run across.

from the water. Manhattan Beach is the most moneyed, family-oriented, and residential of the three. Its 2,300 acres are as developed as a suburban community can be, crowded with smallish homes and yards that typically consist of a square foot of bleached pebbles and a dark green bush. The line of natural dunes hasn't been bulldozed away, and building heights have been held down to a bearable level. These facts, coupled with the town's sudden roller-coaster plunge toward the ocean, allow nearly all who live here an invigorating view of the Pacific Ocean. You feel the ocean in Manhattan Beach. It's like a permanent drive-in movie to help relieve the stress of the gridlock to the east.

Inside the snug city limits of Manhattan Beach (population 36,500) are 13 churches, five parks, and two libraries; one of the parks provides the setting for Sunday afternoon concerts during the summer. Most of the commerce is concentrated around the intersection of the two main drags, Manhattan Beach Boulevard and Highland Avenue.

LOS ANGELES COAST

"CATCH A WAVE": A BRIEF HISTORY OF SURF MUSIC

In the early 1960s, the state of California infiltrated rock and roll with a sound that could have come from nowhere else: surf music. The Beach Boys, Jan and Dean, and Dick Dale launched a nationally popular music scene out of the sun-dappled wonderland of Southern California. It was a movement that was well established before the Beatles made their first stateside splash with "I Want to Hold Your Hand."

The Beach Boys are principally deemed responsible for popularizing the California myth – a harmony-rich musical outlook based on the holy trinity of sun, surf, and girls – although Jan and Dean (with "Surf City") and the Mamas and the Papas (with "California Dreamin'") certainly warbled a few anthems of their own. The promise of a beatific adolescence in the Golden State transcended the foursquare suburban reality of cow towns like Hawthorne and Torrance. As Brian Wilson, the Beach Boys' founder, explained in a 1976 interview: "It's not just surfing; it's the outdoors and cars and sunshine; it's the society of California; it's the *way* of California."

Southern California was the wellspring of the California myth. For those plowing acreage in the Plains states or buried to their knees in winter snows in the Northeast, it was a potent come-on. The California myth promised everything: health and longevity beneath a bountiful sun that shone warmly year-round; prosperity in a job-filled environment catering to the burgeoning aeronautics and communications industries; and, finally, a relaxed approach to life that had "fun, fun, fun" as its first commandment.

Until the Beach Boys came along, surf music was the domain of instrumentalists such as Dick Dale, the "king of the surf guitar." According to Dale, "Real surfing music is instrumental, characterized by heavy staccato picking on a Fender Stratocaster." A surfer could listen to one of his solos and feel the surging power of the ocean as it hurtled him toward shore. Such numbers as "Let's Go Trippin'," "Surf Beat," and "Miserlou" promoted a sense of identity within the surfers' ranks.

Although surf music primarily functioned as party music for surfers in this locale, the genre left its mark on the national charts with songs by the Surfaris ("Wipe Out") and the Chantays ("Pipeline"). Both were released in 1963. The Chantays, a five-man garage band from Santa Ana, rode "Pipeline" all the way to #4. The Surfaris, a quintet from Glendora, saw "Wipe Out" soar to #2. A tumbling wave of tom-tom rolls and

The local businesses squeezed in here are the sort of nonfranchised shops that obsessive consumers love to believe they've discovered for themselves, bearing such names as Pour Moi! La Boutique, Foote Fetish, and Le Chat. Parking isn't necessarily a problem, but it isn't cheap and it isn't easy. Street meters run 24 hours and cost $0.25 for 15 minutes, with a five-hour limit. They take quarters only. Where is somebody supposed to come by that many quarters?

There are some nagging signs that Manhattan Beach may be losing its grip on growth. A 187-acre business park has been relegated to the eastern edge of town in the flight path of Los Angeles International Airport and next to a smoke-belching power plant. With it has arrived an army of nouveau riche who have driven up land values with their real estate schemes. This has caused longtime residents to skirmish with developers.

A young woman who lives in Manhattan Beach told us that the town has developed an attitude that is lacking in the more laid-back Hermosa Beach. That attitude, one supposes, comes from the money it costs to live here. One local realtor—whose slogan is "I have the right energy to sell your house"—advertised frenzied guitar breaks, "Wipe Out" remains the premier instrumental surf hit of all time. The Marketts made their mark with "Surfer's Stomp" and "Balboa Blue." Then there were the Pyramids, from Long Beach, who recorded the surf classic "Penetration." These gonzo freaks performed with shaved heads and arrived at shows in helicopters and atop elephants.

However, it was the Beach Boys who triggered a nationwide mania for surf and hot-rod music. The Beach Boys spread the gospel of surfing "even in places where the nearest thing to surf is maybe the froth on a chocolate shake!" (to quote the liner notes of *Surfin' USA*, their second album). With their earliest songs, "Surfin'" and "Surfin' Safari," the Beach Boys made a magical, intuitive leap – bridging Chuck Berry and the Four Freshmen and adding their own libretto about surfing and the California way of life.

Jan (Berry) and Dean (Torrance) were the other major minstrels in the car-and-surf-song sweepstakes. With "Surf City," a tune cowritten by Brian Wilson, Jan and Dean had the first #1 surfing song in 1963. The real-life "surf city" they had in mind was Huntington Beach, which has taken to promoting itself with that handle in modern times.

Other singing surf and car groups from the 1960s included the Fantastic Baggys ("Tell 'Em I'm Surfing," "Summer Means Fun"), the Rip Chords ("Hey Little Cobra," "Three Window Coupe"), and the Sunrays ("I Live for the Sun"). At mid-decade a new wave of Southern California-based acts swept the Top 40. Among them were the Turtles, Gary Lewis and the Playboys, Paul Revere and the Raiders, the Mamas and the Papas, the Byrds, the Monkees, and the Grass Roots.

In 1967 California would enter a whole different stage when psychedelic music would become all the rage during the "summer of love." The seeds of this revolution can be traced back to five Pendleton-shirted Beach Boys and their idea to sing about surfing. As the late Carl Wilson of the Beach Boys once told us, "People wanted to hang out at the beach. It was really an early hippie thing." In a way, it still is.

If you want the best possible overview of California surf music, then lay your hands on Rhino Records' *Cowabunga! The Surf Box*, a lovingly assembled various-artists box set that tells the story perfectly. Incidentally, the Beach Boys are scattered about, and only Brian Wilson is alive among the three Wilson brothers who formed the core of the band. In late 2008 he released a concept album, entitled *That Lucky Old Sun*, an affectionate ode to Southern California and all that makes it special.

this bargain: "A classic beach home on the walk streets with fabulous ocean views." Translation: A modest wooden box with an upstairs balcony located blocks off the ocean. Asking price: $699,000. Of the mega-moneyed set that has just about displaced the beach bums, one longtime resident said, "The vibe here is spoiled, arrogant, impatient...as if their pampered lives are so pressured. Oh yes, and greedy."

Still, as you near the beach, all pretensions disappear in a blaze of tanned, libidinous glory. Relaxed bars, taverns, and restaurants near the pier on Manhattan Boulevard help sustain the friendly cacophony that is at the heart of the Southern California beach experience.

For more information, contact the Manhattan Beach Chamber of Commerce, 425 15th Street, Manhattan Beach, CA 90266, 310/545-5313, www.manhattanbeachchamber.net.

BEACHES

Manhattan Beach's two-mile oceanfront is completely residential (i.e., no motels, few affordable rentals). The clean, sandy **Manhattan County Beach** is bisected by a 900-foot pier (at the west end of Manhattan Beach Boulevard) and backed by a seawall adorned with tasteful murals and less tasteful graffiti. The water is subject to occasional rough currents but is well patrolled by a bevy of lifeguards. Beach volleyball is not just a sport, it's a religion here. From the pier, sand volleyball courts and nets extend down toward Hermosa Beach. North of Manhattan Beach is **El Porto Beach.** You can walk to it from Manhattan Beach or park near the ramps at 41st and 44th Streets. El Porto has full facilities and volleyball nets, but the scene here tends to be loud and uninviting.

19 MANHATTAN COUNTY BEACH

Location: the Strand at Manhattan Pier in Manhattan Beach
Parking/Fees: metered street and lot parking
Hours: 6 A.M.-sunset
Facilities: concession, lifeguards, restrooms, and showers
Contact: Los Angeles County Lifeguard Service, Southern Section, 310/832-1179

20 EL PORTO BEACH

Location: end of 45th Street in Manhattan Beach
Parking/Fees: metered street parking
Hours: 6 A.M.-sunset
Facilities: lifeguards, restrooms, and showers
Contact: Los Angeles County Lifeguard Service, Southern Section, 310/832-1179

ACCOMMODATIONS

Lodging isn't Manhattan Beach's strong suit. The closest you can get to the beach is three steep uphill blocks away from the action on Highland Avenue. The **Sea View Inn** (3400 Highland Avenue, 310/545-1504, www .seaview-inn.com, $$) is the most appealing of a handful of choices. It has only eight rooms, but these surround a swimming pool away from the noise of the busy thoroughfare.

COASTAL CUISINE

The most celebrated restaurant in town was H_2O, but the award-winning nouvelle cuisine venue has evaporated. One that is garnering

Manhattan County Beach

© PARKE PUTERBAUGH

similar raves is **Rock 'N Fish** (120 Manhattan Beach Boulevard, 310/379-9900, $$), where the healthy preparations of seafood are as impressive as the extensive wine list. **Fonz's Steak and Seafood** (1017 Manhattan Avenue, 310/376-1536, $$$) seems to get the spillover from Rock 'N Fish.

NIGHTLIFE

A clear sign of the upscaling of Manhattan Beach is the fate of La Paz, once considered to be the "king of the beach bars" and "Animal House at the beach" by the usual reliable sources of surfers and local beach bums. It was a sloppy, wonderful, ramshackle place that we feel privileged to have visited on a previous trip. La Paz is gone now, replaced by a municipal parking lot beside the pier. Bars picking up the slack include **Beaches** (117 Manhattan Beach Boulevard, 310/545-2523), which used to be the rowdy Sunsets and is more restaurant than bar now, though it has won "best dance club" honors from a local weekly; **Manhattan Beach Brewing Company** (124 Manhattan Beach Boulevard, 310/798-2744), with designer home brew; and the **Shellback Tavern** (116 Manhattan Beach Boulevard, 310/376-7857), which is the closest in spirit to La Paz you'll find on the beach. It serves pretty good tacos and burgers, too. Just two blocks up a steep hill from the beach is **Baja Sharkeez** (3801 Highland Avenue, 310/545-6563), the most popular surf bar in town. "If I were single," one surfer confided, "this is where I'd come. At night you can't move without knocking someone with an elbow." Sawdust on the floor, surf videos and sports on screens, old flotsam hanging from ceilings, and the best fish taco and veggie burrito within five miles—Baja Sharkeez has it all.

El Segundo

Like San Pedro, El Segundo (population 16,300) is an integral part of Los Angeles, but it is mostly overlooked or ignored. It is home to a sprawl of oil refineries, oil piers, the Hyperion Sewage Treatment Plant (the Grand Coulee Dam of sewage plants), and the Scattergood Steam Generating Station. Hyperion is the "largest activated sludge plant in the world," its 330 million gallons of sewage a day treated and dumped, as sludge, in off-shore canyons. El Segundo is also directly beside Los Angeles International Airport. This bathes the town in a toxic-industrial-aeronautic cacophony that blends perfectly with the boom boxes that reign along the shore.

For more information, contact the El Segundo Chamber of Commerce, 427 Main Street, El Segundo, CA 90245, 310/322-1220, www.beach-web.com.

BEACHES

In spite of the surrounding environment, El Segundo has two of the broadest beaches in the Los Angeles area: **Dockweiler State Beach** and **El Segundo Beach.** Together they comprise a six-mile stretch of sand that would make any other beach town sorely envious. Although there's beach access and large parking lots off El Segundo Boulevard and at the end of Grand Avenue, the best way to see El Segundo and Dockweiler State Beaches is by bicycling along the shoreline-hugging South Bay Bicycle Trail. Almost anywhere along this stretch you can pull off the bicycle trail and the beach is all yours.

It's an odd sensation to be on a beach so huge on a picture-perfect summer day, all of five miles from the center of Los Angeles, and find the place nearly deserted. As long as you don't look shoreward at the oil refineries and sewage plant, or fret too much over the gangsta rap blaring from the direction of the parking lot, you'd swear this was as perfect a beach as you could hope to find. Dockweiler State Beach has the added incentive of a 117-site campground, for RVs only, at its south end. Dockweiler is so long that it encompasses the oceanfront in both El Segundo and neighboring Playa del Rey. To make things even more disorienting, Dockweiler is considered a state beach, though it is leased to the City of Los Angeles and operated by the County of Los Angeles.

21 EL SEGUNDO BEACH

🚴 🏄 🌐

Location: Grand Avenue at Vista del Mar Boulevard in El Segundo
Parking/Fees: $7 entrance fee per vehicle
Hours: 6 A.M.-10 P.M.
Facilities: lifeguards and restrooms
Contact: Los Angeles County Lifeguard Service, Southern Section, 310/832-1179

Playa del Rey

Playa del Rey is a largely residential town built along streets that dead-end into a lagoon at sea level and run on top of towering bluffs that look out over the beach. The chief calling card is Dockweiler State Beach, a wide, white-sand beach extending from Del Rey Lagoon south to the RV campground in El Segundo. Across the lagoon lies Venice Beach; behind it, along constructed waterways, Marina del Rey. It is due west of Los Angeles International Airport.

The drive out to Playa del Rey, west from Lincoln Boulevard through the last unblemished wetlands in Los Angeles, is relatively pleasant. It might not have been, however, had Steven Spielberg and pals had their way with the proposed (and now abandoned) Dream-Works SKG project, which would have defiled 1,087 acres of this oasis for their studio. However, the massive Playa Vista development has a bright side: despite all the new homes and office space, 70 percent of the property has been dedicated to open space.

For more information, contact the LAX Coastal Area Chamber of Commerce, 9100 South Sepulveda Boulevard, Suite 210, Westchester, CA 90045, 310/645-5151, www .laxcoastal.com.

BEACHES

The word "wide" does not even begin to describe the sandy expanse at **Dockweiler State Beach,** which is shared by Playa del Rey and neighboring El Segundo. Dockweiler and adjacent beaches in Los Angeles County have been extended seaward with sand dredged from the site of the Hyperion Sewage Treatment Plant and the Scattergood Steam Generating Station. They can handle all eager beachgoers, all summer long. Even with all of mighty Los Angeles knocking at the back door, such beaches as Dockweiler, Venice, and Santa Monica seldom reach the saturation point. Not that they're terrifically attractive, but they are indisputably large. They are also prone to closure when the waters of Santa Monica Bay become polluted with storm-drain runoff.

22 DOCKWEILER STATE BEACH

🚴 ⛺ 🌐

Location: Vista del Mar Boulevard at Imperial Highway in Playa del Rey
Parking/Fees: $7 entrance fee per vehicle; camping fees $16.35-26.35 per night
Hours: 6 A.M.-10 P.M.
Facilities: concession, lifeguards, restrooms, showers, and picnic tables
Contact: Los Angeles County Lifeguard Service, Southern Section, 310/832-1179

Marina del Rey

Marina del Rey can be summed up in two words: *yachting* and *eating.* It is the world's largest recreational small-craft harbor, consisting of eight basins that collectively contain 6,100 boat slips. It also claims to have the greatest concentration of restaurants in a single square-mile area this side of New York City. The place is a magnet for money.

It's hard to imagine that until the mid-1950s

WANT TO BE AN L.A. COUNTY LIFEGUARD?

If week after week of watching the flesh parade on reruns of *Baywatch* has you eager to join the ranks of Los Angeles County lifeguards, then bear in mind that the reality of landing the job is a little tougher than showing up with a Screen Actors Guild card. In fact, to make it into rookie school at the Lifeguard Training Academy, you must meet the following conditions right off the bat: 1) you must have uncorrected vision of 20/30 or better; 2) you must be able to complete a 1,000-meter ocean swim race (approximately three-fifths of a mile); 3) you must be 18 years of age or older; and 4) you must have a valid California driver's license and high school diploma.

There is a difference between pool and beach lifeguards. In order to become a beach lifeguard, one must first accumulate 600 hours of experience as a pool lifeguard. Candidates for beach lifeguard positions must undergo a 60-hour training program.

Lifeguard trials are held once yearly in September and draw roughly 250 applicants. If chosen, new recruits begin as part-timers, making $19.32 per hour, and attend a hundred hours of "rookie school." They learn first aid and safety and rescue techniques. Recertification is required every year. The county employs 132 year-round lifeguards and hires 650 seasonal lifeguards. It hires roughly a hundred pool lifeguards a year, as they move up or out of the system.

For more information, call the **Los Angeles County Lifeguard Administrative Headquarters** (323/881-2411) or the **Lifeguard Training Academy** (310/939-7200). Los Angeles County lifeguards earn their pay, collectively making 10,000 ocean rescues a year along the 72 miles of the county coastline. There are four section headquarters (at Hermosa Beach, Marina del Rey, Santa Monica, and Zuma Beach), 158 lifeguard stands, and ten Baywatch boats.

However seriously you may or may not take it, *Baywatch* has indirectly saved lives. According to the Guinness Book of World Records, *Baywatch*, which aired from 1990 to 2001, was the most widely watched TV show around the world. (How else would Borat have become so enamored of Pamela Anderson?) Its influence, then, has been positive, raising the level of lifeguard competence in cities all over the world. Case in point: Barcelona, Spain. After city officials flew Los Angeles County lifeguards over for consultations, the beaches of Barcelona were demonstrably safer. On one weekend in 1993 (before the consultations), there were 14 drownings on its beaches. During the first nine *months* of 1994 (after the consultations), there were none.

the area was a swampy lagoon at the mouth of Ballona Creek. Progress, you say? Well, maybe. The construction of the marina has not been without problems. Although the East Coast has an abundance of natural harbors, the California coast has few of them, necessitating the construction of harbors, involving jetties, breakwaters, and the dredging of marinas. After opening, Marina del Rey faced a series of design-related problems. First, under a certain set of wave conditions outside the marina, the original design enabled the spread of destructive standing waves inside the marina, resulting in damaged boats and lawsuits. To rectify this, designers hastily added a 1,200-foot, detached offshore breakwater in 1962. The marina has also seen the recurring problem of sand shoaling up against the north jetty and forming a bar across the southern entrance channel, which has required expensive dredging on a regular basis.

All the same, the marina generates more money than it costs to maintain, so most everyone is happy, especially L.A. boat groupies. Like a hand with eight fingers, the yacht basin at Marina del Rey reaches inland, grabbing Los Angeles by the seat of the pants. In addition to the 6,100 boat slips in the water, it can store another 3,000 vessels in dry dock. There are nearly as many boats in Marina del Rey as there are residents. Admiralty Way runs in a semicircle around the harbor. It connects with Via Marina (on the west side) and Fiji Way (on the south side) to form a great horseshoe around the octet of boat basins. It is in this watery world-within-a-world that the moneyed heart of Marina del Rey can be heard to beat. Some people live on their boats. A few have died on them. Dennis Wilson of the Beach Boys drowned here while diving for discarded souvenirs in a boat slip where he used to live with a former wife.

Over the past three decades, Marina del Rey (population 8,900) has blossomed like a cactus flower out of its desert-like surroundings. An impressive retail industry of waterfront restaurants, luxury hotels, dance clubs, and specialty shops has grown around the harbor. In Marina del Rey you can, as a brochure proclaims, browse for everything "from socks to solid gold." Signs heralding one's arrival in Marina del Rey offer this menu of options: Apartments, Berths, Chandlery, Hotels, Launching, Maintenance, Moorings, Motels, Restaurants, Shops, Sportfishing, Town Houses, Yacht Sales. As you spiral closer to Admiralty Way from the outside world—passing through the buffer zones that isolate Marina del Rey from the less glamorous neighboring communities of Culver City, Playa del Rey, and Venice—an oasis of boats, buildings, and greenery emerges out of nowhere. If you look and listen closely, you might even hear ducks quacking and waddling around a large lake that's part of a nature preserve. Off-road bike paths wind around the marina. The South Bay Bicycle Trail leaves the beach at the mouth of Ballona Creek and passes through the marina, reemerging by the ocean at Venice Pier. Four small parks within the marina add a note

of greenery and tranquility. **Burton Chase Park,** at the end of Mindinao Way, is a six-acre green space from which one can watch boats enter and exit the marina. The retail area known as **Fisherman's Village** is one of the more convincing of the nautical-themed, New England–style shopping complexes we've seen, right down to its cobblestone walks. The whole of Marina del Rey has the privileged, dreamlike aura of a mirage. It's a great mirage, if you've got the monetary means to enjoy it.

For more information, contact the LAX Coastal Area Chamber of Commerce, 9100 South Sepulveda Boulevard, Suite 210, Westchester, CA 90045, 310/645-5151, www.laxcoastal.com.

BEACHES

In this case the proper heading would be the singular *beach*. Because it is a protected inland harbor, Marina del Rey by definition has no ocean beaches. The marina does have one beach at the end of Basin D: **Mother's Beach,** where water-lovers can swim, windsurf, and sail on a sandy, lifeguarded stretch of sand where no waves roll ashore. Maybe that's why choosy mothers choose Mother's as a place to bring their kids to frolic in relative safety. In any case, this mushroom-shaped lagoon enables both calm-water swimming and wind-free sunbathing. The drawback is water quality. Would you want to swim in a man-made lagoon routinely fouled by boat fuel, bilgewater, and storm runoff?

23 MOTHER'S BEACH

Location: Basin D on Panay Way in Marina del Rey
Parking/Fees: $6
Hours: sunrise–10 P.M.
Facilities: lifeguards, restrooms, showers, and picnic tables
Contact: Marina del Rey Parks, Beaches, and Harbors, 310/305-9503

ACCOMMODATIONS

The selection of hotels and restaurants in Marina del Rey makes it the Neiman-Marcus of beach communities. Starting from the top, the vaunted **Ritz-Carlton** (4375 Admiralty Way, 310/823-1700, $$$$) brings a touch of Old World elegance to the land of new money. This 14-story masterpiece affords a choice of harbor or ocean views, swaddling guests in comfort (for a price) in a veritable island of first-class amenities: lighted tennis courts, heated outdoor pool, yacht charters, and so on.

The **Marina Beach Marriott** (4100 Admiralty Way, 310/301-3000, $$$$) offers comparable upscale accommodations in a 10-story tower that looks like a giant sand dune from the street. The balcony views—of the Malibu coastline to the north, of Palos Verdes Peninsula to the south—are majestic, especially around sunset. With a ninth-floor cocktail lounge, ground-floor California-cuisine restaurant (Stones), outdoor garden café and pool, and sumptuous rooms decorated in muted pastels and accented with brass and marble, you won't lack for pampering here.

If money is a consideration, nearby Culver City is loaded with cheaper chain motels. You'll save a bundle, which you can blow on dinner and nightlife in the marina.

COASTAL CUISINE

A few years back one of us had Sunday dinner with rock 'n' roll pioneer Little Richard at **Aunt Kizzy's Back Porch** (4325 Glencoe Avenue, 310/578-1005, $$), a soul-food eatery in the Villa Marina Shopping Center. Not only can Richard sing and pound the piano, the man knows how to pick a restaurant. The culinary style is Deep South and down-home: mounds of fried chicken, pork tenderloin, homemade mashed potatoes and biscuits, stewed vegetables, fruit cobblers, and other fresh desserts. Aunt Kizzy's food is so good it's enough to give you religion, if you haven't got it already.

On the waterfront **Edie's Diner** (4211 Admiralty Way, 310/577-4558, $) does a big

business in burgers, fries, and pie. It's done up in diner chic, from the gleaming ceramic tile to the retro rock tunes on the booth-side jukeboxes, and the burgers are everything you'd want in a slab of ground cow: big, sloppy, and good. Edie's does breakfast as well.

Coffee-holics will want to head over to **Joni's Coffee Roaster Cafe** (552 Washington Boulevard, 310/305-7147, $$), a favorite gathering place of Venice-Marina bohemians and wealthy mavericks. One leather-clad wannabe biker casually ordered a glass of chardonnay and an Anchor Steam beer before the sun was up. "What the heck," he told the nonplussed clerk, "it's Monday morning." In addition to espresso, cappuccino, and pastries, the café offers healthful breakfasts, lunches, and dinners. Hit **Noah's Bagels** (548 Washington Boulevard, 310/574-1155, $) next door, and you're good to go.

NIGHTLIFE

A night on the town in Marina del Rey begins with a fruitless search for a parking space. The way they've got it rigged, there's next to nothing in the way of legal street parking, leaving one with no choice but to hand the keys to a valet at the club or restaurant of your choice. We despise valet parking.

In this vexatious spirit we drove around Marina del Rey looking for parking. After cruising for a while, we tried the lot at a shopping center just outside the marina, but it was filled with signs warning that all cars belonging to non-customers would be towed. We took our chances all the same and left the car, hiking to a place called—it hurts just to type a name this stupid—Moose McGillycuddy's. Moose's is now called **Waikiki Willies** (13535 Mindinao Way, 310/574-3932), but is essentially the same animal as before. It's an indoor/outdoor pub, grub, and disco venue that claims the same sort of crowd that used to jam the Red Onion, a now-defunct singles-bar chain that, in its own way, helped further the 1980s population boom in Southern California.

At Willies, a young crowd hopped to the

fascistic beat of the latest synthetic dance hits. Some lined up to be plastered with free temporary tattoos, which was that evening's big promotion. A salty dog who looked like the Skipper on *Gilligan's Island* circulated with a wicker basket full of plastic-wrapped Moonie roses, cutting an odd figure. In the bathroom a guy removed the sweaty T-shirt in which he'd arrived and changed into a trendier leisure-wear ensemble, looking like a discofied Clark Kent who'd come to dazzle the ladies with his sartorial Kryptonite. At one table a mutually infatuated couple took turns grooming each other, like Rhesus monkeys, with combs and brushes. We stationed ourselves at the Pop-a-Shot concession, vainly trying to impress the locals with our shooting ability and finally retreating to the outdoor patio.

The **Baja Cantina** (311 Washington Boulevard, 310/821-2252) was hopping all night long. Maybe hot chilies were warming up the patrons in this popular Mexican restaurant and watering hole. You come in, put your name on the list, belly up to the bar, grab a Mexican beer, and wait for a table in tight quarters with what seems like half of Los Angeles. The Baja Cantina is noisy and fun, with its socio-cultural ambience best suggested by two of the celebrities whose framed, autographed pictures hang on the wall: actor Tony Danza and porn star Christy Canyon.

Venice

In the 1993 film *Falling Down,* the Michael Douglas character—an everyman driven to psychopathy by the stress of living in Los Angeles—cuts a swath westward across the city to Venice, committing a rash of demented crimes on his way. The police track him down, forcing a final stand at the end of Venice Pier. As he dies, falling over the pier railing after absorbing a point-blank blast from Robert Duvall's service revolver, he gives Venice a last befuddled backward glance and then splashes into the beautiful blue Pacific.

In Venice, life doesn't just imitate art. It defines it. If it's cutting edge, chances are it started in Venice—and it probably will end here, too. Venice is many things: fascinating human zoo, nasty urban war zone, and just about everything in between.

Take the hard-luck Venice Pier, for instance. Built in 1997, it had to be closed down for several years due to structural concerns. (It reopened in 2006.) Like the Michael Douglas character, many alienated people gravitate to Venice to make an escape. On the other hand, many who come here—us, for example—have given it a befuddled backward glance as they headed out of town.

It's easy to trash Venice. Not for nothing is it known as the home of $2 sunglasses, $3 T-shirts, $4 Tarot readings, and $5 stress massages. New Age prophets walk shoulder to shoulder with old-age homeless. Runaway children seek shelter in group houses, and gangs bring their hideous territorial squabbles to the shore. Cops walk the beat, half amused and half afraid.

It's easy to allow preconceptions to unfairly blind a first-time visitor to Venice's peculiar appeal. The source of that appeal goes right back to the town's roots. Venice began as the dream of a man named Abbot Kinney, who made his millions on cigarettes and spent them all in 1900 purchasing 160 acres of marshland south of Santa Monica. For some reason (nicotine frenzy perhaps), he saw similarities between his new property and the site on which Venice, Italy, was built. He commissioned two architects to design a "thoroughly equipped" city with streets, hotels, houses, and canals—15 miles of cement-bottomed canals. By June 1905, the canals were filled with water. All Kinney needed for his new Venice was people to build their dream homes beside his waterways.

Like any good businessman, Kinney lured folks here with a gimmick: gondolas and gondoliers. He imported some of Italy's finest oarsmen and had them serenade prospective buyers while rowing them up and down the canals to inspect the empty lots. He persuaded merchants to build hotels, restaurants, and shops in the architectural style of the Venetian Renaissance. He also oversaw the construction of a lecture hall, pavilion, and theater. Provocative speakers were brought in, first-rate plays were staged, and blue-ribbon orchestras performed. All the while, the gondoliers kept singing.

Kinney's noble experiment failed, culminating in a poorly attended and abbreviated run of *Camille* starring Sarah Bernhardt, the greatest stage actress of her day. Visitors to Venice, it turned out, preferred sand and sidewalks to the interior of a concert hall. To salvage his enormous investment, the dauntless Kinney did an about-face, filling in a number of his festering, plant-choked canals and bringing in sideshow freaks, street theater, and a roller coaster. A miniature railroad was built to run along with the Ocean Front Walk, turning the town into an amusement park by the sea. In 1925 the little town became part of Los Angeles. By 1939 Kinney's conversion was complete, with Venice known as "the Playland of the Pacific" and "the Coney Island of the West."

Venice has since undergone other transformations. It was covered with oil wells, low-income housing, and boarded-up slums in the 1940s. It was adopted by beatniks in the 1950s, hippies in the 1960s, artists and fitness freaks in the 1970s, and gentrified homeowners—the original audience Kinney had dreamed of for Venice—in the 1980s and 1990s. Venice still lives in a dream, as it always has, perceiving itself as some sort of impervious Left Bank, but one beset by problems.

Granted, certain aspects of Venice's surreal sideshow are real and fascinating. There's the endless parade of oddballs who entertain for spare change along Ocean Front Walk, the cement boardwalk that runs along the backside of Venice Beach. Although this pedestrian thoroughfare is only seven-tenths of a mile long, it is light-years beyond whatever else passes for cutting edge elsewhere in America. The best place to start a walk-through is at the Windward Avenue access, the halfway point in the human parade. Here you'll find the classic *Venice on the Half Shell* mural, which captures the spirit of the procession. It may sound like a cliché, but you really are likely to see anything out here. The following are just some of the things we've witnessed: guy in a turban chewing glass; guy on a unicycle juggling knives; another unicyclist juggling chainsaws; legless, armless dwarf dancing on his stumps to Latin disco music; assortment of Michael Jackson impersonators, with proud mamas pocketing the donations; "post tribal artist"; cabalistic Tarot reader; a village shaman offering a spoken "love revival"; a gypsy performing "three-day dissolving marriage ceremonies"; folk performers with purple hair; ancient black woman shrieking incoherent blues while strumming an electric guitar lent her by a well-meaning college kid; body piercers; hair braiders; X-rated comedians; conceptual artists; mural artists; caricaturists; acrobats; animals performing stupid pet tricks; transvestites; leather freaks; Rastafarians; punks, drunks, and punch-drunks; and some people who are really and truly insane.

Along this same route you'll find a few passable bars, some decent take-out food stalls, a good book shop, and a museum of Native American art. Hang around long enough and you'll also absorb the prevailing Venetian outlook: a healthy and well-cultivated disregard for chicness, big money, and normal ways of doing things.

Away from the curious clamor on Ocean Front Walk, Venice reveals another side of itself—a pleasant residential community of 50,000 filled with proud homeowners who casually enjoy the placid life along the town's back canals. In the past few years, the more secluded canals have been cleaned up, and fish are even seen in the no-longer-murky waters. The Canal Walk—between Washington Boulevard and Rose Avenue—is part of the Venice Canal Historic District, which is listed on the National Register of Historic Places. Walking here is an enjoyable and quiet diversion as you observe the fascinating and eclectic architecture and the commendable lengths that the residents have gone to turn the tiniest plots of land into gardening masterpieces.

LOS ANGELES COAST

THE DANDELION UNDER THE PILLOW

Tell someone to put a dandelion under their pillow to cure dandruff and they'll elect you President...of anything.

Henry Morgan, interviewed in *The Realist*, 1960

Some years back, a local news story captured the nation's imagination. A Los Angeles woman lost her cat on a flight from New York's La Guardia Airport to LAX. A California psychic was called in for the cat hunt. The psychic picked up some feline vibes – our theory is litter-box odor – in the cargo bay. Tracking the vibes, the psychic pinpointed the cat's location. That is, the psychic pointed to the section of the cargo bay where the cat was later found. With that, California's booming alternative industry racked up yet another success story.

California is the holy land for spiritual, medical, personal, and political alternatives. This is the state that gave us the Summer of Love and the Monterey Pop Festival – but also the Altamont disaster and the Manson family. It has produced great alternative literature and groundbreaking music. It has also given rise to taxpayer revolts and Pebble Beach. It has coughed up Jim Jones and Ronald Reagan, the Black Panthers, Jerry Brown, the SLA, Patty Hearst, and cults too numerous to name. One of them committed mass suicide one night, believing they would all thereupon hitch a ride upon a comet as it passed closest to earth's orbit. And who can forget former First Lady Nancy Reagan, whose reliance on a California astrologist directed the fate of the country for a spell.

A veritable smorgasbord of healers, shamans, counselors, holistic therapists, ministers, colon irrigators, foot reflexologists, and other assorted gurus make their homes in California. This is especially the case along the coast, where the sea breezes and unchanging weather help foster a meditative, anti-mainstream turn of mind. Every single one of these alternative healers is an expert on something. Some are quacks, while others have legitimately helped people beyond the reach of mainstream medicine while also serving to loosen the fascistic grip that the medical establishment has on our nation's health care system.

One way to get a handle on available alternative services is to consult the myriad free weekly publications devoted to this subject. How can so many people, we wondered, ply their trade in this alternative market? And if indeed they do find enough customers to make a lucrative living, why is the state still so bedeviled? If Los Angeles, for instance, is filled to bursting with self-actualized, self-empowered, and healthy people with their chakras in a row who eat the right organic foods and sip healing herbal teas all the livelong day, why is the city such a dysfunctional smog-choked sprawl that its saner citizens can't wait to flee when a better opportunity elsewhere comes along?

It's not our intent to knock alternatives. In fact this guide is intended to be an alternative to the fulsome, skin-deep prose that fills most travel books and virtually all travel websites. Still, as one peruses the alternative reference tools, the notion begins forming that many of these experts are peddling false hope. At their most innocuous, however, they provide an entertaining sideshow.

Here's a random sampling of those doing business in the alternative healing arts along the California coast:

- "OPENING TO THE GODDESS ENERGY: Explore and heal the denied feminne *(sic)* within...$80 advance, $100 at the door."

- "SINGING, MOVING THROUGH THE FEAR, FOR NON-SINGERS WHO MUST SING: reasonable rates." (Don't karaoke bars provide this service free of charge?)

- "ENHANCED SEXUALITY TRAINING: Sexual meditation. Extended orgasm. Soul union and enlightenment. No overt sexual activity." (What a tease!)

- "PAST LIFE REGRESSION. Explore past lives for: Curiosity, Removing Blocks, Soul Cleansing. Affordable sessions. Sessions led by a metaphysical minister."

- "CLEAR KARMA NOW: Commander A_ S_ offers 'Karma clearings by phone.'"

- "TRAVEL AROUND THE NATIVE AMERICAN AND CELTIC MEDICINE WHEEL...different journeys each week...$20 session."

- "AN EVENING WITH XANDO, channeled by G_. Donation. XANDO is a composite of six angelic beings."

- "POWER NEGOTIATION SKILLS. You will learn to: Formulate and dovetail outcomes for Win-Win results. Preserve the relationship while achieving your outcome. Apply these skills to business, personal, and family issues...$250 at the door." (In other words, learn to manipulate others blind.)

- "GRANDFATHER OF THE NEW AGE REVEALS MYSTERIES: Now nearing 70 years of age, N_ is considered the leading expert on crystal skulls...They are thought to be at least 10,000 to 20,000 years old. A three-day retreat will cost $149, plus transportation to and from Arizona, plus $25 a night at the Healing Center, plus $5 for breakfast and lunch, plus $7 dinner."

- "LOVESTAR INSTITUTE. Holistic Health Psychologist Thanatologist (grief) Counselor." (Good grief!)

- "I AM A CLAIRVOYANT CHANNELER OF MULTIDIMENSIONS: Sit in the presence of Ascension and Dolphin energy attunement while receiving important messages and answers to your delicate and urgent questions."

Heard enough? If not, contact Whole Life Times, P.O. Box 1187, Malibu, CA 90265, 310/317-4200. Tell them Xando sent you.

LOS ANGELES COAST

LOS ANGELES COAST

Community leaders regularly organize cleanups, and ad hoc action, block parties, and neighborhood watches have made inroads on crime prevention. Venice is not about to let the town go to seed as it did in the past.

The best way to see the full tableau that Venice has to offer is to book a walking tour through the **Venice Historical Society** (310/967-5170). The tour costs around $7.50, and reservations must be made ahead of time.

Although the fear of crime is less intense now, and neighborhood pride and vigilance is at an all-time high, Venice still has a ways to go. There are parts of town that even the police have been hesitant to patrol. During one of our visits, a group of Los Angeles's finest staged a protest at being transferred to the Venice beat.

We were warned repeatedly about a trend in urban crime that has been particularly prevalent in Venice: bike-jacking. Meanwhile, a beachside pavilion smells of human waste and is so thick with graffiti that you have to look closely to make out this sign: Notice—Defacing Park Property May Result in a Maximum Penalty of $500 Fine and Six Months in Jail. At the south end of Venice Beach, the gazebos along Ocean Front Walk have not been closed down but might as well be to anyone who doesn't regularly urinate outdoors. We met a Dutch fellow who had a word for the less savory side of Venice: *onguur*. Though he claimed it was untranslatable, his facial expression told us all we needed to know. Venice can be real *onguur* sometimes.

None of this stems the flow of onlookers in Venice. Perversely, the sense of forbidden danger seems to add to its appeal. And so goes Venice, into the setting sun of the California dream, once delicious and golden, and now... Well, we'll close with a quote from one of Venice's stellar residents, Orson Bean, who wrote in *Venice* magazine: "Venice of America dares you to be happy. Someone once wrote that the most revolutionary act possible might be three straight days of continuous happiness. People walk in Venice. They roller-skate and bicycle and skateboard. They rally to save ducks. They don't mind looking like fools. They figure everyone else enjoys it when they look like fools, so why shouldn't they?"

For more information, contact the Venice Chamber of Commerce, P.O. Box 202, Venice, CA 90291, 310/822-5425, www.venice.net.

BEACHES

Venice City Beach has never looked better. It is an amazingly wide sheet of sand, running for two miles north from Venice Pier to Santa Monica Pier. People use this beautiful, wide porch of sand for all the normal activities—swimming, sunning, hanging out—but the dimensions of the beach are so large that their numbers seem deceptively small.

The beach itself is spiked by three enormous jetties and was widened by sand dredged from the site of the massive Hyperion Sewage Treatment Plant. The most intriguing area is at the north end, where a weightlifting area attracts body freaks and has earned the name "Muscle Beach." Some incredible games of basketball are played on the nearby blacktop, with occasional visits from pro stars. The paddle-tennis games are as intense as any matches at Wimbledon. The beach can be accessed from any of the main east–west streets in Venice (Washington Street, Venice Boulevard, Rose Avenue, Windward Avenue, Park Boulevard) or from anywhere on the Ocean Front Walk promenade. Metered parking is available along any of these thoroughfares as well.

24 VENICE CITY BEACH

Location: Washington Boulevard at Ocean Front Walk in Venice
Parking/Fees: $7-10
Hours: 5 A.M.-10:30 P.M.
Facilities: concession, lifeguards, restrooms, showers, and picnic areas
Contact: Los Angeles County Lifeguard Service, Central Section, 310/394-3264

ACCOMMODATIONS

No matter how cutting edge you feel, you do not want to stay in Venice. For one thing, it's unpredictable and sometimes unsafe after dark. For another, there's really not much to choose from in the way of accommodations, unless you rent a beachfront villa by the week (and that is shockingly expensive). Visit for the day and buy a T-shirt, hot dog, and a slab of pizza. Watch the street performers, then quietly take your leave, preferably back to the hotels of Marina del Rey.

All things considered, we fared okay the one time we did stay in Venice. We found a room at the **Venice Beach Cotel** (25 Windward Avenue, 310/399-7949 or 888/718-8287, $). "Cotel" is short for "community hotel," and it is primarily for international travelers on a tight budget. A hostel, if you will, only a notch nicer. The rooms are spartan but clean, with shared bathrooms and no TV or air-conditioning, and the security is reassuringly tight (you must be buzzed in). Most of the foreigners we met at the hotel claimed to be afraid to leave it. They weren't shrinking violets, by any means; we're talking hale and hardy Europeans in their 20s who had seen their share of world travel. After experiencing Venice at night, though, they preferred the hotel's hospitality room—now expanded into "the Interclub"—to the bars and clubs on the streets below. After a few night moves of our own around Venice, we saw their point and gladly joined them.

The best compromise between Venice access and a safe and quiet stay is the **Inn at Venice Beach** (327 Washington Boulevard, 310/821-2557, $$). The rooms are clean and cheerful, and continental breakfast is served in an airy courtyard. Europeans are smitten with this place. And it's just three blocks from Venice Pier.

COASTAL CUISINE

In Venice you take the bad with the good. And some good old reliables are still around. During the day the **Sidewalk Cafe** (1401 Ocean Front Walk, 310/399-5547, $) is the best vantage point from which to observe the human circus. The items on the menu have been given literary names, because the café adjoins the excellent Small World Bookstore. Breakfast, for example, can consist of an omelet named after Gertrude Stein, Carlos Castaneda, or Jack Kerouac. Lunch could be a burger named for Charles Dickens, Pablo Neruda, or James Michener. (The latter, logically enough, features pineapple and ham.) The best place for coffee and conversation is **The Cow** (34 Washington Boulevard, $), a local hangout.

Two arrivals in Venice worth considering are the **West Beach Cafe** (60 North Venice Boulevard, 310/823-5396, $$$) and **Nikki's** (72 Market Street, 310/450-3010, $$$). The former is a crowded, casual establishment specializing in California cuisine. Nikki's has developed a more hip-hop vibe than it used to have as its former incarnation, 72 Market Street.

NIGHTLIFE

We first read about aromatherapy, a New Age form of healing, in a Venice weekly devoted to planetary health. This therapy is based on the belief that your nose takes in "essential oils" vital to your well-being. When unhealthy, you simply need to inhale the proper mix of oils until you're good as new. Depression, for example, can be cured by inhaling the following herbs: basil, bergamot, chamomile, clary, lavender, marjoram, rosemary, and ylang-ylang.

After sampling Venice, both by day and night, we have devised our own form of aromatherapy, which we'd like to share with anyone who has grown sick and tired of life back home. Go to the south end of Venice City Beach at the end of a long, hot summer day. Stand anywhere along Ocean Front Walk and breathe deeply, keeping your mouth closed so as to maximize the essential oils your nose takes in. We promise that you'll be exclaiming, "There's no place like home" in short order.

If you wish to pick through the olfactory minefield of Venice after dark, the **Town House** (52 Windward Avenue, 310/392-4040) is the place to rock out. Large and loud enough for the rowdiest bike gang, the Town House features live rock and roll most nights in summer. If you're looking for a more civilized alternative, amble up Washington Street in the direction of Marina del Rey, where you'll find coffeehouses, sports bars, and cantinas galore.

Hinano (15 Washington Boulevard, 310/822-3902) is a "brasserie de Tahiti," a fancy way of saying "friendly beach bar." Pool tables in one room, booths in the other room, Hinano is what a locals' hangout ought to be. Help yourself to free popcorn out of an old machine, order a pitcher of beer, and sit a spell.

Santa Monica

The most "urban" of Los Angeles's beach communities, Santa Monica (population 87,500) is a showcase for much of the best, and some of the worst, that the city has to offer. The town has a temperate, even climate—perfect for those who live outdoors or play so much in it that they might as well be living outdoors. After the "June gloom" has run its course, the weather in Santa Monica is dependably good the rest of the year.

Santa Monica's beach is where the heart and soul of Los Angeles comes to have fun in the summer. It serves as the steam-release valve for Los Angeles's vast and diverse population, a no-frills playland that attracts close to 15 million visitors a year. That's about a quarter of the total load borne by all the beaches in Los Angeles County. Santa Monica is easily accessible to all. Perhaps for this reason it suffers in comparison to its more glittery neighbors up toward Malibu and down by Manhattan Beach. At Santa Monica it's just good people having a high old time at the beach, many of whom speak English only as a second language. Without Santa Monica in the summertime, Los Angeles would be one big, smog-laced pressure cooker.

In the process of serving as the city's back door to the beach, Santa Monica somehow manages to maintain a character and charm all its own. Grandeur and squalor are mixed here in unequal proportions, creating an appealing blend of tropical rot and urban cool that Raymond Chandler captured in his detective novels. (His fictional "Bay City" was modeled after Santa Monica.) Chandler's subterranean noir universe is but a flickering image now, seen in the architectural splendor of some of the older apartment buildings and the art deco facades of the theaters. The city is in what might be called a period of transition, as it has been for several years. Many buildings are boarded up, some are being torn down, and other marginal properties await the inevitable.

An attempt has been made to revive downtown Santa Monica, adding pedestrian shopping malls and multi-screen cinemas in hopes of bringing back the healing plasma of money that fled to the hills in the 1980s. It seems to have worked. At last count we found over 70 museums and galleries, 12 book shops, and more coffee shops than Dublin has pubs in Santa Monica's 8.3 square miles. The epicenter of this downtown renewal is the Third Street Promenade. This brick pedestrian walkway courses through four blocks of storefronts, from Colorado Avenue to Wilshire Boulevard, running parallel to the beach from three blocks back.

Though this mall dispenses the usual trendy consumer flotsam, the experience of walking through it is spiced by some unique street performers. In fact, these performers lend the promenade a flavor more distinctive than the shops. The Third Street brigade is more talented, and less scatological and dangerous, than the ragtag army in Venice. A string quartet composed of conservatory students plays Vivaldi beautifully. A small ensemble cranks out a huge big-band sound. A lonely jazzman offers mournful blues on the vibes. An old man with an ashen face sings Willie Nelson's "On the Road Again" and yodels while standing on his head in a chair. Awesome! An atheist and a born-again Christian rant at each other through microphones; it is hard to decide who is the more repellent. Two silver-painted characters do coordinated, robotic choreography to hip-hop blaring from their boom box. Weird!

The overwhelming feeling one gets while strolling Third Street is nostalgia for the grandeur that Santa Monica once represented. Many of the promenade businesses trade on nostalgia, re-creating the 1950s and 1960s. The most popular eatery is a faux 1950s diner. The hippest clothier is a thrift shop manqué that sells used clothing at boutique prices. (Ragged-looking T-shirts for $18—what a concept!) The bars are upscale pool halls filled with yuppies slumming as bikers. The nicest theater is a beautifully restored 1940s film palace. Third Street is ultimately a mirage of fake evocations: The upscale, chrome-railed pool hall serves gourmet pizza, the 1950s diner gleams with an antiseptic aura, and the mock-bohemian coffeehouses collect 18 dimes (instead of one) for a cup of coffee.

Only the presence of the homeless milling about soils the mood of sentimental yearning (unless you're nostalgic for the Great Depression). The collision of Santa Monica's downward mobility with its last-ditch attempts at creating an urban island of crime-free consumerism makes for an odd mélange on the streets. We saw some strange scenes indeed. An executive in a designer running outfit was spitting orders into a mobile phone while roller-skating past a haggard woman on a bench who was flicking at invisible bugs, her belongings arrayed in bulging bags at her feet. It was hard to tell which of these two characters was more insane. Then there was the wraithlike, barefoot woman who punched the air like Fred Sanford, intimidating a striding stream of Dockers shorts and Polo shirts into stepping out of her way. At a yogurt café she walked in, looked around, and snatched some food right

off the plate of a startled German tourist. To curb such excesses in the city once known as "People's Republic of Santa Monica," stiff new laws on vagrancy, loitering, and overnight sleeping on the beach have been instituted.

In many ways Santa Monica remains the most appealing and unique place in Los Angeles. Certainly it is among the last bastions of kindness, egalitarianism, and liberalism. Still, it is life lived at its extremes. On the one hand homeless occupy the parks and promenades, and proletarian hordes roam the beach and pier. On the other, luxury hotels overlook the ocean, and stores cater to people with too much disposable income. As is the case in most American cities these days, there is no longer much in the way of a middle class or a happy medium.

For more information, contact the Santa Monica Convention and Visitor Bureau, 1400 Ocean Avenue, Santa Monica, CA 90405, 310/319-6263, www.santamonica.com; or the Santa Monica Chamber of Commerce, 1234 6th Street, Suite 100, Santa Monica, CA 90401, 310/393-9825, www.smchamber.com.

BEACHES

Santa Monica State Beach is easily accessible from downtown Los Angeles via the Santa Monica Freeway (I-10) or one of several primary east–west arteries (Pico, Wilshire, Santa Monica). Any number of bus lines start and end here as well. The dimensions of this beach are amazing: It is 3.3 miles long and several football fields wide. Generally it attracts a close-packed crowd of Hispanic families who bring beach towels and picnic baskets. South of Santa Monica Pier the blankets and bodies thin out. Two concrete walkways run parallel some distance back from the ocean. One ferries pedestrian traffic, while the other transports those on wheels. An army of mobile twenty- and thirty-something cyclists and in-line skaters can be seen leaving vapor trails on the South Bay Bicycle Trail. You can park

BEACH FLICKS

Endless Summer II, released in 1994, didn't capture the imagination of young America the way the original *Endless Summer* did in 1966. Of course the Beach Boys, the Ventures, Dick Dale, and Jan and Dean had musically paved the way for Bruce Brown's first documentary on surfing.

Even before Brown's watershed flick, there were several attempts to capture the burgeoning surf culture on celluloid. Most were stilted and hokey, though these movies did help infuse California and Hawaii with a sort of mythical, siren-like power. In hindsight, these California "beach flicks" – think Frankie Avalon (who was actually from New Jersey) and Annette Funicello (a former Mouseketeer) – have a so-bad-it's-good kind of appeal. The great majority of them were released in 1964 and 1965, after which point a rising countercultural tide would wash away all traces of Frankie, Annette, and their ilk. But thanks to them, everyone who came of age in that time wanted to live beside a California beach – and many, in fact, took pains to make it happen.

Here are capsule summaries of some of the best and worst of the beach flicks, arranged by year:

- **Blue Hawaii** (1961) – Elvis Presley stars in this sandy epic, the most intriguingly perverse aspect of which is the soundtrack, boasting winners like "Slicin' Sand," "Beach Boy Blues," and "Ito Eats." Angela Lansbury plays his mama.

- **Beach Party** (1963) – The first in the Frankie and Annette beach sagas, this had the redeeming presence of Dick Dale & the Del-Tones, plus some of the world's first surf punks, led by notorious Erich Von Zipper. This movie also had an original plot idea: An anthropologist studies surf culture through a telescope. Maybe this is where Tom Wolfe got his inspiration for *The Pump House Gang!*

- **Beach Ball** (1964) – A hokey rip-off of *Beach Party* with a threadbare plot having to do with a music-store owner and a band called The Wigglers, it stars Edd "Kookie" Byrnes and features performances by the Walker Brothers, Jerry Lee Lewis, the Four Seasons, the Nashville Teens, the Righteous Brothers, and the Supremes.

- **Bikini Beach** (1964) – Here's another Frankie and Annette vehicle lacking a full tank of gas, although it turns on a potentially hilarious idea – spoofing the Beatles via a teen idol named the Potato Bug. Little Stevie Wonder performs "Fingertips."

- **Muscle Beach Party** (1964) – Frankie and Annette (again) meet bodybuilders and

in state-run fee lots or take your chances feeding the meters on the streets.

The center of the action is **Santa Monica Pier,** which is among the best in the Golden State. The pier, originally built in 1874, is an antiquated slice of Americana, a West Coast Coney Island stocked with gaming arcades, T-shirt vendors (four for $10, rivaling Venice for, uh, value), fast-food stalls, and incongruously chic restaurants. This incarnation of the pier was built in 1909 but underwent a full-scale $12 million renovation completed in 1997. Tiny arcades flare off from the main concourse, creating an atmosphere not unlike the midway at a state fair. All the ingredients are here for kids to have a good time and for parents to get nostalgic about their own gloriously misspent youth: Skee-Ball, basketball shoots, Wedges/Hedges, bumper cars, rocking horses, an antique carousel, and a gift shop where one can purchase a plaster cast of Elvis stranger than any to be found in Memphis.

Once part of a huge playland, replete with a glamorous ballroom and famous "Blue Streak an Italian countess. Dick Dale & the Del-Tones and Little Stevie Wonder provide musical context.

- *Surf Party* (1964) – Set in Malibu, with songs by the Astronauts, the Routers, Bobby Vinton, and Jackie DeShannon.

- *Beach Blanket Bingo* (1965) – Buster Keaton makes an appearance, rescuing this Frankie Avalon and Annette Funicello farce, based on the latter's reaction to the former's crush on a bimbo named Sugar Cane.

- *How to Stuff a Wild Bikini* (1965) – Frankie, Annette, and Erich Von Zipper reprised. Frankie hires a witch doctor to keep an eye on Annette while he is in the Navy Reserves. Mickey Rooney and Buster Keaton make cameos.

- *Girls on the Beach* (1965) – A sorority tries to raise funds with a rock concert. They want the Beatles to perform, but they settle for the Beach Boys, with equally happy results. It also includes songs by the Crickets and Leslie Gore.

- *Wild on the Beach* (1965) – The best thing about this lame beach-sploitation flick is the music: songs by Colorado's Astronauts ("Little Speedy Gonzalez," "Rock the World," "Snap It") and "Drum Dance," by the great Sandy Nelson.

- *Ghost in the Invisible Bikini* (1966) – Monsters go to the beach, with Boris Karloff and Basil Rathbone trading spooky taunts amidst the beach blankets.

- *Paradise – Hawaiian Style* (1966) – Although the hula dancers were required by film code to cover their navels under their hula skirts, the movie does have Elvis singing "Queenie Wahine's Papaya."

- *It's a Bikini World* (1967) – Tommy Kirk is a poor man's Frankie Avalon. The Animals play "We Gotta Get Out of This Place." We assume they meant this film.

- *Catalina Caper* (1967) – Set on the island off the coast of Los Angeles, this soundtrack's most improbable moment: Little Richard singing "Scuba Party."

- *Clambake* (1967) – Elvis Presley bakes some clams, makes some clams, and goes to Las Vegas afterward to make even more. He's a water-ski instructor in this turkey.

- *Back to the Beach* (1987) – Frankie, Annette, and the gang, which now included the likes of Bob Denver (a.k.a. Gilligan) and Pee Wee Herman (a.k.a. "mud"), attempt to re-create the spirit of their early-1960s beach flicks in the late-1980s. They should've heeded the words of author Thomas Wolfe when he wrote, "You can't go back to the beach again." Or words to that effect.

Racing Coaster," the old outlying structures fell to the wrecking ball some years ago, and all that remains is the pier. New cafés are planned for the future. For now, the fast-food stands are guaranteed to bring back memories of indigestion. Step right up for tacos, hot dogs, cotton candy, fried dough, and fish 'n' chips. Then head home for a large, cool drink of Alka-Seltzer.

We took our Skee-Ball prizes (two tiny plastic rats and a thimble-sized trophy) and headed to Back On the Beach. Yes, that's the name of a wonderful piazza on the sand, an invigorating half-mile hike north of the pier. A former private beach club and now a café with a seating capacity of 200, **Back On the Beach** (445 Palisades Road, 310/393-8282) is a quintessential L.A. beach experience. You can eat a salad as an antidote to the pier food or simply sit back with a beverage and watch the passing parade on the South Bay Bicycle Trail. President Clinton chose this spot for his morning jog when he was in the city, and Al Pacino is regularly seen here. Even more telling is the fact that several episodes of *Beverly Hills 90210* were filmed here. Volleyball nets and playground equipment are nearby, for further diversions.

As for swimming, the waves at Santa Monica State Beach are sufficient to excite the tiny tots on their Styrofoam boards but not large enough to attract serious surfing. Several hundred yards south of the pier is the original **Muscle Beach,** where, since the 1930s, Conan-like men and women have been hoisting barbells all day long while lesser mortals stand around in the sand and applaud. Jack LaLanne and Steve Reeves flexed their pecs here, and Mr. America and Mr. Universe contests have been held here. Down toward Venice you'll come to a sprawl of basketball and paddle-tennis courts, with grandstands beside them. Rest a spell and marvel at the athleticism of the men and women sweating in the sun.

The physical setting of the beach is almost as muscular as the weight lifters. Backed by a long, undeveloped bluff, Santa Monica's beach somehow seems tranquil even when thousands are jammed on the sand below—a glorious sight! Atop the bluff is Palisades Park, a shaded 26-acre jewel that runs for 14 city blocks from Colorado Avenue to Adelaide Drive. This green, shady buffer between the sand and the city is filled with benches and shuffleboard courts, and it's popular with Santa Monica's large contingent of senior citizens. It is also popular with the homeless. The two groups seem to coexist peacefully, though.

Given a city the size of Los Angeles, there are bound to be problems with its most popular beach. In the late 1980s Santa Monica Bay became a colostomy bag for the city's then sick body. The Hyperion Sewage Treatment Plant, a gargantuan facility that serves four million people and was once the pride and joy of Los Angeles (earning rapturous accolades from Aldous Huxley, of all people), broke down. Millions of gallons of raw sewage poured directly into Santa Monica Bay. This set off a chain reaction that brought the county sewage

system and city government to near collapse. The mayor called for voluntary water conservation, but the filthy rich in Westside and the San Fernando Valley didn't go along with it, filling pools and watering lawns in protest. Water became even scarcer, exacerbating tensions with Arizona and Northern California. But, on the bright side, the pollution of the Santa Monica Bay provided the impetus for a slow-growth and eco-minded grassroots movement that has gained strength ever since. An organization called Heal the Bay has gone a great distance toward doing just that through environmental education and direct action.

25 SANTA MONICA STATE BEACH

Location: Ocean Avenue at Colorado Avenue in Santa Monica

Parking/Fees: $5-8 entrance fee per vehicle, or metered street parking

Hours: 6 A.M.-sunset

Facilities: concession, lifeguards, restrooms, showers, and picnic tables

Contact: Los Angeles County Lifeguard Service, Central Section, 310/394-3264

ACCOMMODATIONS

It is possible to stay near the beach in Santa Monica. Many hotels and motels, large and small, line Ocean Avenue a block or two from the pier and a pedestrian bridge away from the beach. Staying here also solves your biggest beach problem, which is parking. Leaving your wheels in a hotel garage sure beats battling experienced, have-you-hugged-my-bumper-today natives, who will beat you to any available slot. There's only one drawback: Ocean Avenue can be loud, even at night. We learned this the hard way one year when we were younger and poorer, taking a room at the least expensive motel on the strip: a $40 jobbie. The price was cheap because it was a four-walled cell with rancid bedcovers and thin, lifeless pillows. Caveat emptor. These fleabags litter the roadside like yesterday's papers.

A money transfusion in recent years has transformed the beachfront. Along with the older, dependable **Holiday Inn at the Pier** (120 Colorado Avenue, 310/451-0676, $$$), high-rise luxury hotels now tower over the Santa Monica Beach south of the pier. The cream of the crop is the **Loews Santa Monica Beach Hotel** (1700 Ocean Avenue, 310/458-6700, $$$$). It's an attractive, upscale tower that somehow exudes a casual sort of class. (The additional parking charges aren't classy or casual, though.) The lobby alone is worth a look-see. You can hear the waves roll in from your balcony and watch the human parade roll by on the bike paths. At night milk and cookies are brought to guests' doors, providing a nice bedtime touch worthy of Mom.

Another recent arrival at Santa Monica Beach is **Le Merigot** (1740 Ocean Avenue, 310/395-9700, www.lemerigothotel.com, $$$$), a J. W. Marriott Beach Resort. It's an opulent resort done in neutral tones. You're a block back from the beach, which is easily accessible via the pool area. The rooms and furniture are upscale and functional. A lobby bar and terrace make a good place to hang out and eavesdrop on conversations. One afternoon we heard a bartender carry on about the way things are in Los Angeles: "Unlike back home, it's not enough just to say that you like a movie out here," he animatedly told an attentive imbiber while cleaning wine glasses. "You have to know the director and his previous work, who the key grip was, who cut the deal, how many theaters it opened at, and on and on. That's just the nature of the business out here. Everybody knows all the smallest details." We wondered how many hundred times he had jovially imparted this memorized speech, these same pearls of wisdom, to other strangers at the bar.

The spa at Le Merigot is not to be missed. A roomful of bikes and cardio machines, another full of free weights, and locker areas with eucalyptus steam room can all be used free of charge by guests. There's also an extensive menu of spa services. For a great workout, warm up on a stationary bike, use the Cybex machines and free weights, finish with an off-property run on the South Bay Bicycle Trail (down to Venice and back is about three miles), and then sit in eucalyptus-scented steam for as long as you can stand it. We did exactly that and had a very pleasant chat with Bill Bridges, a former pro basketball player for the L.A. Lakers. Known as a tough defender who snagged a lot of rebounds, Bridges talked hoops with us for half an hour—a great guy, and this was just one of those encounters that seems to happen in Los Angeles.

The **Bayside Hotel** (2001 Ocean Avenue, 310/396-6000, www.baysidehotel.com, $$) earns the honor of being closest to the beach, which sits just across from it on a quiet loop road in an otherwise residential neighborhood. Nearby, the **Santa Monica Travelodge** (1525 Ocean Avenue, 310/451-0761, $$) offers the usual mid-scale chain amenities.

The retro-coolest place is **Hotel Shangri La** (1301 Ocean Avenue, 310/394-2791, www.shangrila-hotel.com, $$$$), a seven-story art deco landmark built in 1939. It's gracefully anonymous, which is probably why people like Bill Murray and Diane Keaton stay here. Straight out of Miami's Art Deco District, the **Georgian Hotel** (1415 Ocean Avenue, 310/451-3374, www.georgianhotel.com, $$$) is an architectural wonder.

COASTAL CUISINE

The Lobster (1602 Ocean Avenue, 310/458-9294, $$$$) has one of the finest settings anywhere, overlooking the Santa Monica Pier, the Pacific Ocean, and the Santa Monica Mountains. It goes without saying that you want to be here at sunset. But that's far from the only reason you'd come here. The food is sensational. The namesake lobster preparations cannot be beat. One of us ordered a pan-roasted 1.5-pound lobster served atop a bed of tomato risotto. The dish was not inexpensive ($45), but the splurge was worth it. You might get Pacific spiny lobster when they're in season (usually September through February); otherwise, your crustacean will be from Maine. Another of us had seared ahi served atop lightly sautéed greens, mushrooms, artichoke slivers, and more. Aside from being an incredible blend of flavors, it makes one feel instantly healthier.

It's hard to make a rational choice from a menu that is so appealing from top to bottom. The clams and mussels, served in a tasty, briny broth that can be eaten like soup or sopped up with bread, is a top entrée. And the desserts! After eating heartily, we recommend something fruity and fresh like Ciao Bella sorbet (a homemade strawberry sorbet served with berries) or blueberry cobbler. Beyond the superb food and view, the people-watching is not to be missed. Pay attention and you'll get a sense of how Los Angeles ticks: movers and shakers on the make, either sealing deals via cell phone or charming their consorts at the table. The energy level at the Lobster is high, the experience of dining here memorable.

The best quick bite is down at **Back On the Beach** (445 Palisades Road, 310/393-8282, $$), and a convenient quick morning hit can be had at **Starbucks** (Third Street Promenade, 310/260-9947, $). At the latter, Charles Bukowski wannabes nurse bottomless mugs and work on their angst. Dinner is another matter. Santa Monica is home to some of Los Angeles's finest dining. Famed chef Wolfgang Puck's **Chinois On Main** (2709 Main Street, 310/392-9025, $$$$) is a celebrated bastion of haute cuisine blending French, Chinese, and Japanese elements. **Rocken Rolls,** chef Hans Rockenwagner's fast-food kiosk at the Third Street Promenade, is as popular as the French contemporary cuisine at his **Rockenwagner** restaurant and bakery (2435 Main Street, 310/399-6504, $$$$).

But we wanted seafood. We found it, sort of, at **Chez Jay** (1657 Ocean Avenue, 310/395-1741, $$). It's a longtime popular beach hangout run by a guy who once hunted pirate treasure. His signature dish is "spuds

fried with bananas"—real surfer food that, along with his steaks, chops, and seafood, has been pleasing palates for 35 years. Nearby, another oceanfront landmark, **Ivy at the Shore** (1535 Ocean Avenue, 310/393-3113, $$$), serves American fare in a tropical setting adjacent to the ocean. Down toward Venice, two blocks from the ocean, is **Enterprise Fish Company** (174 Kinney Street, 310/392-8366, $$), housed in an impressive ivy-covered warehouse. All the entrées, especially the local catches, are nicely prepared.

We couldn't resist a drive inland for some stargazing and schmoozing, so we did as the Clampetts did, loading up our wallets and going to Beverly...Hills, that is. The Elysian Fields of schmoozing is **The Palm** (9001 Santa Monica Boulevard, 310/550-8811, $$$), in West Hollywood. It's a piece of Manhattan at the end of California's rainbow, and we were told, "If you sit at the bar for a week in the Palm, you will meet anyone you care to know." We didn't have a week, but we did lunch and met Sandy Koufax. Enough said.

One of our old favorites from Malibu, the **Reel Inn** (1220 Third Promenade, 310/395-5538, $$), has opened what to our taste buds is the best food joint on Third Street Promenade. You order at the front, picking your fresh line-caught fish from the display case (try the Cajun-blackened halibut or the simply grilled ahi tuna), then retreat to a picnic table until your name is called. They slop some good stuff, like Cajun rice, home fries, and coleslaw, next to it, and you're in business. Entrées start at $7.95, making the Reel Inn a real bargain. Real upscale seafood is found at Shutters on the Beach Hotel, which has the stylish **One Pico** (1 Pico Boulevard, 310/587-1717, $$$), as well as the pleasant **Pedals Cafe** right on the bike path. Pedals is a great brunch spot on weekends, with indoor and outdoor dining areas and menu choices that range from creative omelets to grilled salmon. Look both ways before crossing because the path narrows in front of Pedals, and bikers and skaters rarely slow down.

NIGHTLIFE

Santa Monica is only one boulevard (Sunset, Wilshire, or Santa Monica) away from Hollywood. Pick up the latest copy of *L.A. Weekly*, *L.A. Reader*, *Rave!*, or the *Los Angeles Times* to find out what's doing in town. The detailed listings for each night of the week will give you some idea of what the term "free will" means. It's difficult to comment in much detail about a scene as extensive as the one in Los Angeles. To a pair of beach bums who have been denied good music in more beach towns than we care to count, Santa Monica and Los Angeles are almost too much of a good thing. If only it could be spaced out evenly over both coasts . . .

The biggest musical waves on the beachfront can be ridden at **Rusty's Surf Ranch** (256 Santa Monica Pier, 310/393-7437), which offers "alternative funk," "masterful power pop," and other hip goodies (as well as pool tables and a full menu) nightly. When we were in town, an adult musical comedy called "Butt Pirates of the Caribbean" was also being presented, no doubt starring a bunch of very jolly Rogers.

We next direct your attention to the vicinity of upper Santa Monica Boulevard, where the old guard clubs are still rocking the City of Angels—**Club Lingerie, Whiskey a Go-Go, the Roxy, McCabe's,** the **Palomino.** We unhesitatingly recommend the **House of Blues Sunset Strip** (8430 Sunset Boulevard, 323/848-5100), less exuberantly the Johnny Depp–owned **Viper Room** (8852 Sunset Boulevard, 310/358-1880). Every night in Los Angeles is a who's who of musicians. Closer to the beach, your main alternative is to stroll the Third Street Promenade (between Colorado Avenue and Wilshire Boulevard). Nondrinkers will dig the outdoor cafés, used book shops, street musicians, cinemas, and dessert places. Imbibers flock to **Yankee Doodles** (1410 Promenade, 310/394-4632), a sports bar that epitomizes all that is faux-gettable about going out these days: overpaid yuppies affecting pirate kerchiefs and $1,000 leather jackets while playing pool and scarfing gourmet pizza. The

drinks are overpriced. One large draft Fosters and a cranberry juice cost almost $10! We retreated to a corner and shot at the electronic basketball concession until our quarters ran out. You would do better to walk a little farther and seek solace at **Anastasia's Asylum** (1028 Wilshire Boulevard, 310/394-7113), a hip coffeehouse in the best sense. There's no cover charge, the local atmosphere is genuine, and there's live entertainment and a vegetarian menu.

Pacific Palisades

This community, nestled in the foothills of the Santa Monica Mountains from Chautauqua Boulevard to Malibu, is not a beach town, but it does look down on one of the loveliest stretches of the Pacific coast. Originally populated in the 1920s by Methodists who founded it as their "new Chautauqua," Pacific Palisades (population 23,000) is now the exclusive domain of the very rich. The streets, most of which branch off Sunset Boulevard, are winding, shaded routes, many ending in cul-de-sacs. Parts of Pacific Palisades are included on Hollywood celebrity bus tours.

We had another reason for visiting Pacific Palisades—a motive not unlike our quest for the ghost of Charles Bukowski in San Pedro. Henry Miller retired here after Big Sur became too unnavigable for his aged body. He spent his happiest golden days riding "his best friend" (a bicycle) around these lovely streets. It was while pursuing the vision of this sweet old man that we stumbled upon the **Self-Realization Fellowship Lake Shrine** (17190 Sunset Boulevard, 310/454-4114), a 10-acre "wall-less temple," bird sanctuary, sunken garden, and altar to the "five major religions of the world." Fitting, somehow, that Henry Miller spent his final days nearby.

For more information, contact the Pacific Palisades Chamber of Commerce, 15330 Antioch Street, Pacific Palisades, CA 90272, 310/459-7963, www.palisadeschamber.com.

BEACHES

Pacific Palisades puts its ocean frontage to good use. It is the site of a state beach named after our most famous cowboy-philosopher. **Will Rogers State Beach** is a sandy swath three miles long that's a favorite of sun-bronzed locals who are serious about their volleyball game and their tans. Its proximity to Hollywood makes it one of the more popular beaches in Los Angeles County. Furthermore, it is the starting point for the South Bay Bicycle Trail, which ends 26 miles later down at Torrance County Beach. That said, we'd take Zuma State Beach, up in Malibu, over Will Rogers any day. The scenery is better and the distance from the highway madness makes Zuma more appealing.

Incidentally, if you want to dig further into the life of the man who never met a man he didn't like, Rogers's 187-acre ranch is open to

THE CITY GETS AN (L)A FOR EFFORT

The state of California is ahead of the rest of the nation on many things, good and bad, but mostly good. And the city and county of Los Angeles, California's largest population center, finally seem to be walking the walk. In addition to a massive tree-planting campaign, communities in the 462-square-mile area are taking stands that should be emulated nationwide. To wit:

- Malibu and Manhattan Beach banned businesses from using plastic carryout bags, in May and July 2008 respectively. Other beach communities will likely follow suit. The Los Angeles County Board of Supervisors, however, bowed to lobbyist pressure, voting for a half-baked measure to delay plastic-bag bans in the Greater LA area. The City Council, perhaps in an effort to shame the county, unanimously approved a ban of all plastic bags by 2010 and, until then, imposed a $0.25 surcharge per bag. Hooray.

- The California Coastal Commission and Heal the Bay, an exceptionally active nonprofit based in Santa Monica, led the 24th annual California Coastal Cleanup Day on September 20, 2008. Lots of plastic bags were found, of course.

- In March 2008, the Los Angeles Water Board put 20 coastal towns on notice that they would be fined $10,000 until they stopped "continually" surpassing federally mandated daily limits of bacterial discharge into the ocean. Among those put on notice were Santa Monica, Long Beach, and Malibu. Malibu has exceeded bacteria limits at its beaches since September 2006. The importance of the Water Board's action can not be overstated. It is the first time in the nation that an oversight body has threatened fines to ensure compliance with beach bacteria limits and clean water standards.

- In February 2007, the California Coastal Conservancy funded the removal of a disused and harmful roadway, aptly named Texas Crossing, from Malibu Creek, freeing a previously blocked mile of new habitat for fish.

- Santa Monica installed three monofilament fishing-line recycling bins on Santa Monica Pier to reduce the damage done by fishing line in the ocean waters. The bins are a prototype for those that will, we hope, soon be appearing up and down the state's coast. Fishing line is virtually invisible in the water, lasts 600 years in the environment, and is responsible for virtual maritime genocide. Derelict fishing gear (nets, rods, traps, hooks, etc.) that has been pitched into the ocean is another problem that is being addressed.

the public as **Will Rogers State Historical Park** (1501 Will Rogers State Park Road, 310/454-8212). Tours of the main house and grounds are offered daily, and one can also hike through the vast natural area or ride on equestrian trails.

26 WILL ROGERS STATE BEACH

Location: 16000 block of Highway 1 in Pacific Palisades
Parking/Fees: $7 entrance fee per vehicle
Hours: 8 A.M.-7 P.M.
Facilities: concession, lifeguards, restrooms, and showers
Contact: Los Angeles County Department of Beaches and Harbors, 310/305-9503

COASTAL CUISINE

Pacific Palisades has got little, if anything, to offer travelers in the way of accommodations and nightlife, being a predominantly ritzy and privacy-hoarding residential community. However, it's got a dandy restaurant on the beach that ranks among the best on the coast. **Gladstone's of Malibu** (17300 Pacific Coast Highway, 310/459-9676, $$$$) is indeed the place to go "4 fish" in Los Angeles County. It's worth the drive, worth the wait, and worth the price. Barrels of peanuts are set out for waiting patrons to crack open and munch, and the oceanside location makes for superb sunset-watching. The portions are huge and the menu expansive at Gladstone's. Prime seafood entrées run in the $25 and up range and include such items as mesquite-grilled sea bass and ahi rolled in Cajun spices, then seared and cooked rare. Appetizers include plump, cold Pacific oysters, as well as ceviche salad and marinated calamari. A sashimi dinner offers a filling platter of raw seafood delights. King and queen crab legs (the latter are slightly saltier and smaller, though still huge) are worth the $30 or so you'll plunk down for

them. What you can't eat at Gladstone's will be wrapped by your server in gold foil and twisted to resemble a seabird or fish—a signature touch that completes a very satisfying dining experience.

Malibu

Malibu might seem to the outside world to be some ultra-chic celebrity enclave accessible only to camera crews from *Lifestyles of the Rich and Famous,* but nothing could be further from the truth. The fact is, there are really two Malibus. The better known of these is the "inner" Malibu—the film colony, the celebrity sandbox, the glamorous private world behind locked gates about which the rest of the world likes to fantasize. The "outer" Malibu is a 27-mile stretch of rugged coastline, plunging canyons, and towering mountains, running along the Pacific Coast Highway from Coastline Drive to the Ventura County line. Local boosters refer to the PCH through Malibu as "the longest main street in America." We like to think of it as Little Big Sur. This side of Malibu—a wild, winding corridor physically bounded by the Santa Monica Mountains and Pacific Ocean—is accessible to all and yet is generally less familiar than the minuscule world of celebrity intrigue that makes Malibu an instant buzzword with readers and viewers of tabloid media.

The reality of Malibu (population 13,000) is very different from popular conceptions of it. Much of it is unforgiving and desolate. Steep mountains plunge to the sea, which crashes angrily against the rocks. The elements hang in precarious balance here, not infrequently tilting over into destructive chaos. Malibu is particularly subject to what native Southern Californians wearily refer to as their four seasons: fire, flood, mudslide, and earthquake. One must drive through Malibu ever vigilant for fallen rocks. Some of the cliff faces along the Pacific Coast Highway are raw where mighty chunks have torn loose and crashed

© PARKE PUTERBAUGH

Malibu Pier

onto the roadway. Narrow ridgetops zigzag northward. Houses are hidden in the canyons between them. The hills are covered with dry, brown vegetation that turns green only when the winter rains come. The threat of fire is constant. Lightning, arson, or a careless match can ignite a blaze that, propelled by hot Santa Ana winds, is capable of racing toward the seaside colony at speeds of 100 miles per hour. The other calamity is mudslides: slow, brown waves of muck, rock, and debris that swallow up everything in their path, houses included. The elements play no favorites here. No matter how much clout they may have in Hollywood, those who live in Malibu have no control over the periodic disasters that plague the seaside colony. Nature does not obey directors' cues.

Still, those who make their residence here derive a perverse sort of pleasure from the challenges of living on the edge. Writer Joan Didion captured its allure in her 1978 essay "Quiet Days in Malibu," in which she wrote: "I had come to see the spirit of the place as one of shared isolation and adversity, and I think now that I never loved the house on the Pacific Coast Highway more than on those many days when it was impossible to leave it, when

fire or flood had in fact closed the highway." A dissenting opinion was rendered in a *People* magazine cover story, which averred: "The plain truth is that [Malibu residents] are getting a noisy, shabby, perilous, and polluted pseudo-paradise."

The extent of the affront includes fecal pollution of the ocean (from untreated sewage and overflowing septic tanks) and not-infrequent offshore oil spills. Damaging waves from winter storms flood homes along eroded beaches in Malibu Colony. There is no beach out back of the Malibu Beach Inn.

Beach closures along Malibu's coast are not uncommon, due to high bacterial counts from human-generated sources of pollution. Breaches of Malibu Lagoon following heavy storms often send ribbons of foul, dark-stained water streaming into the waters near Surfrider Beach, causing mini-epidemics of nausea, vomiting, and diarrhea among surfers. One 21-year-old wave-rider—Erik Villanueva, a student at Pepperdine University, on the hills above Malibu—contracted Coxsackie B virus after paddling through a "dark stain" of pollution off Surfrider Beach in 1992. He has had two heart-transplant

THE PALMS HAVE GOTTA GO

Los Angeles will soon be a city without its most famous visual icon: the palm tree. Since at least the 1940s, tourists have associated palms with the relaxed wealth of sunny Southern California. Image may be everything in the make-believe world of Hollywood, but in the real world, palm trees are an ecological and budgetary disaster.

To begin with, they were never indigenous to Southern California. Not only do palm trees provide little, if any, shade, they do not remove carbon monoxide from the city's car-polluted air as well as other, shadier trees do. They also require frequent expensive maintenance, and their fronds become dangerous spears during winter's Santa Ana winds, bashing windshields and even injuring pedestrians.

Consequently, the city of Los Angeles is planting very few new palm trees once an old one dies off – which they are doing in abundant numbers these days. Instead, sycamores, crepe myrtles, and other indigenous species are being planted throughout the city. The only exceptions will be the relatively few palms that line such tourist routes as Sunset Boulevard and Hollywood Boulevard. In other words, just enough palms will remain to fake out the tourists.

operations and is convinced ocean pollution is to blame. Such events have led to a frenzy of heavily funded studies looking for sources of pollution in the Malibu Creek watershed, studying illness among beachgoers throughout the bay, and monitoring the genetic material of pathogens found in the lagoon. This is another way of saying that life is not always a beach in Malibu. Surfrider Beach receives failing grades when tested for bacterial contamination.

All of this is in large part a consequence of the accelerating pace of development in Malibu. The colony has changed considerably since the late 1970s, when author Joan Didion wrote (in the essay cited earlier): "In a way it seems the most idiosyncratic of beach communities, 27 miles of coastline with no hotel, no passable restaurant, nothing to attract the traveler's dollar." Now, like every other conquered corner of America, there are plenty of hotels, tons of passable restaurants, and lots of places to spend your money, including sprawling malls that would have been unthinkable a decade ago.

In 1986 the California Coastal Commission adopted a land-use plan for Malibu that permitted significant retail growth in three areas: the Malibu Civic Center, the Point Dume/Paradise Cove area, and Pepperdine University. The same plan also okayed the construction of up to 6,582 new dwellings, nearly doubling the number that existed at that time. Many Malibu natives fought the plan, and one local activist griped, "They want to allow undisciplined, unbridled growth in Malibu." That seems to be what they're getting. In 1990 Malibu officially approved its incorporation as a city, something that had been rejected in ballot initiatives dating back to 1950.

The Malibu of today is a collage of the upscale and low-rent, plain and fancy, old and new. In certain ways Malibu still has an Old California feel to it, a wayback-machine aura evident in the unpretentious taverns and food stands that squat by the road, refusing to bend to trends. At the same time recent arrivals on the scene, most evidently the flashy Malibu Colony Mall, have altered the landscape so that it looks more like a Los Angeles suburb than the Malibu of old.

The real appeal of the place remains the elemental collision of geological opposites: ocean basin and mountain ridge. A drive up

POLLUTION REPORT CARD:
L.A. COUNTY BEACHES

So you've made it to Malibu and would love to lay eyes on one of the many celebrities from the entertainment community who make their home here. But you discover that their exclusive Malibu Colony is a gated and off-limits fortress. There's just no way for an ordinary peon from Pasadena or Peoria to slip past security. Not to worry! Just head on over to Surfrider Beach, one of Malibu's most popular spots to surf and swim, and hop in the water. You may wind up indirectly having a close encounter with a celebrity, or a whole bunch of them, when fecal coliform bacteria from overflowing septic tanks in the private colony washes into the ocean and travels with the currents to the beaches due south.

Gross as it sounds, this is exactly what happens in the waters off Surfrider Beach, where a combination of sources that the government hasn't the time, money, or inclination to untangle has been fouling the water with bacteria and sickening those who swim there with a variety of ailments that range from ear and eye infections to gastrointestinal bugs. The city of Malibu has exceeded bacteria limits on its beaches for roughly 500 days since September 2006, according to Los Angeles Water Board, which has threatened fines of $10,000 a day until they cease. The chief culprit is outflow from Malibu Lagoon, which serves as a catch basin for all sorts of disgusting muck. In addition to the septic tanks of Malibu Colony, culprits include excrement from waterbirds, urban runoff from the 110-square-mile watershed that drains into Malibu Creek, runoff from soil tilling and animal waste, and refuse from homeless encampments near Malibu Civic Center. Unlike the vast majority of beaches that border Santa Monica Bay, bacterial levels at Surfrider generally remain high during both wet and dry weather. A new water treatment facility was installed at the mouth of Marie Canyon in Malibu in October 2007, but the city of Malibu continues to exceed federal limits on bacterial discharge into the ocean.

The picture improves somewhat down the coast. Will Rogers State Beach, in Pacific Palisades, had always been another pollution hot spot. For many years industrial operations such as the Chevron oil refinery and Hyperion Sewage Treatment Plant were to blame. But under pressure from environmental groups like Heal the Bay, they've gone a long way toward cleaning up their act. Chevron voluntarily extended its wastewater discharge pipes from 300 to 3,000 feet offshore and also provided funding for a pilot epidemiological study to determine the causes and prevalence of illness among bay-area beachgoers.

The guiltiest contributors to the bay's bacterial stew these days are the citizens of Los Angeles themselves. Fertilizer runoff from lawns, oil and antifreeze dumped into sewers, and garbage tossed into streets and gutters all find their way into the bay via storm drains during periods of rain. Piers are another source of human-generated contaminants that stress the bay. Eight native species of fish have been found to be contaminated with DDT and PCBs, severe and persistent toxins dumped into the bay during the 1960s. They are slow to break down in the cold, mucky bay bottom where they reside, and consequently are still working their way up through the food chain.

National organizations such as the Natural Resource Defense Council (NRDC) and Oceana have joined California-based advocacy groups like Heal the Bay and the Surfrider Foundation in calling for solutions to ocean pollution. As an attorney for NRDC noted, "A relaxing day at the beach may actually be a hazard to your health." If you're concerned, take a stand and get involved. By law the beaches belong to everybody and, by God, everyone should be upset about what's happening to them.

Heal the Bay
1444 9th Street
Santa Monica, CA 90404
310/451-1500
www.healthebay.org

Heal the Bay is an increasingly powerful foundation that started out in a living room and grew to an organization with 10,000 volunteers, all upset with the condition of Santa Monica Bay. Their goal is to achieve a "fishable, swimmable, surfable" bay, and they do it by lobbying, educating the public, and barraging the media with facts, figures, and photographs. They have proven that you can indeed "fight city hall" and win the battle. They were responsible for stopping the county of Los Angeles from dumping sewage sludge into the bay and they have pressured the city of Los Angeles to ban plastic bags and begin treating the bay as a vital source of life and health for the entire community. This is a remarkable group, worthy of your donations of money and time.

Surfrider Foundation
P.O. Box 6010
San Clemente, CA 92674
949/492-8170
www.surfrider.org

In 1984 this environmental action group was founded in Malibu by surfers who saw their beloved ocean growing filthier by the day. As former executive director Jake Grubb told *Rolling Stone:* "When I started surfing these waters in the early 1960s, they were green and blue. Today, they're gray or brown." Their ranks have swelled to 35,000 members in 60 chapters, with headquarters in San Clemente. Their high-profile victories have included successfully suing pulp mills for polluting Humboldt Bay and halting plans to construct a mile-long breakwater off Imperial Beach. Their Blue Water Task Force collects ocean samples for water-quality testing. They'd rather be surfing (who wouldn't?), but they've responded to the mandate for action.

Oceana
1350 Connecticut Avenue, N.W., 5th floor
Washington, DC 20036
202/833-3900
www.oceana.org
Pacific Office: 99 Pacific Street, Suite 155C
Monterey, CA 93940
831/643-9266

In 1987, after successfully fighting oil companies on offshore drilling, Ted Danson founded American Oceans Campaign. The Santa Monica-based organization warned people about ocean and beach pollution and educated policymakers and the public about the need to preserve and restore our shorelines. "Oceans and beaches used to be visually pleasing," Danson said in a 1995 interview. "They took your breath away and made you feel good about being alive. Now they're lined with wall-to-wall condominiums. Because of the sheer number of people, water supplies are overburdened and breaking down." Danson's American Oceans Campaign merged with the Washington-based Oceana. This larger international advocacy organization exists "for the sole purpose of protecting the world's oceans to sustain the circle of life." Global in scope, they now have 300,000 members in 150 countries. Oceana's West Coast office is located in Monterey.

LOS ANGELES COAST

ART AND HISTORY IN OLD MALIBU

In search of art and history? There are two Malibu-area attractions to satisfy your hunger. The first is the J. Paul Getty Museum at the **Getty Center** (1200 Getty Center Drive, 310/440-7300, www.getty.edu). The much-hyped Getty Center, a cultural mecca, opened in 1997. This 110-acre "campus" is nestled in the Santa Monica foothills, overlooking Brentwood. The museum reflects Getty's lifelong interests as a collector of Greek and Roman antiquities, Renaissance and Baroque paintings, and European decorative arts. The museum building is a re-creation of the Villa dei Papiri, an ancient Roman country house, and the gardens are filled with plants and trees that might have been found there 2,000 years ago.

Since our last visit, the provenance of many Getty antiquities have been at the center of a legal case that has roiled the international art waters. Marion True, the former chief antiquities curator, was indicted in Italy on charges of conspiring to acquire artifacts that were illegally removed from that country's soil. The Greek government pressed similar charges against True but dropped them when the Getty agreed to return four artifacts. The criminal charges in Italy against True are still active. Visitors are advised to visit the Getty Museum ASAP in case any more of their collection is deemed ill-gotten cultural booty. The museum is open 10 A.M.–6 P.M. Tuesday–Thursday, 10 A.M.–9 P.M. Friday–Saturday, and 10 A.M.–6 P.M. Sunday. Admission to the museum is free, but parking costs $10.

Another curious diversion worth checking out is the historic **Adamson House and Malibu Lagoon Museum** (23200 Pacific Coast Highway, 310/456-8432, www.adamsonhouse.org), located a quick left turn north of Malibu Pier. The house and grounds formerly belonged to the Adamson family, daughter and son-in-law of the last owners of the Malibu Spanish Land Grant. Built in 1929, the house is a classic Moorish-Spanish Colonial Revival-style residence that serves as a museum of ceramic art and design. The fantastic flower gardens on the premises were created by covering the natural dunes with a layer of humus.

History buffs should note that a historical marker commemorates this establishment as the probable site of explorer Juan Rodríguez Cabrillo's New World landing in 1542. He disembarked to greet the canoe-paddling Chumash and to claim all the lands of "Alta California" in the name of the king of Spain. Large-scale real-estate transactions such as this one were apparently a simple matter back then. You just stepped up to the counter, so to speak, and ordered. The Adamson house and Malibu Lagoon Museum are open to the public 11 A.M.–3 P.M. Wednesday–Saturday. Admission is $5 for adults and $2 for children ages 6-16.

the Pacific Coast Highway through Malibu—particularly above Point Dume, where the development subsides—is a stunning and humbling encounter with nature in the raw. The unfolding panorama of beaches yields one remarkable vista after another.

As for the highway, it's something of a bane in Malibu. At various points, especially along a four-mile stretch north of Topanga Canyon, it is subject to mass movements (falling rocks, landslides) from the unstable cliffs that were cut to build it. Traffic tramples through town on the four-lane Pacific Coast Highway like a stampede of cattle. On weekends the road jams to a standstill with carloads of Angelinos headed to their favorite north county beaches or to play with the boats they keep in Ventura County's yacht basins. Beach parking lots fill up quickly, and the overflow lines the highway shoulders in both directions. For pedestrians, dashing across the highway is a bit like playing Russian roulette.

A beach access point we attempted to reach during one such crossing nearly rendered us roadkill. All that risk to check out a cement walk between buildings—one of the narrow accesses the California Coastal Commission has waged costly battles to establish, much to the chagrin of Malibu residents. Officially it is known as the Zonker Harris Access-way, after the *Doonesbury* cartoon character. Malibu is a thorn in the side of the Coastal Commission, as it is the most privatized stretch of California's coast and one near its largest population center.

On either side of it lies private property. You're reminded not to trespass, although California law does grant citizens the right to walk along the beach shoreward of the mean high-tide line. We did just that, ambling in the direction of the Malibu Pier past all manner of sunbathers (including some seminude beauties) who paid us no mind. The pier at Malibu is an old, broad-planked affair with a restaurant on the shore end. You can buy bait and tackle, obtain a fishing license, and charter a sportfishing boat at **Malibu Sport Fishing Landing** (23000 Pacific Coast Highway, 310/456-8030). At one time the modest commercial heart of Malibu, the pier area has been overtaken by all the new commercial development several miles north, near the fabled and private Malibu Colony.

The canyons of Malibu are cut with tortuous roads that wind through the Santa Monica Mountains. A drive up one of the canyon roads is a great way to pass a few hours, offering a mix of ocean vistas and mountain scenery as you make the jagged ascent. We went up Topanga Canyon Road and returned via Malibu Canyon Road, passing in a short time from cool sea level to broiling higher altitudes. Lay hands on a map of Malibu and design your own up-and-back route.

Beyond these suggestions you are more or less on your own in Malibu. Sometimes you can be made to feel as unwanted as a stray dog shuffling along the side of the road. Unless you have a ton of money or know someone who lives here—say, Brad Pitt or Goldie Hawn—you'll have a hard time fashioning any sort of extended vacation on the Malibu coastline other than a camping trip. But we'd rather be tenting beneath a stand of sycamores at Leo Carrillo State Park than attempting celebrity sightings at Paradise Cove any day. When we think of Malibu, we think of the land, not the famous landowners.

For more information, contact the Malibu Chamber of Commerce, 23805 Stuart Ranch Road, Suite 100, Malibu, CA 90265, 310/456-9025, www.malibu.org.

BEACHES

Because the terrain is so rugged, with the Santa Monica Mountains plunging steeply into the sea, the geography of the coastline makes for some amazing beaches along Malibu's 27 miles. About half of the Malibu coast (12.5 miles) is given over to state and county beaches, while the rest is under development. Surfrider, Zuma, and County Line are all names familiar to beachgoers and surfers worth their sea salt. But there are literally two dozen or so named beaches in Malibu. We'll hit the highlights.

Malibu's beach-erosion problems along the more developed areas southeast of Point Dume continue to worsen, as the ocean chomps hungrily at some of the most expensive real estate in the country. Out behind Gladstone's 4 Fish Restaurant, straddling the line between Pacific Palisades and Malibu, breakers tenaciously whittle away the beachfront. A rock jetty built to keep the vanishing beach from retreating is fighting a losing battle as the sea steadily advances upon the establishment.

The first real beach in Malibu is **Topanga County Beach,** at the south end of Malibu, which runs for just over a mile. Like many in the area, it is narrow and rocky, set at the base of steep, eroding bluffs. Surfing is popular at the mouth of Topanga Creek, but there are too many rocks to allow for safe swimming along most of the beach. Above it is **Las Tunas County Beach,** a narrow, unimproved beach beneath the bluffs that holds a special attraction to surf casters.

Surfrider Beach is right up from the Malibu Pier. The beach covers 35 acres, including nearly a mile of ocean frontage. Its waves are perfectly formed and, even when small, carry surfers a good distance. The waves we've seen in summer are unspectacular in size but fascinating in form. Riding them, the surfers look as if they're walking on water, almost moving in slow motion, gliding in on perfectly shaped, long-cycle waves for what seems like an eternity. The beach is at the head of a dramatic, U-shaped cove. Kiddies, bronzed Adonises, and big-bellied men, plus the usual crew of noble surfers, pack the place. Ravishing California girls watch the guys work out on the volleyball courts or in the waves, which are fought over and claimed by the most skillful surfers. The only bum note is water quality, with bacterial contamination making wave-riding here tantamount to surfing in a Petri dish. Adjacent to Surfrider is the small Malibu Lagoon Museum and Adamson House. The museum, Malibu Lagoon (at the mouth of Malibu Creek), Surfrider Beach, and the 700-foot Malibu Pier all fall within the boundaries of **Malibu Lagoon County Beach.** The lagoon is subject to contamination, and though the warm, protected waters are attractive to young children, it can be pretty scummy. Not for nothing does the county post advisories against swimming here.

Between Malibu Lagoon and Point Dume lie several small beaches worthy of mention. **Paradise Cove** is a private fee beach in the heart of Malibu Colony, offering the likeliest chance of celebrity sightings. Unlike whale-watching expeditions, however, a sighting is not guaranteed. The entrance fee lands you on a beach with a short pier and a wonderful view of the opposing sandstone bluffs of Point Dume and the Santa Monica Mountains. **Escondido Beach,** at the mouth of Escondido Creek, can be reached via a stairway near Malibu Cove Colony Drive; it's a good diving area but otherwise not worth the trouble. Close by is **Dan Blocker County Beach** (formerly

Corral State Beach), a lifeguarded beach (in season) that draws some surfers and divers. The beach is narrow and rocky, there are few facilities, and only roadside parking. But it's a great spot for scuba enthusiasts.

Much like the coastline in Laguna Beach and La Jolla, Malibu's is intercut with coves, many of them accessible by stairways and paths if you know what you're looking for. Keep your eyes open for some of these spots between Topanga Beach and Paradise Cove (they are numerous). Also, be prepared to park on the highway and deal with hazardous crossings. Just for the record, there are public-access stairways to the beach on the following numbered blocks of the Pacific Coast Highway: 20000, 20350, 24318, 24434, 24602, 24714, 25118, 31200, and 31344.

Around the tip of Point Dume is **Point Dume County Beach** (a.k.a. Westward Beach), on Westward Beach Road. Nearby **Zuma County Beach** is the ultimate Southern California beach: wide, wild, extending for miles, and inhabiting a stupendous natural setting. It is the largest county-owned beach, with no fewer than eight parking lots and a $6 parking charge, avoided by many who use the shoulders of the Pacific Coast Highway. The beach here deserves its reputation for danger, as the waves form close to shore, rising out of nowhere to back-breaking height before crashing noisily and sending tongues of seawater and foam scurrying up the sloping beach face. It's the perfect recipe for rip currents, necessitating frequent heroics from the lifeguard stands. Contrary to notions that primo Malibu beaches such as this one are peopled only with perfect specimens awaiting casting calls from soap-opera producers, Zuma is chock full of families and normal-looking folks on summer weekends. With the invigorating clean air, the azure ocean's churning fury, and the breathtaking backdrop of steep-sided, brushy mountains, Zuma County Beach makes it possible to understand why residents risk life, limb, and earthly possessions to live in Malibu. Zuma comes equipped with food stands at both ends of its four-mile expanse along the Pacific Coast Highway, from the western side of Point Dume to Broad Beach Road. There is also a huge area given over to volleyball courts. West of Zuma, stairways along Broad Beach Road lead to secluded **Broad Beach.**

Next up is **Robert H. Heyer Memorial State Beach.** In fact, it is a trio of small cove beaches accessible by path and stairway. Moving west, the three beaches are **El Matador, La Piedra,** and **El Pescador,** occupying 18, 9, and 10 acres, respectively. The attraction is isolation from the madding crowd. Parking is by the honor system; you're asked to stuff $2 into a collection box. Switchback paths are carved into the crumbly cliffs. No wonder Malibu has mudslides in the rainy season; the hills are nothing more than loosely consolidated dirt clods. The beaches and offshore waters are strewn with sizable, steep-sided sea stacks. Come here for a taste of the wild side of Malibu's coastal geology. Approximately two miles west of El Pescador is **Nicholas Canyon County Beach,** slightly larger (at 23 acres) than the trio preceding it. Keep your eyes out for the turnoff down to the fee parking lot, which is directly across from the Malibu Riding and Tennis Club. You can also hike down from Leo Carrillo State Park, which adjoins it. Formerly known as Nicholas Beach—surfers referred to it as Point Zero—it is less crowded than many Malibu beaches and relatively free of wave-hogging surf punks. It is informally used as a nude beach, though authorities try to discourage it.

27 TOPANGA COUNTY BEACH

Location: 18500 Pacific Coast Highway in Malibu
Parking/Fees: $7 entrance fee per vehicle
Hours: 6 A.M.-sunset
Facilities: concession, lifeguards, restrooms, showers, and picnic tables
Contact: Los Angeles County Lifeguard Service, Northern Section, 310/394-3264

28 LAS TUNAS COUNTY BEACH

Location: 19400 Pacific Coast Highway in Malibu
Parking/Fees: $7 entrance fee per vehicle
Hours: 6 A.M.-sunset
Facilities: lifeguards and picnic tables
Contact: Los Angeles County Lifeguard Service, Northern Section, 310/394-3264

29 SURFRIDER BEACH

Location: Pacific Coast Highway at Malibu Pier
Parking/Fees: $7 entrance fee per vehicle
Hours: 6 A.M.-sunset
Facilities: concession, lifeguards, showers, and restrooms
Contact: Los Angeles County Lifeguard Service, Northern Section, 310/394-3264

30 MALIBU LAGOON COUNTY BEACH

Location: Pacific Coast Highway at Malibu Creek
Parking/Fees: $7 entrance fee per vehicle
Hours: 6 A.M.-sunset
Facilities: lifeguards, restrooms, showers, and picnic tables
Contact: Los Angeles County Lifeguard Service, Northern Section, 310/394-3264

31 DAN BLOCKER COUNTY BEACH

Location: 26000 Pacific Coast Highway in Malibu
Parking/Fees: limited free roadside parking
Hours: 6 A.M.-sunset

Facilities: lifeguards and restrooms
Contact: Los Angeles County Lifeguard
Service, Northern Section, 310/394-3264

32 ESCONDIDO BEACH

Location: path at Escondido Creek near Malibu
Cove Colony Drive in Malibu
Parking/Fees: limited free roadside parking
Hours: sunrise-sunset
Facilities: none
Contact: Malibu Division of the Angeles
District of the California Department of Parks
and Recreation, 310/457-8140

33 PARADISE COVE

Location: 28128 Pacific Coast Highway in
Malibu
Parking/Fees: $25 entrance fee per car
Hours: sunrise-sunset
Facilities: concession, lifeguards, and
restrooms
Contact: Paradise Cove, 310/457-2511

34 POINT DUME
COUNTY BEACH

Location: end of Westward Beach Road, on the
north side of Point Dume, in Malibu
Parking/Fees: $7 entrance fee per car
Hours: 6 A.M.-sunset
Facilities: lifeguards, restrooms, and showers
Contact: Los Angeles County Lifeguard
Service, Northern Section, 310/394-3264

35 ZUMA COUNTY BEACH

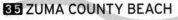

Location: four miles north of Malibu at 30000
Pacific Coast Highway

Parking/Fees: $7 entrance fee per vehicle
Hours: 6 A.M.-sunset
Facilities: concession, lifeguards, restrooms,
and showers
Contact: Los Angeles County Lifeguard
Service, Northern Section, 310/394-3264

36 BROAD BEACH

Location: stairways lead to the beach from
Broad Beach Road at Highway 1 in Malibu
Parking/Fees: limited free street parking
Hours: 6 A.M.-sunset
Facilities: none
Contact: Los Angeles County Department of
Beaches and Harbors, 310/305-9503

37 EL MATADOR STATE
BEACH

Location: six miles north of Malibu at 32350
Pacific Coast Highway
Parking/Fees: $2 entrance fee per vehicle
Hours: 6 A.M.-sunset
Facilities: restrooms
Contact: Malibu Sector, Angeles District,
California State Parks, 310/457-8143

38 LA PIEDRA STATE BEACH

Location: seven miles north of Malibu at
32700 Pacific Coast Highway
Parking/Fees: $2 entrance fee per vehicle
Hours: 6 A.M.-sunset
Facilities: restrooms
Contact: Malibu Sector, Angeles District,
California State Parks, 310/457-8143

El Matador State Beach

39 EL PESCADOR STATE BEACH

Location: 7.5 miles north of Malibu at 32900 Pacific Coast Highway
Parking/Fees: $2 entrance fee per vehicle
Hours: 6 A.M.-sunset
Facilities: restrooms
Contact: Malibu Sector, Angeles District, California State Parks, 310/457-8143

40 NICHOLAS CANYON COUNTY BEACH

Location: nine miles north of Malibu at Nicholas Canyon Road and Highway 1
Parking/Fees: $7 entrance fee per vehicle
Hours: 6 A.M.-sunset
Facilities: lifeguards, restrooms, and picnic tables
Contact: Los Angeles County Lifeguard Service, Northern Section, 310/394-3264

ACCOMMODATIONS

Malibu has exactly one luxury ocean hotel along its 27 miles, the fabulous **Malibu Beach Inn** (22878 Pacific Coast Highway, 310/456-6444, www.malibubeachinn.com, $$$$). This three-story, pink-stucco wonder is perched beside—and, at high tide, directly above—the ocean. When they say oceanfront, they're not exaggerating. You can open the balcony doors of your room and let the sounds of the churning, crashing ocean lull you to sleep. The complimentary breakfast buffet includes wonderful pastries, fresh fruit, cereal, and coffee. You can carry it to an outdoor sundeck and enjoy the morning meal over a copy of the *Los Angeles Times*. The rattan furniture and contemporary California decor enhance the sense of a relaxed getaway at the ocean's edge. And rooms are a princely $490–675, with suites going for $875–1,350. Oh yes, for that extra touch, you can pay $20 to get a "rose petal turndown."

If you're going to pay top dollar for a place at the beach, you will find no nicer spot to do it than the Malibu Beach Inn. We have our own homemade souvenirs of the visit, incidentally: cassettes of waves breaking on the beach below, made with our portable recorders. The inn has won Robin Leach's seal of approval (check out the handwritten note just inside the lobby), and who better knows about refined lifestyles than he? Situated a short distance down from Malibu Pier, the inn can, incidentally, arrange delivery of a meal from Alice's Restaurant, a long-standing landmark at the base of the pier.

COASTAL CUISINE

Granita (23725 West Malibu Road, 310/456-0488, $$$) is the hands-down standout on the Malibu dining scene. This star attraction in celebrity chef Wolfgang Puck's arsenal of California restaurants has won over even jaded Malibu natives, who are wowed by its beachside proximity, its underwater fantasy decor (done in handmade ceramic tile and etched glass), and such dishes as Mediterranean fish soup, lobster club sandwich, spicy shrimp pizza, and seared scallops over black-pepper fettuccine. Dress is Malibu casual: informal but neat. You may need to call up to a week in advance for a reservation, especially on weekends.

Another popular hangout is **Coogie's Beach Cafe** (23750 Malibu Road, 310/317-1444, $$), a spacious, high-ceilinged restaurant in a shopping center. Coogie's serves Malibu-style cuisine (indulgent and creative but healthy) at fair prices. All the salads are good, as are items like fresh Alaskan salmon patties with dill, served with a plate of eggs any style. It's a very Malibu kind of place, and you're likely to be surrounded by any number of Hollywood notables slumming in their casual wear. No one pays them (or you) any mind; that's part of the unspoken code of civility in celebrity-thick Malibu.

You can't get anything you want at **Alice's Restaurant** (Malibu Pier, 23000 Pacific Coast Highway, 310/456-6646, $$$), but your choices range to such satisfying selections as red snapper or shrimp sautéed with garlic, shallots, and tomatoes. And, of course, the B52 cocktail, for which the bartenders are famous; it apparently gets you "bombed." The **Reel Inn** (18661 Pacific Coast Highway, 310/456-

8221, $$) is a favorite of locals (especially surfing locals) who step up to the counter for everything from fresh fish to tacos.

Up at the opposite end of Malibu, directly across the street from County Line Beach, is a restaurant and fresh-seafood shop with the promising name **Neptune's Net** (42505 Pacific Coast Highway, 310/457-3095, $). It's the kind of place that we tend to romanticize—off the beaten track, filled with local color, offering fresh, nonfranchised food. In reality, much more could be done with it. Still, the location is unsurpassable.

NIGHTLIFE

Nightlife has never been a big proposition up in Malibu, the whole idea being that it is an enclave for people who prefer not to be recognized. Nonetheless, a good time can be had at the **Malibu Inn** (22969 Pacific Coast Highway, 310/456-6060), a riotously fun restaurant and saloon. Its ceiling is bedecked with a bizarre collage of metal wheels, surfboards (one serrated with shark-teeth indentations), baseball mitts, and bric-a-brac. You can order food, if you wish, through a huge, red pair of plastic lips. There's a pool table, bar, some tables, and a sawdust-strewn wood floor in the main part of the saloon. The Malibu Inn is as down to earth as it gets. Lest you think Malibu is all reclusive celebrities and pricey cafés, duck in here for a brew with the surfing clan.

Finally, in the interest of cultural history, we recommend a visit to **Moonshadows** (20356 Pacific Coast Highway, 310/456-3010). It was here, in August 2006, that Mel Gibson got so sloshed that, when pulled over by the police on his way home, he felt duty-bound to lecture them on Middle East history, biblical ideas, and female anatomy. He excoriated "the Jews," called one of the arresting officers "Sugar Tits," and then went into rehab, as they all do after behaving abysmally.

The tabloid press and paparazzi would go into a serious tailspin without celebrities to trail in Malibu—making note of hard and flabby bods on its beaches, monitoring the latest drunk-driving arrests on Pacific Coast Highway, and stalking their prey's every move, including the most banal daily visits to Starbucks. How boring our world would be without celebrity cellulite to cluck about, new serpentine tattoos to ogle, rumored affairs to lose sleep over, and, of course Britney Spears's latest outrage, right? Wrong. Get a life, America.

Leo Carrillo State Park

Malibu's marvelous procession of beaches reaches its crescendo with Leo Carrillo State Park. The 3,000-acre park encompasses two sections of beach, separated by Sequit Point, and a 139-site campground arrayed along a loop road in a scenic, fragrant canyon on the landward side of the Pacific Coast Highway. Nestled amid eucalyptus and sycamore groves, the campsites here are absolutely enthralling. Few other parks in the country can offer access to beach and mountains in such proximity. You are on the geological cutting edge of California's tectonic assembly line here.

For more information, contact Leo Carrillo State Park, 36000 Pacific Coast Highway, 818/880-0350. www.parks.ca.gov.

BEACHES

Leo Carrillo State Park's 1.5 miles worth of beaches are steeply sloped with coarse brown sand. When we visited, little kids were getting waxed on the beach by crashing breakers, while big kids who bobbed in the offshore kelp beds atop surfboards were also being slammed to the mat by the waves' decisive crashes. The surf here is not for the inexperienced or faint of heart, but the setting is as magnificent as any you'll find on either coast, offering sea

caves and tidepools to explore, acres of sand to spread out on, and a scenic mountainous backdrop to gaze upon. For surfers there are good southerly swells, though the offshore and onshore rocks are intimidating.

Up by the Ventura County line vans and cars line the road, and surfers scamper down the steep, reddish-brown bluffs. **County Line Beach** is a favorite of Southern California surfriders, accorded a status on par with such legendary breaks as Rincon and Windansea. And this is where Malibu and Los Angeles County finally come to an end.

41 LEO CARRILLO STATE PARK

BEST (

Location: one mile south of the Ventura County line at 36000 Pacific Coast Highway
Parking/Fees: $10 entrance fee per vehicle; camping fees $20-25 per night, plus $7.50 reservation fee
Hours: 8 A.M.-sunset
Facilities: concession, lifeguards, restrooms, showers, and picnic tables
Contact: Leo Carrillo State Park, 818/880-0350

42 COUNTY LINE BEACH

Location: Pacific Coast Highway at Ventura County line
Parking/Fees: limited free roadside parking
Hours: 8 A.M.-sunset
Facilities: none
Contact: Leo Carrillo State Park, 818/880-0350

VENTURA COAST

It's little wonder that Ventura County has become a port of call for urban dropouts from Los Angeles who yearn for safe, sane, and smogless suburbs. Vacationers, tired of battling the Southern California throngs, have also begun pointing their rental cars toward the 42 miles of coastline in Ventura County.

Once rural and still primarily agricultural—the Oxnard Plain, which dominates the eastern part of the county, is among the most fertile areas in the nation—Ventura County began growing at the point where U.S. 101/Ventura Freeway meets Highway 1/Pacific Coast Highway, near the conjoined cities of Oxnard and Ventura. Perhaps because of a concerted slow-growth movement that's been fighting sprawl, Ventura in particular retains something of a recognizable personality and neighborly, small-city feel.

The Santa Monica Mountains separate Los Angeles County from the Santa Barbara Coast both sociologically and geographically. As a state of mind, the Central Coast begins here, even though Southern California physically extends up to Santa Barbara, by general consensus.

The beaches of Ventura County illustrate the yin and yang of California's coastal geography. Some of these beaches, such as McGrath State Beach and San Buenaventura State Beach, are as wide and inviting as any you'll find. Others, especially those fronting the string of small, sea-walled communities at the north end of the county—Solimar, Seacliff, Faria, Hobson, Mussel Shoals—are seemingly down to their last grains of sand.

But one should not overlook Ventura, an attractive small city that serves as a gateway to the Channel Islands, or Oxnard, which has an appealing harbor. These adjacent communities' beaches would be the envy of many a sand-depleted beach town farther south.

All are at least worth a peek, for different

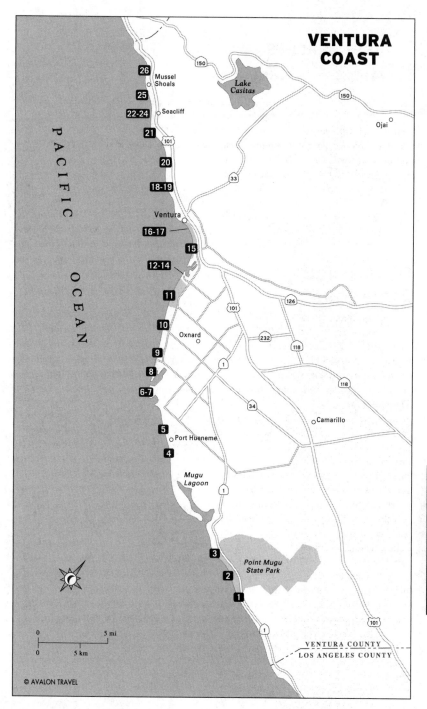

VENTURA COAST

PACIFIC

OCEAN

26 Mussel
    Shoals

25

22-24 Seacliff

21

20

18-19

Ventura

16-17

15

12-14

11

10 Oxnard

9

8

6-7

5 Port Hueneme

4

Mugu
Lagoon

3 Point Mugu
2 State Park

1

Lake
Casitas

Ojai

Camarillo

VENTURA COUNTY
LOS ANGELES COUNTY

0   5 mi

0   5 km

© AVALON TRAVEL

BEST BEACHES

⟨ McGrath State Beach, page 216

---

reasons. And while you're looking around, we would like to direct your attention toward the horizon, where the Channel Islands—a chain of eight pearly isles that have been called America's Galápagos—lie approximately 20 miles offshore of the Ventura Coast. Five of the Channel Islands collectively form one of our most prized national parks and marine sanctuaries.

Point Mugu State Park

Point Mugu (pronounced "ma-GOO") State Park is found at the south end of Ventura County. The five-mile shoreline is just one facet of Point Mugu's appeal. The 15,000-acre park provides the lure of excellent hiking trails and campgrounds at Sycamore Canyon and Thornhill Broome Beach. A 70-mile network of hiking trails centers around Sycamore Canyon, which serves as a popular hikers' hookup to the Santa Monica Mountains. Here, majestic sycamores reach 80-foot heights. Deer and coyotes make appearances on some trails, such as the nine-mile Big Sycamore Canyon Loop, which leads to stunning ocean overlooks.

Incidentally, "Mugu" derives from the Chumash Indian word "Muwu," which means beach. Both actual and mythological tragedy are associated with Point Mugu. In 2000 an Alaskan Air jet crashed into the ocean just offshore, killing all 88 passengers and crew. More fancifully, there's an Indian legend about a Princess Hueneme, who flung herself from the rock after her husband left her for a spell-casting minx.

For more information, contact Point Mugu State Park, 9000 West Pacific Coast Highway, Malibu, CA 90265, 818/880-0363, www.cal.parks.ca.gov.

BEACHES

Sycamore Cove Beach is Point Mugu's main oceanfront day-use area, and it is stocked with everything one could want for a day at the beach, from a grassy picnic area to a sandy beach. Across the highway is Sycamore Canyon, which has a shaded, 55-site campground (no hookups). A mile and a half up Highway 1 is **Thornhill Broome Beach,** a beachside campground that does not accommodate daytrippers. Roughly the same distance further will land you at **Mugu Beach,** where you'll find a gravel lot with no facilities and a cheap ($4) day-use fee. Mugu Beach is near Mugu Rock, an often-photographed monolith created when a path for Highway 1 was dynamited through the mountain. People climb Mugu Rock and whale-watch from its summit.

The campgrounds at Sycamore Canyon and Thornhill Broome are popular with families, booking far ahead on weekends. Sycamore Cove is a sandy, crescent-shaped beach with an amazing backdrop of cool, shady sycamores running up into the folded foothills. As a setting, it simply cannot be beat.

◻ SYCAMORE COVE BEACH

Location: six miles north of the Los Angeles County line on Pacific Coast Highway in southern Ventura County

Parking/Fees: $10 entrance fee per vehicle; camping fees $20-25 per night, plus $7.50 reservation fee

Hours: 7 A.M.-10 P.M.

Facilities: lifeguards, restrooms, showers, and picnic tables

Contact: Point Mugu State Park, 818/880-0363

② THORNHILL BROOME BEACH

🏕 🏃 ⛷

Location: 1.5 miles northwest of Sycamore Cove Beach on Pacific Coast Highway in southern Ventura County
Parking/Fees: accessible to campers only; camping fees $11-15 per night, plus $7.50 reservation fee
Hours: 7 A.M.-10 P.M.
Facilities: lifeguards, restrooms, showers, and picnic tables
Contact: Point Mugu State Park, 818/880-0363

③ MUGU BEACH

🏕 🏃 ⛷

Location: three miles northwest of Sycamore Cove Beach on Pacific Coast Highway in south Ventura County
Parking/Fees: $4 entrance fee per vehicle
Hours: 7 A.M.-10 P.M.
Facilities: none
Contact: Point Mugu State Park, 818/880-0363

Point Mugu Naval Base

The U.S. Navy has realigned operations in Ventura County, consolidating various commands into two operating facilities: Point Mugu and Port Hueneme. Between them there is a naval air station, air and surface warfare centers, a satellite operations center, an early-warning wing, and the famous 31st "Seabees" group. The navy is the county's largest employer, directly or indirectly responsible for 15,000 jobs.

All very fascinating, but how does that pertain to this book? Well, the Point Mugu facility occupies a chunk of coastland. And while you can't visit the beach here, for obvious reasons of national security, it might interest you to learn that threatened least terns nest on the sandy peninsula at Point Mugu. Also, there's a beach motel out here—but you've got to be affiliated with the military to use it.

For more information, contact Naval Base Ventura County, 311 Main Road, Suite 1, Point Mugu, CA 93042, 805/989-1704, www.cnic.navy.mil.

ACCOMMODATIONS

The "morale, welfare, and recreation" department of the U.S. Navy's Southwest Region offers beachside lodgings at its Point Mugu installation for active and retired military personal, reservists, and Department of Defense civilians. You can stay at the **Beach Motel** (Point Mugu, Naval Base Ventura County, Building 774, 805/283-4240, $) or the **RV Park** (Point Mugu, Naval Base Ventura County, Building 770, 805/283-6123, $). At ease, soldier!

Port Hueneme

The word *hueneme* is pronounced "why-NEE-mee," as if the town is inquiring or whining about its own identity. Lying uprange from the largest missile testing ground on the West Coast, one can't blame the locals for asking questions. Within the town limits, approaching from the south on Highway 1, farmland abounds. Scientific and uniform, row upon row and mile after mile of green stubs protrude from fields, with migrant workers bending and stooping under picked loads. A heavy industrial presence is also evident, with Kaiser Aluminum and a paper mill spewing smoke out their stacks.

Port Hueneme (population 21,500) is packed with quiet, symmetrical neighborhoods where homes and apartment complexes

VENTURA'S MOST WANTED

This may seem hard to believe, but one of us is a fugitive from justice in Ventura County, having failed to pay a fine for the crime of...jaywalking. There is, no lie, a bench warrant for his arrest. That would, by extension, make the other beach bum guilty of harboring a fugitive or aiding flight to avoid prosecution. The story of how a pair of innocents like us came down on the wrong side of the law follows.

The sordid saga starts in Marina del Rey, where we dined on raw oysters and sushi from a buffet one Friday night back in 1988. Because the raw seafood morsels had, for some reason, been left incubating beneath warm lights, they were a perfect medium for bacterial contamination. Not knowing any better, we dove into this all-you-can-eat buffet. The restaurant in question no longer exists, and we came close to no longer existing ourselves in the days that followed.

The next day we both took profoundly ill, projectile vomiting as if possessed by demons. Our gastrointestinal distress, now bordering on delirium, reached its nadir in Ventura. Of course, we didn't bother to see doctors. Like fearless surfers, we decided to ride out the waves of nausea. That night in Ventura one of us walked into a glass balcony door in his tenth-floor hotel room. Both of us passed miserable, sleepless nights. At 6 A.M., the other decided to get out of bed and buy a newspaper.

Admittedly appearing a bit rough around the edges, the sick, sleep-deprived beach bum exited the lobby of the hotel. He crossed the deserted street on this silent Sunday morning to purchase a newspaper from a vending box. He was accosted by an officer of the law, who appeared from nowhere, as if lying in wait. He could barely comprehend the officer's spiel about having crossed the street while the Don't Walk sign was flashing, and he thought he was dreaming when the cop pulled out a pad and began writing up a ticket for jaywalking – on Sunday at 6 A.M. on a quiet, carless street in Ventura.

The fine was $10. The slip of paper was chuckled over by both beach bums (providing a rare bit of levity in a week's work of illness) and quickly went missing. We were writing a book on the road while sicker than dogs and had other priorities. Although forgotten by the perpetrator, the petty offense remained in the files of the Ventura Police Department. Over the years, follow-up notices were sent to the home of the beach bum's mother in North Carolina. One tendered an offer of amnesty if the fine (which had by then been jacked up with late-payment surcharges) was paid. The next was a bench warrant, which would be rescinded only upon payment of the fine, which had ballooned to $200.

Let's get real. The "guilty" beach bum has a few words to say. Thousands of motorists speed on the Ventura Freeway with no legal consequences, many with cell phones pressed to their ears. Don't you think a jaywalking ticket deserves to be forgiven? Surely the officers of this fine community have something better to do than troll for early-morning jaywalkers. This is the sort of trivial offense that would be noticed and ticketed only on the slowest day in the fictional town of Mayberry RFD. Weren't there any unsolved murders or burglaries to which they could have better devoted their time?

It is no fun being wanted by the law. And so the wanted beach bum asks, from the bottom of his now-healthy GI tract, for forgiveness of this ridiculous and now unaffordable ticket. In return, he won't ever jaywalk in Ventura again. Promise.

are laid out not unlike the rows of crops that lead up to them. This anonymous uniformity is explained by the military presence, with the Naval Base Ventura County occupying sites at Point Mugu and in Port Hueneme. The U.S. Navy's Construction Battalion Center, Port Hueneme takes up the sea lion's share of coastal access around the town center.

For more information, contact the Port Hueneme Chamber of Commerce, 220 North Market Street, Port Hueneme, CA 93041, 805/488-2023, www.hueneme chamber.com.

BEACHES

At the west end of Surfside Drive is **Hueneme Beach Park,** site of a broad beach and handsome, 1,240-foot pier. Parking is self-pay, and the pier is open 24 hours a day, with cutting tables and sinks provided for filleting catches. The sand is grayish brown, wide, and dotted with volleyball nets, barbecue rings, and picnic tables. The beach ends at the south jetty of the naval complex. It is claimed to be the only city-owned beach park in Ventura County. Every year in mid-August the city holds a weekend-long Hueneme Beach Festival. It's a good excuse to pig out and play.

4 HUENEME BEACH PARK

🚲 ⛵ 🏄 🌐

Location: end of Surfside Drive in Port Hueneme
Parking/Fees: metered parking lot
Hours: sunrise–10 P.M.
Facilities: concession, lifeguards, restrooms, showers, and picnic tables
Contact: Port Hueneme Recreation and Community Services, 805/986-6542

Oxnard

While parts of town belie Oxnard's claim to being "the city that cares," much of its shoreline is a pleasant surprise. Blessed by a beautiful setting, comfortable year-round climate, large and scenic harbor, strong prevailing winds, and wide, big-duned beaches, it's a place with a lot of potential. At the same time, certain less charming areas bear the hallmarks of poverty that one associates with migrant labor and low-ranking military personnel. Nonetheless, they've been working to position Oxnard as a pro-business mecca, proudly heralding it as "the most business-welcoming community in Ventura County." Reading between the lines, there is a faint hint of desperation in those words.

The town takes its awkward name from Henry Oxnard, a mogul whose sugar-beet empire was located hereabouts. With a population of 185,000, Oxnard is a medium-sized city in the middle of the fertile Oxnard Plain, where crop fields extend as far as the eye can see. This agricultural delta was created by the once-mighty Santa Clara River (whose mouth has been reduced to a trickle by agricultural withdrawals). The river was dammed, the delta became a plain, and the plain gave way to the multicolored fields that run to the east as far as the Santa Monica Mountains. Oxnard calls itself the Strawberry Capital of the World. California supplies 80 percent of the world's strawberries, and Oxnard celebrates with a Strawberry Festival on the third weekend in May. Other crops—such as lemons, corn, and broccoli—are grown here, too. Trucks and trains haul off Oxnard's bounty to supermarkets the world over.

But Oxnard's "lower 40" is also filled with new middle-class housing and bank buildings—the things one associates with an up-and-comer. Literature from the local chamber of commerce has proclaimed Oxnard "the fastest growing area in the state." It is a sentiment offered without irony, as though this were great news. Oxnard wears its recent growth as well as can be expected. Signs of it are obvious along Highway 1 on the outskirts of town, a suburbia of predictable sterility. But the beach areas, accessed via Harbor Boulevard, are low-key to the point of isolation. Oxnard's beaches are so beautiful and healthy it's surprising they haven't been exploited like those farther south.

Perhaps this is owing to the fact that the upscale side of Oxnard caters primarily to a boating crowd. The scenic harbor and surrounding area offer biking and hiking trails, picnic tables, tennis courts, playgrounds, and a safe, secluded harbor beach. The entire coastline is situated at the proper angle to receive wind and water currents vital to a rising watersports capital. Channel Islands Harbor was dredged into existence in 1965 and modeled after a New England seaport, with 2,600 boat slips and a restaurant row.

It is not hard to figure out how Oxnard's incongruous overlap of suburbia and farmland occurred. It lies 60 miles northwest of Los Angeles, where the Ventura Freeway meets the ocean, making it a logical area for stressed Angelenos to plunder after they've maxed out their own turf. What kind of changes might they bring to the landscape? Well, we saw a sign staked in a field filled with crops and farm workers whose curious message read: Thanks, Oxnard, for Destroying This Farmland.

For more information, contact the Oxnard Convention & Visitors Bureau, 1000 Town Center Drive, Suite 130, Oxnard, CA 93036, 805/385-7571, www.oxnardtourism.com; or the Oxnard Chamber of Commerce, 400 East Esplanade Drive, Oxnard, CA 93036, 805/983-6118, www.oxnardchamber.org.

BEACHES

As if to reinforce the uniqueness of the coast in these parts, the 50-mile stretch from Oxnard State Beach north to Gaviota State Park (above Santa Barbara) has been given its own name—the Channel Coast, a reference to the windswept Channel Islands, which lie 20 miles offshore and are visible on clear days.

From the south, the first beach inside Oxnard's town limits is **Ormond Beach**. It's an environmentally controversial spot that's off the beaten track. To get there, take Highway 1 to Hueneme Road. You'll pass acres of farmlands, eventually making a left on Perkins Road, which leads to the beach via a corridor of warehouses and industrial plants. Park at the cul-de-sac and catch a whiff of the paper mills. The beach itself is healthy, with a full dune structure and not much human visitation. It's understandable why few come here except to sit in cars on their lunch hour and drink beer from brown bags.

Ormond Beach, as the Sierra Club noted, has traditionally been used by the city of Oxnard as "the site to locate industrial development it did not want elsewhere." But Ormond Beach is a sensitive wetlands area, and with more than 90 percent of California's coastal wetlands long since destroyed, the remaining ones are hotly contested by environmental groups whenever a developer comes along with a proposal that will result in their damage or loss. That's exactly what's happened at Ormond Beach, where Occidental Petroleum wishes to site its first liquid natural gas terminal in California. So now the city of Oxnard is trying to pull a rabbit out of the hat by pleasing everybody with regard to the "Ormond Beach Redevelopment Area." Here are its objectives:

- Conserve, protect, and enhance the natural environment by restoring severely degraded wetlands and establish a fully functioning restored tidal connection and saltwater marsh ecosystem.

- Improve recreational and tourism opportunities.

- Strengthen market conditions and enhance economic opportunity in the city.

To this pie-in-the-sky set of competing directives, all we can say is, "You can't have your wetlands and mistreat them, too."

North of the U.S. Navy's Port Hueneme site lies **Silver Strand Beach**. To find it requires a circuitous route around the naval base: north on Ventura Road, left on Channel Islands Boulevard, left on Victoria Avenue, and left again on Ocean Drive to the Sawtelle Avenue access. Silver Strand is a free beach with lifeguards in the summer. A shipwreck, the SS *La Jenelle*, does duty as a fishing jetty at the south end of the beach. Be careful when casting, though, because it's slippery and the surf can get rough.

The best way to access Oxnard's more commendable beaches is via Harbor Boulevard. **Hollywood Beach** is a quiet city beach off Harbor Boulevard at the corner of La Brea Street and Ocean Drive; it has volleyball nets and summer lifeguards. There's a little swimming beach near the harbor, locally known as **Channel Islands Harbor Beach.** A park runs around the harbor's inner flank, offering grassy picnic sites and bike paths.

North of Hollywood Beach, also off Harbor Boulevard, is **Oxnard Beach Park,** a great day-use facility for families and large groups. The park comprises 62 acres of athletic fields, picnic tables, barbecue pits, pedestrian and bike paths, and a trail system that leads over dunes to a stretch of sand so wide it will take your breath away. The surrounding residential area, Oxnard Shores, strikes a nice balance between nature and human habitations, with low-lying architecture divided by canals, not unlike those in Venice Beach. Nonetheless, it's oddly devoid of human presence, as if a neutron bomb has gone off, leading us to wonder if these might be often-empty second homes for Los Angelenos.

Next up is **Mandalay Beach County Park,** a swath of sand whose jurisdiction and fate had been in dispute for some years; the beach is once again open and accessible. Set in an upscale subdivision that's crowned by Embassy Suites Mandalay Beach Resort, it's good to see that Mandalay's broad apron of sand isn't just being hoarded by the hoi polloi. It's a good place to go fly a kite—really!

The most precious of Oxnard's treasures is **McGrath State Beach.** This hidden jewel is one of the most appealing of the state's coastal parks. McGrath is on the north side of Oxnard at the Santa Clara River bed. McGrath State Beach offers 174 wind-protected and shaded campsites, a visitor center, nature trails, an estuary, mountainous dunes, and two miles of wide, windswept beaches. If you want to camp at McGrath, be advised that reservations fill up quickly (especially in summer), and stays are limited to one week.

Since the ocean currents are particularly strong here and the waves break on a deep, sloping shoreline, swimming is not recommended (though a lifeguard is on duty in summer). This beach is best for walking or surf casting, and the park is a living lab of natural wonders. The dune structure at McGrath is among the healthiest left in Southern California. They are nonetheless fragile and should be traversed only on designated paths. Dunes are formed when ocean currents and winds move sand around, and they are held in place when colonized by plants. These plants are easily broken or dislodged by human disturbances: feet, mountain bikes, mopeds, Jeeps, and all-terrain vehicles.

The northern 160 acres of McGrath constitute the **Santa Clara Estuary Natural Preserve,** which protects the habitat of the California least tern and the Belding's Savannah sparrow. A self-guided half-mile trail accesses a portion of the preserve, offering glimpses of the freshwater and saltwater plants and animals that intermingle in this precious ecosystem. The murky water is a rich nursery of nutrients. Shrimp feed on plankton, fish eat the shrimp, and shorebirds devour the fish. All the while the next generation spends its formative months in this protected, nurturing habitat.

5 ORMOND BEACH

Location: Hueneme Road to end of Perkins Road in Port Hueneme
Parking/Fees: free parking lot
Hours: 24 hours
Facilities: none

Contact: Oxnard Department of Parks and Facilities, 805/385-7950

6 SILVER STRAND BEACH

Location: Ocean Drive at Sawtelle Avenue in Oxnard
Parking/Fees: free parking lot
Hours: 24 hours
Facilities: lifeguards and restrooms
Contact: Oxnard Department of Parks and Facilities, 805/385-7950

7 CHANNEL ISLANDS HARBOR BEACH

Location: San Nicholas Street at Ocean Street in Oxnard
Parking/Fees: free street parking
Hours: 24 hours
Facilities: lifeguards and restrooms
Contact: Oxnard Department of Parks and Facilities, 805/385-7950

8 HOLLYWOOD BEACH

Location: 501 Ocean Drive in Oxnard
Parking/Fees: free parking lot
Hours: 24 hours
Facilities: lifeguards, restrooms, and showers
Contact: Oxnard Department of Parks and Facilities, 805/385-7950

9 OXNARD BEACH PARK

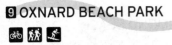

Location: Harbor Boulevard between Beach Way and Falkirk Avenue in Oxnard
Parking/Fees: $0.75 per hour or $4 per day
Hours: sunrise-sunset

Facilities: lifeguards, restrooms, and picnic tables
Contact: Oxnard Department of Parks and Facilities, 805/385-7950

10 MANDALAY BEACH COUNTY PARK

Location: end of Mandalay Beach Road in Oxnard
Parking/Fees: $0.75 per hour or $4 per day
Hours: sunrise-sunset
Facilities: none
Contact: Ventura County Department of Parks and Recreation, 805/654-3951

11 MCGRATH STATE BEACH

  BEST

Location: off Harbor Boulevard at Santa Clara River, between Oxnard and Ventura
Parking/Fees: $8 entrance fee per vehicle; camping fees $20-25 per night, plus $7.50 reservation fee
Hours: 8 A.M.-8 P.M.
Facilities: lifeguards, restrooms, showers, picnic tables, and barbecue grills
Contact: McGrath State Beach, 805/968-1033

ACCOMMODATIONS

There are less costly places to stay in Oxnard than the **Embassy Suites Mandalay Beach Resort** (2101 Mandalay Beach Road, 805/984-2500, $$$$), but none that are so close to the beach. It is directly on Mandalay Beach, and this is one good reason to stay here. It goes beyond Oxnard's wildest dreams of luxury, though at a budget-smashing price tag of $239 a night and up. It is constructed along the lines of a Spanish estate, with grottoes, fountains, gardens, and waterfalls. Buried among the manicured acreage is what is claimed to be the largest free-form swimming pool in Southern California, plus two tennis courts. Per the Embassy Suites norm, they throw in a full, cooked breakfast in the Surf Room each morning and drinks at night.

Similar comforts can be found in a less expensive harborside setting at the **Casa Sirena Hotel and Marina** (3605 Peninsula Road, 805/985-6311, www.casasirenahotel.com, $$), a three-story, 275-room resort. Tennis courts, exercise room, and patios and balconies overlooking the marina are a few of the amenities. There's also a fine restaurant, the Lobster Trap, on the premises.

COASTAL CUISINE

The best way to check out Oxnard's showpiece, Channel Islands Harbor, is from a restaurant window, especially toward sundown when the sailboats are returning to port. The waterside **Lobster Trap** (3605 Peninsula Road, 805/985-6361, $$) is on the extensive grounds of the Casa Sirena Hotel and Marina. Established in 1969, the Lobster Trap flies in live Maine lobsters almost daily. Even more appealing are local seafood specialties, such as crusted halibut.

Oxnard is otherwise largely choked with fast-food franchises. Consider the following to be our fair warning as to the dimensions of this culinary dead zone. Within the borders of Oxnard are 15 Subways, eight McDonald's, seven El Taco de Mexicos, four Jack in the Boxes… you get the idea. Oxnard and Ventura have 18 doughnut shops between them. That is in addition to countless nonfranchised *taquerias* and Chinese take-out joints. Something is rotten in the heart (not to mention stomach) of Oxnard, and we suggest the Surgeon General send in a SWAT team before the entire city requires bypass surgery.

Channel Islands

A string of eight pearl-like clusters that dot the horizon off California's Central Coast, the Channel Islands are part of a geological chain that includes Santa Catalina Island. Each of

the Channel Islands has a unique ecosystem kept in changeless isolation by protective ocean boundaries. Five of the islands (Anacapa, Santa Cruz, Santa Rosa, San Miguel, and Santa Barbara) and the nautical mile that surrounds each (125,000 acres of submerged marine habitat) make up Channel Islands National Park. The other three islands are San Nicolas, San Clemente, and Santa Catalina.

The five islands of the National Park are not nearly as accommodating as Catalina—at least not in the conventional sense. It takes careful planning to reach them. Visitors must arrange transportation to and from the islands, and they must have a burning desire to rough it at primitive campsites and on rugged trails. The islands do not lend themselves to quick look-sees. They require hardy souls (not to mention soles), as they can be windswept, forbidding places. On the other hand, a visit to any of them will reward you with memories to last a lifetime. We spent a day on Santa Cruz Island that was as warm and welcoming as it could possibly be.

The Channel Islands were originally inhabited by the Chumash tribe (*chumash* means "island people"), who ventured off-island in their sturdy *tomols* (canoes) to trade with other tribes on the mainland and harvest the rich marine life in the waters of the Santa Barbara Channel.

In 1542 Europeans began to arrive. The Spanish explorer Juan Rodríguez Cabrillo came first, wintering on San Miguel. He, in fact, died here—the result of a fall from a steep incline. (He was allegedly buried on San Miguel, but his grave has never been discovered.) By the early 1800s the Chumash were packed off to missions on the mainland, and Europeans used the islands for hunting, grazing sheep and cattle, and growing grapes for California's earliest wines. The Channel Islands have since served as defense installations, as well as living labs for scientific inquiries of the Darwinian kind. The islands were made part of the National Park System in 1980.

Because each island offers unique treasures,

ADVENTURING ON THE CHANNEL ISLANDS

Island Packers (1865 Spinnaker Drive, 805/642-1393), has been leading excursions to the Channel Islands for 40 years, and it has been the exclusive authorized vendor for this national park for as long as we've been coming to California. It's an efficient operation with an informed, pleasant crew, which includes an on-board naturalist. The company offers trips of varying types – kayaking, sightseeing, whale-watching, and camping – to all five of the park's Channel Islands. We opted for an all-day trip to Santa Cruz, the largest and most diverse island of the group.

If we had more time, we would have liked to put down tent stakes near Prisoner's Harbor – a camping area at mid-island among oak trees 1,500 feet above the ocean. Instead, we got dropped off at Scorpion Ranch, on the eastern end of the island. On the trip out to Santa Cruz Island, we saw numerous sea lions, some hanging out on the buoys, and learned that there are 140,000 sea lions in the Santa Barbara Channel. We also passed oil platforms, a reminder of the car culture we were happily leaving behind. Since the boat ride gets bumpy, we recommend bringing Dramamine or buying ginger snaps at the Island Packers office to avoid seasickness.

The eight isolated islands (five of which make up Channel Islands National Park) teem with biodiversity. They are pristine havens for more than 2,000 species of animals and plants, 145 of which are found nowhere else on earth. Just how pristine? Well, in 1970, when it was learned that DDT had been washing into the ocean and killing brown pelicans, only one chick survived on little Anacapa island. Through the banning of DDT and other legal measures, the endangered pelican was given a fighting chance. Today, there are 6,000 nesting pairs of brown pelicans on West Anacapa each year – the largest rookery on the Pacific Coast. The boundary of the park extends a mile out from each island underwater.

A genial park ranger lives on the island. As our skiff rumbled toward the rocky beach at Scorpion Cove, he jitterbugged over to offer a greeting and an orientation to Santa Cruz Island. He also explained the rules, which weren't terribly hard to follow: "You can go anywhere you want on the island. Just stay off the tops of the cliffs and be nice to the birds. They're friends of mine."

The island scrub jay, a species native to the Channel Islands, is particularly friendly, which has tempted some visitors to feed them. Please resist this temptation. There are also anywhere from 5,000 to 7,000 wild pigs on the island, as well as some island

and the logistics for reaching them differs, the five are described individually. Some general information, however, applies to all of them. First, the headquarters for Channel Islands National Park is on the harbor in Ventura. Even if you don't plan to visit the islands, a trip to park headquarters is worthwhile. The museum offers an excellent exhibit detailing the rich panoply of life offshore. You can also grab useful literature in the museum and shop. The best time to explore the islands is March–July, though they're open to visitation year-round.

Although you can arrange transportation to the islands with any licensed pilot, most people choose to book passage at **Island Packers** (1865 Spinnaker Drive, 805/642-1393), next door to park headquarters. As the official park concessionaire, they regularly schedule departures to and from the five islands and are well-versed in the ways of the land. Fares vary for travel to each island, as do schedules and trip duration. For instance, you can book full-day (7–8 hours), half-day (3.5 hours, no landing), or in-between (5–6 hours) trips to Anacapa Island, which is the closest to the mainland.

The only place to stay overnight on the islands is in a tent, and camping requires a foxes and wild horses. Santa Cruz Island is also home to one of the world's largest sea caves (Painted Cave), which is filled with bats. The bats, pigs, and foxes poke their snouts out only at night, so camping here will open a whole different world than a day trip.

The first thing you notice is the quietude. We took to the high trail. Either it's mislabeled "moderate" or we're losing our edge, because it's pretty tough slogging part of the way. The trail goes from sea level to an elevation of 1,200 feet in half a mile, but the climb is worth every ounce of energy expended, offering an amazing view for 30 miles in all directions. Bring food and water, but pack light. We took sardines, crackers, fruit, and bottled water and had a memorable lunch atop Santa Cruz Island, lolling afterwards in the sun like the sea lions in Santa Barbara Channel.

You can also explore the tidepools among the gigantic rocks at the south end of Scorpion Landing. Each ever-changing pool is a window into the teeming riches inhabiting the waters of these pristine islands. Watching the starfish, anemones, snails, and crabs scuttle, crawl, and wobble in the waves is a hypnotic way to pass an hour or two.

On the trip back, we saw a blue whale. The captain had seen him feeding earlier, so he headed in that direction, cut his engines and waited. After a while, the blue whale breached spectacularly about 400 yards ahead of the ship. We watched as he blew a few toots out his blowhole and then, *whoosh*, dove headfirst into the krill patch he had discovered (the largest blues consume six tons of krill a day). According to the captain, this was an unusually "friendly" blue whale. He was seemingly oblivious to our presence and not averse to swimming in our direction. Sure enough, when the whale breached a second time, he was less than a hundred yards from our ship. When he dove, he lifted his fluke high above the surface, "sounding" in order to give himself more speed on the dive.

The blue whale is the largest animal that's ever lived on our planet. Adults average 100 feet in length and weigh 400,000 pounds. At birth, they weigh 7,000 pounds! The blue whale's average life span is 70 years. Its heart is as big as a Volkswagen Bug and its tongue is larger than an entire elephant. On a less amusing note, it has been hunted to near extinction, and the only population that's been making any sort of comeback is the 2,000 or so that summer in the waters off the central California coast. We hit this one right at the start of their feeding cycle in the channel waters. We were lucky. And how.

permit from the National Park Service. A nightly fee of $15 is charged, and there is a camping area on each of the five islands. Reservations can be made at 877/444-6777 or www.recreation.gov. (Try reserving six months to a year ahead.) Just so you know, there are seven campsites on Anacapa, 40 on Santa Cruz (plus a new backcountry campground), 15 on Santa Rosa, seven on Santa Barbara, and nine on San Miguel. If you camp on any of the Channel Islands, you must bring fresh water, because there are no facilities (except for latrines). A park ranger is on-site in case of emergencies.

Anacapa: Actually three small islands in one, Anacapa is five miles long but covers only a single square mile of land. East Anacapa is 11 miles from Ventura, and the passage takes 75 minutes. Boats dock at Landing Cove, and the first hike a visitor takes is straight up—154 steps to the top of the bluff, where the land levels out. From here you can visit the Anacapa Island Lighthouse, which overlooks a rocky hangout of a healthy California sea lion population. You can also take the Loop Trail, a daunting 1.5-mile hike around the island whose highlights include sea caves, sea cliffs, and incredible bluff-top views. The terrain is rocky and the vegetation sparse on

Anacapa—there are no trees—and the winds can be fierce. There are no sandy beaches, either, but on calm days you can swim at Landing Cove and dive at Cathedral Cove along the north shore. There are seven tent sites on East Anacapa (with a total capacity of 30 people), and stays of up to 14 days are permitted. West Anacapa, the largest and westernmost of the three islets, is off-limits, being the primary nesting spot for the brown pelican. Middle Anacapa has a landing spot at East Fish Camp. The cost of a day trip to Anacapa, depending on the type and length of the trip, is $45 per adult ($58 if camping).

Santa Cruz: This is the largest of the Channel Islands. Santa Cruz Island is 24 miles long and occupies 96 square miles of land. It is also the most varied in terrain and the most blessed with sandy beaches among its 77 miles of shoreline. It's home to more than 650 plant species found among 10 distinct plant communities and 140 bird species. The western 76 percent of the island is owned by the Nature Conservancy, a few scattered property owners, and the Santa Cruz Island Preserve. Structures built by French settlers in the 1890s have been preserved, including a chapel, slaughterhouse, winery (but of course!), and barns. There's a 40-site campground at Scorpion Valley and a new backcountry campsite (Del Norte) 3.5 miles inland. The fare to Santa Cruz Island is $48 per adult ($64–60 if camping), and the crossing takes two hours. (Note: For more information on this particular island, contact the Nature Conservancy, Santa Cruz Island Project, 213 Stearns Wharf, Santa Barbara, CA 93101, 805/962-9111; or Santa Cruz Island Preserve, P.O. Box 23259, Santa Barbara, CA 93121, 805/962-9111.)

Santa Rosa: The second largest of the Channel Islands (15 miles long, 10 miles wide, occupying 53,000 acres), Santa Rosa is the best bet for overnight stays. It has great hiking trails, mountains, canyons, the largest marsh on the islands, and a varied shoreline with sandy beaches on which harbor seals breed. Bird-watchers, kayakers, hikers, pho-

tographers, beachcombers, and rare-animal spotters (the Channel Island fox and spotted skunk are endemic to Santa Rosa) all love this island. It's also home to a rare stand of Torrey pines. There are only 15 campsites, so reserve a site at least one year in advance. Boat trips take 3.5 hours each way ($65 per adult, $90 if camping). Camping on Santa Rosa's beaches is allowed for "experienced kayakers and boaters on a seasonal basis."

San Miguel: The farthest island from the mainland, San Miguel might be the most fascinating of the bunch. It is certainly the most primitive. The middle of the five islands in terms of size (eight miles long, five miles wide), it is whipped by ferocious winds that sculpt the sand into natural monoliths, a form of mineral sand-casting known as "caliche forests." A 15-mile hiking trail cuts through a raw landscape rounded by the wind from the beach at the landing all the way to Point Bennett at the western tip. En route, you can spot seals and sea lions on the beach (upwards of 30,000 have been counted in the summer), rare birds, and ground vegetation. Historians visit the island for its 500 archeological sites and the possibility of stumbling over Cabrillo's skeleton. Boat trips take upward of four hours each way ($75 per adult, $108 if camping)—and, to our thinking, there is no reason to come all the way out here if you are not camping. There are nine tent sites with a total capacity of 30 people.

Santa Barbara: The smallest of the Channel Islands (640 acres) lies the farthest south, necessitating a three-hour boat ride ($60 per adult, $90 if camping). A visit to Santa Barbara Island demands an overnight stay to take advantage of the 5.5 miles of hiking trails. It's a particularly rewarding perch for bird-watchers, while snorkelers are often joined by playful seals. There are no shade trees and only eight primitive campsites on the island.

For more information, contact Channel Islands National Park, 1901 Spinnaker Drive, Ventura, CA 93001, 805/658-5730, www.nps .gov/chis. For boat-trip reservations, contact

Island Packers, 1867 Spinnaker Drive, Ventura, CA 93001, 805/642-1393, www.islandpackers.com. For camping reservations, contact the National Recreation Reservation Services, 877/444-6777, www.recreation.gov.

Ventura

The full, legal, incorporated name of Ventura is San Buenaventura—a title officially bestowed in 1866—which is Spanish for "City of Good Fortune." Indeed, Ventura (population 108,000) does possess the good fortune of not being anywhere near Los Angeles, from which it is separated by the Santa Monica Mountains and a one-hour freeway ride (assuming no traffic delays). Ventura is separated from Oxnard by the dry bed of the Santa Clara River, and in some ways, the two towns bear a family resemblance. Both are twin peas in the fertile pod of Ventura County and have beautiful, uncrowded beaches and breezy harbor areas. However, as far as history, charm, and personality are concerned, Ventura shines more brightly than its neighbor.

The name San Buenaventura derives from the Catholic mission established here in 1782 by Father Junipero Serra. The original mission, chapel, and grounds have all been beautifully restored and maintained, as has the downtown Old Historic District that surrounds it. The **San Buenaventura Mission** (211 East Main Street, 805/643-4318) is open for tours 10 A.M.–5 P.M. daily. The entire town has internalized the lesson that historic preservation is a key to self-preservation. Other historic buildings open for touring include a pair of adobes, the **Ortega Adobe** (215 West Main Street, 805/648-5823) and the **Olivas Adobe** (4200 Olivas Park Drive, 805/644-4346). Ortega is typical of the adobes that were found along Main Street in the 1800s, and from here in 1897 the "Pioneer Ortega Chili" business was launched. The Olivas Adobe is a two-story hacienda built around 1849 and run today as a historical park by the city of Ventura. Both are open daily, and are free of charge to tour.

Next door to the San Buenaventura Mission is the **Albinger Archaeological Museum,** which houses artifacts spanning 3,500 years and five native cultures: Native American, Spanish, Mexican, Chinese, and American. Drop by **San Buenaventura City Hall** (501 North Poli Street, 805/654-7837) or the **Museum of Ventura County** (89 South California Street, 805/653-0323) to pick up a walking tour guidebook of these and other historic attractions. The museum is in a temporary storefront location while its permanent home (at 100 East Main Street) is renovated and expanded. City Hall, built in 1914 of simulated white marble, is an impressive piece of architecture in its own right. Even Ventura's post office is worth a look. Three blocks from City Hall on Santa Clara Street, the post office houses a fascinating mural painted by Works Progress Administration artist Gordon Grant, who spent most of 1936 and 1937 working on this tribute to the heroism of the common laborer and farmer.

Certainly, Ventura offers enough in the way of history, archeology, and architecture to keep anybody busy for a few days. But there's more for the educated browser as well: bookstores—five of them in a two-block radius! Among them is the cooperative **Book Mall of Ventura** (105 South Oak Street, 805/641-2665), a 15-dealer bonanza of used, rare, and out-of-print books. Main Street Ventura is also stocked with art and antique stores, as well as a disproportionate number of thrift shops, which is bound to please that intrepid soul in search of the perfect bowling shirt. Then there's downtown Ventura's abundance of coffeehouses. They can be found all along California and Main Streets.

In all respects Ventura operates at a more civilized and leisurely pace than the Southern California norm. You begin to sense a real break between the Southern and Central California sensibilities. Ventura has got aspects of both: the compulsive physicality and cutting-edge

"DON'T DO ANYTHING RATIONAL"

One beautiful morning while jogging up to Surfers' Point in Ventura, we came upon a seventy-something character seated on riprap alongside the dry mouth of the Ventura River. He sported a floppy tennis hat, snow-white beard, and rueful expression. We decided to make his acquaintance, asking about the chewed-up condition of the path beside the ocean.

A big winter storm took it out a decade or so ago, he said, and the only person who tried to remedy the situation, by depositing some rocks without official approval, was put in jail. The salty dog chuckled bitterly and let loose with a series of nasty invectives in the general direction of local politicians, developers, and the California Coastal Commission.

He grew up a half mile from where he was sitting, and he still lives in his family's house. He played on the sand at Emma Wood State Beach, long before the sand washed away. He fondly recalled that beach when it had curvaceous dunes among which were housed World War II–era gun emplacements to fend off an anticipated Japanese land invasion. Now he worries over other invasions that have occurred since what he described as a bucolic childhood: developers, yuppies, greedy rich people, immigrants, SUVs, and the government.

"I've seen too much change in Ventura," he said. "And all of it is horrible."

At that point, one of his boyhood friends joined us.

"Yes," he agreed, gently ribbing his curmudgeonly pal. "And you are talking to one of the horrible changes right here, gentlemen."

But then, they both bemoaned the fact that developers have bought up all the farmland hereabouts. This happened when the state began taxing farmers at the same rate as residential developments, which is to say their farmland was taxed at its "potential" value as real estate.

"What could be more valuable than this farmland?" one mournfully asked. "It's some of the most fertile in the world."

No disagreement from us.

Next they worried over the distant hills behind Ventura, an uncluttered backdrop that gives the city its out-of-the-way feel. "What's going to happen when they start building up in the hills?" wondered the old guy, warming up to the subject. "All of that shit is going to just run downhill right into the ocean."

We agreed with them that most developers should be sent to prison or banished to a distant island. They added that there were simply too many people in the world. Again, we agreed. We felt like we were talking to older versions of ourselves.

Eventually the salty dog got up and limped back out to the walking trail, continuing his wobbly morning workout. Over his shoulder he said, "Have a good rest of the day. Don't do anything rational."

cultural preoccupations of the Southland, and the less-harried and somewhat provincial outlook of the Central Coast. It was on the streets of Ventura, for instance, that we saw our first real cowboy, a strapping fellow swathed in denim and crowned with a cowboy hat who politely asked us for spare change.

Ventura admittedly faces growth issues, as ever-more escapees from Los Angeles flee their crisis-ridden city, opting to commute from or retire to Ventura County. Much of the growth has been absorbed by Oxnard, which has swelled like a goiter along the U.S. 101 corridor. This buffer has thus far tempered the impact of Los Angelization upon Ventura. Its streets are still clean. The air itself is more breathable. You don't have to keep your guard up quite so reflexively.

Ventura is trying to decide which of its identities will best attract new visitors and vacationers. Among the nifty options offered to visitors are:

- **Ventura River Trail,** a bike/hike path that follows an old railroad right of way for over six miles along a newly restored river estuary
- **"Fun and Free By the Sea,"** an annotated list of "48 free things to do in Ventura in 48 hours"
- **Historic walking tours** through the "old town" area that include "Murder Most Foul," "Lost Adobes of Main Street," "Victorian Ventura," and "Erle Stanley Gardner's Ventura" (based on the author and native son's travels around the county)
- A diverse array of museums, everything from the **Oil Museum** to the (whoa, dude!) **Skatelab Skateboarding Museum & Park**

The brightest news in the first decade of the twenty-first century was the 2002 opening of California State University Channel Islands, the first four-year public university in Ventura County. We could imagine far worse ways to pass four years than to study environmental science and resource management in these old Spanish Revival buildings a mere three miles from the Pacific Ocean. By 2025, CSU Channel Islands projects it will have 15,000 full-time students.

If downtown Ventura is the heart of its history and culture, then **Ventura Pier and Promenade** are its recreational centerpieces. On weekends, craftspeople and vendors peddle their wares, and in-line skaters and cyclists pedal their wheels. The wide concrete promenade extends past Surfers' Point, with benches placed at intervals for restful contemplation of the ocean. At 1,200 feet the Ventura Pier is the longest wooden pier in California. It dates back to 1872, when San Buenaventura was a busy harbor into which steamships would come and go bearing cargoes of lumber, oil, and farm products. Between the pier and the harbor lies sandy San Buenaventura State Beach. Just north of the harbor, at the end of Seaward Avenue, is a bustling little neighborhood with a "California beach town" feel to it. On the east end of Ventura's oceanfront is Ventura Harbor, which comes with the obligatory "seaside village" of shops and restaurants. Refreshingly, this one is Spanish in character, with piped-roof, mission-style architecture providing a sharp contrast to the clichéd New England fishing village motif found elsewhere on the coast.

Ventura's beachfront parks attract all kinds of people. On a summer Sunday we saw a gaggle of surf punks cussing like troopers; a family wheezing along on a tandem bike as the kids urged their huffing and puffing dad to pedal faster; a counterculture minstrel curled up at the base of a tree, strumming a guitar; and elderly couples serenely surveying the ocean from park benches. It's always nice to see a representative cross-section of humanity enjoying a day at the beach in their own ways.

For more information, contact the Ventura Visitor and Convention Bureau, 89-C South California Street, Ventura, CA 93001, 805/648-2075, www.ventura.usa.com.

BEACHES

The city of Ventura has some fine beaches within its borders, from Ventura Harbor up to the county fairgrounds at the north end. **San Buenaventura State Beach** is a formidable two-mile beach possessing good width and a bit of dune structure. Plenty of parking is available in lots and on the street. Crowds don't seem to be a problem. On one gorgeous summer weekend several years back, even with a hefty contingent of bikers on hand for a charity road race, plenty of spaces were available. This long beach is good for swimming and sunbathing.

North of the pier, **Promenade Park** runs along a narrow, rocky, and highly eroded oceanfront. The most inviting feature of this park is the promenade itself, which connects the pier with **Surfers' Point.** At the end of California Street ("C Street" to the locals) at Seaside Wilderness Park, Surfers' Point sits near the mouth of the Ventura River. As the name suggests, surfers take advantage of the city-run park facilities and free parking. (Pay parking is available nearby for those not lucky enough to snag a spot.)

The point gets wrapped with winter swells from the north, with a healthy helping of distant storm-generated "juice" pushing the surf up to 20 feet on the outside break. In conditions like these, Surfers' Point is not for neophytes or the faint of heart. And don't come here to swim, as there is no beach, just moss-covered rocks. The California Coastal Commission has been hoping that the severely narrowed beach will regenerate naturally, and its inaction has rankled some locals.

There are also small beaches on the peninsulas that flank Ventura Harbor. **Marina Park,** on the north side of the harbor, is a playland of boat docks, volleyball and basketball courts, a fishing pier, and picnic area. Protected by jetties, **Harbor Cove Beach** is considered the safest in the area for kiddies, including the added incentives of a child's play area and big picnic lawn. **Surfers' Knoll** faces the ocean's waves from the opposite side of Spinnaker Drive.

12 SURFERS' KNOLL

Location: west end of Spinnaker Drive, on the ocean side of road, in Ventura
Parking/Fees: free parking lot
Hours: 24 hours
Facilities: restrooms
Contact: Ventura City Department of Parks and Recreation, 805/652-4550

13 HARBOR COVE BEACH

Location: west end of Spinnaker Drive, across the harbor from Marina Park, in Ventura
Parking/Fees: free parking lot
Hours: 24 hours
Facilities: restrooms
Contact: Ventura City Department of Parks and Recreation, 805/652-4550

14 MARINA PARK

Location: south end of Pierpont Boulevard in Ventura
Parking/Fees: free parking lot
Hours: 24 hours
Facilities: restrooms and picnic tables
Contact: Ventura City Department of Parks and Recreation, 805/652-4550

15 SAN BUENAVENTURA STATE BEACH

Location: San Pedro Street at Pierpont Boulevard in Ventura
Parking/Fees: $8 entrance fee per vehicle, or metered street parking
Hours: 24 hours
Facilities: concession, lifeguards, restrooms, showers, and picnic tables
Contact: Channel Coast District of the California State Parks, Gaviota Sector, 805/968-1033

16 PROMENADE PARK

Location: Ventura Pier to Surfers' Point in Ventura
Parking/Fees: free parking lot
Hours: 24 hours
Facilities: concession, restrooms, and picnic tables
Contact: Ventura City Department of Parks and Recreation, 805/652-4550

17 SURFERS' POINT

Location: Figueroa Street and Promenade at Seaside Park in Ventura

Parking/Fees: free parking lot and nearby pay parking lot ($1 per hour or $5 all day)
Hours: 24 hours
Facilities: restrooms and showers
Contact: Ventura City Department of Parks and Recreation, 805/652-4550

RECREATION AND ATTRACTIONS

- **Bike/Skate Rentals:** Cycles 4 Rent, 239 West Main Street, Ventura, 805/652-0462
- **Boat Cruise:** Pacific Sailing, 1967 Spinnaker Drive, Dock D-10, Ventura, 805/658-6508
- **Dive Shop:** Ventura Dive 'n' Sport, 1559 Spinnaker Drive, Suite 108, Ventura Harbor Village, Ventura, 805/650-6500
- **Ecotourism:** Channel Islands National Park, 1901 Spinnaker Drive, Ventura, 805/658-5730
- **Marina:** Ventura Harbor, 1583 Spinnaker Drive, Ventura, 805/642-8538
- **Pier:** Ventura Pier, 668 Harbor Boulevard, Ventura
- **Rainy Day Attraction:** San Buenaventura Mission, 211 East Main Street, Ventura, 805/643-4318
- **Shopping/Browsing:** Ventura Harbor Village, Spinnaker Drive, Ventura, 805/644-0169
- **Sportfishing:** Harbor Village Sportfishing, 1449 Spinnaker Drive, Ventura, 805/658-1060
- **Surf Shop:** Waveline Ventura, 154 East Thompson Boulevard, Ventura, 805/652-2201
- **Vacation Rentals:** Harbor Realty, 1106 South Seaward Avenue, Ventura, 805/648-3068

ACCOMMODATIONS

The place to stay in Ventura for the beach-obsessed is the **Crowne Plaza Ventura Beach** (450 East Harbor Boulevard, 805/648-2100, $$$). This 10-story tower offers the best views of and closest proximity to the beach, beside Ventura Pier and U.S. 101. You couldn't ask for a better location, and the rooms take full advantage of this with balconies that overlook the water. It's a high-rise hotel, but the prices are reasonable ($160 and up a night) for California oceanfront standards, especially compared with what you'd shell out for similar digs in Los Angeles County. One caveat: It's a contest between nearby U.S. 101 and passing trains (at 5 A.M.!) as to which noise source will most interrupt your sleep. The hotel offers earplugs to drown out the disturbances.

A modest notch down in location—and a modest step up in amenities—is the **Marriott Ventura Beach** (2055 East Harbor Boulevard, 805/643-6000, $$$). A block from the south end of San Buenaventura State Beach in a neighborhood removed from the downtown bustle, the rooms at this former Doubletree Hotel are spacious and well appointed, and a huge pool and hot tub are the attractive centerpieces of the interior courtyard. Just about any need can be met on the premises, from a drink at the Borneo Bar to a meal at the Gallery Restaurant.

Another respectable choice is the venerable **Pierpont Inn** (550 San Jon Road, 805/643-6144 or 800/285-4667, $$), on seven beautifully landscaped acres atop a bluff overlooking Pierpont Bay. Built in 1908 and operated by the same family since 1928, the Pierpont Inn has east and west wings, plus the Bluff House, an eight-room building perched on the bluff directly overlooking the ocean, and two private cottages. Garden-view rooms go for $145–195 and suites go for $195–250. The inn's 77 rooms include working fireplaces for those nights when the cold westerly winds blow off the ocean. The grounds are thick with flowers, and a path runs down the hill and under the freeway to the beach. A local landmark, the Pierpont attracts a faithful clientele.

Inn on the Beach (1175 South Seaward Avenue, 805/652-2000, www.innonthebeachventura.com, $$) is moderately upscale with 24 Victorian-style guest rooms decorated with

VENTURA COAST

French/Italian antiques and patios or balconies that overlook the ocean. At the south end of Seaward Avenue, it's just feet from the beach.

Finally, if you're traveling on a budget, the **Vagabond Inn** (756 East Thompson Boulevard, 805/648-5371, 800/522-1555, $) is clean, comfortable, and close enough to the action to have a footbridge to the beach and pier.

COASTAL CUISINE

If it's really, really fresh seafood you want—so fresh it hasn't even been cooked—step up to **Sushi Marina** (120 South California Street, 805/643-5200, $$). It's the most swinging sushi bar this side of Hermosa Beach. When we ate there it stayed packed till its 10 P.M. closing with a young crowd of raw-fish addicts. Sushi Marina serves some of the finest and freshest sushi we've had on the coast. The sushi dinner consists of six pieces each of California and tuna roll, plus half a dozen assorted sushi items, including such personal favorites as bonito, the roast beef of the sea. Sushi Marina has plenty of cooked selections, including teriyaki and sukiyaki, as well.

Out on Ventura Pier is a seafood restaurant where those without poles can still land a big fish. **Eric Ericsson's on the Pier** (668 Harbor Boulevard, 805/643-4783, $$$) grills some of the most bodacious fish fillets in Ventura. A refrigerated case filled with long, gigantic slabs of fish at their rainbow-hued finest—glistening crimson ahi, meaty white halibut, bright orange salmon—catches your eye as you enter. Another good view, onto Ventura Pier and the surrounding beach, awaits guests in the glassed-in dining room. Any number of fish specials—orange roughy, swordfish, halibut, salmon, ahi tuna, Pacific red snapper, mahimahi—are listed daily. Entrée prices average around $20, which includes chowder or salad, rice or potato, and vegetable. This is, you may notice, a full dinner. You are now on the Central Coast, which means that tab-inflating à la carte charges have, for the most part, been left behind, along with smog and traffic, in Los Angeles County. However, the large number of fried items at Eric Ericsson's

is a tip-off that you've dropped a notch into another culinary zone. Our advice: Stick to the fresh fish and seafood specials.

For lunch, try **Franky's Place** (456 East Main Street, 805/648-6282, $), especially if you're poking around Ventura's Old Historic District. The booths are separated by pieces of sculpture set on pedestals, and the red-brick walls are covered with original oil paintings. The quality of the food matches that of the art—and it's healthy, to boot. Serving natural foods with a vegetarian emphasis, Franky's offers pita and croissant sandwiches, heaping salads, and great homemade soups.

Ventura Harbor has an unusually vibrant scene of its own, above and beyond the amenities on hand for the boating set. A boardwalk affords strollers a pleasant way to fantasy-window-shop for yachts. It also offers more reality-based shops, a cute little play arcade (featuring Skee-Ball, our favorite waste of time at the beach), friendly pubs, and open-air waterside eateries. We hooked an invigorating lunch at **The Greek at the Harbor** (1583 Spinnaker Drive, Suite 101, 805/650-5350, $$$), which has a magazine-sized menu of Greek staples (as well as belly dancing most nights and dancing waiters on weekends). The Aphrodite salad (jumbo shrimp, tomatoes, avocado, mushrooms, artichokes) was tasty and filling, and the golden calamari hit the spot. The Greek's musical soundtrack gave the scene a pleasant Mediterranean air.

NIGHTLIFE

Away from Southern California, the term "nightlife" generally takes on a less lustrous glow. Yet while downtown Ventura is no Sunset Boulevard in the party-down department, it's not entirely bereft of good times after dark. The restored **Majestic Ventura Theater** (26 South Chestnut Street, 805/653-0721) books a steady stream of middling popular national acts, heavily tilted toward punk and metal, indie rock and world music (e.g., the Deftones, Rancid, Yellowman, the Hives).

VENTURA COAST

On the bar/club scene, we were pointed to a number of places, which we dutifully checked out. Our first stop was **Bombay Bar & Grill** (143 South California Street, 805/643-4404), where you might shake thy booty to loud rock and hip-hop records spun by a dude with a handle like DJ Pleazure. We passed.

Blues, swing, and novelty acts like the Man-eaters and the Atomic Dogs are the fare served at **Nicholby's** (404 East Main Street, 805/653-2320), which has been voted "Ventura's #1 nightclub." Also popular is **Karma Lounge** (281 West Main Street, 805/641-9090), where a hair metal band called Steel Panther was wowing them on our last visit. For a mellower vibe, try the courtyard setting of **Zoey's** (451 East Main Street, 805/652-1137), which has mostly acoustic acts, some of national renown, as well as blues and bluegrass.

There are a baker's dozen coffee houses in Ventura, including three Starbucks, where one can have a civilized good time in less hysterical surroundings. Several are clustered downtown on or near Main Street, including the **Busy Bee** (478 East Main Street, 805/644-4864), **Cafe Bella** (79 South California Street, 805/643-2171), and **Bagel Rock Cafe** (2781 East Main Street, 805/648-7625). And how can you not like a java joint called **Bad Ass Coffee Company** (204 East Thompson Boulevard, 805/643-6700)?

Emma Wood State Beach

Emma Wood State Beach is attached to the north end of Ventura where U.S. 101 meets Old Rincon Highway. Emma Wood has campsites directly on the beach. The southern section of the park—designated Emma Wood **Group Camp** and located at the end of Main Street in Ventura—has four group sites for tent campers that can accommodate up to 30 persons each, plus an RV group site for up to 50 RVs. If you plan on coming, especially during the warmer months, a prior reservation through ReserveAmerica (800/444-7275) is an absolute necessity.

The **North Beach** section of the park has roughly 75 campsites along a threatened beach at which waves lap hungrily at a concrete seawall. It looks as if the campsites could easily be inundated by a big wave. Still, the place is often full because rarely does one get to sleep this close to the ocean. Plus, there's good surfing and fishing. Anglers cast for perch, cabezon, and corvina. At low tide, kids and amateur biologists study the marine life in the tidepools. Bird-watchers find grebes, cormorants, curlews, willets, sandpipers, pelicans, and even a few songbirds and red-tailed hawks in the marsh at the southwest end of the beach.

The beach and campground are fascinating objects of study in and of themselves, as both appear imminently threatened by the ocean's merciless advance upon them. Huge chunks have been chewed out of the seawall, and tree-sized drift logs have been hurled like toothpicks onto the beach. A ranger detailed all of the expensive fixes that have had to be done just to keep the place operative. We found ourselves wondering not if but when the state would have to cut its losses and forfeit Emma Wood State Beach to the elements.

BEACHES

18 GROUP CAMP

Location: along the Pacific Coast Highway, three miles north of Ventura
Parking/Fees: $8 entrance fee per vehicle; camping fees $20 per night, plus $7.50 reservation fee
Hours: 8 A.M.-11 P.M.
Facilities: restrooms, showers, and picnic tables
Contact: Emma Wood State Beach, Group Camp, 805/648-4610

VENTURA COAST

19 NORTH BEACH

Location: along the Pacific Coast Highway, three miles north of Ventura
Parking/Fees: $8 entrance fee per vehicle; camping fees $20 per night, plus $7.50 reservation fee
Hours: 8 A.M.-11 P.M.
Facilities: lifeguards, restrooms, showers, and picnic tables
Contact: Emma Wood State Beach, North Beach, 805/648-4807

Solimar Beach

At the south end of this tiny community, two miles north of Emma Wood State Beach along Rincon Parkway (a.k.a. Old Pacific Coast Highway), glimpses of "Old California" can be seen. Empty cars line the shoulder of the highway beside a mile-long seawall, their owners straddling surfboards in the frothing ocean. There's no day-use fee, nor is there an official coastal access, because at the north end of the seawall lies the private "beach colony" of **Solimar Beach.** The not-so-pacific ocean waters beat relentlessly against the seawall and the thinning beach, leading one to suspect that this is an inevitably doomed stretch of road—not unlike patches of Old Pacific Coast Highway south of here that now rest in the big drink. Meanwhile, surfers paddle out to Solimar Reef, about 300 yards offshore, which provides a six-foot swell in winter.

BEACHES

20 SOLIMAR BEACH

Location: five miles north of Ventura, along Rincon Parkway/Old Pacific Coast Highway, in Solimar
Parking/Fees: free roadside parking
Hours: sunrise-sunset

Facilities: none
Contact: none

Faria Beach

This minute town just north of Solimar Beach on Rincon Parkway/Old Pacific Coast Highway consists of a string of 30 residences facing the hungry ocean. The ocean's waves break directly on the cement wall upon which these doomed structures foolishly sit.

Faria Beach County Park offers 42 campsites in a dirt lot above the boulders that vainly hold back the ocean's encroachment. Faria (pronounced "fa-REE-ya") is a popular beach campground. Again, the access is almost too good. The nightly camping fee of $30 seems steep for what you get: a strip of sun-baked asphalt on a wave-rocked perch with no sand to stroll on. At the north end, the litter can get as thick as a town dump. On our latest visit, the pile of debris blowing about was a foul and shameful sight. This was despite the presence of a graffiti-festooned dumpster for trash disposal. Worse, a lot of non-camping ne'er-do-well youths looked to be engaged in some sort of *Porky's*-style weekend party antics. In all respects, the scene at Faria Beach is not our idea of a good time at the beach.

Surfers pay for day use to try their luck off Pitas Point. They make the strenuous hike up to the point with their boards. The "outside" break is for experienced hands, the "inside" for beginners. Sea kayakers were spied paddling around. But be forewarned: There are no lifeguards and there is no swimming, because there is no beach.

BEACHES

21 FARIA BEACH COUNTY PARK

Location: State Beach exit from U.S. 101 north of Ventura and follow the Rincon Parkway/Old Pacific Coast Highway into Faria Beach

© PARKE PUTERBAUGH

Faria Beach

Parking/Fees: $4 entrance fee per vehicle; camping fees $45 per night with hookups, $30 per night without hookups
Hours: sunrise-sunset
Facilities: restrooms, showers, and picnic tables
Contact: Ventura County Department of Parks and Recreation, 805/654-3951

Seacliff

Rincon Highway passes through Seacliff, yet another private "beach colony." Public access is at **Hobson County Park,** which has a small, 31-site campground and picnic facilities. RVs are jammed so close together that privacy seems impossible. SUVs park at crazy angles, making it hard to negotiate the oval drive through the park. (The world, in our view, was not created with SUVs in mind.) Generators whir, kids shout, and music blares, but the campers seem blissfully unaware of these seeming annoyances. Beach erosion is severe here, and the park actually closes during heavy storms. In fact, Hobson looks to us to be one good meteorological jolt away from permanent closure. The reef here makes

for good tidepool exploration at low tide, but swimming is out of the question.

The surfing is good at Seacliff, but it's a half-mile swim out to Seacliff Reef. Between Seacliff and Faria, **Rincon Parkway North** serves as a linear campground for RVs, which are allowed to pull over for the night for a modest charge. It's a bumper-to-bumper refugee camp of RVs—it's claimed there are 127 spaces, but it looked like more to us—squeezed onto a narrow shoulder of asphalt mere feet from highway traffic and overlooking an unusable, inaccessible beach. Pressed between traffic and a seawall, this is not beach camping at its most idyllic. Some folks just sit in chaise lounges and hang fishing poles over the seawall. Whatever floats your boat.

BEACHES

22 RINCON PARKWAY NORTH

Location: Seacliff exit from U.S. 101 north of Ventura to Rincon Parkway/Old Pacific Coast Highway north between Faria and Hobson

VENTURA COAST

NOLLAN V. CALIFORNIA COASTAL COMMISSION

James Nollan, a Ventura County landowner, made national headlines in 1987 by taking his property-rights case to the U.S. Supreme Court and winning. The verdict in the case of Nollan v. California Coastal Commission was seen as a victory for developers and property owners, and as a setback for the commission by restricting one of its key strategies for providing more public beach access.

The site that ignited the legal imbroglio was a 3,600-square-foot beachfront lot in Faria Beach in rural northern Ventura County. On it sat a decrepit beach cottage owned by James and Marilyn Nollan. In 1982 the couple applied for permits to raze and replace it with a two-story beach bungalow. The California Coastal Commission (CCC), empowered to grant or deny permits for development along the ocean, had routinely demanded public easements of landowners. In exchange for a permit, the CCC required the Nollans to grant a right of public access along a lateral strip of beach between the high-tide line and a seawall on their property. The area in question was 10 feet wide and ran the length of their property. The CCC wanted to make it easier for the public to pass between a public beach a quarter mile north of the Nollans' property and another that lay one-third mile south.

Under California law, the public owns the shoreline up to but not above the mean high-tide line. That is to say, you can legally walk along the part of the beach that is always or occasionally inundated by waves, but not above it. The dry-sand part of the beach can be privately owned, and crossing it without prior permission is an act of trespass, if the landowner is so inclined. The CCC, in accordance with its mission to protect the state's coastline "as a natural resource belonging to all people," had for years imposed public-access dedication requirements upon permit-seeking property owners as a means of increasing public access to the beaches. Such conditions had been imposed upon 1,817 property owners through the end of 1984. Then came Nollan.

In Ventura County Superior Court, the Nollans challenged the CCC-issued development permit with the contested condition. After the Nollans won their case, the CCC appealed. The California State Court of Appeal reversed the earlier decision.

Parking/Fees: free roadside parking; camping fee $25 per night
Hours: 24 hours
Facilities: none
Contact: Ventura County Department of Parks and Recreation, 805/654-3951

23 HOBSON COUNTY PARK

Location: Seacliff exit from U.S. 101 north of Ventura to Rincon Parkway/Old Pacific Coast Highway, follow north to Hobson
Parking/Fees: $4 entrance fee per vehicle; camping fees $45 per night with hookups, $30 per night without hookups

Hours: sunrise–sunset
Facilities: concession, restrooms, and showers
Contact: Ventura County Department of Parks and Recreation, 805/654-3951

Oil Piers Beach

Among the more fascinating and eerie spectacles along the California coast are these four privately owned piers belonging to oil companies whose platforms you see on the offshore horizon. The longest pier leads to a man-made island, gussied up like a tropical paradise to disguise the oil-drilling pumps.

Oil Piers Beach stretches south and north of the largest pier and provides some of the best

Supported by the conservative Pacific Legal Foundation, the Nollans appealed to the U.S. Supreme Court, arguing that under the terms of the Fifth Amendment of the U.S. Constitution the CCC's demands for an easement constituted an unwarranted "taking" of private property. The clause in question comes at the end of the Fifth Amendment: " . . . nor shall private property be taken for public use without just compensation."

On June 26, 1987, in the last ruling handed down in the 1986-1987 term, the Supreme Court held in favor of the Nollans. By a vote of 5-4, with Justice Antonin Scalia writing the majority opinion, the court ruled that granting public access to private property without compensation must be tied to a specific, justifiable public purpose. A condition placed on development, such as a grant of public easement, fails to pass the test of constitutionality if it "utterly fails to further the end advanced as the justification for the prohibition," said Scalia. In simpler language, if the CCC "wants an easement across the Nollans' property, it must pay for it."

The decision was a pivotal one in the area of private-property rights, pursued with vigor by the Rehnquist court with Justice Scalia at the forefront. Dissenting justices mustered strong arguments of their own, but the tilt of the conservative court opposed government limitations on private property development. The decision forced the CCC to reconsider its methods – which may have been more commendable in principle than constitutional in reality.

In the intervening years the Nollan case has turned out to have less severe impact on government regulation than some had initially feared. Even the CCC tried to put a positive spin on the Supreme Court verdict. Its executive director claimed, "We're pleased the courts explicitly upheld the right of local and state governments to require public access and dedication as long as they can show a direct relationship between the project and the conditions."

As for the Nollans, it was all more a matter of principle than practice. They had been allowing people to cross their property for years and said they would continue to do so, even after the court decision. "As long as the people are not obnoxious, we would give them permission to walk back and forth," said Mr. Nollan.

Case closed.

---

surfing in California. (In fact, that's the only action these beaches attract.) It's something of a rite of passage to surf in the shadows of such industrial might. For those curious to catch a glimpse of this spectacle, park alongside Rincon Parkway/Old Pacific Coast Highway and poke your nose over the crest of the hill.

BEACHES

24 OIL PIERS BEACH

Location: along Rincon Parkway/Old Pacific Coast Highway at the north end of Seacliff
Parking/Fees: free roadside parking

Hours: sunrise-sunset
Facilities: none
Contact: none

Mussel Shoals

Unlike the residential "colonies" to the south, Mussel Shoals is an actual town that sits on either side of the Pacific Coast Highway between Oil Piers Beach and the Santa Barbara County line. It's a threatened setting, with the surf literally rumbling the earth below one's feet. Abandoned segments of Old Pacific Coast Highway can be seen here, affording a sobering glimpse of what lies ahead for coastal planners.

BEACHES

North of **Mussel Shoals Beach** lies La Conchita Point, where the surf breaks close to the pier and onshore rocks. Needless to say, this one is for fearless experts only. The sight of someone taking a wave here is, like kung fu fighting, both exciting and a little frightening. North of the point is **La Conchita Beach**, which can be reached off the U.S. 101 shoulder via a riprap revetment. Plenty of surfers park beside the highway between La Conchita and Rincon Point and lug their boards down to the beach. For everyone else, it's just not worth the trouble.

25 MUSSEL SHOALS BEACH

Location: 11 miles northwest of Ventura on U.S. 101 in Mussel Shoals
Parking/Fees: limited free street parking
Hours: sunrise-sunset
Facilities: none
Contact: Ventura County Department of Parks and Recreation, 805/654-3951

26 LA CONCHITA BEACH

Location: north of Mussel Shoals on U.S. 101 at La Conchita
Parking/Fees: limited free roadside parking
Hours: sunrise-sunset
Facilities: none
Contact: Ventura County Department of Parks and Recreation, 805/654-3951

ACCOMMODATIONS

For those who relish out-of-the-way overnight destinations, Mussel Shoals has a funky inn perched above the ocean. The name of this surfside haven is **Cliff House** (6602 West Pacific Coast Highway, 805/652-1381 or 800/892-5433, $$$). At $150–250 per night, the rates are on the high side for surfers on safari but affordable for venturesome city sorts looking to make a romantic getaway. Crash here and you'll be lulled to sleep by waves that break against a seawall at the end of a grassy backyard festooned with tropical plants. There's a pool and ping-pong table out back and a restaurant (The Shoals) on-site.

SANTA BARBARA COAST

If you took all the finest ingredients that go into making a great beach—sand, sun, surf, and scenery, along with good dining and lodging options near the water—and tossed them in a big pot filled with kelp and salt water, you'd have the recipe for the Santa Barbara Coast. Even factoring in such negatives as offshore oil platforms, this area has been graced with an abundance of coastline to crow about and recreate upon. With the exceptions of an area around Point Conception (private ranchland) and Vandenberg Air Force Base (military installation), the 140-mile Santa Barbara Coast is remarkably accommodating. For that matter, even Vandenberg AFB is hospitable in its own way, allowing anglers with a permit to toss a line from its shore.

In terms of scenery, culture, climate, and beaches, the city of Santa Barbara is as close to ideal as any we've encountered.

If our book royalties suddenly spiked upward, we would happily move out there with our respective families to sunbathe, read books, swat volleyballs, fall off surfboards, and watch time pass on Santa Barbara's famed courthouse clock tower for the rest of our days.

Tucked away in the nether regions of the Santa Barbara Coast are some truly wonderful spots. Guadalupe, a speck of a burg, provides access to the tallest sand dunes on the West Coast, and there's timeless isolation to be found at Point Sal State Beach. A holy trinity of state beaches—El Capitán, Refugio, and Gaviota—are worth their weight in golden sands. These beaches are so valuable, in terms of ecology and relative lack of development, that the federal government has been looking at preserving 72 miles of coastline as Gaviota Coast National Seashore. We'd certainly support that proposal.

COURTESY OF THE SANTA BARBARA CONFERENCE VISITORS BUREAU AND FILM COMMISSION

VENTURA COUNTY
SANTA BARBARA COUNTY

Los Padres
National Forest

San Luis Obispo County

New Cuyama

Sierra Madre Mountains

San Rafael Mountains

Santa Ynez Mountains

Lake Cachuma

Santa Ynez

Carpinteria   1-2
3-4
Montecito   5
6
7
Santa   8-10
Barbara   11-13
14
15
Goleta   16
Isla Vista   17-19
20

PACIFIC OCEAN

21
22
Gaviota State Park   23-24

Solvang
Buelton
Santa Ynez River

Santa Maria
Orcutt
Guadalupe
Lompoc

Vandenberg Air Force Base

25
26-27

29-30   28

SANTA BARBARA COAST

SAN LUIS OBISPO COUNTY

10 mi
10 km

© AVALON TRAVEL

BEST BEACHES

◖ East Beach, page 247

Rincon Point and Rincon Beach County Park

Rincon is one of the best surfing spots in California. It used to be hard to access because of beach-hogging private homes in the area. However, there are now two well-maintained public accesses that will get you from the highway to the beach with relative ease and total legality. They are Rincon Point and Rincon Beach County Park.

BEACHES

The long, centipede-like parking lot at **Rincon Point**—the more southerly of the two Rincon accesses, designated as a unit of Carpinteria State Beach—is a godsend to surfers. A well-graded dirt path at its south end worms its way between U.S. 101 and all the private beachfront homes en route to a U-shaped cove with a splendid view of the rugged mountains. One must then walk west around the point—which is just inside Ventura County and also accessible via Rincon Point Parkway—to find the waves for which Rincon is fabled.

Rincon is a classic right-point break. It is also one of the best winter surf areas in the world because seasonal swells make for flawlessly shaped waves. You've got to know what you're doing, though, as the surf gets so rough that even paddling out can be problematic. South of Rincon Point, a second and third point aren't as crowded and have the added feature of tidepools to explore if the waves aren't breaking. The cobblestone beach out here is pretty to look at but not conducive to wading or swimming. However, you don't have to come with the intention of surfing or

swimming to appreciate the scenic beach and the shaded hike down to it. Bring a lounge chair and cooler, and watch a real-life surf flick unfold before your very eyes.

Directly across from the turnoff to Rincon Point is **Rincon Beach County Park,** a county-run facility with an overlook, picnic tables, and access to the beach via a winding wooden stairwell that descends a cliff face. Swimmers take the plunge north of the stairwell bottom, where a sign designates that 220 yards of beach have been set aside for swimmers only. Note that there are no lifeguards here. Nude sunbathers disrobe at the far north end of the beach. It's a mixed crowd (old, young, gay, straight) and a congenial scene.

1 RINCON POINT

Location: Rincon Parkway/Old Pacific Coast Highway at Ventura County line
Parking/Fees: limited free roadside parking
Hours: sunrise-sunset
Facilities: none
Contact: none

2 RINCON BEACH COUNTY PARK

Location: Bates Road, off U.S. 101, three miles east of Carpinteria
Parking/Fees: free parking lot
Hours: 8 A.M.-sunset
Facilities: restrooms and picnic area
Contact: Santa Barbara County Department of Parks and Recreation, 805/681-5650

© PARKE PUTERBAUGH

Rincon Beach County Park

Carpinteria

Many a coastal civic group has proclaimed its sandy land grant to be the "world's safest beach," but Carpinteria just might be the first beach to have been so ordained. Way back in 1602, Spanish explorers described it as *cosa segura de buen gente,* or "the safest beach on the coast." Nestled against the Santa Ynez Mountains on a fertile plain, Carpinteria is a small town (population 13,700) with big assets: beautiful, uncluttered beaches; pleasing Mediterranean climate; and a commanding view of the Channel Islands. The slope of the beach is gentle, with no sudden drop-offs or riptides, making for worry-free swimming.

The original inhabitants of the Carpinteria Valley were the Chumash, who utilized the extensive tar pits for pitch to seal their canoes. Their canoe-building enterprise gave rise to the town name, as Spanish conquistadors referred to it as a "carpentry shop." Carpinteria sits atop a huge pool of the black gold. Beneath the fertile soil in the valley lies a thick layer of tar, and below that, a sea of oil. Much industry in and around Carpinteria is related to petroleum production. Seven oil platforms are visible

offshore, and many more fill the rich Santa Barbara Channel. Agriculture is pursued with equal gusto.

To a vacationer's eye Carpinteria has the appeal of a quiet town with rural, slowpoke ways and naturally protected beaches. Some might even argue that Carpinteria is the last great undiscovered beach town in California. It's actually lost a small percentage of population since the beginning of the decade. Unfortunately, a privatizing of the shoreline for wealthy snobs is evident in the 12-mile stretch from Carpinteria to Santa Barbara. Much of it is blocked off by egregious mansions, residential "colonies," and gated communities. (Isn't that an oxymoron?) One place, Padaro, seems inordinately smitten with self-importance. The walls and trees surrounding it are peppered with "Absolutely No Trespassing" signs, and coils of razor-edged barbed wire top their castle walls.

One note of consolation: It seems that Padaro and its like are walled in on both sides. What glimpses we could catch of their shore revealed a lot of protective riprap and precious little beach. The town of Carpinteria itself, though, is unpretentious and laid back. It is so pleasantly livable that the less we say about it, the better for those who live there already.

Several years ago we noticed a sign—a small billboard, actually—staked into a grassy headland south of town. It read, Buy the Bluffs: Small Town, Big Dreams. A grassroots group, the Citizens for Carpinteria Bluffs, worked to save the bluffs from developers and Union Pacific Railroad, which wanted to build a siding there. A drive up the bluffs, ending at a dirt lot, revealed why the locals were so interested in preservation. We got out of the car, walked to the edge of the cliff, and beheld one of the most stunning beach vistas in California—and one of the last tracts of coastal open space in southern Santa Barbara County.

In 2002, a 52-acre tract of Carpinteria Bluffs that had been acquired by the group was officially dedicated in a day of celebration. This is great news, not just for this particular open-space parcel, but as evidence of what a committed group of individuals can accomplish, even in the face of strong business and political interests that oppose preservation.

For more information, contact the Carpinteria Valley Chamber of Commerce, 5285 Carpinteria Avenue, Carpinteria, CA 93013, 805/684-5479, www.carpchamber.org.

BEACHES

Carpinteria State Beach is a 50-acre park with a mile-long sandy beach, large dunes, healthy tidepools, and 261 made-in-the-shade campsites. A pretty river courses through the park, descending from mountains that provide a scenic backdrop. It's Shangri-La at the shore, pure and simple. The only drawback is that passing trains can awaken sleeping campers in the middle of the night. An interpretive display on the Chumash is on the premises.

Adjoining it to the north is **Carpinteria City Beach.** A "bathing beach" at the end of Linden Avenue, this municipal beach is particularly safe because an offshore reef acts as a natural breakwater, preventing rip currents from forming. The broad, tree-backed beach bans dogs and surfing, but it's family friendly

and has picnic tables and volleyball nets. You'll have to park at metered spaces on the surrounding streets or in a pay lot ($1 per hour or $5 all day). Some of the tar bubbling beneath the ocean floor (60 feet below the surface) seeps into the water and ends up on the bottoms of human feet, thus explaining the ubiquitous packets of "Tar Off" seen around town. Not to worry; it's part of a natural process, not an oil spill.

On the north side of Carpinteria, accessible via Santa Claus Lane, is **Padaro Beach** (a.k.a. Santa Claus Beach). Here's the drill: Park your car on the side of the road, cross railroad tracks, and work your way over a wall of boulders and then through a small sand fence to get out onto the beach. A pretty beach it is, too: nice and flat, with coarse brown sand, looking north at the private colony of Padaro, protected from human invaders and the ocean's incursion by more boulders. Even with all that money, it's like they're living in some sort of prison. On the beach side, they're walled in by rocks, while on Padaro Lane, coils of razor wire prevent unwarranted access to the playpens of the rich and paranoid. Hey, they can have it—and here's hoping the next El Niño takes it.

A county beach access, **Loon Point Beach,** has been added in recent years, with a free parking lot among eucalyptus trees on Padaro Lane. It's a bit of a traipse to the beach that involves walking beside railroad tracks and then gingerly negotiating a rutted, gullied path down to the water. A quarter mile later, you're on a beautiful beach backed by yellow sandstone cliffs. The headland above it looked to be under development—no doubt another "luxury gated community."

3 CARPINTERIA STATE BEACH

Location: Casitas Pass Road exit from Highway 1 in Carpinteria; right on Carpinteria Avenue and left on Palm Avenue into the park

Parking/Fees: $8 entrance fee per vehicle; camping fees $30-44 per night beachside,

Carpinteria bluffs

$20-34 inland, plus $7.50 reservation fee; "Hike and Bike" sites $5 per night
Hours: 7 A.M.–sunset
Facilities: lifeguards, restrooms, showers, and picnic tables
Contact: Carpinteria State Beach, 805/968-1033

4 CARPINTERIA CITY BEACH

Location: end of Linden Avenue in Carpinteria
Parking/Fees: metered street and lot parking
Hours: sunrise–11 P.M.
Facilities: lifeguards
Contact: Carpinteria Community Services, 805/684-5405

5 PADARO BEACH

Location: Santa Claus Lane in Carpinteria
Parking/Fees: free roadside parking
Hours: sunrise–11 P.M.
Facilities: none

Contact: Santa Barbara County Department of Parks and Recreation, 805/681-5650

6 LOON POINT BEACH

Location: end of Padaro Lane in Padaro
Parking/Fees: free parking lot
Hours: 8 A.M.–sunset
Facilities: restrooms
Contact: Santa Barbara County Department of Parks and Recreation, 805/681-5650

ACCOMMODATIONS

Many overnight visitors to Carpinteria camp in the state park, one of the most scenic and well-shaded in all of coastal California. The town also gets its share of day-trippers at the city beach on summer weekends. Motels are few and scattered, but their number will no doubt increase as word gets out about this charming town. As it is, no motel sits directly on the beach, though you can make yourself comfortable several blocks away at the **Best Western Carpinteria Inn** (4558

Carpinteria Avenue, 805/684-0473, $$) or **Prufrock's Garden Inn** (600 Linden A venue, 805/566-9696, $$$$).

The latter, a romantic seven-room B&B, indeed takes its name from T. S. Eliot's elliptical poem "The Love Song of J. Alfred Prufrock." One does not expect to encounter abstruse literary references in modest Carpinteria, but we're not complaining. Rates are not cheap at either place, and rooms at the inn run in the stratospheric $200–300 range. If you're looking for cheaper digs in the same neighborhood, **Motel 6** (5550 Carpinteria Avenue, 805/684-8602, $) will leave the light on for you.

COASTAL CUISINE

The usual assortment of pizza joints, taco huts, cafés, and delis typify Carpinteria's plain-cloth dining scene. You can charbroil your own fish at **The Palms** (701 Linden Avenue, 805/684-3811, $$$). The **Fish Barrel** (509 Linden Avenue, 805/684-2391, $$) specializes in diversity, offering fish 'n' chips and Thai food on the same menu. The **Coffee Grinder** (910 Linden Avenue, 805/867-6015, $) will get your day off to a good start. If the coffee doesn't jolt you, the folk art will. For anything more ambitious, head north to nearby Santa Barbara, which is one of California's culinary capitals.

Summerland

The seaside village of Summerland (population 1,800) is a cat's whisker east of Montecito. The name summons visions of a place where everyone is on permanent vacation and the sun's always shining. Though small, Summerland has a pair of nice bed-and-breakfast inns, a good restaurant, a few antique shops, and a county park worth dropping by if you're passing through.

For more information, contact the Santa Barbara Conference and Visitors Bureau, 1601 Anacapa Street, Santa Barbara, CA 93101, 805/966-9222 or 800/549-5133, www.santa barbaraca.com.

BEACHES

Lookout County Park offers the option of picnicking on the wooded bluff top above or playing on the sandy beach below. This semi-isolated spot is the only public beach of any consequence between Carpinteria and Santa Barbara. Lifeguards are on duty on summer weekends only. Because of the isolation, nude sunbathers congregate on the sands south of here, unofficially known as Summerland Beach.

7 LOOKOUT COUNTY PARK

Location: end of Lookout Park Road in Summerland
Parking/Fees: free parking lot
Hours: 8 A.M.-sunset
Facilities: lifeguards (weekends only), restrooms, and picnic tables
Contact: Lookout County Park, 805/969-1720

ACCOMMODATIONS

The **Inn on Summer Hill** (2520 Lillie Avenue, 805/969-9998 or 800/746-7930, $$$$) is a 16-room hotel/inn offering ocean views, full breakfast, canopy beds, and English country decor in its suites. Rates start at $209 per night for rooms, $370 for suites. The yellow clapboard **Summerland Inn** (2161 Ortega Hill Road, 805/969-5225, $$) has fewer amenities than its competitor, but its 12 comfortable rooms go for about half the price ($85–190 in season, $30 less than that in the off season). It's a great deal, almost a bargain, on this pricey part of the coast.

COASTAL CUISINE

Quaint and casual, the **Big Yellow House** (108 Pierpont Avenue, 805/565-4889, $$) is comfortably situated in a century-old Victorian mansion, offering home-style meals (steak, seafood, and pasta) and appetizing ocean views. Its culinary orientation is California-style home cooking, and it serves three meals daily.

SANTA BARBARA COAST

Montecito

The main reason to come to the upscale village of Montecito is to stay at one of its several splendid hotel-resorts. From beachside beauties like the Four Seasons Biltmore Santa Barbara and the Miramar to the San Ysidro Ranch in the steep hills, the bywords here are money and luxury. If Santa Barbara is perceived as a bastion of high life brimming with comfort and money, then Montecito is an even more exclusive enclave. Coast Village Road is Montecito's Rodeo Drive, lined with expensive shops that bear names like Angel, Mischief, and Objects. On the real estate market, unspectacular homes costing a cool million are not unusual, and $4 or $5 million for a house and lot with a view doesn't raise an eyebrow.

At one time a minor coda appended to Santa Barbara's seaside symphony, Montecito is now a full-fledged fugue in its own right. Currently the population is listed at around 10,000. You can gauge the community's wealth not only by its inflated real estate prices but by such everyday things as the cost of gas or a cup of coffee, and the lost-pet ad we saw affixed to local telephone poles. Instead of a beloved mutt or housecat, the heartbroken owner was looking for an exotic red-billed parrot that had flown the coop.

For more information, contact the Santa Barbara Conference and Visitors Bureau, 1601 Anacapa Street, Santa Barbara, CA 93101, 805/966-9222 or 800/549-5133, www.santa barbaraca.com.

BEACHES

Miramar Beach is accessible from and named after the Miramar Resort Hotel, which fronts 500 feet of prime, uncrowded ocean frontage. Trails lead to **Hammond's Beach,** a public beach slightly west of Miramar. These two beaches are mainly enjoyed by guests of the hotel or locals who want to escape the crowds in Santa Barbara. Both lie well off the beaten path. To get to Miramar and Hammond's Beaches, take Eucalyptus Lane to a small park-ing area at its end. Miramar is right here, while a trail leads from here to Hammond's Beach.

Butterfly Beach lies along Channel Drive between the "Biltmore Wall" (in front of the Four Seasons Santa Barbara Biltmore) and the end of Butterfly Lane. Butterfly Beach isn't much of a beach. In past years, it's been so eroded that we've seen the ocean lapping at the retaining wall. In 2002, there seemed to be a bit of a beach in place here. (We suspect beach renourishment.) In recent years, the beach has held its own and is one of the few purely west-facing strands in this part of the coast, adding to its appeal with locals. In any case, an impressive contingent of young women reposed in the sand. Behind the beach, the green, lovely grounds of the Biltmore provided a resplendent backdrop.

Incidentally, bicycling is a great way to get out and see the Montecito and Santa Barbara beachfront. A bike path runs from the Biltmore to the harbor area just north of Stearns Wharf, a distance of about four miles. Most hotels stock bikes for their guests. Alternatively, rent one at **Beach Rentals** (8 West Cabrillo Boulevard, 805/963-2524), across from Stearns Wharf in Santa Barbara.

8 MIRAMAR BEACH

Location: at Miramar Resort Hotel, 1555 South Jamison Lane, in Miramar
Parking/Fees: limited free street parking
Hours: 8 A.M.-sunset
Facilities: none
Contact: Santa Barbara County Department of Parks and Recreation, 805/681-5650

9 HAMMOND'S BEACH

Location: trail to beach from end of Eucalyptus Lane in Montecito Park
Parking/Fees: free parking lot
Hours: 8 A.M.-sunset
Facilities: none

Contact: Santa Barbara County Department of Parks and Recreation, 805/681-5650

10 BUTTERFLY BEACH

Location: along Channel Drive, between Four Seasons Biltmore and Butterfly Lane, in Montecito
Parking/Fees: free limited street parking
Hours: sunrise-10 P.M.
Facilities: none
Contact: Santa Barbara City Department of Parks and Recreation, 805/897-1983

Butterfly Beach

ACCOMMODATIONS

You'll find Santa Barbara's topmost hotels and resort properties in Montecito. The **Four Seasons Biltmore Santa Barbara** (1260 Channel Drive, 805/969-2261, $$$$) ranks at the top of the list. It is so posh and well established that it publishes its own folio-sized, book-length history. The premises teem with orange trees and fragrant botanical gardens, and the rooms are palatial. Graceful arches and brick walkways connect the villa-style buildings. The grounds are covered with Monterey cypress, blue gums, and parlor palms. The Four Seasons Biltmore feels like a world unto itself—which, in a sense, it is, being situated directly on Butterfly Beach, out of range of traffic and in-town bustle. Amenities include a fully equipped fitness center, heated 50-meter outdoor pool and hot tub, and two on-site restaurants. Twelve-speed mountain bikes are cheaply rented to guests, which is good since standard room rates run—gulp—$600-870 nightly. Two nights at the Biltmore would pay our respective monthly mortgages!

Up the road a piece, a few miles into the mountains off San Ysidro Road, is the legendary **San Ysidro Ranch** (900 San Ysidro Lane, 805/969-5046, www.sanysidroranch .com, $$$$). It is a 540-acre resort ranch whose chief claims to fame are that Vivien Leigh and Laurence Olivier were married on the grounds and that JFK and Jackie honeymooned there. These events are preserved in framed clippings hung in the lobby area. Rest and relaxation without pomp or pretense is the philosophy here. The rooms are in bungalows strewn around the sprawling estate. Some have their own hot tub on a private deck. Nothing comes cheaply here: Nightly rates range from $500 for a "canyon room" to $1,000 for a "deluxe cottage" to $1,350 for a two-bedroom suite to $2,995 for the "Kennedy Suite." If you've really got loot to burn, the Warner Cottage goes for $5,995 (no typo!) per night.

The ranch has its own stables, and guests can opt for any kind of horse ride, from a trail ride into the mountains to a "meditation walk" around the grounds. On the latter you close your eyes, bliss out, and let your equine bodhisattva lead you on a journey to the center of the mind. The ranch also offers spa services, such as massage, aromatherapy, and skin treatments. A menu of these, ranging from an hour-long massage to a full two-day schedule of indulgent therapies, will set you back anywhere from $145 to more than a grand.

Pets are welcomed and, somewhat ridiculously, pampered to the max. The "privileged pet" program includes peanut-butter canine cookies at check-in, VIP gifts upon arrival (rawhide chews, squeaky toys, personalized bowl), the pet's name hung on a wood-burned sign outside the cottage, doggie turn-down service, and Perrier for pets. Sound a bit excessive? It did to us, too. But maybe not to Pokey, Smoke, Chloe, Rexford, Fresca, and Sprite—some of the pooches whose names were entered in the pet guest register at the front desk.

The **Miramar Resort Hotel** (1555 South Jamison Lane, 805/969-2203, $$$) claims the technical distinction of being the only hotel on the beach in the area. That is to say, there's not even a street to cross to get to the sand. The hotel offers lodgers a choice of rooms, cottages, and bungalows at numerous price points, ranging $85–835.

Closer to town, the **Montecito Inn** (1295 Coast Village Road, 805/969-7854, www .montecitoinn.com, $$$$) has a bit of showbiz history attached to it. Charlie Chaplin and (though brochures don't mention him) the scandalized Fatty Arbuckle established the Montecito Inn in 1928. Its 53 rooms are decorated in French provincial style, while the lobby is a lake of Italian marble. The inn is three blocks from the beach. Chaplin's Little Tramp couldn't have afforded to stay here, but if you're solvent to the tune of $245 and up per night, they'll roll out the welcome mat.

A final word: While the standard rates quoted at the higher-end resorts might seem way out of your league, it's worth trolling around for special packages and deals. At the Montecito Inn, for instance, a "midweek special" will net you a room with a queen bed for $149 a night Sunday–Thursday.

COASTAL CUISINE

All the best dining in Montecito is in the resorts and hotels. The menu at the **Stonehouse** at the San Ysidro Ranch (900 San Ysidro Lane, 805/565-1700, $$$$), for instance, will help you "rediscover the great foods of America," as the dining room's motto proclaims. Many of the herbs and vegetables used are organically grown on the premises. Entrées run about $25–50.

The Four Seasons Biltmore Santa Barbara has its own fine on-premises dining rooms as well: **La Marina** (1260 Channel Drive, 805/969-2261, $$$$) specializes in California regional cuisine (read: surf and turf items with creative, high-end sauces and accompaniments), such as roast sea bass with three vegetable purees, morel mushrooms, and fava beans in a potato cage (let me out!). The more casual **Patio Restaurant** ($$$) serves a decadent Sunday-brunch spread from its glass-enclosed atrium.

NIGHTLIFE

The **Four Seasons Biltmore Santa Barbara** (1260 Channel Drive, 805/969-2261) has a nice, civilized lounge with a pianist. If you want anything more from your evening than the sounds of a well-groomed gent tickling the ivories amid the clinking of cocktail glasses, you'll have to head into downtown Santa Barbara, where you'll find nightlife to last till sunrise.

Santa Barbara

If you were to feed into a computer all the variables that govern quality of life, Santa Barbara might just top the list. All it takes is a day or two of exposure to the beaches, mountains, towering palm trees, Spanish architecture, and convivial bustle to become convinced that this is America's most nearly perfect setting for a city. This is true despite the very real problems that have beset the community over the years.

The reasons for Santa Barbara's good fortune are many, and geography is not the least of them. Santa Barbara (population 86,200) is encircled by the Santa Ynez Mountains, which cradle the city, staving off winds that blow down from the north. Twenty miles offshore, the Channel Islands intercept the Pacific swells, protecting the coastline. Santa Barbara is the only city in California that faces due south, running along a figurative east–west ceiling that divides the Central and Southern California coasts. It is the northernmost city that maintains that sunny SoCal climate and vibe. The climate is moderate year-round: comfortably cool in summer, never too cool in winter, shirt-sleeve weather almost every day. Located between Los Angeles (92 miles southwest) and San Francisco (332 miles north), Santa Barbara embodies elements of both cities without suffering the extreme urban angst common to them. Even better, Santa Barbara isn't suffering growth pains common to so many American cities. Quite the opposite: Its population has dropped by 4 percent since the beginning of the decade.

This city is a human parade that makes State Street, the primary artery, seem like a nonstop Cinco de Mayo celebration. Our most recent visit to Santa Barbara coincided with this Mexican holiday, which has become, like St. Patrick's Day, another excuse for Americans to drink and party. College kids were out in force at happy hour and late into the night, although this is nothing unusual in Santa Barbara. Their whooping and whistling could be heard the length of State Street.

Other groups commingle in this open-air bazaar from first rays to last call. You'll see families on vacation, hooting happily as they pedal tandem bikes or duck into ice-cream shops for sugar fixes. Well-mannered, broad-bellied bikers navigate gleaming, screaming Harleys. Perfectly togged yuppie couples stroll the streets on romantic getaway weekends. Young, free-spirited foreign visitors are drawn to Santa Barbara's figurative fountain of youth. At night, older folks turned out in dark suits and formal gowns make their way to the symphony or theater after dining at one of State Street's tony restaurants. You'll also see lots of homeless people.

We will grant you this: The homeless of Santa Barbara are more resourceful than the typical down-at-the-heels spare-changers in places like Santa Monica and San Francisco. On one of our visits, a homeless entrepreneur had constructed a folk-art installation on the sandy beach beside the pier. Decorative motifs included a tiny mirrored ball, sparkly adornments on flags, sawed-off plastic soda jugs, and half-buried beer cans (possibly drained by the artist himself). The words "Welcome to Santa Barbara" were spelled out in raised block letters in the sand. We saw him chomping on a big hunk of watermelon when we first passed his environment; on our return, he lay prone inside a pup tent with his feet protruding from the end. He had placed a wicker basket below the pier railing to catch the change that grateful art lovers could lob into it from above. For better or worse, this sort of scene has become part of the city's landscape.

Many who live here are activist-aesthetes who have made a mission of keeping their city clean, green, and out of the hands of those who'd turn it into an urban Disneyland. Public consensus ensures progressive stands on such issues as controlled growth and habitat preservation. Consequently, there's always some kind of battle being waged—city-hall caucuses and grassroots crusades aimed at saving parks and heading off the latest nefarious development proposal. Nonetheless, Santa Barbara can be a restful city. At least two beachcombers burned out from months of rambling around the lion's den of Southern California have found it to be so.

Santa Barbara exists in relatively easy harmony with its environment. Tourism is the closest thing to an industry. Block after block is filled with museums, galleries, theaters, libraries, bookstores, and historic buildings. Following a 1925 earthquake, the city council established an architectural board of review that drafted a design code. Consequently, Santa Barbara was rebuilt in an appealing style that reflects the city's 200-year Spanish and Mexican heritage. Even gas stations and fast-food joints adhere to the stringent architectural code. Pipe roofs, terra cotta tile sidewalks, vanilla stucco walls, colorful mosaic

THE OTHER SIDE OF PARADISE

Santa Barbara is a wonderful city. Seldom will you find such varied beauty – mountains, beaches, vineyards, hot springs – in such proximity, and with a perfect climate to top it all off. But the city, for all its magnificence, doesn't exist in a glass bubble. It is subject to the myriad stresses and strains that bear upon all American cities in these troubled times. It has fought many issues with the sort of diligence one wishes every community in America would muster. Nonetheless, this earthly paradise has had its share of problems.

Fire – The California wildfires of 2007 and 2008 did not leave Santa Barbara unscathed. Even though fire didn't threaten the city directly, smoke filled the air, affecting respiratory health and keeping tourists away at the height of the summer season. Back in 1990, an arsonist set a fire on the western outskirts of Santa Barbara that consumed 4,900 acres, destroyed hundreds of homes, and caused $238 million worth of damage. Hills, canyons, and neighborhoods in northern Santa Barbara and Goleta were blackened.

Drought – In the 1970s Santa Barbara elected not to tie into water supplies imported from the Sierra via the State Water Project, fearing that more water would mean more unwanted development. It has paid a heavy price for its self-reliance, suffering periodic drought. As California entered its fourth year of drought in 1990, for instance, with the dry summer season still to come, one of Santa Barbara's reservoirs dried up and another was only one-quarter full. The crisis forced the city to impose severe water conservation measures. Its green parks and gardens then turned a dry, dead brown.

Freeways and malls – For years Santa Barbara stubbornly defied progress by refusing to do anything about U.S. 101, which cut through the center of town. Residents also hotly debated the construction of a downtown shopping mall. The city spent millions and convened nine civic commissions to study the mall and freeway projects. Their eventual implementation was a comedy of errors. By the time the city finally okayed the U.S. 101 project, the state had temporarily run out of funds to pay for it. By dragging its heels on the downtown mall, the city lost commitments from key stores. Both projects were finally addressed. Freeway snarls are in the past, and

blocks, arcades and walkways, wrought-iron railings, and flower-filled gardens confer a unified architectural signature. Even the benches are adobe.

The most visible example of this style is **Mission Santa Barbara** (2201 Laguna Street, 805/682-4713, www.sbmission.org), established in 1786. Dubbed the "Queen of the Missions," it sits on a knoll overlooking the town. At close range it almost appears two-dimensional, like a Hollywood movie set. The grassy square before it is a greener green and the sky a bluer blue than your most vivid Kodachrome fantasy. The graceful Spanish Colonial facade is dressed in pink and white tones;

behind it rise twin bell towers. The grounds include a museum and flower garden. Of the 21 Franciscan missions established throughout California, Mission Santa Barbara is one of the few that remains active as a parish church.

Continuing into the hills along Mission Canyon Boulevard, you'll come upon **Santa Barbara Botanic Garden** (1212 Mission Canyon Road, 805/682-4726). The botanical garden encompasses 65 acres and 1,000 species of native California trees, flowers, shrubs, grasses, and annuals. The grounds are divided into environmental biomes (canyon, desert, arroyo, meadow, and woodland), each with its own trails. This lovely park plunges visitors the downtown mall is an improvement over what it replaced. But the projects did traumatize and divide the community for years.

Homelessness – Thanks to its temperate year-round climate, Santa Barbara attracts a sizable indigent population. They gather beneath the beach's palm trees, watching the passing parade. Political correctness aside, their presence blights the area. The hue and cry over homelessness has gone on for many years and made national news in 1986, when an ordinance banning overnight sleeping in public was challenged by the late homeless activist Mitch Snyder. The city council amended the ordinance to permit the homeless to sleep in vacant lots and parked cars – a move hailed as an act of "reasonableness and courage."

Offshore drilling – Oil rigs have physically polluted Santa Barbara's beaches and visually polluted the horizon. Nearly two-thirds of California's offshore oil and 85 percent of its natural gas is pumped from beneath the ocean in Santa Barbara and Ventura Counties. In 1969 Santa Barbara made national news and galvanized the environmental movement when a catastrophic spill from an offshore oil rig befouled 150 miles of shoreline. Fishers in the Santa Barbara Channel subsequently lost half of their trawling grounds. Fast forward to 2002, when the Bush administration pushed for 36 approved but undeveloped oil leases off Santa Barbara County's coastline. The state of California, Santa Barbara County, San Luis Obispo County, and 10 environmental groups jointly sued the Department of the Interior over the leases. Even when they're functioning properly, oil platforms produce pollution – each generating the equivalent of 7,000 cars driving 50 miles a day. When they come down, there are additional problems, such as what to do about heavy metal and hydrocarbon-contaminated shell mounds scraped off old platform legs.

Dirty beaches – Many of Santa Barbara County's beaches have had poor or failing grades for water quality. Creek-mouth beaches are problematic during wet periods, when nonpoint source pollution washes into streams and out to sea.

Housing – There has been a serious affordable-housing crisis in Santa Barbara. Much is made of the "chronic scarcity of well-designed, appropriately located housing for middle- and lower-income residents." When it comes to housing, Santa Barbara County is the least affordable in the state. Not only residents but businesses are being forced out by the squeeze. The median price for a home in Santa Barbara County's "South Coast" reached $629,000.

back into pre-European, pre-condominium California. Inside the redwood grove everything is stilled to a profound, cathedral-like silence beneath huge boughs. Five miles of pathways wind through the garden. Admission is $8 for adults, $4 for kids.

The **Santa Barbara Museum of Natural History** (2559 Puesta del Sol Road, 805/682-4711) offers geology and biology exhibits: a 33-foot model of a giant Pacific squid, planetarium, replica of a Chumash priest doing the "Seaweed Dance" (variations of which are performed nightly at the rock clubs down on State Street), and much more. Founded in 1916, it's impossible to miss: Just look for the place with

the 72-foot whale skeleton out front. Admission is $10 for adults and $6 for kids.

A walking tour of Santa Barbara's Red Tile District is recommended. Visitors can view 20 downtown buildings of historical and architectural interest in a 12-block stroll. (For a map and guide drop by the tourist information center at 1330 State Street.) One of the downtown "must-visits" is **El Presidio de Santa Barbara State Historic Park** (123 East Canon Perdido Street, 805/966-9719). Built in 1782, this was the northernmost of four military fortresses constructed by the Spanish along the coast. Two sections of the original Presidio quadrangle have survived earthquakes and are preserved as a park that forms the heart of Santa Barbara's El Pueblo Viejo Historic District.

Santa Barbara boasts arts-and-crafts galleries, plus a smattering of theater, symphony, and ballet. The city also has much to offer college kids and lower-rung culture vultures like ourselves. The heart of Santa Barbara—in terms of retail shops, restaurants, and nightlife—is State Street, from Los Olivos Street to Cabrillo Boulevard (on the waterfront). State Street has its share of pool halls, dive bars, and tattoo parlors, but for the most part it is in tune with the real-life needs of its collegiate, retiree, and tourist patrons. Recreationally, some of the most competitive volleyball in the state is played on the sand courts of East Beach. Within the county's borders are 20 U.S. Forest Service, California State Park, and Santa Barbara County Park campgrounds.

Down at West Beach, at the foot of State Street, lies **Stearns Wharf,** an old, broad-planked commercial pier on which the public can walk or drive. It is the oldest commercial pier on the West Coast. All day long, cars rumble slowly out and back along the weary timbers of the wharf. (You can park for a fee at pier's end.) The pier is home to a disappointing collection of long-lived seafood restaurants and shops, but it is worth a visit to catch a seabird's-eye view of the beach by day or a romantic glimpse at the twinkling lights of the city at night.

Last of all we'll mention the courthouse. If Mission Santa Barbara is the religious symbol of the community, then **Santa Barbara County Courthouse** (1100 Ancapa Street, 805/962-6464) is the town's most impressive secular landmark. Built in an elaborate Spanish Moorish style and occupying a full city block, it looks more like a palace than a courthouse. This turreted treasure must be toured to be believed. It would indeed be an honor to pay a traffic ticket here. The crowning touch is the clock tower ("El Maridor"), atop which an observation deck offers a sweeping panorama of Santa Barbara.

Pondering the city from this vantage point, one cannot help but reflect on the perfect yin-yang of the setting: mountains and ocean, warm sun and cool breezes, college kids and golden oldies, Spanish Colonial architecture and contemporary Americana.

For more information, contact the Santa Barbara Conference and Visitors Bureau, 1601 Anacapa Street, Santa Barbara, CA 93101, 805/966-9222 or 800/549-5133, www.santa barbaraca.com.

BEACHES

Santa Barbara's south-facing beach runs in a long arc along Cabrillo Boulevard. Its 2.5 miles are divided into the plainly named **East Beach** and **West Beach.** These are calm-water beaches whose inland fringe is lined with huge, towering palms that list ever so slightly landward. You really can't improve on this setting, with the mountains, penetrating sunlight, and a hard-blue sky for a backdrop. There's ample parking in huge lots, but for a breezy, bracing, and gas-free tour we recommend the bike path that snakes along the beach zone. The beaches are sandy and broad, litter-free, and well patrolled by lifeguards. Most everyone pedals or jogs the bike path at a relatively unhurried pace, savoring the sights. In-line skating moms can be seen pushing jogging strollers.

There are more sand volleyball courts on East Beach than anywhere else in California—except maybe Manhattan Beach. East Beach is also the site of Cabrillo Pavilion, a recreational center, bathhouse, and architectural landmark dating from 1925. Volleyball players, many of whom are seriously good, turn out in droves on weekends. On one Sunday in late spring, we saw kids braving the waves, shouting as they splashed around in frigid 60-degree water. Oil platforms are still visible offshore, though they are gradually being retired. Parking at East Beach costs $2 for up to three hours or $7 for all day. You're supposed to self-pay, and don't think for a second they won't ticket you.

Some locals will cop an attitude and disparage these big, wide, breezy beaches as being "too touristy," but there's enough beach here for everybody. Landward of the bike path is a landscaped, grassy ribbon known as Palm Park. It's an appealing green complete with picnic tables and a lawn that's trimmed, weedless, and more comfortable than shag carpeting—just ask the homeless who while away the hours sitting in the midday sun.

West Beach, which is on both sides of Stearns Wharf, is wide but generally less used for sandy recreation than East Beach. At the far end of West Beach, around the 1,000-slip harbor and breakwater that protects it, the coast gets hillier, and small beaches are tucked into coves at creek mouths. **Leadbetter Beach,** off Shoreline Drive, adjacent to Santa Barbara Harbor, is a good board and windsurfing beach. It also makes a swell spot to pass the time watching boats sail in and out of the harbor. It's a popular place to party, and locals who avoid East and West Beaches claim it as their own. West of Leadbetter Beach, off Shoreline Drive at the end of Mesa Lane, is **Mesa Lane Beach** (a.k.a. 1,000 Steps Beach), another locals-only spot that maintains a comfortable distance from the hubbub of downtown Santa Barbara.

Two miles farther west, **Arroyo Burro Beach County Park,** which is known to locals as Hendry's Beach, lies beneath the cliffs at the edge of a mesa at the mouth of Arroyo Burro Creek. It's a pretty spot, and a pretty popular one, complete with a picnic area, a surprisingly good restaurant (the Brown Pelican), and a sandy, crescent-shaped beach. Hang gliders launch from the cliffs above at Elings Park. The scene, particularly the striking geography, is like a scaled-down version of Black's Beach/Torrey Pines State Beach in San Diego County.

11 EAST BEACH

BEST (

Location: East Cabrillo Boulevard, between Niños Drive and State Street, in Santa Barbara

Parking/Fees: metered lot and street parking
Hours: sunrise–10 P.M.
Facilities: lifeguards, restrooms, showers, and picnic tables
Contact: Santa Barbara City Department of Parks and Recreation, 805/897-1983

12 WEST BEACH

Location: State Street at Stearns Wharf in Santa Barbara
Parking/Fees: metered lot and street parking
Hours: sunrise–10 P.M.
Facilities: concession, lifeguards, and restrooms
Contact: Santa Barbara City Department of Parks and Recreation, 805/897-1983

13 LEADBETTER BEACH

Location: Shoreline Drive, north of the Santa Barbara Harbor, in Santa Barbara
Parking/Fees: metered parking lot
Hours: sunrise–10 P.M.
Facilities: concession, lifeguards, restrooms, and picnic tables
Contact: Santa Barbara City Department of Parks and Recreation, 805/897-1983

14 MESA LANE BEACH

Location: stairwell to beach at end of Mesa Lane in Santa Barbara
Parking/Fees: free street parking
Hours: sunrise–10 P.M.
Facilities: none
Contact: Santa Barbara City Department of Parks and Recreation, 805/897-1983

15 ARROYO BURRO BEACH COUNTY PARK

Location: two miles west of Santa Barbara, off Cliff Drive
Parking/Fees: free parking lot
Hours: 8 A.M.–sunset
Facilities: concession, lifeguards, restrooms, and picnic tables
Contact: Arroyo Burro Beach County Park, 805/687-3714

RECREATION AND ATTRACTIONS

- **Bike/Skate Rentals:** Beach Bike Rentals, 22 State Street, Santa Barbara, 805/966-2282

- **Boat Cruise:** Santa Barbara Sailing Center, 133 Harbor Way, Santa Barbara, 805/962-2826

- **Ecotourism:** Captain Don's Whale Watching, 219 Stearns Wharf, Santa Barbara, 805/969-5217

- **Fishing Charters:** Sea Landing Sportfishing, 301 West Cabrillo Boulevard, Santa Barbara, 805/963-3564

- **Marina:** Santa Barbara Harbor, 805/564-5433

- **Pier:** Stearns Wharf, State Street at West Cabrillo Boulevard, 805/564-5526

- **Rainy Day Attraction:** Santa Barbara Museum of Natural History, 2559 Puesta del Sol Road, 805/682-4711

- **Shopping/Browsing:** La Cumbre Plaza, State Street and Hope Avenue, Santa Barbara, 805/687-6458; El Paseo, 812 State Street, Santa Barbara (California's oldest shopping mall)

- **Surf Shops:** A-Frame Surf, 3785 Santa Claus Lane, Carpinteria, 805/684-8803; Channel Islands Surfboards, 29 State Street, Santa Barbara, 805/966-7213; Surf Country, 5668 Calle Real, Goleta, 805/683-4450

- **Vacation Rentals:** Coastal Getaways,

1086 Coast Village Road, Montecito, 805/969-1258

ACCOMMODATIONS

Santa Barbara is not a cheap place to visit or vacation, so come prepared for some degree of sticker shock. An oceanfront favorite is **Harbor View Inn** (28 West Cabrillo Boulevard, 805/963-0780 or 800/755-0222, $$$$). The beautifully landscaped mission-style inn overlooks Stearns Wharf and has its own outdoor pool and sundeck, plus an exercise room and sauna. The grounds are gorgeous and the renovated rooms large, airy, and appealing. There's marble everywhere, especially in the spacious, well-appointed bathrooms. Rates aren't cheap, running $350–590 per night in summer. Whatever you pay, keep in mind that you're right by the beach, the wharf, and the action along State Street. You could not be better situated in Santa Barbara, in terms of location and amenities.

The **Santa Barbara Inn** (901 East Cabrillo Boulevard, 805/966-2285 or 800/231-0431, www.santabarbarainn.com, $$$$) is a good choice within sight of the beach. Located east of the downtown bustle, it's quiet at the Santa Barbara Inn. Rooms are spacious and comfortable, and you're only a crosswalk away from East Beach and Cabrillo Pavilion. The three-story hotel has a sundeck, pool, and whirlpool.

A good distance away but well worth mentioning is **El Encanto Hotel and Garden Villas** (1900 Lasuen Road, 805/687-5000, $$$$). Nestled in the foothills overlooking Santa Barbara, El Encanto is a European-style inn brimming with informal elegance; it's worth the drive up the mountain. At night the town below glimmers like a distant field of flickering candles. Spread out on the grounds of El Encanto are the garden villas. A large pool and Japanese koi pond are set among a thick tangle of flowers and shrubs. A touch of class graces every aspect of El Encanto, where a casual California ambience tempers the European formality to a glow as rosy as a Pacific sunset. Room rates start at $209, and a deluxe suite can top $500 per night.

Having changed owners, El Encanto Hotel and Garden Villas is undergoing restoration and refurbishing. It is now under the ownership of Orient-Express Hotels. Expect bigger things (including prices).

Between the mountaintops and ocean's edge are some less expensive motels where one can lie in for under $125 a night, but that is about the bottom-line limit in Santa Barbara. Our choice for the budget-minded, largely because of its location (a half block from the beach, across from City Park), is **Santa Barbara Beach Travelodge** (22 Castillo Street, 805/965-8527, $$). Other serviceable and less costly beachside motels in the vicinity of West Beach include **Ocean Palms** (232 West Cabrillo Boulevard, 805/966-9133, $$), **West Beach Inn** (306 West Cabrillo Boulevard, 805/966-3904, $$), and **Best Western Beachside Inn** (336 West Cabrillo Boulevard, 805/965-6556, $$).

In the summer of 2008, winds blew smoke from huge forest fires into Santa Barbara, impacting tourism with unhealthful air and reduced visibility. National and international news coverage only fanned the flames, so to speak, keeping visitors away.

COASTAL CUISINE

Every chef worth his or her salt mill wants to open a restaurant in Santa Barbara, which explains why there are somewhere in the neighborhood of 500 of them, from humble taco huts to formal fine dining. They publish brochures, flyers, and entire magazines about dining in Santa Barbara. Restaurants come and go on this highly competitive scene. The competition is ultimately too intense to allow everyone to make a go of it.

One solid survivor of the food wars is **Downey's** (1305 State Street, 805/966-5006, $$$$). Quality will always win out, and chef-proprietor John Downey's philosophy of serving fine dishes made with fresh ingredients and no corner-cutting has served him well. It's a small restaurant, with about a dozen tables. Specializing in "sophisticated California

cuisine," it has been judged by the Zagat Survey to be among the top 25 restaurants in California. Dinner here is meant to be an unhurried experience, lingered over and savored. Appetizers of note might include fresh deep-sea Santa Barbara mussels, served on the half shell in a smoky bacon vinaigrette. Entrée items can run the gamut from fresh catches, such as an extraordinary grilled Hawaiian escolar (a deep-sea dweller that occasionally turns up in tuna fishers' nets) to sliced breast of duck, grilled to a turn and served in cabernet sauce. Santa Barbara County wines are spotlighted on the wine list.

Original Enterprise Fish Company (225 State Street, 805/962-3313, $$$), a few blocks back from the beach on the west side of State Street, is our favorite place for seafood. The menu is a changeable list of fresh fish by location and type. It may include Alaskan halibut, Pacific swordfish, Hawaiian ahi, and Costa Rican mahimahi. The halibut, prepared your choice of four ways, is particularly affordable ($16.95, including salad, bread, and side item) and delicious. We tried it two ways—in a ginger-soy beurre blanc and crusted with sesame seeds and topped with spicy fruit salsa—and both were excellent. The restaurant occupies a cavernous old building with brick walls and exposed steel beams. The open cooking area at the center, with two huge smoking grills, is a show in itself. On our latest trip we had dinner at the Enterprise and then returned for lunch the next day. We would've eaten there again if duty didn't demand we check out some other places.

Brophy Bros. Clam Bar and Restaurant (119 Harbor Way, 805/966-4418, $$$) is Santa Barbara's other great fish house. Its waterside location makes it a good place to head at sunset. **Piranha Restaurant & Sushi Bar** (801 State Street, 805/884-1190, $$$$) is the locals' choice for sushi. Over on Stearns Wharf, the **Harbor Restaurant** (210 Stearns Wharf, 805/963-3311, $$$) specializes in oak-grilled fish and seafood and offers the best ocean view in town.

Joe's Cafe (536 State Street, 805/966-4638, $) merits commendation for very different reasons. If you can appreciate an old-time saloon with padded booths, checkered tablecloths, and a long bar where food and drink are served in generous quantities, you'll love Joe's. Serving supper since 1928, it is Santa Barbara's oldest restaurant. The matchbook motto says it all: "Proud to be local and proud of our past." Mounted deer and moose heads look down on hungry diners awaiting the arrival of heaping, home-cooked blue-plate specials. More than once have we enjoyed the solid, stick-to-the-ribs grub: hot open-faced roast beef sandwiches, brisket of beef, combination seafood plates, and more. Take our clichéd advice and "Eat at Joe's."

A strong Mexican influence pervades Santa Barbara, and State, Haley, and Milpas Streets are lined with Mexican cantinas. Have at it, amigos, and may the best burrito win. For a hot tip on great, cheap Mexican eats, try **Super-Rica Taqueria** (622 North Milpas Street, 805/963-4940, $). Incidentally, the best day starter or eye opener is **Santa Barbara Roasting Company** (321 Motor Way, 805/962-5213, $), just three blocks from the beach near the corner of State Street and West Gutierrez. Great coffee—especially iced drinks (try a white chocolate "Fred")—and baked goods are served in a relaxed, jazz-tinged atmosphere.

Of course, we haven't begun to cover the culinary possibilities in this cultured pearl of a town. Write the Santa Barbara Conference and Visitors Bureau or drop by the Information Stand at 1330 State Street for more detailed listings.

NIGHTLIFE

State Street in downtown Santa Barbara is a veritable Whitman's Sampler of fun after dark. Just wander by all the bars and clubs emitting decibels into the night and listen for something that catches your fancy. The street is a nonstop block party. Nobody seems to give a hoot about how loud the hoopla gets, and this laissez-faire attitude is a welcome change from the usual opprobrium.

We polled some local waitresses to get a reading on the hottest nightspots on Santa Barbara's changeable scene. They recommended **Velvet Jones** (423 State Street, 805/965-8676) for live music and **Q's Sushi A Go Go** (409 State Street, 805/966-9177) as the best place to party. Velvet Jones is a rock club that's made its reputation presenting shows by the likes of Dishwalla, Hoobastank, Alien Ant Farm, TSOL...you get the idea. Occupying a historic (ca. 1885) building, Q's has a dance floor, sushi bar, booths, and pool tables on its three floors. It has a sushi menu and a sick-of-sushi ("SOS") menu, too. Be forewarned of hefty covers and long lines.

In our experience over the last 20 years, the supply of suds and sounds along State Street is dependably endless. You'll hear a little bit of everything while making the rounds of **Sharkeez** (416 State Street, 805/963-9680), **The Spot** (389 Linden Avenue, 805/684-6311), **Calypso Bar & Grill** (514 State Street, 805/966-1388), the **Press Room** (15 East Ortega Street, 805/963-8121), the **Beach Shack** (651 Paseo Nuevo, 805/883-1939), and **O'Malley's** (523 State Street, 805/564-8904). We particularly like the eclectic CD jukebox at O'Malley's. Santa Barbara's nightlife choices just go on and on. Techno rules at the **Madhouse Martini Lounge** (434 State Street, 805/962-5516). There are also deejays at **Club 634** (634 State Street, 805/564-1069) and **Zelo** (630 State Street, 805/966-5792). Although it might seem as if there is nothing but techno and hip-hop being blasted into the ears of deaf (and dumb) college kids, there are alternatives, such as **Rocks** (801 State Street, 805/884-8485).

Home-brewed suds and good eats are found at **Santa Barbara Brewing Company** (501 State Street, 805/730-1040), where beer-making equipment is on view. Among the offerings, Santa Barbara Blonde and State Street Stout were to our liking. From the menu, we enjoyed the shrimp steamed in home brew. The place draws an attractive crowd of smiling faces.

At some point during your nighttime wanderings, angle out onto Stearns Wharf. This three-block wooden pier, built in 1872, widens into an over-the-water parking lot for all the people who have come to shop and dine at its restaurants. The longest-lived place on the wharf is the **Harbor Restaurant** (210 Stearns Wharf, 805/963-3311). Upstairs, the Harbor dispenses drinks and entertainment. Years ago it was described to us as a "one-night romance kind of place" by a bellhop who appeared to be in the know. Indeed, we later saw him off in a corner, deep in negotiations for a one-night romance. As for us, we were approached by a deranged woman who called us "fake preppies," insulted our clothes, refused to believe we weren't locals, asked for identification to prove otherwise, put one of our driver's licenses in her mouth, threatened not to return it, then made it abundantly clear she was available for the evening. One more story for (and from) the road.

Goleta

Goleta is an example of what we refer to as the "evil twin theory." For every lovely town that reins in development and maintains a high standard of living, there is another lurking nearby that lets such principles fall by the wayside. Santa Barbara's flip side is Goleta. With a population of 29,500, this next-door neighbor doesn't attract a fraction of its publicity. In contrast to Santa Barbara's international reputation, Goleta is all but unknown to the outside world. That is because Goleta functions as a repository for those things Santa Barbara wishes to keep outside its city limits—mainly the University of California at Santa Barbara, the Santa Barbara Airport, and people whose salaries and/or investments don't reach six figures.

This ain't no knock on higher education, you see. UC Santa Barbara is a fine school that turns out a lot of engineers, physicists, and surfers. But such is the nature of Goleta that the university located here nominally chooses to align itself with a city eight miles away. Goleta is essentially a seaside student colony. Its streets are dusty, its storefronts are generic, and the town has an overall look of plainness. The university is unquestionably the main attraction. The student body studies and lives here, and some of them surf at the base of the bluffs along which the school is situated. But for the most part they head into Santa Barbara to have fun. You should take their cue and do likewise.

For more information, contact the Goleta Valley Chamber of Commerce, 271 North Fairview, Goleta, CA 93117, 805/967-2500 or 800/646-5382, www.goletavalley.com.

BEACHES

A terrific county park beach provides an oasis of escape from the strip-mall blues of Goleta. **Goleta Beach County Park** is a great spot in a gorgeous setting. Parking is free, and people come to picnic, play volleyball, toss horseshoes, and frolic in the water. Tables, hibachis, and open-air shelters are provided. The 29-acre park includes a long, thin pier; wide sandy beach; and more green acres than Hooterville. All in all, it's a very pleasant surprise.

16 GOLETA BEACH COUNTY PARK

Location: 5990 Sand Spit Road in Goleta
Parking/Fees: free parking lot
Hours: 8 A.M.-sunset
Facilities: concession, lifeguards, restrooms, and picnic area
Contact: Goleta Beach County Park, 805/967-1300

ACCOMMODATIONS

Your lodging choices in Goleta are pretty much brand-name chains, including a few nicely tended properties like the **Best Western**

South Coast Inn (5620 Calle Real, 805/967-3200, $$) and the **Holiday Inn** (5650 Calle Real, 805/964-6241, $$).

However, a major five-star luxury resort has arrived on the scene. Four miles northwest of UCSB, **Bacara Resort & Spa** (8301 Hollister Avenue, 850/968-0100, www.bacara resort.com, $$$$) has its own beach away from the hubbub. Set along a rugged stretch of coastline 13 miles north of Santa Barbara—and technically in Goleta—Bacara is among the rarest of California species: a luxury resort built directly on the beach. Bacara is situated on two miles of coast. Its shoreline remains a wild beach—no grooming or cleanup—in deference to rare and endangered species like the globose dune beetle, the red-legged frog, and the monarch butterfly.

The Spanish mission–style buildings at Bacara are set back from the beach. You'll still get a nice view of the ocean, but the buildings don't infringe upon the dunes ecosystem. The resort was designed to suggest the glamour of "old Hollywood" in the 1940s. This is most evident in the palatial lobby; the circular, clubby Bacara Bar; and the main pool. The approach to the pool, with the ocean behind it, is one of the more visually arresting sights at any California resort. We were impressed by the fact that on a spring weekend when the hotel was filled to capacity, the grounds were peacefully uncongested.

Room rates are what you'd expect at such a place, starting at $475 and soaring from there, depending on location, room size, and view. You can, for instance, spend $2,500 nightly to stay in a "signature partial ocean-view suite." (We could easily make that much money last a few weeks on the road.) The rooms are full of extra touches—robes, slippers, wide balconies, gas fireplaces. The Spa at Bacara occupies 42,000 square feet of pricey pampering (e.g., massages that cost $3 per minute).

The Bacara was built with wealthy executives and entertainment-industry types in mind. Even with a listing economy, there will always be an upper crust who can afford places like the Bacara and desire its rarefied air. We saw hip, Gatsby-esque types strolling to dinner at **Miro,** the fine-dining restaurant that displays three original Miro sculptures, plus wall-sized paintings executed after the style of great artists. In contrast to the mannerly old-money types who still don suits and ties for dinner, we saw a lot of L.A. playboys garbed in black with slicked-back hair and cell phones at the ready.

We've rubbed elbows with the rich and famous and have stayed at many of America's finest resorts. Even when we don't belong, we've gotten good at faking it. However, we felt somewhat out of our element at Bacara. No one made us feel that way; everyone was perfectly charming and gracious. It was just something we knew: Serious money comes to let its hair down here. As they put it, "old Hollywood glamour" meets "new California dreaming" at Bacara.

COASTAL CUISINE

Goleta Beach County Park has its own neat little restaurant, the **Beachside Bar Cafe** (5905 Sand Spit Road, 805/964-7881, $$). It overlooks the water and serves fresh catches like local sea bass and ahi, plus everything from sandwiches to salmon *en papillote.*

Isla Vista

Isla Vista backs right up against Goleta, and indeed the two are so inseparable that everything we said under "Goleta" suffices to cover Isla Vista as well in all categories—except beaches, of which Isla Vista has more options. Both Isla Vista and Goleta share campuses of the University of California at Santa Barbara. The main campus is at Goleta Point, in Goleta; the west campus is in Isla Vista, at Coal Oil Point. The town of Isla Vista (population 20,500) and its several beaches lie between the two points.

For more information, contact the Goleta Valley Chamber of Commerce, 271 North Fairview, Goleta, CA 93117, 805/967-2500 or 800/646-5382, www.goletavalley.com.

THE BATTLE OVER HASKELL'S BEACH

Mention the words "Haskell's Beach" to Santa Barbara locals, and they might start looking wistful. For decades, Santa Barbara County residents knew a paradisiacal stretch of coast above Goleta as Haskell's Beach. It was a little slice of undefiled coastal habitat – a remote coast getaway enjoyed by those in the know. Now it is home to the ritzy Bacara Resort & Spa. You'd never guess from strolling the grounds of this pricey resort that it was the site of a major battle between developers and environmentalists.

The debate over Haskell's dated back to a 1975 proposal by the Wallover Corporation (which bought the parcel in 1969) to build 153 townhouses on its coastal holdings. Wallover had been purchased by a New York banker and developer named Alvin Dworman, who was determined to develop the 73-acre coast parcel that came with his acquisition of the company.

After a futile attempt by the state of California to acquire the land for public recreation purposes in the late 1970s, Wallover partnered with the Hyatt Corporation, and a new proposal for a 524-room luxury destination resort was made in 1983. The Santa Barbara County Board of Supervisors was complicit in what followed, as they endorsed the rezoning of Haskell's Beach in 1985 as "Visitor-Serving Commercial." This action extended the Goleta urban planning area all the way out to this formerly deserted beach. While in the planning stages, the proposed development was called "the Santa Barbara Club Resort and Spa." In 1997, Hyatt – having grown wary of the economic risk – pulled out of the deal. Dworman forged onward, taking on all comers.

The fight to build or block the resort pitted Dworman and local pro-development forces against environmental and grassroots groups. Arguments against development included the fact that several protected and endangered species occupied the area. It became a battle royale. When the dust cleared, Dworman (a former Golden Gloves boxer) emerged victorious, albeit with bloodied reputation. The brawl had been ugly and costly. All told, there were 50 public hearings and three major lawsuits. The developers spent $11 million on public relations, legal fees, and permits.

The 360-room, $220 million Bacara Resort & Spa opened in September 2000. As for the environmental aftermath, one demoralized activist wrote, "Despite our best efforts, Haskell's Beach, as we know it, is gone. It is doubtful that it could be restored to its former beauty, were it possible to try. A tragedy of great magnitude has occurred at Haskell's Beach."

BEACHES

For approximately 2.5 miles between Goleta Point and Coal Oil Point, the coast runs on a near-perfect east–west axis. Sand beaches are beneath the bluffs, beginning with **Isla Vista Beach,** accessible via stairways at several street ends. A grassy bluff-top park, **Isla Vista County Park,** overlooks the beach. At this park you can lounge, read, and gaze seaward from ocean-facing wooden platforms.

One of Santa Barbara County's most recent coastal acquisitions is **Santa Barbara Shores,** 118 acres of open space that abuts a golf course. Hiking trails skirt the coastal bluffs. You can access another beach, though not without difficulty, at the university-owned **Coal Oil Point Natural Reserve.** You need a special West Campus parking permit, available by calling 805/893-5092. The permit is a bargain ($3) and serves a useful purpose of limiting the numbers here. The reserve comprises mostly protected coastal wetlands, though the beach below the frontal dunes—plainly referred to as **Sands Beach**—is available

SANTA BARBARA COAST

to the public. Surfers call it Devereaux's (that's the name of the slough). All of these Isla Vista beaches are enjoyed by surfers who relish the fact they don't have to fight crowds to get super rides.

Just outside the Bacara Resort & Spa on Hollister Road is a new beach access, **Bacara Beach.** No doubt it was provided as part of the deal to construct Bacara Resort & Spa. These days, coastal development typically requires some kind of quid pro quo in the form of deeded public access by the developer. Bacara Beach occupies part of an area formerly known as Haskell's Beach, at least some of which wound up in public hands.

17 ISLA VISTA COUNTY PARK

Location: Del Playa Drive at Camino Corto in Isla Vista
Parking/Fees: free street parking
Hours: 8 A.M.-sunset
Facilities: picnic tables
Contact: Santa Barbara County Department of Parks and Recreation, 805/681-5650

18 SANTA BARBARA SHORES

Location: south of Hollister Road in Isla Vista
Parking/Fees: free parking lot
Hours: 8 A.M.-sunset
Facilities: none
Contact: Santa Barbara County Department of Parks and Recreation, 805/681-5650; City of Goleta, 805/961-7500

19 SANDS BEACH

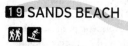

Location: end of Storke Road in Isla Vista, on the campus of the University of California at Santa Barbara

Parking/Fees: $3 entrance fee per person; park in Isla Vista and walk across campus, or reserve a campus parking permit by calling the Natural Reserve System Director's office, 805/893-5092
Hours: 24 hours
Facilities: none
Contact: Natural Reserve System Office, Marine Science Institute (Trailer 342), University of California at Santa Barbara, 805/893-5092

20 BACARA BEACH (A.K.A. HASKELL'S BEACH)

Location: off Hollister Road five miles west of Goleta
Parking/Fees: free parking lot
Hours: 8 A.M.-sunset
Facilities: restrooms and showers
Contact: Santa Barbara County Department of Parks and Recreation, 805/681-5650

NIGHTLIFE

When you're done hitting the books, head to **Study Hall** (6543 Pardall Road, 805/685-0929). That is, if you're old enough.

El Capitán State Beach

North of Goleta, private ranchland dominates the terrain on both sides of U.S. 101. This prohibits any viable beach access, unless you savor the idea of being mauled by a steer while loping with your beach towel toward a stunning headland. Take time out instead to notice how your surroundings change as you proceed north. The distant peaks are higher, more jagged. The land is open, with rolling pasture between the ocean and mountains. The air seems more breathable, and the winds blow with greater force. Road signs warn of "Gusty Winds." Even the beaches seem wilder.

For more information, contact El Capitán State Beach, c/o Channel Coast District, California State Parks, 1933 Cliff Drive, Santa Barbara, CA 93109, 805/899-1400, www.parks.ca.gov.

BEACHES

Between Santa Barbara and Point Conception, the coastline runs along an east–west axis, and the beaches face due south. This keeps northern swells at bay, and anything else unpleasant is fended off by the Channel Islands. Ocean swimming is ideal here, and three of California's most appealing state beaches—El Capitán, Refugio, and Gaviota—can be found in a row along a nine-mile stretch.

The first of these is **El Capitán State Beach,** 15 miles northwest of Santa Barbara. To get there you'll pass beneath the U.S. 101 overpass and through a lovely grove of sycamore and oak trees, ending at a sizable campground. Nature lovers will enjoy exploring the many facets of this 133-acre park, including sea cliffs, tidepools, meadows, marine terraces, and canyons. A central stairwell cuts along the bluff to the beach below. It's a healthy strand with teeming tidepools. Swimming is safe, and good surfing is possible on winter swells. Surf-casting catches include perch, bass, and halibut. A trail for cyclists and hikers runs along the bluff top for 2.5 miles north to Refugio State Beach. A camp store is on the grounds, just in case you forgot sunscreen, potato chips, or "Tar Off" packets. There's also a boat launch ($5 per boat).

El Capitán State Beach was named for Jose Francisco de Ortega, the Spanish captain who scouted for the Portolà expedition of 1769. Part of Ortega's old rancho serves as **El Capitan Canyon Campground** (11560 Calle Real, Goleta, CA 93117, 805/685-3887), a privately owned resort in a canyon on the other side of the highway. You can bunk down in a "deluxe safari tent" for $145 a night or opt for cabins that range $255–350 per night. Incidentally,

the old Reagan Ranch is buried in the hills behind El Capitán.

21 EL CAPITÁN STATE BEACH

Location: 15 miles northwest of Santa Barbara, off U.S. 101
Parking/Fees: $8 entrance fee per vehicle; camping fees $20-25 per night, plus $7.50 reservation fee; "Hike & Bike" sites $5 per night
Hours: 8 A.M.-sunset
Facilities: concession, lifeguards (seasonal), restrooms, showers, and picnic tables
Contact: California State Parks, Channel Coast District, 805/899-1400, or 968-1033

Refugio State Beach

The name of the park comes from Spanish explorer Jose Francisco de Ortega's once extensive rancho, La Nuestra Señora del Refugio ("Our Lady of Refuge"). From this refuge Ortega traded with pirates and smugglers until a band of French buccaneers came ashore, looted his mansion, and then burned it down. In the 1930s a chap named Nelson Rutherford opened a campground here. He built a house that still stands and granted public access to a mineral spring on the beach. When his private campground became too much for him to handle, he sold it to the state in 1950.

For more information, contact Refugio State Beach, c/o Gaviota Sector, California State Parks, 10 Refugio Beach Road, Goleta, CA 93117, 805/968-1033, www.parks.ca.gov.

BEACHES

More than anything else, **Refugio State Beach** is a scaled-down version of El Capitán State Beach. Located 18 miles northwest of Santa Barbara and three miles above El Capitán, Refugio offers 80 tent campsites and a slightly rockier shoreline, with rich tidepools, a 1.5-mile-long beach, and a beautiful view of the Channel Islands from the bluff above the campground. Refugio has an added botanical distinction: enormous banana palm trees line Refugio Creek to the east, lending the land a tropical feel that is rare this far north. In recent years cliff erosion has threatened the sacred palms, 20 of which have been replanted farther inland. On one visit we saw a knot of surfers getting some good long rides up at the western end of the beach. We also saw people swimming in the freshwater lagoon formed where Refugio Creek enters the ocean.

22 REFUGIO STATE BEACH

Location: off U.S. 101, 17 miles northwest of Santa Barbara
Parking/Fees: $8 entrance fee per vehicle; camping fees $20-25 per night, plus $7.50 reservation fee; "Hike & Bike" sites $5 per night
Hours: 8 A.M.-sunset
Facilities: concession, lifeguards (seasonal), restrooms, showers, and picnic tables
Contact: California State Parks, Channel Coast District, Gaviota Sector, 805/968-1033

Gaviota State Park

Gaviota State Park lies six miles up the road from Refugio State Beach and 24 miles from Santa Barbara. It provides the last user-friendly access to the coast until Pismo Beach, 60 miles north. It's also the last viable glimpse of the Southern California coast before the elemental rawness of the Central Coast takes over on the far side of Point Conception. Gaviota takes its name from the Spanish word for seagull. It is here that Portola's gang came ashore and shot a seagull. (Don't get any ideas of your own.)

Gaviota offers full camping facilities (including showers and restrooms), isolation without danger, natural wonders, 5.5 miles of coastline, and easy access to the beach. The setting of this large and varied park is as unusual as it is beautiful. The rusting hulk of an ancient railroad overpass towers majestically over the beachhead, spanning two sheer walls of rock.

For more information, contact Gaviota State Park, c/o Gaviota Sector, California State Parks, 10 Refugio Beach Road, Goleta, CA 93117, 805/968-1033, www.parks.ca.gov.

BEACHES

Located where Gaviota Creek empties into the ocean, the beach at **Gaviota State Park** is great for fishing, swimming, and beachcombing. A fishing pier offers a three-ton hoist used to launch or haul powerboats from the water. Near the water 54 campsites are available, 36 of which have RV hookups.

Away from the ocean, Gaviota's 2,700 acres provide extensive hiking possibilities among the hills to the east. Hikers and backpackers can make their way to hot springs offering body-temperature water. An 11-mile trail crests at Gaviota Peak, a 2,458-foot promontory from which intrepid climbers can collect breathtaking coastline views as a reward for having made their way to the top.

A half-mile southeast of the main entrance to Gaviota State Park, adjacent turnouts have trails leading to clothing-optional cove beaches called **San Onofre Beach** and **Vista del Mar Beach.** Both lie on state-park property and do not offer facilities.

23 SAN ONOFRE AND VISTA DEL MAR BEACHES

Location: 0.5 mile southeast of the main entrance to Gaviota State Park, off U.S. 101
Parking/Fees: free roadside parking
Hours: 8 A.M.-sunset
Facilities: none

Contact: California State Parks, Channel Coast District, Gaviota Sector, 805/968-1033

24 GAVIOTA STATE PARK

🔺 🚶 ⚓ 🚻

Location: 20 miles northwest of Santa Barbara off U.S. 101
Parking/Fees: $8 entrance fee per vehicle; camping fees $20-25 per night, plus $7.50 reservation fee
Hours: 8 A.M.-sunset
Facilities: lifeguards (seasonal), restrooms, showers, and picnic tables
Contact: California State Parks, Channel Coast District, Gaviota Sector 805/968-1033

Point Conception

Traveling north from central Santa Barbara County's trio of state-beach jewels—El Capitán, Refugio, and Gaviota—you have a choice. You can continue hugging the relatively inaccessible shoreline via Highway 1, or you can hit the freeway (U.S. 101), which cuts an inland swath.

If you choose Highway 1, you will be rewarded with Point Conception, a formidable jut of land 50 miles northwest of Santa Barbara that signals the geographical end of Southern California. There is no direct access to Point Conception, because private ranches swallow the Point Conception headland. These ranches—Bixby and Hollister—are notoriously nasty to intruders, so be forewarned: We will not provide bail money should you be arrested with our book in hand. Still, getting to Point Conception is worth the difficult trek. As long as you stay below the high-tide line, you are within your legal right to walk to Point Conception via the beach. That doesn't mean you won't be hassled by the sentinels at Hollister Ranch, though. The best way for a determined surfer to gain legal access to the waves at Point Conception is by boat. Intrepid beach hikers

who want to see the point up close and personal can walk five miles south from Jalama Beach County Park.

Jalama Beach County Park

Jalama Beach County Park is very much out of the way, lying 55 miles northwest of Santa Barbara. One must turn west from Highway 1 onto Jalama Beach Road and drive 14 desolate miles to the park. Jalama draws anglers, surfers, windsurfers, hikers, bird-watchers, and whale-watchers. Surfers love Jalama Beach in the summer and often trek south to Point Conception in search of a perfect wave.

For more information, contact Jalama Beach County Park, Star Route, Lompoc, CA 93436, 805/736-6316 (recorded information) or 805/736-3504 (park office), www.santa barbaraparks.com.

BEACHES

The beach at **Jalama Beach County Park** is small (a half mile, at most), but the campground is fairly large (110 sites, all overlooking the ocean) and set among 28 acres. If you savor the thrill of beach hiking, you'll be in heaven here. A mile north is Vandenberg Air Force Base (watch for missile fragments while beachcombing), and five miles south is Point Conception. The trail to Point Conception retraces the route of Juan Bautista de Anza, who brought 250 colonists from Mexico through here in 1775–1776. Notably, they ended up founding San Francisco.

It is safe to walk this trail only at low tide. The beach trail starts out wide but thins and disappears at times, forcing one to straddle seawalls and railroad tracks. Just north of the point is Point Conception Coast Guard Lighthouse, which has been warning boats away from this hazardous stretch of coast since 1856. Because it is a still-active lighthouse on government property, it is not a climbable landmark, so keep on trucking.

25 JALAMA BEACH COUNTY PARK

Location: Take Highway 1 five miles north of Lompoc, turn west onto Jalama Beach Road and follow for 10 miles
Parking/Fees: $8 entrance fee per vehicle; camping fees $20-30 per night
Hours: 8 A.M.-sunset
Facilities: concession, lifeguards, restrooms, showers, and picnic tables
Contact: Jalama Beach County Park, 805/736-3504

Lompoc

If you're up for another adventure after Point Conception, head out to Ocean Beach County Park. To find it, follow Highway 1 through the sweet-smelling, flower-filled fields of Lompoc (pronounced lom-POKE), which merits it the nickname "Valley of the Flowers." Lompoc has a not-insubstantial population of 44,200. There's a high-security federal prison in town, and Vandenberg Air Force Base is close by.

Highway 246/Ocean Park Road cuts west from the center, leading through Vandenberg Air Force Base. The road becomes curvier and bumpier with each of its 10 miles, finally giving out in a parking lot. Stop, look, and listen. Rusted railroad cars sit on an abandoned piece of track. The wind whistles through the sandy fields. You are officially in the middle of nowhere.

For more information, contact the Lompoc Valley Chamber of Commerce and Visitors Bureau, 111 S. I Street, Lompoc, CA 93436, 805/736-4567 or 800/240-0999, www.lompoc.com.

BEACHES

Ocean Beach County Park comprises 28 wetlands-bounded acres, embracing a broad, sandy beach and a lagoon at the mouth of the Santa Ynez River. The river mouth serves as a fragile riparian habitat for the California brown pelican and the least tern. A half-mile dirt path leads under the Southern Pacific Railroad trestle to a beach with healthy-sized sand dunes.

26 OCEAN BEACH COUNTY PARK

Location: 13 miles west of Lompoc, via Ocean Park Road/Highway 246, in the town of Surf
Parking/Fees: free parking lot
Hours: sunrise-sunset
Facilities: restrooms and picnic tables
Contact: Ocean Beach County Park, 805/934-6123

Vandenberg Air Force Base

The fishing access at Vandenberg Air Force Base Fishing Access is the hard-core angler's El Dorado. Its beaches are reached out of a tiny blip on the mapmaker's radar, called Surf, at the mouth of the Santa Ynez River. Vandenberg offers limited access (50 people per day, weekends only) to an eight-mile stretch of coast from the river to Purisima Point. No swimming or surfing—only fishing.

For more information, contact Vandenberg Air Force Base, 805/606-3595, www.vandenberg.af.mil.

BEACHES

To obtain a permit to visit **Vandenberg Air Force Base Fishing Access,** call the base's game warden (805/606-6804). Be prepared to give your name, license plate number, vehicle identification number, and a fishing license number for every occupant in your car. Fishing access permits are given to callers on a first-come, first-served basis for the coming weekend beginning the prior Monday morning. No calls are taken after noon on Friday.

27 VANDENBERG AIR FORCE BASE FISHING ACCESS

Location: Vandenberg Air Force Base, off Highway 1
Parking/Fees: free weekend fishing access pass available from Vandenberg Air Force Base Game Warden; valid driver's license and California fishing license required
Hours: sunrise-sunset Saturday-Sunday
Facilities: none
Contact: Vandenberg Air Force Base, 805/606-3595

Point Sal State Beach

Another spot for the lonesome traveler in northern Santa Barbara County is Point Sal State Beach, a free day-use-only beach that takes nerves of steel and sturdy hiking boots to reach. To get to this windswept, two-mile stretch of coastal wilderness, take unpaved Brown Road (just south of Guadalupe) to Point Sal Road. Since 1998, the latter has been closed past a certain point, having been reclaimed by nature during a period of heavy rain. This closure necessitates a 4.5-mile one-way hike to the beach—that is, providing Vandenberg Air Force Base isn't denying access because of a missile launch or for some other reason. If you do make it out to the beach, you might as well continue hiking north along the beach for another two miles to Mussel Point. In its elemental wildness and beauty, the area resembles Big Sur. Bring a camera, dress for a bracing wilderness hike, and bring plenty of snacks and water.

In May 2008, the county came to terms with Vandenberg Air Force Base on a plan to repair the Point Sal Road, thereby immeasurably improving access to Point Sal for those who cannot fathom a nine-mile round-trip hike. "Efforts to develop a long-term access plan to Point Sal State Beach are continuing," according to the California State Parks website.

For more information, contact Point Sal State Beach, c/o La Purisima Sector, 2295 Purisima Road, Lompoc, CA 93436, 805/733-3713, www.parks.ca.gov.

BEACHES

Point Sal State Beach is a good surf casting spot and, during the winter migration, a great whale-watching point. It is protected from the northwesterly winds that buffet the sand-dune ranges to the south. In other words, you don't have to hike the beach at a 45-degree angle.

An excellent hiking trail can be found at Point Sal. This vertigo-inducing five-mile trail can be treacherous, too, as it tiptoes along the tops of bluffs a hundred precipitous feet above the water. Down below, you can spot seals and sea lions on the rocks and hear them barking above the roar of the surf.

28 POINT SAL STATE BEACH

Location: nine miles west of Guadalupe via Point Sal Road
Parking/Fees: free parking lot
Hours: 8 A.M.-sunset
Facilities: none
Contact: California State Parks, Channel Coast District, La Purisima Sector, 805/733-3713

Guadalupe-Nipomo Dunes Preserve

North of Lompoc, sand dunes rise along the coast like bare white mountains for 20 miles. They reach their highest peaks west of the ramshackle town of Guadalupe, and the highway doesn't go anywhere near them. En route to them, Main Street passes the town cemetery, a few rugged fields, and an open range where cows graze, oblivious to the gusty winds, chilly temperatures, and sand.

GUADALUPE DUNES DISASTER

The Guadalupe Dunes have been frequented by relatively few visitors over the past 30 years. That is because the Union Oil Company of California (a.k.a. Unocal) maintained a 2,700-acre oil field among the Guadalupe-Nipomo Dunes dating back to the 1960s. At its peak, the oil field contained 215 wells. Before the operation was shut down in 1994, a spill was detected that had been going on for quite some time – perhaps three decades. Estimates of the amount of petroleum product leaked into the sand range 8-20 million gallons, making it twice as big as the oil spill caused by the *Exxon Valdez* in Alaska.

Unocal was charged with criminal activity for covering up the spills at its Guadalupe oil field while continuing to pump black gold from the ground. Once state officials and environmental groups got wise to the corporate malfeasance, lawsuits flew. In July 1998, Unocal ended five years of negotiating with the state and agreed to pay $43.8 million, one of the biggest settlements ever negotiated by the state attorney general's office. The money would cover penalties, natural resource damages, and injunctive relief to secure site cleanup. The Surfers Environmental Alliance has described the settlement as a "paltry token to the public" compared to the $425 million Exxon had to pay on its 1989 crude oil spill. Nonetheless, Unocal completed its mandated five-year cleanup in 2001, after having been granted more than 1,000 separate permits by the California Coastal Commission.

The cleanup required Unocal to bulldoze an area the size of two football fields and dredge deep into the dunes to remove all the contaminated sand. They had to destroy the dunes in order to save them, in other words. Public and private landholders with a stake in the dunes' continued preservation came together to form **The Dunes Center** (1055 Guadalupe Street, Guadalupe, CA 93434, 805/343-2455), which has a visitors center near the entrance to the preserve.

BEACHES

To access the dunes, follow Main Street/Highway 166 for eight miles out of Guadalupe to its end at the beach. A small parcel of beach is given over to **Rancho Guadalupe Dunes County Park,** where you'll find not much more than portable toilets, a parking lot, a seawall, and lots of wild, wind-blown beach.

Sand is everywhere. Sand blows over the road, obscuring it in places. Sand covers the parking lot. Sand forms a buffer between you and the beach. Sand gets in your eyes. This area—the first of three dune fields that make up a range of sand mountains known collectively as the **Guadalupe-Nipomo Dunes Preserve**—is owned and protected by the Nature Conservancy, which provides trail information and interpretive brochures. Since 1987, the conservancy has acquired 3,117 acres

of dunes habitat. The area is of high ecological interest because of its overlap of southern and northern California coast habitats. Within these dune fields is a complex ecosystem made up of dune hollows, lakes, wetlands, and scrublands.

Meditative strolls can be taken among the dunes at various points along the 18 miles of coastline from here to Pismo Beach. Somewhere among all that sand is Mussel Rock, the highest dune on the West Coast. It is all sand, not rock, and stands 500 feet tall, give or take a few shifting grains. An arduous, ankle-sinking two-mile hike is required if you wish to see the biggest sand dune in the West. That might be your only recreation, because the ocean at the Guadalupe entrance to Nipomo Dunes is too rough for immersion. We saw no surfers, no swimmers, no picnickers, no fishers, and no lifeguards—nothing

Guadalupe Dunes

but sand, sand, sand. Enough to make Lawrence of Arabia feel at home.

In addition to the Guadalupe entrance off Highway 166, the Nature Conservancy maintains a second access point to the dunes and several hiking trails at Oso Flaco Lake. Four miles north of Guadalupe on Highway 1, turn left on Oso Flaco Lake Road and drive about four miles to the preserve. Parking costs $4, and the Nature Conservancy provides a map of the area at the entrance kiosk. A boardwalk through Nipomo Dunes leads 1.5 miles to the beach. Another trail, a seven-mile round-trip, winds along the shore of this pristine lake, which provides habitat for ducks, herons, and pelicans. Oso Flaco derives its name from the Spanish for "skinny bear," which is exactly what Portola's men killed here in 1769. There are no bears left, but there is a particularly secluded spot with a musical name, Hidden Willow Valley, where willows grow between the dunes. Bring a canteen and wear a hat.

This coastal preserve is one of the most remarkable in California, and because it's in the right hands, we can all sleep better. The entire Nipomo Dunes area has a history as fascinating as its terrain. These sands have been shifting for 20,000 years, embracing and covering any and all attempts at human habitation. Back in the 1930s, the dunes were home to the "Dunites," a ragtag army of artists, hermits, nudists, and writers who inhabited shacks among the ephemeral sands and published their own *Dune Forum* magazine. The area indeed lends itself to solitary artistic activity, and after an hour or so of hopping about shifting ground cover, one is put in mind of Kobo Abe's disturbing but brilliant novel *Woman in the Dunes*. Reading that book is as close as we'd like to come to living among all this golden sand, as glorious as it is to look upon. Perhaps because of the deep isolation and rich legacy, Guadalupe Dunes attracts the occasional nude sunbather.

The Nature Conservancy operates the Dunes Center, a visitors center in Guadalupe that is open noon–4 P.M. on Friday, Saturday, and Sunday. Staff members serve as docents for hikes and bird walks into the dunes, sponsor workshops and other educational events, and work to preserve the dunes.

SANTA BARBARA COAST

For more information, contact the Dunes Center, Guadalupe–Nipomo Dunes Preserve, 1055 Guadalupe Street, Guadalupe, CA 93434, 805/343-2455, www.dunescenter.org.

29 RANCHO GUADALUPE DUNES COUNTY PARK

Location: eight miles west of Guadalupe, via Main Street/Highway 166
Parking/Fees: free parking lot
Hours: 8 A.M.-sunset
Facilities: restrooms
Contact: Ocean Beach County Park, 805/934-6123

30 GUADALUPE-NIPOMO DUNES PRESERVE

Location: accessible through Rancho Guadalupe Dunes County Park (eight miles west of Guadalupe, via Main Street/Highway 166) or Oso Flaco Lake (four miles north of Guadalupe via Highway 1, then four miles west via Oso Flaco Lake Road)
Parking/Fees: free parking lot
Hours: by reservation only
Facilities: restrooms
Contact: Dunes Center, Guadalupe-Nipomo Dunes Preserve, 805/343-2455

PISMO BEACH AND THE CENTRAL COAST

One of the great joys of beach travel is visiting—and in our case, revisiting—a stretch of coastline that has everything going for it and has been largely bypassed by the thundering herd. So it is with the Central Coast and its unassuming towns: humble Pismo Beach, lovely Morro Bay, quiet Cambria, quaint Cayucos, and historic San Simeon.

This area of coastline is bounded by the remarkable Nipomo Dunes at the south end, and the Hearst Castle, in San Simeon, to the north. In some ways, San Luis Obispo—a town that isn't even on the ocean—is the real heart of the Central Coast. It's a scaled-down version of Santa Barbara set in an agricultural valley. From this jumping-off point, a visitor can easily access the area's extraordinary beaches.

Bunched together at the south end are the "Five Cities": Arroyo Grande, Oceano, Grover Beach, Pismo Beach, and Shell Beach. The largest of these, Pismo Beach, is best known for the Pismo clam. The area is also renowned for its broad dune fields, which are among the most extensive in the state. Oceano Dunes State Vehicle Recreation Area is the only place in California where one can legally drive on the beach. Shell Beach and Avila Beach offer enticing, cliff-hugging views and splendid cove beaches.

Morro Bay looks out on the visually arresting monolith of Morro Rock. Romantic Cambria's calling card is the inspirational seclusion of Moonstone Beach. In between is the Western-themed town of Cayucos, which seems frozen in time. Rolling hills and green valleys, clean air and comfortable temperatures, and more than 30 inland wineries in the Edna and Arroyo Grande Valleys serve to complement the outstanding array of beaches on the coast.

© PARKE PUTERBAUGH

THE CENTRAL COAST

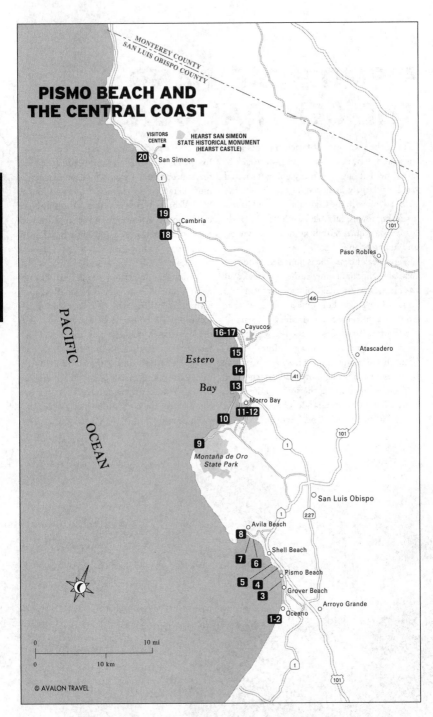

PISMO BEACH AND
THE CENTRAL COAST

MONTEREY COUNTY
SAN LUIS OBISPO COUNTY

VISITORS
CENTER

HEARST SAN SIMEON
STATE HISTORICAL MONUMENT
(HEARST CASTLE)

20 San Simeon

1

101

19 Cambria
18

Paso Robles

1

46

16-17 Cayucos

Estero **15**

14

Atascadero

Bay **13**

41

Morro Bay

11-12

10

101

9

Montaña de Oro
State Park

1

PACIFIC

OCEAN

San Luis Obispo

1   227

Avila Beach

8

Shell Beach

7   **6**

Pismo Beach

5   **4**

3   Grover Beach

Oceano   Arroyo Grande

1-2

1

101

0   10 mi

0   10 km

© AVALON TRAVEL

BEST BEACHES

(Pismo Beach, page 271   (Moonstone Beach, page 289

Arroyo Grande

The 50-mile stretch of U.S. 101 from Santa Barbara to Pismo Beach passes through some extraordinary interior scenery, from the flower fields of Lompoc Valley to the forest surrounding Guadalupe. Suddenly, in a swooping series of hairpin turns, the highway descends to the coastal plain again, heading back toward the beach with the precision of a heat-seeking missile. Before reaching the ocean, the highway passes a crossroads called Arroyo Grande (pronounced "ah-ROY-yo GRAN-dee").

At this point, there is absolutely no question that you have left Southern California and entered the Central Coast. More Western than Californian, these towns are filled with less narcissistically body-conscious folks who go in for cowboy boots and motorbikes. Their homes aren't featured in *Architectural Digest,* nor do their wardrobes turn up in the pages of *GQ* or *Vogue.* Tentlike gingham dresses are spied as frequently as taut bare midriffs on the women. Even the mountains that press against the towns are different, softer in tone and texture, less jagged, and covered with gray-brown whiskers.

Pismo Beach, as a municipal entity, is five towns that incorporated into one. They call this mid-coast mini-metropolis "the Five Cities." Moving north along U.S. 101, they are Arroyo Grande, Oceano, Grover Beach, Pismo Beach, and Shell Beach. Four are directly on the coast, while Arroyo Grande is a few miles inland. The manners, appearance, and style vary from town to town. At the extremes, Shell Beach represents the most overt stab at gentrification while Pismo Beach is cut from plainer cloth. Think of Pismo Beach as denim to Shell Beach's silk.

Arroyo Grande has been used as a backdrop for Hollywood film shoots. No wonder: It has a pleasantly authentic hometown feel. The town center contains a few blocks of Victorian-era architecture, and its antique shops do a brisk business. On its periphery, things get a little more contemporary, which is to say franchised. Above Arroyo Grande, after its inland swing, the Pacific Coast Highway shoots back toward the beaches. Keep rolling up PCH and the ocean will soon come back into view.

For more information, contact the Arroyo Grande Chamber of Commerce, 800 West Branch Street, Arroyo Grande, CA 93420, 805/489-1488, www.arroyograndecc.com.

ACCOMMODATIONS

Relative to Southern California, room rates drop along the Central Coast. If you're laying over in Arroyo Grande, the **Best Western Casa Grande Inn** (850 Oak Park Boulevard, 805/481-7398, $) is an attractive and affordable option. For us, after a long day of driving, it was a veritable oasis, and we made use of every amenity, from the pool and spa to the free breakfast.

Oceano Dunes

Oceano Dunes is the only place on the California coast where it is legal to drive on the beach. From Oso Flaco at the north end of Nipomo Dunes to Grover Beach—a distance of over four miles—cars are permitted on the beach. They call this the "Sand Highway." Its official name is Oceano Dunes State Vehicle Recreation Area, and it consists of 4,000 sandy acres of dunes and beaches.

It can be accessed from Grover Beach and

Oceano, two otherwise unzoned, unregulated sprawl spigots whose elected officials should be ashamed of themselves. Once you're on the sand, however, you're in another world. The speed limit on the Sand Highway is 15 miles per hour, and you must drive in the hard-packed sand near the ocean's edge. Beginning at Post 2 in Oceano, all-terrain vehicles (ATVs) and off-highway vehicles (OHVs) are permitted on the dunes themselves, which stretch for almost a mile inland. Cars are not permitted on the dunes.

The tallest dunes have no vegetation holding them in place, and thus drift with the winds. Therefore, a bunch of ATVs stir-ring up the sand aren't going to cause any damage—unless those driving them roll over and injure themselves, that is. Although the state maintains other off-road recreational areas, Oceano Dunes is the only one directly on the coast. Thus, brigades of ATVs, OHVs, and "street legal" vehicles converge on the park during summer weekends. Therefore, when visiting Oceano Dunes, be prepared and always look both ways before crossing the beach.

For more information, contact the Oceano Dunes State Vehicle Recreation Area, 576 Camino Mercado, Arroyo Grande, CA 93420, 805/473-7230, www.parks.ca.gov.

THE GEOLOGY OF SAND DUNES

The sand dunes in the Nipomo and Oceano area are the most extensive coastal dunes remaining in California. The material that forms these piles is washed into the ocean by rivers and creeks in the surrounding watershed. Deposits from this rich lode are carried by shore-paralleling ocean currents and then shaped into dunes by onshore winds. The prevailing winds here push sand particles into wavy crests that run north-south. The slope is gentle on the windward (west) side, steep on the leeward (east) side. As sand grains are blown over the crest of the dune from west to east, the high crests collapse, sliding leeward in what are called "slip-face" slopes.

The most stable dunes are those with vegetative cover – wildflowers, shrubs, and grasses that hold the sand in place by breaking the force of the prevailing winds. At Oceano Dunes, the holdfast vegetation on the smaller, more stable dunes includes arroyo willow, California sagebrush, sand verbena, and bush lupine, as well as a non-native European beach grass.

Most coastal vegetation is fragile and must survive in a harsh environment of desiccating wind, hot sun, and deep water table. These plants can be easily dislodged if disturbed by contact with visitors' feet or wheels. Once the top of the vegetative cover has been severed, the extensive root system that holds the sand in place dies off and the dune becomes vulnerable to massive shifting.

The key to keeping dunes in place is to leave them undisturbed. That is, do not blaze trails among the vegetation, and stick to areas that have already been traveled. Maybe we're just weird, but we've always wondered what kind of person could enjoy trampling vegetation while scooting around dunes atop a sputtering, gas-guzzling, noise-making machine.

On dunes like those at Pismo Beach, the biggest piles of sand are those that won't support vegetable cover. It is these places where all-terrain vehicles should be used (but not abused). Anyone caught driving through dune grasses deserves to be chopped up and fed to the Pismo clams.

TURN OFF THE ATV!

ATVs and OHVs are those three-wheeled gizmos that look like big-wheeled riding lawn mowers but are capable of considerably higher speeds. Like the Satanic ski-mobiles and Jet Skis, these vehicles have become the scourge of park managers and lovers of quietude and undefiled nature everywhere. Nonetheless, ATVs are as common as sand fleas in Oceano Dunes State Vehicle Recreation Area. They pointlessly churn the sand as their red-faced operators tear around the dunes while risking rollovers, which are not uncommon. Rather than dismiss them without trying them, however, we decided to price and size up the machines at a couple of rental places in Oceano.

We had every intention of taking them out for a spin until we discovered these things rent $40-70 per hour! You can rent a car for an entire weekend for that. The big ones – recommended to us "beginners" – have five gears and no hand-clutch. Smaller ones go for $48 for two hours (there's a two-hour minimum at most places). No wonder all the fun-loving yahoos truck their own in on trailers.

Out on the beach, the speed limit of 15 mph is obeyed no more than the posted speed on any highway. Whether riding around the soft, hilly dunes in an ATV or on the flat hard beach in a car, no one drives 15 mph or under. We got in a veritable traffic jam going at least 35, unable to slow down lest we be rear-ended. And one obnoxious SUV owner decided to cut diagonally past all the other cars toward the exit ramp. He had to be going 55 by the time he hit the asphalt. Someone could get killed out here! Too bad it wasn't him. The moral of the story is: Keep your eyes open and look both ways before driving or strolling at Oceano Dunes.

BEACHES

Oceano Dunes State Vehicle Recreation Area offers thousands of acres of the most spectacular sand piles on the West Coast. You won't believe your eyes, especially when you're steering your car directly toward the ocean. Driving on the beach has a strange appeal, especially since it allows you to quickly leave the crowds behind and find a quiet stretch of shoreline that's more to your liking. Keep an eye on your car, though. Some people fall asleep when high tide rolls in and…well, you can guess the rest. Also, be careful if you decide to go in the water, because there are no lifeguards.

1 OCEANO DUNES STATE VEHICLE RECREATION AREA

Location: access ramps at the end of Grand Avenue in Grover City and Pier Avenue in Oceano

Parking/Fees: $6 entrance fee per vehicle; camping fee $10 per night, plus $7.50 reservation fee

Hours: 8 A.M.-5 P.M.

Facilities: restrooms

Contact: Oceano Dunes State Vehicle Recreation Area, 805/473-7230

ACCOMMODATIONS

You can camp among the Oceano dunes, but you are advised to make reservations in advance. The sites are primitive—basically, wherever you throw down your tent—and the number of campers allowed here at any one time is 1,000. You really don't need wheels to have fun. Plenty of excellent hiking trails traverse the dunes, inland lagoons, and a fascinating array of terrain.

You can also pitch a tent at several other campgrounds in the area: two of them at Pismo State Beach, and a 64-siter in Oceano Memorial County Park (on Pier Avenue in Oceano).

Pismo Beach, Oceano, Grover Beach, and Shell Beach

Pismo Beach is the heart and soul of the "Five Cities." The other four—Arroyo Grande, Oceano, Grover Beach, and Shell Beach—banded together with Pismo Beach some years back to form a collective municipality known as...Pismo Beach. The area mascot is the Pismo clam. Both the towns and the clam are humble but majestic souls that have survived bad times and emerged with bright futures.

Visitors are greeted by a spaceship-like sculpture of the Pismo clam at the Price Street exit off U.S. 101. The Pismo is the town's pride and joy, being one of the largest and most delicious clams on the West Coast. Euell Gibbons, in his beach survival guide *Stalking the Blue-Eyed Scallop*, called it "a clam refined to the absolute ultimate." In fact, it's too tasty for its own good. By the mid-1980s the beleaguered bivalve had been clammed to the brink of extinction. For five years a law forbade any clamming of the Pismo, allowing them to replenish.

Other than the temporary loss of its clam, Pismo Beach has been blessed with natural gifts—dunes to the south; wide, hard-packed sand beaches in town; perfect year-round climate; and unsurpassable vistas from jagged headlands that spread north into Shell Beach. The biggest problem has been its image as a down-on-its-heels honky-tonk town. Take Shell Beach. This wealthier community ostensibly changed its name to get a separate post office (though it retains the same zip code and falls within Pismo Beach city limits). According to a local businessman, however, it really wanted to distance itself from Pismo Beach.

Another local, a Shell Beach businesswoman with Beverly Hills pretensions, theorized that what's keeping Pismo from becoming a major vacation destination is its lack of an upscale shopping district. "Oh, you can buy things there," she allowed, "but . . ." Her unfinished sentence hung in the air, implying that there's no upscale, New England seaport–themed shopping village in Pismo Beach. Maybe because shopping remains a low priority for us, we're unable to grasp how a lack of overpriced boutiques, shoe stores, and knickknack emporiums is a drawback.

Our own theory about the town's image problem has nothing to do with shopping. It's the name. "Pismo" doesn't exactly roll off the tongue. But the name comes legitimately with the territory. As it turns out, *pismo* is a Chumash word meaning "blobs of tar wash up on the beach." By the time the Spanish arrived, the Chumash had inhabited the area for 9,000 years. The Spanish had no problem with the name because in Spanish *pismo* means "a place to fish." Thanks to this semantic convergence, the town has a unique but not exactly mellifluous name.

Happily, Pismo Beach (population 8,500) focuses on its many natural blessings. The folks who flock here in the summer from the sweltering valleys aren't complaining. When the temperature exceeds 100 degrees inland, Pismo might as well be named Paradise. The hotter it gets in the valleys, the cooler it is in Pismo. The inland swelter draws moist air off the ocean, bathing Pismo Beach in cool marine fog. This makes for endlessly varying cloud patterns and beautiful sunsets. Who wouldn't love such a setting, whatever the name?

BEACHES

Pismo State Beach is a vast and lengthy swath of sand with access points covering 23 miles of coast and four of the "Five Cities." The state beach includes two campgrounds, **Oceano Dunes** and **North Beach.** Cars are allowed on the beach to the south, making it California's answer to Daytona Beach, Florida, without the bathing beauties. Thankfully, the beaches in Pismo Beach and Shell Beach are pedestrian only, with plenty of room for swimming, tanning, fishing, and surfing. The latter has grown so popular that an annual tournament is now held in Pismo. The

© PARKE PUTERBAUGH

THE CENTRAL COAST

Shell Beach

namesake clam, meanwhile, slowly continues its comeback.

At the center of this modest scene is the **Pismo Beach** Pier, a 1,250-foot structure at the end of Pomeroy Street that is perfect for surf casting and surfer watching. The south side of the pier is one of the best surf spots in the county. What makes it so great is that it breaks left on the left side of the pier and right on the right side of the pier. Winter storms during El Niño events over the past decade have inundated the beach, lapping at the bases of buildings and the street-end turnarounds, but Pismo Beach has been building up again and looks little the worse for wear.

The sea cliffs become more pronounced toward Shell Beach, where coves have been given names like Turtle Beach and **Pirate's Cove.** Several overlooks dot the bluff tops along Seacliff Drive, and four of them have been designated city parks: **Margo Dodd, Ocean,** Memory, and Spyglass. Stairwells from the first two, on the southern edge of Shell Beach, lead down to small, secluded cove beaches.

On a final note, we've lifted this pertinent quotation from a Pismo Beach Chamber of Commerce brochure, of all unlikely places. It is taken from "Childe Harold's Pilgrimage," by that legendary poet and beach bum, Lord Byron:

> There is rapture on the lonely shore,
> There is society, where none intrudes,
> By the deep sea, and music in its roar:
> I love not man the less, but Nature more.

For more information, contact the Pismo Beach Visitor Information Center, 581 Dolliver Street, Pismo Beach, CA 93449, 805/773-4382, www.pismobeach.org.

❷ OCEANO DUNES AND NORTH BEACH

Location: along Pier Avenue in Oceano
Parking/Fees: $6 entrance fee per vehicle; camping fees $20-25 per night Oceano Dunes, $29-34 per night North Beach, plus $7.50 reservation fee
Hours: 8 A.M.-5 P.M.

THE CLAM THAT MADE PISMO BEACH FAMOUS

No less an authority than Euell Gibbons honored the Pismo clam (*Tivela stultorum*). In his 1964 beachcomber's bible *Stalking the Blue-Eyed Scallop*, he wrote, "At the first bite I became a full-fledged convert to the Cult of Pismophagists, and I knew why Californians come year after year to do battle with the waves in order to get a bag of Pismos."

Since Gibbons sang his praise of Pismos, they were almost eliminated, due to over-clamming and shortsighted greed. Even then, he'd heard tales: "There are stories of local farmers gathering these clams by the wagon load by opening furrows across the beach at ebb tide with horse-drawn plows. Some...were sold on the market, but many a wagon load went back to the farms to fatten the pigs and chickens...To hear of the way this vast wealth of clams was squandered is enough to make one weep."

But then so is the taste of a Pismo clam. Its flavor, plenitude, and size – it is one of the largest clams in the world – are what made it so popular. After a total ban on Pismo clamming in the mid-1980s, they have begun to return. The Pismo clam requires a rock-free sand beach and constant exposure to ocean waves. The beaches from Oceano to Morro Bay are ideal, with their pure sand and gradually sloping shoreline.

Pismo clams reach a length of five inches and weigh about a pound at maturity, after 4-7 years. A seven-incher is at least 15 years old. Some have lived to the age of 20 and weighed as much as five pounds. They are found in 1-3 feet of water at low tide, burrowing about a half-foot beneath the hard, wet sand. Finding them requires probing every few inches of the ocean floor with a clam fork, one with a five-inch clamming gauge. If a clam smaller than five inches is taken, it should be replaced with its shell opening toward the horizon.

The fun of Pismo clamming is that you have to spend your time knee deep in water. This means you get slapped around by the waves, too. "Ordinary clam digging might be poor sport," wrote Gibbons, "but this seeking the Pismo in the surf was wildly exhilarating. Not that the clams fight back. They don't need to. The clams merely lie quietly...and let the waves above do their fighting."

Now for the bad news. You cannot take any Pismo clams at any time in designated clam preserves, which include Pismo Beach and the Oceano Dunes and Nipomo Dunes areas. Pismos can be taken in Monterey and Santa Cruz Counties in season (September 1-April 30) with a limit of ten and a five-inch minimum size. In short, you can take Pismo clams just about anywhere but Pismo Beach. And you're required to have a saltwater fishing license.

For information on the latest regulations regarding the taking of Pismo clams, contact the **California Department of Fish and Game,** Marine Region, 20 Lower Ragsdale Drive, Suite 100, Monterey, CA 93940, 831/649-2870.

Facilities: concession, restrooms, showers, picnic tables, and visitor center
Contact: Pismo State Beach, 805/489-1869

3 PISMO BEACH

BEST (

Location: end of Pomeroy Street, at Pismo Beach Pier, in Pismo Beach
Parking/Fees: $6 entrance fee per vehicle and metered street parking
Hours: 24 hours
Facilities: restrooms and showers
Contact: Pismo State Beach, 805/489-1869

4 MARGO DODD PARK

Location: off Seacliff Drive in Shell Beach
Parking/Fees: free parking lot
Hours: sunrise-sunset
Facilities: none
Contact: none

5 OCEAN PARK

Location: off Seacliff Drive in Shell Beach
Parking/Fees: free parking lot
Hours: sunrise-sunset
Facilities: none
Contact: none

6 PIRATE'S COVE

Location: Avila Beach Road exit from U.S. 101 south of San Luis Obispo, follow for two miles; left on Cove Landing Road, follow to dirt parking lot on right; trail leads to beach
Parking/Fees: free parking lot
Hours: sunrise-sunset
Facilities: none
Contact: none

THE CENTRAL COAST

Pismo Beach

RECREATION AND ATTRACTIONS

- **Bike/Skate Rentals:** Wheel Fun, 640 Dolliver Street, Pismo Beach, 805/773-0296
- **Dive Shop:** Scuba Adventures Diving Center, 1039 Grand Avenue, Arroyo Grande, 805/473-1111
- **Ecotourism:** Sub Sea Kayaks, 699 Embarcadero, Morro Bay, 805/772-9463; Kayak Horizons, 551 Embarcadero, 805/772-6444
- **Marina:** Morro Bay Marina, 699 Embarcadero #11, Morro Bay, 805/772-8085
- **Piers:** Pismo Beach Pier, Pismo Beach; Port St. Luis Pier, Avila Beach
- **Rainy Day Attraction:** Hearst Castle, Hearst San Simeon State Historical Monument, San Simeon, 805/927-2020 or 800/444-4445
- **Shopping/Browsing:** East Village, Cambria
- **Sportfishing:** Virg's Landing, 1215 Embarcadero, Morro Bay, 805/772-1222
- **Surf Shop:** Central Coast Surfboards, 855 Marsh Street, San Luis Obispo, 805/541-1129
- **Vacation Rentals:** Beachside Reservations, 330 Main Street, Pismo Beach, 800/700-1254, http://beachsidereservations.com

ACCOMMODATIONS

Lodgings in Pismo Beach and environs run the spectrum from seedy motels to affordable mid-grade chains to luxury beach resorts. Most of the deluxe lodgings are found in Shell Beach, although a notable one is in Pismo Beach proper.

SeaVenture Resort (100 Ocean View Avenue, 805/773-4994, $$$$) is an ambassadorial representative of the kind of tony, upscale getaway that's been popping up along the Central Coast, even in formerly honky-tonk towns like Pismo Beach. A few blocks from the pier at the end of quiet Ocean View Avenue, the SeaVenture is on a broad, sandy beach, but the rooms are so exceptional that one is almost tempted not to leave them. The walls and carpets are a soothing, deep green. Louvered doors open out onto balconies, each of which has its own hydrotherapy spa. Each room also has a fireplace with gas logs, wet bar, and CD and DVD players. A continental breakfast is brought to each room, based on a checklist of preferences hung by guests on their doorknobs the night before. Bring some movies and CDs, eat on premises, hang out on the beach, and you can forget about the car after check-in. Considering what you receive, rates (which begin at $179) are fair—especially when you consider what you'd pay for equivalent location and amenities in Southern California.

The Cliffs Resort (2757 Shell Beach Road, 805/773-5000 or 800/826-7827, $$$) is a five-story cliff-top resort that offers luxury without excess. The setting—100 feet above the sea stacks on Turtle Beach—speaks for itself. The various on-premises amenities (large heated outdoor pool, sauna, well-groomed grounds and gardens, café and restaurant) complete the experience. Beach access is via a stairwell along the cliff face. Rates run roughly $159–209 per night for double rooms.

The **Best Western Shore Cliff Lodge** (2555 Price Street, 805/773-4671 or 800/441-8885, $$) is another well-tended hotel on stunning grounds. It comes with a heated pool. Not surprisingly, the three hotels mentioned so far also have some of the best restaurants in town attached to them. Rates run roughly $229–249 for double rooms.

The **Sea Crest Motel** (2241 Price Street, 805/773-4608 or 800/782-8400, $$) is the best of the less expensive places. It's on the north side of Pismo, atop a cliff. A steep wooden stairwell leads to the sand. The grounds encompass a number of jagged promontories upon which one can watch the sun slip into the rough and tumble ocean.

The **Pismo Beach Hotel** (230 Pomeroy Street, 805/773-4445, $$) has been a local institution since 1937, but it's also been out of commission for a long time. Renovated and reopened in this decade by a new owner, it has the air of a European lodge, sans the high price tag (rooms run $100–200). Moreover, it shares an address with the hippest coffee shop in town, the **Black Pearl** (230 Pomeroy Street, 805/773-6631, $), and it's just 200 yards from Pismo Beach Pier. Rates for a double room run about $129 in season.

COASTAL CUISINE

It used to be that in the Esperanto of road hunger, "Pismo" meant "mediocre." That is no longer true, as excellent dining spots are now serving fine fare from panoramic dining rooms. The **Shore Cliff Restaurant** (2555 Price Street, 805/773-4671, $$), in the Best Western Shore Cliff Lodge, offers good, fresh seafood in a glassed-in dining room that takes in a sweeping view of the ocean from its perch. Order the calamari Galantine (squid stuffed with crabmeat) or the fresh catch. Shore Cliff has the best clam chowder in town. It's not the typical thick, floury stew, but more of a soup that lets the good taste of Pismo's finest shine through.

Fine dining can be had at the **Sea Cliffs Restaurant** (2757 Shell Beach Road, 805/773-3555, $$) in the Cliffs at Shell Beach resort. Without much fanfare, the Sea Cliffs Restaurant chefs prepare some of the tastiest seafood on the Central Coast. Most of the seafood dishes are cooked on a mesquite grill. The Sunday brunch is a local favorite.

The **SeaVenture Restaurant** (100 Ocean View Avenue, 805/773-4994, $$$$) specializes in Cal-Asian cuisine: things like ginger-soy sauces and such high-maintenance entrées as seared halibut with shiitake risotto and cashew pesto, Asian vegetables, red pepper coulis, and crispy soba. (Ye gads!) Other popular entrées are champagne prawns and freshly shucked scallops. Get here early and receive a break on

price with the Sunset Dinner menu. You'll also enjoy a great view of the ocean from the third-floor dining room. Happy hour (4 P.M.–7 P.M. daily) is a happening time here.

Finally, if you want a good, simple plate of fish 'n' chips—and you should, now and again—head to **Pismo Fish & Chips and Seafood Restaurant** (505 Cypress Street, 805/773-2853, $$), where the fish is lightly battered and fried. Pismo Fish & Chips and Seafood Restaurant has been run by the same Danish family for decades, and they know their fish 'n' chips, fish dinners (13 kinds!), fish tacos, etc.

If you crave a break from fried fish, just say "Mo"—**Mo's Smokehouse** (221 Pomeroy Street, 805/773-6193, $$), that is. Mo's is a regional chain based in San Luis Obispo. They serve Virginia shredded pork, Memphis pork ribs, and hickory-smoked chicken in various combinations. It hit the spot as a break from our research-driven seafood inquiries, but Mo's fare frankly pales next to the real thing back East. Just to set the record straight, shredded (actually, the correct term is *minced*) pork barbecue is a North Carolina specialty. We ought to know; we went to college there and gorged on the stuff.

The surfers and inlanders who come to Pismo Beach to play have their own routine of longstanding. According to an acquaintance from San Luis Obispo, the perfect day in Pismo Beach goes like this: Hang out on the beach and surf by the pier, have clam chowder in a sourdough bowl for lunch, hit the beach again in the afternoon, and then chow down at McClintock's for dinner. **F. McClintock's Saloon and Dining House** (750 Mattie Road, 805/773-1892, $$$), which has a huge carved cowboy out front, serves great steaks as well as local favorites like onion rings with salsa and turkey nuts. (Yes, you read correctly.)

Lest we forget, you are now entering wine country. Numerous wineries are within an hour's drive of Pismo Beach; ask for recommendations.

THE CENTRAL COAST

A final tip: For breakfast, grab a cinnamon roll at **Old West Cinnamon Rolls** (861 Dolliver Street, 805/773-1428, $). It may not do your diet any good, but you'll thank us just the same.

NIGHTLIFE

The daytime is really the right time in Pismo Beach. The town's social life centers around the pier and surrounding streets. The liveliest night spot in Pismo is **Harry's Cocktail Lounge** (690 Cypress Street, 805/773-1010), which has horseshoes for door handles and features live music—formerly country-and-western, then contemporary rock bands, and now cost-cutting karaoke, two-man bands, and so-called live acts like a "retro disco" tribute band from Los Angeles called Rollercoaster. To be frank, we jadedly view the entire club scene these days as a giant roller coaster that's plunged into ear-splitting dance-music oblivion and would rather forgo the torture for a good night's sleep and an early start on the day.

Harry's claim that "every night rocks" is a bit hackneyed by now, but it is the most popular nightspot in the area. Besides, many years ago football commentator John Madden met his wife at Harry's, and look how big he is now.

Avila Beach

Around the corner from Shell Beach, on the other side of San Luis Obispo Bay, is Avila Beach, a small village of about 300. Until the environmental disaster brought about by Unocal, Avila served as the sun-and-fun capital for students from California Polytechnic State University in San Luis Obispo. Then it became a veritable ghost town for two years, with Avila State Beach surrounded by construction fencing as bulldozers excavated oil-soaked sand to a depth of 80 feet. Having known what this beach looked like in happier times, it was disturbing to see it in critical condition, like a car-wreck victim hooked up to life-support machinery. Happily, it's out of the intensive care unit and is presently on the mend.

North of Avila Beach is Port San Luis Recreation Area, which includes launching access at Olde Port Beach, a commercial fishing pier, and a coastal hiking trail. This 10-miler stretches from Avila to Montaña de Oro State Park. It crosses land owned by Pacific Gas and Electric, which opened its Diablo Canyon nuclear facility in 1986 after years of litigation and engineering snafus. The Diablo Canyon Plant, like the one down in San Onofre, is on an earthquake fault. As a concession to the public (for jeopardizing its very existence?), PG&E has provided the Pecho Coast Trail. It can be accessed in Port San Luis, off Harford Drive.

Along the trail you can see the **Port San Luis Lighthouse** (circa 1890), known as the "Victorian Lady" to locals. The Nature Conservancy leads hikes to the lighthouse (reservations required; call 805/541-8735). A half-day hike goes to the lighthouse, and a full-day hike goes all the way to Rattlesnake Canyon. One noteworthy part of the trail is an oak grove dedicated to Pat Stebbins, a California Coastal Commission director who died in 1990 after years of advocacy for public use of beaches.

The unsightly oil tanks that once dominated the backdrop from the highest peak above the town have been removed. The Unocal-polluted sand along the beachfront has been exhumed and hauled away, replaced by trucked-in sand. The beachside promenade that had to be dismantled has now been replaced by a nice new boardwalk, attractive decorative planters, and numerous stairwells leading down to a beach so wide that it seems bionic. Volleyball nets have been restrung and expanded, and playground swings and a slide have been added for the wee ones. A portion of Front Street is now blocked off for pedestrians only.

All of these changes, of course, will not entirely solve the problems related to Unocal's malfeasance, but they at least relieve the scene of its most ominous symbols and restore Avila Beach's visual appeal. From our perspec-

AVILA BEACH'S OILY PAST

One of the more sordid environmental sagas ever to take place along the California coast is the desecration of lovely Avila Beach by the Union Oil Company of California (Unocal), the same people who polluted the Guadalupe Dunes down the coast and curried favor with the Taliban to build a pipeline across Afghanistan back before 9/11. Unocal has long had its way with this relatively defenseless village of 350. Were it just a matter of an oil leak and some contamination, the situation would be sad but solvable, perhaps serving as a cautionary tale that might make things better in the future.

Just as we suspected on our first visit to Avila Beach – at one time among our favorite beach towns on the Central Coast – the petroleum "tank farm" that once sat high atop a bluff above the town was not just an aesthetic blight but a ticking time bomb. The first detonation took place in 1989, when it was determined that the tanks had for years, if not decades, been dripping diesel and crude oil and gasoline from underground pipes leading to Unocal's industrial pier at Avila's harbor. The oil mixture built up beneath the postcard-perfect cove beach that defines this town, creating a toxic mound 10 stories high.

The cleanup, negotiated over a long period and finally begun in 1998, was completed, for the most part, by the summer of 2001. It necessitated Unocal's removal of 400,000 gallons of petroleum leakage and 100,000 cubic yards of sand, as well as the near closure of the only road into and out of the community (essentially shutting the town down for a year). Unocal also agreed to pay $18 million for cleanup and restoration. In addition, 20 beachfront homes and businesses – the down-home establishments that gave this town its appealing quaintness – were demolished. All of this cleanup was much more than Unocal was initially prepared to do.

The greatest fear of many longtime residents was not necessarily whether the environmental problem could be mitigated. It was what would be constructed on all that prime oceanfront real estate to replace what had been lost. After all, Unocal not only ruined the life of this village, it was allowed to buy the land on which the demolished houses stood while retaining its tank farm and pier. In other words, Unocal could have reaped a profit from all this devastation. As one resident speculated back in 1998: "It's going to be high-rises."

Well, it's not a high-rise, but Avila Lighthouse Suites (550 Front Street, 805/627-1900 or 800/372-8452, $$$$), which opened in spring 2008, is Avila Beach's first "all-suites luxury hotel." Of course it comes with a "beautiful new spa" and "state-of-the-art fitness room." Bah. We checked rates for a fall weekend, and they were $329-379 per night. Sorry, but this is not what we had in mind for Avila Beach's reconstruction.

tive, just seeing Avila open to visitors again is enough to warm the bivalves of our heart.

For more information, contact the Pismo Beach Chamber of Commerce and Visitor Information Center, 581 Dolliver Street, Pismo Beach, CA 93449, 805/773-4382, www.pismobeach.com.

BEACHES

To get to **Avila Beach** from either Shell Beach or U.S. 101, take Avila Beach Drive. It is the only road in and out of a circuitous rural stretch that requires your full attention. The collegians call it "Bust Road," because the cops wait along the shoulder after the bars close. While Avila Beach was off-limits for its cleanup, the college kids began hanging in greater numbers out at Pirate's Cove, a clothing-optional beach between Pismo Beach and Avila Beach. Now they're back in all their bikini-clad splendor on the new, improved Avila Beach.

A short distance north of Avila Beach is a crescent of darkened sand identified as **Olde Port Beach**. Keep driving and have a meal at the Olde Port Inn Restaurant on the Port San Luis Pier.

7 AVILA BEACH

Location: Front Street between San Rafael Street and Harford Drive in Avila Beach
Parking/Fees: free street parking
Hours: sunrise-sunset
Facilities: concession, lifeguards, restrooms, and showers
Contact: San Luis Obispo Port Authority, 805/595-5400

8 OLDE PORT BEACH

Location: one mile north of Avila Beach, just south of Port St. Luis Pier
Parking/Fees: free parking lot
Hours: sunrise-sunset
Facilities: restrooms
Contact: San Luis Obispo Port Authority, 805/595-5400

ACCOMMODATIONS

Away from the ocean, among the woods along Avila Beach Drive, is a spa and resort worth seeking out. **Sycamore Mineral Springs Resort** (1215 Avila Beach Drive, 805/595-7302, www.sycamoresprings.com, $$$) is many things—gourmet restaurant (Gardens of Avila), place to stay, botanical haven, and a spiritual way station. But it is primarily a mineral-spring spa and has been since 1897. One can receive a professional massage ($75 for 30 minutes, $110 for an hour, $140 for 90 minutes), plus unlimited access to the natural hot springs. Right away, the friendly staff makes you feel comfortable, and an hour later you will be too relaxed to get back in the car. This may mean staying overnight and eating dinner, which we'd also recommend. There's a Spa Escape Package that includes three days, two nights, and $440 worth of spa treatments for $759 (weekdays) and $899 (weekends). The rooms are up in the woods, and each comes with its own mineral spa in a redwood tub. Pure bliss.

The **Inn at Avila Beach** (256 Front Street, 805/595-2300, $$$) is the town's venerable beachfront mainstay. Rooms are not cheap ($200 and up), but they offer packages and specials (such as $50 gas card enticements). Having weathered the Unocal storm, the place deserves to thrive now. A pink stucco beach house featuring ocean-facing suites with balconies, it is the best bird's-eye perch onto the sands of Avila Beach.

COASTAL CUISINE

The **Gardens of Avila** (1215 Avila Beach Drive, 805/595-7365, $$$) is at the lush Sycamore Mineral Springs Resort. The eclectic menu offerings range all over the globe, including coriander-crusted ahi tuna with steamed baby bok choy. Being on the grounds of a spa, there's an extensive health and wellness menu. Many ingredients are local. Seafood items are the best bets, as the catch comes straight off the pier at Port San Luis. Be forewarned, unmarried couples: The readers of a local publication recently voted Gardens of Avila "best place to propose."

The **Olde Port Inn Restaurant** (Port San Luis Pier 3, 805/595-2515, $$$$) serves fish straight from the boats, too. Literally, you get the catch of the day. The restaurant's founder is Leonard Cohen (no relation to the poet/singer). Cohen started the California Cio-Pinot Cook-off, an annual cioppino and pinot noir contest that benefits local charities. Dinner prices for seafood entrées start at $17.95, although fish and chips and fish tacos from the à la carte menu run $8.95. The house special cioppino runs $23.95. And the view from the pier—well, you can't put a price on that.

By the way, Cohen has turned the restaurant over to his son, also named Leonard. He has brought in a new chef who is introducing items like Cajun-blackened halibut with mango salsa. Not to worry, stalwart Olde Port fans: Old standbys like fish tacos, shrimp quesadillas, and fish and chips are still on the menu.

Locals head to **Fat Cats Cafe** (3920 Avila Beach Drive, Port San Luis, 805/595-2204, $) for breakfast, which is served 24 hours a day. Order huevos rancheros (ranch-style eggs) or a build-your-own omelet and enjoy the view of sailboats on the bay from the brick patio. Fat Cats serves lunch and dinner, too, and prices are very reasonable.

P.S.: If you want seafood right off the boat to cook in your suite, Avila Bay Pier is the best place to shop.

San Luis Obispo

Like Santa Barbara, San Luis Obispo is the sort of town you don't want to just visit—you want to live there. The natural setting—a valley 2,000 feet below the Santa Lucia Mountains, bisected by a small river—blends perfectly with the culture and cuisine.

Although it is not directly on the beach, San Luis Obispo (pronounced "San LOO-iss Oh-BISS-poh" and called "S.L.O." for short) is a jumping-off point for numerous Central Coast getaways, including Pismo Beach, Avila Beach, Morro Bay, Cambria, and San Simeon. It is also a worthy destination in and of itself. The city has its own symphony and opera company, chorales, Mozart Festival, theater companies, and arts and crafts galleries.

That's just the half of it. San Luis Obispo (population 43,500) has an indefinable quality that transforms it from an otherwise pleasant crossroads into a real honey of a place. Perhaps it's the presence of California Polytechnic State University, with its hip, eco-minded student

body of 11,000. In a college town the continuous stream of fresh blood and new ideas guarantees that daily life won't get stale. There are also the surrounding agricultural valleys, which once earned S.L.O. a reputation as a cow town. These days, the massive greenbelt seems downright magical, contributing to the healthy bustle of the town. Every Thursday a farmers market sets up on Higuera Street, and virtually the entire town attends. One can only hope that San Luis Obispo—located roughly halfway between Los Angeles and San Francisco—will continue to preserve the natural treasures that make it so unique.

Once the heart of Mission San Luis Obispo de Tolosa, the town has deep historical roots. The mission was the first in California to use red-tiled roofs as fireproofing against Native Americans' flaming arrows. The mission's church (782 Monterey Street, 805/543-6850) has been restored, and the nearby **San Luis Obispo County Historical Museum** (696 Monterey Street, 805/543-0638) contains Native American and early settlement artifacts. Much of the rest of the town's architecture dates from the Victorian period. Careful planning and refurbishing has kept growth within tasteful bounds.

Walking is the best way to see the local history and architecture. Two suggested hikes offer a larger perspective on this setting. The first is a 1.5-mile round-trip trek up to Bishop Peak, which provides views of the town and the valley. The second is a one-mile walk through Poly Canyon on the university campus. Park across from the Fisher Science Building on Perimeter Road and roam among the wildflowers.

Another kind of touring is rewarding for those folks who, to paraphrase the late Orson Welles, drink no wine before its time. Forty wineries and vineyards are located in San Luis Obispo County. Among the best known of the bunch are **Edna Valley Vineyard** (2585 Biddle Rand Road, 805/544-5855) and **Corbett Canyon Vineyard** (2195 Corbett

Canyon Road, 805/544-5800). Both are in the greater San Luis Obispo city limits. To find the rest, pick up a brochure at any area restaurant or motel.

For more information, contact the San Luis Obispo County Visitors & Conference Bureau, 811 El Capitan Way, Suite 200, San Luis Obispo, CA 93401, 805/541-8000 or 800/634-1414, www.sanluisobispocounty.com.

ACCOMMODATIONS

You may not look out upon sand and surf, but you will get a nice view in San Luis Obispo, no matter where you stay. For romantic getaways there are three excellent, slightly quirky places to consider. The **Madonna Inn** (100 Madonna Road, 805/543-3000, $$$) is best known for the simple reason that there's no other place like it in California (or in the country, for that matter). Every one of its 109 rooms is decorated in a different style, and the architecture of the lodge itself is part Elizabethan, part gingerbread, part Victorian, part…You get the idea. It's unabashedly eccentric, and the grounds are fun to stroll. Rooms run $179–250.

Equally delightful is the **Garden Street Inn Bed & Breakfast** (1212 Garden Street, 805/545-9802, $$). Built in 1887 on land once owned by the mission, the Garden Street Inn is an Italianate Queen Anne–style house that's historic without being musty. It's also right in the center of the downtown historic area. Finally, the **Apple Farm Inn** (2015 Monterey Street, 805/544-2040 or 800/255-2040, $$$) re-creates Victorian times with country classic styling, an attached mill house, and a restaurant that serves things like chicken and dumplings and apple pie.

For budget-minded families, the **Vagabond Inn** (210 Madonna Road, 805/544-4710, $) offers a continental breakfast and the come-on that "kids under 19 stay free." Kids under 19?

COASTAL CUISINE

Pete's Southside Cafe (1815 Osos Street, Railroad Square, 805/549-8133, $$) has the right pedigree. It began as a small café in Avila Beach. Now it's thriving as a fine diner that has an upstairs tamale bar. Its hallmark is Caribbean and Latin American entrées, including a killer fish Veracruz. The paella Valencia wins "best of" awards yearly.

NIGHTLIFE

Nightlife in S.L.O. is anything but slow. It's a town full of college bars, with laughter, music, and mug-clanging good times ringing out from every door front after dark. The most popular in town, **Mother's Tavern** (725 Higuera Street, 805/541-8733), charges a cover from those lured inside by the deejayed dance music. Here you'll see valley cowboys trying to connect with Cal Poly coeds in a noisy setting not designed for easy traffic flow—not our cup of cabernet, to be honest. Mother's is a restaurant by day.

Live music can be had at the **Downtown Brewing Company** (1119 Garden Street, 805/543-1843). "Fine ales, food, and live music" are the calling cards. These days at Downtown Brewing Co., live music means a mix of hip-hop, reggae, and aggressive and old-school rock. Everyone from Digable Planets and Steel Pulse to Eddie Money and Horror Pops were on the docket on our latest pass-through. We're pretty particular about our music, but with 11 home brews on tap, just about anything would sound good in this place.

The best dance club, by general consensus, is **The Graduate** (990 Industrial Way, 805/541-0969), where "every night is an adventure." Each night features a different type of music and dancing. For instance, Wednesday is "College Hump Night," Thursday is "Country Night," and Friday is "Hot Latin Night!"

Montaña de Oro State Park

Just south of Morro Bay, near the small bayside towns of Los Osos and Baywood Park, Montaña de Oro State Park spreads out across an immense swath of land. It faces the ocean for seven miles, from the Morro Sand Spit south. Spanish explorers named the area Montaña de Oro (Mountain of Gold) because of the golden poppies that cover its hills and terraces. Monarch butterflies nest in the eucalyptus from October to March, adding to the gilded appearance. Today this 8,400-acre wilderness park is one of the great treasures of California's state-park system.

We quickly ran out of superlatives when trying to describe the park's assets and acreage. Simply ponder what is here: sand dunes, jagged cliffs, rocky coves, sea caves, and shallow reefs. There are 50 miles of trails for hiking, biking, and horseback riding. These trails traverse the inland canyons and mountains as well as the shoreline, and provide a self-guided laboratory of geological and botanical diversity. On a clear day from the 1,845-foot summit of the Valencia Peak Trail, one can see 90 miles of coastline. People also come to fish, scuba dive, and tidepool along the rocky shore. For an unforgettably scenic four-mile round-trip hike, take the Bluff Trail, which runs from the visitors center to Grotto Rock, passing tidepools and cove beaches along the way.

Montaña de Oro is a primitive park, with only 50 unimproved campsites and minimal facilities. There is a special area for equestrian campers, which must be reserved in advance. One deterrent to heavy visitation is that there is no potable water inside the park. That is precisely what keeps it pristine, despite increasing visitation as word gets around. And thus, we quietly encourage you to visit.

For more information, contact Montaña de Oro State Park, c/o San Luis Obispo Coast District, California State Parks, 1150 Laurel Lane, San Luis Obispo, CA 93401, 805/528-0513, www.parks.ca.gov.

BEACHES

The beaches at **Montaña de Oro State Park** are as wild as an unbroken colt, choked with rocky outcroppings and sea caves and pounded by a frothy, roiling surf. The coarse salt-and-pepper sand is not conducive to sunbathing, but the park and its coastline are ruggedly beautiful. Indefatigable surfers sometimes hike through the woods to the small beach at well-named Hazard Canyon, where dangerous surf awaits.

The best beach is the sandy crescent at **Spooner's Cove** (named for the rancher and dairyman who was the former landowner), where there's a primitive campground. The cove takes up nearly half a mile of coastline and is worth a full day of exploration in itself. At the south end is a black, pebbly sand beach wide enough to sunbathe on. Bring a pad to put under your towel, though, because the rocks will work their way into your back and buttocks. Splitting the cove in the middle is a rocky proscenium that allows the unique experience of walking out among the ocean

Montaña de Oro State Park

COURTESY OF SAN LUIS OBISPO COUNTY VISITORS & CONFERENCE BUREAU

THE CENTRAL COAST

waves and yet remaining high and dry, though this is not recommended for those with vertigo problems.

Just to the north is another rocky cove beach backed by an enormous sea cave that begs to be explored. Signs warn of the possibility of entrapment by fast incoming tides. Farther back from Spooner's Cove, you can see the limestone layers, hundreds of thousands of years old, from which this land was carved, and a trickling coastal stream, gurgling its pristine cool, clear water toward the ocean. This is as majestic an assortment of natural treasures as we've seen on any of our beach wanderings.

9 MONTAÑA DE ORO STATE PARK

Location: From north of San Luis Obispo take Highway 1 to the Los Osos/Baywood Park exit and drive west on Los Osos Valley Road, which becomes Pecho Valley Road, to the park entrance. From south of San Luis Obispo, take U.S. 101 to the Los Osos/Baywood Park exit. Proceed 12 miles west on Los Osos Valley Road, which becomes Pecho Valley Road, and follow to the park entrance.
Parking/Fees: free parking lots; camping fees $11-15 per night, plus $7.50 reservation fee
Hours: sunrise-sunset
Facilities: restrooms and picnic tables
Contact: Montaña de Oro State Park, 805/528-0513

Los Osos and Baywood Park

The conjoined towns of Los Osos and Baywood Park (population 15,000) have grown in recent years, and they now risk overdoing it as badly as the "Five Cities" franchise thicket in the Pismo Beach area. For now, though, Los Osos is an appealing stopover for visitors to Montaña de Oro who don't fancy primitive camping.

For more information, contact the Los Osos/Baywood Park Chamber of Commerce, 781 Palisades Avenue, Los Osos, CA 93402, 805/528-4884, www.losososbaywoodpark.org.

Morro Bay

Morro Rock is an enormous monolith that sits just offshore from the town of Morro Bay. This volcanic remnant—what geologists call a volcanic neck—is the pet rock of the Central Coast and the "Gibraltar of the Pacific," and it dominates the landscape in these parts. It is an awesome, commanding sight. The rock is so iconic that its likeness appears on anything having to do with Morro Bay, from postcards and tourist brochures to ashtrays and motel-room trash baskets. The Portuguese explorer Juan Cabrillo dubbed the rock El Morro ("domed turban") when he sailed into Estero Bay in 1542.

From a distance it looks like a bare, brown geodesic dome. It is one of seven volcanic peaks, known as the Seven Sisters, that run in a nearly straight line from San Luis Obispo to Morro Bay. Morro Rock is the most northwesterly of them. Because it is offshore, it stands in bold relief and is the most spectacular to behold. Morro Rock rises 578 feet above sea level and weighs 20 million tons. Dating from the early Miocene period, it is estimated to be between 22 and 26 million years old.

Black Mountain, another of the Seven Sisters, rises close by in Morro Bay State Park. A paved road leads to **Black Mountain Lookout,** which, at 865 feet, is the highest point in the park. From here you are treated to a sweeping view of the coast. With its many different lithologies arrayed in a confounding hodgepodge, this area of the Central Coast has been referred to as a "geological mulligan stew."

Morro Rock is composed of hard igneous rock that has outlasted the metamorphic rock of the Franciscan formation into which it intrudes. It looms above the landscape surrounding it, standing undaunted after millions of years. The

KEEPING COUNT OF CALIFORNIA'S SEA OTTERS

In June 2002, biologists and vacationers began taking note of large numbers of dead sea otters washing up on the beaches of California's Central Coast. These sad sightings occurred shortly after the state's spring otter count had found that the species' populations were down from 2001, continuing a downward trend that dates back seven years.

The otter population peaked in 1995 and bottomed out in 1999. Biologists suspected that the high death rates were due to starvation, disease, pollution, entanglement in fishing gear, and even shooting deaths. Something does smell fishy about the fact that most of the dead otters were young adults, the age group most vital for replacing the once plentiful numbers of this threatened species.

Some good news, for a change: The counts for 2006, 2007, and 2008 saw a slight increase in sea otter numbers, though not enough to take them out of "threatened" status. They're hovering at around 2,200 along the Central Coast.

To keep abreast of otter news and to assist with increasing their numbers, contact **Friends of the Sea Otter,** P.O. Box 223260, Carmel, CA 93922, www.seaotters.org.

only real threat to its well-being is humankind. Between 1891 and 1963 quarrying operations robbed Morro Rock of its sharp peak and some of its elevation. The volcanic rock and talus quarried off the rock were used to build breakwaters here and at Avila Beach, and to construct a causeway linking Morro Rock with the mainland. (It formerly stood 1,000 feet offshore.) After all that, it was discovered that Morro's lava rock doesn't hold up to constant pounding by the sea. Moreover, quarrying was beginning to affect the fragile Morro Rock ecosystem. Nesting grounds for the rare and endangered peregrine falcon were being destroyed and the rock itself was losing its shape and height. By the time local residents demanded a halt to quarrying, more than a million tons of rock had been hauled away. Morro Rock was designated a State Historical Landmark and a Peregrine Falcon Reserve in 1968. These days you can drive halfway around its base, but climbing Moro Rock was banned in 1973, in deference to the falcons.

The Morro Bay Power Station is another massive feature on the landscape. Its three 450-foot-tall smokestacks are directly across the road from Morro Rock, but you won't see them pictured on postcards or promotional brochures for Morro Bay. They resemble enormous filter-tipped cigarettes, make a noise not unlike the drone in the film *Eraserhead,* and warm the nearby water by a few degrees. Between San Diego and Morro Bay we'd seen two nuclear power stations built on fault lines and now a power plant sited by one of the most wondrous natural features on the coast. Ah, the folly of mankind—when will we ever learn?

Its smokestacks aside, Morro Bay is a charming community of 10,350 friendly souls. People come to this less harried part of the coast to kick back and relax and recreate in the outdoors. You can hike the state-park trails and Morro Bay's sandy spit or book a deep-sea fishing trip. With a sizable sport- and commercial-fishing fleet operating out of the breezy harbor, Morro Bay has the authentic flavor of a fishing village with minimal tourist trappings.

A number of outfitters operate along the Embarcadero, Morro Bay's waterfront avenue. **Virg's Landing** (1215 Embarcadero, 805/772-1222) reels in the most anglers. It bustles like the floor of the stock exchange. Folks are constantly coming and going, booking trips and consulting the experts. A full-day trip runs $89; a half day $59. When the albacore are running, eager anglers flock to Morro Bay, and fishing fever takes over the town.

Every day, the commercial fleet sails in with fresh catches of salmon, albacore, ling cod, Pacific snapper, Alaskan halibut, and thresher shark. Morro Bay is one of the five largest estuaries in California and a biologically rich habitat. Visitors can partake of its bounty by boarding a water taxi from Virg's to the **Morro Sand Spit,** the four-mile peninsula that separates Morro Bay from the ocean. The hundred-yard crossing will deposit you on a sand bank. It can be a mite uncomfortable on the spit "if the wind's blowin' like snot," according to our plainspoken skipper, so dress accordingly or wait for a calmer day. Once on the spit, you can hike, dig for clams, surf cast, or bird-watch.

Still more soul-satisfying, nature-oriented activity can be found at **Morro Bay State Park,** attached to the southeastern end of town. It's a multiple-use recreation area with everything from campsites and hiking trails to a resort and a needless 18-hole golf course. A museum of natural history contains dioramas on nature, wildlife, and the area's early Chumash inhabitants. The marsh, located where Los Osos Creek enters Morro Bay, is home to 250 species of birds. The park is the site of a six-acre eucalyptus grove that serves as a rookery for great blue herons, which nest in the treetops from January to August. You can rent a canoe and paddle the quiet waters of the estuary or row out to the spit.

The Embarcadero runs for about a mile from Morro Rock to Morro Bay State Park. It is a highly walkable mile, passing bait-and-tackle shops and fish and chip stands (serving *local* fish, they emphasize). At the corner of Morro Bay Boulevard and Market Street is the Centennial Stairway. This impressive redwood staircase descends to Fisherman's Memorial, a small harborside park with a 7,000-pound anchor as its centerpiece. The town's pride and joy is its giant chessboard, an outdoor game board whose dimensions are straight out of *Alice in Wonderland.* The redwood chessmen stand three feet tall and weigh 18–20 pounds each.

Morro Bay has been trying to pursue a slow-growth policy in the face of strong developmental pressure. As people flee Southern California with bulging retirement accounts and golden parachutes, keeping a lid on growth has proven difficult. The issue isn't just the usual desire to preserve an unhurried way of life and an unspoiled landscape. Water, or the lack of it, is the real limiting factor. Officials are concerned that overuse of dwindling water resources could cause underground aquifers to draw in salty seawater, ruining local water tables.

Meanwhile, migrating Southern Californians have been steadily pricing Central Valley residents out of Morro Bay's housing market. Housing prices jumped 40 percent in one memorable year. With their deep pockets the Southlanders have simply outbid all other comers. Given the markets they're used to, they are paying prices that feel like bargains. Already the hills west of Main Street are crowded with homes.

Morro Rock itself presides benignly over the human activity at its base. It will still be standing long after the last fish 'n' chip shop has closed its doors. More than most communities, Morro Bay takes a philosophical cue from this monolith, endeavoring to safeguard its essential qualities as a serene locale. The town refers to itself as a place "where the sun spends the winter."

No matter what season, the view from Morro Bay is a fine one when the setting sun drops into the ocean. As the sun falls, train your eyes on Morro Rock, which takes on a bewitching range of hues and auroras. One evening around twilight we spied a small violet cloud hovering around the top of Morro Rock like a halo. Exquisite!

For more information, contact the Morro Bay Chamber of Commerce, 845 Embarcadero, Morro Bay, CA 93442, 805/772-4467, www.morrobay.org.

BEACHES

If you love the beach, bay, and ocean, you will find Morro Bay an ideal place to drop anchor.

Morro Spit, the sand spit that extends like an arm north from Montaña de Oro State Park, ends with a fist-shaped protrusion that nearly chokes the narrow neck of the bay. It runs for four miles and can be reached via water taxi (boarded along the Embarcadero in downtown Morro Bay) or by four-wheel drive from the south, where it joins the mainland at Montaña de Oro. The spit is formally known as the **Morro Dunes Natural Area.** Dunes on the spit reach 85 feet in height.

Morro Bay State Park is situated on Morro Bay Lagoon but not directly on the ocean. So while it has a host of other amenities—camping, hiking, golf course, museum—don't come expecting beach access, at least from the park property. A town park on Bayshore Drive sits off the south end of Main Street. **Bayside Bluffs Park** abuts Morro Bay State Park; a stairway and graded path lead from the bluff-top picnic area to the beach.

Morro Rock and Beach, a small, crescent-shaped beach behind the breakwater, lies at the base of Morro Rock itself. Sun worshippers head here. Cataracts of spray fly off the top of the breakwater as waves thunder against it, but the water on the protected beach behind it is as calm as a rippled lake. Our advice: Enjoy the beach, but leave the breakwater alone. If you're tempted to scale the rocks for the view from the top, consider our experience.

One afternoon years ago we hoisted ourselves up the breakwater's slippery, wet staircase of boulders. As we neared the top we noticed a longer-than-usual pause between waves. Suddenly, a monster wave crested high above us, like a creature from a Japanese horror film. In the eerily quiet seconds before it broke, washing us down the wall of rock to the ground, we said our prayers. The gods were with us that day; we only got soaked, not severed on the rocks. Wetter than a pair of sea otters but otherwise unhurt, we changed into dry clothes and permanently swore off climbing breakwaters.

Morro Strand State Beach is divided into two sections. The south section, formerly known as Atascadero State Beach, offers a 104-site campground. The smaller north section lies three miles north of town, off Highway 1. The beach is wide and runs for nearly two miles. RVs jam the campground, but the lack of shade might make Morro Strand State Beach (South) a little tough on tenters, who are better advised to check out Montaña de Oro State Park. Morro Strand is an inviting day-use beach. Large waves roll lazily toward shore for a good distance, making for long rides. You can do everything on the beaches of Morro Strand but dig for clams, which is prohibited.

10 MORRO DUNES NATURAL AREA

Location: access dunes via water taxi from Embarcadero in Morro Bay
Parking/Fees: none
Hours: sunrise-sunset
Facilities: none
Contact: Morro Bay State Park, 805/772-2560

11 MORRO BAY STATE PARK

Location: From Highway 1 north of San Luis Obispo, take Los Osos/Baywood Park exit and drive west on Los Osos Valley Road for one mile. Turn right into park, which is along State Park Road in Morro Bay.
Parking/Fees: $6 entrance fee per vehicle; camping fees $29-34 per night with hookups, $20-25 per night without hookups, plus $7.50 reservation fee
Hours: sunrise-sunset
Facilities: concession, restrooms, showers, picnic tables, and visitors center
Contact: Morro Bay State Park, 805/772-2560

THE CENTRAL COAST

THE CENTRAL COAST

12 BAYSIDE BLUFFS PARK

Location: west end of Bayshore Drive at Main Street in Morro Bay
Parking/Fees: free parking lot
Hours: sunrise–sunset
Facilities: picnic tables
Contact: Morro Bay Parks Department, 805/772-6278

13 MORRO ROCK AND BEACH

Location: near Morro Bay Harbor, at the end of Coleman Drive in Morro Bay
Parking/Fees: free parking lot
Hours: sunrise–sunset
Facilities: lifeguards and restrooms
Contact: Morro Bay Harbor Department, 805/772-6254

14 MORRO STRAND STATE BEACH (SOUTH)

Location: along Highway 1 between Yerba Buena Avenue and Atascadero Road in Morro Bay
Parking/Fees: free parking lot; camping fees $20-25 per night, plus $7.50 reservation fee
Hours: sunrise–sunset
Facilities: restrooms and picnic tables
Contact: Morro Strand State Beach, 805/772-2560

ACCOMMODATIONS

Located halfway between Los Angeles and San Francisco, Morro Bay is an ideal rendezvous point for residents of the two metropolises. The town is equipped with accommodations in all price ranges, from modest park-at-your-door motels to more resort-oriented facilities. The golden mean in Morro Bay would be someplace like the **Best Western Tradewinds** (225 Beach Street, 805/772-7376, $$), which is the closest lodging to Morro Rock itself and only one short block from the waterfront.

COURTESY OF SAN LUIS OBISPO COUNTY VISITORS & CONFERENCE BUREAU

Morro Rock

The lodging of first choice is the **Inn at Morro Bay** (60 State Park Road, 805/772-5651, $$$). Located inside Morro Bay State Park, the inn is set back from the modest bustle of the Embarcadero. A luxury resort with a romantic atmosphere, its 100 guest rooms feature cathedral ceilings, gas fireplaces, country French decor, and outdoor decks overlooking the bay. The suite-sized rooms are filled with heavy, hand-carved furniture, and the brass-fixture bathrooms come with a complimentary assortment of French soap. As lavish as it sounds, the Inn at Morro Bay has a cozy, country-inn-style atmosphere. They also offer package deals, with the added enticement of gas cards.

Another fine choice is **Embarcadero Inn** (456 Embarcadero, 805/772-2700, $$), on the bay at the south end of town. The rooms are large, and the furniture cushiony. There are DVD players in the room and DVDs at the front desk. Most rooms have a gas fireplace and an outdoor balcony, and the inn has a pair of indoor saunas. Rooms go for $120–185. With its slate-colored, weathered-wood exterior, the Embarcadero Inn is the most distinguished-looking lodge on the waterfront.

The town of Morro Bay is outfitted with a number of plainer but perfectly comfortable and inexpensive motels. The Days Inn–owned **Harbor House Inn** (1095 Main Street, 805/772-2711, $) and **El Morro Masterpiece Motel** (1206 Main Street, 805/772-5633, $) are both attractive, nicely maintained properties within walking distance of the waterfront.

COASTAL CUISINE

Improvements are steadily being made along the waterfront as fading mom-and-pop joints inevitably give way to something more contemporary and, frankly, nicer. You'll find such successful newer arrivals as the **Otter Rock Cafe** (885 Embarcadero, 805/772-1420, $), a high-quality fast-food spot where you order at the window and carry your food to tables that look out over the water. At Otter Rock, baskets of fried seafood (fish, squid, oysters,

scallops) and chips are served for less than $10. Otter Rock Cafe also has a full bar and live entertainment on weekends.

Old reliables on the scene include the **Harbor Hut** (1205 Embarcadero, 805/772-2255, $$$) and the **Great American Fish Company** (1185 Embarcadero, 805/772-4407, $$$). Both are operated by longtime residents and serve freshly caught seafood. The Harbor Hut was the first restaurant on the waterfront in Morro Bay. It opened in 1948, serving chili and chowder in a small Quonset hut. Today it's a prosperous local institution where oysters are fixed a half-dozen ways. Daily catches, from snapper to swordfish, are fried, broiled, steamed, or sautéed, and combination surf-and-turf platters will assuage hearty appetites. From an unfancy dining room overlooking Morro Harbor, the Great American Fish Company serves its namesake fish in mostly simple ways—i.e., grilled over mesquite or fried. The former option is indisputably healthier and arguably tastier, especially when you're talking about locally caught fish. Red snapper (moist, tender) and halibut (meaty, firm) are generally the freshest offerings caught by the local fleet, and a simple mesquite grilling (or Cajun-style blackening for $1 extra) is preferred. Fish entrées run in the $12–15 range and come with a choice of two side dishes. Don't pass up the smoked albacore appetizer—a generous helping served with red-onion rings, crackers, and three sauces.

Moving upscale and away from the beach, the dining room at the **Inn at Morro Bay** (60 State Park Road, 805/772-5651) serves Cal-nouvelle cuisine with a subtle French flair. You can count on fresh ingredients, superb preparation, a respectable wine list, excellent service, and a spectacular view of the bay. Entrée selection might include something like crab-crusted halibut with wild mushroom and asparagus ragout or lobster brûlée.

A perennial award winner on Morro Bay's waterfront is **Windows on the Water** (699 Embarcadero, 805/772-0677, $$$), a great place for romancing couples. The restaurant's acronym is WOW, and that's what you'll be saying when you dig into such entrées as roasted salmon, especially if you've managed to snare a reservation at sunset.

Fish fans can indulge their yen for sushi at **Harada Japanese Restaurant and Sushi Bar** (630 Embarcadero, 805/772-1410, $$$). The must-stop place for breakfast is **Carla's Country Kitchen** (213 Beach Street, 805/772-9051, $), which serves knockout scrambled-egg dishes.

NIGHTLIFE

If you're hankering for a good dinner or a good time after dinner, go to **Rose's Landing Restaurant and Cocktail Lounge** (725 Embarcadero, 805/772-4441), a steak-and-seafood restaurant on the water that offers live entertainment on certain summer nights.

Cayucos

Cayucos is tucked into the head of a V-shaped cove formed where Cayucos Creek empties into the ocean. This town of 3,000 is an anomaly on the Central Coast. It doesn't look like it could give a hoot about tourism. It has the feel of an Old West town—which, in fact, it is. Its saloons look like real Old West saloons, because they are.

No enormous infusions of cash have been pumped into Cayucos to restore, refurbish, revive, or revise. You'll find one central street (Ocean Avenue), with angle-in parking on both sides. Antique and gift shops predominate. An auto-repair garage on the north side of town has been here since 1932, which qualifies as ancient history on the West Coast. An enormous mobile-home park squats nearby. People come here to fish, decide they like the place, and stick around for a while.

Cayucos Pier, an old, planked affair that has all kinds of personality, has been around since 1875. Vendors push carts around the beachfront, selling such things as "churros" (long, greasy, fried Mexican pastries rolled in sugar—mmm mmm, bad). In Cayucos, hot dogs and hamburgers outsell nouvelle cuisine. An unforgettable juxtaposition of signs that we noticed several years ago speaks volumes about the town. One by the town library announced the hours it was open: a mere two days a week. Next to it was a sign for a sporting-goods store, whose wares included "tackle, bait, amo *(sic)*, scuba gear."

Cayucos looks out over the placid waters of Estero Bay onto majestic Morro Rock, some five miles away. The little town lies in the proverbial shadow of Morro Rock and, hence, largely gets overlooked by those passing through the area. The Hearst Castle brings crowds to San Simeon, Morro Rock attracts tourists to Morro Bay, and romantic bluff-top B&Bs draw couples to Cambria. However, nothing but empty ranchland and the town of Harmony (population 12) fill the 15 miles between Cayucos and Cambria.

Cayucos is not a vacation destination per se, but if you want to experience a California beach town that has largely been left untouched, it fits the bill. In the words of a local who escaped a rat-race life decades ago, "What we offer is peace and serenity from the stresses of big-city life."

For more information, contact the Cayucos Chamber of Commerce, P.O. Box 346, Cayucos, CA 93430, 805/995-1200 or 800/563-1878, www.cayucoschamber.com.

BEACHES

Approaching Cayucos from the south, you'll first encounter **Morro Strand State Beach (North).** This is the smaller, less developed section of the park. **Cayucos Beach** is at the residential south end of the town proper and can be accessed via nine stairwells along a 22-block stretch of Pacific Avenue.

Cayucos State Beach is where the action is, near the modest commercial district. It has good waves and looks to be popular with boogie boarders, whom we've seen pitched into forceful forward rolls by sizable breakers. Anglers are in their glory on the 940-foot Cayucos Pier (built in 1875), which is surrounded by bait-and-tackle shops and lit at night.

Between Cayucos and Cambria along Highway 1 there are eight vista point turnouts where one can catch breathtaking ganders of the beautiful Central California coast.

15 MORRO STRAND STATE BEACH (NORTH)

Location: Studio Drive at 24th Street in Cayucos
Parking/Fees: free parking lot
Hours: sunrise-sunset
Facilities: restrooms and picnic tables
Contact: Morro Strand State Beach, 805/772-2560

16 CAYUCOS BEACH

Location: access via nine stairwells along Pacific Avenue, between First and 22nd Streets, in Cayucos
Parking/Fees: free street parking
Hours: sunrise-sunset
Facilities: none
Contact: San Luis Obispo County Department of Parks and Facilities, 805/781-5930

17 CAYUCOS STATE BEACH

Location: Ocean Drive at Cayucos Road in Cayucos
Parking/Fees: free street and lot parking
Hours: sunrise-sunset
Facilities: concession, restrooms, and picnic tables
Contact: San Luis Obispo County Department of Parks and Facilities, 805/781-5930

ACCOMMODATIONS

Don't come to Cayucos expecting to find pools, fireplaces, and late-afternoon wine-and-cheese hours. Most of the places here seem designed to meet the uncomplicated demands of those who have come to fish. Hence, kitchenettes are included with most rooms, so you can cook your catch. A couple of motels south of the town center rise above the no-frills standard. The most inviting of these is the **Beachwalker Inn** (501 South Ocean Avenue, 805/995-2133 or 800/750-2133, $$$). Prices seem a bit steep ($130–220 in summer), but you're only a block from the beach.

COASTAL CUISINE

For seafood, try **Bill & Carol's Sea Shanty** (296 South Ocean Avenue, 805/995-3272, $), which posts daily fresh-fish specials and is open seven days a week. Open since 1983, the Sea Shanty qualifies as a Cayucos institution that's popular with locals and vacationers alike. **Schooner's Wharf** (171 North Ocean Avenue, 805/995-3883, $$$) changed ownership, and the chef has made interesting changes to the menu, adding items like "surf trip halibut."

NIGHTLIFE

Old Cayucos Tavern (130 North Ocean Avenue, 805/995-3209) has been serving cowboys and cowgirls since 1906. The atmosphere alone is priceless in this day and age of generic dance clubs and retro-chic bars. The tavern offers live music most nights.

Cambria

If there's a prettier setting for a beach in all of California than Cambria, we have yet to find it. Lying between Cayucos and San Simeon, Cambria is a shy princess knocking at the back door of Hearst Castle. Its motto says it all: Where the pines meet the sea. A century ago Cambria was a thriving community of 7,000 souls who worked at whaling, mining, and farming. Today it numbers slightly less than that, and there's little more going on than agriculture, arts and crafts, and a modest tourist trade.

Those who visit here are mostly the spill-over from San Simeon, plus enlightened travelers and couples on romantic getaways who can tell a genuinely quaint village from a contrived imitation. Part of the attraction of Cambria is its seclusion and wildness, and the townsfolk work to keep it that way. "Most of the residents have a slow-growth policy," explained a local innkeeper. "Some would call it a no-growth policy."

Many of the later arrivals are retiring creative sorts—artists, writers, and craftspeople—who have given Cambria something of the flavor of Laguna Beach without the hectic pace of Southern California. The town is divided by Highway 1 into East and West Villages. East Village is older, with many of its historic homes dating from the days when Cambria was known as "Slabtown," after the rough-hewn boards from which they were built. It has all the shops and galleries, and it's a good place to while away the hours on a foggy morning as you're waiting for the sun to break through.

West Village is where the beaches are. To get there, disengage from Highway 1 at Moonstone Beach Road. Immediately you're in another world. You can see the steep, plunging mountains of Big Sur to the northwest, against a backdrop of flower- and grass-filled meadows. A string of cozy B&B-style motels and inns lines the landward side of Moonstone Beach Road. The preeminent feature in this landscape is the grassy, wildflower-strewn mesa that overlooks the beach. Trails crisscross the area right to the bluff edges, and people stroll at all hours. Take your pick—early morning, mid-afternoon, ruddy sunset, or by the light of the silvery moon. The scenery is always beautiful, and the variegated light plays on the panorama, revealing its many subtle facets.

Indeed, Cambria is the perfect spot for beach and nature lovers who don't feel compelled to engage in athletic endeavors involving special equipment and sportswear. All you need in Cambria are walking shorts, a light sweater, tennis shoes, and a point-and-shoot camera. (It is hard to take a bad picture here.) Nature will take care of the rest. So come with your significant other, and prepare to savor some of the most breathtaking sunsets and scenery on the California coast.

Set among a native Monterey pine forest, Cambria is the sort of town that vigilantly eschews aesthetic breeches in the armor of good taste. Back in the 1990s, for instance, the townsfolk were up in arms about the possible arrival of a McDonald's. Reaction to this unwanted invader filled the front page of the local newspaper, spilling over into editorials and letters. One outraged local expressed the majority opinion: "The notion that something so insidious as a McDonald's chain restaurant may come to Cambria fills me with shock, anger, disgust, and disappointment."

More recently, Cambrians have banded together to check development before it chokes them. Two signs along Highway 1 approaching Cambria from the south read: Cambria Land Conservancy and Friends of the Ranchland. Both serve to indicate that Cambrians want to protect their golden egg before the yoke's on them. If this strikes outsiders as "burn the bridges" mentality, then so be it. Someone has to draw a line in the sand and say "enough." We thank God for towns like Cambria, Carmel, and Santa Barbara, which are diligently preserving their magic so that future generations can enjoy it.

Weather-wise, summer months are foggy. It's not the best time to visit the Central Coast, unless you're an inland native who's trying to escape the interior heat. September and October are usually picture-perfect: mild and clear, without blustery winds and choking fog. By the way, if you don't want to be pegged as a tourist, pronounce the town name "CAM-bree-ah," with a short "a" and the accent on the first syllable.

For more information, contact the Cambria

Chamber of Commerce, 767 Main Street, Cambria, CA 93428, 805/927-3624, www .cambriachamber.org.

BEACHES

Moonstone Beach runs for two miles until it tags up with San Simeon State Beach to the north. The coastline is rugged, with gnarled driftwood limbs and tangled mats of seaweed that have been driven ashore. Moonstone Beach is best accessed at Leffingwell Landing, a quarter mile west of Moonstone Beach Drive's southern intersection with Highway 1. Moonstone Beach takes its name from the polished jade, agate, and quartz pebbles that collect in mounds here. On certain parts of the beach there is no sand, just heaps of these pea-sized stones.

A bluff-top trail wanders above Moonstone Beach, extending from end to end. At some points, eroded indentations in the coastline have brought the ocean precariously close to the roadside. The paths above Moonstone Beach have been redirected to adapt to the shoreward slumping of bluff materials. Waves rise in perfect form, then crash mightily on the rocks, sweeping over the stony shoreline. Surfers congregate up toward a point at the beach's south end. Everyone else just walks and watches. Who could ask for anything more?

18 MOONSTONE BEACH

BEST (

Location: Moonstone Beach Drive between Leffingwell Landing and Highway 1 in Cambria
Parking/Fees: free roadside parking
Hours: sunrise-sunset
Facilities: restrooms and picnic tables
Contact: San Simeon District, California State Parks, 805/927-2020

ACCOMMODATIONS

Cambria is the Central Coast's most romantic coast hideaway, and Moonstone Beach is the site of the choicest accommodations. All are in proximity to one another, and the decor, prices, and quality are fairly uniform among them. They all cost more or less the same: $100–200 or more a night, depending on time of year and demand for rooms. Nearly all advertise "Pool,

© PARKE PUTERBAUGH

Moonstone Beach

Fireplace, HBO" on their outdoor signs. And all are well maintained, quiet, and comfortable. We're partial to the **Sea Otter Inn** (6656 Moonstone Beach Drive, 805/927-5888 or 800/966-6490, $$), which has gas fireplaces in all rooms, a heated pool, TVs with DVDs, and films for rent at the desk.

The **Best Western Fireside Inn** (6700 Moonstone Beach Drive, 805/927-8661 or 888/910-7100, $$$) has the most units, and they are modern and well kept. Others that offer similar appeal and amenities include **Fog Catcher Inn** (6400 Moonstone Beach Drive, 805/927-1400 or 800/425-4121, $$$), **Cambria Landing** (6530 Moonstone Beach Drive, 805/927-1619, $$$), and **Sand Pebbles Inn** (6252 Moonstone Beach Drive, 805/927-5600 or 800/222-9970, $$$). Sand Pebbles boasts English country decor, canopy beds, and a tearoom where continental breakfast is served. Cambria Landing has the benefit of being next door to Moonstone Beach Bar and Grill, which will meet your restaurant and nightlife needs quite adequately.

A relative newcomer to Moonstone Beach Drive, **Pelican Cove Inn** (6316 Moonstone Beach Drive, 805/927-1500, $$$) might just be the nicest hideaway of all. Formerly Cambria's Pelican Suites, it is definitely the most elegant, featuring high beds with canopies. Comforters, carpeting, and wall coverings are coordinated in mauve and chocolate tones. A fine continental breakfast is served in the inn's warm, luxurious lobby. Cambria's Pelican Suites also gets a nod from us for spending $200,000 to save the riparian creek that runs through the property, which has been expanded in recent years. All that and an extra-friendly staff add up to a winner in our book.

It pays to price-shop among these generally interchangeable B&B-style motels along Moonstone Drive. By doing so on an early Sunday afternoon in May, for instance, we landed a deal. For $75—well below the listed price—we got a comfortable room, free breakfast, and a decent bottle of chardonnay.

COASTAL CUISINE

A plentiful selection of nonfranchised restaurants can be found around town, both in East Village and out by Moonstone Beach. As one local put it, "We've already got **Main Street Grill**" (603 Main Street, 805/927-3194, $). "Who needs McDonald's?" Another East Village favorite is **Robin's** (4095 Burton Drive, 805/927-5007, $$), a gourmet vegetarian restaurant serving ethnic dishes prepared with locally grown organic produce.

Out on Moonstone Beach, the **Sea Chest Oyster Bar** (6216 Moonstone Beach Drive, 805/927-4514, $$$) does a raging business serving generous portions of Alaskan crab legs, among other things, to crowds that happily pile in to break bread and crab legs. The **Moonstone Beach Bar and Grill** (6550 Moonstone Beach Drive, 805/927-3859, $$$), formerly the Moonraker, serves a variety of fare, but the best bet is the ever-popular pesto shrimp pasta and fresh mahimahi.

Sadly, a longstanding favorite for visitors to Cambria, Brambles Dinner House, closed in 2008. Its owners are planning to open another restaurant in San Luis Obispo, which we'll eagerly review in the next edition of this book.

NIGHTLIFE

Go to **Moonstone Beach Bar and Grill** (6550 Moonstone Beach Drive, 805/927-3859) if you're thirsty for a nightcap. In general, though, like most villages on this wild and scenic stretch of coastline, more noise is made by ocean waves than human beings after 10 P.M. Knock off early and save your strength for an early-morning beach hike.

San Simeon

Its owner christened it La Cuesta Encantada (The Enchanted Hill), but the world knows it better as Hearst Castle. The state park system formally refers to it as **Hearst San Simeon State Historical Monument**. Whatever you want to call it, the 165-room palace overlook-

TOURING HEARST CASTLE

Four completely different daytime tours are offered of Hearst Castle, and in the spring and fall, evening tours are also available. The spruced-up visitors center includes the National Geographic Theater, which runs the large-screen companion movie *Hearst Castle – Building the Dream*. The state is to be commended for keeping admission fees reasonable. All tours involve about a half mile of walking and between 150 and 400 steps, and in our experience the Hearst Castle tour guides have been well-informed and engaging. Here's a quick overview of each tour, all of which also include the indoor ("Roman") and outdoor ("Neptune") pools:

* **Tour 1:** This is the General Tour, recommended for first-time visitors. It covers the ground floor of the main building, one of the guest houses ("La Casa del Sol"), and part of the gardens. Admission also includes a 40-minute National Geographic documentary film.

* **Tour 2:** On the Private Quarters Tour, visitors explore the upper floors of the main building, including two suites, study, guest rooms, library, kitchen, and pantry.

* **Tour 3:** The North Wing Tour consists of three floors of guest suites, one of the guest houses ("La Casa del Monte"), and a short film.

* **Tour 4:** The Garden Tour guides you through Hearst's gardens, as well as a guest house ("La Casa del Mar"), the wine cellar, and the "hidden terrace." The main building is not entered. This tour is offered April-October.

* **Tour 5:** The Evening Tour provides a nighttime glimpse of the castle on Fridays and Saturdays, March-May and September-December, as well as every night during some holiday periods, such as Easter and Christmas. The tour includes highlights from Tours 1, 2, and 4, and lasts two hours and 10 minutes.

Make Hearst Castle tour reservations at 800/444-4445 or www.hearstcastle.com. You can also book tours at ReserveAmerica at 800/444-7275 or www.reserveamerica.com. Tickets for Tour 1 – "Hearst Experience," which includes the National Geographic film – are $20-24 ($10-12 for those under 17). Tours 2, 3, and 4 cost $15 ($10 for those under 17), and evening tours run $30 ($15 for those under 17). Tickets may also be purchased at the Hearst Castle ticket office, open daily 8 A.M.-4 P.M. Reservations can be made up to eight weeks in advance for individuals and 12 weeks in advance for groups. Reservations for wheelchair-accessible tours can be made directly with Hearst Castle by calling 805/927-2020 at least 10 days in advance.

ing the ocean from the Santa Lucia Mountains is the Central Coast's architectural centerpiece. It's as simple as this: No visit to the area is complete without a tour of Hearst Castle.

San Simeon is castle country. Everything else—sun, sand, sea, and the mountains that roll down to it—plays second fiddle to the incomprehensible grandiosity of Hearst Castle. The mid-coast mountaintop hideaway was built by newspaper magnate William Randolph

Hearst as a "carefully planned, deliberate attempt to create a shrine of beauty." One million people visit San Simeon every year, making it California's foremost state-run attraction.

Hearst was one of America's wealthiest men when he commissioned work on the castle, portrayed as the tomblike "Xanadu" in Orson Welles' classic film *Citizen Kane*, the barely fictionalized biography that is a cornerstone of every college-level film-appreciation course.

Born in 1863, Hearst was the sole heir to the nation's third largest fortune. His father, George Hearst, made his millions speculating in gold and silver mines, including the Comstock Lode. The elder Hearst turned his attention to real estate in the 1860s, gobbling up ranchland at $0.65 an acre. By acquiring adjoining land grants in the San Simeon area, he amassed a spread of 275,000 acres.

In the later years of the 19th century, the family often embarked on summer retreats to San Simeon, living in a tent pitched on top of a 1,600-foot mountain they called Camp Hill. William Randolph Hearst decided to build his dream castle on this site. He had not done badly for himself, thanks to his father's largesse. Hearst was given the *San Francisco Examiner* on his 24th birthday—nice present, that—and went on to inherit the $11 million family fortune. He oversaw a vast media empire that grew to include 30 newspapers, 15 magazines, six radio stations, and several film companies. In all, Hearst owned 94 businesses that employed 40,000 people. Yet history largely remembers him as a yellow journalist whose papers' hysterical reportage helped start a war and elect a president. (We cannot help but avoid pointing out—citing Fox News, George W. Bush, and the Iraq War as evidence—that things really haven't changed all that much since Hearst's time.)

Hearst's private passion for art collecting was greater even than his public passion for journalism and politicking. Hearst reportedly spent $1 million a year on artwork alone for 50 consecutive years. Some pieces date back 3,500 years, to the 18th Egyptian dynasty. He intended his castle to be a Louvre-like repository for his priceless collection of Mediterranean Gothic and Renaissance paintings, tapestries, and antique ceilings. Work was undertaken on the buildings and gardens in 1919. Hearst enlisted Julia Morgan, a renowned Berkeley-trained architect, to work for and with him. She agreed to devote two weekends a month to the Hearst manse, a project that kept her occupied for 20 years.

Hearst indulged every whim and desire that could be conceived, given virtually boundless economic resources. The crowning glory of the hilltop estate is La Casa Grande, the 115-room main house. It includes the gargantuan Refectory and Assembly Room (each filled with priceless art and artifacts), two libraries, and a movie theater. There's no place like home, especially when home is surrounded by 123 acres of exotic gardens, plus a line of hundred-foot Mexican fan palms. Three guest houses—Casa del Mar, Casa del Sol, and Casa del Monte—adjoin the big house, as do huge indoor and outdoor swimming pools. Hearst, an animal fancier, made a virtual nature preserve of his estate, importing 90 species from around the world and allowing them to roam the hills and fields. To this day, zebras and Barbary sheep, remnants of this bestiary, wander the grounds.

There is no end of jaw-dropping facts about the castle and tales about the celebrity aristocracy who were Hearst's constant guests during the gilded age of the 1920s and 1930s. Artifacts on display include Greek and Roman temple relics, 2,000-year-old sarcophagi, mille fleur tapestries from the north of France, and a Spanish castle ceiling (shipped overseas in a hundred crates and reassembled at San Simeon). You hear of a storage room filled with fur coats, provided as a courtesy for female guests wary of catching a shiver in the cool mountain air after stepping out of the 345,000-gallon heated outdoor pool.

America is fascinated with big money, and that's partly what keeps the tourist buses chugging up the mountain day in and day out. Though we don't have a king and queen, we do have a palace, and its name is San Simeon. Seven years after Hearst's death in 1951, his heirs turned over the estate to the state of California in exchange for $56 million in tax breaks. Today, tours run like clockwork 8:20 A.M.–3 P.M. (later in summer) every day of the year but Christmas, Thanksgiving, and New Year's Day. Tickets for the introductory "Hearst Experience" cost $24 (peak season) or $20 (off-peak season). Admission for kids under 17 drops to $12 (peak season) and $10 (off-peak season). Evening tours cost $30 for adults and $15 for kids under 17, regardless of time of year.

Each tour lasts just under two hours and involves nearly equal amounts of walking and gawking. Visitors are shepherded around the grounds by smiling guides who remind you not to step off the indoor-outdoor carpet runners that keep tourist hoof prints off the priceless marble, tile, and wood floors. One of us was chided like a misbehaving ten-year-old for stepping off the carpet. A word to the wise: Castle tours might be a little boring for fidgety young kids and culturally lowbrow adults. However, we'd recommend it without hesitation to travelers possessing any level of interest in art, architecture, or (of course) lifestyles of the rich and famous. Incidentally, the Hearst Corporation endures as a vast media empire, controlling newspapers, magazines, and book-publishing houses—not to mention 80,000 acres of land surrounding Hearst Castle.

The tiny village of San Simeon (population 250) lies beside the coast at the foot of Hearst's mountain. It exists mainly to serve tourists, and beyond a modest motel row, there's not much here. If you're planning on touring San Simeon—and it should be on your itinerary, if you've never done it—we'd recommend staying in Cambria, a short hop down the road and a more scenic and interesting place to bunk down.

For more information, contact the San Simeon Chamber of Commerce, 250 San Simeon Avenue, Suite 3A, San Simeon, CA 93452, 805/927-2020, www.sansimeonchamber.org; or San Simeon State Park, 750 Hearst Castle Road, San Simeon, CA 93452, 805/927-2020, www.parks.ca.gov.

BEACHES

Although Hearst Castle eclipses everything around it, two public beaches in San Simeon offer something else to do in the area.

San Simeon State Park lies between two creeks (Santa Rosa and San Simeon), abutting queenly Cambria to the south and providing 187 campsites and a day-use beach. Surfing is hit or miss, and swimming is for polar bears only, but diving is dependably good.

William R. Hearst Memorial State Beach lies at the foot of the Hearst property. San Simeon Point protects Hearst Beach from the ocean's onslaught, but the real attraction is a 1,000-foot fishing pier, where anglers cast for snapper and rockfish or charter boats for deep-sea fishing trips.

In terms of beaches, there are two sides to Hearst. North of the pier is a wide, protected cove beach backed by shade trees, a setting especially appealing to picnicking families. The blue-green water here is calm enough that small craft and sailboats anchor right offshore. South of the pier is a longer, rockier beach with rougher surf. This is more appealing to surfers and naturists.

From this vantage point you're in the often bypassed village of San Simeon. Formerly a whaling village, it is now just a small cluster of buildings on a short spur road off Highway 1. There's not much more here other than an old schoolhouse and the oldest store in the state, Sebastian's General Store, which also houses the local post office.

19 SAN SIMEON STATE PARK

Location: San Simeon Creek Road at Highway 1
Parking/Fees: free parking lot; camping fees $15-25 per night San Simeon Creek, $11-15 per night Washburn, plus $7.50 reservation fee
Hours: sunrise-sunset
Facilities: restrooms, showers, and picnic tables
Contact: San Simeon District, California State Parks, 805/927-2020

© PARKE PUTERBAUGH

William R. Hearst Memorial State Beach

20 WILLIAM R. HEARST MEMORIAL STATE BEACH

Location: 750 Hearst Castle Road, end of San Simeon Road off Highway 1 in San Simeon

Parking/Fees: $2 entrance fee per vehicle

Hours: sunrise–sunset

Facilities: concession, restrooms, and picnic tables

Contact: San Simeon District, California State Parks, 805/927-2020

ACCOMMODATIONS

The first motel in the area was **San Simeon Lodge** (9520 Castillo Drive, 805/927-4601, $). Built in 1958, the year in which the state acquired the Hearst Castle, it offers serviceable accommodations and reasonable, family-friendly prices. A whole strip of motels has grown up alongside the year-round industry of castle touring. The **Best Western Cavalier Resort** (9415 Hearst Drive, 805/927-4688, $$) is the only oceanfront motel in San Simeon, boasting 900 feet of coastline, plus fireplaces, balconies, and other upscale amenities more common to Cambria than San Simeon. Rooms rent for $150–300.

The **Orchid Inn at San Simeon** (9215 Hearst Drive, 805/927-3878, $$) puts a bit of Cambria's B&B-style amenities (country English decor, fireplaces, canopied beds) close to Hearst Castle. Formerly the Seacoast Lodge, the Orchid Inn adds special touches, such as delivering breakfast to your door. For the budget-minded, **Motel 6** (9070 Castillo Drive, 805/927-8691, $) offers economy, convenience, and clean, comfortable rooms.

COASTAL CUISINE

Because they feed more than a million mouths a year, the restaurateurs of San Simeon take a similar approach toward hungry tourists: Herd 'em in, fill 'em up, and move 'em out. They arrive by the busload before or after touring the house that Hearst built. One restaurant manager bragged to us about her restaurant's ability to feed thousands of hungry mouths a day. The secret is to induce them into ordering the serve-yourself buffet. "Don't even let 'em see a menu," she confided. "They might get ideas."

San Simeon Restaurant (9520 Castillo Drive, 805/927-4604, $$), which adjoins San Simeon Lodge, has been around the longest and has mastered the art of feeding the masses. One must heave open a veritable castle door to get inside. The dining room is filled with San Simeon memorabilia. The house specialty is prime rib, which suits the transient meat-and-potatoes crowd just fine.

NIGHTLIFE

William Randolph Hearst is dead, and after dark so is San Simeon. However, one very viable choice is an evening tour of Hearst Castle.

BIG SUR AND MONTEREY

Big Sur, the stunning geographical centerpiece of the California coastline, has never failed to awe and inspire all who pass through it. Intrepid travelers savor the sometimes white-knuckled drive along cliff-hugging Highway 1. Making this 90-mile trek is a rite of passage for vacationers who want the real, uncut California coast experience. Let's put it this way: There's no more scenic drive in America than Highway 1 through Big Sur.

Driving Big Sur is not unlike riding through the geographical equivalent of the Louvre, with one masterpiece after another passing before your awestruck eyes. Each sight is sufficiently varied in shape, size, and beauty to keep the passage consistently breathtaking. The cove beaches of southern Big Sur meld into the raw contours and lofty peaks of the Ventana Wilderness along Big Sur's midsection and the exquisite beauty of northern Big Sur. It's all too beautiful.

Big Sur has inspired more verbiage than a dozen Norton anthologies. Poetry, prose, proclamations, postcards—all that and more have been written about Big Sur, one of the last great untamed, unregulated wilderness areas in the lower 48 states. Maybe it's the jagged rocks in the water. Or the crashing waves flinging cataracts of foam in the air. Or the portentous fog that hangs over land and sea. Or the enticing mystery of nature at its most inhospitable—a raw ocean backed by the Santa Lucia Mountains and Los Padres National Forest. "Harsh and lovely," wrote local novelist Lillian Bos Ross, "held fast to their ancient loneliness by a sheer drop of 5,000 feet by a shoreless sea."

Whatever it is, one is never at a loss for words when describing Big Sur. Robinson Jeffers wrote his most heroic verse while living there. Novelist Richard Brautigan also mythologized the area, as did noted photographers Edward Weston

© PARKE PUTERBAUGH

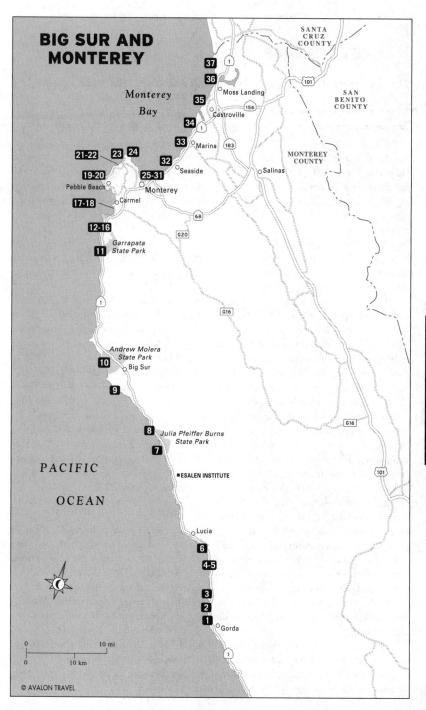

BIG SUR AND MONTEREY

Monterey Bay

37
36
35   Moss Landing
34   Castroville
33   Marina
32
21-22 23 24
19-20   25-31   Seaside
Pebble Beach   Monterey   Salinas
17-18   Carmel
12-16
11   Garrapata State Park

Andrew Molera State Park
10   Big Sur
9

8   Julia Pfeiffer Burns State Park
7

ESALEN INSTITUTE

PACIFIC

OCEAN

Lucia
6
4-5
3
2
1   Gorda

SANTA CRUZ COUNTY
SAN BENITO COUNTY
MONTEREY COUNTY

0   10 mi
0   10 km

© AVALON TRAVEL

BEST BEACHES

(**Pfeiffer Beach, page 310**

(**Asilomar State Beach, page 329**

and Ansel Adams, their visual record of Big Sur gracing many a coffee table. Nouveau salon painters continue the tradition of freeze-framing Big Sur, their efforts filling many a trendy gallery on the California coast. And now we'll give it our best shot. So climb in the car and join us for a ride up the coast through Big Sur.

North of Big Sur, the coastline enfolding Monterey Bay offers much in the manner of the muse, as well—inspiring epic poems, novels, photographs, paintings, spiritual retreats, and nature cults. The populous Monterey Peninsula has a storehouse of treasures: the steep-sloped, blinding white-sand beach at Carmel; the calming stands of pine in Pacific Grove; and the strollable bayside in Monterey, with its pier, marina, and aquarium.

Each of these cities has its own personality and purpose, as well. Carmel is a tony village whose shopping district serves well-heeled visitors, but it is otherwise a quiet, retiring place—especially after the sun goes down. Pacific Grove is unpretentious and mainly residential. Although it is the least tourist-oriented of the three, you'll still find the best bed-and-breakfast inns, as well as a number of agreeable restaurants, out this way. Monterey, put simply, serves the tourist trade, but it does so about as well as one might hope. It's grown on us over the years, which is saying a lot, given our curmudgeonly bent. One place we won't wax poetic about is Seaside, which in a previous edition we characterized as "a boil on the ass of Monterey." Enough said.

Farther up the road, off the peninsula and along the bay, the population thins out, giving way to the wilderness beaches of rural Moss Landing and the fertile farmland surrounding Castroville. Some of these less-visited locales have a rustic appeal of their own. So don't just whiz through like some typically harried, hot-footed tourist. Stop and smell the roses—and taste the artichokes, while you're at it.

Point Piedras Blancas

At the south end of Big Sur is Point Piedras Blancas, a vista point turnout you will not want to bypass. Although this detour offers no public beach access, it does offer a unique opportunity on the California coast to study the behavior of sea lions and seals in the wild. Adult elephant seals—so large they almost resemble manatees—are spotted here from late November to March. More frequently, the beach below the viewing spots is dotted with the prone, twitching, snoozing, and honking bodies of weary California sea lions and harbor seals, as well as a few baby elephant seals (known as "weaners").

This Point Piedras colony of elephant seals is the fastest growing on the mainland of California. Informative placards describe the life cycles of these endangered sea mammals, and viewing perches let you peer nearly straight down at them in action. One placard described the fighting that often occurs among male elephant seals who are trying to protect their harem of females. A photograph of two bloodied studs accompanies the description, which prompted one young boy to ask his father if they were going to fight while we were watching them.

"No, they only do that during mating season," the father explained.

"What's *mating* mean?" the son queried.

There followed a brief silence, then a studiously considered response: "That's when they are, uh, trying to find a girlfriend."

As we are both fathers of young children, we noted the skill of this dad, for future use.

For more information, contact the Friends of the Elephant Seal, Central Coast, P.O. Box 490, Cambria, CA 93428, 805/924-1628, www.elephantseal.org.

Big Sur

We completely understand all the aesthetes' fascination and fixation with Big Sur. We happened to drive its length on one of the most glorious days in all creation. The sun was high, the sky hard blue, everything green and blooming, the air so clear that everything had a high definition almost to the point of hyper-realism. The natural world seemed more of a marvel and sanctuary than ever. Even the most devout atheist would have to give some ground to the notion of a divine creator in such a setting on such a day as this.

The Santa Lucia Mountains, which rise with near verticality from the waters edge, are harrowing and awesome to behold at any time, under any conditions. Yet they were particularly majestic on this day. Every turn in the road brought a new overlook onto the ocean or scene of topographic wonder jutting above us. The forms are so incredible in their relation to one another that you sometimes feel as if you're wearing 3D glasses.

Written large on a landscape that is inhospitable to habitation and highways—including that perilous marvel, Highway 1, etched into the cliffs and forever being repaired or rebuilt—it delivers a lesson in humility to a species that foolishly believes it can conquer all. Humankind will never tame this corner of creation—nor should we even dare to try. All efforts should henceforth be directed at preservation, not development.

From either end, the initial ascent into Big Sur is a roller-coaster ride like no other. You go up, up, up and then down, around curves and loop-de-loops, only to emerge with a vista that makes you feel as if you're on top of the world. Numerous turnouts make it possible to study the splendor. On a nice day, you might pull over and drink in nature's majesty for an

© PARKE PUTERBAUGH
Big Sur

BIG SUR AND MONTEREY

LIVING ALONG BIG SUR

Glimpses gleaned from Henry Miller's later writings and conversations with a few long-time residents have fueled our fascination with what life in Big Sur must be like year-round. The idea of a community of 1,600 enlightened souls evenly spaced out along 90 miles of precipitous ridges and rugged coastline does hold some appeal, though the reality is no doubt more difficult than our utopian notions.

With habitations out of sight of the road, chance encounters with Big Sur residents are pretty remote – that is, until we happened to meet a loquacious local at a Big Sur restaurant one evening. She was our server, and when we told her of our longtime curiosity, she gladly entertained and enlightened us with tales of her life there. Articulate, witty, self-effacing, and yet self-assured, she came off as the kind of neighbor we'd like to have.

She came from Pittsburgh, earning a degree in social work that led to employment as a resident counselor at a state prison. Deciding her long blonde hair and gentle spirit were not suited to work in prison surroundings, she came to Big Sur, where she has resided ever since. She has had many homes, hopping from one rental to another and camping in a tent when none was available. She even had the ultimate Big Sur experience of living in Henry Miller's former home on Partington Ridge. She was, in short, immersed in this seemingly invisible community, a gregarious soul living among hermits. She took painting lessons from an elderly woman who served as a sort of guru, and she wanders the hills with her easel like Van Gogh at Arles. "So much comes up when you put oil on canvas," she says. "Who needs a psychiatrist?"

She also earns money from "body work" – nutrition, health, hygiene, and massage – and makes medicinal potions from home-grown herbs and English lavender. In Big Sur no one agonizes over the issue of age as we do in the "real world." Wrinkles betoken wisdom. What people do care about is privacy. And though it's not apparent to the naked eye, our server insisted that things are changing in changeless Big Sur. Upon one back ridge, 25 new homes have been built where there was just one when she first arrived. Rumors fly about celebrities buying property.

She bemoaned the high property taxes, reflected in her monthly rent, which force her to work three shifts at the restaurant. Then there's the summertime flood of tourists, snarling along the Pacific Coast Highway. Worst of all, her latest rental would soon be coming to an end. She'd been there five years, and "this was the first year the roof hasn't leaked," she said, exasperated but not embittered. She'd be okay, she insisted. She has enough hooks in the community to keep a roof over her head. She could always go back to the tent life. "That was okay when I was young, but . . ."

It doesn't seem fair. People like our server, who have the lowest impact on the environment, are always the renters. They're the ones who realize that life is temporary and therefore don't try to make piles of money and buy up everything they can lay hands on. Beyond Big Sur's heavenly natural setting, people like her make the area even more special. May she continue to keep a roof (or tent) over her head.

MARGARET W. OWINGS: AN ENVIRONMENTAL LEGACY

When Margaret Wentworth Owings died in 1999, California lost one of its greatest and most tireless coastal and ocean conservationists. Found dead of heart failure at Wild Bird, her clifftop home in Big Sur, she had just finished compiling her complete writings and artwork. The results were published as *Voice from the Sea: Reflections on Wildlife and Wilderness.* For the past 50 years, Owings fought to keep developers away from Big Sur and sat on the council of the Big Sur Land Trust.

The turning point in her activism, she once said, was when she saw a man shoot a sea lion for no reason but pointless bloodlust. Owings was founder and first president of Friends of the Sea Otter. She led a successful lobby to end bounty hunting of mountain lions in California. She was also a member of the Point Lobos League, which helped save the beaches between Carmel River and Point Lobos State Preserve. In addition, this tireless servant sat on the council of the Save the Redwoods League and was a member of the California Parks Commission (1963-1969), a trustee of Defenders of Wildlife (1969-1974), a board member with the National Parks Foundation (1968-1969), a trustee of the African Wildlife Leadership Foundation (1968-1976), a trustee of the Environmental Defense Fund (1972-1982), and founder of the Rachel Carson Council.

In 1998 the National Audubon Society listed her among the 100 individuals who've done the most to shape the environmental movement, placing her in such stellar company as Jacques-Yves Cousteau, Lady Bird Johnson, and Morris Uddall. Almost everyone who visits Big Sur falls in love with it. Owings was one of those rare individuals who loved Big Sur so much she devoted her life to preserving it.

A suggestion from two appreciative beach writers: Name a Big Sur beach after her.

BIG SUR AND MONTEREY

hour or more. You might also choose to take a cigarette break, as many sadly seem to do, especially nicotine-addicted European travelers. What a waste of fresh air!

Each turn of the geographic kaleidoscope brings a new perspective. Green, folded mountainsides rise like fertile pinnacles toward heaven. The colors of the mountains change with the light and time of day, as does that of the water. Looking down on one cove, we saw brown, volcanic sand on the beach; agitated near-shore waters that had turned a sediment-stirred whitish-brown; a band of jade-colored water that reminded us of Florida's emerald coast; and, finally, the steely azure that typifies the deeper Pacific.

Some sights are surreal. Certain offshore rock formations look like they were dropped here from outer space. Sheer mountain faces constantly cough up rocks onto the road, and

yellow-and-black signs warn of slides. Work crews struggle to keep Highway 1 passable, especially after the winter rainy season, when running water further destabilizes nonvegetated cliff faces. There have been years when the road has been closed for months while CalTrans crews deal with cataclysmic rock slides or the necessary re-bridging of some seemingly unbridgeable chasm. In places, the road looks like it's been Krazy Glued back together, and we could smell fresh asphalt on a few stretches. Highway 1 is high maintenance, and in some future decade, we imagine, they'll have to throw in the towel on it. On a per mile basis, Highway 1 is the costliest stretch of blacktop to maintain in all of California.

For all these reasons, CalTrans has found it necessary to devise a Big Sur Coast Highway Management Plan (CHMP). This is what they have to say about it: "The Big Sur CHMP...will establish a framework for continued safe and efficient operation of Highway 1 in a manner that preserves, restores, and maintains the natural and scenic characteristics of the corridor… While intensive efforts are required to keep the highway open and safe, over time, some of the strategies employed are seen as having the potential to degrade the overall quality of the corridor. The management plan strives to achieve a consensus-based approach to developing sustainable management strategies that will ensure the long-term preservation of the special qualities that make Big Sur unique."

In other words, hope to hell that someone doesn't turn off the funding spigot, or Highway 1 is history.

Notably, the flattest stretch, and the one that remains closest to sea level, is designated Pacific Valley. It lies between the communities of Gorda and Lucia, a distance of roughly eight miles. We could rhapsodize at length about every blessed mile of Big Sur, but we'll leave it to you to make your own discoveries, which is as it should be. The necessary stops, in our opinion, are Julia Pfeiffer Burns State Park and Andrew Molera State Park. Beyond that, just pull the car over whenever the mood and the view seize you. Make sure your camera's batteries have enough juice in them to record the numerous pictures or lengthy videos you'll no doubt want to make. When the batteries for our digital camera gave out just as we were entering Big Sur, we were forced to pay through the nose at a roadside shop. Don't let this happen to you! The same holds true for gas, which is both more expensive and less available in Big Sur than in the communities at either end.

On a cultural note, you'll want to stop at the Coast Gallery, which exhibits the watercolors of Henry Miller and prints of Marc Chagall. Miller, a Big Sur denizen for decades (he lived on Partington Ridge), was best known as a writer, though he painted with an almost religious zeal toward the end of his life. Filled with rainbow-like hues, his celebratory paintings project a childlike wonder that is perfectly in keeping with his exuberant spirit. The Coast Gallery also sells lots of pricey, sleek animal sculptures, as well as books, gifts, coffee mugs, and decorative knickknacks; there's even a café. In terms of food, though, we'd recommend that you save your appetite for Ventana (if you want a great meal) or Nepenthe (if you want a great view).

Despite its obvious magnetism for artists and writers, it was not until itinerant savant and Brooklyn native Miller settled on Partington Ridge in 1944 that Big Sur began gaining widespread notice. The same man who sparked obscenity trials with his erotica turned to watercolors here. About his new Canaan he wrote: "At dawn its majesty is almost painful to behold. That same prehistoric look. The look of always. Nature smiling at herself in the mirror of eternity."

Another writer, Jack Kerouac, came to Big Sur seeking solitude, briefly encamping here in 1960 to escape the wages of fame. He lit out for a shack in a Big Sur canyon and managed to capture a piece of it in his novel *Big Sur:* "Big elbows of rock rising everywhere, sea caves within, seas plollicking all around inside them crashing out foams, the boom and pound on the sand, the sand dipping quick (no Malibu Beach here). Yet you turn and see the pleasant woods winging upcreek like a picture in Vermont. But you look up into the sky, bend way back, my God you're standing directly under that aerial bridge with its thin white line running from rock to rock and witless cars racing across it like dreams! From rock to rock! All the way down the raging coast!" The band Death Cab for Cutie used this novel, and by association this exceptionally beautiful area, as the springboard for their stirring 2008 release, *Narrow Stairs.* In fact, frontman and songwriter Ben Gibbard wrote the album's songs while holed up in Big Sur.

Enough of artistic inquiry. A few geographic facts are in order to distinguish Big Sur the place from Big Sur the state of mind. Big Sur stretches, roughly, from the San Luis Obispo County line to the Carmel River, just above

BIG SUR LAND TRUST

The future of Big Sur is a topic so hot that the locals have been burning up over it for the last two decades. At present Big Sur is an untamed wilderness, geographically and politically. The coastal lands are largely in private hands, while the interior mostly falls under federal jurisdiction as Los Padres National Forest. Despite efforts to have Big Sur declared a National Seashore – and thus, theoretically, protected in perpetuity – it is not presently controlled by any governmental body.

Flying in the face of those who say Big Sur should be federally protected, the Big Sur Land Trust (BSLT) works toward the goal of "retaining the land in its natural state" and "creating an effective private-sector alternative for land preservation." To that end, BSLT has devised various creative ways by which locals can donate or set aside land without shafting their next of kin – i.e., through conservation easements, charitable remainder trusts, and life estates. To date, more than 30,000 acres of the Big Sur coast and the Monterey Peninsula have been protected by BSLT. A huge success story was the purchase by the Land Trust – with help from the Nature Conservancy and the state of California – of the Palo Corona Ranch, a 9,898-acre tract south of Carmel that is the "gateway to Big Sur."

This success notwithstanding, arguments on both sides of the issue carry merit. The locals don't want Big Sur to become another National Park playland like Yosemite and Yellowstone, overrun with tourists and RVs. They also don't want to be told what to do with their own land by outsiders – even well-known ones like Robert Redford and the late Ansel Adams, both of whom led battles on Capitol Hill to annex Big Sur in the 1980s. As a show of good faith, BSLT has adopted the stringent guidelines of the California Coastal Commission to ensure that no desecration of the land takes place. Still, the signs are there – For Sale signs on plots of land in southern Big Sur, that is – and the potential for exploitation exists with the private sell-off of land.

Although we agree in spirit with Big Sur locals, whether or not the Land Trust can exert any real control over the actions of private landowners, when push comes to shove, is very much a matter of concern. On the other hand, as one local resident put it, "Why disturb what's perfect? Private property is a worthwhile idea in this area."

For more information, contact the Big Sur Land Trust, P.O. Box 221864, Carmel, CA 93922, 831/625-5523, www.bigsurlandtrust.org.

Point Lobos, a distance of 90 miles. It extends to the east beyond Ventana Wilderness. All told it covers 300 square miles (192,000 acres). The population of the region hovered around 1,000 for decades, a stability attributable to the high price of available land, scarcity of water, and the near impossibility of getting new structures approved under strict local ordinances. (The number of residents is now a whopping 1,600.) The largest part of coastal Big Sur—the part that most visitors see along the cliff-hugging Pacific Coast Highway—is privately owned. The town of Big Sur is not really a town but a sparsely settled strand of inns, restaurants, and residences, most of which are hidden on backcountry ridges. No Trespassing and No Beach Access signs are common, because the locals are hermits who don't want to be bothered.

The name Big Sur derives from a rare meeting of English and Spanish. "Sur" is taken from El Pais Grande del Sur, which means "The Big Country to the South." The name was bestowed by the Spanish at Carmel Mission in the late 1700s, denoting the impassable region along the coast. But many moons before the missions were built, the Esalen tribe inhabited the region. Their villages along the Big Sur Valley date back 3,000 years. They discovered an abundance of earthly delights

THE HENRY MILLER LIBRARY

Could there be a more perfect setting than Big Sur for a literary legacy as exuberant as Henry Miller's? For years, even after Miller left Big Sur to live in semi-seclusion in Pacific Palisades (where he died in 1980), his good friend Emil White created and ran the Henry Miller Library out of his Graves Canyon home. The library still exists there today – a glimpse of green serenity along a dusty curve in the Pacific Coast Highway in Big Sur. White's archive included his personal collection of Miller's books, mementos, and watercolors. A charming raconteur, White screened Miller's endless army of admirers. In some ways, his congeniality made him the unofficial greeter for the Big Sur community.

When White died in 1989, the Henry Miller Library was bequeathed to the Big Sur Land Trust. In 1997 the library became an independent organization whose mission is to champion Miller's literary and artistic legacy while also serving as a "cultural resource center" for artists, writers, musicians, and students. Concerts, workshops, and exhibits are held at the natural redwood amphitheater on the grounds, while readings and lectures are staged in the library. In keeping with Miller's renegade spirit, the West Coast Regional Championship Poetry Slam has been held here.

Too many literary shrines are as stiff as the writer's cadaver. A painful shuffling of feet ensues while a wooden tour guide recites vital statistics as you stroll past the writer's roped-off pen-and-pencil set. There's no such formality here. The Henry Miller Library is a sort of "serve yourself" kind of place, the spirit of which is found in a "Notice to Visitors" that Miller wrote and posted on his own door. A facsimile of Miller's note sits outside the Miller library, gently offering such words of wisdom as, "When you come, be so kind as to check your neuroses and psychoses at the gate. Gossip may be exchanged during the wee hours of the morning when the gremlins have left...Let us do our best even if it gets us nowhere. In the midst of darkness there is light."

The Henry Miller Library is at Milepost 29.7S/61.3N. It is open 11 A.M.–6 P.M. Wednesday-Monday. There is no charge to enter, and a small gallery and bookshop are on the premises. For more information, contact the Henry Miller Library, Highway 1, Big Sur, CA 93920, 831/667-2574, www.henrymiller.org.

at their disposal—plenty of fish and meat, as well as hot springs. Then the Spanish came to convert the contented Esalen to Christianity. The tribes died off soon thereafter. Today, one of the tribes' sacred springs is the centerpiece of the Esalen Institute, a spiritual organization that's blazing new trails in self-awareness.

The first-time visitor to Big Sur will take Highway 1 in and out. For all intents and purposes, this is the only road through here. Though a few back roads exist, only one—the sometimes inaccessible Nacimiento-Fergusson Road—actually pierces the mountains, connecting with U.S. 101, which lies 30 miles east. Other roads in the area are little more than dirt

tracks, barely large enough for one car and best suited for four-wheel-drive vehicles.

The 91-mile passage through Big Sur on Highway 1 is as legendary as it is exhilarating. As a driving experience it is unsurpassed. In 1966 Lady Bird Johnson proclaimed it the nation's first Scenic Highway. Today, more cars and RVs lumber through Big Sur than Yosemite National Park each year. Like a naturally occurring roller coaster, Highway 1 varies in elevation from 20 to 1,200 feet, in width from 18 to 24 feet, and in scenic splendor from "Oh, wow!" to "Don't get too close!" to "Oh my *god!*"

Various points of interest along the road are

designated not by address but by milepost from the south or north boundary. For example "Milepost 28S/63N" means that you are 28 miles from the northern boundary and 63 miles from the southern boundary. Since the winter storms of 1997–1998, the highway has taken major hits from floods and rock slides, and portions of it have been made one-lane only in order to do "seismic retrofit work." Be extra careful and patient. Hey, cut the ignition and dig the scenery.

Before embarking on this epic drive, take a few precautions. Fill the gas tank. Make sure the tires and brakes are in good shape. Drive from north to south, if possible—the most breathtaking views are seen that way. Let the passengers do all the ogling. If you want a closer look, 300 turnouts have been carved into the roadside for that purpose. Don't needlessly pass slowpokes; as the billboard says, "Risking Is Losing."

En route, the constantly changing landscape will captivate and enrapture you. At points the road might even nauseate you. Bring or stop for crackers, soda, and motion-sickness medication in case of carsickness. (Cokes and Saltines are part of our pre–Big Sur packing ritual.) Some places, particularly a handful of beaches, are well worth a side trip off Highway 1. Budget enough time to savor the sights and make some side trips. You're in heaven; there's no hurry. Simply strap in and enjoy the ride of a lifetime.

Much of Big Sur, including beaches and campgrounds, falls under the jurisdiction and ownership of the U.S. Forest Service. For more information, contact Los Padres National Forest, 6755 Hollister Avenue, Suite 150, Goleta, CA 93117, 805/968-6640, www.fs.fed.us/lospadres.

For specific information on Ventana Wilderness—the 150,000-acre unit within Los Padres National Forest that includes part of the Big Sur coast and much of the Santa Lucia Mountains—contact the Monterey Ranger District Office, U.S. Forest Service, 406 South Mildred Avenue, King City, CA 93930, 831/385-5434.

A detailed topographic map of Ventana Wilderness and a map of the entire Los Padres National Forest—including campgrounds and hiking trails—are available by mail from the Monterey Ranger District Office for $4.25 each. Specify which map(s) you are requesting, and make checks payable to BSNHA.

For more information on Big Sur in general, including recreation, lodging, and restaurants along Highway 1, contact the Big Sur Chamber of Commerce, P.O. Box 87, Big Sur, CA 93920, 831/667-2100, www.bigsurcalifornia.org; or Big Sur Station, Big Sur, CA 93920, 831/667-2315.

BEACHES

The beaches of Big Sur include everything from rocky, sandless strips to coves whose sands range from beige to deep volcanic brown to coal black. You can view some of these coves from roadside turnouts, and they are as appealing as they are inaccessible. That is to say, some of the most amazing beaches in California cannot be physically reached, but they can be visually enjoyed from above.

Because we've organized this guidebook from south to north, the wonders of Big Sur will be described in that direction. (Both north and south mileposts are provided in the practical beach information, however.) It will help immeasurably to carry a map of Big Sur. A good one can be found in *El Sur Grande*, a newspaper-style guide that identifies all pertinent landmarks. Pick up a free copy while you're in the area; it's widely available.

Another good way to obtain Big Sur information is by calling **Big Sur Station** (831/667-2315). This multi-agency information service of California State Parks, the U.S. Forest Service, and CalTrans is housed in a brochure-filled office about 25 miles south of Carmel along Highway 1 in Big Sur. Of course, you'll want to be outfitted with the necessary maps and info before you reach that point.

Some of the easiest coastal access in Big Sur can be found along a four-mile marine terrace at the south end, between Willow and Wild Cattle Creeks. **Willow Creek Picnic Area** and **Jade Cove** offer a scenic overview of the region's geologic treasures. Willow Creek is primarily a spot for a quick lunch. An access trail leads to a rocky cove beach, and the sizable rocks offshore are impressive to study. Jade Cove is worth a longer pause.

At the Jade Cove access, you scale a stepladder over a fence and hike across a field of wildflowers to a dirt path that leads, via stumbling and sliding steps, down to a rocky beach. Visitors can scan the rocks and pebbles on shore for the mineral jade, specifically nephrite jade ("the stone of heaven"). Anything below the high-tide line is up for grabs, and some people make off with handsome hauls. As is always the case with a golden goose, though, people will pluck all the eggs. That is, amateur rock hounds and gallery-bound artists have picked so much of the nephrite, according to state authorities, that the Lands Commission is considering stepping in to monitor the activity. In 1971 divers took a 9,000-pound jade boulder worth $180,000.

Across the road from Jade Cove is the 43-site **Plaskett Creek Campground,** a National Forest facility that costs $16 per night. You'll need to make reservations as far in advance as possible if you wish to camp here. A half mile north of Jade Cove is **Sand Dollar Picnic Area and Beach.** Its tree-shaded picnic tables and cove can be reached by hiking across a field. The beach got stripped of its sand during a run of storm-filled winters. Natural processes have replenished it, and it is one of Big Sur's real shoreline treasures—maybe the finest of the relatively rare number of accessible beaches along its southern 50 miles.

A similar setting exists at **Mill Creek Picnic Area,** although the beach is a bit rockier and the trail leading to it steeper. Another Forest Service campground can be found a half mile up Highway 1 at Kirk Creek. Nestled against the Santa Lucia Mountains four miles south of a little burgh named Lucia, **Kirk Creek Campground** sits on bluffs overlooking the ocean. A steep, serpentine road leads to a small lot and a smattering of tables. You can scramble down a short path to a rocky shoreline with a sandy crescent just to the north. Trails also lead up into the Ventana Wilderness, where some long, satisfying hikes can be taken. Just make sure you've planned any trek so that you're back before nightfall. Being stuck in the dark on a primitive trail in the mountains of Big Sur when the animals start their stalking and screeching can be harrowing, especially for those lacking outdoor survival skills.

Two miles north of Kirk Creek is **Limekiln State Park.** Formerly a private campground, Limekiln was acquired by the state and opened to the public in 1995. Campsites are scattered in the redwoods and by the beach beneath a bridge at the mouth of Limekiln Creek, named for the remnants of lime kilns that lie a short distance up the creek (and can be hiked to). Frankly, the campsites aren't much—picnic tables and hibachis in a gravel lot directly beneath the bridge—but the natural setting is beyond compare. Limekiln Creek gurgles out of the mountains and then crosses a flat bed of gravel before emptying into the sea. Hiking trails extend into the mountains. Picnic tables at the ocean's edge make an enticing day-use area of Limekiln, too.

After a dozen or so miles of hairpin turns, you come upon **Julia Pfeiffer Burns State Park.** A 3,580-acre day-use park whose chief scenic attraction is **McWay Falls,** it is arguably the most spectacular and photographic spot on the Big Sur coast. Finding it requires a short hike along McWay Creek, which ends up plummeting 50 feet to the beach below. It is the only place on the California coast where a waterfall empties directly into the ocean. McWay Falls is a major photo op, and a lovely cove beach to boot. Divers submerge joyfully into the 1,680-acre underwater reserve. Two environmental campsites are available, requiring a half-mile hike out to a bluff overlooking the ocean. Fires and rockslides in 2008 have caused the closure of all park trails east of Highway 1. They remained closed as we went to press and will stay that way until further notice.

Partington Cove is the site of a 110-foot tunnel burrowed into the rock in the 1880s by pirates, who stashed their booty here. Later it served as a landing point for the early settlers and as a place for Prohibition-era bootleggers to bring liquor to shore. There is no official beach access at Partington Cove, but visitors can scoot down a steep path to the small beach. It is marked by an iron gate and black mailbox on the ocean side of the highway, 1.8 miles north of Julia Pfeiffer Burns State Park.

Two miles up the road is the **Coast Gallery** (Milepost 33S/52N, 831/667-2301), where local artists exhibit their work. What makes the Coast Gallery special is its extensive collection of original Henry Miller lithographs and watercolors. Miller devotees should also visit the **Henry Miller Memorial Library** (Milepost 29.7S/61.3N, 831/667-2574), a few hundred yards up the road.

The first of Big Sur's truly great beaches lies five miles farther up the road. A marked turnoff at Sycamore Canyon Road (Milepost 27.1S/63.2N) leads downhill to **Pfeiffer Beach.** A two-mile road passes through inhabited Sycamore Canyon. Makeshift homes list among the trees like pine cones, mutely testifying to the rough life still to be found in the wilderness (and a cautionary note to those who fantasize living along Big Sur to be a day at the beach). From the parking lot, a quarter-mile path leads through cypress trees to the beach. Miracle of miracles, Pfeiffer Beach is a wide sandy beach, battered by waves that rush through sea caves and arches to the shore in foamy torrents. A strong undertow discourages swimming. No camping or fires are allowed, either.

A U.S. Forest Service day-use area, Pfeiffer Beach underwent major road repair and site improvements several years ago, including new restrooms, paved parking, beach access trail, landscaping with native plants, and interpretive signage. The improved Pfeiffer Beach day-use area is well worth visiting.

Another mile yields **Pfeiffer Big Sur State Park** (Milepost 26.0S/63.7N), a splendid 821-acre retreat along the east side of Highway 1, at the foot of the Santa Lucia Mountains along Big Sur River Gorge. Set among redwoods, oaks, and meadows, the park beckons campers and hikers. There are half a dozen trails in the park, ranging up to four miles in length. There's also an inn (Big Sur Lodge). Be advised that the forest fires of 2008 have necessitated closure of many trails east of Highway 1 throughout Big Sur, including Pfeiffer Big Sur State Park, so inquire at the office about the status of any trail you wish to hike before setting out.

Some of the ancient, stately trees here predate the signing of the Magna Carta. Others, long dead, lie like toppled Greek columns in backwoods groves. One of the more memorable hiking trails leads to lovely Pfeiffer Falls. The Pfeiffers, whose names adorn so much around here, were the first European immigrants to permanently settle in this area, arriving in 1869.

Five miles north is **Andrew Molera State Park,** another great parkland. Molera allows public access to the ocean along a portion of Big Sur that is otherwise mostly held by El Sur Cattle Ranch, which restricts public access with barbed-wire fences and off-putting signs. Andrew Molera State Park was named for the grandson of Juan Bautista Roger Cooper, the original owner of the ranch at Molera Point. It is speculated that Cooper used his "Ranch of the South" to import goods without paying the high customs in Monterey. Beyond that, Molera was a legitimate dairy man, famous for his Monterey Jack cheese. The largest state park in Big Sur, Andrew Molera's 4,800 acres feature scenic trails through former pastureland and alongside the Big Sur River, an area rich with bird life. However, a natural calamity struck here in summer 2008 when fires raged out of control, forcing the temporary closure of Andrew Molera, Julia Pfeiffer, and Limekiln State Parks, as well as units of Los Padres National Forest abutting Big Sur.

BIG SUR AND MONTEREY

The beach at Andrew Molera is one of the few walkable sand strips in Big Sur. It is pounded by rough surf that makes for hazardous swimming. Some years back, the beach got washed away due to flooding on the Big Sur River. It has since recovered, but nature can exert her will at any time. Flooding can damage the pedestrian footbridges over creeks to the beach at Andrew Molera, making the trek an adventure in pioneer-style stream-fording. Just realize you're in a place that's rawer and more subject to the whims of the elements than the usual beach park.

The seclusion seems to inspire a loss of inhibition, explaining a smattering of nudity at Andrew Molera State Park (as well as Pfeiffer Beach). A 60-site tent-only campground lies right above the ocean. Campers must pack in all gear on the half-mile trek from the parking lot. The campground is a big, grassy common area; there's a formal limit of 350 campers per night, but they try not to turn anyone away. Trails in the park allow for riverside, lagoon-side, meadow, headland, and bluff-top hikes.

A private horse stable conducts guided trail walks along what they call the "most spectacular ride in America." What's fun for the riders, however, is not so much fun for beach walkers. Out on the beach, you may find yourself amid a minefield of horse droppings, as the nags leave their filthy calling cards all over the place. The state-park overseers might wish to consider the environmental consequences of trail rides or find a way to diaper the equine offenders so as not to foul the beach. (For reservations and information, call **Molera Trail Rides** at 831/625-5486.)

Five miles north of Andrew Molera, the **Point Sur Lightstation** shines a beacon on coastal history and continues to warn oceangoing vessels of the treacherous waters off Point Sur. Built in 1889 on a volcanic rock 361 feet above the pounding surf, Point Sur is the only functioning lighthouse on the California coast with all of its original buildings intact. The Stanton Center in Monterey displays its original Fresnel lens (it could be seen 23 miles out to sea); today the U.S. Coast Guard manages the station's automated light and fog signal. Guided tours of the lighthouse, which is on the National Register of Historic Places, are given by docents on weekends. (For information, call 831/625-4419.)

Closer to the northern boundary of Big Sur—5.4 miles above Point Sur, to be exact—Highway 1 crosses Bixby Bridge, one of the West Coast's most photogenic spans. This concrete arch, a true engineering marvel, is 700 feet long and towers 260 feet above the creek. It was the longest bridge of its kind in the world when built in 1932. Back when the local sea otter population almost dwindled to extinction, it is believed that the sole surviving male—from whom all others are now descended—lived in the waters beneath Bixby Bridge.

Six more miles bring yet another spectacular Big Sur parkland that beckons passersby who think they've seen it all. **Garrapata State Park** lays claim to more than four miles of coastline among its 2,879 acres. The trails that lead down to the rugged beaches wind through several different kinds of coastal vegetation, including cactus and redwood groves. Garrapata (which means "tick" in Spanish) is not for everyone, however, as the rough trails don't lend themselves to quick jaunts. The park trails are worth every step, offering spectacular views of the ocean, cavorting sea otters, and tidepools. Parking and day-use access to the park is free, but it is primitive. Pull your car over at either Turnout 13 (west side) or Turnout 14 (east side). Unmarked paths from Turnout 13 lead out to Sobranes Point and up to Whale Peak—a prime whale-watching promontory. The beach at Garrapata is another favorite with the clothing-optional set.

The northernmost access point on the Big Sur coast is Point Lobos State Reserve, a locale so extraordinary it warrants its own section.

1 WILLOW CREEK PICNIC AREA

Location: Milepost 61.5S/28.2N on Highway 1 in Big Sur
Parking/Fees: free parking lot
Hours: half hour before sunrise–half hour after sunset
Facilities: restrooms, picnic tables, and fire pits
Contact: Big Sur Station, 831/667-2315

2 JADE COVE

Location: Milepost 59.8S/29.9N on Highway 1 in Big Sur
Parking/Fees: free parking lot
Hours: half hour before sunrise–half hour after sunset
Facilities: none
Contact: Big Sur Station, 831/667-2315

3 SAND DOLLAR PICNIC AREA AND BEACH

Location: Milepost 59.3S/30.4N on Highway 1 in Big Sur
Parking/Fees: $5 entrance fee per vehicle; camping fee at Plaskett Creek Campground $22 per night, $5 per night walk-in or bicycle camping
Hours: half hour before sunrise–half hour after sunset
Facilities: restrooms and picnic tables
Contact: Big Sur Station, 831/667-2315

4 MILL CREEK PICNIC AREA

Location: Milepost 54.5S/35.2N on Highway 1 in Big Sur
Parking/Fees: free parking lot
Hours: half hour before sunrise–half hour after sunset
Facilities: restrooms and picnic tables
Contact: Big Sur Station, 831/667-2315

5 KIRK CREEK CAMPGROUND

Location: Milepost 54.0S/35.7N on Highway 1 in Big Sur
Parking/Fees: free parking lot; camping fee $22 per night, $5 per night walk-in or bicycle camping
Hours: half hour before sunrise–half hour after sunset
Facilities: restrooms and picnic tables
Contact: Big Sur Station, 831/667-2315

6 LIMEKILN STATE PARK

Location: Milepost 52.1S/37.6N on Highway 1 in Big Sur
Parking/Fees: $6 entrance fee per vehicle; camping fees $20-25 per night, plus $7.50 reservation fee
Hours: 8 A.M.-8 P.M.
Facilities: restrooms, showers, and picnic tables
Contact: Limekiln State Park, 831/667-2403

7 JULIA PFEIFFER BURNS STATE PARK

Location: Milepost 37.0S/52.7N on Highway 1 in Big Sur
Parking/Fees: $10 entrance fee per vehicle
Hours: half hour before sunrise–half hour after sunset
Facilities: restrooms and picnic tables
Contact: Big Sur Station, 831/667-2315

8 PARTINGTON COVE

Location: Milepost 35.2S/54.5N on Highway 1
Parking/Fees: free limited roadside parking
Hours: half hour before sunrise–half hour after sunset
Facilities: none
Contact: Big Sur Station, 831/667-2315

9 PFEIFFER BEACH

                    BEST

Location: from Highway 1 in Big Sur, turn west onto Sycamore Canyon Road (Milepost 27.1S/63.2N), follow for two miles
Parking/Fees: $5 entrance fee per vehicle
Hours: half hour before sunrise–half hour after sunset
Facilities: restrooms
Contact: Big Sur Station, 831/667-2315

10 ANDREW MOLERA STATE PARK

Location: Milepost 21.4S/68.3N on Highway 1 in Big Sur
Parking/Fees: $10 entrance fee per vehicle; camping fee (tents only) $10 per night, plus $7.50 reservation fee
Hours: half hour before sunrise–half hour after sunset
Facilities: restrooms and picnic tables
Contact: Big Sur Station, 831/667-2315

11 GARRAPATA STATE PARK

Location: turnouts 13 and 14, just north of Garrapata Creek Bridge, on Highway 1 in Big Sur
Parking/Fees: free roadside parking
Hours: half hour before sunrise–half hour after sunset
Facilities: none
Contact: Big Sur Station, 831/624-4909

Andrew Molera State Park

BIG SUR AND MONTEREY

© PARKE PUTERBAUGH

ACCOMMODATIONS

A complaint we've often heard about Big Sur is that it's hard to get a foot in the door, so to speak. That is, people who don't want to rough it by camping but still want to check out Big Sur are intimidated by the prospect of staying here. Fear not—there are plenty of places to stay. They're just expensive and have been mandated into near invisibility. Built off the road, they blend into the landscape so well that if you speed through on the Pacific Coast Highway, you'll miss them. Do not look for glowing Best Western or Holiday Inn signs jacked 50 feet in the air. There are absolutely no brand-name motel chains to be found between San Simeon and Carmel.

Accommodations run the gamut from primitive campsites to luxury lodges. There are 10 campgrounds on national forest or state park land. We've already discussed six of them that are set along or close to the ocean. Do take pains to reserve all accommodations in Big Sur, campsites included, well in advance. The best month to visit, everyone seems to agree, is October.

Pfeiffer Big Sur State Park offers 217 developed campsites along the pristine Big Sur River. They cost $20–35 per night, plus a $7.50 reservation fee. Call Reserve America at 877/444-6777 for camping reservations at Pfeiffer Big Sur and all other California state parks, as well as for U.S. Forest Service campgrounds, including the coastal campgrounds along Big Sur at Plaskett Creek and Kirk Creek.

For those who don't want to camp but still want to give nature a great big bear hug in the morning, the 62-unit **Big Sur Lodge** (Milepost 26.0S/63.7N, 831/667-3100 or 800/424-4787, $$) is the answer. It's actually a number of semiprivate cottages—duplexes, triplexes, and larger—scattered among the trees in Pfeiffer Big Sur State Park. Clean and comfortable, the rooms come with fireplaces, and some have kitchens. There's even a heated swimming pool, a comfortable place to soak in the cool air and redwoods. Rates for standard rooms can go as high as $300 per night in season, as we discovered the hard way in the summer of 2008. You pay extra for a fireplace, kitchen suite, or both. Rates drop some after Labor Day.

Another isolated haven is **Lucia Lodge** (62400 Highway 1, 831/667-2391, $$), comprising 10 spartan but well-maintained cottages that cling to the southern coast of Big Sur. Cabins are available on a first-come, first-served basis, with no reservations taken. No need to go elsewhere to eat, as there's a pleasant restaurant on the property.

Anywhere else but in Big Sur, the **Glen Oaks Motel** (Milepost 66N/25S, 831/667-2105, $) would be just another nondescript motel. Its ordinariness makes it stand out here. Actually, it's a clean "post adobe" not unlike any other roadside mom-and-pop motel, with 15 rooms and two cottages. Speaking of mom, some years back we had a tough time convincing the congenial matron to honor our reservation for a room with two beds. She eventually solved the problem with some last-minute room-shuffling. The two guys who pulled in after us weren't so lucky. They decided to make do with one bed, vowing to maintain "a discreet and dignified distance." Later we saw one of them dragging a chaise lounge into the room. Prices are very affordable for Big Sur.

Then there's Ventana, a resort that exists on a whole other plane. Do you want a splendid retreat from everything, including the usual romantic resort affectations? If the answer is yes, then the **Ventana Inn & Spa** (Milepost 62.7N/28.3S, 831/667-2331, $$$$) is your window on the wilderness and one of the finest resting spots anywhere. Everything is arranged to enhance the embrace of solitude, from the exposed wood architecture to the fireplaces in the rooms, the meditative grounds strung out across two heaven-focused ridge tops, the serenade of birds, the almost noiseless leaping of deer through the underbrush. At check-in guests are issued a white, hooded terry cloth robe. After a day spent wandering around in your robe, you'll feel a little bit like a Zen master. No wonder the motto here is "Nourish your spirit." Follow your bliss, while you're at it!

Further nourishing can be had at Ventana's health club, sauna, and library. An extensive array of massage services will cleanse away all worldly dust within you. A dozen or so masseuses are available, each with his or her own special expertise. One advertised being "certified in postural integration deep tissue work," while another promised to "sculpt your body using a blend of techniques from deep tissue to subtle cranial work and energy balancing." Decisions, decisions!

Needless distractions are kept at a minimum, which explains the ambivalence toward kids as guests. In the words of the innkeepers: "Ventana was designed and is operated as a retreat for adults. We do not have any activities for children and therefore we do not encourage people to bring them here…Many people have come here for a few days expressly to get away from their own children." Ah, if only all resorts purporting to be "escapes" were so enlightened—and honest.

If you want company, a continental breakfast and afternoon wine-and-cheese buffet are served in the library and lobby. It's a spread of delights the likes of which you won't encounter anywhere else, including the best granola we've ever had. Given the peerless amenities and priceless peace and quiet, room rates at Ventana are certainly not reasonable. They start at $399 a night; there are 60 units in 12 buildings. As we left, we pondered a Zen koan of our own devising: What is the sound of two beach bums smiling?

The latest arrival in Big Sur—and new arrivals are a glacial occurrence out here—is **Post Ranch Inn** (30 miles south of Carmel on Highway 1, P.O. Box 291, 831/667-2200, $$$$). It opened for business in 1992, becoming the first new resort along the Big Sur coast in more than two decades. The 30 cabins are spread among the redwoods along a ridge overlooking the ocean; some are designated "ocean houses," others "tree houses," for obvious reasons. Take your pick—woods or water?—and come prepared to pay handsomely for this splendid hermitage: Room rates run $555–2,185 (you read correctly) per night. Ouch!

If the prospect of staying in Big Sur in anything other than a tent is prohibitively expensive, here's a suggestion: Stay in a more affordable inland town along U.S. Highway 101, such as Gilroy. It's barely an hour from Big Sur, and you can save big bucks at night while enjoying Big Sur during the day.

COASTAL CUISINE

The **Ragged Point Inn** (19019 Highway 1, 805/927-4502, $$$) is located five miles north of San Simeon, on the southern end of Big Sur. The setting is hard to beat, and the food—especially the seafood entrées—is commendable as well. The Ragged Point Inn also rents rooms. Most overlook the shoreline, which lies 350 feet down below the cliffs. All of this makes Ragged Point a great spot for a sedentary getaway.

If you're staying at Ventana, there's no reason to get back in the car to go to dinner. No before-dinner stroll can top the ten-minute walk from your room at the inn to the **Restaurant at Ventana** (Milepost 62.7N/28.3S, 831/667-2331, $$$$). Lit by small, shoe-level bulbs, the path crosses a woodland and ascends a ridgetop with moon and stars above and wild game loping into the brush at ground level. The restaurant setting extends this sense of natural communion. Its understated elegance is conveyed in the lovely varnished wood and exposed beam interior. The dining room is surrounded by windows (*ventana* means "window" in Spanish) that look out on the 800-acre spread. It is staffed by folks who seem positively clairvoyant about your needs. In the summer of 2008, they remained open, even while fires from the west crept ever closer to the edge of Ventana's property. Views from the windows were especially ghostly and memorable as Big Sur lay enveloped in smoke and fire.

An 18-page wine list offers rare and interesting California vintages, plus well-chosen and affordable ones, including a custom Ventana-label Chardonnay and Riesling. The ever-changing menu is kept to a manageable size, offering artfully prepared appetizers and main courses. We supped contentedly on petit filet mignon with a fresh corn pudding, and grilled rainbow trout with fresh spinach and new potatoes. And we slept contentedly afterward. In fact, we paused on the pathway back to the inn to lie on our backs and gaze up at the night sky, with the moon shining brightly. Pure magic.

At **Nepenthe** (Milepost 62.2N/28.8S, 831/667-2345, $$), the burgers roll out of the kitchen like beer barrels in Milwaukee. They're especially large patties made from ground steak, for which reason the menu calls them Ambrosiaburgers. Beat generation author Jack Kerouac referred to them as Heavenburgers in his underrated later novel *Big Sur.*

Nepenthe was originally an adobe and red-wood house built by a student of Frank Lloyd Wright and bought as a wedding gift for Rita Hayworth by Orson Welles. It has been run by the same family since 1949. People come to Nepenthe (it means "no sorrow" in Greek) for more than the heavenly hamburgers. They also come for the heavenly view, overlooking the ocean from a dazzling perch 808 feet above sea level. In fact, it is the view you're largely paying for, since no hamburger is worth $13.50, nor is a side of fries worth $6.75. In addition to Ambrosiaburgers, Nepenthe serves a decent smoked salmon salad with lemon vinaigrette. For an appetizer, try the Castroville artichoke, poached, chilled, and served with balsamic vinaigrette. You can sit indoors, but unless a tempest is raging there is no reason not to dine out on the deck, with its matchless view and gratis servings of fresh air.

Two other old reliables are **Deetjen's Big Sur Inn** (Milepost 60.8N/30.2S, 831/667-2378, $$$) and the **River Inn** (Milepost 66.5N/24.5S, 831/667-2700, $$$). Deetjen's is the more offbeat of the two, with a shrine to Robinson Jeffers taking up one entire corner. The Norwegian-style complex includes a 14-room inn and a restaurant that serves breakfast

and dinner. The River Inn lies in the Big Sur Valley, where the Big Sur River discharges into the ocean. If you're driving from north to south, plan for an early-morning chowdown at the River Inn. Try the trout and eggs, as one of us did many years ago before an unforgettable sojourn in the cool blue light of morn. The River Inn also includes an 18-unit motel, gas station, gift shop, and grocery store.

NIGHTLIFE

Nepenthe (Milepost 62.2N/28.8S, 831/667-2345) is as close to a public meeting spot as there is in this notoriously hermitic community. People nurse their drinks on the art-bedecked patio, warm their hands over a fire, and enjoy gazing at the ocean and artwork, including a driftwood angel sculpture and eerie mosaic that are, like the restaurant, total originals.

Beyond quaffing a drink at Nepenthe, as, Kerouac poetically stated in *Big Sur,* "There's the laughter of the loon in the shadow of the moon." In other words, stay put, wherever you are, and savor the sounds of nature.

Point Lobos State Reserve

A rugged, primeval headland jutting out into the fierce sea south of Carmel, Point Lobos State Reserve is billed as the "crown jewel of the California State Park system," a claim that's hard to dispute. The name derives from a much longer Spanish appellation that trans-lates as "point of the sea wolves." In the 1700s and 1800s, it variously served as a livestock pasture, abalone cannery, whaling station, and shipping point for coal mined nearby.

At one point developers planned to subdi-vide it as Point Lobos City. Its purchase by a farsighted owner, A. M. Allan, forestalled such a fate. In 1933 Point Lobos was acquired by the Save the Redwoods League and donated to California to maintain as a parkland. Today it is jointly run by the state and the Point Lobos Natural History Association, whose

BIG SUR AND MONTEREY

volunteers lead nature walks and staff the reserve's information station. Trailers and campers are prohibited, as is any kind of camping.

The reserve is open 9 A.M.–6 P.M. daily and closes later in summer. They've doubled the entrance fee to $10 since our previous visit, which wasn't all that long ago. In defense of the state-park system, part of the logic behind raising coastal-park entrance fees to $8 or $10 is to regulate visitation, so that the parks don't physically deteriorate from overuse. Moreover, the parks' administrative and maintenance costs are ever soaring in cash-strapped California. At the same time, we hate to see the state-park system pricing itself beyond the means of ordinary people. After all, isn't it ordinary people's taxes that fund the parks?

Plan to arrive early, as the reserve has a "carrying capacity" of 450 people, and latecomers must wait to gain entrance. The reserve occupies 554 land acres and 750 submerged acres. With the addition of the latter in 1960, Point Lobos became the first underwater reserve in the nation. Roads take you only so far into the park, which is fine, since Point Lobos begs to be explored on foot. Pick up a detailed map, which outlines 14 possible hikes, at the entrance station. The Cypress Grove Trail, a three-quarter-mile loop, leads to the granite cliffs overlooking Pinnacle Cove and passes through one of two remaining natural stands of Monterey cypress in the world. The reserve was originally established to protect these gnarled wonders.

Skittering ground squirrels, fields of yellow lizard tails and apricot-colored sticky monkey flowers, and offshore rocks acrawl with sea lions and harbor seals are but a few of the sights to enjoy in this wild place. Hikers who wish to traipse the perimeter should allow at least three hours to cover the six-mile trek from Bird Island to Granite Point.

For more information, contact Point Lobos State Reserve, Highway 1, Box 62, Carmel, CA 93923, 831/624-4909, www.parks.ca.gov.

BEACHES

Acessible beaches are tucked into coves along Point Lobos' southern flank. Imagine our surprise to turn a corner on Bird Island Trail and catch sight of emerald green **China Cove Beach,** a hundred feet below down a long staircase. At the mouth of Gibson Creek, where the Bird Island and South Plateau Trails run out, you'll find **Gibson Beach.** It's separated from China Cove by Pelican Point and is another swell spot for launching a dive or braving a swim in frigid waters. Both can be reached via wooden staircases.

The one-mile South Shore Trail yields its own bounty of rocky, shell-strewn beaches between Sea Lion Point and the Bird Island parking area, including **Hidden Beach, Weston Beach,** and **Sand Hill Cove.** Just be careful while wandering out on the rocks, and keep a mindful eye on the always unpredictable ocean.

12 CHINA COVE BEACH

Location: along Bird Island Trail at Point Lobos State Reserve, located off Highway 1 on Riley Ranch Road, three miles south of Carmel
Parking/Fees: $10 entrance fee per vehicle
Hours: 8 A.M.-one hour after sunset
Facilities: restrooms
Contact: Point Lobos State Reserve, 831/624-4909

13 GIBSON BEACH

Location: along Bird Island Trail at Point Lobos State Reserve, located off Highway 1 on Riley Ranch Road, three miles south of Carmel
Parking/Fees: $10 entrance fee per vehicle
Hours: 8 A.M.-one hour after sunset
Facilities: restrooms
Contact: Point Lobos State Reserve, 831/624-4909

14 HIDDEN BEACH
🏃🏃

Location: along South Shore Trail at Point Lobos State Reserve, located off Highway 1 on Riley Ranch Road, three miles south of Carmel
Parking/Fees: $10 entrance fee per vehicle
Hours: 8 A.M.-one hour after sunset
Facilities: restrooms
Contact: Point Lobos State Reserve, 831/624-4909

15 WESTON BEACH
🏃🏃

Location: along South Shore Trail at Point Lobos State Reserve, located off Highway 1 on Riley Ranch Road, three miles south of Carmel
Parking/Fees: $10 entrance fee per vehicle
Hours: 8 A.M.-one hour after sunset
Facilities: restrooms
Contact: Point Lobos State Reserve, 831/624-4909

16 SAND HILL COVE
🏃🏃

Location: along South Shore Trail at Point Lobos State Reserve, located off Highway 1 on Riley Ranch Road, three miles south of Carmel
Parking/Fees: $10 entrance fee per vehicle
Hours: 8 A.M.-one hour after sunset
Facilities: restrooms
Contact: Point Lobos State Reserve, 831/624-4909

Carmel

Among small American towns, Carmel is a celebrity. It can't travel to New York to appear on *The Late Show with David Letterman,* but in every other respect it fits the bill. Carmel is well known for being well known. It is a de rigueur stop on California bus-tour decath-

lons. Carmel's fame went into orbit when its most famous resident, Clint Eastwood, served a two-year term as mayor in the late 1980s. As is usually the case with a celebrity, strangers are drawn to it, desiring to bask in Carmel's limelight, as if proximity might confer some mysterious luster upon them as well.

Given its popular perception as a see-and-be-seen kind of place, Carmel can get mighty crowded. Cars gridlock the village streets and buses discharge an endless cargo of sightseers who clog the sidewalks. Attracted by its air of sophistication, foreigners descend on Carmel in droves, chattering in heavily accented English or their native tongues. However, the universal truth that binds all visitors is that beyond a visit to an established historical landmark such as the Carmel Mission, no one can really figure out what to do in Carmel. Most visitors amble up and down Ocean Avenue, munch on sweets, pose for pictures in front of rocks and trees, duck into quaint shops to ogle overpriced goods, and pause thrice daily for meals.

So why all the fuss? For starters, Carmel is a gorgeous village, blessed with a natural setting that could turn any gutter-mouthed Dirty Harry into a beatific babbler like native son Robinson Jeffers. Carmelites refer to their community as "a village in a forest"—and that brief description neglects to mention the roiling ocean that crashes on the sugar-white sand of cypress-dotted Carmel City Beach. Nowhere in the world is the margin where land and sea meet as spectacular as it is in Monterey County from Carmel south through Point Lobos and Big Sur. That isn't just the lofty rhetoric of two itinerant beach bums; it comes close to being a verifiable truth. Moreover, the residents of Carmel are well-educated, arts-savvy, and genuinely appreciative of their natural bounty.

So what's the problem? As bucolic as it may seem, the village of Carmel is swimming in contradictions. The election of "Mayor Clint" back in 1988 let only some of the most obvious ones out of the closet. Issues constantly being debated in this contentious community boil down to development vs. preservation, old (stodgy) vs. young (progressive), tourists vs. natives, and arts vs. sports. The last of these refers to what we perceive as an undeclared war between painters and golfers for the soul of Carmel, and the outcome will determine whether its future will be one of visionary preservation or a banal triumph of capitalism's shark-like appetite to consume everything in its path.

From a visitor's standpoint this can lead to mixed messages. They want you, but they don't want you. Or, put another way, they don't want you but they do need you. Carmel derives 60 percent of its operating revenue from tourism, while homeowners—mostly retirees—provide a meager 11 percent. Many Carmelites frankly and publicly disdain the locustlike invasions that overrun their streets. Yet tourism is a necessary evil in Carmel, so they've reluctantly made a deal with the devil in the interest of keeping the money flowing and the community solvent.

Traffic coming into town is pure hell, backing up to Highway 1 as testy motorists inch their way along, engines and tempers overheating. Parking is scant. Buses are not allowed past a certain point, so they wheeze down a side street to a special bus-berthing spot, discharging their blinking passengers into the brilliant sunlight to hoof it about hilly Carmel. Wheezing themselves after a few paces, this army of day-trippers marches obediently into the business district, only to discover that the principal diversion in this faux country village is shopping. Ocean Avenue is a miracle mile of bakeries, bistros, galleries, and gift shops where you can score anything from gold chains to goat cheese.

The setup appears to go something like this: They want you to breeze into Carmel in the morning, while away the day dropping loot on gifts, antiques, clothing, and meals, and then blow out of town before night falls. If you haven't taken the hint, Carmel rolls up the sidewalks after dark. Off of Ocean

Avenue you'll find few streetlights to guide your steps, and the signs identifying street names are almost deliberately small, as if to confound and frustrate outsiders. Despite the tug of war between pro-growth, slow-growth, and no-growth factions, Carmel zealously guards its privacy while its denizens espouse a political outlook that comes closer to libertarianism than either of the mainstream political parties.

The denizens of Carmel are wealthy. They strongly defend their right to acquire and preserve without interference and regulations (except for those they impose on others). They have essentially burned their bridges to the outside world, leaving a narrow footpath into the village accessible only to those bearing the passport of a credit card and/or ready cash. Though such an outlook may seem peevish and elitist, even we cannot argue with the results, although we'd quibble with the philosophy. They have tended their community well, keeping vulgar commercialism at arm's length. For that you'll have to head up the peninsula, to Monterey or Seaside. Having viewed the entire coastline at close range, we'll concede that in certain cases enlightened despotism may be preferable to the unregulated rule of market forces. You see, they simply want Carmel to remain a pleasant seaside village. *Theirs.*

To that end Carmel has been buttressing itself against growth and development since day one. Carmel got its start in 1906 as a seaside colony populated by artists and academics who had been displaced by San Francisco's Great Earthquake. The village attracted a literary elite that included Jack London, Upton Sinclair, Sinclair Lewis, and Robinson Jeffers. Artists came as well. All were enchanted by the refreshing climate, gossamer sunlight, pine-forested hills, rugged cliffs, and powdered-sugar beaches of the Monterey Peninsula. From the beginning the citizens of Carmel banded together to ensure that their way of life would be preserved. Restrictive zoning ordinances passed in the 1920s outlawed things that have become commonplace everywhere else, like tall buildings and neon signs.

In 1929 Carmel wrote its guiding philosophy into the city charter: "The city of Carmel-by-the-Sea is…predominantly a residential city, wherein business and commerce are… subordinated to its residential character." Words alone are not enough to ensure such an outcome, so the town requires a permit for just about everything, from cutting down a bush to filming a movie scene. The result is governmental gridlock where nothing is granted, nothing gets done, and therefore nothing much changes.

Consequently, Carmel has the look—although crowds deny it the feel—of a rural English village. The same determined spirit not to yield to unchecked growth has remained viable throughout the century, although the composition of the town has shifted from artists to retirees. This is a polite way of saying that Carmel is evolving into a community that reveres golf tournaments more than Bach festivals. Still, there is a continuity between generations in that both resist the forces of change. Today, village preservation is pursued with an even greater twinge of fanaticism, since so much more can go wrong in the slipshod modern world. There are no street numbers in Carmel, for instance. No numbers means no addresses and, therefore, no mail delivery. The atavistic Carmelites must personally collect their mail at the local post office. When a small movement to number the houses of Carmel surfaced, an outspoken local newspaper and barometer of community opinion headlined its disparaging editorial, "What, a Subway Next?" When such issues arise, the battle cry becomes, "Save Carmel from Santa Cruz-itis!"

Carmel is a village of roughly 4,000 well-to-do souls—less than one-tenth the size of Santa Cruz—tucked into the lower left-hand corner of the Monterey Peninsula. It occupies exactly one square mile. The town starts at the top of a hill, where Ocean Avenue intersects Highway 1, and plunges steeply toward the ocean. It is along Ocean Avenue, as well as a block or two off the streets it crosses, that most of Carmel's upscale shops can be found. Inns and bed-and-breakfasts materialize closer to the water. Ocean Avenue gives out by Carmel City Beach, but the steep gradient continues down a hillock of pure white sand to the water's edge.

Because traffic tends to snarl both in town and on weather-beaten Highway 1, particularly on weekends in season, you're best advised to park on the outskirts and walk into town. Be further advised that the retail shops in Carmel are not for the faint of pocketbook. Most of the older mom-and-pop shops and restaurants—such as a lamentable recent casualty, the Clam Box—have been squeezed out by places that can deal with $20,000 monthly rents for commercial space. A retailer must sell a hell of a lot of cashmere sweaters or pastel wall hangings to make ends meet, and you'd better believe that the cost of doing business in Carmel is passed along to the consumer.

Amid all this upscale merchandise, the old **Carmel Mission** (3080 Rio Road, 831/624-1271) remains an eminently worthwhile place for travelers to stop, rest, refocus, and reassess priorities. Its full name is San Carlos Borroméo de Carmelo Mission. Constructed from 1793 to 1797, it was the personal favorite of the nine missions founded by Father Junípero Serra throughout California. The ambitious padre is, in fact, buried here. Architecturally, the mission is notable for its large, arcaded quadrangle, but there are also attractive gardens, informative exhibits, and a museum on the premises. A small donation is suggested. It is well worth dropping a few bucks into the box for the peace to be found inside the mission walls. Just think of how many more bucks you'll be dropping along Ocean Avenue in Carmel.

Carmel is indisputably a beautiful place, nestled among stands of pine and cypress against the ocean's indigo backdrop. It is a smogless village whose only drawback may be that too many people want to share in its natural bounty. For the lucky visitor who comes to stay for a few days or a week, Carmel makes a relaxing place to recharge the batteries in splendid surroundings. Day-trippers with harried itineraries will catch only a fleeting glimpse of what makes Carmel special. Natives condescendingly abide the influx of outsiders while trying to control their numbers and minimize the impact on Carmel's sacred quality of life. The question is, how do you moderate the crowds without creating bad feelings and severing the economic jugular that allows the town to endure in its visitor-subsidized prosperity? They're debating that very question day by day, issue by issue, in Carmel.

For more information, contact the Carmel Business Association and Visitor Information Center, San Carlos Avenue between Fifth and Sixth Avenues, P.O. Box 4444, Carmel, CA 93921, 831/624-2522, www.carmelcalifornia .org; or the Monterey Peninsula Convention and Visitors Bureau, 401 Camino El Estero, Monterey, CA 93940, 877/666-8373, www .montereyinfo.org.

BEACHES

A wide crescent between forested points, **Carmel City Beach** is among the most stunning settings for a beach on any coast, in any part of the world. The first glimpse of this shoreline is unforgettable. As it nears the water, Ocean Avenue slopes sharply downhill, ending at a sandy circle with a Monterey cypress in the center. A heart-stopping plunge down steep-sloped dunes leads to the ocean. Carmel City Beach will mesmerize you with the clarity of the air and vivid brightness of the light; the impregnable points of land that jut out on either side, framing the beachfront; the wind-sculpted cypress trees perched atop the dunes, their agonized contortions a testament to adaptive fortitude; the metallic blue surface of the indomitable, churning sea; and, finally, the resounding cymbal crash of huge, unforgiving waves.

It is a rough beach to swim on, but a beautiful one to look at. The beach forms a sandy

amphitheater upon which people sit and watch the sun set, listen to the crashing breakers, and enjoy a breathtaking tableau of sun, sea, sky, and cypress. People just tend to stare out to sea, mesmerized. Beachgoers spread out towels and blankets and sun themselves on windless indentations on the high dunes. Had we been plopped here unawares, we might have believed ourselves to be on a beach along the Côte d'Azur. On a sadder note, Carmel City Beach suffered mightily at the hands of the repeated destructive shoreline surgery of several successive El Niño events. At its worst, the beach looked like a wedding cake that had been half-eaten by an angry giant. It's become steeper and narrower, as if the ocean is advancing upon the town. But what nature taketh away, nature giveth back, too, in a continual cycle of advance and retreat that's been going on long before human beings laid eyes on this shoreline.

If you're up for a walk, Scenic Road runs parallel to the ocean, affording bluff-top views and occasional access to the beach via staircases. The southernmost of these leads to **Carmel River State Beach,** a 100-acre sanctuary on both sides of the mouth of the Carmel River. More beach access can be gained south of here, off Ribera Road and Highway 1. As the surf is hazardous and unpredictable, swimming is discouraged. Divers, however, enjoy exploring the offshore Carmel Bay Ecological Reserve. The Monterey pines and Monterey cypress are, incidentally, found nowhere else in the world.

17 CARMEL RIVER STATE BEACH

Location: Scenic Road at Carmel Street, off Highway 1, one mile south of Carmel
Parking/Fees: free parking lot
Hours: sunrise-sunset
Facilities: restrooms
Contact: Monterey District, California State Parks, 831/649-2836

18 CARMEL CITY BEACH

Location: end of Ocean Avenue in Carmel
Parking/Fees: metered street parking
Hours: sunrise-10 P.M.
Facilities: restrooms and picnic tables
Contact: Carmel Department of Forests,
Parks, and Beaches, 831/624-3543

ACCOMMODATIONS

La Playa Hotel (Camino Real at Eighth Avenue, 831/624-6476, $$$) easily makes our short list of best places to stay at the beach in California. It is a comfy, sun-dappled paradise by the sea. On a quiet side street, with the hotel on one side and roomy bungalows on the other, La Playa sprawls across some of the choicest commercial real estate in Carmel. Purple bougainvillea crawls across the rooftops. The gardens outside the bungalows are a riot of flowers and greenery. An interior courtyard, fragrant with floral scents, encloses a pool. Carmel's amazing beach is a few short blocks away.

In the style of the finest lodging places, La Playa creates the feel of a serene world-within-a-world that immediately relaxes visitors and drains away cares. The slapping of waves on the shore is audible from the open windows of the cottages. We stayed at a guest cottage named Log Haven, a two-story wooden house with a pair of sizable bedrooms, high-ceilinged living room with a fireplace and hardwood floors, fully equipped kitchen, upstairs sitting room, and lots of storage alcoves. The guest cottages run quite a bit more than rooms at the hotel but offer enough room to accommodate several couples or a large family with no problem.

Another well-tended inn is the **Colonial Terrace Inn** (San Antonio and 13th Avenue, 831/624-2741, $$$). It's as close as any hotel gets to the beach here, and the rooms are $190–250, which is a virtual steal in Carmel. The inn's seven buildings are decorated with heritage furnishings in the colonial style, and no two are alike. All rooms have gas fireplaces, some look out on the ocean, the gardens are beautiful, and a complimentary continental breakfast is served each morning.

Several enticingly low-key inns can be

BIG SUR AND MONTEREY

© PARKE PUTERBAUGH

Carmel

found in the heart of Carmel, along Ocean Avenue near the beach. Nestled amid the oaks and pines of old Carmel, **Lobos Lodge** (Monte Verde at Ocean Avenue, P.O. Box L-1, 831/624-3874, $$) is rustic on the outside and modern on the inside. Each of the 29 units is decorated differently, and all have fireplaces and patios. Rooms are reasonable at $125–185, suites at $185–255.

Some of Carmel's heart-of-the-village inns verge on the cutesy, such as the **Lamp Lighter Inn** (Camino Real and Ocean Avenue, 831/624-7372, $$), which is straight out of fairy-tale land. Its nine cottages have names like Hansel and Gretel and the Blue Bird Room and are painted to resemble gingerbread houses. The owner extends the fantasy by talking about the elves that play in the garden and referring to her associate as an "elf's helper." We were not certain she was playing with a full deck, but the Lamp Lighter Inn seems charming enough.

Up the hill from the beach, San Carlos Street is lined with inns and inn-like motels, such as the **Dolphin Inn** (San Carlos Street and Fourth Avenue, 831/624-5356, $$). Rooms are quiet and comfortable; extras like a pool, continental breakfast, and afternoon snacks are welcome; and it's a treat to be able to park your car and explore Carmel on foot from such a convenient location. The Dolphin Inn, incidentally, is one of seven "Inns by the Sea," an assemblage of personable, well-tended inns along the Monterey Peninsula with five properties in Carmel and one apiece in Monterey and Pacific Grove. Call 800/433-4732 for more information about special rates.

South of Carmel, high on a hill overlooking the ocean, is **Highlands Inn** (120 Highland Drive, 831/620-1234, $$$$). The inn is a historic property, built in 1916 but renovated and modernized in modern times. Lately it has been swallowed up by the Hyatt chain, which is somewhat disappointing. It is a smooth-running, first-class resort popular with honeymooners (1,000 weddings are performed here annually) and anyone looking for a great escape in the rural highlands overlooking the ocean along the Central Coast.

The view of the Pacific from the inn's Grand Lodge is splendid; it's as if you're on the bow of a ship suspended over the ocean. Each room is outfitted with a fireplace and vista deck. You will pay dearly for such pampering: Rooms start at close to $500 a night and top off close to $800. Yes, you read that correctly. It is indeed a sharp upward climb to the Highlands Inn, both for the car and the pocketbook, but worth it if both are running smoothly.

A note for those seeking to travel economically: Room rates in Carmel drop substantially during weekdays in winter. And you can always stay elsewhere more cheaply on the Monterey Peninsula and drive over to Carmel for the day.

COASTAL CUISINE

We're partial to a couple of restaurants outlying the village of Carmel proper. **Rio Grill** (Rio Road and Highway 1, 831/625-5436, $$$) is a popular Southwestern-themed restaurant in the Crossroads Shopping Center, a mile or so outside the village where the land begins dropping to the Carmel Valley floor. Caricatures by celebrity folk artist George Rodrigue—a relocated Cajun painter whose trendy "blue dog" is a recurring motif—fill the walls of the bar and lobby area. A jar of crayons on each table encourages adults to doodle and scrawl on paper tablecloths. And what food! Most entrées are grilled or cooked in a wood-burning oven. Selections range from hearty fare like rabbit, duck, chicken, and ribs to daily seafood specials.

We'd be neglectful if we didn't mention the culinary houses of worship co-owned and operated by Carmel's most famous citizen, Clint Eastwood. By now all the world knows about **Hog's Breath** (San Carlos Street and Fifth Avenue, 831/625-1044, $$), the restaurant and saloon that is an in-town landmark. If you didn't know about Eastwood's involvement, the menu would quickly tip you off. Selections include the Dirty Harry Burger, the Sudden Impact (sausage, peppers, and cheese on a French roll), the Eiger Sandwich (roast beef), and the For a Few Dollars More steak dinner. (Hey, why not "Magnum Forcemeat"?) Tourists crowd in during the daytime and crane their necks in the unlikely hope of glimpsing Carmel's former mayor and Hollywood's favorite filmmaker and action hero.

Eastwood is also invested in **Mission Ranch** (26270 Dolores Street, 831/625-9040, $$$$), a historic property on the Carmel River. The house specialties are stick-to-the-ribs ranch food. The menu is heavy on steaks—barbecue, prime rib—though you'll find a few catch-of-the-day specials as well. The prime rib comes in either a regular or "ranch" cut, the latter suggested for Paul Bunyan appetites only.

Inside the village area Carmel is the site of pricey, intimate restaurants hidden on side streets—places like **Anton & Michel** (Mission Street, 831/624-2406, $$$), an established eatery serving gourmet European cuisine in a cozy, romantic setting. Another restaurant of long-standing, this one with a strong seafood emphasis, is **Flaherty's Seafood Grill** (Dolores Street and Sixth Avenue, 831/625-1500, $$$). At Flaherty's the fish and shellfish come right off local boats or are flown in fresh.

The **Grill on Ocean Avenue** (Ocean Avenue between Dolores and Lincoln Streets, 831/624-2569, $$$) offers an eclectic array of creative dishes—French and California cuisine with Japanese grace notes—bringing yet another unique range of flavors to the discriminating palates of Carmel.

We've saved the best, or at least our favorite, for last: **Flying Fish Grill** (Carmel Plaza, 831/625-1962, $$$) serves some of the most inventive seafood dinners we've had on either coast. The Flying Fish is stylish without calling attention to itself, and the menu is short but sweet. We've had eye-watering sashimi and lightly seared oysters for appetizers, and escolar with roasted garlic and shiitake mushrooms and the crowd-favorite almond-crusted sea bass for entrées. Other tempting choices

include black bean salmon and catfish. A reasonably priced wine list is offered, as are artistically rendered desserts. Flying Fish is open for dinner only.

Would you like to dine at the same table at which Vincent Van Gogh broke bread? If so, then come to **Casanova** (5th Street between Mission and San Carlos, 805/625-0531, $$$). Yes, they really do have Van Gogh's table. Better yet, they have really good food. Casanova is deceptively small from the outside; open the doors and it's a bright, bustling place with several dining rooms serving cuisine inspired by the south of France and north of Italy. Our first choice among many fine menu offerings: *Pave de Saumon Citronette*—herb-crusted, pan-roasted wild salmon in a mustard-citrus sauce. For dessert, the warm chocolate cake with Armagnac ice cream.

NIGHTLIFE

While wandering the darkened streets of Carmel one foggy night in search of **Hog's Breath** (San Carlos Street and Fifth Avenue, 831/625-1044), we ran into a wizened old soul looking like the ghost of Ernest Hemingway. We asked for directions and he instructed us to follow him.

"I've lived here 30 years, and I still get lost," he said. We trailed the kindly codger as he wound his way through back streets and alleyways. All the while he kept up a steady stream of chatter, muttering about Eastwood's restaurant-cum-watering hole, which he variously referred to as "Hog's Butt" and "Clam Breath." We followed him through a rear entrance into the courtyard of Hog's Breath. Without turning around or breaking stride, he bade us farewell for the night and exited through the front door.

There is virtually no other nighttime activity in the village of Carmel than the quiet boozing going on at Hog's Breath. It closes around 1 A.M., a little earlier or later depending on the crowd. We planted ourselves on the outdoor patio, where giant tree trunks gnarl their way out of the ground. The restaurant's interior is more intimate, with tables set off in alcoves for romantic tête à têtes. After a civilized drink or two, we groped our way back through the dark and fog to our inn, recalling the words of our self-appointed sage and sherpa: "The nightlife around here is strictly for the newly wed and nearly dead."

Pebble Beach

We're not overly fond of Pebble Beach and the excessive privatization of its splendid coastline, so we'll be painlessly brief in our opprobrium. Pebble Beach is known for its two resorts (the Pebble Beach Lodge and the Inn at Spanish Bay), five golf courses (notably the Pebble Beach Golf Links), and the 17-Mile Drive. The origins of Pebble Beach as a resort date back to 1887, with the construction of the grand Del Monte Hotel and a private scenic drive that circled the property. In 1915 the grand-nephew of telegraph inventor Samuel Morse oversaw a full-tilt series of "improvements" to the property, including the construction of the Lodge at Pebble Beach, the laying out of the Pebble Beach Golf Links, and the paving of the 17-Mile Drive.

Millionaires built seaside mansions on the property; the owner of one marble-faced palace went so far as to heat her private beach with underground pipes. In 1946 Bing Crosby began crooning a new tune as the impresario of an annual pro-am tournament played here that bore his name. (These days it's the AT&T–Pebble Beach National Pro-Am Golf Championship.) In 1979 the Pebble Beach Company was sold to 20th-Century Fox. Then it went to a Japanese firm. Now it's in the hands of a consortium headed by Pete Ueberroth (former baseball commissioner and 1984 Summer Olympics organizer), Dick Ferris (former United Air Lines chairman), Clint Eastwood (actor, ex-mayor, hard-line right-winger), and Arnold Palmer (former pro golfer). This gang of four has had environmentalists in an uproar with their plans for

an extensive expansion that would encroach on the Del Monte Forest.

In 2001, the Pebble Beach Company filed ten Development Project Applications with the Monterey County Planning Department. Among other things, these include plans for a new 18-hole golf course with clubhouse, restaurant, parking lot, maintenance facility, pro shop, and 11 new hotel buildings that will house "golf cottages." The construction of the course and other projects would require the removal of approximately 17,000 trees. The Pebble Beach plunderers are also calling for major building additions at their Spanish Bay Resort and a new driving range and golf-teaching facility. They want to add a new building with 63 guest rooms at the Pebble Beach Lodge. They proposed new residential lots and subdivisions around the property. The list goes on and on.

"We view this as the largest project with the most devastating coastal impacts proposed in decades," Mark Massara, director of the Sierra Club's California coastal programs, told *USA Today* in 2005. "We're fully committed to ensuring that it doesn't go forward."

What makes it all so egregious is that Pebble Beach sits on the western side of the Monterey Peninsula in the middle of the Del Monte Forest, which is by far the largest and healthiest stand of Monterey pine forest left in the entire world. Pebble Beach is private and restricted, accessible only through five pay-to-enter gates along the 17-Mile Drive. As it is, 6,000 people live in the disappearing forest in and around Pebble Beach.

In spite of the ecological value of this priceless island of Monterey pine forest, the Pebble Beach Company wants to develop almost all their remaining holdings in Del Monte Forest. If approved, it would have been the largest single development in the history of the Monterey Peninsula in terms of homes, acreage, and destroyed pine forest. The population of Pebble Beach would increase by another 1,000 golf geeks, bringing with it additional environmental stresses.

THE 17-MILE DRIVE: A MUST TO AVOID

If you're headed to the Monterey Peninsula, chances are the 17-Mile Drive is on your itinerary. Almost everyone succumbs, believing that it is a not-to-be-missed scenic drive "through pine forests and groves of Monterey cypress and along a coastline of singular beauty."

You are wasting time and money if you shell out for the 17-Mile Drive. It would be a time-consuming bore if it were free, but the greedheads who live in Pebble Beach charge $9.25 for the dubious privilege of driving through their "private community." This is highway robbery. The money is not funneled into state or county coffers, nor does it benefit some worthy environmental cause. Instead, it goes to the private Pebble Beach Company. To add to the bottomless greed of it all, the brochure we were handed at the gate turned out to be a retail catalog for pricey golf wear from the Pebble Beach Lodge.

Year after year, the 17-Mile Drive remains a large draw, recommended as one of the top attractions on the Monterey Peninsula. The scenery is not nearly as striking as the hundreds of miles of public highways along California's coastline that can be driven for free. The drive through Big Sur – 90 miles of mountainous coastal wonders without golf courses to distort the natural environment – puts the 17-Mile Drive to shame and doesn't cost a penny. Ditto for Sunset Drive in the adjacent congenial community of Pacific Grove.

When informed of our book venture, the crabby old gatekeeper barked: "If you quote from anything in the brochure, you've got to ask permission." Here's a quote from the brochure that says it all: "Fulfill your shopping desires by choosing from the ultimate in golf and tennis gear, jewelry, women's designer fashions, art, gift items, and more." We did not ask permission. Furthermore, we urge you to steer clear of Pebble Beach and stick to those parts of the coast that are, as they should be, free to all.

In fact, we'll save you the entrance fee into 17-Mile Drive. Climb in the car with us as we pay the $9.25, drive through the gate, and see the sights. First, you pass miles of what looks like any well-to-do suburban neighborhood in America, trailing fuming buses and a line of hoodwinked motorists. Along a stretch where the road hugs the coastline, they've erected signs pointing to photo ops like the "Restless Sea" and "Point Joe," which are attractive overlooks but nothing out of the ordinary for the Central Coast. But because the Pebble Beach Company has assigned names and numbers and charged money to drive past them, people believe they're experiencing something unique and worthwhile. Or maybe they don't, judging from some of the comments we overheard.

Eventually, you pass the Pebble Beach Golf Links, a study in the fine art of turning a pristine and endangered coastal forest into a denuded plain of heavily fertilized, close-cropped grass. We cruised onward. The sights were more sightless by the minute: earth-moving equipment, average-looking homes, charred trees. Even the "Lone Cypress" – the signature attraction of the 17-Mile Drive and the pride and joy of Pebble Beach (it's part of the corporate logo) – is down on its heels, having become ridden with termites.

It seems that vandals tried to burn the tree, proving that there's no crime so perverse that someone won't eventually think to attempt it in California. Now termites have invaded the tree's charred, weakened, ocean-facing side. Not to worry! The Pebble Beach Company's resource department is nursing a replacement Lone Cypress in a secluded spot while doing their best to shore up the original.

After a while, we couldn't wait to exit. We had a parting taunt ready for the gatekeeper, but a sign on the way out said Do Not Stop at Gate, presumably sparing the hired hands a chewing out from hotheaded tourists.

The slate of proposed projects would develop more than one square mile—an area equal in size to the adjacent town of Carmel. If this sounds as ill-advised to you as it does to us, join the Concerned Residents of Pebble Beach and Monterey County in voicing your opinion to county supervisors. To learn more, point your browser to the nonprofit group's website at www.cr-pb.org.

Now that we've gotten you all exercised over the fate of Del Monte Forest due to the boneheads at the Pebble Beach Company, we're pleased to say we've got a happy ending—at least for now. In June 2006, the company abruptly withdrew its plan, one day before the California Coastal Commission was to vote on it. The 168-page environmental impact study prepared by the commission indicated that a favorable vote would not have been a likely outcome for the Pebble Beach Company.

"The major part of what they were proposing clearly was inconsistent with the Coastal Act," said Peter Douglas, the commission's executive director. "My hope is they revise the plan to delete the golf course and some of the other inconsistent features."

Then, in 2007, the commission finally put the kibosh on a revised proposal, voting against the needed changes to the county's land-use plan required to move forward. Thank God. It was reported that "no further discussions about the project are scheduled."

For more information, contact the Pebble Beach Company, 2700 17-Mile Drive, Pebble Beach, CA 93953, 800/654-9300, www.pebble-beach.com.

BEACHES

Believe it or not, there are actually some public beaches around Spanish Bay. No doubt they were a grudging concession from the developers exacted by the California Coastal Commission in exchange for permit approvals. From the junction of Asilomar Boulevard and Sunset Drive in Pacific Grove, a biking and hiking path called the Spanish Bay Recreation Trail leads through the forest behind the Inn at Spanish Bay, joining up with 17-Mile Drive and its procession of small cove beaches a short distance later. It also intersects a boardwalk that leads from the hotel lobby over the dunes and out to North and South **Moss Beach,** where you can sun yourself without spending a fortune (or a night).

The best surfing is found at **Spanish Bay**—"a half-mile of smooth beach surf," according to longboard guru Bank Wright—which frugal surfers get to by hiking from Asilomar State Beach. One of Pebble Beach's more notable cove beaches is **Fanshell Beach,** a north-facing sugar-textured sand beach at Signal Road and 17-Mile Drive. On the southern end of 17-Mile Drive—just north of Carmel City Beach—is another publicly accessible point, called **Stillwater Cove.** It has a tiny sand beach but is noted for its pier, which has a boat hoist. This is accessible via the Lodge at Pebble Beach parking lot. Call 831/625-8507 for boat information.

19 STILLWATER COVE

Location: south end of 17-Mile Drive in Pebble Beach
Parking/Fees: $9.25 entrance fee per car to nonguests or nonresidents of Pebble Beach and its lodges
Hours: sunrise-sunset
Facilities: none
Contact: Pebble Beach Company, 831/647-7500 or 800/654-9300

20 FANSHELL BEACH

Location: Signal Hill Road at 17-Mile Drive in Pebble Beach
Parking/Fees: $9.25 entrance fee per car to nonguests or nonresidents of Pebble Beach and its lodges
Hours: sunrise-sunset
Facilities: none
Contact: Pebble Beach Company, 831/647-7500 or 800/654-9300

21 MOSS BEACH

Location: north of Point Joe along Spanish Bay Road in Pebble Beach
Parking/Fees: $9.25 entrance fee per car to nonguests or nonresidents of Pebble Beach and its lodges
Hours: sunrise–sunset
Facilities: none
Contact: Pebble Beach Company, 831/647-7500 or 800/654-9300

22 SPANISH BAY

🚴 🏃 ⛷️

Location: behind the Inn at Spanish Bay, along the Spanish Bay Recreation Trail, in Pebble Beach
Parking/Fees: $9.25 entrance fee per car to nonguests or nonresidents of Pebble Beach and its lodges
Hours: sunrise–sunset
Facilities: none
Contact: Pebble Beach Company, 831/647-7500 or 800/654-9300

ACCOMMODATIONS

If you've won the lottery or made a killing in the market—or not been killed by the market—perhaps you can afford to stay at the **Lodge at Pebble Beach** (1700 17-Mile Drive, 831/647-7500 or 800/654-9300, $$$$). Room rates range $675–2,125 per night. Playing a round of golf on its justly famous Pebble Beach Golf Links costs $495 for 18 holes. Dinner at Club XIX, the lodge's premier dining room, averages $120 per plate. So if you share a standard ocean-view room ($965 per night), game of golf, and dinner for two, the cost of your one-night stay will total $2,195, plus drinks, taxes, and gratuities. On the plus side, they will refund the $9.25 charged to pass through the 17-Mile Drive toll gate if you're staying at one of the lodges. That brings the pretax total of a one-night, one-meal, one-game stay down to $2,185.75.

The new kid on the block is the **Inn at Spanish Bay** (2700 17-Mile Drive, 831/647-7500, $$$$), where you will not lack for comfort. Like the Lodge at Pebble Beach, it has a private beach, golf courses, tennis, pools, bikes, horses, health club, hiking trails, restaurants, stores, picnic tables, patios, balconies, and fireplaces. (The Lodge at Pebble Beach goes one further with a post office and bank.) Are we leaving anything out? The Inn at Spanish Bay is described as the more "casual" of the two, which means you get a slight break on the room rate: $595–850 a night for a double room.

COASTAL CUISINE

The celebrated restaurants at the Pebble Beach resorts are **Club XIX** (Lodge at Pebble Beach, 831/624-3811, $$$$) and the **Bay Club** (Inn at Spanish Bay, 831/647-7500, $$$$). Club XIX serves a French country menu, while the Bay Club tends toward northern Italian. Both are quite good, needless to say, and so expensive that (as the cliché goes) if you have to ask how much it is, you probably shouldn't be here. Dinner for two will cost around $240, exclusive of drinks, taxes, and tips.

Pacific Grove

Pacific Grove is the shy but beautiful daughter of the Monterey Peninsula. Hidden by trees and cooled by steady winds off Monterey Bay, this modest seaside village values a sensible regimen of spiritual nourishment, moderate exercise, fresh food, and lots of beauty rest. She's not a bit covetous of her peninsular siblings' popularity. Pacific Grove is content to let Carmel, Pebble Beach, and Monterey deal with the vulgarities of fame.

This attitude comes with the territory. More hometown than boomtown, Pacific Grove has led a quiet, ascetic life since her birth in 1875 as a "Christian seaside resort." The original hundred acres of pine-, oak-, and cypress-covered wilderness that make up the central grid of the town were marked off by the Methodist Episcopal Church for use as a

© PARKE PUTERBAUGH

Pacific Grove

camp-meeting retreat. The first camp meeting was held on August 8, 1875, and the lots were sold in 30- by 60-foot increments—large enough to accommodate a substantial tent. But a crowd of 450 worshippers turned out, more than had been anticipated, and in the ensuing years still more arrived. When summer rolled around, Pacific Grove became a virtual tent city. At summer's end the wooden frames were left standing while the tents were unfurled and stored in Chautauqua Hall, a utilitarian wood structure built in 1879 for the "presentation of moral attractions."

With this many people seeking it out for solace, Pacific Grove could not remain a simple religious retreat for long. In 1889, a permanent, year-round population of 1,300 incorporated a square-mile area of woodlands, and the town was created. The tents disappeared, replaced by tiny board-and-batten cottages, some built directly on the old frames. Larger Victorian dwellings were also built. These homes, along with the original churches, Chautauqua Hall, and the Point Pinos Lighthouse, still stand in Pacific Grove as unpretentious reminders of a quiet past. Most of the homes have plaques on the front door that identify the original owner and the year of its construction. Today Pacific Grove's population hovers around 15,000.

In terms of area, Pacific Grove embraces a choice corner of the wild Monterey Peninsula. You enter the town through a forest, and by the time you reach the seaside retreat you might as well have stepped back a century in time. This is not to imply that Pacific Grove is an old spinster living among dusty hymnbooks and faded memories. On the contrary, her original homes are in good repair and constant use as residences, inns, and offices—and their rising real-estate value has begun pricing this "last hometown" almost out of the reach of the middle-class folks that have always been its mainstay.

A full day can be spent hiking around Pacific Grove, admiring her restorations and resilience. An especially rewarding experience is the Pacific Grove Historic Walking Tour, an entertaining packet dispensed by the Chamber of Commerce from its neat little office at Forest and Central Avenues. Your efforts will be rewarded with a healthy perambulation and a thorough knowledge of Victorian-era California trivia.

PAELLA FANDANGO

Here's a recipe for Paella Fandango, one of the signature dishes served at Fandango in Pacific Grove. Fandango is among our favorite restaurants on the California coast. Chef Pierre Bain's recipe for this classic Spanish dish is easy to prepare and simply delicious. According to our paella guru, "If you follow the recipe, it turns out perfectly every time."

$1/2$ cup olive oil
1 large onion, chopped
2 cloves garlic, chopped
2 large tomatoes, diced
1 each red and yellow bell pepper, cut in strips
2 cups uncooked white rice
8 cups chicken broth
3 tablespoons fresh parsley, chopped
2 large pinches saffron threads
2 chicken breasts, cut into 4-5 pieces each
$1/2$ pound chorizo sausage, cut into $1/2$-inch slices
$1/2$ pound scallops
$1/2$ pound shrimp, peeled with tails intact
$1/2$ pound calamari
8-10 little neck clams
8-10 mussels
1 cup peas, fresh or frozen
salt, pepper, cayenne

In a Dutch oven, heat olive oil and add onion, garlic, tomatoes, and peppers. Sauté until limp. Add white rice and chicken broth, and bring to a boil. Add the parsley and saffron and cook for 20 minutes at a simmer. Add the remaining ingredients and cook until done, about 20-40 minutes. Season to taste with salt, pepper, and cayenne. Serves 8.
Recipe courtesy of Fandango.

BIG SUR AND MONTEREY

The most informative tour stop is the **Pacific Grove Museum of Natural History** (165 Forest Avenue, 831/648-5716). Founded in 1881, it's one of the best of its size in the country. It's also free of charge, though you'll be moved to give a donation. In two floors of gallery space, every facet of Monterey County's rich natural history is showcased. This includes insects, rodents, birds (400 species), fish, reptiles, rocks, fossils, Native Americana, and the town's evocative symbol, the monarch butterfly *(Danaus plexippus).*

A more appropriate mascot could not be found for Pacific Grove, which, when it gets the slightest bit of boosterism, bills itself as "Butterfly Town, USA." Every year, thousands of orange-and-black monarchs migrate to the

pine groves nearby. They arrive on November 1 and leave by March 1. On dull winter days they hang in thick clusters from the trees, but on warm, sunny days they swoop all over town. The city protects these fluttering critters, imposing fines of up to $1,000 for "molesting butterflies." This same ordinance asks citizens to "protect the butterflies in every way possible from serious harm and possible extinction by brutal and heartless people." If you don't want to be assaulted by a mob of angry matrons wielding antique butter churns, then you'd better leave the sweet little things be.

On the other hand, you may never see a monarch butterfly. They're gone by summer and are sometimes undetectable in winter. Their wings fold inward, so that only their neutral-colored undersides are visible. The distinctive, lovely markings are seen only by those with the patience to look closely. The same is true of Pacific Grove. The closer you look at it, the more its charming detail and coloring will be revealed.

The entire town gathers visitors in its warm, fuzzy embrace. Even at a gas station on Lighthouse Avenue, where we stopped to ask for directions, the beaming, Ward Cleaver–like proprietor put his arms around our shoulders and said, "That would normally cost you a dollar, but I'm running a special today."

For more information, contact the Pacific Grove Chamber of Commerce, Central and Forest Avenues, 584 Central Avenue, P.O. Box 167, Pacific Grove, CA 93950, 831/373-3304, www.pacificgrove.org; or the Monterey Peninsula Visitors and Convention Bureau, 401 Camino El Estero, Monterey, CA 93940, 877/666-8373, www.montereyinfo.org.

BEACHES

For so understated a town, Pacific Grove is actually quite large in terms of area. Whereas the old historic neighborhoods can be pleasantly strolled in an afternoon, the ruggedly beautiful shoreline goes on for miles, especially in and around Asilomar State Beach. The beaches beg to be explored on bicycle. In fact, Pacific Grove is a peninsula within a peninsula. The terrain out here is relatively flat, the roads less traveled by cars, and the neighborhoods safer than in Monterey.

The **Pacific Grove Bicycle Trail** will solve all your beachcombing problems. It starts at the south near Spanish Bay, cuts through Asilomar, Point Pinos, and Lover's Point, and then hooks up with the more heavily trafficked Monterey Bay Recreational Trail near the Monterey Bay Aquarium. The best place to rent wheels is **Adventures by the Sea** (299 Cannery Row, 831/372-1807), directly on the beach at Lover's Point, just off the bike trail, which also rents kayaks, diving gear, and so forth for those who want to brave the bay. From there one can continue north, through Monterey and up to Seaside—quite a haul, though it gets progressively less peaceful with each passing mile.

Back at Spanish Bay one comes face to face with the enmity that other Monterey Peninsula residents feel toward their Pebble Beach neighbors. This was once the most exquisite cove beach in the area, a favorite with locals, surfers, artists, and photographers. Now it's the backdrop for a luxury resort (the Inn at Spanish Bay and its adjoining golf course, the Links at Spanish Bay), which, after years of heated legal dickering, was finally approved by the local zoning board. They must have been out of their sand bunkers! Given this golf resort's extensive privatization, we wonder why they don't just complete the deal by building a crocodile-infested moat around the compound. Ansel Adams, whose gallery is in Pebble Beach, would have been livid.

There is a way to circumvent this privacy. Take the hiking trail at nearby Asilomar State Beach that leads, via a wooden boardwalk, to the Inn at Spanish Bay's parking lot. Continue walking, pausing long enough to thumb your nose at the resort. You will soon hook up with the Coastal Bluff Hiking Trail, which leads to Point Joe, the most scenic spot on the overly hyped 17-Mile Drive. You will be standing on the beach itself—not viewing it from some overlook—and you will have saved the $9.25 fee that's levied to enter the 17-Mile Drive by car. The view? Imagine Ansel Adams's finest photograph.

Off Sunset Drive/Highway 68 and Asilomar Avenue, **Asilomar State Beach** is a meditative mix of rocky headlands, tidepools, and cove beaches. The beach is a half mile of sand backed by healthy grass-covered dune fields that stretch for hundreds of yards toward the Asilomar Conference Grounds. It's popular with surfers, divers, kite fliers, and sunbathers. Parking and day use are free at Asilomar State Beach.

The bike trail courses around the rocky headlands at Point Pinos and the Pacific Grove Shoreline Marine Refuge, a feast for the eyes.

The beaches here are more for browsing than swimming, with many rich tidepools but sand and pebbles too coarse for bare feet. Pretend you're a seagull soaring above this buffet, which is probably what all those birders sitting in their cars with binoculars are doing. The waves create a teeming stew of fish, shells, kelp fronds, sea grapes, starfish, and sea grass. These are the same tidepools that inspired John Steinbeck and his hero, Doc Ricketts, in the novel *Cannery Row.*

Steinbeck: "It is a fabulous place: when the tide is in, a wave-churned basin, creamy with foam…but when the tide goes out the little water world becomes quiet and lovely, fantastic with hurrying, fighting, feeding, breeding animals."

Steinbeck's grandparents had a house nearby, which is now the modest **John Steinbeck Memorial Museum** (222 Central Avenue, 831/373-6976). Speaking of literary inspiration, Robert Louis Stevenson spent many ecstatic hours in Pacific Grove, too. He sat out at Point Pinos—the entrance to Monterey Bay—perhaps staring longingly toward Tahiti.

The **Point Pinos Lighthouse,** built in 1855, is the oldest light station in continuous service on the West Coast, guiding navigators through these sometimes rugged waters. The building, lenses, and prisms are all original, and they can be viewed by the public on Saturdays and Sundays, 1 P.M.–4 P.M. (For information, call the lighthouse at 831/648-5716.)

Although surfers love Asilomar State Beach in the winter—when waves reach heights of eight feet—the heaviest bombers come to Point Pinos. Between Point Pinos and Lover's Point is an area known as "Boneyards"—though its official name is **Perkins Park**—where the surf breaks perilously close to the rocky headlands. Sit on one of the bluff-top benches and watch the show, as do-or-die surfers consider this spot a must, especially at high tide.

Families gravitate to **Lover's Point,** a large, grassy area with volleyball courts, babies' swimming pool, snack bar, restrooms,

and sandy beaches. (Singer John Denver fatally crashed his experimental plane into the bay here in 1997.) The surf here is nowhere near as rough as that at Point Pinos. The entire area is lined with parks set on bluff tops above the shore, along which runs the Monterey Bay Recreational Trail, a paved pathway for walkers and cyclists. This linear bayfront green passes and encompasses a series of small parks set back from the bay—including Berwick Park, Greenwood Park, and Andy Jacobsen Park. Collectively, they are known as **Shoreline Park** and offer access to pebbly pocket beaches here and there via short, sloping trails. Benches provide strollers with ample rest stops, offering further proof that Pacific Grove may indeed be the Monterey Peninsula's last real hometown. Finally, this same area—from Asilomar to Lover's Point— is a great promontory from which to watch whales migrate in the winter.

Also in the immediate area is a golfing opportunity par excellence, one of the few we wholeheartedly endorse at the beach. **Pacific Grove Municipal Golf Links** (77 Asilomar Avenue, 831/648-5775) is a pleasant, low-key alternative to Pebble Beach's overpriced courses. It's truly a public course with the same stunning scenery. The fairway of the 16th hole, for example, runs alongside the Point Pinos Lighthouse. The greens fees are reasonable ($40–45 for 18 holes, as opposed to $495 at Pebble Beach), the staff is friendly, and the manners are refreshingly unpretentious.

23 ASILOMAR STATE BEACH

BEST (

Location: Sunset Drive between Asilomar and Jewel Avenues in Pacific Grove
Parking/Fees: free street parking
Hours: sunrise-sunset
Facilities: restrooms and showers
Contact: Asilomar State Beach, 831/646-6440

BIG SUR AND MONTEREY

24 LOVER'S POINT

Location: Ocean View Boulevard at 17th Street in Pacific Grove
Parking/Fees: free parking lot
Hours: sunrise–10 P.M.
Facilities: restrooms and picnic tables
Contact: Pacific Grove Parks Department, 831/648-3130

25 SHORELINE PARK

Location: Ocean View Boulevard between Lover's Point and Point Cabrillo in Monterey
Parking/Fees: free street parking
Hours: 6 A.M.–10 P.M.
Facilities: none
Contact: Monterey Parks Department, 831/755-4895

ACCOMMODATIONS

The **Asilomar Conference Center** (800 Asilomar Avenue, 831/372-8016, $$) might just be the best bargain on the Monterey Peninsula. Don't let the name put you off. A conference at Asilomar is as likely to be a quiet family retreat as a meeting of corporate eager beavers spouting sales figures and studying pie charts.

Founded in 1913 by the YWCA as the premier "chautauqua" in California, the Asilomar Conference Center is now run on a nonprofit basis by the California State Park System. The original 11 buildings (all National Historical Landmarks) were designed by Julia Morgan, the San Francisco architect responsible for Hearst Castle at San Simeon. They're spread out among 105 acres of Monterey pines and cypress, with wooden walkways leading across the dunes to the state beach. Facing due west, Asilomar is treated to stunning sunsets, and its 28 woodsy lodges have appealingly rustic names like "Willow Inn" and "Oak Knoll." Though conference facilities are available,

guests need not be part of a group to come here. A full breakfast, served cafeteria-style in a large hall, comes with the room. It's like being back at camp.

The rest of the town's accommodations are similarly neat, trim, low-key, and/or historic, making Pacific Grove the ideal place to stay if you're laying over on the peninsula. Options range from small motels, like the **Larchwood Inn** (740 Crocker Avenue, 831/373-1114, $$), to the **Lighthouse Lodge and Suites** (1249 Lighthouse Avenue, 831/655-2111, $$). The former is next to Asilomar, while the latter is set among the shady acres close to Point Pinos Lighthouse, virtually guaranteeing a quiet vacation. Cute little mom-and-pop motels proliferate in the area around Asilomar, furthering the hometown ambience of Pacific Grove. Any one of them would make a fine place to drop your bags for a stay.

Pacific Grove is probably best known as a happy hunting ground for bed-and-breakfast inns, original Victorian homes that have been lovingly converted into lodgings. Several excellent ones include **Green Gables Inn** (301 Ocean View Boulevard, 831/375-2095, $$$) and **Gosby House** (643 Lighthouse Avenue, 831/375-1287, $$$). The Green Gables, a Queen Anne mansion built in 1888, is situated on a quiet cove, while the Gosby House is on the town's main thoroughfare. Both provide ideal escapes from modern civilization, offering more privacy than the average B&B amid trappings of quaint Victorian splendor that the old queen herself would definitely have approved.

Gosby House has been an inn since it was built in 1887, its earliest guests having been pilgrims to the camp meetings. One of us was so smitten with the place that he actually spent part of his honeymoon here. Gosby House has a quiet garden and courtyard, and the 22 rooms (seven with private entrances) are filled with period furnishings, artwork, stuffed bears, and McGuffey's Readers. Both inns are reasonably priced ($155–225 per night at the Gosby House in season, $135–225 per night at the Green Gables Inn), considering what you get.

COASTAL CUISINE

The Monterey Peninsula is now marketing itself, in a low-key way, as the "Provence of California," and indeed a revised approach to cuisine is developing around the abundant fresh local produce and seafood. It's little wonder, when 80 percent of the world's broccoli is grown in the vicinity, as are large percentages of artichokes, grapes, lettuce, and ranch-raised game.

Fandango (223 17th Street, 831/372-3456, $$$) is the first of several restaurants to add to your dinner wish list. Run by the ever-pleasant (and present) Pierre Bain, Fandango resembles a villa in the south of France. Not surprisingly, the owner comes from a family restaurant tradition dating back 250 years in the Basque region. Prior to opening Fandango with his wife Marietta, Bain worked at Pebble Beach.

The experience of eating here is top of the line, the menu prices eminently fair and affordable. As an appetizer, the Veloute Boula Boula—a soup made of peas, consommé, and sherry—is hard to top. The house specialty is Paella Fandango, a veritable fishing boat of goodies including littleneck clams, scallops, calamari, shrimp, mussels, chicken, and much more. Well worth the $26.95 they charge. Other specialties include rack of lamb Provençal, Basque-style lamb shank, and mesquite-grilled salmon and swordfish.

The locals' favorite seafood venue is **Fishwife at Asilomar Beach** (1196 Sunset Drive, 831/375-7107, $$). The freshest catches are served with a Caribbean flavor and consistently win "Best Seafood" awards for the entire peninsula. The house specialties are snapper Cancun (seasoned with achiote and topped with salsa brava), prawns Belize, calamari abalone-style, fish chowder, and key lime pie. The setting is casual, the prices are right, and the line is often out the door.

We recently visited Fishwife for an early lunch, slipping in before the line formed. The daily grill special featured wild Monterey Bay salmon, which has a rich, distinctive flavor. The pastas were tempting, too. Pasta Alfredo is cooked in a shellfish-based veloute sauce,

sautéed with shallots, butter, and cream, and combined with crab, scallops, or shrimp (or in combination). The Portofino combines crab, shrimp, scallops, baby clams, calamari, and fresh fish. The dinner menu is expanded with a mouthwatering group of "fisherman's bowls" that include the Bahamian bowl (snapper rubbed with Coral Key spices), Bayou bowl (catfish or snapper), Mazatlan bowl (jumbo shrimp), Cozumel bowl (tilapia), and others.

The Fishwife is so successful that the owners opened a second restaurant in Seaside (**Fishwife Seafood Cafe,** 789 Trinity Avenue, 831/394-2027, $$), the nondescript oceanfront town grafted onto the flanks of Monterey. Fishwife also publishes a popular collection of its recipes.

Another longtime favorite is **Tinnery at the Beach** (631 Ocean View Boulevard, 831/646-1040, $$), right on the water at Lover's Point. It's not exactly gourmet cuisine, but by Pacific Grove's standards it's affordable family dining. The Tinnery is staffed by friendly, wholesome locals, and the dining room has a peerless bay view. At sunset you can watch fishing boats returning to Monterey, and on clear days you can see as far as Moss Landing and Santa Cruz, on the far side of the bay. After you're as stuffed as a halibut, take an after-dinner stroll along Lover's Point before retiring to your room at the inn.

Yet another longtime resident of the Pacific Grove dining scene is the **Old Bath House** (620 Ocean View Boulevard, 831/375-5195, $$$$), a pricey place that does unusual things with seafood and game dishes. Eclectic appetizers include tempting exotica such as house-cured salmon with pistachio-crusted goat cheese, and grilled prawns and wild boar sausage.

The aptly named **Passionfish** (701 Lighthouse Avenue, 831/655-3311, $$$) is making waves for its proclaimed dedication to "serving sustainable seafood." Cooks use only line-caught local fish—catches like wild Monterey Bay salmon—and local produce. On the night we visited (it's open for dinner only), six of 11 menu items were seafood, including wild salmon, halibut, escolar, and mahimahi. The artfully spartan interior design is a perfect complement to the fare, and the wine list has won awards from *Wine Spectator*.

To open your day, and perhaps even your mind, hit **Bookworks** (667 Lighthouse Avenue, 831/372-2242, $), Pacific Grove's best bookshop and a relaxed coffeehouse in the bargain. The shop has a decent collection of contemporary literature, classics, history, and travel books, plus one of the largest and most passionately annotated displays of "staff picks" we bookworms have ever seen. In other words, they love the printed word at Bookworks.

NIGHTLIFE

Your after-dinner stroll along Lover's Point (originally "Lovers of Jesus Point") should suffice for nightlife in Pacific Grove. More by silent agreement than by local ordinance—though it was "dry" until 1972—Pacific Grove has no bars. Nor will you find pool halls, nightclubs, discos, or beer joints here. About all you can do is quaff a drink to tepid lounge music at the Tinnery and the Old Bath House (described under *Coastal Cuisine*). For anything livelier than this, head over to Monterey. In the ascetic spirit of Pacific Grove, we chose to pass up an evening of square dancing at Crocker Hall in the Asilomar Conference Center. It just seemed too darned wild.

Monterey

If the Monterey Peninsula were a baseball team, Carmel would lead off and play second base, Pebble Beach would be the overpaid designated hitter, and Pacific Grove would be the utility infielder who exerts a stabilizing influence on the bench. Monterey would be the cleanup hitter, because that's exactly what it does. It cleans up after the tourists. This is no accident. By design Monterey draws the tourist hordes, who roam the streets, starving, hysterical, clad in goofy clothing, looking for an angry fix of clam chowder. (Apologies to the late Allen Ginsberg for our antic revision of the opening line from his classic poem "Howl.")

Nothing is wrong with tourism. It gives people something to do two weeks a year and helps keep our temperamental economy afloat. It is also a "clean industry," for the most part, having a relatively low impact on the environment. Monterey's rich history, the restoration of the canneries, and the magnificent **Monterey Bay Aquarium** (886 Cannery Row, 831/648-4800) are all part of the attraction. Unlike many tourist traps, Monterey actually has something to offer other than shopping and eating.

In years past, we've felt that Monterey was more of a tourist trap than it needed to be. To give the town its due, Monterey has been changing for the better, especially on the water. Today an excursion to Monterey is worthwhile, particularly when it's combined with side trips to Big Sur, Carmel, and Pacific Grove.

One of our biggest gripes is that it's not exactly easy to find your way around the town of Monterey. It's the biggest town on Monterey Peninsula, but the layout of its streets and the web of exits that lead into it are confusing. It can be hard just to get from downtown to Cannery Row (or vice versa), even though they're close to each other. Our advice: Bring a map with you and study it beforehand. You'll still make a wrong turn, we wager.

Spread out around the curve of a harbor and groping inland, Monterey (population 28,500) is a contoured combination of the old and the really old. The center of the latter is historic Old Town, which can be toured with a decent pair of sneakers and a map. This section of Monterey has been taken over by the California State Park System (in conjunction with the Monterey History and Art Association), which does these sorts of things right. An excellent self-guided walking tour has been laid out, called "the Path of History," which allows visitors to explore the meticulously restored adobes, chapels, theaters, and pubs that make Monterey "the most historic city in California."

MONTEREY NATIONAL MARINE SANCTUARY

Monterey Bay is the centerpiece of the largest protected marine area in the United States. Encompassing one-fourth of California's coastline, the Monterey National Marine Sanctuary stretches from the waters off San Simeon all the way up to the Golden Gate Bridge in San Francisco (with a 71-square-mile "raw sewage exemption zone" off San Francisco). In all, 5,312 square nautical miles – 1.5 times the size of the largest national park in America – are protected from offshore oil and gas development, ocean dumping, sub-sea mining, agricultural runoff, and untreated sewage disposal. That is because the rich ecosystem of Monterey Bay is:

* The permanent or seasonal home to 27 species of sea mammals, including endangered whales and threatened sea otters;

* Home to 345 species of fish, most of California's species of algae, and among the world's richest assemblages of invertebrate life;

* The nesting area or sanctuary to 94 species of seabirds, including endangered species.

We learned firsthand about the bay's invertebrate population one night. After an obligatory swing through Monterey's clubs and bars, we returned to our car, parked along Cannery Row's waterfront. Just offshore, we spied a veritable navy of fishing vessels. Pitch dark though it was on shore, it was bright as day on the bay. A circle of boats with powerful, mounted klieg lights illuminated the surface of the water. They were fishing for squid, and this technique – using light to throw off their prey's biological clocks – draws them to the surface in search of food. Instead of finding food, these unsuspecting squid become food themselves, winding up as fried calamari strips on tourists' plates at Fisherman's Wharf.

The Monterey National Marine Sanctuary is a center for international research on marine life and marine ecology, encompassing 11 research institutions. Its mission is to monitor all activities impacting the marine area, including effluent from ships and land, development, and recreational uses, as well as monitoring the populations of aquatic species. Monterey Bay and surrounding waters became a sanctuary in 1992, during the Clinton administration, when the federal government designated it as such after a 15-year wrangle. At present the sanctuary is managed by the National Oceanic and Atmospheric Administration (NOAA), but management may be transferred to a joint public-private venture.

Monterey has several histories rolled into one. Founded in 1542 by Juan Cabrillo, it has been the capital of California on three separate occasions. It has also served as an international trading center, whaling mecca, giant industrial sardine cannery, and, finally, the place where the state of California was born. This historic event transpired at the Constitutional Convention of 1849, held in the still-standing Colton Hall. Soon after, gold was discovered up north. San Francisco swiftly became the preeminent city in Califor-

nia, leaving Monterey to ponder its past. The best place to begin a tour of the wonderful remnants of Old Town—and to pick up all the available free literature—is the **Monterey State Historic Park Visitor Center** (20 Custom House Plaza, 831/649-7118). Stop there to get acclimated, then start walking.

On the Path of History you'll see the original Custom House, where all imported goods were brought ashore and inspected before permission was granted to unload. Many a sea captain averted this procedure by off-loading

THE MONTEREY BAY AQUARIUM

The Monterey Bay Aquarium opened in 1984 with the expressed goal of "expanding public interest and knowledge and concern for the marine life of Monterey Bay and the ocean environment." It has more than achieved that goal and is a yardstick by which environmental education ought to be measured. With regularly changing exhibits, tanks full of living specimens, video and film footage, and live presentations, the aquarium re-creates the rich underwater habitat of Monterey Bay, which sits right outside its back door. A relief map we'd seen at the Pacific Grove Museum of Natural History showed how the bay plunges 300 feet straight down into an underwater canyon that eventually reaches 8,400 feet in depth. This nutrient-rich canyon nourishes a wide variety of marine species from which the aquarium draws its exhibits.

State of the art does not mean virtual reality at Monterey Bay Aquarium. It means actual reality! That is, kids are allowed to watch animals do their things – everything from octopuses and sharks to sea slugs and barnacles. There's a kelp forest, sandy shore, coastal stream, reef, and bat-ray tank. There's also a touch pool – the underwater equivalent of a petting zoo.

Among the regular activities that visitors most enjoy is the daily feedings of sea otters (at 10:30 A.M., 1:30 P.M., and 3:30 P.M.). They are indeed cute little critters. A sea otter, we learned, eats one-third of its weight in food every day. According to ongoing surveys, only 2,200 of these otters are left in California. The otters who reside and cavort at the aquarium to the immense delight and relief of all were once injured or orphaned.

One of the most fascinating exhibits is "Mysteries of the Deep," a display of deep-sea creatures taken from depths of over 3,000 feet in the bay. Normally, such creatures do not survive in captivity, but the aquarium spent $5 million and a decade of research to replicate the deep-sea environment, where no sunlight reaches, water temperature is close to 40 degrees, food is scarce, and water pressure is crushing. Up to 40 such rare species are on display now.

There's also a superlative book and gift shop. An on-premises restaurant, the Portola Cafe (831/648-4870, $$), serves crab cakes, calamari, prawns, grilled fish – that is, if the sight of cooked seafood doesn't repulse you after having just admired them alive and well in their native habitat.

Admission to Monterey Bay Aquarium isn't cheap ($24.95 for adults, $22.95 for students and seniors, $15.95 for kids 3-12), but the facility warrants the tariff and is good for at least a half-day's studious wandering. You'll want to return year after year, too. The best deal is to become a member of the Monterey Bay Aquarium for $120, which allows an entire family – two adults plus all children or grandchildren 3-21 – unlimited admission for a year. At the north end of Cannery Row in Monterey, the Monterey Bay Aquarium is open daily 10 A.M.-6 P.M. (from 9:30 A.M. in summer).

For more information, contact the Monterey Bay Aquarium, 886 Cannery Row, Monterey, CA 93940, 831/648-4800, www.mbayaq.org.

CANNERY ROW, THEN AND NOW

One path of history that you should avoid in Monterey is the one that leads through Cannery Row. Its past is indeed fascinating, but you will not find a genuine legacy here. With the shining exception of the Monterey Bay Aquarium, you will find a monument to bad taste and rampant consumerism. You will also find a degraded shopping zone that shamelessly trades on the name of John Steinbeck. You will, in fact, find everything but a genuine tribute to the hardworking blue-collar spirit of yesteryear.

Originally, Cannery Row was a line of pack houses where sardines were weighed, sorted, counted, and canned by guys and dolls who never dreamed that what they were doing to make ends meet would be glamorized decades later. The first canneries were built in the 1890s. By the late 1940s they were shut down because the bay and ocean were overfished and polluted.

This was the place Steinbeck wrote about in his novel of the same name. Published in 1945, *Cannery Row* caught Monterey at the peak of its canning days, when 4,000 workers canned 237,000 tons of sardines in a year. Steinbeck saw Cannery Row as "a poem, a stink, a grating noise, a quality of light, a tone, a habit, a nostalgia, a dream. Cannery Row is the gathered and scattered, tin and iron and rust and splintered wood, chipped pavement and weedy lots and junk heaps."

This is not what exists along Cannery Row today. The shops here are the sort of thing that you'd find at an amusement park: creamy fudge, jelly beans, and taffy. The "olde" arcade – one of the faithfully restored structures – has a depressingly musty feel. Toward the end of his life, Steinbeck returned to see what had become of the Monterey he knew. "They fish for tourists now," he said forlornly. As if to echo Steinbeck's thoughts, the National Trust for Historic Preservation has listed Cannery Row among the nation's most endangered historic places.

BIG SUR AND MONTEREY

on one of the islands south of Carmel, returning later to pick up the untaxed cargo. Also on the path is the state's first theater, still producing live drama when not serving ale and food under the name **Jack Swan's Tavern.**

Other highlights include the **Pacific House** (an 1847 military storehouse, now an excellent museum of California history), the state's first kiln-fired brick house, the old whaling station, and the **Robert Louis Stevenson House.** Built in 1847, the Stevenson House is where the author lived when he was courting Fanny Osbourne, a married woman who vacationed here. Civil War buffs can see the house where William Tecumseh Sherman lived from 1847 to 1849, back when he was a man about town (before he torched Georgia).

Even the historic houses that are not official stops on the path have been commandeered for other functions—investment firms, real estate offices, law offices, Mexican restaurants—

leading us to turn an old cliché on its head: The more things stay the same, the more they change in Monterey.

One welcome addition to the waterfront that has rekindled interest in Monterey's history is the **Stanton Center.** This 18,000-square-foot structure is devoted to the rich maritime and European colonial history of the peninsula. Its centerpiece is the **Maritime Museum of Monterey** (5 Custom House Plaza, 831/375-1643). The museum focuses on the town's history as California's premier port, re-creating life aboard a ship, inside the Custom House, and at a lighthouse. Original artifacts, vintage photographs, and excellent documentary footage are used to convey these settings. The treasure is a two-story, five-ton Fresnel lens that served as the beacon at Point Sur Lightstation for 100 years. A modest admission fee is charged, but the seven exhibit areas are a good return on investment.

FULL MOON OVER MONTEREY

It was not our day. Or, should we say, night. Due to an error on the itinerary we drew up, we showed up in Monterey late on a Saturday afternoon without hotel reservations. Every road experience, even a bad one, somehow proves useful, or at least instructive, in the long run. The bad ones often turn out to be the most fun to write about. Perhaps you can benefit from our misfortune in Monterey. The lesson is twofold: 1) Do not show up in popular vacation destinations without confirmed reservations; and 2) Double-check your itinerary for accuracy before leaving.

Our botched Saturday night went down like this. A day of reveling in the beauty of Big Sur had left us exhausted, so we were eagerly anticipating the turn of a key in a hotel room door and the opportunity to drop bags and collapse. Fatigue weighed heavy on us. We inadvertently showed up in Monterey without a reservation and quickly found the entire peninsula was booked solid. In Pacific Grove, Carmel, and Monterey, the No Vacancy signs were glowing at every turn. When we asked where to find a room, we were told, "Go east, young men." East to Salinas, that is.

Salinas is 20 miles inland from Monterey. It is Steinbeck country, population 100,000. Imagine our dismay to learn that even the hotels and motels in Salinas were full. No room at the Comfort Inn. No room even at fleabag motels you'd hold your nose just driving past. There was one vacancy at the Holiday Inn Express: a smoking room with one bed for well over $100. No thanks; we weren't that desperate. We agreed that we would sleep in the car before paying that kind of money in Salinas. We continued checking one motel after another and all were full. Our heavy-lidded eyes noticed cowboys hollering "yee-haw" in parking lots. As we later learned, Salinas was hosting the 85th annual California Rodeo that very weekend.

After chasing No Vacancy signs for what seemed like forever, we conceded defeat and swung out of Salinas. By now we were cruising past the broccoli fields of the Salinas Valley in a state of confused exhaustion as the day's final rays streaked the darkening night sky with a brilliant blaze of orange. We completed a circuitous loop

Next to the center in the outdoor plaza a performance space stages historic skits for the kids. The entire area is a successful compromise between doing justice to history and meeting tourist needs—a balance that Monterey itself has needed to strike for years.

The Stanton Center and its environs have gone a long way toward improving downtown Monterey, which was drastically altered by all the corporate development wedged onto the waterfront in the 1980s. The logjam of growth reconfigured the old street grids into a maddening and confusing maze. Ironically enough, this corporate strangulation discouraged locals from frequenting the downtown area. In the words of one entrepreneur, the ill-planned growth "castrated the town, sapping the vitality out of Alvarado Street, where things were once hopping all the time." But

now the downtown is coming back, even if the electrical current that kept Alvarado humming has been short-circuited by obstructive hotel complexes.

To us there's no mystery about it. We've seen it a hundred times, in nearly every American beach town. If a community plays to its strengths—ocean, sand, and sun—it will never lose. If it goes too far toward accommodating entrepreneurial greed, replacing genuine atmosphere with gold-plated fakery, it will eventually pay the price for lost authenticity with diminished interest.

Take the two best-known attractions in town...please. They are Fisherman's Wharf and Cannery Row. Situated on opposite sides of a Coast Guard facility and 10 minutes apart by foot, they are similar in appeal—twin strips of tourist flypaper around which buzzes through the area. We had begun in Monterey, proceeded to Salinas, and then headed northwest to Castroville and Watsonville before returning dejectedly to Monterey. This redundant trek added 100 pointless miles to our car.

And still we pressed on. We tried the city of Marina, home to the decommissioned Fort Ord. The Travelodge, the Inn Cal – both large, both full. Grimly we drove south to Seaside, Monterey's downtrodden neighbor, where we found another strip of motels flashing No Vacancy signs. The proprietor of one flyblown dive, chattering on a cell phone, said he'd heard there was one room left at another fleabag motel across the way. "Go, go!" he urged like a football coach sending us in to run a key fourth-down play. Alas, we moved too slowly. Some other sucker snapped it up.

Good fortune smiled on us at last. The Bay Breeze Motel had one room left, for $65. The room was spartan but clean. It would do. We rested on our respective mattresses, reflecting on the automotive nightmare of the last several hours. This is the darker side of traveling, the part where you pine for the comfort and safety of your bed back home.

Bay breezes blew cooling gusts of air through the window. The same breeze also carried the sounds of a couple who were arguing in Spanish in the parking lot. They were joined in disharmony by two more squabbling lovebirds.

What was going on? Just then, we beheld a radiant full moon in the night sky. That explained why all hell was busting loose. Under the circumstances, we weren't going to get to sleep anytime soon, so we headed into Monterey for a bite to eat. We parked along Cannery Row, disembarking just in time to watch a yuppie couple fighting on the street. They loudly traded insults and accusations. "Bullshit!" he screamed, backing her against a wall. People turned toward them and froze, as if playing statues. A stray dog added a loud, reproving *woof*.

Cannery Row offered a miserable choice of dining options whose cheap scents drove us up the street to a family-run Italian restaurant. Refueled by an eight-topping pie, we made our way back to our motel in Seaside. We woke up to a new morning, sun shining brightly. Maybe it was all just a bad dream.

an endless procession of dazed and confused humans, trailing clam chowder and souvenir baubles. Both were once the haunts of working men, clanging machinery, and ladies of the night. In short, they were raw places with a peculiar history all their own.

These days **Fisherman's Wharf** is easily the more appealing of the two areas, having been spruced up in recent years. Originally built by slave labor as a safe harbor for cargo-laden schooners rounding the horn from the east, the old Fisherman's Wharf was the center of the West Coast whaling industry. Since the late 1800s it has been the domain of a fleet of Sicilian fishermen whose efforts made Monterey the sardine capital of the world.

The seafarers have erected a shrine at the mouth of the harbor in honor of Santa Rosalia, their patron saint. Most of the old-family Italians who settled here eventually made a fortune in real estate. Oddly, the wharf doesn't exactly feel like a wharf. Walking its planks is more like strolling a downtown street, because shops and restaurants line both sides in an unbroken wall. Monterey's Fisherman's Wharf is unique among California pier/wharves because of this "closed in" feeling.

Cannery Row, on the other hand, has for years been a largely dubious tourist attraction, though the most excessive tourist bilking has begun to wane. You will want to poke your nose into the Coast Guard facility. Sea lions can be observed from the Coast Guard Pier, basking in the sun on the breakwater. These lazy-looking, heavy-lidded beasts lounge around like overfed tourists on a motel-room bed. Appearances are deceptive, though. The breakwater here is just a resting place on their annual migrations between Mexico and Canada. Feeding them is forbidden; they must catch their own calamari.

For more information, contact the Monterey Peninsula Chamber of Commerce, 380 Alvarado Street, Monterey, CA 93940, 831/648-5360, www.mpcc.com; or the Monterey Peninsula Visitors and Convention Bureau, 401 Camino El Estero, Monterey, CA 93940, 877/666-8373, www.montereyinfo.org.

BEACHES

Visitors come to Monterey for many reasons, but beaches are the least of them. Better beaches lie elsewhere on the peninsula (in Pacific Grove and Carmel) and directly above it (in Seaside and Marina). The surf along the beaches of Monterey is too cold and hazardous for swimming, and the wind blows nearly nonstop, so don't wear that wacky straw hat you bought on Cannery Row, unless you want to see it wind up on the head of a sea lion.

Still, there is some coastal access and much in the way of watery recreation. Scuba diving, deep-sea fishing, ocean kayaking, sailing, and windsurfing are all popular pastimes, and local merchants can set visitors up with equipment rentals and instruction. The best spots for diving are **Macabee Beach, San Carlos Beach Park** (accessible along Cannery Row), and **Coast Guard Pier,** where you can swim alongside the sea lions and explore the rich marine life of Monterey Bay. And let's not forget the dive-bombing pelicans, who hit the water with a snappy report that sounds like a fastball smacking a catcher's mitt.

The best place for kids to get wet is **Del Monte Beach,** along a lake in El Estero Park, on the other side of Del Monte Boulevard from the ocean. Ducks and migratory birds come here, and canoes and kayaks can be rented. There's also a toddlers' wading pool and the aptly named Dennis the Menace Play Area, designed by Hank Ketcham, the creator of that famous comic strip. It features innovative equipment and a real train engine for firsthand exploration.

Monterey State Beach offers several access points. A narrow stretch of sand known as **Windows on the Bay** can be found north of Fisherman's Wharf #2 (a municipal wharf built in 1926 for commercial fishing). Another unit lies a mile northeast, at the end of **Sand Dunes Drive.** This one is broader, sandier, and "dunier" than the first. Between these two points is **Beach Way Access,** which has a small free parking area at the end of Beach Way, but no facilities.

The Monterey Bay Recreational Trail, a five-mile shoreline bike path that takes in the Monterey waterfront between Pacific Grove and Seaside, is a great way to get a ground-level feel for the town and the bay. We've biked it, hiked it, and run its length, and never get tired of coming back for more. The trail is particularly pleasant between San Carlos Beach Park and Fisherman's Wharf, passing through Fisherman's Shoreline Park.

26 MACABEE BEACH

Location: Prescott Avenue at Cannery Row in Monterey
Parking/Fees: metered street parking
Hours: 6 A.M.–10 P.M.
Facilities: none
Contact: Monterey Parks Department, 831/755-4895

27 SAN CARLOS BEACH PARK

Location: end of Reeside Avenue, between Cannery Row and Coast Guard Pier, in Monterey
Parking/Fees: metered street parking
Hours: 6 A.M.–10 P.M.
Facilities: picnic tables
Contact: Monterey Parks Department, 831/755-4895

28 DEL MONTE BEACH

Location: Park Avenue at Del Monte Boulevard near Wharf #2 in Monterey
Parking/Fees: limited free street parking
Hours: 6 A.M.-10 P.M.
Facilities: restrooms
Contact: Monterey Parks Department, 831/649-2836

29 WINDOWS ON THE BAY

Location: north side of Wharf #2 off Del Monte Boulevard in Monterey
Parking/Fees: limited free street parking
Hours: 9 A.M.-half hour after sunset
Facilities: restrooms
Contact: Monterey State Beach, 831/649-2836

30 BEACH WAY ACCESS

Location: end of Beach Way, off Del Monte Boulevard, in Monterey
Parking/Fees: free parking lot
Hours: 9 A.M.-half hour after sunset
Facilities: none
Contact: Monterey State Beach, 831/649-2836

31 SAND DUNES DRIVE

Location: south of Monterey Beach Hotel, at the end of Sand Dunes Drive off Highway 1, in Seaside
Parking/Fees: free parking lot
Hours: 9 A.M.-half hour after sunset
Facilities: restrooms
Contact: Monterey State Beach, 831/649-2836

RECREATION AND ATTRACTIONS

- **Bike/Skate Rentals:** Adventures by the Sea, 299 Cannery Row, Monterey, 831/372-1807
- **Boat Cruise:** Baywatch Cruises, 437 Figueroa Street, Monterey, 831/372-7151
- **Dive Shop:** Aquarius Dive Shop, 2040 Del Monte Avenue, Monterey, 831/375-1933, and 32 Cannery Row, Monterey, 831/375-6605
- **Ecotourism:** Chris' Whale Watching Tours, Fisherman's Wharf, Monterey, 831/375-5951
- **Lighthouse:** Point Pinos Lighthouse, 165 Forest Avenue, Pacific Grove, 831/648-5716
- **Marina:** Monterey Marina, foot of Figueroa Street, Monterey, 831/646-3950
- **Rainy Day Attraction:** Monterey Bay Aquarium, 886 Cannery Row, Monterey, 831/648-4800
- **Shopping/Browsing:** Carmel Village, Carmel Business Association, Carmel, 831/624-2522
- **Surf Shop:** On the Beach Surf Shop, 693 Lighthouse Avenue, Monterey, 831/646-9283
- **Vacation Rentals:** San Carlos Agency, Inc., 26358 Carmel Rancho Lane, Carmel, 831/624-3846

ACCOMMODATIONS

More than any other town on the peninsula, Monterey has welcomed large corporate hotels to set up shop. In fact, the former Doubletree Hotel, now the **Portola Hotel and Spa at Monterey Bay** (2 Portola Plaza, 866/711-1534, $$$$), the **Monterey Marriott** (350 Calle Principal, 831/649-4234, $$$$), and the **Hyatt Regency Monterey Resort & Spa** (1 Old Golf Course Road, 831/372-1234, $$$$) have been accused of undermining the town's essential character. We'd agree that they've done nothing for Monterey but fatten the tax base. But to be fair, Monterey attracts tourists in sufficient numbers that these hotels' presence isn't exactly the obscenity it would be in Carmel or Pacific Grove. This is a convention and tourist town, after all.

By far the best of the larger non-franchised luxury hotels is **Hotel Pacific** (300 Pacific Street, 831/373-5700, $$$$), which blends in nicely with its neighborhood and is within easy walking distance of many attractions. Done up in peach tones, the Hotel Pacific has mastered the art of relaxed opulence. The architecture reflects the California mission style that is Monterey's architectural heritage. Even the layout is like that of a mission, with a series of discrete buildings constructed around four courtyards and linked with terra-cotta-tiled pathways that pass beneath archways and beside adobe gardens.

The accommodations feel less like a hotel room than a real, open living space. Floors are either hardwood or adobe tiled. The second-floor library, where the hotel serves continental breakfast in the morning and wine and cheese in the afternoon, contains a better selection of true literature (as opposed to best-selling dreck) than we've ever seen at a hotel or inn. An outdoor hot tub is hidden off to the side on an upper-floor landing.

The town of Monterey itself spreads out on all sides, begging to be strolled. Yes, you pay for such convenience and elegance ($279–419 per night). But the Hotel Pacific, unlike some of its high-priced neighbors, exudes genuine warmth and personality. It is the only place we've stayed where, in addition to the standard Gideon's Bible, a copy of *The Teachings of Buddha* had been placed in the nightstand.

The most enjoyable bed-and-breakfast in town is the **Old Monterey Inn** (500 Martin Street, 831/375-8284, $$$$). Parental discretion is advised because this is a couples' getaway. Built as a private residence in 1929, it is set amid beautiful gardens of roses, begonias, ferns, and rhododendrons and a forest of giant California live oaks. It is an English country cottage whose 10 unique rooms have been given evocative, offbeat names (such as "Serengeti" and "Tattershall").

The proprietors, Ann and Gene Swett, are delightful hosts who make you feel that this is not just their home (as it has been for 30 years) but yours as well. When we arrived, we asked, "Where's the office?" Gene paused, reflected, smiled, and threw his arms out as he announced, "There is no office here." We immediately loved the place. Room rates include an elaborate home-cooked breakfast and a spread of wine and cheese in the afternoon. The Swetts know the area intimately, and their inn has won numerous awards.

The best beachfront hotel—indeed, the only place to stay on a sand beach in Monterey—is the **Best Western Monterey Beach Hotel** (2600 Sand Dunes Drive, 831/394-3321, $$). It is a banquet-sized lodge nestled among the healthy dunes beside Monterey State Beach, a formidable stretch of sand that extends north of here. The hotel was built in 1969, before the California Coastal Commission began automatically nixing such projects. As such it is an anomaly: a real beach hotel. It surely could not be built so close to the water in this day and age. Garden- and ocean-view rooms are available. Downtown Monterey is about two miles away. Waves crash with particular vigor here—all the better for lulling you to sleep at night.

Monterey Bay Inn (242 Cannery Row, 831/373-6242, $$$) is a pleasant, low-key lodge at the north end of Cannery Row. It nestles atop a rocky fold of land overlooking San Carlos Beach Park. From our balcony we could watch sea otters frolicking in the shallows, birds flitting among the rocks, and divers plumbing the endlessly fascinating visual feast. The inn provides binoculars in each room (a nice, novel touch), free continental breakfast, hot tub and sauna, and safe parking space in a ground-level garage. It is very conveniently located. You're right on Cannery Row, and Fisherman's Wharf is only a ten-minute stroll up the bike path from the inn.

Of course there are scads more hotels and motels and inns all over Monterey. We've written about some of our favorites; if you would like a more extensive listing, contact the chamber of commerce and request a *Monterey Peninsula Hotel & Motel Guide.*

Incidentally, a flock of budget motels can be found in the vicinity of Seaside and Marina, the low-end burgs that lie along Highway 1 north of Monterey. None are as inviting or as economical as they would have you believe. Mostly, they're a shabby row of generics held together by spackling compound. They do good business only when hotels and motels fill up to capacity in the more desirable communities around the peninsula.

COASTAL CUISINE

In years past Monterey did not have a dining scene worthy of its history as an international trading center. Mostly, it was run-of-the-mill fried fish, calamari strips, and "world-famous clam chowder" so pasty and thick a spoon would stand up in it. That all-you-can-eat mentality has magically transformed in recent years. The most telling sign can be witnessed on Old Fisherman's Wharf—that former dead zone for hunger pangs—where you can now get a decent, well-prepared meal.

Of course, some folks who have a reflexive aversion to places that tourists throng will avoid Fisherman's Wharf on principle, no matter how good the food. But don't let that deter you from visiting. You may not have the meal of a lifetime, but you will likely leave happy.

The dish of choice for tourists still seems to be that horrid chowder, served in hollowed-out "bowls" of Italian bread. Nonetheless, we did quite well for ourselves, stumbling on **Liberty Fish Company** (43 Fisherman's Wharf, 831/375-5468, $$), where the salmon smoking on the grill looked too good to pass up. It was excellent, perfectly singed and flavored, and served with a fresh salad. The marinated octopus salad was good, too.

A few steps down the wharf is **Cafe Fina** (47 Fisherman's Wharf, 831/372-5200, $$), which is one step up in cuisine. The service surprised us with its quality, as did the house specialty, pasta Fina, a healthy and hearty plateful of shrimp over linguine.

Domenico's (50 Fisherman's Wharf, 831/372-3655, $$$) is an Italian classic of long standing on the wharf. Seafood and pasta, often in combination, are the primary entrées. Grilled sea bass, Dungeness crab, Monterey Bay prawns—you really can't go wrong.

At **Gilbert's Red Snapper** (30 Fisherman's Wharf, 831/375-3113, $$$), the seafood comes reasonably priced and well-prepared—especially the namesake red snapper ($12.95), which is grilled, and that Central Coast staple, fish 'n' chips ($10.95).

Rappa's End of the Wharf (101 Fisherman's Wharf, 831/372-7562, $$$$) has been around since 1932. In addition to excellent seafood (pan-fried sand dabs, blackened red snapper, flame-broiled salmon, all local), the tableside views of the bay are great, and there's a free observation deck for those just passing through.

Elsewhere around Monterey, the cuisine has blossomed into a world-class act. The two most interesting we've found—though there are many others—are **Fresh Cream** (99 Pacific Street, Heritage Harbor, 831/375-9798, $$$) and **Tarpy's Roadhouse** (2999 Highway 68, 831/647-1444, $$$). Fresh Cream serves French cuisine with a California touch (e.g., sautéed salmon with an artichoke puree), and it overlooks Monterey Bay, making it the most romantic dining spot in town. Chef Gregory Lizza has established a peerless reputation and has earned every possible accolade. Entrées are always inventive, and the restaurant begs repeated visits to properly sample such memorable preparations as sautéed halibut with sweet onion sauce, cabernet reduction, and infused oil, and pan-seared ahi tuna with pineapple rum sauce.

Tarpy's Roadhouse serves up hearty American fare a few miles outside of town, on the road toward Salinas. Executive chef Michael Kimmel describes his culinary approach as "Californian American country cuisine," which fortunately does not exclude seafood. In keeping with the setting, the menu choices are "from the ranch" (duck, beef, chicken) and "from the sea" (salmon, prawns, and two weekly catches). A recurring item on Tarpy's seafood menu is herb-crusted salmon with tomato-cucumber relish and lemon butter.

During our visit, the Dungeness crab cake and oak-grilled eggplant appetizers sent our taste buds soaring. The oak-grilled ribs and bourbon-molasses pork chop are house specialties, but you're safe ordering any of the filling fare served here. There's even a meatloaf unlike any you've ever tasted; it's served with marsala-mushroom gravy on roasted-garlic whipped potatoes. The stone-house setting is as original as the eclectic art that lines the walls. The restaurant, incidentally, was named for Matt Tarpy, a local landowner from the 1800s who died protecting his property.

A favorite of locals is **Flavors Cafe & Grill** (807 Cannery Row, 831/646-8488), on Cannery Row. It's inexpensive and nonfranchised. Another well-kept secret beloved by locals is the **Trailside Cafe** (500 Wave Street, 831/649-8600, $), which is accessible only from the Monterey Bay Recreational Trail. It's a great spot for lunch or a cup of coffee, and you can eat inside or out.

We always take a meal at **Gianni's Pizza** (725 Lighthouse Avenue, 831/649-1500, $). The best way to find this institution is to follow your nose a few blocks up the hill from the dining dregs of Cannery Row. Family-owned since 1974, Gianni's smells of homemade pasta, rich sauce, and fresh, oven-baked goods. While waiting for your pizza, try the homemade garlic and cheese breadsticks—two or three of these will set you right! Gianni's is a family-style place in the very best sense, and if you need a break from seafood and/or expensive menus, come here.

NIGHTLIFE

Monterey will always hold a special place in the hearts of rock 'n' roll fans. The first true rock festival took place here in 1967, two years before Woodstock. It was immortalized in D. A. Pennebaker's documentary *Monterey Pop*. Eric Burdon wrote a hit song about the event ("Monterey"), extolling the virtues of Flower Power. But the Monterey Pop Festival was a one-shot deal. It was the bastard son of the Monterey Jazz Festival, which is still held here each September at the Monterey Fairgrounds, a 24-acre field surrounded by oak trees. Blues fans gather for their own festival each June as well.

As for ongoing nightlife, Monterey holds the flickering candle for the entire peninsula. Those who just want to sip a variety of suds should head to **Peter B's** (2 Portola Plaza, 831/649-4511), a microbrewery featuring six tasters for one flat fee. Another option is "barking seal karaoke"; feel free to investigate.

The closing of Fort Ord—former home to thousands of restless military weekend party animals—has toned down the wildest excesses of Monterey's club scene. The two viable venues for live rock and roll are **Doc's** (95 Prescott Street, 831/649-4241) and **The Planet Ultra Lounge** (2110 North Fremont Street, 831/373-1449). Doc's, known for years as Doc Ricketts' Lab, is in the bottom of what was once the marine-life collecting lab of Doc Ricketts himself, the main character in John Steinbeck's *Cannery Row*. Besides being one of the few Cannery Row structures that possesses a legitimate connection with Steinbeck's legacy, Doc's features rock bands on a regular basis. The happy specimens who dance here nightly are a testament to the rejuvenating power of live rock and roll. The Planet Ultra Lounge, formerly Planet Gemini, used to feature live rock and roll but has widened its stance to include country, comedy, and "Italian Night."

Sly McFly's Refueling Station (700 Cannery Row, 831/372-3225) also offers live entertainment most nights and a full menu. Sly has won "Best Blues Club" honors three years running—not that there's a slew of competition hereabouts for that particular niche. The area's most eclectic music venue (rock, blues, jazz, reggae) is the **Blue Fin Cafe & Billiards** (685 Cannery Row, 831/375-7000), a third floor club/restaurant/pool hall that serves a decent full menu of burgers, pasta, and seafood, and 22 types of beer. It also serves up a mixed bag of music, some live, some deejayed.

One night years earlier this decade we went to Planet Gemini. The entertainment was an Eagles tribute band from Reno, Nevada. Ordinarily we'd drop an anecdote as old as this account from a new edition, but this one is too amusing to omit. They were called Heartache Tonight (after one of the Eagles' songs), and they performed eerily accurate human-jukebox re-creations of the Eagles' old hits. Their performance was exacting, right down to their ten-gallon hats and the buzzard skulls and Old West totems that littered the stage. Some months later, one of us saw the Eagles perform on an overpriced, overhyped reunion tour. The upshot is that we paid a measly $3 cover to see Heartache Tonight play the Eagles' songs better than the Eagles did themselves for $100.

In downtown Monterey, we found a British-style pub, **Britannia Arms** (444 Alvarado Street, 831/656-9543), that proved to be a good spot to end a very long evening. It assuaged both our hunger pangs and our need to chill out after a full weekend of club-hopping. Decent music played at reasonable volume as we ordered mugs of black and tan and plates of fish 'n' chips. So authentic were the grog and grub that we almost felt compelled to speak in faux British accents. **The Crown & Anchor** (150 West Franklin Street, 831/649-6496) is another even more authentic British pub. Other popular downtown hangouts are **The Mucky Duck** (479 Alvarado Street, 831/655-3031), another British-themed pub; **Cibo** (301 Alvarado Street, 831/649-8151), an Italian restaurant and jazz bar renowned for its martinis; and **Viva Monterey** (414 Alvarado Street, 831/646-1415), a small but popular rock and roll club.

Monterey's nightlife is among the liveliest between Santa Barbara and Santa Cruz. With part of Fort Ord having been converted into a branch of the state university system, the town is hopping like never before. For an overview of Monterey's prolific club scene, pick up a copy of *Coast Weekly*, a free alternative paper distributed all over the peninsula.

Seaside

The town of Seaside straddles the coast between Monterey and Fort Ord like a fat flea sucking blood from its unwilling host. Believe it or not, Seaside (population 34,000) is actually larger that Monterey. In every other way, however, it is Monterey's inferior. The only reason a visitor would need to know about it is if there is no lodging to be found anywhere else on the Monterey Peninsula.

Full of one-star motels, fast-food stands, liquor stores, and a big-box retailer or two, Seaside looks like a Salvation Army warehouse for all the things that Monterey, Pacific Grove, and Carmel did not want.

For more information, contact the Seaside/Sand City Chamber of Commerce, 505 Broadway Avenue, Seaside, CA 93955, 831/394-6501, www.seaside-sandcity.com.

BEACHES

Units of **Monterey State Beach** are in Seaside, flanking each side of the Best Western Monterey Beach Hotel. It's part of the same wild, woolly, and windy beach that extends down from Marina, and you can't argue with the price—it's free.

32 MONTEREY STATE BEACH

Location: north of Monterey Beach Hotel off Highway 1 in Seaside
Parking/Fees: free parking lot
Hours: 9 A.M.-half hour after sunset
Facilities: restrooms
Contact: Marina State Beach, 831/384-7695

Sand City

News alert: The population of Sand City has doubled since the previous edition of this book. That is to say, this tiny community has jumped from 184 to 363 souls who inhabit its narrow strip of sand between Highway 1 and the ocean. Presumably, you have to really like sand to live in a place called Sand City.

For more information, contact the Seaside/Sand City Chamber of Commerce, 505 Broadway Avenue, Seaside, CA 93955, 831/394-6501, www.seaside-sandcity.com.

Marina

Marina is most notable for being home to Fort Ord, which lays claim to 28,500 acres of prime California coastland. Until 1993, when Defense Department budget cuts forced the phased closing of the base, the army infantry training center was home to thousands of service personnel and their families. It also encompassed two golf courses, shopping centers, housing developments, and miles of beaches.

Obviously, the departure of so many military personnel has taken a toll on the local economy. But tourism has picked up some of the slack.

It still has a ways to go on this count. The towns of Seaside and Marina, between which Fort Ord is sandwiched, are pretty shoddy, as is the military installation itself. But Fort Ord's decommissioning has, in some ways, turned out to be a blessing. In fact, the Monterey Peninsula might be better off in the long run. Another branch of the state university system—California State University, Monterey Bay—opened in 1995 on the site of the former army base. Fort Ord's 18-hole courses now belong to the town of Seaside. As for the four miles of beaches that belonged to the military, these are now part of Fort Ord Dunes State Park.

For more information, contact the Marina Chamber of Commerce, 3170 Vista del Camino, Marina, CA 93933, 831/384-9155, www.marinachamber.com.

BEACHES

With its golden-brown sand, gently rising dunes, and absence of jagged rocks along the shoreline, **Marina State Beach** is as close to

Marina State Beach

© PARKE PUTERBAUGH

WAITING FOR FORT ORD

Good news! **Fort Ord Dunes State Park** is open. Well, sort of. The park was slated to open in 1998. Ten years later, it began opening ever so slowly, like a reluctant abalone shell.

Let's backtrack a bit. In 1994, the population of the Monterey Peninsula shrank by tens of thousands when the Department of Defense closed Fort Ord, a U.S. Army base located between Seaside and Marina. The 28,500-acre military installation – a site roughly the size of San Francisco – was home to the 7th Infantry Division. The combined population of base personnel and family members topped 35,000, making Fort Ord the largest city on the peninsula. After decommissioning, the empty base commanded some of the most coveted real estate on the California coast, including four miles of coastline. An 885-acre chunk of this sandy bounty was slated to become Fort Ord Dunes State Park. Unfortunately, it took fifteen years for this to happen.

One reason for the delay is that Fort Ord was a toxic waste dump. Throughout Fort Ord – which was an infantry training base and battle simulation center – ominous portents of contamination included razor fencing, concrete roadblocks, barbed wire, and countless Restricted Area signs. There were grim warnings about unexploded bombs, rockets, mortar shells, grenades, and bullets, as well as chemical spills. The military housing is off-limits, too, and probably beyond rehabilitation because of lead-based paint and asbestos used in its construction. Much of the housing is still boarded up, awaiting environmental remediation before it can be razed.

Fort Ord is home to 4,000 college students at California State University, Monterey Bay (CSUMB). The University of California Santa Cruz was itself given 1,100 acres of the property, which they plan to use for a research center. Monterey Peninsula College is building an emergency training facility on the base for the future homeland-security police state in the making. Most of the rest of the development on the Fort Ord campus is, in the words of one expert, "a typical California beach town revival, with hotels and single-family housing tracts winning out over innovative planning and affordable housing." Big plans had been touted, including the construction of a giant New Urbanism–style community. Instead, the towns of Seaside and Marina squandered most of the 5,200 acres of land they were given on housing subdivision and shopping centers – in other words, more suburban sprawl. Very disappointing.

But back to Fort Ord Dunes State Park. For years, the park remained hung up with the state's budget crisis and therefore was not actually transferred in ownership from the federal government to the state. Finally and officially, Fort Ord Dunes State Park opened on March 3, 2009. The deed of transfer from the federal government went through, and now California has its newest state park, complete with four-mile coastline, boardwalk, and bluff-top viewing platform.

the look of a Southern California beach as you'll find along Monterey Bay. During the summer, when temperatures hover around 100 degrees in the valleys and deserts to the east, Marina State Beach is packed with sunbathers.

The surf here is too rough for swimming, and the wind whips ferociously at times, explaining the hang-glider ramp that sits atop a big brown whale of a dune at the beach's center. A 2,000-foot boardwalk leads across the dunes to the beach. It is a compelling place to stroll and learn about dune vegetation; accompanying charts explain the "good" (sand verbena, primrose, sagewort, lizard tail) and the "bad" (Hottentot fig, European dune grass) vegetation. Most items on the "bad" list are exotic species that were introduced for purposes of dune stabilization but overran the place, altering native ecosystems.

33 MARINA STATE BEACH

Location: end of Reservation Road in Marina
Parking/Fees: free parking lot
Hours: 8 A.M.-half hour after sunset
Facilities: restrooms
Contact: Marina State Beach, 831/384-7695

34 FORT ORD DUNES STATE PARK

Location: from Highway 1 in Marina take the 12th Street Exit (from the north) or Light Fighter Drive Exit (from the south). Turn onto Divarty Street, then turn right on 1st Avenue and follow signs into park.
Parking/Fees: free parking lot
Hours: 8 A.M.-half hour after sunset
Facilities: restrooms
Contact: Fort Ord Dunes State Park, 831/384-7695

Castroville

Castroville lies a whisper to the east of the beach. It's not on the coast per se, but it's close enough to merit mention. Besides, we're fond of artichokes, and Castroville (population 6,724) is the artichoke heart of America.

"What we do here in Castroville is grow artichokes," is how a local chamber of commerce representative plainly put it to us.

The entire town marches to the beat of a different vegetable. They are completely devoted to the 'choke, which is a tasty, if unusual, vegetable. (Actually, it's a flower.) Between Monterey and Half Moon Bay, we've enjoyed many a Castroville artichoke, dunking them in mayonnaise, butter, or vinaigrette.

If you're in Castroville, you should stop and eat artichokes. The main house of artichoke worship is the **Giant Artichoke** (11261 Merritt Street, 831/633-3501, $$). The cooks do everything that can be done to an artichoke. They serve it fried with garlic mayonnaise, steamed with butter, boiled into artichoke soup, placed atop beef patties with Monterey Jack cheese (the Castroville Burger), and baked into quiches. If you're a serious chokehead, the Artichoke Sampler is the only way to go. But don't pass up the seafood entrées as well: calamari, snapper, you name it. And by all means buy a Giant Artichoke T-shirt and confound the folks back home.

The produce and seafood in the area couldn't be fresher. We whiled away part of an afternoon at local produce stands, savoring the sights and smells of just-picked vegetables bulging in the bins. We felt healthier just looking at them. Every year Castroville hosts the Artichoke Festival. Posters scattered around town urge support for various candidates for the title of Artichoke Queen. Don't laugh. Would you believe that Marilyn Monroe won the title of Artichoke Queen back in 1947?

For more information, contact the Castroville Chamber of Commerce, 10683 Merritt Street, Castroville, CA 95012, 831/633-2465, www.northmontereycounty.org.

SALINAS: A SIDE TRIP TO STEINBECK COUNTRY

Though Salinas is not on the ocean, it makes a great day trip for visitors to the Monterey Peninsula, primarily because it was the hometown of John Steinbeck, perhaps best known for the time he spent along Cannery Row. The half-hour drive east on Highway 68 cuts through massive agricultural tracts and enters this pleasantly cluttered "cow town" at the heart of fertile Salinas Valley. The setting of many of Steinbeck's novels – including *East of Eden* and *Tortilla Flat* – Salinas is an authentic slice of Western life that has grown into a sizable city but has changed relatively little in atmosphere from the days when the author lived there.

The best place to start is the **National Steinbeck Center** (1 Main Street, 831/796-3833), a state-of-the-art museum devoted to the life of one of our greatest writers. In addition to having the definitive collection of Steinbeck artifacts, exhibits on his life, and guides to walking and driving tours of Salinas, the center has artifacts from the master's life. For example, his camper, "Rocinante" (featured in one of our favorite road books, *Travels with Charley*), is on permanent display, as are stage settings that bring the other books to life. The museum is open 10 A.M.–5 P.M. daily; admission is $10.95 for adults, $7.95 for children ages 13-17, and $5.95 for those ages 6-12. These prices were inflated for the Steinbeck centenary in 2002 and have continued to inexplicably climb since.

Not far away is the **John Steinbeck House** (132 Central Avenue, 831/424-2735), the Victorian-era home dating from 1897 where Steinbeck was born (in 1902) and raised. In addition to the preserved shrine (entrance is $4 for adults, $2 for kids), a dandy little restaurant is on the premises. There are two seatings for lunch, at 11:45 A.M. and 1:15 P.M.; call ahead for reservations.

Serious Steinbeck scholars will want to visit the **John Steinbeck Library** (350 Lincoln Avenue, 831/758-7311), a full-fledged public library with the author's archives housed in a separate wing. These include books, manuscripts, tapes, correspondence, clippings, and photographs. The library is open Monday–Saturday, and the archives can be viewed by reservation only.

To celebrate its native son, Salinas holds an annual **Steinbeck Festival** during the first week of August. It includes lectures, films, tours, panel discussions, and live dramatizations of his work. Another wildly popular event in Salinas is the **California Rodeo,** held the third week in July. One of the nation's largest and most celebrated, the rodeo packs the peninsula every year.

Finally, for lovers of roadside oddities, check out the sculpture on the lawn of the **Salinas Community Center** (940 North Main Street). Created by Claes Oldenburg and entitled *Hat in Three Stages of Landing*, it features three cowboy hats, each weighing 3,500 pounds.

For more information on Salinas, contact the **Salinas Valley Chamber of Commerce,** 119 East Alisal Street, P.O. Box 1170, Salinas, CA 93902, 831/424-7611, www.salinaschamber.com.

BIG SUR AND MONTEREY

Moss Landing

There's not much to Moss Landing, a harbor-front community of about 800 in northern-most Monterey County. It is quickly passed through, unless you're hunting for beaches. Three state beaches—Salinas River, Moss Landing, and Zmudowski—lie within striking distance. So does Elkhorn Slough, which stretches seven miles inland, harboring a variety of wildlife.

Visitors can tour Elkhorn Slough via guided sea-kayak trips and marine-biologist-led pontoon-boat tours ($32 for adults, $24 for kids 13 and under). You'll see harbor seals, sea otters, shore birds, and more. Contact **Elkhorn Slough Safari** (831/633-5555) for information and reservations. Moss Landing also has a safe, T-shaped harbor that's used by pleasure boaters.

For more information, contact the Moss Landing Chamber of Commerce, 8071 Moss Landing Road, P.O. Box 425, Moss Landing, CA 95039, 831/633-4501, www.mosslanding chamber.com.

BEACHES

Just south of Moss Landing, beach mavens will find **Salinas River State Beach.** It is a haunting, windswept location that is fairly inhospitable unless you come dressed and prepared for it. A wooden walkway leads from the parking lot to the beach. A sign warns, Swimming and Wading Unsafe, and the heavy chop on the water does look daunting.

The beach is broad and sandy, with steep dunes. On one visit we saw a few intrepid anglers braving gale-force winds while a sailboat seemed on the verge of capsizing. All we saw on a return visit several years later was a shivering group of migrant workers and a clump of college coeds who were dancing in gale-force winds. The former were drinking and the latter grooving to the music on their boombox.

The 518-acre Salinas River Wildlife Refuge adjoins the beach to the south. Though Salinas River State Beach occupies a very rural setting, the smokestacks of a nearby power plant are visible.

Next up is **Moss Landing State Beach,** which offers access to Elkhorn Slough, rewarding nature lovers with a close look at coastal wetlands. The beach itself is broad and windswept, the surf rough and dangerous, the view (onto power-plant smokestacks) not the best. But Elkhorn Slough is not to be missed.

The sign pointing the way to **Zmudowski State Beach,** the last beach in Monterey County, lies a few miles north of Moss Landing. Be forewarned: When you make the turn-off from Highway 1, you're still quite a ways from the water. The road to Zmudowski skirts fields of artichokes and Brussels sprouts. On the beach a sign warns, Danger: Intermittent Waves of Unusual Size and Force. That is in addition to blasts of wind of unusual size and force.

Zmudowski, like Moss Landing State Beach, is a good place for clamming and surfing. If you come to picnic, you'll run the risk of getting sandblasted silly. For your average beachgoer, Zmudowski really isn't worth the effort it takes to get here. Though, of course, we're always grateful for the gesture of beach access wherever it is provided.

35 SALINAS RIVER STATE BEACH

Location: Portrero Road at Highway 1, one mile south of Moss Landing
Parking/Fees: free parking lot
Hours: 8 A.M.-half hour after sunset
Facilities: restrooms
Contact: Marina State Beach, 831/649-2836

36 MOSS LANDING STATE BEACH

Location: Jetty Road at Highway 1, north of Moss Landing Harbor, in Moss Landing
Parking/Fees: $2 entrance fee per vehicle
Hours: 6:30 A.M.-half hour after sunset
Facilities: restrooms
Contact: Marina State Beach, 831/649-2836

37 ZMUDOWSKI STATE BEACH

Location: end of Geiberson Road north of Moss Landing; follow signs from Highway 1 to beach
Parking/Fees: free parking lot
Hours: 8 A.M.-half hour after sunset
Facilities: restrooms
Contact: Marina State Beach, 831/649-2836

COASTAL CUISINE

The hot spot for seafood in Moss Landing is **Phil's Fish Market and Eatery** (7600 Sandholdt Road, 831/633-2152, $$$). You can get charbroiled salmon, shark, ahi, albacore, halibut, and more, or grilled snapper, sole, sand dabs, and squid steak. The "lazyman's cioppino" is justly famous, as are the clam chowders.

Specialties at **Moss Landing Deli Cafe** (421 Moss Landing Road, 831/633-3355, $$) include squid and eggs, crab cakes, and deep-fried artichokes. Don't leave town without trying the oysters and prawns, served with homemade sauces, at **Moss Landing Oyster Bay** (413 Moss Landing Road, 831/632-0119, $$). Prices are fair, portions are large, and the ambience is local. The restaurant serves some of the best seafood in Monterey County, and the crab sandwiches (made with Dungeness crab) are a total treat.

BIG SUR AND MONTEREY

SANTA CRUZ COAST

The coastline in and around Santa Cruz varies from upscale villages in the south to the vastness and isolation at the north end of the county. Santa Cruz itself is a boardwalk town, with an amusement park right beside its main beach. In that respect is the closest thing to the New Jersey shore in the state of California. In all other respects, Santa Cruz is a world apart. The University of California at Santa Cruz (UC Santa Cruz, for short) sets the tone of defiant unconventionality. Alternative lifestyles rule here, although there's been something of a tug of war for the soul of Santa Cruz with all of the Silicon Valley millionaires who have sent real estate prices soaring (and dreadlocked neo-hippies packing). Santa Cruz and environs also serve as a coastal playpen for the populated cities of the Santa Clara Valley, including San Jose, located up and over the Santa Cruz Mountains.

Even so, the city of Santa Cruz remains one of the most liberated places on the planet, in terms of lifestyles. It's the urban equivalent of one of those "mystery spot" tourist traps where gravity supposedly doesn't behave the way it does elsewhere. (Perhaps not coincidentally, there is a mystery spot three miles north of town.) Cut off from the rest of the world by geography, Santa Cruz has evolved a distinct character of its own—one in which the alternative has become mainstream.

The shapes and sizes of the numerous beaches in Santa Cruz and throughout Santa Cruz County vary as widely as the people who populate them. There exists everything from tiny coves that only privileged handfuls know about to broad, sandy expanses where hard-fought volleyball games get played while surfers compete for wave-riding privileges.

For beachy symbolism you can't beat this fact: The first east–west road encountered in southern Santa Cruz County is called Beach

© PARKE PUTERBAUGH

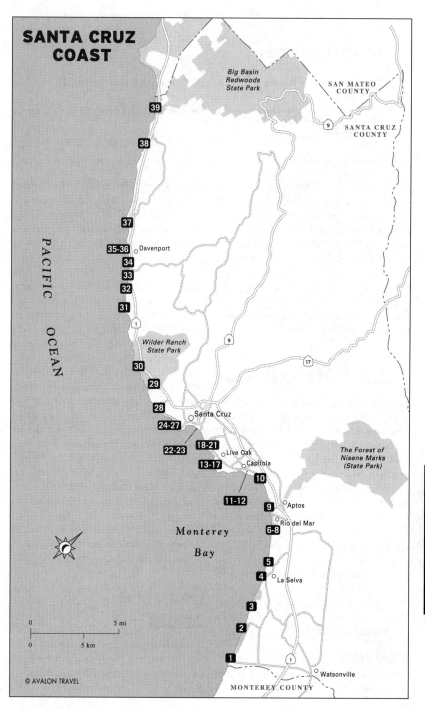

SANTA CRUZ
COAST

Big Basin
Redwoods
State Park

SAN MATEO
COUNTY

39

38

SANTA CRUZ
COUNTY

9

PACIFIC

OCEAN

37

35-36 ○ Davenport

34

33

32

31

1

Wilder Ranch
State Park

9

17

30

29

28

24-27 ○ Santa Cruz

18-21

22-23   ○ Live Oak

13-17   ○ Capitola

The Forest of
Nisene Marks
(State Park)

10

11-12

9 ○ Aptos

6-8 ○ Rio del Mar

Monterey

Bay

5

4 ○ La Selva

3

0   5 mi

2

0   5 km

1

○ Watsonville

© AVALON TRAVEL

MONTEREY COUNTY

BEST BEACHES

(Seacliff State Beach, page 356

(New Brighton State Beach, page 357

(Seabright Beach, page 371

(Bonny Doon Beach, page 377

Road, and it leads to Palm Beach. The beach due north of it is called Sunset Beach. Santa Cruz County is something of a throwback to the beachy look and mindset of Southern California. You start seeing things like rowdy dive bars, a surfer's shrine and museum, a seaside amusement park, and people of all ages wearing anything from tentlike bathing suits to daring two-pieces to nothing at all. Yes, naturism is rampant, especially on the remote beaches north of Santa Cruz.

Sunset State Beach

Santa Cruz County is a wonderland of unspoiled beaches in jaw-dropping settings. Some are confined to coves, while others run for great distances along a regular shoreline. Beaches are pressed against staggering backdrops that include sheer cliff faces and steep, vegetated dunes.

From the county's south end, the party starts with Palm Beach, a subunit of Sunset State Beach. Palm Beach borders the Pajaro River Bike Path, a nine-mile route that runs along the watercourse that divides Santa Cruz and Monterey counties. Close by is Pajaro Dunes, a development of condos and homes too near this unspoiled beach for our liking.

For more information, contact Sunset State Beach, 201 Sunset Beach Road, Watsonville, CA 95076, 831/763-7062, www.parks.ca.gov.

BEACHES

Getting to Palm Beach requires a bit of time and patience. Taking the Beach Road turnoff from Highway 1, you'll traverse five miles of bumpy back roads that pass farmers' fields. **Palm Beach** is well off the beaten track and offers two completely different settings separated by a whale of a dune ridge. The first is a grove of eucalyptus trees whose limbs provide a fragrant canopy for a scattering of picnic tables. It is a calm, shaded environment protected from stiff winds by high, humpbacked dunes. Cross the dunes and it's a different scene: warm sun, wide sandy beaches, and breakers rolling ashore in perfect sets, urged along by seemingly ceaseless breezes.

Up the road lies the main entrance to **Sunset State Beach.** It has more facilities—paved parking lots, covered picnic tables, and developed campsites. A cliff-hugging road zigzags down to the campground and the beach. Cultivated fields border the park. Monstrous silver drift logs have washed ashore. Whether you're looking down at the beach from the vantage point of the bluffs or up from the water's edge, Sunset State Beach offers breathtaking scenery. It's lifeguarded and popular with day visitors and overnight campers alike. The surf, alas, is hazardous, but that doesn't deter crowds from frolicking on the ample strand.

1 PALM BEACH

Location: from Highway 1 in Watsonville, follow Beach Road five miles west to the beach
Parking/Fees: $8 entrance fee per vehicle
Hours: 7 A.M.-half hour after sunset

© PARKE PUTERBAUGH

Sunset State Beach

Facilities: restrooms and picnic area
Contact: Sunset State Beach, 831/763-7063

2 SUNSET STATE BEACH

Location: from Highway 1 in Watsonville, turn
west onto Sunset Beach Road and follow it to
the beach
Parking/Fees: $8 entrance fee per vehicle;
camping fee $25 per night, plus $7.50
reservation fee
Hours: 7 A.M.-half hour after sunset
Facilities: lifeguards, restrooms, showers, and
picnic tables
Contact: Sunset State Beach, 831/763-7063

La Selva

A little community that's snug as the proverbial
bug in a rug nestles off Highway 1 between the
wilds of southern Santa Cruz County and the
reappearance of civilization in Aptos. La Selva
boasts its own public library and surf shop. You
may see (as we did) handwritten signs urging you
to slow down. You can't get to the beach directly
from town, but a bluff-top park offers a spectacular coastal overlook. We watched a group of
horses and riders gallop around free as the breeze
on the wide, sandy, private expanse below.

For more information, contact the Santa Cruz
County Conference and Visitors Council, 701
Front Street, Santa Cruz, CA 95060, 831/425-
1234 or 800/833-3494, www.santacruzca.org.

BEACHES

Manresa State Beach is a dual-access park.
The **Manresa Uplands** unit offers walk-in
tent camping in a scrub-and-shrub setting
and beach access from a smallish parking lot.
Stretch those calf muscles before sallying forth,
because 170 steps lead down the stairs to the
beach. Crumbly, light brown sandstone bluffs
loom behind the beach. The main entrance to
Manresa is more accessible—a mere 55 steps
down to the beach. Lots of youthful folks
surf and sunbathe and giggle and chatter in
the sand.

Next up is private La Selva Beach, and
above it is **Lundborgh Beach,** which lies in

front of a train trestle. It is public, but you can get to it only by walking north from Manresa State Beach, being careful while crossing La Selva Beach, lest you rile the locals who own the property.

3 MANRESA UPLANDS

Location: end of Sand Dollar Drive, off San Andreas Road, in La Selva
Parking/Fees: $6 entrance fee per vehicle; camping fee $25 per night, plus $7.50 reservation fee
Hours: 7 A.M.-half hour after sunset
Facilities: restrooms, picnic tables, and showers
Contact: Manresa Uplands State Beach, 831/761-1795

4 MANRESA STATE BEACH

Location: end of Manresa Beach Road, off San Andreas Road, in La Selva
Parking/Fees: $8 entrance fee per vehicle

Hours: 7 A.M.-half hour after sunset
Facilities: lifeguards and restrooms
Contact: Manresa State Beach, 831/761-1795

5 LUNDBORGH BEACH (A.K.A. TRESTLE BEACH)

Location: park at Manresa State Beach, off San Andreas Road, in La Selva, and walk north
Parking/Fees: none
Hours: sunrise-sunset
Facilities: none
Contact: none

Aptos

Eight miles south of Santa Cruz, Aptos is a study in contradictions. It's a charming, quiet village, and a bustling, harried town (population 9,500). It's a friendly place but one whose inhabitants can display flashes of temper when something gets in their way. Shortly upon arriving in Aptos one afternoon, we butted heads with an unhelpful clerk at

Manresa State Beach

the local post office who turned surly and confrontational when we asked for a piece of tape to seal a box we'd just bought. Then we encountered an impatient driver who leaned on his horn and flashed the lights of his imported gas-guzzler because we apparently interfered with his God-given right to exceed the speed limit on Highway 1. Now, these were random encounters and we're familiar enough with statistics to know that two events do not define an entire community. But, still, we felt something in the air here... call it angst.

Nerves jangled by our brief foray into the part of Aptos that lies east of Highway 1—the part where all the strip malls are—we rolled down Rio Del Mar Boulevard's long incline, which deposited us on Rio Del Mar Beach. This side of Aptos is just what the doctor ordered—a flat, open beach; pretty neighborhoods tucked into green, vine-covered hills; and a handful of motels and restaurants within view of the water. But even here, shortly after finding our way onto the sand, we were startled to witness a punk punching down a plastic barrier meant to keep cars off the beach while his pals yahooed and cheered.

For more information, contact the Aptos Chamber of Commerce, 7605-A Old Dominion Court, Aptos, CA 95003, 831/688-1467, www.aptoschamber.com.

BEACHES

Rio Del Mar Beach is the center of the action in Aptos. Located at the end of Rio Del Mar Boulevard, the sand is so wide you'll work your calf muscles into oxygen deficit traipsing across it to the water's edge. If you wish to escape the summer crowds, a turn from Rio Del Mar Boulevard onto Summer Avenue or Townshend Drive will lead to **Seascape Park** and **Hidden Beach**, respectively. These two county parks plopped among residential developments merit the names "Hidden" and "Seascape." Parking is minimal—20 spaces at Seascape and eight at Hidden Beach—but if you can snag a spot, you'll be rewarded with

access to the less visited side of Aptos' lengthy strand. Both parks also have playgrounds and picnic tables.

Lying a short, hikeable distance above Rio Del Mar Beach is **Seacliff State Beach.** This is the site of a real curiosity: the *Palo Alto*, an old World War I supply boat that never saw active duty and now serves as an extension of the fishing pier. Towed here in 1929, it was a kind of pleasure palace—dining, dancing, what have you—before going financially bust two years later and then literally breaking up in a storm. Lashed to the end of the fishing pier, it's open to visitors, who can mount a few rusty steps onto its deck and toss a line into the water or just poke around.

Seacliff is heavily used by anglers, picnickers, and campers. Commercial facilities include a bait-and-tackle shop and snack bar that dispenses homemade sandwiches. The beach is reached by a steep, winding road. It has 26 choice campsites with full trailer hookups right by the water, and you'd better believe they are rarely vacant. A bike path links Rio Del Mar and Seacliff State Beach.

6 HIDDEN BEACH

Location: from Rio Del Mar Boulevard in Aptos, turn left on Townshend Drive, left on Cliff Drive, follow it to park
Parking/Fees: none
Hours: sunrise-sunset
Facilities: restrooms and picnic tables
Contact: Santa Cruz County Parks Department, 831/454-7901

7 SEASCAPE PARK

Location: from Rio Del Mar Boulevard in Aptos, turn left on Sumner Avenue and follow to beach
Parking/Fees: free parking lot
Hours: sunrise-sunset
Facilities: restrooms and picnic tables

Contact: Santa Cruz County Parks Department, 831/454-7901

8 RIO DEL MAR BEACH

Location: end of Rio Del Mar Boulevard in Aptos
Parking/Fees: $6 entrance fee per vehicle
Hours: sunrise-10 P.M.
Facilities: restrooms and showers
Contact: Seacliff State Beach, 831/685-6442

9 SEACLIFF STATE BEACH

 BEST (

Location: end of State Park Drive, off Highway 1, in Aptos
Parking/Fees: $8 entrance fee per vehicle; camping fee $25 per night, plus $7.50 reservation fee
Hours: sunrise-10 P.M.
Facilities: concession, lifeguards, restrooms, showers, and picnic tables
Contact: Seacliff State Beach, 831/685-6442

ACCOMMODATIONS

Beach lovers flock to the **Rio Sands Motel** (116 Aptos Beach Drive, 831/688-3207 or 800/826-2077, $$), which takes pride in being "100 steps to the beach." Give or take a few footfalls, that seems accurate. An unusually comfortable motel, the Rio Sands is on a quiet side street. Some rooms are actually suites with small kitchens, comfy bedrooms, and living area with couch, TV, and balcony. An outdoor spa nestles in a peaceful courtyard garden. All that for only $119–159 a night in season qualifies as a bargain on the California coast. They even post lower-priced "specials" on their website from time to time.

The **Seascape Resort** (1 Seascape Resort Drive, 831/688-6800, $$$$) perches on bluffs overlooking the ocean. As if the setting weren't sufficient, the resort gilds the lily with golf, tennis, spa, and other ways to drop a bundle. "Gild" is the operative word, as the rates run $300–600 per night.

COASTAL CUISINE

For starters, Aptos has one of the finest restaurants in Santa Cruz County, the **Bittersweet Bistro** (787 Rio Del Mar Boulevard, 831/662-9799, $$$$). The look is casual elegance, the style is American bistro with Mediterranean influences, and the sauces and presentation are exquisite. Freshly caught seafood and organic local produce are highlighted.

You can't get any closer to the ocean than **Cafe Rio** (131 Esplanade, 831/688-8917, $$$), a modern-looking wood-and-neon place that has good fresh seafood and is a stone's throw from the beach. Then there's **Cafe Sparrow** (8042 Soquel Drive, 831/688-6238, $$$), a cozy continental hideaway that offers grilled chicken, lamb, and veal dishes, and a solid wine list.

NIGHTLIFE

Most night moves are made in the direction of Capitola and Santa Cruz. Aptos maintains more of a village atmosphere than its noisy neighbors. Still, **Cafe Rio** (131 Esplanade, 831/688-8917) does have a nice bar and a semblance of life after dark.

New Brighton State Beach

Between Aptos and Capitola lies New Brighton State Beach, which is reachable via the Park Avenue exit off Highway 1. Signs point the way into a tree-shaded glen, beyond which lie high, grass-covered dunes and a flat, sandy beach.

For more information, contact New Brighton State Beach, 1500 Park Avenue, Capitola, CA 95010, 831/464-6330, www.parks.ca.gov.

BEACHES

Because **New Brighton State Beach** faces due south, it is spared the prevailing winds that mercilessly wrack other stretches of the Santa

Cruz coast. This area was originally known as China Cove or China Beach, from a time in the late 1800s when Asian fishermen dragged the water with fishing nets. Tall beach grasses and thick, scrubby vegetation hold the steep dunes in place.

At the foot of the dunes is a gravel road used by joggers, and hiking trails line the cliffs. New Brighton has a mile's worth of coastline, which is excellent for surf fishing and clamming. Behind the dunes, 112 developed campsites burrow beneath stands of pine and cypress.

10 NEW BRIGHTON STATE BEACH

 BEST (

Location: end of Park Avenue, off Highway 1, between Aptos and Capitola
Parking/Fees: $8 entrance fee per vehicle; camping fee $25 per night, plus $7.50 reservation fee
Hours: sunrise–10 P.M.
Facilities: concession, lifeguards, restrooms, showers, and picnic tables
Contact: New Brighton State Beach, 831/464-6330

Capitola

Many who work in Santa Cruz prefer to live in Capitola, Aptos, or Soquel, the upscale villages that lie just southeast of town. These seaside towns look like botanical gardens compared to parts of Santa Cruz. Capitola—or Capitola-by-the-Sea, to be accurate—is south of Highway 1 and east of 41st Avenue, a heavily trafficked road lined with shopping centers and gas stations. The easiest way to get to the heart of Capitola and its city beach is to take the Bay Avenue exit off Highway 1 and proceed south until you start smelling suntan lotion.

Capitola (population 9,500) is built around a broad, sandy cove. The Esplanade runs along the water, and Capitola Avenue parallels it for a few blocks. All the town's best shops, restaurants, and action can be found here. After a few laps around the shopping district, it becomes clear that Capitola is a mélange of well-to-do young professionals, coffee-drinking bookworm/artist types, and beach bums and bunnies who have driven down for the day from UC Santa Cruz, San Jose, and points further inland. Indeed, Capitola and Santa Cruz are the northernmost outposts of the classic California beach life.

There's only one snag when it comes to enjoying this cold-water Acapulco, and it's a big one: parking.

"Going to Capitola today?" a Santa Cruz merchant asked with raised eyebrows. "Good luck finding a parking space."

Prepare to drive in circles and then pounce like a wild cat when a car pulls away from a meter. Considerable gas is wasted by a wagon train of frustrated drivers playing musical parking spaces. There's a large, metered public lot on Capitola Avenue a few blocks from the beach behind City Hall, but that too fills quickly and you may find yourself driving in circles waiting for someone to leave. Moreover, the spaces are too narrow to fully accommodate today's wide-bodied SUVs.

If you're not up for an extended hunt for a parking space, miles of state beaches run from Capitola down to the Monterey County line. Incidentally, we had the thought that being a tow-truck driver in Capitola would make a lucrative occupation.

There used to be a lot more beach in Capitola than there is now. The beach profile changed with the construction of jetties at the Santa Cruz Small Craft Harbor in 1985. Due to alterations in the littoral current, Capitola's beaches washed away during the first winter following the harbor's arrival. Capitola City Beach was subsequently restored with trucked-in sand and protected by a jetty built south of Capitola Fishing Wharf. But that jetty has itself triggered a domino effect, starving beaches beneath the Grand Avenue cliffs (south of Capitola City Beach) and causing erosion and property loss. All of which goes to prove you'll never create anything but disaster by tampering with nature. The business types who run everything never learn this lesson.

Capitola is a pretty village, with attractive homes nestled into the hills and ravines along Soquel Creek. Way back in 1869 Capitola came to life as a campground retreat. In 1894 came the Grand Capitola, a palatial resort hotel comparable in its heyday to San Diego's Hotel del Coronado. Financial troubles prompted the hotel to close in 1929, and some suspected arson when a fire destroyed the building that December.

Today, Capitola supports a modest tourist industry and entertains large numbers of Santa Clara Valley day-trippers fleeing the scorching summer heat. On pleasant weekend afternoons—and except for stormy winter days, just about all of them are—Capitola swells to overflowing. It's a great beach town in miniature, with a small, crescent-shaped public beach, modest 600-foot fishing wharf, and a lagoon near the mouth of Soquel Creek known as "Little Venice," where paddleboats can be rented.

For more information, contact the Capitola Soquel Chamber of Commerce, 716-G Capitola Avenue, Capitola, CA 95010, 831/475-6522, www.capitolachamber.com.

BEACHES

We're a little concerned about Capitola. The beaches are shrinking, while traffic to and people on them keep growing. Still, when it's healthy or recently replenished with sand, **Capitola City Beach** is one of the more appealing beaches in a county blessed with an abundance of them. Jam-packed with bodies, it attracts surfers, collegians, families, valley girls and guys, and more. The beach is about a quarter mile long and 100 yards at its widest point. At times, every square foot is packed with sprawling, lounging bodies and volleyball players.

The surrounding shopping area is full of stores that display trendy merchandise (designer swimwear, arts and crafts) and tend to the hunger pangs of the perambulating beach crowd. You might see musicians playing for spare change or artists displaying their wares (e.g., watercolors of beach scenes) along the walkway by the beach. Occasionally the ocean water gets bacterially contaminated by runoff from Soquel Creek, but this is not usually a problem in the dry months of May through September.

Generally, Capitola City Beach is clean and safe. Folks even hang out at night. Concrete benches line the Esplanade, and strollers come to breathe the salt air and meditate to the musical mantra of the sea's waxing and waning. One evening we spied a man wearing only a red Speedo and a shower cap bolt across the beach on a mission: a midnight swim. Disbelieving spectators shouted advice and encouragement as the polar bear disappeared into the inky darkness where night and ocean meet: "Buddy, you're gonna freeze." "Go, go!" "Damn, he went in." He returned none the worse for wear, climbing into his van and turning on the heater.

Capitola also has another sandy crescent, known as **Hooper's Beach,** just west of its fishing wharf at the end of a stairwell. It's been dog-friendly since 2000, after the locals clamored for a legal beach for all their friendly Fidos to frolic on.

11 CAPITOLA CITY BEACH

Location: along the Esplanade, at end of Capitola Avenue, in Capitola
Parking/Fees: metered street and lot parking
Hours: sunrise–sunset
Facilities: lifeguards, showers, and restrooms
Contact: Capitola Public Works Department, 831/475-6522

© PARKE PUTERBAUGH

Capitola Fishing Wharf

12 HOOPER'S BEACH

Location: foot of Wharf Road in Capitola
Parking/Fees: metered street and lot parking
Hours: 24 hours
Facilities: none
Contact: Capitola Public Works Department, 831/475-6522

ACCOMMODATIONS

Capitola isn't exactly a vacationers' mecca, but there are a few places to stay. Two are side by side near the Capitola Fishing Wharf, overlooking the beach and bay. One of them, the **Capitola Venetian Hotel** (1500 Wharf Road, 831/476-6471, $$), has an interesting history. It's next door to the Venetian Court, California's first condominium development. At the time of its construction in 1920, the word "condominium" didn't exist to describe the concept of individual ownership of apartment-style, stucco-and-tile cottages. Over the years the Venetian—at the mouth of Soquel Creek, an area known as "Little Venice"—has

taken its share of direct hits during winter storms. Still, most owners seem determined to remain and rebuild, probably because you can't get any closer to the ocean or the heart of Capitola. And the units are beautiful, as are the flowery grounds around them.

Adjacent to the Capitola Venetian is the 10-unit **Harbor Lights Motel** (5000 Cliff Drive, 831/476-0505, $$), which provides balconies, deck chairs, and complete kitchens. If you don't mind not being right on the ocean, the **Inn at Depot Hill** (250 Monterey Avenue, 831/462-3376, $$$$) is a sumptuous hillside bed-and-breakfast.

COASTAL CUISINE

All conversations about dining in Capitola inevitably begin and end with **Shadowbrook** (1750 Wharf Road, 831/475-1511, $$$), a romantic dining spot that's been around since 1947. Set along Soquel Creek in a quiet, residential part of Capitola, Shadowbrook serves seafood, prime rib, and other tasty fare in an elegant yet comfortable setting.

Getting there is half the fun. To reach the restaurant you must park in a lot above it and then make the descent via a red cable car that's been a fixture since 1958. There are half a dozen different dining rooms, including the Wine Cellar and the garden-view Greenhouse. Speaking of wine cellars, Shadowbrook has an extensive one—amazingly, the restaurant lost only a bottle or two in the huge earthquake of 1989, thanks to prescient quake-proofing only a year or so earlier—and bartenders also mix some tasty liqueur-spiked coffee beverages.

If you're looking for gourmet takeout, head to **Gayle's Bakery and Roticceria** (504 Bay Avenue, 831/462-1200, $). It's worth fighting the crowds to peruse the selection of sandwiches, salads, meats and cheeses, appetizers, and desserts.

As for the beach scene, **Ristorante Il Pirata** (201 Esplanade, 831/462-1800, $$$) is the place to be on busy weekends, by the look of the crowded deck and long line out front. With reasonably priced items like *pesce* *alla griglia* (grilled fish) going for $16.50, we can see why.

NIGHTLIFE

At night the area surrounding Capitola City Beach becomes a popular promenade. Several square blocks of Spanish-style stucco exteriors are bathed in cursive neon script. Couples stroll shoulder to shoulder with youths who wander between coffee shops, pizza parlors, and the beach. By 9 or 10 P.M., several mild-mannered restaurants make a Clark Kent–style changeover into nightclubs.

Two old reliables are **Margaritaville** (231 Esplanade, 831/476-2263) and **Zelda's** (203 Esplanade, 831/475-4900). The former was the liveliest place we ducked into, having the decided plus of an outdoor deck overlooking the water. Down the street is Zelda's, a restaurant that offers live entertainment once the kitchen shuts down. One night we heard a local singer-guitarist have a respectable go at the blues.

Live Oak

The private community of Live Oak has a string of beaches—mainly larger named and smaller unnamed coves—between 41st Street in Capitola and the Small Craft Harbor in Santa Cruz. Live Oak is a leafy, tree-lined burg nestled between Capitola and Santa Cruz. Because it is residential in nature, it escapes most of those towns' traffic problems.

On the other hand, East Cliff Drive can get pretty congested on weekends as surfers and beachgoers vie for limited parking. Their solution to this is a "parking by permit only" system. That is to say, you can't park at any of the Live Oak beaches without paying for a permit. They can be purchased from a white van parked on East Cliff Drive at Ninth Avenue. It's marked "Parking Permits Sold Here." Nonresident parking permits cost $5 per day or $25 per year.

For more information, contact the Santa Cruz County Conference and Visitors Council, 701 Front Street, Santa Cruz, CA 95060, 831/425-1234 or 800/833-3494, www.santacruzca.org.

BEACHES

Live Oak does its best to make the beach-going experience difficult for outsiders. The following sign can be seen all along East Cliff Drive in Live Oak:

WELCOME TO LIVE OAK BEACHES
- No Glass Containers
- No Littering ($1,000 Fine)
- No Alcoholic Beverages
- No Fire on Beaches
- No Camping
- Dogs on Leashes
- No Burning Pallets

If you can find a spot to park, and observe all the rules, this is a pleasant stretch of cove beaches, with benches overlooking the ocean from East Cliff Drive and paths or stairs leading down to the sandy crescents below. Many are outposts for surfers and tidepoolers. Live Oak Beach is the most accessible and widest drape of sand hereabouts, but do have that parking permit in hand and good luck finding a space.

Beaches can be accessed via paths or stairs at the ends of avenues along East Cliff Drive in Live Oak, between the Santa Cruz Small Craft Harbor and 41st Avenue. **The Hook** is a premium wave-riding spot at 41st Avenue; ditto for **Pleasure Point,** at 32nd Avenue. The bluffs above make a premium surf-watching spot as well.

Around Pleasure Point lies **Moran Lake Beach and Park,** the next sizable drape of sand. People come here mostly to sunbathe and walk dogs; its flat expanse is protected from the wind by large rocks at either end. **Corcoran Lagoon Beach** is backed by the body of water that provides its name. Tidepools can be found on the east side, accessible from a path at East

Cliff Drive and 21st Avenue. **Sunny Cove** draws bodysurfers and boogie boarders, while **Lincoln Beach** attracts picnickers and more contemplative sorts.

13 THE HOOK

Location: East Cliff Drive at 41st Avenue in Live Oak
Parking/Fees: metered street and lot parking
Hours: sunrise-sunset
Facilities: restrooms, picnic tables
Contact: Santa Cruz County Parks Department, 831/454-7901

14 PLEASURE POINT

Location: East Cliff Drive at 32nd Avenue in Live Oak
Parking/Fees: free parking lot and permit-only street parking
Hours: sunrise-sunset
Facilities: restrooms and showers
Contact: Santa Cruz County Parks Department, 831/454-7901

15 MORAN LAKE BEACH AND PARK

Location: East Cliff Drive at 26th Avenue in Live Oak
Parking/Fees: free parking lot and permit-only street parking
Hours: 8 A.M.-sunset
Facilities: restrooms, showers, and picnic tables
Contact: Santa Cruz County Parks Department, 831/454-7901

16 CORCORAN LAGOON BEACH

Location: East Cliff Drive between 22nd and 23rd Avenues in Live Oak
Parking/Fees: permit-only street parking
Hours: sunrise-sunset
Facilities: restrooms
Contact: Santa Cruz County Parks Department, 831/454-7901

17 SUNNY COVE

Location: East Cliff Drive at 17th Avenue in Live Oak
Parking/Fees: permit-only street parking
Hours: sunrise-sunset
Facilities: none
Contact: Santa Cruz County Parks Department, 831/454-7901

18 LINCOLN BEACH

Location: East Cliff Drive at 15th Avenue in Live Oak
Parking/Fees: permit-only street parking
Hours: sunrise-sunset
Facilities: restrooms
Contact: Santa Cruz County Parks Department, 831/454-7901

Santa Cruz

Santa Cruz marches to the beat of a different drummer. It is one of the most free-thinking, footloose, and liberal communities in the world. In order to decipher the various drumbeats, one really has to get to know the area, and that takes time. Although we pride ourselves on being able to size up a town pretty quickly, we'd have to admit that Santa Cruz

SCENES FROM SANTA CRUZ

A community as fluid and freewheeling as Santa Cruz is hard to explain. That is to say, it can't truly be "captured" in a conventional essay. So we're offering this mosaic, based on things we've seen and heard on our many visits.

A homeless man who looks like Popeye begs for change from a guy with his nose buried in a book at a sidewalk café. The bookish coffee-drinker ignores the pleading, which prompts the derelict to press his case even harder. A middle-aged earth mother at another table chides the homeless man for bothering the coffee-drinker who wants to be left alone. She then hands the bum some change and they say "God bless you" to each other. Another homeless man, who's muttering nonsense as he drifts down the sidewalk, pauses to lean over the rail and purrs "You're beautiful" to a college girl, who scowls and looks disgusted.

Two extremely hirsute hippies in ponchos and jeans are playing the Beatles' "Across the Universe" on flute and guitar for strollers on Pacific Avenue. Up the street, beside a faded old Volkswagen bus whose door has been slid open, one hippie dude strums madly on an acoustic guitar while his pal bangs time on the VW's side panel. Over in Capitola, yet another musical duo is trolling for change by playing spacey fare like Pink Floyd's "Wish You Were Here." A smoldering cigarette hangs from the heavy-set keyboardist's lips.

Three sushi chefs at a popular Japanese restaurant take a break from their knives to admire a vintage automobile that has entered the parking lot. "Wow...a 1968," one exclaims before they resume carving raw fish fillets.

A lanky fellow sporting a giant plastic pig nose pedals a bicycle down Front Street. He is wearing a white sanitation worker's uniform. The words "Make Your Mark" are scrawled on the back in green paint.

Santa Cruz's answer to the Addams Family enters a restaurant at dinner hour. The glowering, taciturn dad has the rugged, unsmiling demeanor of a bounty hunter. The tall, witchy mother sports black capri pants more befitting a teenager's figure. A silver ring pierces the goth-girl daughter's lower lip, and a web of tattoos covers every inch of her arms. And you thought the Osbournes were a case study in psychopathology.

"Everybody's being nice and mellow out there in traffic today," exclaims a deejay on a jam-packed Sunday afternoon. "There's been some fender-benders down in Monterey, but nothing to report in Santa Cruz. Keep it up!"

A couple of teenage skateboarders are attempting the pointless feat of riding a

gradually unveils itself in layers, resisting hasty or expeditious conclusions. To understand Santa Cruz you must get in the flow and go with the flow. But which flow to go with? That's the problem.

The social geography of this city, like the physical terrain in the area, varies according to location. The municipal wharf, boardwalk, and main beach area, for instance, combine the Southern California beach-town mentality and the Jersey Shore boardwalk sensibility. Imagine Asbury Park, New Jersey, coupled with Huntington Beach, California. Surfing and volleyball rule on Cowell Beach, just west of the boardwalk by the Santa Cruz Municipal Wharf. Beach volleyball games go on from sunup to sundown on this favored spot, where world-class volleyball tournaments are staged. Meanwhile, surfers vie for large, tubular waves that roll ashore on this south-facing beach.

We witnessed a scene at Cowell that will be forever emblazoned in our memories. Two beach babes were carrying surfboards. They forded the knee-deep mouth of the San Lorenzo narrow rail that runs beside a drugstore. Not surprisingly, one takes a hard fall and winds up face down on the sidewalk, writhing in pain.

A spare-changer on a park bench is deep in conversation with another. He earnestly queries, "Why are all the whores suddenly going to church?"

A local paper asks people on the street a topical question each week, printing selected responses. One such question: "Has the sex scandal involving priests affected your view of the Catholic church?" A UC Santa Cruz student replied, "I think they are using the scandals to create a media hype to distract people from the real issues of war."

On Santa Cruz Boardwalk, the screams of riders being hurled around the Hurricane compete with the strains of "Hanky Panky," by Tommy James and the Shondells, blaring in the gaming arcade. Whining children tug at the sweatpants of their mothers, begging for quarters.

Two hip, young, German couples check into a motel on Ocean Street, overpaying without complaint. Do these fun-seeking foreigners head for the beach and boardwalk? No. They are later spied huddling around the two-star motel's tiny, kidney-shaped pool, looking bored and confused.

Three surf bums are carrying surfboards from their cheap, utilitarian motel room. With visions of Steamer Lane no doubt dancing in their heads, they climb into a van, turn the key in the ignition, and – *nothing*. Dead battery. Someone left the interior light on all night long. Talk about a turn-down day.

A young boy marches ahead of his family toward the ocean, carrying a toy boat. He suddenly drops the boat, holds his nose and exclaims, "PU! It smells like the beach."

Signs of the Times

* "Trespassers will be eaten." – sign on a chain-link fence surrounding a house near the beach

* "MUMI NATION...Santa Cruz art phunk...bring beer goggles, photon beams, and dancing shoes...$3." – flyer affixed to telephone pole

* "Free" – one-word offer taped to discarded box springs propped against a fence

* "No Skateboarding." – a jagged line has been scratched through these words on a sign listing forbidden activities in a hotel parking lot

* "Is It Too Old-Fashioned to Have Integrity?" – graffiti

River and then walked along Santa Cruz's Main Beach between West Cliff and East Cliff Drives. We watched incredulously as the girls, wearing only bikinis while most of the guys were zipped into wet suits, paddled out to the waves at Cowell Beach. What made their immersion so remarkable was the fact that, on this windy afternoon in late March, the water temperature registered only 51 degrees. We'd always heard that 20 minutes exposure to 55-degree water provokes the onset of hypothermia. Deciding to test the waters, we waded up to our calves. This caused leg numbness followed by shooting pain. How did they do it? Is it a simple matter of growing accustomed to frigid water, or were these young women some sort of bionic aliens with surfboards? Forget the surfer-girl flick *Blue Crush;* these Santa Cruz hotties were the real deal.

A late-afternoon run along West Cliff Drive was more our speed. It is here that Santa Cruzans' intense pursuit of fitness can best be observed. West Cliff Drive is an ideal place for strolling, running, skateboarding, in-line

THE BEST OF SANTA CRUZ

Each year, *Metro Santa Cruz*, the city's excellent arts and entertainment weekly, publishes "The Goldies" – a listing of readers' best-of choices in numerous categories. We've written about places and things we like in Santa Cruz, so now we'll let the folks who actually live there have their say. Here are the 2008 Goldies that were awarded in categories of interest to us and our readers, reprinted from *Metro Santa Cruz*. All are in Santa Cruz, unless otherwise noted.

Beaches/Outdoors

Best Beaches: Seabright, Twin Lakes, Seacliff
Best Bike Rides: West Cliff Drive, Wilder Ranch, Nisene Marks
Best Boardwalk Rides: Giant Dipper, Fireball, Carousel
Best Hiking Spots: Wilder Ranch, Nisene Marks, Pogonip Greenbelt
Best Sunset-Watching Spots: West Cliff Drive, Natural Bridges, East Cliff/Seabright Beach
Best Surf Spots: Steamer Lane, Pleasure Point, Cowell Beach

Stores

Best Bookshops (used): Logos Books and Records, 1117 Pacific Avenue, 831/427-5100; Bookshop Santa Cruz, 1520 Pacific Avenue, 831/423-0900; Capitola Book Cafe, 1475 41st Street, Capitola, 831/462-4415
Best Record/CD Stores: Streetlight Records, 941 Pacific Avenue, 831/421-9200; Logos Books and Records, 1117 Pacific Avenue, 831/427-5100; Metamusic Records, 320 Cedar Street, 831/466-9027
Best Surf Shops: O'Neill Surf Shop, 110 Cooper Street, 831/469-4377; Pacific Wave, 1502 Pacific Avenue, 831/458-9283; Arrow Surf and Sport, 2322 Mission Street, 831/423-8286

skating, dog-walking, surfing, surfer spectating, people-watching, and reverent contemplation of one of nature's grandest temples: the wild, steep, and fluted edge of the Pacific Ocean.

For all these reasons West Cliff Drive is one of the can't-miss highlights of the California coast. Seemingly everyone has a bicycle, surfboard, skateboard, or revered animal companion in tow. Those who don't are jogging or gazing meditatively upon the ocean from park benches.

West Cliff Drive follows the undulating coastline of Santa Cruz, with steep, indented cliffs and cove beaches at their bases. Signs read, Warning! Cliff Edges Are Dangerous, as if the danger weren't self-evident. Protective steel barriers keep the public from getting too close to the edge along some sections of West Cliff Drive.

This is the site of Steamer Lane, one of the most legendary surf spots on the West Coast. Surfers by the score bob atop boards at various localized breaks, tightly clustered and divvying up rides according to a rigid pecking order. Small pocket beaches (e.g., Its Beach) can be accessed via stairways, and these are particularly popular with dog owners. In fact, it's a veritable canine free-for-all on some of these sandy crescents, as dogs bark and bask and scamper and test the water and check one another out.

The other part of Santa Cruz where the social geography's a little different is downtown along Pacific Avenue. This is where the town's

Nightlife

Best Bars: Red Restaurant and Bar, 200 Locust Street, 831/425-1913; Clouds, 110 Church Street, 831/429-2000; Poet and Patriot, 320 Cedar Street, 831/426-8620
Best Dance Clubs: Club Dakota, 1209 Pacific Avenue, 831/454-9030; Blue Lagoon, 923 Pacific Avenue, 831/423-7117; Moe's Alley, 1535 Commercial Way, 831/479-1854
Best Microbreweries: Seabright Brewery, 519 Seabright Avenue, 831/426-2739; Santa Cruz Mountain Brewery, 402 Ingalls Street, 831/425-4900; Boulder Creek Brewing Company, 13040 Highway 9, Boulder Creek, 831/338-7882
Best Dive Bars: Asti, 715 Pacific Avenue, 831/423-7337; Rush Inn, 113 Knight Street, 831/435-9673; Brady's Yacht Club, 413 Seabright Avenue (no phone)
Best Happy Hours: El Palomar, 1336 Pacific Avenue, 831/425-7575; Crow's Nest, 2218 East Cliff Drive, 831/476-4560; Clouds, 110 Church Street, 831/429-2000
Best Live Music Clubs: The Catalyst, 1011 Pacific Avenue, 831/423-1336; Moe's Alley, 1535 Commercial Way, 831/479-1854; Kuumbwa Jazz Center, 320 Cedar Street, 831/427-2227

Restaurants

Best Cheap Eats: Charlie Hong Kong, 1141 Soquel Avenue, 831/464-2739; Taqueria Vallarta (three locations in Santa Cruz); Palomar Taco Bar, 1336 Pacific Avenue, 831/425-7575
Best Coffeehouses: People's Coffee, 1200 17th Avenue, 831/429-9804; Lulu's, 1545 Pacific Avenue, 831/429-9804; Cafe Pergolesi, 418 Cedar Street, 831/426-1775
Best Seafood: Stagnaro Bros., 59 Municipal Wharf, 831/423-2180; Crow's Nest, 2218 East Cliff Drive, 831/476-4560; Riva's Fish House, 500 Municipal Wharf, 831/429-1223
Best Sushi: Mobo Sushi, 105 River Street, 831/425-1700; Shogun, 1123 Pacific Avenue, 831/469-4477; Takara, 1800 Soquel Avenue, 831/457-8466

alternative heart and soul beats loudest. It lies at the figurative intersection of Woodstock Nation and Desolation Row.

The area is known as Pacific Garden Mall, and it is Santa Cruz's answer to Venice, California, or the Lower East Side of Manhattan. Here, penniless urban bohemians must countenance increasing incursions by upscale merchants. Franchises for the upwardly mobile, like The Gap, lie close to bars and coffeehouses where the less prosperous nurse mugs for hours. Out on the street the downright destitute congregate in packs or mill solitarily. Human nut cases can frequently be seen muttering and gesticulating wildly to no one in particular. Santa Cruz is benignly tolerant of its homeless population, a fact of life here,

though we've detected a subtly increasing impatience with their presence.

Some of the kids who aren't yet homeless look as if they're apprenticing at it. You'll find more wool caps on the streets of Santa Cruz than anywhere this side of Saskatchewan. There are also acres of tattooed skin, sadistic metal piercings, hair sprouting from every orifice (though often shaved right off the head), oversized thrift-shop clothing, lit cigarettes, and vacant or malcontented stares. These are the visible retorts of the economically disfranchised—some by circumstance, others by choice.

All the same, Pacific Avenue has received a partial makeover during the dot-com and Dow-driven prosperity of the 1990s and the new millennium. Lights have been strung in the trees that line the street, making nighttime glimmer like Christmas, and big construction projects bring new parking garages and office space to downtown Santa Cruz. All of this makes the contrast between the high and low end, with relatively little in between, that much more pronounced.

At the height of Santa Cruz's real-estate bubble, *New York Times* reported that extremely modest one-bedroom "starter homes" were going for half a million dollars. Even though the bursting of the dot-com bubble in the 1990s and the bank collapses and stock market plunges of 2008 and 2009 have reduced America to near barter-society status, Santa Cruz remains an almost prohibitively expensive place to live. How does a student or surfer dude make ends meet here?

Like a salmon swimming upstream, Santa Cruz somehow resists the currents of mainstream American life. It is indeed a puzzling, intriguing, and contrary place—even Highway 1 can't make up its mind what to do, boldly entering the city from the south and then becoming a confusing maze of turns and exits. Suffice it to say that Santa Cruz—which means "Sacred Cross"—is many things. It's a patchwork of lifestyles, politics, landforms, and roads that converge to make up the largest seaside resort north of Santa Barbara. The base population of 55,500 swells on weekends with crowds from Silicon Valley, San Jose, and San Francisco.

From the start the town was marked by mysterious events. The mission built here in 1791, Misíon la Exaltación de la Santa Cruz, vanished without a trace. It was somewhere near the San Lorenzo River and was perhaps swallowed by it. To this day the river is subject to destructive flooding. A replica of the mission has been built outside of town, but few go out of their way to see it. That is just as well, because Santa Cruz turned away from spiritual matters in 1865, when the first public bathhouse was built on the beach. A boardwalk, dance hall, and casino were added, bolstered by a lucrative logging economy

that transformed the quiet town into a resort. A roller coaster and carousel followed. The crowds began arriving when the railroad company feverishly promoted a "Suntan Special," which deposited visitors from San Francisco and San Jose on the main beach at Santa Cruz. This inspired railroad stations to be built up and down the coast, paralleling what is today Highway 1. The original roller coaster and carousel—the latter with beautiful mounts designed and painted by Charles Looff in 1911—are still in service, and many of the fine Victorian homes of the logging moguls still stand.

The San Lorenzo River snake-dances through town before emptying into the ocean south of Main Beach. Santa Cruz is a busy proletarian beach resort at this end of the river. Upriver, Santa Cruz is more upscale and suburban. Everywhere else, the town is a hotbed of liberalism and laissez-faire lifestyles. New Age free-thinkers seem to hold sway here to a greater degree than any other community in California (save, perhaps, Bolinas). We took a political/philosophical reading from two bumper stickers spied on different cars within minutes of each other: "Visualize Industrial Collapse" and "Never Drive Faster Than Your Angel Can Fly."

Still, for a supposedly peaceable haven, you don't always feel safe in Santa Cruz, especially after dark. The city has an underside, as do most places where eccentricities are not only tolerated but encouraged. We overheard unnerving snatches of conversation around town on such subjects as urban warfare. You'll see squadrons of loiterers affecting a punkish hippie look that bespeaks poverty and defiance. It's the same all over: tousled cataracts of hair spilling out from under wool caps; morgue-like black clothes draped over hunched shoulders; wispy nature trails of facial hair; metal piercings affixed to lips, nostrils, cheeks, and other anatomical parts. One night, we spied a gaggle of such specimens outside a club where a band was mangling a Jimi Hendrix song—all too appropriately, "I Don't Live Today."

Here's another scene we'll never forget. One afternoon, we watched a 1960s acid casualty

ROOM RATE ROULETTE

There's a game that gets played in Santa Cruz in the summer months and on warm, clear weekends the rest of the year. We call it "room rate roulette." It's a game of chance in which motels and guests each look to secure the best price, from their perspective. Motels want to charge as much as they can get, while guests want to spend as little as they can. There is nothing unusual about this. What makes the situation in Santa Cruz unique is the fluidity of the prices. It verges on being a barter system. Realizing this, you might save some money.

A Santa Cruz motel owner tipped us off to this years ago. There are a lot of motels in Santa Cruz. Sometimes there are more visitors than rooms, and other times it is the other way around. Things can get interesting either way. When rooms are tight, people scramble from motel to motel checking out availability and happily paying inflated prices for a roof over their heads. When rooms are readily available, they will patiently shop for the lowest price. If you've come without reservations, you'll quickly discover whether it's a buyer's or seller's market.

For instance, on a sunny spring Saturday afternoon, Vacancy signs were up all over town. Motel lots looked to be half to two-thirds full. Occupancy rates were high enough that motels weren't giving rooms away but not so full that lodgers couldn't afford to check out their options. It made for an interesting dynamic. We had a room, but as an experiment we inquired about prices at a number of motels along Ocean Street and Riverside Avenue. Many others were doing likewise. We'd run into the same faces in different lobbies.

It soon became clear that prices were negotiable. "What are you looking to pay?" was a refrain we'd hear while leaving a lobby after receiving a rate quote. It was a bit like the song and dance on a car lot. We were quoted prices ranging $65-130. The cheapest rate was at Inn Cal, a perfectly fine chain motel on Ocean Street a half mile from the beach and boardwalk. The highest rates were in the immediate vicinity of the beach. Rooms were $129 at the AAA-rated Carousel, ideally situated on the corner of Riverside Avenue and Beach Street. The Super 8 Motel, a bottom-feeding chain, wanted $99-129. The median price in Santa Cruz on this particular weekend was $89.

So if you don't like posted room rates in Santa Cruz and the motels are not full, then feel free to shop around and barter, if you've got the stomach for it. It's kind of like an in-person version of the Priceline.com approach. Just so you know, room rates drop during the week, especially outside the summer months. They must have long winters in Santa Cruz. The sign outside a Travelodge advertised "low winter rates"; the date was May 13. It should also be pointed out that Santa Cruz is a popular beach town. Don't come expecting a Ritz-Carlton or even a three-star Holiday Inn. People come to Santa Cruz to party, and motel rooms reflect this reality. They're not filthy or uninhabitable, but they've seen a lot of use by family vacationers and hordes of party people. It's not a far cry from the scene at boardwalk towns along the New Jersey shore or in Myrtle Beach, South Carolina. In terms of the California coast, however, Santa Cruz stands alone in this regard.

offer running, unsolicited commentary on a young street musician's performance: "It's not that you can't play, man. You play pretty good. It's just that you're not utilizing your talent to any creative, original purpose." The fact that the singer was wearing a red clown's nose as he strummed his earnest covers of familiar folk tunes lent some credence to the hippie elder's critique.

The liberal melting pot in this left-of-center burg is the University of California, Santa Cruz, which occupies a green, 2,000-acre campus northeast of town. Founded in 1965, UC Santa Cruz is set on a former cattle ranch that's now home to an arboretum of rare plants and groves of redwood trees. The buildings are hidden among the trees, making this one of the best-concealed institutions of higher learning on the planet. The sports mascot is the banana slug. (John Travolta memorably wore a Santa Cruz Banana Slugs T-shirt in a scene from *Pulp Fiction*.) The campus restaurant is called the Whole Earth (serving "Thai-style Tofu and Veggies"). Narrative evaluations are given instead of grades, and courses taught here have included "The Pursuit of Truth in the Company of Friends" and "Female Masturbation."

All levity aside, it is heartening to find a university that isn't just another mill for business degrees. Student-led tours are available through the admissions office Monday–Friday; for reservations call 831/459-4008. To get to UC Santa Cruz, take Highway 1 to Bay Street, then head north and follow the signs. And now, follow us to the beaches of Santa Cruz.

For more information, contact the Santa Cruz County Conference and Visitors Council, 701 Front Street, Santa Cruz, CA 95060, 831/425-1234 or 800/833-3494, www.santa cruzca.org.

BEACHES

Santa Cruz has numerous beach-access points, though some are in residential areas with limited parking. Only savvy locals know about some of the more hidden coves, and each beach seems to be claimed by a different crowd. Starting on the east side of town, **Twin Lakes State Beach** is a popular 86-acre park that lies between Corcoran Lagoon and the **Santa Cruz Harbor Beach,** at Santa Cruz Small Beach Harbor.

Seabright Beach

On the west side of the yacht basin is **Seabright Beach**—though sentimental locals still prefer the name **Castle Beach**—where the most popular pastimes along the mile-long strand are volleyball by day and bonfires at twilight. There's a small lighthouse at the east end and a rock jetty. Nice, tubular waves break on a sloping, brown-sand beach. There are plenty of families, lots of room, and a little concession stand. We couldn't help but notice, however, that the sand is littered with charred wood chips from beach bonfires.

Despite all the attractive options that lie east of the San Lorenzo River, you'll probably wind up on **Main Beach** if you're not a local. As the name suggests, it's the longest and widest strand in town—the "main" beach—and the famed Boardwalk runs beside it. Accommodations are clustered close by. Touristy though it is, Main Beach and the Boardwalk should be strolled and experienced. It's a real slice of life and a full-tilt fun-time arcade unique along the West Coast.

The **Santa Cruz Boardwalk** has been spruced up since the 1980s. Back then it looked like the setting for a Bruce Springsteen song about hard times on the Jersey shore. Today it's much improved. At Neptune's Kingdom, a clean, if generic, arcade, parents can toss down schooners of beer upstairs while their progeny destroy galaxies on video games downstairs. A "historium" justifies the nautical motif with a few educational placards. Outside in the bright sun, beach bums have their pick of things to ride, eat, and play, including our old boardwalk favorite, Skee-Ball. We copped some plastic skull rings our last time out.

The Sky Glider ski lift carried us high above the frivolity, providing an incredible panorama of the town, beach, and ocean. Caterpillar cars dipsy-doodle on the roller coaster next door, allowing total strangers to share moments of gleeful terror. A multitude of food stalls sell typical beach fare, and an equally large number of rides will help you lose it. The rides have names like Giant Dipper and Chaos. One spinning capsule holds riders suspended upside down at its apo-gee for several seconds, then flings them back to earth in a frightening blur. Do people really pay for this sort of torture? Apparently so, judging from the crowds, laughter, and screams.

If you're buying by the ride, these stomach churners can add up, so go for a day pass. In sum, Main Beach is a classic boardwalk scene that from a distance—say, from Lighthouse Point or Municipal Wharf—conveys an airy, nostalgic quality, almost like it's been frozen in time.

If boardwalk revelry isn't your kids' idea of fun, two options remain. First, lengthy psychological testing. (What child doesn't love being suspended upside down a hundred feet above the ground?) Second, take the **Santa Cruz Steam Train**. It's a turn-of-the-century locomotive that leaves from the back of the boardwalk arcade and travels inland through a redwood forest and along the San Lorenzo River canyon. It stops at Roaring Camp, a former gold-mining area. It's a great half-day excursion. (Call 831/335-4484 for fares and schedules.)

At the north end of the oceanfront, on the other side of the municipal wharf, is **Cowell Beach.** Years ago, a Miss California pageant held here had to be canceled because spectators pelted the contestants and each other with raw meat. Now the main competition at Cowell is an annual volleyball tournament. Volleyball and surfing rule at Cowell. It's almost an unstated imperative that you must be doing something athletic on this beach. Few just lie around.

Some of the best surf California has to offer can be found above Cowell Beach, along West Cliff Drive at a rocky area called **Steamer Lane.** Only the best and bravest surf here, because the swells reach mountainous heights and threaten to hurl their fearless riders against the cliff bases or fillet them on rocks that barely jut above the surface. Surfers who aren't in the water sit on the rocks, waiting their turn. Everyone else stands on the edge of an eroding cliff, watching nervously, taking photographs, and creating an intimate community based on fear or sadism. Waves slam against the shore, sending spray upward. Before the fence was erected, onlookers were occasionally washed over the edge to their deaths.

The state allocated funds to create **Lighthouse Field State Beach,** a ten-acre open space that overlooks Steamer Lane. This spared it from a threatened development (a conference center and hotel, as if there aren't enough of those), which galvanized Santa Cruz environmental groups. An integral part of Lighthouse Field—which stretches west of the bluffs—is the **Santa Cruz Surfing Museum** in the **Mark Abbott Lighthouse** (West Cliff Drive, 831/429-3429). Like the California Surf Museum in Oceanside, this is an imperative stop. Photographs adorn the walls—of people riding hollowed-out 16-foot longboards, of 19 surfers crammed inside a woodie—and videos and news clippings document the sport's rich history. The centerpiece is a shrine where the ashes of 18-year-old Mark Abbott are interred beneath a pile of rocks and shells. This young man challenged the sea and lost, but the war rages on at Steamer Lane. The bookshop here has a great selection of surf and beach publications. Interestingly, Lighthouse Point, on which it sits, is regarded as the northernmost end of Monterey Bay.

Nearby **Its Beach** is popular with dog owners, who are allowed to unleash their canines in the morning and evening. The same goes for **Mitchell's Cove,** another patch of sand that does a disappearing beach trick during winter months when storms scrub the shore clean. Most years it reappears when fair weather rebuilds the beaches.

If you're not yet beached out, follow West Cliff Drive to **Natural Bridges State Beach,** named for an offshore arch. Though no lifeguards patrol the beach, it's considered safe, and chaperoned tots wade giddily in the foaming waves. The 65-acre park includes trails through coastal scrub meadow habitat. Visitors can study marine life at **Joseph M. Long Marine Laboratory and Aquarium** (100 Shaffer Road, 831/459-4308), a working research facility with an aquarium full of sea urchins, sea sponges, abalone, anemones, and starfish. There's also a sea-lion-viewing perch, as well as the skeleton of a blue whale. It's a cheap way to educate the kids and learn something yourself. (The laboratory is open 1 P.M.–4 P.M. Tuesday–Sunday.)

West Cliff is the best place in town to walk, run, bicycle, skateboard, in-line skate, watch surfers, observe sunset, meditate, contemplate, exercise a dog, meet a friend, whatever. We always make a point of running along West Cliff Drive from Cowell Beach to as far as our legs will carry us. Something about the cornucopia of interesting people and the cliff-hugging scenery makes this one of the more exceptional aerobicizing locales in coastal California.

On a final note, lifeguards are on duty at Santa Cruz city beaches from Memorial Day to Labor Day and on weekends only during spring and fall.

19 TWIN LAKES STATE BEACH

Location: East Cliff Drive at Seventh Avenue in Santa Cruz
Parking/Fees: metered street and lot parking
Hours: 8 A.M.-10 P.M.
Facilities: lifeguards and restrooms
Contact: California State Parks, Santa Cruz District, 831/427-4868

20 SANTA CRUZ HARBOR BEACH

Location: East Cliff Drive at Fifth Avenue in Santa Cruz
Parking/Fees: metered street parking
Hours: 9 A.M.-5 P.M.
Facilities: concession, lifeguards, and restrooms
Contact: Santa Cruz Harbor, 831/475-6161

21 SEABRIGHT BEACH

 BEST (

Location: in Santa Cruz at the end of
Seabright Avenue
Parking/Fees: metered street parking
Hours: 6 A.M.–10 P.M.
Facilities: concession, lifeguards, and
restrooms
Contact: Santa Cruz Marine Safety Division,
831/429-2850

22 MAIN BEACH

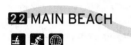

Location: in Santa Cruz along Beach Street,
east of the Municipal Wharf
Parking/Fees: metered lot and street parking
Hours: sunrise–10 P.M.
Facilities: lifeguards and restrooms
Contact: Santa Cruz Marine Safety Division,
831/420-6015

23 COWELL BEACH

Location: in Santa Cruz along Bay Street at
West Cliff Drive, west of the Municipal Wharf
Parking/Fees: metered street and lot parking
Hours: sunrise–10 P.M.
Facilities: lifeguards and restrooms
Contact: Santa Cruz Marine Safety Division,
831/420-6015

24 STEAMER LANE

Location: in Santa Cruz at Lighthouse Point
off West Cliff Drive
Parking/Fees: metered street parking
Hours: sunrise–10 P.M.
Facilities: none
Contact: Santa Cruz Marine Safety Division,
831/420-6015

25 LIGHTHOUSE FIELD STATE BEACH

Location: in Santa Cruz at Point Santa Cruz
along West Cliff Drive
Parking/Fees: metered street parking
Hours: 7 A.M.–sunset
Facilities: restrooms and picnic tables
Contact: Lighthouse Field State Park,
831/429-2850

26 ITS BEACH

Location: West Cliff Drive between Lighthouse
Field State Beach and Natural Bridges State
Beach in Santa Cruz
Parking/Fees: metered street parking
Hours: 24 hours
Facilities: none
Contact: Santa Cruz Marine Safety Division,
831/420-6015

27 MITCHELL'S COVE

Location: West Cliff Drive between Lighthouse
Field and Natural Bridges State Beaches in
Santa Cruz
Parking/Fees: metered street parking
Hours: 24 hours
Facilities: none
Contact: Santa Cruz Marine Safety Division,
831/420-6015

28 NATURAL BRIDGES STATE BEACH

Location: West Cliff Drive at Natural Bridges
Drive in Santa Cruz
Parking/Fees: $8 entrance fee per vehicle
Hours: 8 A.M.–sunset
Facilities: concession, restrooms, picnic
tables, and visitors center
Contact: Natural Bridges State Beach,
831/423-4609

SANTA CRUZ COAST

RECREATION AND ATTRACTIONS

- **Bike/Skate Rentals:** Bike Rental Center, 131 Center Street, Santa Cruz, 831/426-8687
- **Dive Shop:** Aqua Safaris Scuba Center, 6896 Soquel Avenue, Santa Cruz, 831/479-4386
- **Ecotourism:** Venture Quest, 125 Beach Street, Santa Cruz, 831/427-2267
- **Marina:** Santa Cruz Harbor, 135 Fifth Avenue, Santa Cruz, 831/475-6161
- **Pier:** Santa Cruz Municipal Wharf, Beach Street, Santa Cruz, 831/420-6025
- **Rainy Day Attraction:** Santa Cruz Surfing Museum, Mark Abbott Lighthouse, West Cliff Drive, Santa Cruz, 831/429-3429
- **Shopping/Browsing:** Pacific Garden Mall, Pacific Avenue, Santa Cruz
- **Sportfishing:** Santa Cruz Sportfishing, North Santa Cruz Harbor, Dock H, Santa Cruz, 831/426-4690
- **Surf Report:** 831/464-3233
- **Surf Shop:** Santa Cruz Surf Shop, 753 41st Avenue, Santa Cruz, 831/464-3233
- **Vacation Rentals:** Bailey Properties, 106 Aptos Beach Drive, Aptos, 831/688-7009

ACCOMMODATIONS

The motel scene in Santa Cruz, like the scene around the boardwalk and arcade, has steadily been improving. In the past, sobering stories were told about oceanfront motels here—tales of crime, degeneracy, noise, odors, overcrowding of rooms, and substance abuse. Our favorite tale, possibly apocryphal but maybe not: A teenager steps out to get a soda one evening, leaving his grandmother in the motel room with the door unlocked. He lingers a while on the boardwalk. When he returns, he finds a derelict passed out in bed next to Grandma, who has somehow slept through it all. Then, there's the one about the "hippie" (they use that word a lot) who lived for a month inside a hotel elevator.

We've informally inventoried hotels and motels near Main Beach, where rooms plunge to less then $50 in the dead of winter and get jacked up to $150 and more in summer at places with letters missing from their signs. Some Santa Cruz innkeepers are reluctant to quote prices unless you put down your credit card, especially on busy summer weekends, when they charge whatever the market will bear.

The best-situated hotel in Santa Cruz, if not the whole of California, is the **Dream Inn** (175 West Cliff Drive, 831/426-4330, $$$$). This ten-story lodge overlooks the Santa Cruz Municipal Wharf, Cowell Beach, and the Pacific Ocean, whose plunging waves will lull you to a deep, restful sleep. The view alone is worth the price of the rooms, which are not so much extravagant as extremely comfortable.

The ocean-facing deck on the third floor has a heated pool and spa. One memorable night after the sun went down, we watched, transfixed, from the hot tub as a full moon illuminated the night sky. You can't put a price on moments like these, which might be a good thing since room rates run around $300–400 per night. For those on a bit more of a budget, **Holiday Inn Express** (600 Riverside Avenue, 831/458-9660, $$) lies just two blocks away and costs half as much, with a free breakfast thrown in.

We've also stayed at a posh resort that's not on the water but overlooks it from the hills above Santa Cruz. As we made the steep ascent to **Chaminade** (1 Chaminade Lane, 831/475-5600 or 800/283-6569, $$$$), a deer loped in front of our car. It seems as much a nature preserve as a hotel, and it gets high marks for its mountainside setting. We also liked the villa-style rooms and unparalleled quiet within. If Chaminade is a more meditative retreat than your typical hotel and conference center, that's because the compound used to be a monastery. Chaminade's Sunset Restaurant, incidentally, serves an award-winning weekend brunch.

COASTAL CUISINE

Santa Cruz has a varied dining scene—everything from fast food to health food, from seafood restaurants on the wharf to taco stands on side streets. The Santa Cruz Municipal Wharf is the place to go for a seafood meal with a view. This huge, bulky wharf extends 3,000 feet into the ocean. There's usually plenty of parking; you collect a ticket at the entrance gate and pay by the hour. Take your pick of sit-down restaurants with picture windows that face the ocean.

A longtime wharf favorite is **Stagnaro Brothers** (Municipal Wharf, 831/423-2180, $$). A restaurant and a fish market, Stagnaro's motto is "Caught today, cooked today." You can eat your catch in a casual atmosphere or take it to go. Red clam chowder is a house specialty; it's a hearty concoction that cuts the chill when a cold wind is blowing off the ocean.

Though locals might disparage the wharf for being too touristy, they've got no qualms about walking the planks to dine at **Riva Fish House** (31 Municipal Wharf, 831/429-1223, $$), which draws gaggles of residents and visitors alike. We won't elaborate on what the menu at a fish house on a wharf might look like (use your imagination). Just know one thing: If you don't get here early, prepare to leave your name and wait.

Once, on a squalling January afternoon, we had a memorable lunch at the **Miramar Fish Grotto** (45 Municipal Wharf, 831/423-4441, $$). We ate sole meunière, green salad, and fresh bread while watching monstrous winter waves threaten to pound the wharf to smithereens. Gazing out the windows while gale-force winds blew the rain sideways, we could see an ocean kayaker being tossed around like a bath toy. Then came a run of big waves. Each giant breaker struck the pier with a sound like a bowling ball scattering tenpins. The wharf would shudder, and overhead lights swayed. We found ourselves wondering how the pier could survive such abuse. And yet the Santa Cruz Municipal Wharf has been standing since 1914.

Santa Cruz's most popular waterfront restaurant is the **Crow's Nest** (2218 East Cliff Drive, 831/476-4560, $$), near Twin Lakes State Beach and the Small Craft Harbor. It gets its fish from the fleet next door, has easy access to the beach, and is family friendly. Wednesdays it holds a clambake on the beach. Crow's Nest is also a big singles hangout and nightclub.

A favorite eatery near the Boardwalk is **Beach Street Cafe** (399 Beach Street, 831/426-7621, $), a good bet for breakfast or lunch. While basking in the friendly chatter, enjoy the framed collection of Maxfield Parrish prints, one of the largest in the United States. Good coffee, great omelets. For morning muffins, hit **Rebecca's Mighty Muffins** (4125 Portola Drive, 831/462-2990, $). Some are healthy, others are sinfully good, and still others try to be a little of both. Our faves: raspberry poppyseed cheesecake, cranberry orange pecan, and chocolate chip cheesecake.

For killer Mexican food, head to **El Palomar** (1336 Pacific Garden Mall, 831/425-7575, $$), where you can choose from two eating areas: a fancy dining room with high-end Mexican seafood dishes and a stand-up taco and alcohol bar. At the latter, you can scarf down unbelievable snapper and scallop tacos. Soft corn tortillas are hand-pressed before your very eyes from a mound of dough. It's a bustling room in which a terrific quick meal can be made from several soft tacos and a Mexican beer or two.

Another Mexican favorite is **Rosa's Rosticeria** (493B Lake Avenue, 831/429-1223, $), by the Yacht Harbor and very reasonably priced. For something completely different try **Vasili's Greek Food & Barbeque** (1501 Mission Avenue, 831/458-9808, $$), which serves a terrific roast chicken in lemon, olive oil, and artichoke hearts.

The most beloved sushi restaurant in Santa Cruz is **Mobo Sushi** (105 South River Street, 831/425-1700, $$$), where they're reverential of their craft and very creative. Rolls include the Crop Burning (avocado, cucumber, shiitake, cilantro, spicy sauce) and the Pink Caddy (unagi, hamachi, sake, ebi, spicy sauce). A sushi platter will net delicacies like bonito and some of the reddest tuna you'll ever see.

One of the best breakfasts or brunches in town is served at **Zachary's** (819 Pacific Avenue, 831/427-0646, $). How's this for a morning jump-starter: smoked chicken-apple sausage, eggs, home-fried potatoes, and homemade bread.

NIGHTLIFE

Santa Cruz is a party town. People listen and dance to any type of music—live, taped, synthesized, loud, soft, garage, grunge, hip-hop. You might hear everything from Guns N' Roses to Glenn Miller. It doesn't matter. Clubs are scattered around town, catering to a cross section of locals and party animals from over the mountains.

Two of the most popular and longest-lived are the **Crow's Nest** (2218 East Cliff Drive, 831/476-4560) and the **Catalyst** (1011 Pacific Avenue, 831/423-1336). The Crow's Nest turns the second floor of its seafood restaurant into a happy danceteria, and after the plates are put away, it cranks up the volume. Occasionally the club features live acts, but mostly it's decent deejayed music—one night we heard James Brown's "I Feel Good" as we approached from blocks away—and the dance floor is jampacked. It's a thirty-something crowd, though not a somnolent one.

The Catalyst is a former bowling alley transformed into a world-renowned venue for alternative music. More collegiate and liberalized, it's a cavernous clubhouse with two floors, several rooms, and bars everywhere you turn. The Catalyst has a long and storied history. It's a favorite venue of Neil Young, who's been known to break in new material and/or bands here. Good bands, great venue.

Much of downtown Santa Cruz, along Pacific Avenue, had to be rebuilt or renovated after the 1989 earthquake. It's generally an okay place to stroll around. We're not going to romanticize it, though, because the area sometimes has the unnerving aura of an urban DMZ compounded by rampant homelessness. Here's a quasi-amusing vignette: One morning we stumbled upon a half-naked homeless man who was changing clothes on the grounds of our hotel beside a sign that read Panhandlers Are Not Welcome and Will Be Prosecuted. So it goes in Santa Cruz.

Downtown you will find great bookshops, coffeehouses, and bars filled with locals. True to its name, **99 Bottles of Beer on the Wall** (110 Walnut Street, 831/459-9999) offers 99 brands of beer. If you really want to bend elbows with the locals, stroll the lower end of Pacific Avenue, where you'll find such dive bars as the **Asti Cafe** (715 Pacific Avenue, 831/423-7337). The Asti and its neighbors have cold beer, blaring jukeboxes, milling crowds, and an atmosphere as loud and lascivious as the bars where we misspent our college years. The Asti gets extra points for carding one of us.

Wilder Ranch State Park

Wilder Ranch State Park is one of California's most intriguing oceanfront parks. It opened in the early 1990s. For the century prior to the acquisition of nearly 5,000 acres by the state in 1974, the ranch was operated as a farm by the Wilder family. About 900 acres were under cultivation, with one-eighth of the nation's Brussels sprouts grown inside park boundaries. Portions of this farmland have been returned to wetland and riparian habitat, and are now filled with native flora and fauna. Twenty-two acres have been set aside as a cultural preserve, and many of the original Wilder family buildings stand intact.

For more information, contact Wilder Ranch State Park, 1401 Coast Road, Santa Cruz, CA 95060, 831/423-9703, www.parks.ca.gov.

BEACHES

Most of the trails and acreage lie north of Highway 1, up in the hills, which rise to 800 feet. But it's the stretch of Wilder Ranch seaward of the highway that is attractive to beach bums. There are six named beaches inside **Wilder Ranch State Park.** One way to view them is to hike the Ohlone Bluff Trail, a majestic 2.5-mile footpath that runs along the shoreline. From the park office take Old Cove Landing Trail for 1.2 miles to the beach, where it meets Ohlone Bluff Trail. Wilder Beach is an off-limits preserve for the endangered snowy plover. Other beaches appear as separate coves below the bluff top, and the names are as appealing as the scenery: Fern Grotto Beach, Sand Plant Beach, Strawberry Beach, Three Mile Beach, and Four Mile Beach.

Logically enough, **Four Mile Beach** (the most popular) is four miles north of town, off Highway 1. Start measuring the distance from Highway 1 at Mission Street in Santa Cruz, and at four miles look for a rut-filled parking lot. A 10-minute walk across railroad tracks and past a wetlands leads to the beach. Clothed and nude beachcombers and surfers use Four Mile by day, and teen hell-raisers show up after dark.

In addition to Ohlone Bluff Trail, 34 miles of scenic backcountry trails wind through the inland hills and valleys. These trails are popular with horseback riders and mountain bicyclists. No camping is allowed. Guided tours and hands-on demonstrations of ranch life are offered on the weekends; reservations are required.

29 WILDER RANCH STATE PARK

Location: two miles north of Santa Cruz, off Highway 1
Parking/Fees: $8 entrance fee per vehicle
Hours: 8 A.M.-sunset
Facilities: restrooms and visitors center
Contact: Wilder Ranch State Park, 831/423-9703

30 FOUR MILE BEACH

Location: four miles north of Santa Cruz, off Highway 1
Parking/Fees: free roadside parking
Hours: 8 A.M.-sunset
Facilities: restrooms
Contact: Wilder Ranch State Park, 831/423-9703

Red, White, and Blue Beach

For many years Red, White, and Blue Beach was one of California's legendary (and best) nude beaches, located off Highway 1 five miles north of Santa Cruz. Although the red-white-and-blue mailbox of former owner and operator Ralph Edwards still marks the spot, the beach itself has closed for good. Warm, sunny days used to draw crowds of 500 naturists frolicking in the water and around the volleyball nets. And so one of California's premiere nude beaches has, we're sorry to say, bitten the dust...er, sand.

North County Beaches

Beginning about seven miles north of Santa Cruz, a series of cove beaches can be accessed along Highway 1, including Laguna Creek Beach, Panther Beach, Yellowbank Beach, and Bonny Doon Beach. Each requires hiking across a bluff and down to the beach—often a steep scramble down a loosely consolidated sea cliff.

A word of caution about the beaches of northern Santa Cruz County: Their character tends to change after dark from a nude Dr. Jekyll to an intoxicated Mr. Hyde. Nighttime is when young party animals from the Santa Clara Valley come to raise hell. They build bonfires on the beach, drink themselves senseless, and litter the sand with glass, garbage, and puke. One high schooler told a reporter for the San Jose Mercury News, "We party at Bonny Doon. You have to walk down a hill, and cops don't go down there. So you light a bonfire and drink until you can't walk. A lot of times people just spend the night; they're way too drunk to walk back up the hill."

For years authorities have attempted to curb this behavior. They've ticketed cars parked on the shoulders of Highway 1 at night. They've broken up many a beachside bacchanal, some of which have attracted upward of a thousand kids. But there's only so much they can do. Youth must have its fling, and the pagan rituals of partying on the beach after dark are part of it.

The dark side of all this is fights, drunk driving, falling off cliffs, drownings, and murder. Even during daylight hours we've seen some pretty thuggish-looking characters hanging around these north county pullouts. Auto break-ins are another problem—don't leave any valuables inside your car or trunk. Watch your step, watch the company you keep, and don't drink and drive. Don't ever come out here alone. Enough kids have been hurt or died that the authorities and general public are not amused by alcohol-related lawbreaking, even if it is part of the perceived adolescent rites of passage.

BEACHES

The best known of the North County beaches, **Bonny Doon Beach** lies nine miles north of Santa Cruz, at Milepost 27.6 on Highway 1 at Bonny Doon Road. (Up in the hills is the settlement of Bonny Doon. In June 2008, raging fires necessitated its evacuation.) The other named beaches of note—from south to north, **Laguna Creek Beach, Panther Beach,** and **Yellowbank Beach**—lie 7.3, 7.7, and 8.0 miles north of Santa Cruz, respectively.

These are all legendary party spots on weekend nights—especially during full moons, when all-night raves have been staged on the

sands of Four Mile and Panther beaches. Now an officially recognized coastal access, Bonny Doon offers paved, angle-in parking along the ocean side of Highway 1. Signs warn against parking between 10 P.M. and 6 A.M. After crossing railroad tracks and descending a dirt path, you come upon an absolutely stunning beach that resembles a natural amphitheater, with cliffs on either side that keep the winds at bay.

The remoteness of the site and the protection afforded by the encircling cliffs have made Bonny Doon one of the premier nude beaches on the California coast. It is also one of the friendlier haunts of the bare-assed set, who congregate by the cove at the north end. The other beaches in this daisy chain are equally endowed with sheltering cliffs and desirable isolation.

After 40 years of taking it all off at Bonny Doon Beach, its clothing-optional status may be in jeopardy. In 2006, the state of California acquired five miles worth of beaches in northern Santa Cruz County, including Bonny Doon. The naturists fear that state-park rangers will crack down on nudity, as they did at Garrapata State Park, at the north end of Big Sur. On the other hand, there's something called the "Cahill policy," which tolerates nudity where it has long been practiced (i.e., Black's Beach in San Diego County, Grey Whale Cove in San Mateo County).

In any case, a few years after acquiring Bonny Doon, the state-park system has still done very little with it. It's not even listed on their official website. Maybe they've decided to let sleeping nudists lie.

31 LAGUNA CREEK BEACH

Location: Laguna Creek Road at Highway 1, seven miles north of Santa Cruz
Parking/Fees: free roadside parking
Hours: 6 A.M.-10 P.M.
Facilities: none

Contact: Santa Cruz County Parks Department, 831-454-7901

32 PANTHER BEACH

Location: off Highway 1, eight miles north of Santa Cruz; look for turnouts
Parking/Fees: free roadside parking
Hours: 6 A.M.-10 P.M.
Facilities: none
Contact: Santa Cruz County Parks Department, 831/454-7901

33 YELLOWBANK BEACH

Location: off Highway 1, eight miles north of Santa Cruz; look for turnouts
Parking/Fees: free roadside parking
Hours: 6 A.M.-10 P.M.
Facilities: none
Contact: Santa Cruz County Parks Department, 831/454-7901

34 BONNY DOON BEACH

 BEST

Location: Bonny Doon Road at Highway 1, nine miles north of Santa Cruz
Parking/Fees: free parking lot
Hours: 6 A.M.-10 P.M.
Facilities: none
Contact: Santa Cruz County Parks Department, 831/454-7901

Davenport

For such a little place, Davenport (population 200) has several worthwhile attractions. It is home to the Davenport New Cash Store—a one-of-a-kind restaurant, bakery, bed-and-breakfast, and art gallery. In winter and early spring, the town is one of the premier spots in Northern California to watch gray whales as they make their way from feeding grounds in the Arctic to breeding grounds in Mexican lagoons, and back again.

Davenport is also the site of a giant, Depression-era cement plant. The decayed pilings of a

© PARKE PUTERBAUGH

Bonny Doon Beach

SANTA CRUZ COAST

massive, 3,000-foot wharf, from which the plant loaded its product onto ships, list in the water. For beach fanatics, the main attraction is a holy trinity of sandy accesses: Davenport Beach, Davenport Landing, and Scott Creek Beach.

For more information, contact the Santa Cruz County Conference and Visitors Council, 701 Front Street, Santa Cruz, CA 95060, 831/425-1234 or 800/834-3494, www.santacruzca.org.

BEACHES

From the highway it's a short dash to the huge expanse of sand at **Davenport Beach.** The healthy dune structure makes a scenic backdrop for a beach hike, where the only threat to your serenity might be the occasional hang glider leaping from a bluff above. Incidentally, a half mile south is Davenport Cove (a.k.a. Shark's Tooth Cove), a spot frequented by nude beachgoers.

Davenport Landing Beach is accessed via Davenport Landing Road, a loop road one mile north of town. Parking beside the road is permitted 6 A.M.–10 P.M., but there's room for only about 20 cars. It's a lot easier to get to than Bonny Doon and its neighboring

accesses. A short hike leads down a gradually sloping embankment, revealing cliffs at either end of a scenic cove. On a perfect Thursday in July, we had the beach to ourselves.

The prettiest of the three coastal settings in Davenport is **Scott Creek Beach,** where Scott Creek trickles across a sandy delta into the Pacific. When we visited, surf casters were digging the scene (though no fishing is allowed in the creek itself). Windsurfers frequent both Davenport Landing and Scott Creek. There's a lovely pond and wetlands on the east side of Highway 1 at Scott Creek, and the quarter-mile beach lies between bluffs on the west side.

35 DAVENPORT BEACH

Location: off Highway 1 in Davenport, 11 miles north of Santa Cruz
Parking/Fees: free roadside parking
Hours: 6 A.M.-10 P.M.
Facilities: none
Contact: Santa Cruz County Parks Department, 831/454-7901

Davenport Landing Beach

36 DAVENPORT LANDING BEACH

Location: 13 miles north of Santa Cruz off Highway 1 in Davenport
Parking/Fees: free roadside parking
Hours: sunrise-sunset
Facilities: none
Contact: Santa Cruz County Parks Department, 831/454-7901

37 SCOTT CREEK BEACH

Location: 14 miles north of Santa Cruz off Highway 1 in Davenport
Parking/Fees: free roadside parking
Hours: 6 A.M.-10 P.M.
Facilities: none
Contact: Santa Cruz County Parks Department, 831/454-7901

ACCOMMODATIONS

For a weekend getaway, consider booking a room at **Davenport Roadhouse** (1 Davenport Avenue, 831/426-8801, $$), whose rooms are behind the New Davenport Cash Store and above the restaurant. However, you are still on the east side of the highway and the traffic noise will compete with the sound of the waves.

COASTAL CUISINE

The **Davenport New Cash Store** (Davenport Avenue, 831/426-8801, $$$) is a gourmet restaurant, bakery, pottery gallery, and bed-and-breakfast inn rolled into one. The culinary emphasis is on creative seafood and pasta dishes, as well as local wines. Breakfast, lunch, and dinner are served.

Greyhound Rock and Waddell Creek

The angler's Nirvana in these parts is Greyhound Rock Fishing Access, 28 miles north of Santa Cruz in the middle of nowhere. Close by is Waddell Creek Beach, one of a series of wild and lovely creek-mouth beaches that extend from here north into neighboring San Mateo County.

Both Greyhound Rock and Waddell Creek are bounded by Big Basin Redwoods State Park, an enormous parkland (18,000 acres) that extends from the coast up into the Santa Cruz Mountains. An overnight stay in the inland campground is an attractive proposition. (The entrance fee at Big Basin is $7 per vehicle, and the camping fee is $25 per night, plus a $7.50 reservation fee.) Big Basin offers outdoors enthusiasts 80 miles of backcountry hiking trails, waterfalls, and tent sites—145 at base camp, plus 40 walk-in sites.

For more information, contact Big Basin Redwoods State Park, 21600 Big Basin Way, Boulder Creek, CA, 95006, 831/338-8860, www.parks.ca.gov.

BEACHES

Developed by the State Department of Fish and Game, **Greyhound Rock Fishing Access** features a trail and stairwell that lead down to the beach from paved parking lots right off Highway 1. The pathway is a real doozy, descending steeply to the beach. Greyhound Rock sits offshore, deflecting waves that wrap around it in such a way that a triangular beach has formed onshore. There is a picnic table and overlook up top if you don't want to huff and puff down to the water.

Waddell Creek Beach is usually quite windy, making it a favorite spot for windsurfers and hang gliders. A self-guided nature center offers insight on local flora and fauna, including a sobering note about dwindling steelhead and rainbow-trout populations, which once spawned happily in Waddell Creek. One more observation: The parking lot at Waddell Creek

Waddell Creek Beach

is deeply rutted and sits on unconsolidated bluffs that look to be slumping shoreward at an alarming rate. Just above Waddell Creek, Highway 1 passes some of the most menacing, erosion-prone cliffs this side of Big Sur. It's a high-hazard area for slides as the dark brown cliff faces—nearly vertical and shorn of vegetation—periodically slump and fail. A pile of rubble typically accumulates at the bottom. Keep your foot on the gas pedal through here.

38 GREYHOUND ROCK FISHING ACCESS

Location: Highway 1 at Swanton Road, north of Scott Creek, in north Santa Cruz County
Parking/Fees: free parking lot
Hours: 6 A.M.–10 P.M.
Facilities: restrooms and picnic tables
Contact: Santa Cruz County Parks Department, 831/454-7901

39 WADDELL CREEK BEACH

Location: one mile south of the San Mateo County line, along Highway 1
Parking/Fees: free parking lot
Hours: 6 A.M.–10 P.M.
Facilities: restrooms, campground
Contact: Big Basin Redwoods State Park, 831/338-8861

SANTA CRUZ COAST

© PARKE PUTERBAUGH

SAN FRANCISCO BAY AREA

If the Santa Cruz coast is like a mop-topped surfer, his grungy edge tempered by a basically sunny disposition, then the coastline belonging to the county of San Mateo and city of San Francisco is a grizzled veteran of the sea, maybe a steely-eyed fisherman or salty dog. The rocky shoals and heavy fogs along San Mateo county's 55-mile shoreline have long put the fear of shipwrecks in sailors' hearts, and the steep, shifting terrain in the Devil's Slide area has tossed both a coastal railroad and a highway into the Pacific.

The perfectly appealing towns of Half Moon Bay, Princeton, Moss Beach, Miramar, El Grenada, and Montara exemplify the other side of this coastline. There's also the wild isolation of Año Nuevo State Reserve, home to a huge colony of seals and a string of state beaches—Bean Hollow, Pescadero, Pomponio, San Gregorio, Half Moon Bay, and Montara. It is a land of grazing cattle and green fields of vegetables that love the cool fogs that shroud the area.

With San Francisco to the north, San Jose and the Santa Clara Valley to the east, and Santa Cruz to the south, San Mateo County exists in a sort of urban-to-rural transition zone. Despite its proximity to populated areas, geographical isolation makes it a tough commute. That has held in check the explosive growth that is so evident elsewhere on the coast. That's not to say the San Mateo coast, especially Half Moon Bay, isn't growing. Lately, especially on weekends, we've found traffic to be knotty and slow moving all over town—a sure sign of inundation. Let's hope they can keep a lid on it.

The beaches themselves are too cold and hazardous for swimming, and the only beauties you'll see sunbathing here are northern elephant seals at Año Nuevo State Reserve. The blubbery darlings are the largest pinnipeds in this hemisphere, reaching 16 feet

© KATHRYN OSGOOD

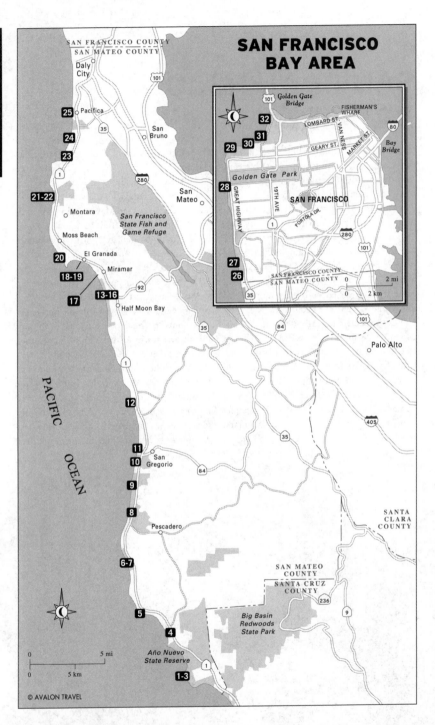

SAN FRANCISCO BAY AREA

SAN FRANCISCO COUNTY
SAN MATEO COUNTY

Daly City

101

25 Pacifica

San Bruno

35

24

23

1

280

San Mateo

21-22

Montara

San Francisco State Fish and Game Refuge

Moss Beach

20 El Granada

Miramar

18-19

17 **13-16**

92

Half Moon Bay

35

84

101

Palo Alto

1

12

405

35

11

10 San Gregorio

84

9

8

Pescadero

SANTA CLARA COUNTY

6-7

SAN MATEO COUNTY

SANTA CRUZ COUNTY

236

9

5

Big Basin Redwoods State Park

PACIFIC OCEAN

4

Año Nuevo State Reserve

0   5 mi

0   5 km

1-3

1

© AVALON TRAVEL

Inset map: SAN FRANCISCO

101 Golden Gate Bridge

FISHERMAN'S WHARF

32

LOMBARD ST.

31

GEARY ST.

VAN NESS

MARKET ST.

80

Bay Bridge

29 **30**

Golden Gate Park

19TH AVE

SAN FRANCISCO

28

GREAT HIGHWAY

1

PORTOLA DR.

280

101

27

26

SAN FRANCISCO COUNTY
SAN MATEO COUNTY

0   2 mi

0   2 km

35

in length. In addition to seal-watching, San Mateo County offers low-impact pastimes—tidepooling, strolling, fishing, camping, birding, and whale-watching—on its raw and elemental shoreline.

Just north of this rugged coastline lies San Francisco, where one can easily leave their heart, but where we left our footprints in the sand. That's right, the city by the bay has an unheralded side to its personality: The eight-mile stretch of ocean coastline from the San Mateo border to the Golden Gate Bridge is all public land, and much of it is fronted by sand.

An ocean beach in San Francisco, you say? Yes, and it is called Ocean Beach, a four-mile strand that stretches from Daly City to an old landmark, the Cliff House. This beach has it all—sand dunes, sea walls (dressed up by WPA murals from the 1930s), walkways, promontories. So where are all the swimsuit-clad beachgoers? Well, the plain fact is that San Francisco's beaches don't see very many days of sunshine or wind-free warmth. During the summer months, the shoreline fog is so thick you need a divining rod to find the water. And when you do, the frigid, tempestuous waves roar their disapproval. The riptide-prone Ocean Beach is flat-out dangerous, having claimed the lives of many unwary swimmers over the years.

If you stay dry and enjoy the view, you'll be fine. No city in America is blessed with such awe-inspiring vistas as San Francisco. The view from the Presidio's coastal trail north toward the Golden Gate Bridge and the Marin Headlands is one that everybody should lay eyes on during their lifetime. There are even a couple of beaches—Baker Beach and China Beach—where one can sunbathe and pass an afternoon in relative comfort, around the protective bend of Lands End.

Año Nuevo State Reserve

Año Nuevo State Reserve is first and foremost a wildlife refuge. It is the mainland rookery of the northern elephant seal and one of their largest gathering spots in the world. Peak population of the playful pinnipeds at Año Nuevo is 3,000. Second, it is a park open to human visitation. Just north of the Santa Cruz County line and 55 miles south of San Francisco, the reserve's 4,000 acres include scrub-covered coastal hills and rocky intertidal beaches. A rustic white barn serves as visitor center, museum, gift shop, and ticket counter for visitor permits and guided seal walks.

Whale-watching, bird-watching, clam-digging, and surf casting are other popular activities. In addition to elephant seals, other marine mammals—harbor seals, northern fur seals, sea lions, and sea otters—make their home here for at least part of the year. California gray whales pass Point Año Nuevo during their winter migration.

The Elephant Seal Viewing Area at Año Nuevo State Reserve can be visited 8 A.M.–3 P.M. daily April–November with a visitor permit, obtainable at the reserve office. Guided walks are offered daily December 15–March 31 and cost $7 per person. For **Año Nuevo Guided Walk** reservations, call 800/444-4445; they can made be starting at 9 A.M. on October 20. The viewing area is completely closed to visitors December 1–December 14. To hear a recorded message about the reserve, call 650/879-0227.

Incidentally, National Geographic's Seal Cam—a live webcam of elephant seals on Año Nuevo Island—went offline for repairs in 2007 but is now back and better than ever (www.video.nationalgeographic.com/video/sealcam). Viewing times are 9 A.M.–9 P.M.; the rest of the time is audio only.

For more information, contact Año Nuevo State Reserve, New Years Creek Road, Pescadero, CA 94060, 650/879-2025, www.parks.ca.gov.

BEACHES

The shoreline at **Año Nuevo State Reserve** consists of sandy coves and rocky headlands, with one of California's largest surviving dune fields bordering the wildlife protection area. Visitors can hike to a point from which they might spy seals playing on the beach or on offshore chunks of rock. One elongated outcrop is particularly surreal, as several abandoned buildings stand on it. Rocks and buildings alike are covered with seals and cormorants and stained with their droppings, giving it the peculiar appearance of a Hollywood stage set overtaken by wildlife.

The tangy air, crashing waves, and barking seals make for an enchanting nature experience. From the parking lot past the entrance station, it's a short hike to the silty, V-shaped, drift-log strewn **New Years Creek Beach,** via the gullied New Years Creek Trail. It's a 1.6-mile hike out to Point Año Nuevo, but the trail has been closed past the 0.9-mile mark. A section of the park south of Cascade Creek is off-limits to visitors during seal-breeding season (December 15–March 31), though guided tours of small groups are conducted by volunteer naturalists at this time. These walking tours cover three miles and take 2.5 hours.

Bight Beach is another seals-only playground by the sea. It lies between South and North Points, backed by a vast dune field covering 350 acres. Humans are allowed out here by permit only April–November.

There are two more beach accesses off Highway 1 at the north end of Año Nuevo's landholdings. You'll see two small lots on the west side of the highway, from which trails lead four-tenths of a mile across a meadow to these **North Año Nuevo Beaches.** There are no facilities here—nothing more than free parking, garbage cans, and sandy, deserted beaches.

Año Nuevo's rocky, south-facing beach runs along a mile of curving coastline. Surfers have been known to catch a wave off the point, which breaks best in summer, but they must face the ever-present threat of shark attacks. Sharks are natural predators of seals, and are therefore found in greater number at Año Nuevo. Is a well-formed wave worth that kind of risk? Apparently, some surfers think so.

■ NEW YEARS CREEK BEACH

Location: New Years Creek Road off Highway 1, 26 miles south of Half Moon Bay
Parking/Fees: $7 entrance fee per vehicle; $7 per person for guided elephant seal walks, offered December 15–March 31
Hours: 8 A.M.-sunset, special restrictions for seal viewing areas; check with park for details
Facilities: restrooms, picnic tables, and visitors center
Contact: Año Nuevo State Reserve, 650/879-2025

■ BIGHT BEACH

Location: New Years Creek Road off Highway 1, 26 miles south of Half Moon Bay
Parking/Fees: $7 entrance fee per vehicle; $7 per person for guided elephant seal walks, offered December 15–March 31
Hours: 8 A.M.-sunset, special restrictions for seal viewing areas; check with park for details
Facilities: restrooms, picnic tables, and visitors center
Contact: Año Nuevo State Reserve, 650/879-2025

■ NORTH AÑO NUEVO BEACHES

Location: New Years Creek Road off Highway 1, 26 miles south of Half Moon Bay
Parking/Fees: free parking lots
Hours: 8 A.M.-sunset, special restrictions for seal viewing areas; check with park for details
Facilities: restrooms, picnic tables, and visitors center
Contact: Año Nuevo State Reserve, 650/879-2025

Gazos Creek Access

Stairs lead to a lagoon and beach by Gazos Creek Bridge, six miles north of the Santa Cruz County line on Highway 1. The creek meanders into the sea at Gazos Creek Access.

For more information, contact Año Nuevo State Reserve, New Years Creek Road, Pescadero, CA 94060, 650/879-2025, www.parks.ca.gov.

BEACHES

The parking lot is on a bluff overlooking the broad, sandy, semicircular cove at **Gazos Creek Beach.** Behind it rise the redwood canyons of Gazos, Whitehouse, and Cascade Creeks, combined into the undeveloped acreage of Año Nuevo State Park. The Pigeon Point Lighthouse is visible to the north.

◖ GAZOS CREEK BEACH

Location: Gazos Creek Bridge at Highway 1, 22 miles south of Half Moon Bay
Parking/Fees: free parking lot
Hours: 8 A.M.–sunset
Facilities: restrooms
Contact: Año Nuevo State Reserve, 650/879-2025

Pigeon Point

The 115-foot-tall **Pigeon Point Lighthouse** has been guiding mariners since 1872. Because so many ships have sunk off the point, the lighthouse remains a vital navigational aid. It is the second tallest structure of its kind in California and the tallest one still in operation. Also on the site is a hostelry where you can stay for a pittance out on the wild edge of the San Mateo coast. The lighthouse and hostel are on Pigeon Point Road, off Highway 1 about 20 miles south of Half Moon Bay and

27 miles north of Santa Cruz. Due to concerns over the lighthouse's structural safety, tours are not currently being given, though the grounds remain open.

For more information, contact Pigeon Point Lighthouse State Historic Park, 210 Pigeon Point Road, Pescadero, CA 94060, 650/879-0633 (hostel), 650/879-2120 (park), www.parks.ca.gov.

BEACHES

There's good tidepooling in the vicinity of **Pigeon Point,** and gray whales can be sighted on their annual migration during spring months.

◗ PIGEON POINT

Location: Pigeon Point Road at Highway 1, 20 miles south of Half Moon Bay
Parking/Fees: free parking lot
Hours: 7:30 A.M.–9:30 P.M.
Facilities: restrooms and showers
Contact: Pigeon Point Lighthouse State Historic Park, 650/879-0633

ACCOMMODATIONS

The **Pigeon Point Lighthouse Hostel** (210 Pigeon Point Road, Pescadero, 650/879-0633, $) occupies bungalows that formerly accommodated Coast Guard families. There are private rooms for couples and families, as well as dormitory-style bunkrooms for travelers who are game for a communal experience (52 beds total). Rates run $22–24 per adult, $10 per child (ages 6–12); a private room costs $55 and up. The former Fog Signal Building now serves as a recreational lounge for overnighters. A big hot tub overlooking the ocean is available for rental. South of the lighthouse, a trail leads to Gazos Creek Beach.

Bean Hollow State Beach

A shelf of rocks divides Bean Hollow State Beach, one of the more wild and scenic stretches of coastline in San Mateo County, into broad coves. Raw, elemental beach wilderness is the main feature at Bean Hollow, which lies 18 miles south of Half Moon Bay.

BEACHES

You'll find mostly rocky surf at Bean Hollow, save for small, sandy coves at **Pebble Beach** and **Arroyo de Frijoles Beach**—which is Spanish for "bean hollow"—at the south end of Bean Hollow.

A nature trail connects Bean Hollow with Pebble Beach, a mile to the north. A helpful brochure, which can be picked up in boxes at either end of the trail, is keyed to numbered posts along the way, and the basic geology, ecology, and marine biology of the area are conveyed in easy-to-follow text. One of the more interesting facts we learned has to do with coastal bluff erosion. Where the sandstone is soft, cliffs can retreat as much as 22 feet per year. Living proof of this can be seen in the rerouting of the trail that's been necessitated by the shoreward retreat of the bluffs.

Pebble Beach derives its name from the crop of smooth, rounded pebbles found at surf's edge. One theory holds that it is the site of a former stream mouth whose pebbly remnants were bound up in the sandstone-conglomerate overlay in the recent geological past. You're encouraged to admire the pebbles but to leave them where they lie. The sandstone in this vicinity takes on a distinctive orange hue. Rare, lacelike formations called tafoni are carved into the coastal rocks. Offshore, the roiling surf whips up an oozy froth.

6 PEBBLE BEACH

Location: 18 miles south of Half Moon Bay off Highway 1
Parking/Fees: free parking lot
Hours: 8 A.M.-sunset
Facilities: restrooms and picnic tables
Contact: California State Parks, Bay Area District, 650/879-2170

© KATHRYN OSGOOD

Pebble Beach

7 ARROYO DE FRIJOLES BEACH

Location: 17 miles south of Half Moon Bay off Highway 1
Parking/Fees: free parking lot
Hours: 8 A.M.-sunset
Facilities: restrooms and picnic tables
Contact: California State Parks, Bay Area District, 650/879-2170

Pescadero State Beach

There are three beach-access points at Pescadero State Beach, a mile-long beach 14.5 miles south of Half Moon Bay. The best access is the northernmost lot at Pescadero Creek, where a small day-use fee is collected. The south one has a larger parking lot perched at bluff's edge, overlooking the raging sea. The parking lot, formerly a bumpy and pothole-riddled disaster, has been scraped and laid with new gravel.

All three lots offer access to **Pescadero**

State Beach Marsh Preserve, on the east side of the highway, where hiking trails wander through one of the most significant freshwater/brackish coastal marshes in California. It is a critical resting place on the Pacific flyway. A bird checklist is available to visitors.

Free ranger-led marsh walks are offered on Saturday at 10:30 A.M. and Sunday at 1 P.M. throughout the year, weather permitting. Meet at the parking lot on Highway 1 just south of Pescadero Creek. Look for a sign that reads: Pescadero State Beach Marsh Preserve. No reservations are necessary.

BEACHES

The beaches of **Pescadero State Beach** represent the San Mateo coast at its wildest: rough surf, rocky beach, nearly leveled headlands that people explore for close encounters with nature in extremis. Breakers violently pound rocky outcrops. The rough-and-tumble setting is perfect for sunset watching, as the ocean's acrobatics provide a dramatic soundtrack for the sun's disappearing act. If you're fearless and sure-footed, stroll out onto the points of rock that extend seaward in defiance of the

© PARKE PUTERBAUGH

Pescadero State Beach

waves' relentless pounding. It is haunting and undeveloped out here, and one roadside sign says it all: Next Gas 35 Miles.

8 PESCADERO STATE BEACH
🚶🚶

Location: 14.5 miles south of Half Moon Bay along Highway 1

Parking/Fees: $6 entrance fee per vehicle at north lot; free parking at central and south lots

Hours: 8 A.M.–sunset

Facilities: restrooms and picnic tables

Contact: Pescadero State Beach, 650/879-2170

COASTAL CUISINE

The "historic" community of Pescadero, a tiny hamlet a few miles inland, is in the heart of a rural area renowned for its trout fishing. At **Duarte's Tavern** (202 Stage Road, 650/879-0464, $$), a former stagecoach-era saloon, locals flock for seafood and gossip. Pronounce it DOO-arts, or they'll know you're from out of town. Hell, they'll probably realize that in half a second anyway.

Pomponio State Beach

Pomponio State Beach lies 12 miles south of Half Moon Bay. It is the smallest of the trio of state beaches located in the sparsely populated midsection of San Mateo County.

BEACHES

The broad, semicircular beach at **Pomponio State Beach** is not as stunning as San Gregorio or as expansive as Pescadero, but neither is it as heavily visited. It is a sandy creek-fed beach flanked by grassy bluffs, with a cove and a narrower strip of sand running north of it. Pomponio takes its name from a Native American outlaw who lived in a nearby cave during Spanish rule. There are picnic tables in the green grass above the beach.

At its southern end, Pomponio is a clothing-optional beach that's a bit hard to reach. If you're walking along the water line, this stretch is accessible from the parking lot only at low tide, lying 0.7 mile to the south. The other way in is to walk north the same distance from Pescadero State Beach.

Pomponio State Beach

© PARKE PUTERBAUGH

⑨ POMPONIO STATE BEACH

🚶 🧺

Location: 12 miles south of Half Moon Bay on Highway 1
Parking/Fees: $5 entrance fee per vehicle
Hours: 8 A.M.-sunset
Facilities: restrooms and picnic tables
Contact: California State Parks, Bay Area District, 650/879-2170

San Gregorio State Beach

San Gregorio State Beach is a great spot for hiking. Scenic paths wander atop mustard-colored sandstone bluffs overlooking the ocean, and the beach itself is wonderfully wide at the mouth of San Gregorio Creek. Away from the creek, it narrows dramatically in both directions, hemmed between ocean and bluff.

The beaches of San Mateo County—and San Gregorio in particular—are amazing to behold. The topography is rugged, the ocean chilly and tempestuous. Solitary beach hiking is an inviting activity, though you are advised to keep an eye on tides and sleeper waves. One evening around sunset in May, we hiked up a trail that skirted the cliff's edge south of the creek. From this awesome promontory, we watched the sun set—a magnificent spectacle that resulted in this sincere—if, in hindsight, overstated—notebook entry: "Greatest experience of life: Sunset over San Gregorio."

BEACHES

On a weekend afternoon in late summer, the broad apron of sand below the parking lot of **San Gregorio State Beach** was packed with all kinds of folks: a church youth group playing games on the beach; families of every ethnic origin gathered around picnic baskets; college students basking in the sun; and little children charging madly about. However, not a soul braved the water. On a windy March weekday in another year, by contrast, San Gregorio was empty, and a bitter wind chilled us to the marrow. A winter's worth of storms had turned the expansive creek mouth beach into what looked like a graveyard for drift logs.

The paved parking lot at San Gregorio costs $6 to enter. Just up the hill, south of the

© PARKE PUTERBAUGH

San Gregorio State Beach

bridge over San Gregorio Creek, people park on the shoulder of Highway 1 and enter for free along paths that lead down to the beach. Being ardent supporters of California State Parks, we encourage one and all to ante up their fair share and spare the crumbling bluffs their destructive footsteps.

10 SAN GREGORIO STATE BEACH

Location: 10.5 miles south of Half Moon Bay on Highway 1
Parking/Fees: $6 entrance fee per vehicle
Hours: 8 A.M.-sunset
Facilities: restrooms, picnic tables, and fire pits
Contact: California State Parks, Bay Area District, 650/879-2170

San Gregorio Private Beach

San Gregorio Private Beach is clothing optional. It's not just any old nude beach, though. San Gregorio Private Beach claims to be America's oldest nude sand beach, having catered to naturists for six decades.

BEACHES

Located below steep bluffs, **San Gregorio Private Beach** offers an expansive stretch of scenic beauty. In addition to true-blue au naturel aesthetes, some prurient opportunists apparently couple in driftwood lean-tos, referred to as "sex condos." There's plenty of beach to go around out here—two long, lonesome miles of it. Crowds numbering upward of 500 let it all hang out on summer weekends. Straight couples and families congregate at the south end.

Some avoid the charges ($5 per car or $2 per person) by parking along the roadside and making the treacherous hike down via trails. Such high-impact intrusions are no doubt responsible for accelerating bluff erosion. Be a sport, ante

up the fee and enter where you ought to. As an alternative, you can hike north along the beach for half a mile from San Gregorio State Beach.

11 SAN GREGORIO PRIVATE BEACH

Location: end of dirt toll road, 100 yards north of junction of Highways 1 and 84 (address on gatepost is 119429 Highway 1)
Parking/Fees: $5 per car or $2 per person
Hours: 10 A.M.-7 P.M. (9 A.M.-sunset on weekends)
Facilities: restrooms
Contact: none

Martins Beach

The fact that science-fiction writer H. P. Lovecraft coauthored a short story called "The Horror at Martin's Beach" shouldn't put you off of this prime fishing spot in San Mateo County.

BEACHES

Martins Beach is a private fishing cove; you pay a $5 toll to enter the road and cast a line. There's an on-site store that's open in summer, plus restrooms and picnic tables.

12 MARTINS BEACH

Location: Martins Beach Road and Highway 1, six miles south of Half Moon Bay
Parking/Fees: $5 entrance fee per vehicle
Hours: 6 A.M.-5 P.M. (to 6 P.M. on weekends and later in summer)
Facilities: restrooms and picnic tables
Contact: Martins Beach, 650/712-8020

Half Moon Bay

Half Moon Bay may soon need to be renamed Full Moon Bay, as suburban sprawl pushes down from San Francisco (30 miles north) and up from Silicon Valley (30 miles southeast). Formerly a nub in the middle of the rural San Mateo Coast, where Highway 1 meets Highway 92, the quaint, seaside town served as an overflow valve for stressed-out urbanites fleeing the congested Bay Area. However, strict coastal zoning regulations, limitations in sewer capacity and water supply, and the hassles of living here—especially commuting anywhere from here—have tempered the influx somewhat.

The community itself has implemented a 3 percent per year ceiling on growth. In its pursuit of slow growth, Half Moon Bay is occasionally assisted by flooding and landslides, which close Highways 1 and 92 from time to time. The long-range view is that Half Moon Bay and its neighboring communities are facing "overwhelming transportation, economic, and environmental problems," according to a report. Already the area is badly bogged down by traffic.

Half Moon Bay is at the heart of an area known as Coastside—a string of towns along the central San Mateo County coast. In addition to Half Moon Bay, Coastside includes El Granada, Miramar, Princeton, Moss Beach, and Montara. The combined population of these and a few inland hamlets is growing. Much of the land along the foggy coast is used for farming artichokes, Brussels sprouts, pumpkins, and flowers. Luxury Cape Cod–style developments have gone up, contrasting with the modest dwellings of agricultural workers. The once-present aura of tranquility has been disturbed, and the future is uncertain. Much depends on how accessible the area becomes as improvements to the primary arteries are made. Already Highway 92 has been widened, and Caltrans plans to bore a 4,200-foot hole through San Pedro Mountain to make Highway 1 more passable through Devil's Slide, between Half Moon Bay and Pacifica. They project that the twin tunnels will open in 2011.

The oldest community in San Mateo Coun-ty, Half Moon Bay (population 12,400) has already been gentrified. Art galleries, trendy boutiques, and sophisticated eateries like Pasta Moon and Sushi Main Street have taken up residence alongside San Mateo County Farm Supply and Cunha's Country Store. Half Moon Bay is an appealing weekend destination, offering comfortable bed-and-breakfasts, urbane restaurants, upscale shopping, and an opportunity to chill out. And we do mean chill out.

Emplaced in a natural setting of waves and sand backed by rolling brown hills and jutting headlands, the Coastside area is appealingly raw and strikingly beautiful. Frequently buried beneath a ceiling of coastal overcast, Half Moon Bay wears a gray, austere look. Heavy fogs carry as much as a million gallons of water shoreward per hour. Temperatures are unvarying: highs in the 60s, lows in the 40s. Precipitation varies radically depending on time of year. May through mid-October is the dry season, while mid-October through April is rainy.

For more information, contact the Half Moon Bay/Coastside Chamber of Commerce & Visitors Bureau, 235 Main Street, Half Moon Bay, CA 94019, 650/726-8380, www .halfmoonbaychamber.org.

BEACHES

Cowell Ranch State Beach, which lies three miles south of town, opened to the public in 1995. Getting to the beach requires a half-mile hike and a descent down a steep staircase, all of which ensures more privacy than you'll find on the beaches up in Half Moon Bay. **Pelican Point Beach,** about two miles south of where Highways 1 and 92 meet in Half Moon Bay, has a bit more to offer. The private campground has 84 campsites for tents and RVs, as well as beach access.

The big enchilada in these parts is **Half Moon Bay State Beach,** a 2.3-mile stretch of shoreline in Half Moon Bay proper. It has four named beach accesses: Francis, Venice,

Dunes, and Roosevelt (from south to north). Theoretically, the six-mile Coastside Trail connects these beaches, running along the marine terrace above the water. It's used by joggers, bicyclists, and walkers. However, the trail is discontinuous, owing to bluff-side erosion and the ocean's encroachment. Attempting to run its length one morning, we found ourselves stymied by sudden endings and reroutings. It's a lovely path, to be sure, but one that is (like the coast itself) under siege, particularly at the north end. An equestrian trail runs parallel to the Coastside Trail. Horses can be rented by the hour at private stables in Half Moon Bay.

Francis Beach is the largest and most popular unit. It is reached by heading west along Kelly Avenue (off Highway 1) and then turning right on Balboa Boulevard, which leads to the gated entrance. A field of grassy short bluffs above the beach is studded with picnic tables. Picnicking families and their victuals draw throngs of hungry shorebirds that squawk for handouts and forage through garbage cans like a scene from Alfred Hitchcock's *The Birds*. Wave erosion and human feet have carved gullied paths down to the beach. From the sandy strand, it's another sharp drop to where the waves wash up. The steep gradient and strong backwash make this look to be an unsafe beach for swimming. Water temperatures hover just above 50 degrees, and hypothermia is almost guaranteed without a wetsuit. Still, crowds descend on Francis Beach to camp, picnic, and frolic.

A gravel road leads out to **Venice Beach,** which has a large parking lot and is a popular spot for horseback riding. **Dunes Beach** and **Roosevelt Beach** are smaller points of entry accessed from the same road (Young Avenue). Between Venice and Dunes is the **Sweetwood Group Camp,** a tent-only group campsite that can accommodate up to 50 persons and 12 vehicles. Close by are **Sea Horse Ranch and Friendly Acres Horses and Rentals** (2150

Highway 1, 650/726-2362), where a guided 90-minute horse ride on the beach costs $65. Early birds can nab a two-hour beach ride at 8 A.M. for only $45—a veritable steal, as these things go.

13 FRANCIS BEACH

Location: end of Kelly Avenue, off Highway 1 in Half Moon Bay
Parking/Fees: $6 entrance fee per vehicle; camping fees $25 per night (Francis Beach), $111 per night per group site (Sweetwood Group Camp)
Hours: 8 A.M.-sunset
Facilities: restrooms, showers, and picnic tables
Contact: Half Moon Bay State Beach, 650/726-8819

14 VENICE BEACH

Location: end of Venice Boulevard, off Highway 1 in Half Moon Bay
Parking/Fees: $6 entrance fee per vehicle
Hours: 8 A.M.-sunset
Facilities: restrooms and picnic tables
Contact: Half Moon Bay State Beach, 650/726-8819

15 DUNES BEACH

Location: end of Young Avenue, off Highway 1 in Half Moon Bay
Parking/Fees: $6 entrance fee per vehicle
Hours: 8 A.M.-sunset
Facilities: restrooms and picnic area
Contact: Half Moon Bay State Beach, 650/726-8819

16 ROOSEVELT BEACH

🚲 🚶 🎿

Location: from end of Young Avenue at Dunes Beach, off Highway 1 in Half Moon Bay, follow park road north to beach
Parking/Fees: $6 entrance fee per vehicle
Hours: 8 A.M.-sunset
Facilities: restrooms
Contact: Half Moon Bay State Beach, 650/726-8819

RECREATION AND ATTRACTIONS

- **Bike/Skate Rentals:** Half Moon Bay Bike Rentals, 648 Kelly Avenue, Half Moon Bay, 650/712-4499
- **Ecotourism:** Pescadero State Beach Marsh Preserve, Pescadero, 650/879-2170
- **Lighthouse:** Pigeon Point Light Station, Pescadero, 650/879-0633; Point Montara Light Station, Montara, 650/728-7177
- **Marina:** Pillar Point Harbor, Princeton-by-the-Sea, 650/726-5727
- **Pier:** Romeo Pier, Pillar Point Harbor, Princeton-by-the-Sea, 650/726-5727
- **Rainy Day Attraction:** gallery hopping, Main Street, Half Moon Bay
- **Shopping/Browsing:** Main Street, Half Moon Bay
- **Sportfishing:** Riptide Sportfishing, 300 Capistrano Road, Half Moon Bay, 415/469-8433
- **Surf Shop:** Half Moon Bay Board Shop, 3032 Cabrillo Highway North, Half Moon Bay, 650/726-1476
- **Vacation Rentals:** Del Mar Properties, 980 The Alameda, Ed Granada, 650/712-6800

ACCOMMODATIONS

The Beach House (4100 North Cabrillo Highway, 650/712-0220, $$$$) is a relative newcomer to Half Moon Bay. It's a modern, well-equipped (with fireplaces and CD changers), inn-like hotel that looks out on Princeton Harbor from the far north end of Half Moon Bay. The Coastside Trail—a scenic godsend to walkers, bikers, and runners—begins right out the Beach House's back door. The rooms are described as "ocean lofts," and they're not quite suites but more spacious than typical digs at hotels or inns. You can prop yourself up on pillows in bed and gaze out the picture window onto the harbor—not an unpleasant proposition. You can also cook a meal, listen to CDs, watch a DVD, or warm up by the fire. In short, all the bases are covered at this ultramodern inn.

The posh **Best Western Half Moon Bay Lodge** (2400 South Cabrillo Highway, 650/726-9000, $$$$) is another recent arrival. Formerly part of the posh Woodside Hotels and Resorts collection, it has taken a step down in yuppie cachet, now being a part of the Best Western chain. Still, rooms have an elegant, European feel and the Half Moon Bay Golf Links (two courses) and the beach are nearby. One cool morning we sat in the gazebo-covered outdoor whirlpool and soaked before heading off to grab the free continental breakfast. It's a relaxing place to de-stress on the San Mateo Coast. And the staff will happily point you to all the best restaurants in town, too.

The old Victorian buildings of Half Moon Bay have been preserved, and a few have been put to use as bed-and-breakfast inns. The most lavish of these is **Mill Rose Inn** (615 Mill Street, 650/726-8750, $$$$), a pricey, overblown but romantic retreat in Half Moon Bay's Old Town district surrounded by an English country garden. They pamper you with "classic European elegance by the sea" here: robes, wine and cheese, tubs for two, outdoor spa in a white gazebo, and so on. Roses are everywhere. Honeymooners, take note. Another denizen of the bed-and-breakfast scene is the **Old Thyme Inn** (779 Main Street, 650/726-1616, $$$), done in Queen Anne style with an herb garden and more affordable prices.

Half Moon Bay also has a couple of newer arrivals in the motel category, namely **Days Inn** (3020 Cabrillo Highway, 650/726-9700, $) and **Holiday Inn Express** (230 South Cabrillo Highway, 650/726-3400, $$). At the other extreme is the lately arrived **Ritz-Carlton Half Moon Bay** (1 Miramontes Point Road, 650/712-7000, $$$$), also by the golf links and perched on bluffs overlooking the ocean. This 261-room lodge, needless to say, is far and away the plushest and priciest resort along the San Mateo Coast—almost inappropriately so, in our opinion.

COASTAL CUISINE

Since the restaurants of Half Moon Bay serve the discriminating palates of many who live (or once lived) in San Francisco, there is a respectable dining scene there. Topping the list is **Pasta Moon** (315 Main Street, 650/726-5125, $$$), where linguine with scallops and other seafood-pasta combos are worth raving about.

San Benito House (356 Main Street, 650/726-3425, $$$) is a turn-of-the-20th-century inn and restaurant known for California cuisine in a French country setting. San Benito was the original name of the settlement at Half Moon Bay. **Cetrella Bistro** (845 Main Street, 650/726-4090, $$$) serves Mediterranean cuisine and has a great bar and wine cellar. Entrée items include local halibut over a corn, fava bean, and cherry tomato succotash (healthy!) and Catalonian shellfish stew.

Gourmet takeout or eat-in fare can be had at **Two Fools Cafe and Market** (408 Main Street, 650/712-1222, $$). **Main Street Grill** (547 Main Street, 650/726-5300, $) serves the best home-cooked breakfast and lunch on the San Mateo coast—everything from omelets and sourdough French toast to burgers and microbrew beers.

Raw fish addicts will want to head to **Sushi Main Street** (696 Mill Street, 650/726-6336, $$$). You can judge a sushi bar by its rolls, and Sushi Main Street's are killer. The local favorites are Half Moon Bay (artichoke heart, avocado, radish, sprouts) and Princeton-by-the-Sea (albacore, ginger, green onion). And dig the Hawaiian special: tuna, avocado, macadamia nuts. The restaurant also has hot entrées (tempuras, teriyakis) and clay pot specials.

On a more budget-conscious note, **Three Amigos** (200 South Cabrillo Highway, 650/726-6080, $$) will have you doing handstands and hat dances over its Mexican food. Go for the chicken fajita burrito, a hearty handful of grilled poultry strips and all the other Mexican essentials stuffed inside a flour tortilla. At first glance, it looks huge enough to feed a party of five, but one hungry gaucho can put it away without much trouble. The Acapulco Burrito (prawns, peppers, onions, and crab) also came highly recommended.

NIGHTLIFE

The **Half Moon Bay Inn** (401 Main Street, 650/726-5997), a dimly lit tavern smack dab in the center of town, is where the locals come to bend an elbow. The bar at the aforementioned **Cetrella Bistro** (845 Main Street, 650/726-4090) is a great place to sip wine or microbrew beer. Alternatives in the communities north of Half Moon Bay include **Miramar Beach Restaurant** (131 Mirada Road, 650/726-9053) and **Moss Beach Distillery** (140 Beach Way, Moss Beach, 650/728-5595).

Miramar

Miramar is more remarkable for what it used to be than for what it is. It was once the site of the Palace Miramar, a seaside resort hotel (circa 1916) with an indoor saltwater plunge. During Prohibition, Miramar served as the drop-off point for bootleg liquor shipped down from Canada. Local rumrunners paddled out to meet the large ships and carry the hooch to shore under cover of darkness. The Miramar Beach Inn (circa 1918) was designed and constructed as a Prohibition roadhouse and, it is rumored, bordello. These days, the same building does business as the Miramar Beach Restaurant, a rustic eatery and music club with great ocean views. Miramar itself (population 400) is a sweet nothing of a town: a few residential streets running parallel to a beach that disappears rapidly as high tide approaches.

For more information, contact the Half Moon Bay/Coastside Chamber of Commerce & Visitors Bureau, 235 Main Street, Half Moon Bay, CA 94019, 650/726-8380, www .halfmoonbaychamber.org.

BEACHES

Miramar Beach adjoins El Granada Beach, which runs up to the breakwater at Pillar Point Harbor. The breakwater, built in 1959, has caused massive erosion on the beaches south of it. It interrupts the natural, shore-parallel movement of sand down the coast and focuses greater wave energy on the beaches, resulting in accelerated sea-cliff erosion. Parts of Mirada Road have been destroyed, and the highly erodable cliffs have retreated an estimated 90 feet since the harbor construction project. Life is a beach, unless you live down-drift of a breakwater or jetty, in which case life is a shrinking beach.

17 MIRAMAR BEACH

Location: end of Mirada Road in Miramar, two miles north of Half Moon Bay
Parking/Fees: free street parking
Hours: half hour before sunrise–half hour after sunset
Facilities: none
Contact: none

ACCOMMODATIONS

The **Cypress Inn** (407 Mirada Road, 650/726-6002, $$$) is a bright, contemporary B&B outfitted in Southwestern decor. The three-story, 12-room inn was built a stone's throw from the ocean in 1989, and every comfortable room has a fireplace, balcony, and view of Miramar Beach.

COASTAL CUISINE

The **Miramar Beach Restaurant** (131 Mirada Road, 650/726-9053, $$$) was revamped some in the 1990s. It still has the sturdy, solid look of dark wood and brass, but the menu has been expanded and updated. In addition to grilled steaks and seafood, you can order linguine with cracked crab and bay shrimp or salmon in puff pastry.

NIGHTLIFE

Surprisingly, for a town that's just a blip on the coastal radar, Miramar boasts two revered music spots. **Miramar Beach Restaurant** (131 Mirada Road, 650/726-9053) tends to book the remnants of San Francisco bands that stood the world on its ear in the 1960s and are somehow scraping by today. During one of our treks through the area, former members of Moby Grape, the Doobie Brothers, and the Sons of Champlin were all booked.

The other side of Mirada's musical coin is the **Bach Dancing and Dynamite Society** (Mirada Road, 650/726-4131), an oceanfront beach house whose owner and impresario, Peter Douglas, hosts 26 Sunday afternoon concerts a year—mainly jazz and the classics. You can bring your own wine and picnic on the deck while the band plays. This eccentric and eclectic place has been hosting music since 1964.

El Granada

El Granada is a mostly residential town of 5,500 arrayed in semicircular roads on the east side of Highway 1. It has a touch of everything for the tourist: a nice, comfy inn that's a five-minute stroll from the beach (**Harbor View Inn,** 51 Avenue Alhambra, 650/726-2329, $$), a good continental bistro that offers live jazz and classical music on weekends (**Cafe Classique,** 107 Sevilla Avenue, 650/726-9775, $$$), and El Granada Beach. The only drawback is noise from nonstop traffic on the highway.

For more information, contact the Half Moon Bay/Coastside Chamber of Commerce & Visitors Bureau, 235 Main Street, Half Moon Bay, CA 94019, 650/726-8380, www .halfmoonbaychamber.org.

BEACHES

El Granada Beach is wide, but the short bluffs behind it suffer erosion when winter storms do their damage. Sometimes the sea chomps through the riprap and into the roadway, necessitating repairs. Pillar Point Harbor has brought increased commerce to Coastside but made a mess of the beaches next door. Still, watersports enthusiasts—boogie boarders, ocean kayakers, and surfers—have fun just below the east breakwater, an area known as **Surfers Beach.**

18 EL GRANADA BEACH

Location: between Mirada Road and East Breakwater at Pillar Point Harbor, three miles north of Half Moon Bay off Highway 1
Parking/Fees: metered parking lot at Pillar Point Harbor
Hours: half hour before sunrise-half hour after sunset
Facilities: none
Contact: none

Princeton-by-the-Sea and Pillar Point

The cliffs of Pillar Point form a protective shield enfolding the development known as Pillar Point Harbor. The Army Corps of Engineers built two breakwaters in 1961, further protecting the harbor and allowing expansion to its present size of 369 berths. Surrounding the harbor is the community of Princeton-by-the-Sea, an unpretentious scattering of Cape Cod–type homes that were here long before the faux New England architectural theme became an overplayed cliché on the California coast. Princeton is a quiet town along Harbor Road, which curves off and rejoins Highway 1. Pillar Point is a real working harbor whose 180-boat fishing fleet lands 10 million pounds of fish a year.

Not surprisingly, there are some terrific seafood restaurants in the area—probably the best grouping of them between San Francisco and Santa Cruz. Still, the harbor complex doesn't appear to be prospering the way its developers might have hoped. A huge, glassed-in harborfront retail complex, complete with cushy hotels and restaurants, never got beyond the planning stages.

BEACHES

Half Moon Bay made headlines in 1994 when Mark Foos, a world-class surfer, was killed while riding a 18-foot wave at a break called Maverick's, offshore of **Pillar Point.** Maverick's is not for the timid or inexperienced, but the word is out—both about the size of waves when they're breaking, and their lethal potential. Unless you're a world-class daredevil, just stay onshore and look for whales or at surfers. Pillar Point is a prime location for whale-watching December–March.

For more information, contact the Half Moon Bay/Coastside Chamber of Commerce & Visitors Bureau, 235 Main Street, Half Moon Bay, CA 94019, 650/726-8380, www .halfmoonbaychamber.org.

19 PILLAR POINT

Location: along Capistrano Road, four miles north of Half Moon Bay off Highway 1
Parking/Fees: metered parking lot
Hours: sunrise-sunset
Facilities: restrooms and picnic tables
Contact: Pillar Point Harbor, 650/726-5727

SURF'S WAY UP AT MAVERICK'S

Maverick's is where the most fearless wave riders in the world come to play Russian roulette with Mother Nature. Hawaiian surfer Mark Foo, considered the greatest big-wave rider of them all, met his match in December 1994, when he disappeared inside an 18-foot wave. His splintered surfboard and 36-year-old body were found floating in the harbor an hour later. Foo's death made national headlines and was the subject of multiple magazine articles that helped put Maverick's, big-wave riding, and "extreme sports" on the map. As a result, the winter wave-riding scene at Maverick's regularly receives national coverage. Now it's been formalized into a competition – bearing the macho name "Men Who Ride Mountains" – underwritten by the surfboard maker Quiksilver.

Maverick's lies beyond the cliffs along the north shore of Pillar Point, near the town of Princeton. Huge swells from far-distant storms create waves as high as 40 feet four or five times a year during the winter storm season. It is a quarter-mile, half-hour paddle out to this open-ocean break. Most surfers get there by boat. Risks associated with Maverick's – aside from the obvious one of falling off a giant wave and being driven to the ocean floor until drowned – include shark attacks and being filleted on the near-shore rocks. The *San Francisco Chronicle* has branded Maverick's "the wildest, heaviest, most dangerous big-wave spot on earth." There's even some risk involved in watching this madness from the slippery cliffs at Pillar Point.

Maverick's is not for inexperienced surfers, which is why it's fortunate the spot has a no-nonsense gatekeeper in Jeff Cook, who discovered it back in 1975. The surfing competition at Maverick's, which runs from the beginning of November to the end of January, is by invitation only, and is limited to 20 – most of them Californians with plenty of prior experience at Maverick's. Still, this is extreme sports *in extremis*: a surfing event where wave height and water temperature reach unfathomably high and low points, respectively, nearly meeting somewhere in the 40s and testing the most indomitable competitor's willpower.

All this danger is endured for what amounts to chump change in the world of professional sports. As Mark Foo griped shortly before his death, "We're out there risking our lives for nothing, or maybe a few thousand bucks, while some overweight guy is standing over a three-foot putt for half a million dollars." Money isn't even a factor in the minds of most who surf Maverick's, however. It's the challenge of those big waves and the indescribable rush of what is almost a certifiable act of insanity.

If you want to watch surfers at Maverick's on big-wave days, take West Point Road to the U.S. Air Force Radar Tracking Station at Pillar Point. Park at the small lot by the marsh and follow the trail out to the bluffs, where surfers will be visible in the distance. If the lot is full (and it probably will be), you might have to park at Pillar Point Harbor and walk an hour to the site. Nothing about Maverick's, you see, is easy.

THE CAPE COD CONNECTION

What seemed like a developmental affectation – trying to make prefab developments on the San Mateo Coast look like Cape Cod fishing villages – might have some basis in reality. The small town of Princeton-by-the-Sea has taken the Cape Cod architectural theme to extremes, and now it seems history has rewarded it with an improbable shot of New England credibility.

In 2008, local historians determined that the nearby lighthouse at Point Montara sat, once upon a time, right on the elbow of Cape Cod, in Wellfleet, Massachusetts. It was built there in 1881 and later moved by the Coast Guard to Yerba Buena, California, then moved once again to Point Montara. Before each move, the metal lighthouse was disassembled, transported by railroad, and reassembled by some truly tireless workers. The lighthouse still functions and also does double-duty as a hostel. And no, they do not give discounts to Red Sox or Patriots fans.

ACCOMMODATIONS

But for the west-facing coastline, the **Pillar Point Inn** (380 Capistrano Road, 650/728-7377, $$$) might make you think this is Massachusetts rather than California. This stately gray Cape Codder B&B has 11 rooms filled with featherbeds and decor accenting local history, and, of course, a view of the water.

COASTAL CUISINE

Princeton scores high marks with regard to food, since seafood makes a quick passage from fishing boats to restaurant kitchens in this area. For tasty fried seafood in comfortably funky surroundings, duck into **Barbara's Fishtrap** (281 Capistrano Road, 650/728-7049, $$). You may have to wait in line, and Barbara's doesn't accept credit cards or reservations. One caveat: Barbara's chowder in this "New England" village is made sans cream or milk.

Another local favorite is the **Half Moon Bay Brewing Co.** (390 Capistrano Road, 650/728-2739, $$$), which proclaims itself "the unofficial watering hole of Mavericks surfers." The building, which formerly housed the landmark Shore Bird Restaurant, is a replica of a house on Cape Cod, copied down to the minutest detail. Overlooking the harbor and surrounded by a garden and a white picket fence, the pub looks more like a prosperous sea captain's home than one of the area's most popular dining spots. The pub also serves fresh, broiled fish preparations.

You really can't go wrong anywhere around the harbor. We made a good, simple midday meal of clam chowder and sourdough bread at **Ketch Joanne's** (17 Johnson Pier, Pillar Point Harbor, 650/728-3747, $$$), a complex that includes a bar/restaurant, fish market, and open-air seafood barbecue grill. The list of fresh catches is extensive.

NIGHTLIFE

You can grab a beer or drink at **Ketch Joanne's Harbor Bar** (17 Johnson Pier, Pillar Point Harbor, 650/728-5566), but for anything more you'll need to head up to Moss Beach or down to Miramar. Hey, see if *you* feel like partying after a hard day of hauling fish onto the deck of a wave-tossed boat.

Moss Beach

Tucked off Highway 1 six miles north of Half Moon Bay, Moss Beach (population 4,200) is another in a string of inviting Coastside communities. It has a New England–village feel, but not in a contrived, voguish way. Remnants of the little town's rum-running history survive at Moss Beach Distillery, a

Prohibition-era roadhouse that's endured as a popular restaurant and landmark. The chief natural attraction of Moss Beach is James V. Fitzgerald Marine Reserve, which runs for three miles below the bluffs between Pillar Point and Montara.

For more information, contact the Half Moon Bay/Coastside Chamber of Commerce & Visitors Bureau, 235 Main Street, Half Moon Bay, CA 94019, 650/726-8380, www .halfmoonbaychamber.org.

BEACHES

We had a queasy feeling about Moss Beach, which is formally known as the **James V. Fitzgerald Marine Reserve.** We tried to enter from the parking lot at Moss Beach Distillery, but a sign announced the closure of the trail into the reserve. Crumbling cliffs, washed-out trails—same old story. We somehow fumbled our way onto the beach, later discovering there's an easy access from the reserve's well-marked parking lot. (Follow signs from Highway 1.) It was a weird stretch of sand that smelled of seaweed and was covered with black gunk that looked like asphalt chunks. At low tide the ocean pulls back to reveal acres of tidepools, the reserve's big draw. You can investigate on your own or take a ranger-led walk. For information on times and places, call the reserve at 650/728-3584.

In the end we discovered that Moss Beach does have its charms. We explored a trail leading up one of the southern cliffs and found ourselves in a large, eerie cypress forest. From there we took a staircase down to a lovely, secluded beach.

20 JAMES V. FITZGERALD MARINE RESERVE

Location: end of California Avenue, off Highway 1 in Moss Beach
Parking/Fees: free street parking
Hours: sunrise-sunset

Facilities: restrooms and picnic tables
Contact: James V. Fitzgerald Marine Reserve, 650/728-3584

ACCOMMODATIONS

The **Seal Cove Inn** (221 Cypress Avenue, 650/728-7325 or 800/995-9987, $$$) is a recently constructed English manor house that overlooks the ocean in a setting of cypress and wildflowers. It's the kind of comfortably luxurious place that draws people who come to decompress from life in the city—you know, kick back, light a fire, read a book, and get sane again.

COASTAL CUISINE

The **Moss Beach Distillery** (140 Beach Way, 650/728-5595, $$$) is celebrated for its great beachside location, its history, and its possession by ghosts. There's a long story that goes with this, centering around the legend of the Blue Lady, a married woman who died in a car wreck en route to meet her lounge-lizard boyfriend here 75 years ago. Now their poltergeists both supposedly haunt the place—as does the lounge lizard's distraught wife, who leapt to her death upon learning of his infidelity.

Beyond this amusing nonsense, which is occasionally goosed up with ghostly "special effects," the Moss Beach Distillery offers a superb coastal view and serves entrées that run the gamut from pasta and steak to a host of fresh seafood specials. The prevailing culinary approach is uncomplicated but serviceable. And don't you just love the address: the intersection of Beach Way and Ocean Boulevard, evoking a figurative paradise by the sea where we should all be so lucky to spend the rest of our days.

NIGHTLIFE

The **Moss Beach Distillery** (140 Beach Way, 650/728-5595) is the place to come for an afternoon libation or a late-evening nightcap. The outdoor patio is stocked with deck chairs and heavy blankets. Order a drink, tuck yourself in, and watch the sunset—if you're lucky enough to catch one. If you eventually start seeing double, it may have nothing to do with ghosts.

Montara

Montara was conceived at the turn of the century as an artists' colony by a bohemian magazine publisher from San Francisco. However, his grand plans for a seaside community of creative types never took hold, and the artists were displaced by bootleggers. Today, Montara has reclaimed some of its intended character. It's another likable link in the Coastside chain—a nice place to visit or live. Unless, of course, you have to commute via Devil's Slide.

As luck would have it, we spent our last day of beachcombing for a previous edition of this book at Montara. The gods were with us that August afternoon, because the sunset we witnessed was one for the ages—our solar going-away present, we figured. For about ten minutes, people spontaneously dropped what they were doing—be it surfing at Montara State Beach or dining on surf-and-turf at the Chart House—to watch the last sublime rays before the sun dropped from sight. Oddly

THE ONGOING SAGA OF DEVIL'S SLIDE

Highway 1 negotiates a treacherous and unstable passage between Pacifica and Montara known as Devil's Slide. It has always been subject to short-term closures for various reasons, but during January 1995, in the midst of a considerable rainy spell, the road at Devil's Slide essentially slipped off its hinges. A four-mile section of Highway 1 through Devil's Slide was immediately closed and remained so for 158 days. This added delays of up to two hours for Coastside commuters who were forced to take Highway 92. Then the debate began: Repair the existing road? Blast a tunnel through the mountain? Build an inland bypass?

Highway engineers and environmentalists have battled over Devil's Slide since the 1960s. CalTrans wanted to pursue the inland option, cutting across McNee Ranch State Park, but the Sierra Club filed suit to protect the parkland. Environmental groups wanted a tunnel drilled through San Pedro Mountain, which separates Montara and Pacifica. CalTrans argued that would be prohibitively expensive and a geological gamble. Environmentalists argued that the bypass would scar the landscape, silt the watershed, and subject drivers to dangerous fog much of the time. The business community viewed the environmentalists as obstructionists and pressed for the 4.3-mile bypass. "We'd much rather have a safe road than another state park," said a restaurant manager.

However, the voters of San Mateo County won the day, overwhelmingly approving the tunnel option by a 76-24 percent margin in November 1996. The California Coastal Commission certified it a year later. CalTrans is constructing a 4,000-foot-long double-bore tunnel through San Pedro Mountain. In 2002 the Federal Highway Administration approved the project's Environmental Impact Statement. At the time, CalTrans guessed that construction would begin in mid-2004 and take three years to complete. Sound the buzzer: *wrong*. It's now scheduled to open in 2011. We'll see.

Once the tunnel begins receiving traffic, the abandoned stretch of Highway 1 at Devil's Slide will be deeded to San Mateo County for use by bicycles and other non-motorized traffic. We look forward to peddling this wild and beautiful stretch of coast someday soon. Meantime, if you're passing through by car, then remember that until the tunnel is built, the devil still has the upper hand at this dangerous slide area.

enough, the sky was cloudy except for a narrow clearing of blue just above the horizon. All of a sudden a brilliant gold band of light appeared between the cloud bank and the ocean. The sun glowed a fiery red-orange as it made its brief but stunning sojourn, dipping behind the horizon with a final flicker and twinkle that drew whoops and applause. It was, we offer with no irony, a religious experience. Ah, California.

For more information, contact the Half Moon Bay/Coastside Chamber of Commerce & Visitors Bureau, 235 Main Street, Half Moon Bay, CA 94019, 650/726-8380, www .halfmoonbaychamber.org.

BEACHES

Montara State Beach is the hippest beach in San Mateo County. That's not saying a lot, really. From Montara south to the Santa Cruz County line, fewer than 30,000 people live along the coast, and relatively few of them are self-consciously hip. Some pick artichokes and Brussels sprouts. Others make real estate deals or work in Silicon Valley. Then there are retirees and the second-home wealthy. Montara, for

some anomalous reason probably having to do with proximity to Pacifica and San Francisco, draws a younger crowd. They play games on the beach—volleyball, Frisbee, paddleball—as if down on Santa Cruz's Cowell Beach rather than knocking on the back door of Fogtown. Waves are good, if inconsistent. The scene is cool, the water cold.

21 MONTARA STATE BEACH

Location: Second Street at Highway 1 in Montara
Parking/Fees: free parking lot
Hours: 8 A.M.-sunset
Facilities: restrooms
Contact: California State Parks, Bay Area District, 415/330-6300

ACCOMMODATIONS

Many years ago, we stayed at the **Farallone Inn** (1410 Main Street, 650/728-8200, $$) back before it got its massive facelift. Suffice it to say that it needed it, and now it's

© PARKE PUTERBAUGH

Montara State Beach

a modernized, refurbished wonder. All nine rooms, which go for $85–195, have decks and hot tubs, yet there are still reminders of its 1908 heritage. **The Goose and Turrets** (835 George Street, 650/728-5451, $$) is a rambling house with a lot of character. You can walk to the beach or lie in the garden hammock, reading and daydreaming about the four-course breakfast that's served every morning. Rooms go for $145–170. If you're living on a shoestring, you can board cheaply at **Montara Lighthouse Hostel** (Highway 1 at 16th Street, 650/728-7177, $), where beds start at $20.

COASTAL CUISINE

Steve's Blue Pacific Restaurant (Seventh Street and Highway 1, 650/728-5209, $$) is the kind of place that locals like to keep to themselves and out-of-towners wouldn't think to visit without being tipped off. Well, consider yourself tipped. Barbecue is the specialty, and the smoked entrées—prime rib, baby-back ribs, beef bones—rule. You can also order charbroiled salmon, halibut, and prawns.

The Foglifter (8455 Highway 1, 650/728-7905, $$) is another locals' favorite whose rather ramshackle facade belies the cozy dining room and excellent seafood and Italian fare within. The local **Chart House** (8150 Highway 1, 650/728-7366, $$$) is a landmark, overlooking and sharing a parking lot with Montara State Beach. It's high-quality surf-and-turf fare from a franchise that's got the best seaside locations in California. When Devil's Slide shuts down Highway 1, this is where the "Road Closed" signs go up.

Gray Whale Cove State Beach

Strange as it may sound, the state of California is a partner in the nude-beach business. Gray Whale Cove State Beach (a.k.a. Devil's Slide) is privately managed on state-owned land as a clothing-optional beach. (It was once known as Edun Beach—i.e., "nude" spelled backwards.)

There are restrooms, pop machines, even a hot-dog stand. It's up to you to bring the buns, if you know what we mean. The beach is a little hard to find. The unmarked road to it is located 1.2 miles north of the Chart House in Montara and 3 miles south of the Denny's in Linda Mar. Once you've parked in the lot, you'll descend a long (146 steps) staircase to the beach. Once you've made it down to the small, 800-foot cove, pay your money, and let it all hang out, if you wish. Lately, however, more people wear swimming suits than don't, and the naturists head to the north end of the cove to avoid gawkers.

BEACHES

22 GRAY WHALE COVE STATE BEACH

Location: between Montara and Pacifica, at Devil's Slide off Highway 1
Parking/Fees: $6.50 entrance fee per person ($7.50 on weekends)
Hours: 8 A.M.-sunset
Facilities: restrooms and picnic tables
Contact: Gray Whale Cove State Beach, 650/726-8819

Pacifica

Pacifica is not just one small city but a conglomeration of nine separate townships and subdivisions that came together in 1957. For this reason it is not your average municipality. There is no center of town, per se, and each area retains something of an independent personality. There is considerable parkland and wonderful ocean views from the upper elevations of Milagra Ridge and Sweeney Ridge. Pacifica's chief problem, as regards tourism, is that it lies in the long shadow of San Francisco.

No one in their right mind is going to make Pacifica (population 37,500) a vacation destination—not with San Francisco's overwhelming abundance of culture, architecture, and activities so close by. Residents of San Francisco who are looking for a weekend getaway simply pass through Pacifica, if at all, en route to the Half Moon Bay area. This is somewhat ironic, since Pacifica's Rockaway Beach served as "the Playground for San Francisco" for a good portion of the last century.

Then there are ever-present problems with Devil's Slide, the high-hazard area that links Pacifica with the rest of San Mateo County. Of all the locations on the California coast, Pacifica was hit hardest by El Niño. In 1998, houses along Esplanade began teetering at the edges of coastal bluffs that had eroded 30 feet shoreward in two weeks. The unstable, rain-soaked cliffs crumbled, and waves lapping at their bases further accelerated erosion. Ten houses collapsed or had to be destroyed.

BEACHES

Pacifica does have a few things going for it: a restaurant-motel complex at Rockaway Beach and a fishing pier at Sharp Park where salmon are there for the taking. Fall and winter are particularly nice times to visit; it's generally sunny, with moderate temperatures.

Some of the biggest winter waves on the Central Coast roll ashore on the cocoa-colored sands of **Rockaway Beach,** whose buildings are protected from the intrusive surf by rip-rap boulders. About a half mile south lies **Pacifica State Beach,** whose light brown sand and calmer waters provide sharp contrast. Pedro Point provides partial protection from another big, dangerous wave break. **Esplanade Beach** (a.k.a. Sharp Park) is a little over a mile north of Rockaway. Drainpipes poke the ocean at either end of the dark-sand beach, adding to the drab setting. A concrete pier that only an angler could love sits up at the north end.

The lure of Sharp Park is fishing, both from the 1,020-foot **Pacifica Pier,** a.k.a.

Reverend Herschel Harkins Memorial Pier (650/355-0690), and the beach. Catches include salmon and striped bass (in summer), plus rock bass, surf perch, and jacksmelt. It is claimed this pier is the only place in California where you can land a salmon without a boat.

For more information, contact the Pacifica Chamber of Commerce, 225 Rockaway Beach #1, Pacifica, CA 94044, 650/355-4122, www .pacificachamber.com.

23 PACIFICA STATE BEACH

Location: Highway 1 between Crespi Drive and Linda Mar Boulevard in Pacifica
Parking/Fees: free street parking
Hours: 24 hours
Facilities: restrooms and showers
Contact: California State Parks, Bay Area District, 415/330-6300

24 ROCKAWAY BEACH

Location: end of Rockaway Beach Avenue, off Highway 1 in Pacifica
Parking/Fees: free parking lot
Hours: 24 hours
Facilities: none
Contact: Pacifica Parks, Beaches, and Recreation, 650/738-7381

25 ESPLANADE BEACH

Location: along Beach Boulevard in Pacifica
Parking/Fees: free street parking
Hours: 24 hours
Facilities: restrooms
Contact: Pacifica Parks, Beaches, and Recreation, 650/738-7381

ACCOMMODATIONS

A complex of motels and restaurants at Rockaway Beach would like to project a resort aura. Yet a certain tentativeness pervades the area, as if they're afraid it all might wash away. And well it might. The longstanding Lighthouse Hotel has had its ups and downs up until its renovation and reincarnation as **Best Western Lighthouse Hotel** (105 Rockaway Beach Avenue, 650/355-6300, $$$). It's a perfectly serviceable, 92-unit motel; prices run $115–225, depending on time of year. There's also a Victorian-style **Days Inn** (200 Rockaway Beach Avenue, 650/359-7700, $$)—one of the nicer franchises in that generally downscale chain—at Rockaway Beach.

COASTAL CUISINE

The Moonraker (105 Rockaway Beach Avenue, 650/359-0303, $$$) has been a romantic favorite for three decades, but lost some of its reputation and fell on hard times for a while. Now it's back as part of the Best Western Lighthouse Hotel complex. **Nick's Restaurant** (100 Rockaway Beach Avenue, 650/359-3900, $$$) takes its fine-dining rep seriously, with a tuxedo-clad wait staff bustling about. A local landmark, Nick's is also attached to a motel (the Seabreeze, a modest little 20-room job). Nick's serves three meals a day, seven days a week.

NIGHTLIFE

In addition to being a restaurant, **Nick's** (100 Rockaway Beach Avenue, 650/359-3900) is a cocktails-and-dancing kind of place, with live music on weekends. It's like stepping into the past, back when Rockaway Beach was San Francisco's playground and not the overlooked footnote it is today.

Daly City

A sizable backdoor suburb of San Francisco, Daly City (population 100,000) offers unsightly evidence of the area's insatiable need for bedrooms. It was Daly City that inspired folksinger Malvina Reynolds to write "Tiny Boxes," a derisive commentary on mass-produced housing projects: "Tiny boxes, little boxes, and they're all made out of ticky-tack."

Not much has changed since Reynolds' lampoon from the 1960s except more tiny boxes have gone up and a verse about cheesy condos could be added. Tightly packed together, running up and down the hillsides, they look like plastic Monopoly houses. Some of them are built right along the San Andreas Fault. Talk about living dangerously!

For more information, contact the Greater Daly City–Colma Chamber of Commerce, 355 Gellert Boulevard, Suite 138, Daly City, CA 94015, 650/755-3900, www.dalycity-colma chamber.com.

BEACHES

Thornton State Beach lies below steep coastal bluffs and is best accessed by walking down from Fort Funston or up from Mussel Rock City Park. A hiking trail follows the bluff top. People sometimes scramble down the cliffs to reach the sand, though this is discouraged because of the area's history of landslides. The main attraction on Thornton Beach is surf casting. The beach is all but useless for any other purpose in the cold, foggy summer months. It does become more hospitable in the fall, when temperatures warm and the sun breaks free of its fog-induced funk.

By the way, Thornton State Beach has been closed for years and its future status remains in limbo. It hasn't recovered from 1982–1983 winter storms that wiped out park facilities and caused the road to the parking lot to drop more than 20 feet. The state park facilities were permanently abandoned.

Daly City has wanted to improve access, via hiking trails, to what is a perfectly fine, if landslide-prone, beach. Don't think about swimming, though: too cold, too dangerous.

San Francisco

To be honest, San Francisco really doesn't merit a great deal of attention in this book. Coming to this magnificent city for its beaches is like going to Las Vegas for its libraries—no doubt they exist, but they hold a very low priority among visitors, and they're far from being the best examples of their kind. The beaches of San Francisco just aren't the sorts of places you'd want to spend a lot of vacation time. The water's cold, the surf rough, the wind stiff, the fog chilling. That said, it's also true that on one of those rare golden days when the sun is out and the wind has subsided to a whisper, there's no more glorious place to be, especially at sunset.

But back to the original point. We would have preferred to bypass San Francisco and leave this splendid city of 765,000 people to the myriad travel books devoted exclusively to its manifold assets and activities. However, the city does have beaches, so we'll dutifully cover that aspect of its geography forthwith. Just don't expect more than a quick overview of San Francisco's waterfront, because there's 400 miles of Northern California coastline yet to cover.

If you're going there, be sure to pack warm clothes. Just because it's summertime, don't think you can get away with wearing shorts and a T-shirt. In the words of Mark Twain, "The coldest winter I ever spent was a summer in San Francisco." Dress as you would for autumn in New England; wear long pants and keep a sweater tied around your neck. And if you venture here in the winter, make sure you pack an umbrella—the rainy season typically runs from November through March.

Before hitting the beaches, we should say a few words about **Fisherman's Wharf,** that working dock turned tourist trap. It's overrun by disposable-camera-toting outsiders and shunned by locals. All the same, there are a few good reasons for dropping by—and an equal number of reasons for not sticking around too long. Come to stroll the bayside streets, dodging the low-rent vendors' plaints if possible.

We're fond of the seafood take-out counters lined outside the wharfside restaurants. For three or four bucks, you can grab a cup of crab, shrimp, lobster, or squid topped with a tangy dollop of cocktail sauce and a squeeze of lemon. The protein will fortify you for hiking around Nob Hill, Russian Hill, and all the other hills in this vertically inclined city when you tire of the waterfront. If you're looking for a more substantial meal, Italian-surnamed seafood restaurants are plentiful.

Shopping opportunities abound, although there is a distinct low-end aspect to the Fisherman's Wharf retail experience. Along Taylor Street, which runs down to the wharf, we had unsettling flashbacks of Venice Beach in Southern California. Sidewalk peddlers hawk T-shirts, sunglasses, and assorted junk and gimcracks. At the other end of the spectrum, visitors with a ready line of credit will want to explore the maze of shops and boutiques at the **Cannery** (a former Del Monte produce-packing plant) and **Ghirardelli Square** (a converted chocolate factory).

East of Fisherman's Wharf is **Pier 39,** a teeming bazaar that draws a zombiefied crowd of browsers and buyers. Overfed sea lions bob around the green water, barking like bratty children for handouts. The crowd-pleasing pinnipeds have mutated from intelligent, vigorously active creatures into slovenly pier bums, much like their human counterparts. This, of course, is no way to experience San Francisco, unless you're completely lacking in imagination and curiosity.

Other wharf-area attractions include ferry rides and tours of islands in the bay, which leave from Piers 41 and 43 1/2. The National Park Service conducts trips to **Alcatraz** (415/546-2805), the small, jutting island on which a grim-looking former federal penitentiary housed America's most hardened felons, including the Bird Man and Al Capone. If you go, be sure to rent one of the audiotape tours available at the park; narrated by former wardens and prisoners, it paints a realistic and compelling portrait of life on the Rock.

406   SAN FRANCISCO BAY AREA

SAN FRANCISCO BAY AREA

Angel Island, a 760-acre island that actually lies within Marin County waters, serves as a more idyllic state park offering panoramic views of San Francisco from a trail that leads to the top of Mount Livermore (781 feet). Picnicking, tent camping, hiking, and biking can all be enjoyed on **Angel Island** (contact the state park office at 415/435-1915 for ferry schedules and fares). Ferries also make frequent crossings to the bay-hugging, picturesque Marin communities of Sausalito, Tiburon, and Larkspur.

On the eastern side of this boxy peninsula, the piers of the Embarcadero take over, offering deep-water berthing in one of the world's great natural harbors.

Highly recommended to all who want to tour the city by automobile is the **49-Mile Scenic Drive.** You can begin at City Hall (Van Ness Avenue and McAllister Street) or pick it up at any other point en route. Just follow the blue-and-white seagull signs and allow plenty of time to eyeball San Francisco's scenic sights and heights. A brochure annotating the route is available.

For more information, contact the San Francisco Visitor Information Center, Hallidie Plaza (lower level), 900 Market Street, San Francisco, CA 94103, 415/391-2000; www.sfvisitor.org.

BEACHES

Much of San Francisco's coastline belongs to the Golden Gate National Recreation Area, the vast tri-county federal parkland that is managed by the National Park Service. This includes the eight-mile stretch from the San Mateo county line to Aquatic Park, east of Golden Gate Bridge. Four miles worth, from the county line to Point Lobos, faces the ocean, running along a nearly perfect north-south axis. Coming up from the south, this area encompasses **Burton Memorial Beach** (which straddles San Mateo and San Francisco Counties), **Fort Funston Beach** (a popular launch site for hang gliders), and **Ocean Beach.**

The last of these is a long, flat stretch of beach paralleled by the Great Highway. People come to Ocean Beach to park and watch the sun set; to fish on the beach or surf the often sizable waves; and to jog, walk, bicycle, and in-line skate along pathways that run on both sides of the Great Highway. Unspoiled and impressively empty, the beach is regrettably unsafe for swimming—too rough and too cold. In fact, a combination of factors create deadly riptides. On the California coast, 88 percent of all lifeguard rescues are attributable to riptides. Ocean Beach, which is the worst for riptides, has no lifeguards!

If all this hasn't convinced you not to swim at Ocean Beach, ponder this observation by Francis Smith, a UC Berkeley graduate student who studied riptides: "Ocean Beach is the most hazardous and dangerous piece of shoreline associated with an urban environment in the whole United States." More than a dozen people drowned there in one recent year alone.

As you drive north from Ocean Beach, the road begins to rise, meeting a San Francisco landmark, the **Cliff House.** A jaw-dropping overview of Ocean Beach can be had from the deck of the Cliff House. Tourist buses choke the area around the Cliff House with gassy fumes. The tourists pile out to gawk at the bird- and seal-covered rocks offshore and browse the shops, museums, and restaurants before moving on to the next stop.

The Cliff House Visitor Information Center, run by the National Park Service, is a good place to stock up on brochures, books, and maps detailing the recreational opportunities of the Golden Gate National Recreation Area, from visiting forts to hiking ridgetops to camping on the beach. Parking is available along Point Lobos Avenue, the Great Highway, and El Camino Del Mar.

The remains of the Sutro Baths, a turn-of-the-century natatorium, lie below the sandstone bluffs. Trails crisscross the knobby area known as **Lands End** between the Cliff House and China Beach. It's a fascinating place to explore, with paths running down to the ocean, through tunnels, and up and over the bluffs. The beach at Lands End is found at the bottom

GOLDEN GATE NATIONAL RECREATION AREA

This amazing park encompasses 75,398 acres (114 square miles) spread across three counties: San Mateo, San Francisco, and Marin. The Golden Gate National Recreation Area (GGNRA) is a veritable urban greenbelt that ensures this growing metropolitan area will never want for recreational lands in natural settings. In conjunction with the similar-sized holdings of Point Reyes National Seashore up north, it puts San Francisco in the enviable position of having more dedicated parkland close at hand than any other major city in the United States. The citizens of San Francisco should be dancing in the streets about this windfall, established by an act of Congress in 1972.

Eight miles of San Francisco's ocean-facing coastline fall under the domain of the GGNRA, providing green space and beaches to urban dwellers. The 1,500-acre Presidio was a former military installation. In Marin County the GGNRA holdings run the length of the county, taking in the Marin Headlands, Muir Woods, Stinson Beach, Olema Valley, and Tomales Bay.

GGNRA holdings include historic sites (Alcatraz Island, the Cliff House, various seacoast fortifications) and scenic treasures (redwood forests, mountains, bays, and beaches). A 1,014-acre tract in San Mateo County, Sweeney Ridge, is a recent addition. In total, there are 28 miles of shoreline and a hundred miles of trails. In addition, the National Park Service conducts regular tours and educational events at sites throughout the system. These can range from guided hikes and bird-watching expeditions to hands-on seminars on crabbing in the bay.

For more information, contact the Golden Gate National Recreation Area, Fort Mason, Building 201, San Francisco, CA 94123, 415/561-4700, www.nps.gov/goga.

There are also GGNRA visitors centers at Fort Point (415/556-1593) and the Presidio (415/561-4323), in San Francisco; on Alcatraz Island (415/705-1042); at Pacifica (650/355-4122); and at the Marin Headlands (415/331-1540) and Muir Woods (415/388-7368), in Marin County.

You can also call GGNRA for information on the weather in Stinson Beach (415/868-1922), boat transportation to Alcatraz Island (415/546-2700), and the National Maritime Museum in San Francisco (415/556-3002).

of a steep path. It's not worth the trouble or the risk to scuttle down, although the paths above it afford good overlooks.

Around Lands End the coastline runs east for a short distance before making a sharp turn north again to the foot of the Golden Gate Bridge. **China Beach** is tucked into a relatively safe, protected pocket cove that is lifeguarded in summer. China Beach lies below all the gorgeous stucco homes that line El Camino Del Mar in the exclusive Seacliff District. Park on the street and make the steep descent via a path or a paved service road (for handicapped parking only) to the beach.

Baker Beach is a 1.5-mile ribbon of sand that runs all the way up to Golden Gate Bridge. The *San Francisco Bay Guardian* called Baker Beach "America's most popular urban nude beach, drawing local residents and tourists whenever the weather is sunny, plus a smattering of winter diehards." We won't argue with them; they've been compiling an annual issue devoted to California's nude beaches for three decades. Wonderful views of the photogenic steel span and the Marin Headlands can be had there. Everyone we saw, though, was otherwise engaged: figures sleeping on the beach, couples groping on the sand, picnickers at tables under the protected windbreaks of cypress groves, and anglers casting lines into the water.

North Baker Beach is an almost exclusively nude beach. Should you happen to wander off in that direction, don't be surprised if you stumble onto a colony of beachgoers as naked as seals. There's no other reason to come here, as the beach itself narrows in this vicinity.

Rounding out the city's shoreline are **Marina Green** (managed by the San Francisco Parks and Recreation Department), **Crissy Field** (a popular launch site for windsurfers east of the Golden Gate Bridge in the decommissioned Presidio), and **Aquatic Park** (a celebration of all things maritime). Marina Green is a broad bayfront green space on which natives bicycle, jog, walk, toss Frisbees, and fly kites. It's San Francisco's latter-day equivalent of the traditional village green, serving as a gathering place for celebrations and rallies, not to mention being a good place to hang out on a nice day.

Aquatic Park lies between Marina Green and Fisherman's Wharf. It's protected by two piers and a breakwater. The 1,850-foot Municipal Pier is populated with anglers. Onshore, there's the **National Maritime Museum** (415/561-7030), tourable ships, more green space, and a small sandy beach. (Don't base your vacation around the latter, though.) The square-rigger *Balclutha*, built in Glasgow in 1886 and docked at **Hyde Street Pier** (415/447-5000), can be toured for a fee. It is one of seven vessels belonging to the maritime museum, which also houses model ships and seafaring artifacts.

It's all part of the **San Francisco Maritime National Historical Park** (415/447-5000, www.nps.gov/safr), headquartered at Hyde and Beach Streets, on the west side of Fisherman's Wharf.

26 BURTON MEMORIAL BEACH

Location: south of Fort Funston at Skyline Boulevard/Highway 35, near San Mateo County line
Parking/Fees: free parking lot
Hours: 6 A.M.-one hour after sunset
Facilities: none
Contact: Golden Gate National Recreation Area, 415/561-4700, www.nps.gov/goga

27 FORT FUNSTON BEACH

Location: off Skyline Boulevard/Highway 35, one mile north of San Mateo County line
Parking/Fees: free parking lot
Hours: 6 A.M.-one hour after sunset
Facilities: restrooms and picnic tables
Contact: Golden Gate National Recreation Area, 415/561-4700, www.nps.gov/goga

28 OCEAN BEACH

Location: Great Highway, between Cliff House and San Francisco Zoo, in San Francisco
Parking/Fees: free street parking
Hours: 6 A.M.-10 P.M.
Facilities: restrooms
Contact: Golden Gate National Recreation Area, 415/561-4700, www.nps.gov/goga

29 LANDS END

Location: from Geary Boulevard in San Francisco turn north onto Merrie Way, park on street; follow Lands End Trail to beach
Parking/Fees: free street parking
Hours: 6 A.M.-one hour after sunset
Facilities: none
Contact: Golden Gate National Recreation Area, 415/561-4700, www.nps.gov/goga

© PARKE PUTERBAUGH

China Beach

30 CHINA BEACH

Location: Seacliff Avenue at El Camino Del Mar in San Francisco; trail leads to beach
Parking/Fees: free limited street parking
Hours: 6 A.M.-one hour after sunset
Facilities: lifeguard, restrooms, showers, and picnic tables
Contact: Golden Gate National Recreation Area, 415/561-4700, www.nps.gov/goga

31 BAKER BEACH

Location: west end of Gibson Road, near southwest corner of Presidio, in San Francisco
Parking/Fees: free parking lot
Hours: 6 A.M.-one hour after sunset
Facilities: restrooms and picnic tables
Contact: Golden Gate National Recreation Area, 415/561-4700, www.nps.gov/goga

32 NORTH BAKER BEACH

Location: walk north from Baker Beach
Parking/Fees: free parking lot (at Baker Beach)
Hours: 6 A.M.-one hour after sunset
Facilities: none
Contact: Golden Gate National Recreation Area, 415/561-4700, www.nps.gov/goga

ACCOMMODATIONS

You want to stay at the beach? We've got just the place for you. It ain't fancy, but it's clean and at the beach—and that's what this book is all about. It's **Roberts-at-the-Beach Motel** (2828 Sloat Boulevard, 415/564-2610, $), where you're invited to "sleep by the sea." Roberts is a block off the Great Highway, near the San Francisco Zoo and Golden Gate Park.

Two blocks farther landward on the same street is a **Days Inn** (2600 Sloat Boulevard, 415/665-9000, $$), offering a modicum of brand-name dependability. Actually, we found our room and its furnishings quite comfortable. Also close to the beach is the **Oceanview**

© KATHRYN OSGOOD

Baker Beach

Motel (4340 Judah Street, 415/661-2300, $), which is unfancy but clean, safe, and accessible to Ocean Beach and Golden Gate Park.

Another find close to the beach—conveniently close, in fact, to the Cliff House, Lands End, and the Presidio—is **Seal Rock Inn** (545 Point Lobos Avenue, 415/386-6518, $$), an older hotel that makes up in location what it lacks in amenities.

Do you want to feel like a rock star? Stay at the **Phoenix Hotel** (601 Eddy Street, 415/776-1380, $$). It's a tropical-themed hotel with a hip restaurant (Bambuddha Lounge) and simple, reasonably priced rooms ($100 and up) whose tasteful tackiness is part of the fun. All of the rock bands have stayed here at one time or another. If you're queasy about location, you may want to look elsewhere, though, as it's on the edge of the Tenderloin district.

Down by touristy Fisherman's Wharf, you'll find a wide range of places to stay. On the high end there are humongous 500-room towers run by **Sheraton** (2500 Mason Street, 415/362-5500, $$$$) and **Hyatt** (555 North Point Street, 415/563-2218, $$$$), as well as less impressive (and less expensive) properties by

Holiday Inn (1300 Columbia Avenue, 415/771-9000, $$$), **Ramada Inn** (590 Bay Street, 415/885-4700, $$$), and **Howard Johnson** (580 Beach Street, 415/775-3800, $$$). You know what you're getting with those kinds of places—a guarantee of quality within a narrow standard of deviation. All are within three blocks of Fisherman's Wharf. You'll pay dearly to stay near the wharf, but you'll pay dearly to stay anywhere else in San Francisco, too.

Slightly outside the area, between Fisherman's Wharf and the Financial District, are four affiliated motor inns that offer a real break on price and value (around $80 a night, year-round). They're strung along busy Lombard Avenue, with **Cow Hollow Motor Inn** (2190 Lombard Street, 415/921-5800, $$) close to Marina Green, and **Lombard Motor Inn** (1475 Lombard Street, 415/441-6000, $$) close to Fisherman's Wharf. In between you'll find **Coventry Motor Inn** (1901 Lombard Street, 415/567-1200, $$) and **Chelsea Motor Inn** (2095 Lombard Street, 415/563-5600, $$).

If you're looking for more of a bed-and-breakfast experience, you might try **Marina Inn** (3110 Octavia Street, 415/928-1000, $$), a 40-room hotel on the corner of Lombard, behind Fort Mason in the Marina District.

For a fuller array of accommodations in the Bay Area, acquire the latest lodging guide published by the San Francisco Convention and Visitors Bureau.

COASTAL CUISINE

San Francisco rightly enjoys a reputation as an epicurean paradise. There are more than 3,300 restaurants in the City by the Bay. Since detailed coverage of a subject so large is well beyond the scope of this book, we've narrowed our commentary to restaurants in the vicinity of Fisherman's Wharf and out by Ocean Beach. Even there we've been selective.

Our top choice out by the beach is the **Beach Chalet Brewery & Restaurant** (1000 Great Highway, 415/386-8439, $$$), where Golden Gate Park meets the ocean. What could be better than knocking back a schooner of home-brewed California Kind Ale or Golden Gate Park Porter on a Friday evening—featuring live music by some of the Bay Area's great bands—after a dinner of seared salmon and sea scallops while you watched the sun set?

Up where Point Lobos Avenue meets the Great Highway sits a San Francisco institution, the **Cliff House** (1090 Point Lobos Avenue, 415/386-3330, $$$). Five different structures have occupied the same site since its inception in 1863. One burned down when a boatload of nitroglycerin crashed into the cliff on which it sits. The latest edifice is physically quite secure, though locals often sniff that its culinary reputation isn't as firmly grounded. Visitors, dazzled by the glorious views and the old San Francisco ambience, don't seem to care. For our part, we've had fine grilled-fish dinners and a particularly memorable bowl of bouillabaisse at the Cliff House, so it gets our thumbs-up.

A $19 million renovation in 2003–2004 restored Cliff House to its original neoclassical look, and the new, two-story Sutro Wing went up next to it. The 1909 structure has been rechristened the Cliff House Bistro, and it retains a more casual atmosphere, while Sutro's at the Cliff House is the place to come if you're aiming to impress. The floor-to-ceiling windows will wow you, as will the menu (and menu prices). Entrées include a $36 bowl of bouillabaisse and fresh catches that average $29–32. The Cliff House Bistro is somewhat lower-priced, offering a $27 bowl of cioppino (fish stew), fresh catches in the $25 range, and fish 'n' chips for $16. The Bistro's new zinc bar is a big deal. We're just glad the Cliff House is back in business, as closure for building-code violations had been threatened by municipal authorities before the renovation.

Also near the beach is a hole-in-the-wall restaurant that turns out the best ribs and barbecue this side of Oakland. **Leon's BBQ** (2800 Sloat Boulevard, 415/922-2436, $$) has a real down-home neighborhood vibe to go with the hearty servings of ribs and 'cue. So come on in for some home-cooked chow and an "I Porked Out at Leon's BBQ" bumper sticker.

The Fisherman's Wharf area has long served as a punching bag for food critics, who insult it directly when they don't ignore it entirely. This is a little unfair. Sure, the area has its tacky side, with a scuzzy commercial presence whose lowbrow aura is more reminiscent of Times Square than a working wharf and fish market. But some of the restaurants of longstanding do an excellent job of serving quality seafood.

A. Sabella's (2766 Taylor, 415/771-6775, $$$), for instance, dates back to the 1920s, when Antone Sabella—whose father ran a retail market on Fisherman's Wharf—opened a restaurant on this spot. Sabella's is still run by Antone Sabella (albeit the founder's grandson). Fittingly, the menu's pièce de resistance is a dish named after the founder: Antone, a swordfish concoction baked in a beurre blanc, stuffed with deviled shrimp, and topped with parmesan cheese and white sauce. The crab legs (sautéed, fried, or Bordelaise) and crab cioppino (simmered with shrimp and shellfish) also are excellent. Sabella's rates high in our book for the food and the view—three stories above the Fisherman's Wharf hubbub, with an unobstructed outlook on the bay.

Another good bet on the wharf is **Scoma's** (Pier 47, 415/771-4383, $$$). San Francisco's highest-grossing restaurant, it attracts crowds for one reason (well, besides location): dependably fresh, well-prepared seafood. Scoma's signature dish is a little bit of culinary inspiration called Shellfish Sec, a symphony of seafood in a light wine sauce. The combination seafood cocktail (crabs and prawns), the Louis salad, and the sautéed entrées are also highly recommended. Scoma's has its own fish-receiving station, complete with off-loading and a processing operation that goes 16 hours a day. You can wander over and look at what might turn out to be your dinner being cleaned and filleted. Al Scoma, the restaurant's owner, died in 2007, but the traditions he instilled at Scoma's live on. Incidentally, there is a second Scoma's Restaurant just across the bay in Sausalito.

Elsewhere on San Francisco's waterfront, seafood fans flock to the **Pier 23 Cafe** (The Embarcadero, Pier 23, 415/362-5125, $$), whose alfresco dining patio and lively atmosphere attract a young, hip crowd on nice days. Other popular spots include **Scott's Seafood Grill,** which has locations in the Marina District (2400 Lombard Street, 415/563-8988, $$$) and in the Financial District (3 Embarcadero Center, 415/981-0622, $$$), and **Cafe Pescatore** (2455 Mason Street, 415/561-1111, $$$), a small Italian seafood restaurant excelling at such creative concoctions as ravioli stuffed with minced scallops and covered with a tomato-garlic cream sauce.

Before we leave the subject of seafood, we have to break our vow about not straying from the water's edge when it comes to restaurants. It's an ironic fact of life that when San Franciscans crave food with fins, they head inland. Here's the lowdown on four of the best fish joints in town: the venerable **Tadich Grill** (240 California Street, 415/391-1849, $$$), which claims to be California's oldest restaurant in continuous operation; its younger neighbor **Aqua** (252 California Street, 415/956-9662,

$$$), a decidedly upscale and pricey Financial District favorite; **Hayes Street Grill** (320 Hayes Street, 415/863-5545, $$$), a more casual Civic Center eatery; and the **Swan Oyster Depot** (1517 Polk Street, 415/673-1101, $$), where a friendly staff plunks down incredibly fresh, simply prepared seafood on its long lunch counter.

Here's a funny fish tale—a true story, in fact—involving one of this book's authors (who shall remain unnamed). While in San Francisco on an unrelated assignment, he was checking out various restaurants for possible inclusion in this book. Worn out at the end of a long day, a wool cap on his head to ward off the foggy chill, he was studying the posted menu and peering through the front window when a waiter abruptly appeared, closing the curtains and locking the door. The intimation was that your humble travel writer was, in fact, an unwelcome vagrant.

Frankly, you'll find excellent and creative seafood dishes in nearly all of the better restaurants in town.

Finally, we can't exit San Francisco without saying a word about sourdough bread. Some of the best mass-produced sourdough bread to be had is at **Boudin Sourdough Bakery & Cafe** (160 Jefferson Street, 415/928-1849, $), which brings us back to Fisherman's Wharf. There are also Boudin locations at Pier 39 and five other places throughout the city.

NIGHTLIFE

San Francisco is often touted as the most cosmopolitan city in America, and it's certainly one of the most open-minded. Contained within its borders is a little bit of Paris, Rome, Vienna, Sodom, and Gomorrah. Everything from ballet dancing to bondage bars can be located on its fog-shrouded streets after dark. You really don't need us to tell you where or how to have a good time in San Francisco, so we'll just offer a few stray observations before calling it a night.

The tavern at the **Cliff House** (1090 Point Lobos Avenue, 415/386-3330) is patronized and enjoyed even by famously tourist-wary San Franciscans (at least when they have out-of-town guests in tow). With its log-burning fireplace and awesome views, this is a must-visit place to drain a coffee mug or wine glass. Down at Fisherman's Wharf, another favorite tourist haunt, **Lou's Pier 47** (300 Jefferson Street, 415/771-5687), presents live blues acts, none of them too darn spectacular.

It's a yuppie world now, and the fact is evident in most every neighborhood, even North Beach, that traditionally working-class, Italian neighborhood that was the old stomping ground of the Beat Generation. (Incidentally, North Beach used to mark the actual shoreline before landfill was used to extend the city half a mile to its present location at Fisherman's Wharf and the Embarcadero.) Today, this landlocked beach is a grab bag of brass-encrusted cafés, coffeehouses, bars, and bookstores. If you'd like to walk in Jack Kerouac's footsteps, try the following, which were beat-generation hangouts in the 1950s and still retain an air of authenticity: **Caffe Trieste** (609 Vallejo Street, 415/982-2605), **Mario's Bohemian Cigar Store** (566 Columbus Avenue, 415/362-0536), **Tosca Cafe** (242 Columbus Avenue, 415/986-9651), and **Vesuvio's** (255 Columbus Avenue, 415/362-3370). The last two establishments are near the famed **City Lights Bookstore** (261 Columbus Avenue, 415/362-8193), still run by the venerable poet and scene patriarch, Lawrence Ferlinghetti (who was San Francisco's poet laureate in 1998).

Looking for a decent rock club in this music-crazed city? Well, **Bottom of the Hill** (1233 17th Street, 415/621-4455) is San Francisco's answer to New York's late, lamented CBGB's. It's the only real mid-sized rock venue in S.F. and, like CBGB's, tends to stack the bill with no-name acts. Still, it gets some good cult favorites, like Lou Barlow (of Sebadoh), Of Montreal, Interpol, Isis, and others known to those who keep their ear to the ground.

Bimbo's 365 Club (1025 Columbus Avenue, 415/474-0365) is a marvelous relic of San Francisco's martini-swilling past, dating back to 1931. Red velvet everywhere, it's the definition of swank, with one of the best sound systems on the West Coast. Catch a show here if you can. The eclectic bookings range from Apples in Stereo to Sergio Mendes—now that's a spread!

Finally, you can hope that someone good is playing at the **Great American Music Hall** (859 O'Farrell Street, 415/885-0750) or **The Warfield** (982 Market Street, 415/421-8497), two premiere rock venues and San Francisco landmarks. If you're ever at the Great American Music Hall, look up and admire the ornate ceiling. By the way, Phil Lesh (the former Grateful Dead bassist) and Friends presented a five-night stand of shows at the Warfield in May 2008 during which they performed two different Dead albums every night—a historic nod back at the years when San Francisco was home base for psychedelia and the counterculture.

Beyond this overview, you're on your own in this great big city. Grab a local paper and have at it.

POINT REYES AND MARIN COUNTY

By general consensus, Marin County signals the beginning of Northern California. The leap over the Golden Gate Bridge marks a psychological and geographical break from the rest of the state. Marin County also heralds the beginning of a particularly stunning stretch of coastline. From the Marin Headlands to Smith River (on the Oregon border), the scenery changes around every mind-boggling bend in the road.

Several divergent factors have shaped Marin County: the San Andreas Fault, which runs through the county; Mount Tamalpais, which forms a formidable barrier to easy access; an entrenched hippie ethos that dates back to a mass exodus from San Francisco's Haight-Ashbury district in the late 1960s; and a tradition of environmentalism that dates back to John Muir, the county's most celebrated citizen.

Because much of the shoreline is federal parkland—either part of Golden Gate National Recreation Area or Point Reyes National Seashore—the Marin County coast is as pristine as you'll ever find close to a major metropolitan area. The expenditure of effort and difficult passage to these beaches make the rewards of arrival all the greater. What this does, as devotees of Marin County know full well, is separate flighty tourists from real travelers. This, in turn, keeps things relatively peaceful for the hardy souls who live in wind-swept west Marin.

Although most San Franciscans in search of beachy fun converge on Stinson Beach, the real spirit of place can be found at Point Reyes Peninsula—truly a land apart from the rest of the continent. And don't overlook Bolinas, a hidden coastal village that's like entering a time warp back to the 1960s.

© KATHRYN OSGOOD

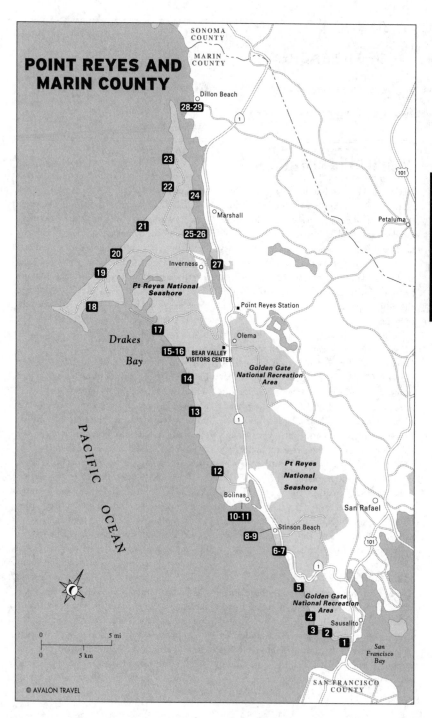

POINT REYES AND MARIN COUNTY

SONOMA COUNTY

MARIN COUNTY

Dillon Beach

28-29

23

22

24

Marshall

21

25-26

20

Inverness

27

19

Pt Reyes National Seashore

18

17

Drakes Bay

15-16

BEAR VALLEY VISITORS CENTER

Point Reyes Station

Olema

14

Golden Gate National Recreation Area

13

PACIFIC OCEAN

12

Bolinas

Pt Reyes National Seashore

San Rafael

10-11

8-9

Stinson Beach

6-7

5

4

3   2

Golden Gate National Recreation Area

Sausalito

1

San Francisco Bay

0   5 mi

0   5 km

© AVALON TRAVEL

SAN FRANCISCO COUNTY

Petaluma

MARIN COUNTY

MARIN COUNTY

Marin Headlands

The Marin Headlands unit of the Golden Gate National Recreation Area (GGNRA) stares down San Francisco from the north side of the Golden Gate Bridge. It used to be U.S. Army land, and the remnants of forts and batteries dot the terrain. For the purposes of this book, we'll provide a brief perusal of the beaches, beginning with Kirby Cove (near the foot of the bridge), proceeding west to Point Bonita, then heading northwest to Muir Beach.

To get your bearings, head to the Marin Headlands Visitor Center, located inside Fort Berry Chapel. To get there from San Francisco, cross the Golden Gate Bridge and take the Alexander Avenue exit from Highway 101. From Alexander Avenue, turn left on Bunker Road. (A brown sign saying Marin Headlands Visitor Center marks the intersection.) Go through the one-way tunnel and drive approximately two miles. Turn left onto Field Road. The visitors center will be on the right.

For more information, contact the Golden Gate National Recreation Area, Marin Headlands Visitor Center, Fort Berry Chapel, Sausalito, CA 94695, 415/331-1540, www.nps.gov/goga/marin-headlands.htm.

BEACHES

The best way to get a handle on the headlands' scenic heights is to follow Conzelman Road. Cross the Golden Gate Bridge into Marin County on U.S. 101, take the Alexander Avenue exit, then make a left turn into GGNRA territory, where you'll pick up Conzelman Road. It is a twisty, windy, sometimes one-way corkscrew that works its way out to Point Bonita Lighthouse, providing some incredible vistas en route.

Kirby Cove is half a mile from where you pick up Conzelman Road. Marin County's geographical counterpart to San Francisco's Baker Beach, it's identifiable by a locked gate in front of a dirt road leading to the beach. There's a narrow, quarter-mile beach and a cave that people like to explore. They also tend to get naked out here, which is pretty much the case with most of the GGNRA beaches. The park service looks the other way, so to speak, unless they get complaints.

There are some fairly difficult-to-find beaches in the vicinity of **Bonita Cove,** which is broken by rocky points into a trio of pocket beaches. Notably, they are composed of wave-pulverized pillow lava. "The more inaccessible, the better" is how nude beach aficionados look at it, and all three beaches are frequented by those who like to recreate in the altogether.

Moving on, **Rodeo Beach** is the most accessible beach in the headlands, but it's just a pebbly cove. The sand is a brown-black color, partly composed of volcanic material, and the beach is dominated by an impressive whitish outcropping at its south end. To the east is pristine Rodeo Lagoon, encircled by hiking trails. A number of disused buildings from the old Fort Cronkite facility complete the coastal tableau, giving the area the sort of frozen-in-time atmosphere of an *X Files* episode.

An inviting coastal hiking trail extends in either direction along the headlands. As we hiked north toward the next beach, Tennessee Cove, we found a group of surfers taking

© PARKE PUTERBAUGH

Marin Headlands

waves into what appeared to be a sheer cliff face. Nearby, a tiny cove invites exploration, though it is reachable (and dangerously so) only by sea.

As we hiked north, the quiet and fog—pierced by the mournful ring of a buoy's bell and the occasional wave breaking in the distance—embraced and intoxicated us. Bird calls and the lonesome sound of wind whipping through the dry vegetation added to the air of mystery. This is the sort of place that explains the fixation by Marin County residents with all things New Age.

How can one not be visited by meditative thoughts when surrounded on all sides by such a paradise? We watched transfixed as waves repeatedly washed over a rock. Could staring at crystals be far behind? The old coast road ends in a gully between Rodeo Beach and Tennessee Cove, an apt reminder of the fleeting nature of human existence. We'll stop before we start sounding like Krishnamurti.

The beach at **Tennessee Cove** is backed by a pond with still more bird life. Getting there requires a two-mile hike from the Tennessee

Valley parking area. The next accessible stretch of sand is Muir Beach. There's plenty more to do in the Marin Headlands—camping, hiking, horseback riding, visiting seacoast fortifications—than this brief synopsis can touch on. The tri-county Golden Gate National Recreation Area is the largest urban park in the world and deserving of a full-length travel guide in its own right.

◼ KIRBY COVE

Location: from U.S. 101 north of Golden Gate Bridge, take Alexander Road exit to Conzelman Road in the Marin Headlands, follow to Kirby Cove

Parking/Fees: free parking lot; camping is free with permit from National Park Service

Hours: 24 hours

Facilities: restrooms and picnic tables

Contact: Marin Headlands unit of Golden Gate National Recreation Area, 415/561-4700

2 BONITA COVE

Location: from U.S. 101 north of Golden Gate Bridge take Alexander Road exit to Conzelman Road; hiking trail from Battery Alexander leads to Bonita Cove at the southwest tip of Marin Headlands
Parking/Fees: free parking lot
Hours: 24 hours
Facilities: none
Contact: Marin Headlands unit of Golden Gate National Recreation Area, 415/561-4700

3 RODEO BEACH

Location: from U.S. 101 north of Golden Gate Bridge take Alexander Road exit to Bunker Road, follow to Rodeo Beach
Parking/Fees: free parking lot
Hours: 24 hours
Facilities: restrooms and picnic area
Contact: Marin Headlands unit of Golden Gate National Recreation Area, 415/561-4700

4 TENNESSEE COVE

Location: end of Tennessee Valley Road, off Highway 1 in Mill Valley; follow trail from parking lot to beach
Parking/Fees: free parking lot
Hours: 24 hours
Facilities: none
Contact: Marin Headlands unit of Golden Gate National Recreation Area, 415/561-4700

Muir Beach

Not only did he have a stand of redwoods dubbed after him, but pioneering environmentalist John Muir rated a beauty of a beach that bears his name. Signs along the impos-

Tennessee Cove

© KATHRYN OSGOOD

sibly serpentine Highway 1 point to Muir Beach, which is within the Golden Gate National Recreation Area and linked to various other Marin Headlands units via the 35-mile Coastal Trail.

Inhabitants of Muir Woods include grosbeaks, warblers, loons, grebes, and gray foxes. A lucky few human intruders have been allowed to build homes on the hillside that overlooks the beach. The architecture is all dark wood and low-scale, like an old California bohemian enclave.

For more information, contact the Golden Gate National Recreation Area, Marin Headlands Visitor Center, Fort Berry Chapel, Sausalito, CA 94695, 415/331-1540, www.nps.gov/goga/marin-headlands.htm.

BEACHES

Framed by a creek and dense, green woods, **Muir Beach** provides a striking setting even when the elements are not hospitable. To reach the beach from the parking lot, which is small and often filled, visitors must cross a rocky field and a bridge that spans a small lagoon called Redwood Creek. In order to protect the fragile

© PARKE PUTERBAUGH

Muir Beach

wildlife habitat, signs in the parking lot direct visitors to use the footbridge instead of finding their own way across the stream.

Frequently windy and draped in fog, Muir Beach does have its serene days—especially during Indian summer, when things warm up. The iffy weather, by the way, hasn't stopped the area from being unofficially partitioned into clothed and clothing-optional beaches. The former is what you walk to from the parking lot. The latter is reached by walking north along the main public beach, across a lagoon, and over a rock pile. It was hard to imagine getting naked on one of our recent summer visits. On a sunny day in late June, the wind was blowing so hard that people were huddled in hooded sweatshirts and jackets.

5 MUIR BEACH

🚲 🚶 🚻

Location: Pacific Way at Highway 1 in Muir Beach
Parking/Fees: free parking lot
Hours: 9 A.M.-10 P.M. (summer); closing hours

vary between 7 P.M. and 9 P.M. the rest of the year
Facilities: restrooms and picnic tables
Contact: Stinson Beach Ranger Station, 415/868-0942

COASTAL CUISINE

Muir Beach is the site of a unique Marin County dining and lodging establishment, **Pelican Inn** (10 Pacific Way, Muir Beach, CA 94965, 415/383-6000, $$$). As authentic-looking as any place in the Cotswolds, the large, Tudor-style building houses a pub and restaurant on the ground floor and seven small guest rooms upstairs. Rooms are snug and appointed with quaint British touches. The pub, as the throng of locals can attest, is just the sort of place you'd want to knock back a pint of Guinness or a warming glass of port on a chilly day. The food is good, hearty (if somewhat pricey) pub fare: bangers and mash (sausage and potatoes), fish 'n' chips, and the like. The Pelican also serves a popular Sunday brunch, and there's a lovely patio out back for alfresco dining on balmy days.

MARIN COUNTY

Steep Ravine Beach

Steep Ravine Beach offers an experience unique on the California coast: tiptoeing into the water at low tide to sit in warm springs that percolate through the ocean floor. Visitors can also tent camp or stay in one of ten rustic cabins here, with prior reservations.

For more information, contact the Golden Gate National Recreation Area, Marin Headlands Visitor Center, Fort Berry Chapel, Sausalito, CA 94695, 415/331-1540, www.nps.gov/goga/marin-headlands.htm.

BEACHES

Steep Ravine is so named for a reason. It's a wild, rocky, sandless beach that necessitates a steep, mile-long hike off Highway 1. To reach the ocean, look for dirt pullouts and a road with a locked gate, two miles south of Stinson Beach. If you're camping, you can drive partway there. If not, you must park along Highway 1 and hoof it.

of Stinson Beach and is identified by a dirt parking lot by the side of Highway 1.

BEACHES

Fairly sizable though it is, we found the lot full, with overflow lining both sides of the road. There are no signs for it, nor is the beach visible from the road. We saw a trail leading down, so we took it. Imagine our surprise to round a corner at the bottom and find ourselves facing a pack of naked bodies. They looked to be having great fun, flinging Frisbees and letting it all hang out. There were more people here, in fact, than at Stinson Beach, the easily accessible public beach we'd just left.

Red Rock Beach is a quarter-mile cove that occupies state-park property. No one bothers the skinny-dippers (or vice versa). The path to the beach is fairly steep and takes about 15 minutes each way to walk. If you wear nothing else, do bring a good pair of walking shoes. Lately, erosion has thinned the beach and, accordingly, the numbers who frolic on it.

6 STEEP RAVINE BEACH

Location: off Highway 1, two miles south of Stinson Beach
Parking/Fees: free limited roadside parking; camping fee $15 per night, plus $7.50 reservation fee; cabin rental $75 per night, plus $7.50 reservation fee
Hours: 7 A.M.-sunset
Facilities: restrooms and picnic tables
Contact: Mount Tamalpais State Park, 415/388-2070

7 RED ROCK BEACH

Location: Highway 1 near Milepost 11, about 1.5 miles south of Stinson Beach; a trail leads to beach from a roadside turnout
Parking/Fees: free limited roadside parking
Hours: 7 A.M.-10 P.M. (summer); closing hours vary between 6 P.M. and 9 P.M. the rest of the year
Facilities: none
Contact: Mount Tamalpais State Park, 415/388-2070

Red Rock Beach

Red Rock Beach has been touted as the coast's friendliest and most popular nude beach. That's friendly as in, "C'mon down, take your clothes off and stay awhile." We stumbled upon it by accident many years ago. It's 1.5 miles south

Stinson Beach

Stinson Beach is where San Francisco goes when it wants to enjoy a day at the beach. Stinson is a flat, sandy, three-mile break in the action between the Marin Headlands and the sea cliffs of Bolinas. Big crowds turn out on weekends when the sun is shining and the air is calm, especially in the months between summer's foggy chill and winter's stormy surliness. There's a bargain aspect to Stinson Beach that no doubt adds to its popularity. It is part of the Golden Gate National Recreation Area, administered by the National Park Service. Unlike the state-park beaches, which charge day-use fees of $6, Stinson is absolutely free.

The beach and the small town that surrounds it are nestled at the base of Mount Tamalpais in a storybook setting. You must earn your passage to this sandy wonderland, and the price to be paid is carsickness. The easiest way here is via Highway 1 (also known as Shoreline Highway or "Dramamine Drive"), which disengages from U.S. 101 near Mill Valley. The road follows the curves and contours of Mount Tamalpais, passing south of Muir Woods. The horseshoe curves will make you queasy. On any given turn you may encounter a snorting Greyhound Ameri-Cruiser or a house-sized RV with its wheels in your lane, so drive carefully. It's worth the risk for the panoramic views along the cliff edges, from which more ocean is visible than anywhere outside of a window seat on an airplane.

A long descent leads into the small town of Stinson Beach (population 800), which has a bit of everything for day-trippers and passers-through: a grocery store, gas station, antiques shop, bookstore, surf shop, restaurants, and a few small roadside motels. With a rise of mountains providing a dramatic backdrop, pure Marin County air to breathe, and a wide white-sand beach to play on, Stinson Beach is well worth the curves that Highway 1 throws in your path to get there.

Indeed, on a nice day Stinson Beach exudes the look and feel of a Southern California beach scene. Nonetheless, it's a community that also leaves itself open to more rarefied pursuits, such as "Shakespeare at Stinson."

For more information, contact the West Marin County Chamber of Commerce, 11431 Highway 1, Suite 15, P.O. Box 1045, Point Reyes Station, CA 94956, 415/663-9232, www.pointreyes.org.

BEACHES

We've seen **Stinson Beach** in all kinds of weather: forbiddingly gray and chilly on the one hand, and sunny and warm on the other. On nice days crowds swell to 15,000 and traffic backs up on Highway 1. Still, the enormous parking lots appear capable of taking on all comers. Stinson is a great spot for surfing and has one of the North Coast's best outfitters, **Live Water Surf Shop** (3450 Highway 1, 415/868-0333). Fall and winter are best for surfing, though we've seen monster waves breaking in summer, too.

Walking north from Stinson Beach, you eventually come to a hidden jewel known as **Seadrift Beach.** (It can also be reached via Seadrift Drive.) This lovely sand beach fronts an upscale subdivision called Seadrift, mostly weekend homes protected by a seawall. Despite local perception, this is not a private beach, so wander it to your heart's content.

MARIN COUNTY

⑧ STINSON BEACH

BEST (

Location: 20 miles north of San Francisco, on Highway 1 in Stinson Beach
Parking/Fees: free parking lot
Hours: 9 A.M.-10 P.M. (summer); closing hours vary between 7 P.M. and 9 P.M. the rest of the year
Facilities: concession, lifeguards, restrooms, and picnic tables
Contact: Stinson Beach Ranger Station, 415/868-0942

⑨ SEADRIFT BEACH

Location: off Seadrift Drive north of Stinson Beach
Parking/Fees: free street parking
Hours: 9 A.M.-10 P.M. (summer); closing hours vary between 7 P.M. and 9 P.M. the rest of the year
Facilities: none
Contact: Stinson Beach Ranger Station, 415/868-0942

MARIN COUNTY

© PARKE PUTERBAUGH

Stinson Beach

RECREATION AND ATTRACTIONS

- **Bike/Skate Rentals:** Dave Barnett's Cycle Analysis, Main Street, Point Reyes Station, 415/663-9164

- **Boat Cruise:** Delta Charters, 310 Harbor Drive, Sausalito, 415/332-3291

- **Dive Shop:** Pinnacles Dive Center, 875 Grant Avenue, Novato, 415/897-9962

- **Ecotourism:** Point Reyes Bird Observatory, Point Reyes National Seashore, 415/868-1221; Muir Woods National Monument, 415/388-2595

- **Lighthouses:** Point Bonita, Marin Headlands, Golden Gate National Recreation Area, 415/331-1422; Point Reyes Lighthouse, Point Reyes National Seashore, 415/663-1092

- **Marina:** Sausalito Harbor, 415/499-5000

- **Rainy Day Attractions:** Bay Area Discovery Museum, 557 McReynolds Road, Sausalito, 415/289-7295; Bay Model Visitor Center, 2100 Bridgeway Boulevard, Sausalito, 415/332-3871

- **Shopping/Browsing:** Bridgeway Boulevard, Sausalito

- **Surf Report:** 415/868-1922

- **Surf Shop:** Live Water Surf Shop, 3450 Highway 1, Stinson Beach, 415/868-0333

- **Vacation Rentals:** Oceanic Realty, 3468 Highway 1, Stinson Beach, 415/868-0717, www.oceanicrealty.com

ACCOMMODATIONS

Our inn of first choice, Casa del Mar, was recently sold by its owners and is now a private residence. This leaves the pickings somewhat lean here, though the 75-year-old **Stinson Beach Motel** (3416 Highway 1, 415/868-1712, $$) is a good choice. It's small (seven units) and features a lush garden setting. Prices fluctuate dramatically from room to room and season to season ($90–225). The location (two blocks from the beach) can't be beat, but what really won us over is the fact that the manager is named Frodo. If your name is Bilbo or Gandalf, you might be eligible for a discount.

A unique place to stay in Stinson Beach is **Patterson Sand Castle Bed and Breakfast Inn** (28 Calle del Pinos, 415/868-1652, $$$), which has all of one room. It's large, airy, romantic, and close enough to the ocean to hear the waves. The house is a landmark, built by the inventor of the Popsicle, Francis Epperson, in 1949. Yes, it looks like a miniature castle. No, it's not built of Popsicle sticks.

Given the lack of accommodations in Stinson Beach, your best bet is to call **Oceanic Realty** (415/868-0717, www.oceanicrealty .com). This company has an extensive listing of beach houses for vacation rental, and many are surprisingly affordable, starting at $700 per week.

COASTAL CUISINE

The Parkside Cafe and Snack Bar (43 Arenal Avenue, 415/868-1272, $$) is a friend to snacking surfers and serious eaters alike. The café serves three meals a day, with dinners tending toward Italian fare. The snack bar's hamburgers have been warming the bellies of beach bums for 50 years.

The **Stinson Beach Grill** (3465 Highway 1, 415/868-2002, $$) is the place to go for that West Marin County favorite, barbecued oysters, as well as pasta and seafood. They also offer live jazz on occasion.

Another casual Stinson Beach eatery, the **Sand Dollar** (3458 Highway 1, 415/868-0434, $$), serves fresh local seafood, and you can dine outside on the patio or inside by the fireplace.

NIGHTLIFE

The **Sand Dollar** (3458 Highway 1, 415/868-0434) has the town's most popular bar and its only real nightlife. The beach itself remains open till 10 P.M. in summer. Since there are fire pits and picnic tables, maybe that is the place to party.

Bolinas

The residents of Bolinas really don't want the world to beat a path to their door, and while they're not openly hostile, neither are they openly hospitable. There's the issue of the road sign, for instance. To get to Bolinas, you must turn off Highway 1 onto Olema-Bolinas Road, just north of Bolinas Lagoon and about 25

miles north of San Francisco. If you don't know what you're looking for, you won't know where to turn. Not only is there no marker pointing to Bolinas, but the very road sign identifying Olema-Bolinas Road is usually missing, a tradition that started in the late 1960s and continues to this day. Between 1970 and 1990, hard-core Bolinas hermits made off with 36 road signs. Transit officials threw up their hands and announced they wouldn't install any more signs.

So who needs signs? To get to Bolinas, turn west from Highway 1 at a fork by the lagoon, approximately five miles south of Olema and four miles north of Stinson Beach. Follow the eucalyptus trees into town. You may notice that many denizens of Bolinas look like survivors who fled the Haight-Ashbury in the late 1960s. Remnants of this lost clan populate the rugged coast from Marin County all the way up to Oregon. Bolinas, lying close to their spawning ground, is one of their strongholds.

Hallmarks of the Haight-Ashbury mentality are everywhere: a multicolored, cabalistic sun painted in the street, bearing the legend "Super Solstice to All"; a bakery/café that prides itself on being the area's "only all-organic flour bakery"; and a fleet of vehicles so ragged it's a miracle their engines turn over. We saw one antique Plymouth with three flat tires and rusty rims. To the windshield was pinned a tow order from the Marin County Sheriff's Office, on which the owner scrawled this response: "If you tow this car there will be trouble." On a nearby billboard was this notice: "'71 VW Bus For Sale. Leaving town and need to sell. $1,700 or best offer."

It's all part of the eccentric appeal of a community that hasn't gone for the corporate land grab and cutesy boutiquing found elsewhere on the California coast. That's "community" in the best sense, with everyone looking after everyone else. The Community Store dominates the main drag and the "Bolinas Community Mural Project" dominates the sides of the old wooden building.

The bulletin board contains snapshots of local surfers and announcements of local events, including "reggae dances" at the local

SAVING BOLINAS LAGOON

The greatest natural treasure of Bolinas is its lagoon, a 1,100-acre tidal estuary that teems with wildlife. Located between Stinson Beach and Bolinas, the lagoon is rapidly filling up with sediment. Although its demise is not imminent, something must be done soon about the problem. Sedimentation is nothing new, having begun in the 1880s when redwoods in the area were logged. But the process has accelerated in the last two decades, as nearby hills are overgrazed and overdeveloped, and runoff from both accumulates in the lagoon.

The Marin County chapter of *Surfrider* describes the situation: "If not corrected, the opening of the lagoon could close off within 50 years. Once the opening closes, the lagoon will stagnate. Vegetation will die, the marine mammals and sea birds will leave, and the sand bars that produce the great waves will disappear." Nobody wants this to happen – not boaters, fishers, swimmers, sunbathers, or surfers – but not everyone agrees on the solution.

The Bolinas Lagoon Ecosystem Restoration Feasability Study has focused on three areas of concern:

- The need to restore critical habitat while determining how to manage and mitigate anthropogenic influences and plan for climate change;

- The significance of Bolinas Lagoon along the Pacific Flyway;

- How Bolinas Lagoon relates to ecosystem sustainability at the local, regional, and national level.

A coalition, the **Bolinas Lagoon Foundation,** is dedicated to saving the lagoon, which is blessed by some of the largest migratory bird populations in Northern California, as well as a healthy population of harbor seals. The foundation has mounted an impressive consciousness and fundraising campaign. Nothing much has happened as of press time, however – just plans to hold more meetings, conduct more studies, and draft more plans.

For more information, contact the Bolinas Lagoon Foundation, P.O. Box 444, Stinson Beach, CA 94970, www.bolinaslagoon.org.

one-room library. Bolinas has a bad rap as a misanthropic enclave. Not true; to a person, the people we met were friendly. They simply desire their privacy, know they live in a special place, and want to keep it that way—as do most genuine communities in America that are ceaselessly pestered by the agents of economic growth and social homogeneity. Peevish though they may appear, the natives of Bolinas are easily understood and forgiven their eccentricity. Long may they live!

There's not much for an outsider to do in Bolinas, particularly tourists looking for shopping malls and golf courses. Still, if you're even mildly curious, Bolinas is worth a side trip. One incentive is **Point Reyes Bird Observatory,** atop Bolinas Mesa. While you're in town, be sure to stop by Bolinas Bay Bakery & Cafe and pick up picnic supplies—sandwiches, salads, wholesome organic goodies—to take out to Point Reyes.

For more information, contact the West Marin County Chamber of Commerce, 11431 Highway 1, Suite 15, P.O. Box 1045, Point Reyes Station, CA 94956, 415/663-9232, www.pointreyes.org.

BEACHES

To get to **Bolinas Beach,** follow Olema-Bolinas Road to Wharf Street, which ends at a

MARIN COUNTY

© PARKE PUTERBAUGH

Bolinas Lagoon

concrete ramp by a pile of riprap that holds a section of the eroding spit in place. If you come out here, make sure you're proficient at three-point turns, because there is no turnaround at the end of Wharf Street. We suspect this is just one more effort to discourage visitation. The south-facing beach looks across Bolinas Lagoon, a nature preserve for migratory waterfowl, toward Stinson Beach. Bolinas Beach ends at a jetty. The shoreline narrows precipitously on the south side of the lagoon, where waves lap hungrily at the base of the bluffs.

Facing the ocean full-on is **Agate Beach,** whose principal attraction is access to Duxbury Reef, an offshore mass of rock where marine and intertidal life can be observed. It can be reached by parking at the end of Elm Road and descending a stairway to the beach. It's evident that the forces of nature are doing more damage to Bolinas than any feared tourist influx. The sea cliffs upon which Bolinas rests are made not of sandstone but mudstone, a more erosive material. Geologist Gary Griggs describes the Bolinas sea cliffs as "one continuous plane of landslides."

10 BOLINAS BEACH

Location: from Highway 1, 4.5 miles north of Stinson Beach, go west on Olema-Bolinas Road to Bolinas; turn left onto Wharf Road and follow to beach
Parking/Fees: free street parking
Hours: 24 hours
Facilities: none
Contact: Bolinas Beach Utility District, 415/868-1224

11 AGATE BEACH

Location: from Highway 1, 4.5 miles north of Stinson Beach, go west on Olema-Bolinas Road to Bolinas; turn left onto Elm Road and follow to beach
Parking/Fees: free parking lot
Hours: 24 hours
Facilities: none
Contact: Bolinas Beach Utility District, 415/868-1224

ACCOMMODATIONS

For all its isolation, Bolinas has a number of inns and guest houses, including **One Fifty-five Pine** (Box 62, 415/868-0263, $$), a beach cottage overlooking the ocean, and **Blue Heron Inn** (11 Wharf Road, 415/868-1102, $$), a small Victorian cottage above a restaurant, lounge, and espresso bar in the center of town. The guest rooms at **Thomas' White House Inn** (118 Kale Road, 415/868-0279, $$) also have funky charm and dynamite coastal views.

COASTAL CUISINE

The aforementioned **Bolinas Bay Bakery & Cafe** (20 Wharf Road, 415/868-0211, $$) takes pains to prepare things the healthy way, using organic flour and greens, and stressing vegetarian preparations. The salads are great: curried tuna, tofu, and eggplant in Asian barbecue sauce, raspberry poppyseed coleslaw—you get the idea. Baked goods include loaves of "Stems and Seeds" bread (a nine-grain, three-seeded whole wheat), sun-dried tomato and Parmesan sourdough bread, and poppyseed custard cake. The owners are not doctrinaire vegans, either. You can order a hamburger (made from Bolinas-raised, natural ground beef) or smoked baby-back ribs (the porkers, too, have had a natural upbringing). They also make great pizzas, pastas, soups, and a pesto croissant stuffed with spinach, walnuts, and six cheeses. Never in our experience has health food seemed so decadent.

NIGHTLIFE

Smiley's Schooner Saloon (41 Wharf Road, 415/868-1311) jumps to the beat of live bands on weekends, many of them survivors of the golden age of the San Francisco scene. You might catch New Riders of the Purple Sage, Commander Cody, Maria Muldaur, or Barry Melton—the former guitarist for Country Joe and the Fish, who now works as a public defender. Incidentally, Smiley's runs a little hotel with guest rooms up the hill from the saloon.

Point Reyes National Seashore

The wilderness area known as Point Reyes is a geological island. It is an island arc that hitched a ride across the Pacific Ocean and slammed into the North American plate, becoming part of what we call California many millions of years ago. The tectonic fun and games continue to this day, as the Pacific and North American plates engage in the geological equivalent of sumo wrestling.

Sooner or later, immense pressure builds along fault lines and the plates slip past each other—an adjustment known as an earthquake. During the cataclysmic San Francisco quake of 1906, whose epicenter was in the Marin County town of Olema, the Point Reyes Peninsula moved 16 feet in 45 seconds. Even when the San Andreas Fault isn't throwing a seismic tantrum, it propels the hook-shaped peninsula northwesterly at the rate of two inches per year. No wonder the National Park Service has made "A Land in Motion" Point Reyes's official slogan.

All this continental drift has helped create California's most unusual coastal landmass. Point Reyes is one of only seven National Seashores in the United States and the only one on the West Coast. It's separated from the rest of California by the San Andreas Fault, which runs through Marin from Bolinas Lagoon to Tomales Bay. Inverness Ridge contributes to Point Reyes's distinct climate zone. East of the ridge the weather is like that of the inland valleys. West of the ridge the land is frequently blanketed in thick, blinding fog, pelted with rains of biblical intensity, and blasted by stiff, chilling winds. They blow as high as a hundred miles per hour out at land's end. It's as if nature is screaming, "You've got all that other land to play with, but this is mine!" At least one Point Reyes lighthouse keeper was driven mad by the relentless winds.

Gusty though it may be, Point Reyes is a land rich in natural beauty, flora and fauna, and history. Before venturing onto the peninsula, stop at **Bear Valley Visitor Center,** the main entrance to the National Seashore, off Highway 1 in Olema. Maps, brochures and visitor info are freely dispensed, and the well-stocked bookshop includes numerous titles about the area. There are visitors centers at Drakes Beach and Point Reyes Lighthouse, too, but Bear Valley is by far the best place to get your bearings and has the most extensive hours.

Bear Valley Visitor Center is open 9 A.M.–5 P.M. on weekdays (from 8 A.M. on weekends and holidays). Point Reyes Lighthouse and Visitor Center are open 10:00 A.M.–4:30 P.M. Thursday–Monday; call 415/669-1534 during operating hours for more information about the lighthouse. Kenneth C. Patrick Visitor Center, at Drakes Beach, is open 10 A.M.–5 P.M. weekends and holidays only.

Incidentally, on weekends and holidays from late December to mid-April, the west end of Sir Francis Drake Boulevard is closed and shuttle buses ferry park visitors from Drakes Beach to the Point Reyes Lighthouse to the Chimney Rock parking lot and back. The buses cost $5 per person over 16 (free otherwise) and run every 20 minutes 9:30 A.M.–3 P.M. Here's the tricky part: The road closes and the buses run *only* on weekends and holidays when the weather's good.

Point Reyes is a hiker's paradise, crisscrossed with 147 miles of trails. To whet your appetite, try the 0.7-mile Earthquake Trail, which traverses the San Andreas fault line outside the Bear Valley Visitor Center. A reconstructed Miwok village is on the grounds. Point Reyes is one of the world's prime bird-watching meccas. Over 450 avian species have been spotted, including curlews, coots, buffleheads, and loons. (Don't they sound like a wacky crew?) At the south end of the shore, accessible from Bolinas, is **Point Reyes Bird Observatory** (415/868-1221), a nonprofit research center with a small museum and database on bird sightings.

On a clear day the drive from Bear Valley to the beaches of Point Reyes is as scenic as any in the state. Around every bend a new and fascinating wrinkle in the land materializes. Forests give way to meadows, which yield to dunes and marshes. Hawks soar above hills and fields, looking for mice rustling in the grass. Herons stand like ghostly sentinels in the wetlands. Deer and elk bound from the shadows. Cows graze stiffly in the buffeting winds. The only signs of human habitations on the peninsula are these still-operating dairy farms, the remnants of the private landholders left from 1962, when the area was declared a National Seashore.

Based on its history, one could argue that Point Reyes is the real New England. In 1579 Francis Drake beached his ship, the *Golden Hinde,* on the peninsula to make repairs and gather supplies before heading back to England with a load of Spanish plunder. He met a peaceful tribe of hunters and gatherers, the Miwok, who'd lived here for centuries. Since the cliffs above the coast vaguely resemble Dover, a homesick Drake dubbed his find "Nova Albion" ("New England"). He claimed the land in the name of Queen Elizabeth and asserted his rights by leaving behind "a plate of brasse, fast nailed to a great and firme post."

That's about as far as the English influence went, because the Spanish were the next to step up to the Pacific plate. In 1603 they swung for the fences, naming the landmass La Punta de Los Reyes (after the Feast of the Three Kings) and pressing the Miwok into forced labor in the missions farther inland. After California became a state in 1850, the land grants were subdivided into ranches, and you still see cattle grazing out here.

Everyone who lives within 200 miles of Point Reyes has their own secret spot. We couldn't possibly do justice to it all, so we'll confine our comments to the beaches and hope that intrepid travelers will ferret out the other goodies that lie inland (creeks, hills, forests, pools, mountain trails). With 74,000 acres of pristine wilderness, there's no end of things to do.

THE MAJESTIC LIGHTHOUSES OF THE CALIFORNIA COAST

Who doesn't love a lighthouse? These isolated, often fog-shrouded structures exert a romantic or adventurous pull on the imagination. Maybe it's the idea that someone is living alone out there on St. George's Light, six miles off the northern California coast, or holed up at the tip of Point Reyes, one of the foggiest spots in the world. Perhaps it's the closet hermit in all of us who loves lighthouses, fantasizing about all that solitude and the lulling of the ocean waves at night.

California has a lot of lighthouses because the rugged coastline and unpredictable shore currents have served as a graveyard for errant sailors. Before gold was found at Sutter's Mill, the state's non-Indian population was 14,000. By 1852, it was 250,000. Most of these new Californians arrived between 1849 and 1852, and they came from all points of the compass. Lighthouses were desperately needed (so were jails, but that's another story), and they began popping up all along the coast. Many of the original structures are still standing, even if the stations themselves have been decommissioned. There are nine lighthouses in the San Francisco Bay alone, including a lighthouse boat in Oakland Harbor.

We've listed only those lighthouses located on or near ocean beaches, with some part of the original structure still existing. They are arranged, like this book, from south to north:

* **Point Loma** – south end of Point Loma at entrance to San Diego Harbor; built 1871; height: 70 feet

* **Long Beach** – Lion's Lighthouse; north side of harbor's entrance; built by Lion's Club in 2000; height: 65 feet

* **Long Beach** – entrance to Long Beach harbor; built 1949; height: 71 feet

* **Los Angeles Harbor** – San Pedro Harbor breakwater; built 1930; height: 69 feet

* **Point Fermin** – San Pedro Harbor; built 1874; height: 30 feet

* **Point Vicente** – Palos Verdes Peninsula; built 1926; height: 67 feet

* **Anacapa Island** – entrance to Santa Barbara Channel, on East Anacapa, 11 miles off Ventura; built 1932; height: 40 feet

* **Point Hueneme** – east entrance, Santa Barbara Channel; built 1941; height: 48 feet

* **Point Conception** – west entrance, Santa Barbara Channel; built 1882; height: 52 feet

* **San Luis Obispo (a.k.a. Port Harford Light)** – Avila Beach; built 1890; height: 40 feet

- **Piedras Blancas** – northern entrance of San Simeon Bay; built 1875; height: 74 feet

- **Point Sur** – Big Sur; built 1889; height: 48 feet

- **Mile Rocks** – half-mile off San Francisco Bay entrance; built 1906; height: 35 feet

- **Point Pinos** – Pacific Grove, south entrance to Monterey Bay; built 1855; height: 43 feet

- **Santa Cruz** – Walton Lighthouse, built on west jetty of Santa Cruz Harbor in 2001; height: 54 feet

- **Santa Cruz** – Mark Abbott Memorial Lighthouse; built in tribute to drowned surfer in 1967; houses a surfing museum

- **Pigeon Point** – southern approach to San Francisco Bay; built 1872; height: 115 feet

- **Point Montara** – at Montara; originally built in Wellfleet, Mass., moved to Montara in 1928; height: 30 feet

- **Fort Point** – San Francisco Harbor entrance; built 1864; height: 27 feet

- **Farallon** – southeast Farallon Island; built 1855; height: 41 feet

- **Lime Point** – San Francisco side of entrance to San Francisco Bay; built 1900; height: 20 feet

- **Point Bonita** – Marin County side of entrance to San Francisco Bay; built 1877; height: 33 feet

- **Point Reyes** – along the Gulf of the Farallons; built 1870; height: 35 feet

- **Point Arena** – two miles north of Point Arena; built 1908; height: 115 feet

- **Point Cabrillo** – between Cape Mendocino and Point Arena; built 1909; height: 47 feet

- **Punta Gorda** – 12 miles south of Cape Mendocino, near Petrolia; built 1912; height: 27 feet

- **Cape Mendocino (old)** – moved to Shelter Cove in 1951; built 1868; height: 43 feet

- **Trinidad Head** – above Trinidad Harbor; built 1871; height: 25 feet

- **St. George Reef** – six miles off the coast from Crescent City; built 1892; height: 90 feet

- **Crescent City (a.k.a. Battery Point Light)** – Crescent City; built 1856; height: 45 feet

MARIN COUNTY

On a sobering note, a huge fire in 1995 charred 12,000 acres on Point Reyes and destroyed 40 homes in Inverness. The Vision Fire, as it came to be known, closed the park for two weeks. It took a firefighting team of 2,000 to bring the blaze under control. To this day, remnants of the fire are visible along Limantour Road.

For more information, contact Point Reyes National Seashore, 1 Bear Valley Road, Point Reyes, CA 94956, 415/464-5100, www.nps .gov/pore.

BEACHES

Beachcombers may find it rough going, but those who like it wild and woolly will be in their glory on this rugged peninsula. There are 30 miles of wilderness beaches on Point Reyes. They're hazardous for swimming but wonderful for hiking, sunning, and seeking solitude. The beaches of Point Reyes can be reached from three park entrances: Mesa Road (off Olema-Bolinas Road), Limantour Road (off Highway 1 near Olema), and Sir Francis Drake Boulevard (off Highway 1 south of Point Reyes Station).

The best and safest beaches are on the southern half of Point Reyes, where they're sheltered by the peninsula's protective hook. The arm that extends back toward mainland California—officially known as Point Reyes—acts as a sort of windbreak and jetty and explains why Drake chose to land here rather than the wild shore to the north. The quickest access to the southern beaches is Limantour Road, a lovely route that winds through the town of Inverness and passes Point Reyes Hostel before ending at Limantour Beach.

Limantour Beach offers good swimming in calm waters and picnicking without gale-force winds. In the 1950s a Carmel-type commercial development (Drakes Beach Estates) was on the drawing board until distressed conservationists intervened to save Limantour, arguably the peninsula's most idyllic spot. Limantour Spit protects the rich and varied Estero de Limantour, and inland trails skirt its shoreline. Bring binoculars for whale- and bird-watching.

Other beaches exist south of Limantour, but they are accessible only by park trails. The first of these wilderness beaches is **Santa Maria Beach,** where the primitive but popular Coast Camp lies behind a sandy ridge. To get there walk south for 1.5 miles from Limantour Beach or hike 2.5 miles over dunes and past marshes along the Coast Trail from its trailhead at Point Reyes Hostel. The Coast Trail stretches for 16 miles, from the hostel to the Palomarin parking area, near Point Reyes Bird Observatory.

Sculptured Beach is 1.3 miles south of Santa Maria, and it too lies off the Coast Trail. It is more of a visual delight than a swimming hole, with sea caves, sea stacks, and crumbling ocher cliffs providing a rugged setting. Be careful not to get stranded against the cliffs by a rising tide. Those who like to live dangerously can proceed around a rubbly point at low tide to another cove, the aptly named **Secret Beach.**

Back on the Coast Trail, **Kelham Beach** lies 2.3 miles south of Sculptured Beach, around Point Resistance. Continue another 0.7 mile and you can crawl through a sea tunnel at Arch Rock (but only at low tide). Wildcat Camp is 3.5 miles farther down the trail. It's ideal for intrepid backpackers. A shorter route to Wildcat Camp starts at Five Brooks Parking Area, five miles south of Olema on Highway 1. The camp is 5.7 miles west of Five Brooks, via Stewart Trail (as opposed to 10.5 miles via the Coast Trail from Point Reyes Hostel). Wildcat Camp occupies a grassy meadow near a small stream. **Wildcat Beach,** another cliff-backed wilderness wonder, lies at the end of a short spur trail.

There's one more named beach on the south flank of Point Reyes National Seashore. **Palomarin Beach** lies west of the Palomarin parking area, just above Bolinas, off Mesa Road. This parking area is the southern trailhead for the Coast Trail. Wildcat Camp is 5.5 miles north and Coast Camp is 13.2 miles north. Got all that? If not, pick up a Point Reyes trail map at Bear Valley Visitor Center. Palomarin Beach is narrow and isolated, and leashed dogs are permitted.

The most popular beach on Point Reyes is **Drakes Beach.** Though located on the peninsula's south side, it is reached by way of a completely different route than Limantour Beach. Backtracking to Inverness, pick up Sir Francis Drake Boulevard and drive 18 miles to Kenneth C. Patrick Visitor Center, a well-appointed facility. From here, easy hikes are available through three different beach habitats—shore, lagoon, and bluff. The beaches and dunes are postcard perfect. Some people even swim here, though we don't have the tolerance for water this frigid.

The second most popular attraction on the peninsula is **Point Reyes Lighthouse.** It's at the end Sir Francis Drake Boulevard, around the bend from Drakes Beach. It's a great and often busy spot for viewing migrating whales and birds, especially at Sea Lion Overlook. The trek out to the lighthouse (built in 1870) requires descending 300 steps. It's not for everyone, and on a foggy, blustery day it's really not for *anyone.*

Another exquisite spot is **Chimney Rock,** which lies at the tip of Point Reyes's hook. Getting here requires a 1.5-mile hike, but it's worth every step. In winter, over 20,000 gray whales have been counted passing this checkpoint. In the teeming waters below the rocks are the remains of countless ships that have wrecked in the smothering fog of Point Reyes, which is the second thickest in America. (Cape Disappointment, in Washington State, has the thickest fog.)

To our thinking, the beaches north of the lighthouse are the hidden treasures of Point Reyes National Seashore. However, be aware that these beaches can be imposing, whipped by wind, waves, and fog. The water is subject to severe undertow and "sneaker waves," and the bluffs are subject to erosion. Be careful when trekking around here, and check tide tables to make sure you won't wind up trapped by high tide. The are no lifeguards out here—just tule elk, who will probably laugh demonically at you like creatures from a Far Side cartoon.

Even so, we strongly recommend visiting these northern beaches. The closest to the lighthouse are **Point Reyes Beach North** and **Point Reyes Beach South,** reachable from accesses several miles apart on Sir Francis Drake Boulevard. Combined, they account for ten miles of raw, unsullied wilderness beach that is given the collective name the Great Beach. When the weather cooperates, the area can be a paradise for walkers, photographers, artists, and picnickers. But be advised that swimmers and surfers are taking their lives in their hands by braving these inhospitable waters.

There are a few more beaches on the north shore. The best swimming in this region is at the beaches of Tomales Bay. The water is much warmer and safer. As for the ocean beaches, the posted warning at the trailhead leading to Kehoe Beach says it all: "The 19-mile northwestern shore of Point Reyes National Seashore is unsafe for swimming, surfing, or wading. Do not enter the water. This warning applies to all beaches from Tomales Point south to the Point Reyes Headland, including McClure's Beach, Kehoe Beach, Abbotts Lagoon, North Beach, and South Beach. Cold water, rough surf, and loose footing make hazardous swimming conditions, but there are more serious dangers. Rip currents, sharks, and sneaker waves are constant threats."

Don't say you haven't been warned. Hiking out to these beaches provides jaw-dropping glimpses of nature in the raw. A bracing two-mile walk leads to **Abbotts Lagoon.** The 0.6-mile path to **Kehoe Beach** passes mountainous dunes, towering bluffs, variegated vegetation, and (if you're lucky) baby-blue skies dotted by silver-lined clouds. Locals prefer Kehoe because dogs are allowed there.

Kehoe Beach has a counterpart across Inverness Ridge on Tomales Bay. **Marshall Beach** is the only bay beach within Point Reyes National Seashore. It's hard to get to, requiring a four-mile drive off Sir Francis Drake Boulevard and a somewhat dreary 1.5-mile hike from the parking lot. It's worth the trouble only if you want to save the niggling entrance fee at Tomales Bay State Park, where you can drive your car right to Hearts Desire Beach.

From the parking lot at the end of Pierce Point Road, a half-mile trail leads to **McClure's Beach**. At low tide explorers are beckoned by tidepools and beautiful water-sculpted driftwood. (A beach to the north, toward Tomales Point, is unofficially known as Driftwood Beach.) Again, be careful while walking the beaches. Stay away from the water's edge, and don't even think about swimming. If the threats of sharks and sleeper waves don't deter you, consider the fact that the average water temperature is a bone-numbing 55 degrees.

12 PALOMARIN BEACH

Location: From Highway 1, 4.5 miles north of Stinson Beach, turn west onto Olema-Bolinas Road and follow it 1.8 miles. Turn right onto Mesa Road and continue 4.5 miles to a gravel parking lot. Hike to the beach from Palomarin trailhead.
Parking/Fees: free parking lot
Hours: 24 hours
Facilities: none
Contact: Point Reyes National Seashore, 415/464-5100

13 WILDCAT BEACH

Location: more than five-mile hike from trailheads at Palomarin, Five Brooks, and Bear Valley Visitor Center at Point Reyes National Seashore; consult park map for details
Parking/Fees: free parking lots; camping fees $15 per site for parties of 1-6, $30 per site for parties of 7-14, $40 for parties of 15-25;

permits required and limited in number, obtain at Bear Valley Visitor Center
Hours: 24 hours
Facilities: restrooms and picnic tables
Contact: Point Reyes National Seashore, 415/464-5100

14 KELHAM BEACH

Location: 4.8-mile hike from Bear Valley Visitor Center at Point Reyes National Seashore; consult park map for details
Parking/Fees: free parking lots
Hours: 24 hours
Facilities: picnic table
Contact: Point Reyes National Seashore, 415/464-5100

15 SCULPTURED BEACH

Location: walk east at low tide only from Santa Maria Beach at Point Reyes National Seashore; consult tide tables and park map for details
Parking/Fees: free parking lots
Hours: 24 hours
Facilities: none
Contact: Point Reyes National Seashore, 415/464-5100

16 SANTA MARIA BEACH

Location: 9-mile hike from Bear Valley Visitor Center or 2.5-mile hike from Point Reyes Hostel at Point Reyes National Seashore; consult park map for details
Parking/Fees: free parking lots; camping fees $15 per site for parties of 1-6, $30 per site for parties of 7-14, $40 for parties of 15-25; permits required and limited in number, obtain at Bear Valley Visitor Center

Hours: 24 hours
Facilities: restrooms and picnic tables
Contact: Point Reyes National Seashore, 415/464-5100

17 LIMANTOUR BEACH

 BEST (

Location: from Highway 1 in Olema, turn onto Bear Valley Road and follow one mile; turn onto Limantour Road and follow to beach
Parking/Fees: free parking lot
Hours: 24 hours
Facilities: restrooms
Contact: Point Reyes National Seashore, 415/464-5100

18 DRAKES BEACH

Location: from Highway 1 in Point Reyes Station, turn west onto Sir Francis Drake Highway, drive 15.5 miles to turnoff for Drakes Beach; follow signs to beach
Parking/Fees: free parking lot
Hours: 24 hours
Facilities: concession, restrooms, showers, picnic tables, and visitors center
Contact: Point Reyes National Seashore, 415/464-5100

19 POINT REYES BEACH SOUTH

Location: from Highway 1 in Point Reyes Station, turn west onto Sir Francis Drake Highway, drive 16 miles to turnoff for South Beach; follow signs to beach
Parking/Fees: free parking lot
Hours: 24 hours
Facilities: restrooms
Contact: Point Reyes National Seashore, 415/464-5100

20 POINT REYES BEACH NORTH

Location: from Highway 1 in Point Reyes Station, turn west onto Sir Francis Drake Highway, drive 13 miles to turnoff for North Beach; follow signs to beach
Parking/Fees: free parking lot
Hours: 24 hours
Facilities: restrooms
Contact: Point Reyes National Seashore, 415/464-5100

21 ABBOTTS LAGOON

Location: from Highway 1 in Point Reyes Station, turn west onto Sir Francis Drake Highway; 2.5 miles north of Inverness, bear right at fork onto Pierce Point Road, drive three miles to Abbotts Lagoon parking lot; two-mile hiking trail leads to beach
Parking/Fees: free parking lot
Hours: 24 hours
Facilities: restrooms
Contact: Point Reyes National Seashore, 415/464-5100

22 KEHOE BEACH

BEST (

Location: from Highway 1 in Point Reyes Station, turn west onto Sir Francis Drake Highway; 2.5 miles north of Inverness, bear right at fork onto Pierce Point Road, drive five miles to Kehoe Beach parking lot; half-mile trail leads to beach
Parking/Fees: free parking lot
Hours: 24 hours
Facilities: restrooms
Contact: Point Reyes National Seashore, 415/464-5100

MARIN COUNTY

© PARKE PUTERBAUGH

Kehoe Beach

23 MCCLURE'S BEACH

Location: from Highway 1 in Point Reyes Station, turn west onto Sir Francis Drake Highway; 2.5 miles north of Inverness, bear right at fork onto Pierce Point Road, drive nine miles to McClure's Beach parking lot; half-mile trail leads to beach
Parking/Fees: free parking lot
Hours: 24 hours
Facilities: restrooms
Contact: Point Reyes National Seashore, 415/464-5100

24 MARSHALL BEACH

Location: from Highway 1 in Point Reyes Station, turn west onto Sir Francis Drake Highway; 2.5 miles north of Inverness, bear right at fork onto Pierce Point Road, drive 1.5 miles and turn right onto L Ranch Road; drive 2.5 miles to Marshall Beach parking lot; 1.5-mile hiking trail leads to beach

Parking/Fees: free parking lot
Hours: 24 hours
Facilities: restrooms
Contact: Point Reyes National Seashore, 415/464-5100

ACCOMMODATIONS

One of the nation's most splendidly sited hostels is **Point Reyes Hostel** (1390 Limantour Spit Road, P.O. Box 247, Point Reyes Station, CA 94956-0247, 415/663-8811, $). It has 44 beds, wood stoves, and complete kitchens. A modest fee of $22 per night is charged per person for shared rooms, and private rooms go for only $58. Be sure to call ahead for reservations, for this is a particularly popular hostel. Other accommodations are readily available in nearby Olema, Point Reyes Station, and Inverness.

COASTAL CUISINE

You can grab a snack at **Drakes Beach Cafe** (Kenneth C. Patrick Visitor Center, 415/669-1297, $), which is open 11:30 A.M.–4 P.M. Friday–Tuesday, "weather permitting." Your only other options lie outside the park at restaurants and grocery stores in the sur-rounding communities.

Tomales Bay State Park

Tomales Bay State Park consists of 1,840 acres adjoining the National Seashore on Point Reyes Peninsula. This super state park lies east of Inverness Ridge along Tomales Bay, which provides safe beaches with calm currents and water that can reach 80 degrees by summer's end. Clamming at low tide (limit of 50 with a fishing license) and surf casting (no license needed) are popular activities. Camping is no longer allowed, and parking overnight is prohibited.

For more information, contact Tomales Bay State Park, 415/669-1140, www.parks.ca.gov.

BEACHES

The most visited of the sheltered, warm-water wonders along Tomales Bay is **Hearts Desire Beach** in Tomales Bay State Park. It is flanked by **Indian Beach** and **Pelican Beach,** which lie north and south, respectively, via half-mile trails.

Farther down is **Shell Beach,** a locally popular destination reached by a four-mile hike from Hearts Desire or a half-mile walk from a nearby parking lot. The 6.5-mile Jepson Trail cuts through one of the few remaining virgin stands of Bishop pine.

On the other side of Tomales Bay, along Highway 1 between Point Reyes Station and Marshall, is the state park's Millerton Point unit. There's a west-facing bay beach, **Alan Sieroty Beach,** and a picnic area.

25 HEARTS DESIRE BEACH

Location: from Highway 1 in Point Reyes Station, turn west onto Sir Francis Drake

Highway; 2.5 miles north of Inverness, bear right at fork onto Pierce Point Road, drive one mile to Tomales Bay State Park entrance
Parking/Fees: $6 entrance fee per vehicle
Hours: 8 A.M.–sunset
Facilities: restrooms, picnic tables, and fire grills
Contact: Tomales Bay State Park, 415/669-1140

26 SHELL BEACH

Location: four-mile hike south along Tomales Bay via Johnstone Trail from Hearts Desire Beach (see earlier entry), or park at end of Camino del Mar, off Sir Francis Drake Highway, and follow half-mile trail to beach
Parking/Fees: $6 entrance fee per vehicle at Tomales Bay State Park; free parking lot at end of Camino del Mar
Hours: 8 A.M.–sunset
Facilities: none
Contact: Tomales Bay State Park, 415/669-1140

27 ALAN SIEROTY BEACH

Location: at Millerton Point on eastern shore of Tomales Bay, 4.5 miles north of Point Reyes Station off Highway 1
Parking/Fees: free parking lot
Hours: 8 A.M.–sunset
Facilities: restrooms and picnic tables
Contact: Tomales Bay State Park, 415/669-1140

Olema

Olema was more populous in the 1870s than it is in the new millennium. Although hardly a bustling metropolis, it is a major West Marin crossroads (Highway 1 meets Sir Francis Drake Boulevard) and gateway to Point Reyes National Seashore. Bear Valley Visitor Center lies one-third mile west of town. The word *olema* means "coyote" in the language of the native Miwok.

The area attracted counterculture types in the 1960s, including the Youngbloods, who recorded a musical retort to country singer Merle Haggard's hippie-baiting "Okie from Muskogee," which they entitled "Hippie from Olema."

This inauspicious crossroads, incidentally, was the epicenter of the San Francisco earthquake of 1906, when the ground jumped 16 feet in less than a minute. A fashion/jewelry store in Olema calls itself The Epicenter. This reality might have something to do with the fact that there hasn't been a population boom out here, which helps keep Olema pleasantly low-key. Horseback riding is available at **Five Brooks Stable** (415/663-1570), located three miles south of Olema.

For more information, contact the West Marin County Chamber of Commerce, 11431 Highway 1, Suite 15, P.O. Box 1045, Point Reyes Station, CA 94956, 415/663-9232, www.pointreyes.org.

ACCOMMODATIONS

The **Olema Inn** (10000 Sir Francis Drake Boulevard, 415/663-9559, $$) has been around since 1876, standing proudly at the crossroads. It's a pretty three-room inn with a garden setting and a pleasant ground-floor restaurant. It merits a literary footnote, too, having been patronized by Jack London and John Steinbeck. Nearby is another bed-and-breakfast, **Roundstone Farm** (9940 Sir Francis Drake Boulevard, 415/663-1020, $$), which occupies a 10-acre horse ranch in the hills overlooking the Olema Valley and Tomales Bay. Built in 1987, this five-room B&B comes with solar heating and skylights. Another recent addition to the local lodging scene, the **Point Reyes Seashore Lodge and Conference Center** (10021 Highway 1, 415/663-9000, $$$) provides travelers and business folk with modern conveniences such as whirlpool baths, wet bars, and a choice of accommodations in luxury cottages or the main lodge.

COASTAL CUISINE

The restaurant at the quaint and inviting **Olema Inn** (10000 Sir Francis Drake Bou-

levard, 415/663-9559, $$$) has a Cal-Mediterranean slant (e.g., calamari with cilantro pesto) and a fine wine list. Tomales Bay oysters, Petaluma duck, and vegetarian dishes are other menu staples. The **Olema Farm House** (10005 Highway 1, 415/663-1264, $$) is an all-American kind of place, serving steak, chicken, and seafood to hungry families.

Point Reyes Station

Point Reyes Station lies along Highway 1, which follows the San Andreas Fault. As you enter from the south, the road makes a sharp left turn, passing a few blocks of stores. This is the heart of Point Reyes Station (population 400), which is the center of provisioning for Point Reyes Peninsula.

Here the New West meets the Old West for a showdown on Main Street, where you'll find art galleries alongside a saddle shop and feed store. Times have changed, as galleries outnumber feed stores. Still, when the noon whistle blows, it's not a whistle but a mechanized "moo." Point Reyes Station makes a convenient, centralized point of entry into the National Seashore. It has a smattering of inns, good restaurants, and even a hint of nightlife.

For more information, contact the West Marin County Chamber of Commerce, 11431 Highway 1, Suite 15, P.O. Box 1045, Point Reyes Station, CA 94956, 415/663-9232, www.pointreyes.org.

ACCOMMODATIONS

Try calling **Inns of Marin** (415/663-2000), a referral-and-reservation lodging service for the West Marin area. You will want to stay in a bed-and-breakfast inn out here. In fact, you have little choice in the matter, as the rural landscape practically mandates the B&B experience. We had a memorable stay at **Thirty-Nine Cypress** (39 Cypress, 415/663-1709, $$), a single-story redwood home overlooking pastures, marshlands, and the fringes of Inverness Ridge. The owner is an expert on the natural history of the seashore. **Holly Tree Inn** (3 Silverhills Road, 415/663-1554, $$) is a four-roomer near park headquarters on a 19-acre estate overlooking Tomales Bay.

COASTAL CUISINE

The **Station House Cafe** (11180 Main Street, 415/663-1515, $$) is one of the most celebrated gourmet restaurants along this stretch of the coast. It's warm, comfortable, and unpretentious on the inside, offering live music on Sunday afternoons and piped-in jazz the rest of the time. The real virtuosity is in the kitchen. For starters, try some oysters. They couldn't be fresher, having been raised close by on Tomales Bay. They're served several ways: broiled in garlic and butter, barbecued with a tasty sauce, and served raw with spicy cocktail sauce. Entrées run from beef, raised organically on a North Coast ranch, to vegetarian plates. Seafood dishes might include salmon broiled with saffron cream sauce or halibut cooked to a delicate turn and served with yellow-pepper vinaigrette. Such accompaniments as pureed beet-ginger tart round out the attractively presented dinner items. Save room for dessert. The lemon pot de crème is a nice grace note to an exceptional meal. Service is friendly and attentive, and the clientele—as is often the case in West Marin County—offers an interesting study in rugged and eccentric individualism. In other words, the joint's got character, as well as great food. The Station House is open seven days a week and serves three meals.

NIGHTLIFE

When the sun is hanging low in the sky, Point Reyes Station resembles the backdrop from the old *Gunsmoke* series. Rather than draw a six-gun and start plugging varmints, head to the **Old Western Saloon** (11201 Main Street, 415/663-1661), a local institution. It has the obligatory long wooden bar with brass rail and gunmetal-gray cash box.

Every now and again (or so we were told) someone ties one on and rides a horse into the

Western. Pool tables, pinball games, and an eclectic jukebox provide other diversions. A bumper sticker above the cash box reminds imbibers that "Nobody's Ugly After 2 A.M." They wouldn't add our McDonald's gift certificate to the grubstake pinned to the wall, but the Western is a very hospitable place. Indeed, Prince Charles and his wife Camilla stopped here for a pint on their last U.S. trip.

The **Station House Cafe** (11180 Main Street, 415/663-1515) is a civilized place to hoist a few and has live weekend jazz to boot. A more recent arrival is **Cafe Reyes Roastery & Pub** (11101 Main Street, 415/663-9493), which also has live entertainment on weekends.

Inverness

In the words of a local innkeeper, "Inverness runs at two speeds: dead slow and stop. Usually, it's the latter." Whether slowed or stilled, Inverness (population 600) provides a convenient and idyllic bayside base for exploring Point Reyes Peninsula. The town offers easy access to Tomales Bay. Contact **Blue Waters Kayaking** (12938 Sir Francis Drake Boulevard, 415/669-2600) about kayak rentals.

For more information, contact the West Marin County Chamber of Commerce, 11431 Highway 1, Suite 15, P.O. Box 1045, Point Reyes Station, CA 94956, 415/663-9232, www.pointreyes.org.

ACCOMMODATIONS

The **Golden Hinde Inn and Marina** (12938 Sir Francis Drake Boulevard, 415/669-1389, $$) offers inn-like comforts (continental breakfast, fireplaces) in a motel setting (comfortable rooms, TVs, showers, pool) directly on Tomales Bay. The adjacent marina serves as a boat launch and berthing spot. The inn also rents kayaks and offers guided kayak tours around Tomales Bay. Rates are reasonable ($110–165), and some units have kitchens, which might come in handy if you catch your own dinner.

MARIN COUNTY

On the bed-and-breakfast front, there's the venerable **Blackthorne Inn** (266 Vallejo Avenue, 415/663-8621, $$$), which has been called a carpenter's fantasy because of its ornate construction from redwood, cedar, and Douglas fir milled right on-site. In addition to its architectural charms, the inn has a 2,500-square-foot sundeck and hot tub, and a glassed-in, upper-story room dubbed the Eagle's Nest. Nearby, **Manka's Inverness Lodge** (Argyle Street, 415/669-1034, $$$) has eight cozy guest rooms and two cabins in a secluded, woodsy setting.

To find out about other inns, cottages, and B&Bs scattered around Inverness and surrounding communities, call **Inns of Marin** (415/663-2000) or **Point Reyes Lodging Association** (415/663-1872). While you're at it, request hiking and day-trip guides.

COASTAL CUISINE

Because the median income of Inverness is relatively high and many of the townsfolk are restaurant-going retirees, the local dining choices are varied and of good quality. They run the culinary gamut from Cal-nouvelle to Czech. At **Barnaby's by the Bay** (12938 Drake Boulevard, 415/669-1114, $$), the restaurant at the Golden Hinde Inn, there are always plenty of freshly harvested mussels and oysters on hand. You'll also find applewood-smoked ribs, chicken, and seafood (including crab cioppino).

Vladimir's Czechoslovakian Restaurant (12785 Drake Boulevard, 415/669-1021, $$$) is interesting because of its owner. A self-proclaimed "mechanical genius" and "extremely hard worker," Vladimir Nevl is a Czechoslovakian expatriate who skied his way to freedom in 1948 after the Communist takeover. He came to Inverness and opened his eatery in 1960. Every entrée bears his name: Vladimir's Garlic Lamb Shank, Vladimir's Beef Tongue, etc.

Another Czech-inspired restaurant is **Manka's Inverness Lodge & Restaurant** (30 Callendar Way, 415/669-1034, $$$). On the site of a former hunting lodge in the hills above the bay, the small, rural-chic restaurant is highly regarded even by snobby San Francisco food critics. It specializes in game dishes (e.g., rabbit-walnut sausage, pan-seared elk loin) and local seafood.

Marshall

Marshall is a blink-and-you-miss-it town of 500 along the eastern shore of Tomales Bay. The seafood specialty in West Marin County is barbecued oysters. More than half the state's commercial shellfish farms are in Marshall.

The local bivalves come in two varieties: Hog Island (mild flavored, best eaten raw on the half shell) and Johnson's (saltier, better suited to roasting and basting with barbecue sauce). You can't lose either way.

For more information, contact the West Marin County Chamber of Commerce, 11431 Highway 1, Suite 15, P.O. Box 1045, Point Reyes Station, CA 94956, 415/663-9232, www.pointreyes.org.

ACCOMMODATIONS

If you want to drop anchor in Marshall, then the **Inn on Tomales Bay** (22555 Highway 1, 415/663-9002, $$$) is your place, as all rooms look out on the bay.

COASTAL CUISINE

Oysters are served in restaurants all over the county, but no one does 'em better than **Tony's Seafood Place** (18863 Highway 1, 415/663-1107, $$). One gray afternoon we sat on the outdoor deck and watched a guy standing over a charcoal brazier, basting the bubbling bivalves with a sweet-spicy barbecue sauce. Were they ever good! Nearby is **Tamal Saka Tomales Bay Kayaking** (11431 Highway 1, 415/663-1743), which offers kayaking classes, rentals, and tours, including a "culinary kayaking adventure."

Dillon Beach

Dillon Beach is the northernmost beach in Marin County. A subdivision of second homes and vacation rentals sprawls upon the hills overlooking the tip of Point Reyes. The big draws are **Lawson's Landing,** a private campground at the mouth of Tomales Bay where you can rent boats and dig for giant clams, and **Dillon Beach Resort,** a private day-use beach with a cafe, cabins, and surf shop.

BEACHES

28 LAWSON'S LANDING

Location: end of Marine View Drive, south of Dillon Beach off Highway 1
Parking/Fees: $7 entrance fee per vehicle; camping fee $23 per night
Hours: 7 A.M.-sunset

Facilities: concession, restrooms, showers, and picnic tables
Contact: Lawson's Landing, 707/878-2443

29 DILLON BEACH RESORT

Location: Beach Avenue in Dillon Beach, off Highway 1 near Sonoma County line
Parking/Fees: $7 entrance fee per vehicle
Hours: 8 A.M.-6 P.M. (to 7 P.M. on weekends)
Facilities: concession, restrooms, and picnic tables
Contact: 707/878-2094

ACCOMMODATIONS

Open-meadow camping is available at **Lawson's Landing** (137 Marine View Drive, 707/878-2443, $). The operators run a barge over to a sand bar at low tides (approximately 7–10 days per month), where folks dig for giant clams. **Dillon Beach Vacation Rentals** (707/878-9011 or 800/447-3767, www.dillon beach.com) is the place to contact for home and cottage rentals in the area.

MARIN COUNTY

SONOMA COAST

The Sonoma Coast affords a travel experience not unlike a slow-motion replay of Big Sur. In this desolate stretch of Northern California, one typically negotiates a series of winding bends along Highway 1 as stunning vistas of rocky headlands and promontories come into view, with the vast ocean churning far below.

Every so often you will come upon a town. Actually the town is likely little more than a fishing village, with a smattering of well-hidden homes and ramshackle tackle huts clinging like barnacles to the rocks above the roaring Pacific or along the banks of a clear, cool river. In other words, the concept of the California coast getaway must be modified along the Sonoma Coast.

The most visible settlements are Bodega Bay and Jenner. Both are former logging and fur-trading centers that fell into blissful sleepiness early in the 20th century, after the supply of trees and otters had been exhausted. Slowly these outposts have reawakened as fishing outposts and coastal retreats to soothe the frayed nerves of urban dwellers, who make occasional pilgrimages here.

That isn't to say Sonoma County has no beaches. On the contrary, the southern third of the county is one large state beach—a 16-mile series of coves collectively known as Sonoma Coast State Beaches. They're excellent for fishing and tidepooling, but not for swimming or even wading; an unexpected wave can easily knock you off your feet and a rip current and hypothermia will quickly finish the job. No lifeguards are posted at any of Sonoma's beaches, so watch your step wherever you comb.

Along the middle third of the Sonoma Coast, a handful of cove and river-mouth beaches are associated with the scattered hamlets along Highway 1. The northern third is unfortunately occupied by Sea

Ranch, a private development. There are several public-access trails leading out to cove beaches along Sea Ranch's property—not obtained without litigation, of course—but the overall feeling is one of profound unwelcome. With so much beach to go around, who needs 'em anyway?

Just in case you're wondering, there are nude beaches in Sonoma County, but they're all along the Russian River, whose waters are considerably more inviting than the frigid, treacherous coastal beaches.

Bodega Bay

After bypassing the Point Reyes Peninsula, Highway 1 rejoins the coast at Bodega Bay, Sonoma County's busiest harbor and pleasure port. So many fishing boats use Bodega Bay that several large marinas are kept active, and the main boat-launching ramp is six lanes wide.

The harbor could not have been planned any better than the way Mother Nature drew it up. Bodega Head is a slug-shaped headland that protects the harbor from the west. The sand spit known as Doran Regional Park extends into the harbor's throat, protecting it from the south. A drive to the top of Bodega Head is an absolute must, as the view is a stunner. Don't let a gale-force wind deter you, either.

Bodega Bay Harbor hasn't always been a smooth-sailing operation. The inner bay, near the warehouses and docks, has had a recurring problem with silting. A deep-water dredge performed in 1943 created a channel that could service a large fishing fleet. By the 1950s Bodega Bay was processing 1,000,000 pounds of fish, 900,000 pounds of crab, and 400,000 pounds of albacore a year.

Nowadays Bodega Bay (population 1,000) primarily serves as a port for recreational and smaller-scale commercial fishing, as its fortunes have waned in tandem with dwindling catches in the overfished ocean. Still, anglers do their best to snare what's left. Deep-sea fishing boats are expelled seaward past Doran Beach, and no

SONOMA COAST SAFETY CHECK

If you want to maintain a healthy relationship with the ocean on the rugged Sonoma Coast, you have to treat it with respect. We came upon the following guidelines for doing just that. They seem so sensible and appropriate to all of Northern California that we've included them here, in abbreviated and paraphrased form, for your safety:

* The ocean is not a large lake or a bubbling creek. It's rough, powerful, and frigid.

* When you're down below a bluff, you can't be seen or heard from above. Children, in particular, should not be allowed to climb down alone.

* Always consult tide tables if you plan to hike along the beach. Advancing tides can pin you to the base of a bluff with nowhere to escape.

* Bluff and headland trails are cut into erodable, soft rock. Before descending any trail to the beach, study the terrain and waves from above. Pay heed to the size and force of incoming waves.

* Never turn your back on the ocean.

* If you are hit by a large sneaker wave, don't try to save anything other than yourself. Drop your camera, backpack, paintbrush, or cell phone and focus on survival.

* Don't go beachcombing or exploring cliff tops alone.

* Beware of poison oak, which thrives all over the North Coast.

resident salmon or rock cod is safe, especially in the waters off Tomales Point.

Bodega takes its name from a Spanish word meaning "resting place." Our idea of rest in Bodega Bay was to let others do the fishing while we ate seafood and hiked the beaches. Incidentally, Bodega Bay was the setting for Alfred Hitchcock's terrifying science-fiction thriller *The Birds*. In fact, you can have a look at the schoolhouse immortalized in the movie.

All visits to Bodega Bay, however, should begin at the wharf, a beehive of activity where you can charter a fishing boat or simply order a seafood dinner at one of the restaurants that continually receive fresh catches.

For more information, contact the Bodega Bay Chamber of Commerce, 850 Highway 1, Bodega Bay, CA 94923, 707/875-3866 or 800/905-9050, www.bodegabay.com.

BEACHES

Doran Regional Park can be reached by turning off Highway 1 onto Doran Park Road. Your landmark will be the Bodega Bay Lodge and Spa. Continue past the hotel, and you'll find a couple of areas to park and play along the bay. The best of these is the Cypress area. It's a picturesque setting, with plenty of small craft at anchor, bobbing on the bright blue water. There are places to picnic, clean fish, and launch boats. Doran Park also features a 112-site bayside campground (no RV hookups).

Westside Regional Park, another county-run facility, is on the inner, harbor-facing side of **Bodega Head.** It has much the same menu of amenities: boat launch, picnic tables, 38 campsites (no RV hookups), sand beach. Sonoma County also obliges hikers with coastal-access trails at **Pinnacle Gulch** (below Bodega Bay, off Highway 1; follow signs to the trailhead) and **Bird Walk Access Point** (on the east side of the bay, along Highway 1).

Trails crisscross Bodega Head. The longest leads through thick dunes to South Salmon

Creek Beach (described later in this chapter). A shorter trail leads east across Bodega Head to **Campbell Cove,** a harbor beach with a boardwalk leading to an observation deck overlooking a small lagoon known as "Hole in the Head." Another trail leads to the top of the headland, providing stunning views of the ocean, bay, harbor, and migrating whales. Aquatic mammals pass south in December and January and return north in March and April. Trails lead down the bluffs to small, scenic coves. Winter waves and weather can be ferocious, so come prepared for a walk on the wild and windy side. Dress warmly!

The University of California operates its **Marine Biological Research Lab** on Bodega Head. It is open to the public for tours on Fridays only 2–4 P.M.; call 707/875-2211 for information.

■ PINNACLE GULCH

Location: 20600 Mockingbird, off Highway 1 in Bodega Bay; trail leads to beach
Parking/Fees: $5 entrance fee per vehicle
Hours: sunrise-sunset
Facilities: restrooms
Contact: Sonoma County Regional Parks, 707/565-2041

■ DORAN REGIONAL PARK

Location: end of Doran Beach Road, off Highway 1 in Bodega Bay
Parking/Fees: $6 entrance fee per vehicle; camping fee $20 per night, plus $8 reservation fee; 707/565-2267 for camping reservations
Hours: sunrise-sunset
Facilities: concession, restrooms, showers, and picnic tables
Contact: Doran Beach Regional Park, 707/875-3540

■ BIRD WALK ACCESS POINT

Location: 355 Highway 1 in Bodega Bay
Parking/Fees: $5 entrance fee per vehicle
Hours: sunrise-sunset
Facilities: none
Contact: Sonoma County Regional Parks, 707/565-2041

■ CAMPBELL COVE

Location: off East Shore Road along the western mouth of Bodega Bay Harbor
Parking/Fees: free parking lot
Hours: 8 A.M.-one hour after sunset
Facilities: restrooms and picnic tables
Contact: Sonoma Coast State Beaches, 707/875-3483

■ WESTSIDE REGIONAL PARK

Location: from Highway 1 in Bodega Bay, turn west onto Bay Flat Road and follow to Westside Road; park entrance is at 2400 Westside Road, next to Bodega Bay Harbor
Parking/Fees: $6 entrance fee per vehicle; camping fee $20 per night; 707/565-2267 for camping reservations
Hours: sunrise-sunset
Facilities: restrooms and picnic tables
Contact: Westside Regional Parks, 707/875-3540

■ BODEGA HEAD

Location: from Highway 1 in Bodega Bay, turn west onto Bay Flat Road and follow to end of Westside Road
Parking/Fees: free parking lot
Hours: 8 A.M.-one hour after sunset

SONOMA COAST

Facilities: restrooms
Contact: Sonoma Coast State Beaches, 707/875-3483

RECREATION AND ATTRACTIONS

- **Bike/Skate Rentals:** Bodega Bay Surf Shack, 1400 Highway 1, Bodega Bay, 707/875-3944

- **Dive Shop:** Bodega Bay Pro Dive, 1275 Highway 1, Bodega Bay, 707/875-3054

- **Ecotourism:** Bodega Head, Westside Road, Bodega Bay, 707/865-3291

- **Marina:** Mason's Marina, 1820 West Shore Road, Bodega Bay, 707/875-3811

- **Pier:** Lucas Wharf, 595 Highway 1, Bodega Bay, 707/875-3522

- **Rainy Day Attraction:** Fort Ross State Historic Park, 19005 Highway 1, Fort Ross, 707/847-3286

- **Shopping/Browsing:** Ocean View Center, 2001 Highway 1, Bodega Bay

- **Sportfishing:** Bodega Bay Sportfishing Center, 1500 Bay Flat Road, Bodega Bay, 707/875-3344

- **Surf Report:** 707/875-3944

- **Surf Shop:** Bodega Bay Surf Shack, 1400 Highway 1, Bodega Bay, 707/875-3944

- **Vacation Rentals:** Bodega Bay and Beyond, 913 Highway 1, Bodega Bay, 800/888-3565

ACCOMMODATIONS

Bodega Bay Lodge and Spa (103 Highway 1, 707/875-3525, $$$) is the largest resort-style lodge on the Sonoma coast. It has 84 rooms, each with its own fireplace. The expansive grounds also offer fishing and access to Doran Beach, a fitness center with full-service spa, a heated swimming pool, and an excellent on-site gourmet restaurant, the Duck Club.

Once you've checked in, there's no real reason to leave. A complimentary wine hour is held in the rustic lobby each day 5–6 P.M. There's a guest library, as well. One of the

more literary inns we've ever stayed at, Bodega Bay Lodge stocks its rooms with books (good ones, too), as well as CD and DVD players. It's equipped as an ideal weekend escape from the harried Bay Area. Vacationers from all over would be well advised to savor the splendid Sonoma-coast scenery from these tony digs.

Inn at the Tides (800 Highway 1, 707/875-2751, $$$) offers peerless water views and the Bayview Restaurant and Lounge. The earth-toned lodge blends nicely into the landscape, and the views of the harbor and Bodega Head make this a cozy hideaway.

Sonoma Coast Villa (16702 Highway 1, 888/404-2255, $$$$) is another luxury enclave in the Bodega Bay area. The 12-room inn's Mediterranean-flavored terra-cotta architecture, terraced gardens, expansive grounds, and numerous amenities (spa, putting green, swimming pool) make it a peaceful hideaway for those who can afford it. Rooms generally run $245–325 per night. Proprietor Cy Griffin has thoughtfully designed a website outlining the best places and activities in Bodega Bay and west Sonoma County. Log onto www.bodegabayvisitors.com for some insightful tips on wine tasting, golfing, horseback riding, gallery hopping, and beach walking.

COASTAL CUISINE

Along the shores of Bodega Bay sits **Tides Wharf** (835 Highway 1, 707/875-3652, $$$), a complex that includes a fish market, restaurant, bar, and gift shop. The complex has a clean, airy look—particularly the dining room, with its big glass picture windows, hardwood floors, and exposed-beam ceiling.

The emphasis is on fresh seafood served with light sauces. Local catches include Pacific red snapper, ling cod, and petrale sole. We sampled the sole, delicate fillets served either pan-fried or dore style (dipped in egg wash and sautéed in a lemon-butter sauce). The sweet, fork-tender calamari steak is prepared parmesan style (with cheese and tomato sauce), but they'll also do it dore style, at your request.

Crab cioppino is a house-favorite stew that consists of a goodly quantity of shellfish (shrimp, scallops, mussels, and a whole Dungeness crab) in a spicy tomato-based sauce that is sopped up with hunks of toasted Italian bread. The appetizer menu includes salmon and albacore, both smoked in-house, and popcorn shrimp: Washington State rock shrimp rolled in herbed bread crumbs, pan-fried, and served with a dipping sauce of butter, wine, garlic, and cayenne.

The wine list is well chosen and reasonably priced, especially the house-label wines, which are made by Adler-Fells. The bar also serves terrific local microbrews, including Russian River Abbey Ale, a ruddy ale that goes down smoothly, and a super-dark oatmeal stout. An extensive dessert listing includes Charleston chocolate truffle, a dense wedge of divine decadence, and New Orleans–style bread pudding topped with praline sauce.

The **Duck Club** (103 Coast Highway, 707/875-3525, $$$) bills its fare as California French cuisine, which means that it freely draws upon two culinary worlds. The large windows of the restaurant open onto windswept dune fields and tidal flats where deer can often be seen wandering. Roast crispy duck with ginger sauce and candied orange is the signature dish, and the chef and sous chef are renowned for innovative combinations of sweet and spicy sauces. For appetizers, you can't miss with Jerusalem artichoke fritters with roast garlic lemon aioli and a cup of Bodega Bay fog chowder. We feasted on ahi tuna with soy, sake, and ginger, and achiote-marinated mahimahi. The fabulous Duck Club cuisine proved the perfect sweet-and-spicy tonic we needed after a long day's drive on the winding roads of the Northern California coast.

A far less fancy, but equally tasty, dining experience can be had at the **Sandpiper Dockside Café** (1410 Bay Flat Road, 707/875-2278, $), which features local seafood and vegetarian dishes.

Bodega Dunes and Salmon Creek Beach

Bodega Dunes is one of the last intact dune fields in California. The sandy wonders have been preserved in a park that includes a 98-site campground where campers can pitch tents or park RVs beneath a canopy of pines and firs. Enormous dunes, covered with a profusion of swaying grasses, protect the campground from offshore winds.

BEACHES

A zigzagging wooden walkway leads over the **Bodega Dunes** to **South Salmon Creek Beach,** which runs for roughly three miles, from the mouth of Salmon Creek to Mussel Point on Bodega Head. Directly connected with the Bodega Dunes, South Salmon Creek Beach is the broader, lengthier strand. Parking is located south of Salmon Creek, while park headquarters is located on the creek's north bank.

North Salmon Creek Beach lies at the bottom end of a lengthy run of Sonoma Coast State Beaches, a grouping of wild and forlorn accesses, each of which has its own turnout and path to a fan-shaped cove beach.

All sorts of compelling reasons are offered against swimming here, including a strong backwash, rip currents, and sleeper waves. The camping is as good as it gets at the beach, but leave the swimsuit at home; the average water temperature along the Sonoma coast beaches is 48–52 degrees. If you don't die of hypothermia or get gnawed to bits by a great white, you might wind up filleted on the rocks by an oversized wave.

So what can you do on a beach like this? Put on a hooded sweatshirt, walk along the shoreline, and "visualize world peace" (to quote a bumper sticker we saw in the parking lot). We did our bit for global harmony by giving a vacationing German family a ride from the beach back to their campsite. They left our car full of sand in return.

A dune restoration project has been completed at South Salmon Creek Beach. After being denuded of their native vegetation, studded with ecosystem-altering invasive plant species, and generally abused for a century, the dunes have mostly been restored. The project involved reshaping the dunes, reintroducing native flora, and laying down boardwalks to minimize damage from humans. A good idea and money well spent; the results speak for themselves.

⑦ BODEGA DUNES

Location: one-half mile north of Bodega Bay, off Highway 1
Parking/Fees: $6 entrance fee per vehicle; camping fee $20 per night, plus $8 reservation fee
Hours: 8 A.M.-one hour after sunset
Facilities: restrooms, showers, and picnic tables
Contact: Bodega Dunes Campground, 707/875-3483

⑧ SOUTH SALMON CREEK BEACH

Location: 1.5 miles north of Bodega Bay, along Highway 1, at mouth of Salmon Creek
Parking/Fees: free parking lot
Hours: 8 A.M.-one hour after sunset
Facilities: restrooms
Contact: Sonoma Coast State Beaches, 707/875-3483

⑨ NORTH SALMON CREEK BEACH

Location: two miles north of Bodega Bay off Highway 1, on the north bank of Salmon Creek
Parking/Fees: free parking lot
Hours: 8 A.M.-one hour after sunset
Facilities: restrooms
Contact: Sonoma Coast State Beaches, 707/875-3483

Bodega Dunes

SONOMA COAST

Sonoma Coast State Beaches

You've heard of ghost towns. Well, Sonoma is a ghost county. Travelers who are sick of crowds, development, and predictable vacations will find the Sonoma coast appealing, but the beaches here can be a bit, well, ghostly. These lonely and wild stretches of sand are pleasurable to ponder from a bluff top but can be daunting at close range, especially in the wrong kind of weather.

For more information, contact the Sonoma Coast State Beaches, 707/875-3483, www .parks.ca.gov.

BEACHES

Collectively known as the Sonoma Coast State Beaches, the 16-mile stretch from Bodega Bay to just north of Jenner offers over 5,000 acres of public land, 1,000 acres of which are dunes and the rest coastal bluffs, with more than 20 units overseen by the state park staff. Here's a list of beach accesses, moving from south to north:

- Bodega Bay
- Campbell Cove
- Bodega Dunes Campground
- South Salmon Creek Beach
- North Salmon Creek Beach
- Miwok Beach
- Coleman Beach
- Arched Rock Beach
- Marshall Gulch
- Carmet Beach
- Schoolhouse Beach
- Portuguese Beach
- Gleason Beach
- Duncan's Cove
- Rock Point
- Duncan's Landing
- Pacific View
- Wright's Beach
- Furlong Gulch
- Shell Beach
- Blind Beach
- Goat Rock Beach
- Russian Gulch

That's an average of one beach-access point every two-thirds mile. To get to each beach requires a hike of varying length and an often-harrowing descent to the shoreline. We've taken a gander at several over the years but have by no means trekked out to all of them. Several, such as Rock Point, aren't beaches at all but headlands overlooking the ocean. The Willow Creek Unit isn't even on the ocean, lying upstream of Willow Creek and several miles from the coast. Granted, it's confusing. We're not sure we've gotten it all completely correct, but our accounting of the Sonoma Coast State Beaches is as comprehensive as any official listing. Incidentally, in deference to the endangered Western snowy plover, dogs are not allowed on any of the Sonoma Coast State Beaches south of Coleman Beach or on Goat Rock Beach.

To make this discussion manageable, we'll focus on units that are more heavily used, have facilities, or are distinctive in some way. From the south, the first Sonoma Coast State Beach access is **Bodega Dunes,** one of the two coast campgrounds (described earlier in this chapter) on state land. The second can be found at **Wright's Beach,** six miles north. There are fewer campsites here than at Bodega Dunes, but they're directly on the beach.

Shell Beach is favored by beachcombers, tidepoolers, anglers—and geologists. Yes, this particular beach stands out among the Sonoma Coast pack for its geological revelations. Dr. Terry Wright has described the rocky coast at Shell Beach as a place "where the complex structure and rocks of the Franciscan Complex lie out like a smorgasbord for hungry geologists. It is a classic field area, world-famous for its perfect exposures of an incredible variety of rocks and structures." Moreover, because it lies along a sheltered inlet, "it is a pleasant place to visit even on the most windswept days."

We walked out to Shell Beach for a good,

NAVIGATING THE TREACHEROUS NORTH COAST

Driving the North Coast of California requires a focused mind and a steady pair of hands to see you safely through. North of Bodega Bay, Highway 1 hugs the rugged, rolling contours of the coastal cliffs, sending vehicles soaring skyward, twisting around hairpin turns, and edging precariously toward cliffs with drops of hundreds of feet and no guardrail.

If the topography doesn't unnerve you, then Highway 1's roaming cattle or fully laden lumber trucks might. Indeed, this section of the Coast Highway is even more treacherous and difficult than the legendary Big Sur. That's not to say it doesn't have its rewards, mainly in the form of unobstructed views of wild, pristine coastline unrivaled anywhere in the world.

Unless God is your copilot, you might want to ponder the following driving tips. We picked them up from local sources and through personal experience on our many coastal forays.

- As Highway 1, a two-lane road, is the only north-south route on the coast, it can bear a fair amount of traffic. Be patient and don't even think about passing anyone. There's a double-yellow line on most of Highway 1 for good reason, and straightaways are scarce. If someone is tailgating you, pull into a roadside turnout or overlook and let them by.

- State law prohibits holding up more than five vehicles in a row. We wonder how many tickets are actually given out for this infraction. If you've got a convoy trailing you, do pull over to the side to let them by.

- Stay alert at night and in the frequent fog. Keep an eye out for wildlife, especially deer and cattle.

- Turn on your headlights in the fog, using normal (not high) beams. This helps you see better and allows oncoming traffic to better see you.

- Watch out for bicyclists. This requires extra caution because there's no real shoulder or margin for error. One small mistake could mean somebody's life. In 1995 a friend of ours died while cycling on Highway 1 in Northern California. He was hit from behind by a car whose driver never saw him.

close look. It's a straight shot off Highway 1 to the parking lot above Shell Beach. From here you can descend the steep, partially paved path to the beach or wander across the bluff tops to Goat Rock Beach via Kortum Trail, a 2.6-mile hike. There are many cormorants in the area; apparently, these dark, long-necked birds like this spot. Human visitors should exercise great caution, though. One sign reads: "The surf at this beach has caused the death of many people who were simply walking the shoreline." Those pesky sneaker waves. There's more: "The cliffs along this coast have caused many deaths." It's

a pretty spot. Just keep an eye on the ocean, the tides, and your footing.

Portuguese Beach is good for rockfishing and surf casting. **Duncan's Landing** is the place to go if you fancy drowning. Otherwise known as Death Rock, it's the single most dangerous spot on California's deadliest stretch of coastline: the 16 miles between Bodega Head and Russian Gulch. **Goat Rock Beach** lies just south of the Russian River mouth. You can walk down to this hard, black-sand beach from Goat Rock Road. Goats used to graze on the massive offshore rock; now Goat Rock is inhabited by harbor seals and seabirds and is off-limits to humans. The best time to visit is April–August, when waves are less menacing and seals are mating.

The other Sonoma Coast State Beaches— **Schoolhouse, Gleason, Miwok, Arched Rock, Carmet, Coleman,** and **Blind Beach**—are more for surf casters and solitary souls. Sure, they're marvelous to look at. But after slipping and sliding down long, steep paths to get at several of them, we're more inclined to pull the car over and enjoy the view from a safe distance.

10 MIWOK BEACH

Location: 2.5 miles north of Bodega Bay, off Highway 1; trail leads to beach
Parking/Fees: free parking lot
Hours: 8 A.M.-one hour after sunset
Facilities: none
Contact: Sonoma Coast State Beaches, 707/875-3483

11 COLEMAN BEACH

Location: three miles north of Bodega Bay, off Highway 1; trail leads to beach
Parking/Fees: free parking lot
Hours: 8 A.M.-one hour after sunset
Facilities: none
Contact: Sonoma Coast State Beaches, 707/875-3483

12 ARCHED ROCK BEACH

Location: 3.3 miles north of Bodega Bay, off Highway 1; trail leads to beach
Parking/Fees: free parking lot
Hours: 8 A.M.-one hour after sunset
Facilities: none

Contact: Sonoma Coast State Beaches, 707/875-3483

13 CARMET BEACH

Location: 3.8 miles north of Bodega Bay, off Highway 1; trail leads to beach
Parking/Fees: free parking lot
Hours: 8 A.M.-one hour after sunset
Facilities: none
Contact: Sonoma Coast State Beaches, 707/875-3483

14 SCHOOLHOUSE BEACH

Location: four miles north of Bodega Bay, off Highway 1; trail leads to beach
Parking/Fees: free parking lot
Hours: 8 A.M.-one hour after sunset
Facilities: none
Contact: Sonoma Coast State Beaches, 707/875-3483

15 PORTUGUESE BEACH

Location: 4.3 miles north of Bodega Bay, off Highway 1; trail leads to beach
Parking/Fees: free parking lot
Hours: 8 A.M.-one hour after sunset
Facilities: restrooms
Contact: Sonoma Coast State Beaches, 707/875-3483

16 GLEASON BEACH

Location: 4.8 miles north of Bodega Bay, off Highway 1; trail leads to beach
Parking/Fees: free parking lot
Hours: 8 A.M.-one hour after sunset

Facilities: none
Contact: Sonoma Coast State Beaches,
707/875-3483

17 DUNCAN'S LANDING

Location: five miles north of Bodega Bay, off
Highway 1; trail leads to beach
Parking/Fees: free parking lot
Hours: 8 A.M.-one hour after sunset
Facilities: none
Contact: Sonoma Coast State Beaches,
707/875-3483

18 WRIGHT'S BEACH

Location: six miles north of Bodega Bay off
Highway 1
Parking/Fees: $4 entrance fee per vehicle;
camping fees $13-16 per night
Hours: 8 A.M.-one hour after sunset
Facilities: restrooms and picnic tables
Contact: Sonoma Coast State Beaches,
707/875-3483

19 SHELL BEACH

Location: seven miles north of Bodega Bay off
Highway 1
Parking/Fees: free parking lot
Hours: 8 A.M.-one hour after sunset
Facilities: restrooms
Contact: Sonoma Coast State Beaches,
707/875-3483

20 BLIND BEACH

Location: along Goat Rock Road, off Highway 1
near mouth of Russian River, south of Jenner

Parking/Fees: free parking lot
Hours: 8 A.M.-one hour after sunset
Facilities: restrooms
Contact: Sonoma Coast State Beaches,
707/875-3483

21 GOAT ROCK BEACH

Location: end of Goat Rock Road off Highway
1 near the mouth of Russian River, south of
Jenner
Parking/Fees: free parking lot
Hours: 8 A.M.-one hour after sunset
Facilities: restrooms and picnic tables
Contact: Sonoma Coast State Beaches,
707/875-3483

Jenner

Jenner's physical setting on the mouth of the Russian River is nothing short of regal, with the town bravely clinging to the cliffs along the river and the curves of Highway 1. From vista points south of town, you can watch this undammed California river roll into the Pacific. Pull over and enjoy an area that is rich in history and scenic beauty. Russian fur trappers originally named the river Slavyanka, meaning "Russian girl," but the name was too much of a mouthful for English-speaking tongues, and it was renamed Russian River.

Later settlers used this stretch of Highway 1, carved into the jagged cliff tops in 1875, as a logging trail. Redwoods were floated down the Russian River toward the sea, where they were loaded onto boats and wagons. If you're interested in learning more, the **Jenner Visitor Center** (10439 Highway 1, 707/865-9433) delves into the Sonoma Coast's history in greater detail. It's open only on weekends.

When leaving town at the north end, drivers ascend Jenner Grade, one of the most dramatic stretches of highway on the California coast. It rivals even Big Sur for vertigo-inducing thrills and chills as one ascends its steeply graded switchbacks. Do we need to add "Fasten your safety belt"? If you'd like to gather your wits before tackling this driving challenge, Jenner and environs offer several fine restaurants and inns burrowed off the highway.

For more information, contact the Sonoma Coast Visitor Information Center, 850 U.S. Highway 1, Bodega Bay, CA 95923, 707/875-3866 or 800/253-8800, www.sonoma.com.

BEACHES

The state owns much of the coastal land north of the Russian River mouth. Several beaches between Jenner and **Russian Gulch,** known as the **North Jenner Beaches,** are reachable by steep coast-access trails down eroding bluffs. **Vista Point** is a relatively new overlook, picnic spot, and beach-access point four miles north of Jenner, where Meyers Grade Road meets Highway 1.

22 NORTH JENNER BEACHES

Location: access trails lead to beaches along two-mile stretch of Highway 1 between Jenner and Russian Gulch
Parking/Fees: free roadside turnouts
Hours: 8 A.M.–one hour after sunset
Facilities: none
Contact: Sonoma Coast State Beaches, 707/875-3483

23 RUSSIAN GULCH

Location: 2.5 miles north of Jenner on Highway 1; trail leads to beach
Parking/Fees: free parking lot
Hours: 8 A.M.–one hour after sunset
Facilities: restrooms
Contact: Sonoma Coast State Beaches, 707/875-3483

24 VISTA POINT

Location: Meyers Grade Road at Highway 1 four miles north of Jenner
Parking/Fees: free parking lot
Hours: 8 A.M.–one hour after sunset
Facilities: restrooms and picnic tables
Contact: Sonoma Coast State Beaches, 707/875-3483

ACCOMMODATIONS

Sea Coast Hide-A-Ways (21350 Highway 1, 707/847-3278, $) is the biggest vacation-home rental agency in town. All the rentals are clean and comfortably furnished, with full kitchens.

Many overnight travelers opt for **River's End** (Highway 1, 707/869-3252, $$), a full-service operation that boasts an excellent restaurant, boat-rental agency, general store, bar, campground, and eight-room lodge. The remodeled cabins at River's End hug the cliffs and offer stupendous ocean views.

Another restaurant/lodge operation is **Murphy's Jenner Inn** (10400 Highway 1, 707/865-2377, $$). You can choose between bed-and-breakfast-style rooms and suites at River House (on the Russian River) or Longfellow's Landing (by a creek). In addition, Jenner Inn rents out a cabin (sleeps eight) and handles private home rentals.

COASTAL CUISINE

River's End (11048 Highway 1, 707/865-2484, $$$) is one of the premier restaurants on the Northern California coast. The fare tends toward hearty game dishes—rabbit, duck, quail, venison—and seafood, all prepared with Germanic flair, assembled with local ingredients, and pungently flavorful. We can heartily recommend the coconut-covered prawns and plump Pacific oysters. A splendid meal is guaranteed, but make reservations well in advance. The view of the ocean from the restaurant and the deck that encircles it is a kind of visual dessert. River's End restaurant

SONOMA COAST

is open Thursday–Monday; the inn is open seven days a week.

Another restaurant of note is **Jenner Inn** (10400 Highway 1, 707/865-2377, $$$), which offers seafood, vegetarian, and beef dishes; a full bar graced by a stone fireplace; and live music on weekends.

Fort Ross

The most historic site in the area is Fort Ross, a 1,160-acre Russian stronghold 11 miles north of Jenner. Not to worry, Joint Chiefs: Fort Ross was abandoned by the Russians in 1841. The original Russian settlers came to the California coast searching for new sources of fur (mainly sea otters) and food for the enrichment of the Tsarist Russian empire. They landed in Bodega Bay in 1809 and held all the coastal land from there to this site, building the fort in 1812 out of local redwood.

Eighty Native American Aleuts and 25 Russian fur trappers kept the Spanish at bay while the job was completed. Fort Rossiya was also a base for growing wheat to supply Russian colonies in Alaska. The Russians, unlike the Spanish, did not try to suppress Native American culture or subjugate the natives. Instead, they intermarried with the local tribe (the Kashaya Pomo) and traded extensively with them. Even today, the largest collection of Pomo artifacts is stored in a museum in St. Petersburg, Russia.

At **Fort Ross State Historic Park** (19005 Highway 1, Jenner, 707/847-3286), restored and reconstructed buildings include barracks, a stockade, a Russian Orthodox chapel, blockhouses, and the commandant's residence. An on-site museum is open 10 A.M.–4:30 P.M. daily. A "Living History Day" is held the last Saturday in July, re-creating a typical day at the fort in 1836. Bring your own Stoli?

BEACHES

Just beyond Fort Ross's front gate is **Fort Ross Cove,** a small beach frequented by

shell collectors. A nearby garden filled with exotic plants is a popular picnicking spot. An underwater park for divers, designated **Fort Ross Reef,** sits offshore. Three miles south is Fort Ross Reef Campground. Trails from the campground lead to coves and beaches in the area.

25 FORT ROSS REEF

Location: eight miles north of Jenner, off Highway 1
Parking/Fees: $6 entrance fee per vehicle; camping fee $20 per night, includes admission to Fort Ross State Historic Park and Salt Point State Park
Hours: 8 A.M.-one hour after sunset
Facilities: restrooms and picnic tables
Contact: Fort Ross State Historic Park, 707/847-3286

26 FORT ROSS COVE

Location: 11 miles north of Jenner, off Highway 1, at Fort Ross State Historic Park
Parking/Fees: $6 entrance fee per vehicle
Hours: 10 A.M.-4:30 P.M. (buildings), sunrise-sunset (grounds)
Facilities: restrooms, picnic tables, and visitors center
Contact: Fort Ross State Historic Park, 707/847-3286

ACCOMMODATIONS

If you want to stay overnight but not inside a tent, the **Fort Ross Lodge** (20705 Highway 1, Jenner, CA 95450, 707/847-3333, $$) offers accommodations with ocean views, fireplaces, patios, hot tubs, complimentary wine, and coastal access.

Timber Cove

Timber Cove is the site of a couple of unrelated and dissimilar operations. One is a restaurant with vacation home rentals, the **Timber Cove Inn** (21780 Highway 1, 707/847-3231, $$$$), at which you'll pay $300–750 for a two-night stay (that's the minimum), though they offer reduced rates in the spring. Timber Cove Inn has 49 rooms in all, spread out on a 26-acre headland. Units range from small cabins to three-bedroom homes; some are down by the ocean, others up in the redwoods. The on-site restaurant has a French Continental menu that's on the expensive side. At the inn you may be shocked to discover a 72-foot obelisk by the late sculptor Benjamin Bufano, entitled *The Expanding Universe.* Ponder that while you're watching whales go by; a major moment of clarity can't be far behind.

The other place to lay over is the **Timber Cove Campground** (21350 Highway 1, 707/847-3278), which has 40 sites for tents and RVs. The campground provides all that's needed for fishing and boating: rentals, launches, licenses, tackle shop.

BEACHES

Timber Cove is another wondrous cove beach poised between striking headlands. Fishing, boating, and whale-watching are the predominant activities. All of the usual warnings about Sonoma Coast beaches apply: Beware of sneaker waves and riptides and don't even think about swimming.

27 TIMBER COVE

Location: 12 miles north of Jenner, off Highway 1
Parking/Fees: $6 entrance fee per person; camping fees $19-21 per night
Hours: 8 A.M.-sunset

SONOMA COAST

WE BRAKE FOR COWS

Highway 1 through Sonoma County is cow country. The critters wander all over the place like acid-dosed Woodstock hippies trying to find the freeway shoulder they parked their van on. During one passage through coastal Sonoma, we were coming around a mountain when we suddenly came screeching to a halt. A big black cow was standing in our lane, staring us down like a Bergmanesque apparition of death. Pea-soup fog was draped around the beast's neck like a shawl, rendering it nearly invisible. We skidded to a stop inches from its steaming nostrils. The cow slowly, carefully appraised the situation, then lumbered aside to let us pass. *Moove,* it seemed to be saying.

We pulled around the bovine obstruction and continued on our journey. Had an RV come rumbling around the bend at that moment, Sonoma would have been one head of cattle poorer and the world one beach book lighter.

On a recent visit, we counted no fewer than nine head of cattle meandering along Highway 1. Three of them clung to an inside curve, barely off the shoulder, pressed against the cliffs. Others nonchalantly clomped across the road. It was a vertical plunge of hundreds of feet to the ocean, and a sheer wall of rock rose high above the road. How did the cows get there? How would they get back to wherever they came from? What is reality?

Clearly the cows pose a danger to unwary motorists, particularly the guy trying to prove how well his new sports car can handle the curves or distracted by a cell-phone conversation with his broker. We had to wonder how many cars have tumbled over the cliffs in Sonoma County over the years, with Elsie's face their last conscious memory.

SONOMA COAST

Facilities: concession, restrooms, showers, and picnic tables
Contact: Timber Cove Campground, 707/847-3278

Stillwater Cove Regional Park

Four miles north of Fort Ross is lovely Stillwater Cove Regional Park, a county-run facility that is usually passed by tourists hell-bent on making Mendocino before nightfall. It's more popular with locals, who are given discounts on the day-use and camping fees. The 17-site campground lies right off Highway 1.

BEACHES

From the campground, a trail follows Stockoff Creek through a small forest and canyon, and down to lovely **Stillwater Cove,** which is frequented by abalone divers.

28 STILLWATER COVE REGIONAL PARK

Location: 16 miles north of Jenner, at 22455 Highway 1
Parking/Fees: $5 entrance fee per vehicle; camping fee $20 per night, plus $8 reservation fee; 707/565-2267 for camping reservations
Hours: sunrise-sunset
Facilities: restrooms, showers, and picnic tables
Contact: Stillwater Cove Regional Park, 707/847-3245.

ACCOMMODATIONS

Near the park is **Stillwater Cove Ranch** (22555 Highway 1, 707/847-3227, $). Coastal accommodations in Sonoma County are few and far between, and rarely are they priced this reasonably. Some units go for $55–65 midweek, a little more on weekends.

"We're for the kind of travelers who can't

afford to stay on this otherwise premium-priced stretch of the coast," said the perky proprietress. Actually, the place is not so much a ranch as an assortment of rustic units and a dairy-barn bunkhouse. The ocean is right across the highway, making this a good spot for fishing, whale-watching, hiking, and enjoying the uncommonly good restaurants between Jenner and Gualala. Stillwater Cove Ranch doesn't serve meals, and all but a handful of rooms lack cooking facilities.

Ocean Cove

Ocean Cove lies between Stillwater Cove Regional Park and Salt Point State Park. It's a private campground built around a cove beach—an inexpensive way for those who love the outdoors to experience the Sonoma Coast. A historic store along Highway 1 is part of the Ocean Cove operation. The cove is open for camping and day use April–November.

For more information, contact Ocean Cove, 23125 Highway 1, 707/847-3422, www.ocean cove.org.

BEACHES

Ocean Cove is a privately owned beach and bluff at which guests can camp, fish, and dive for abalone.

29 OCEAN COVE

Location: 17 miles north of Jenner, off Highway 1
Parking/Fees: $7 entrance fee per vehicle; camping fee $19 per night
Hours: 9 A.M.-6 P.M. weekdays, 8 A.M.-8 P.M. weekends
Facilities: concession, restrooms, showers, and picnic tables
Contact: Ocean Cove Store and Campground, 707/847-3422

Salt Point State Park

This is another heaven-sent state park, the perfect way station on the North Coast for those who want a bit of everything. Among its 5,970 acres, Salt Point State Park has seven miles of rugged shoreline with dozens of hard-sand cove beaches, as well as hiking trails that head inland and reach elevations of 1,000 feet in the foothills. There are both coastal (Gerstle Cove) and upland (Woodside) campgrounds. The former is situated by the **Gerstle Cove Underwater Reserve,** a diving and tidepooling spot with 30 improved sites. The latter is a bit farther removed, offering 109 sites, both improved and primitive.

BEACHES

A rewarding hike from a roadside parking lot leads out to **Stump Beach.** It's a two-miler that meanders along the bluff tops to a lovely cove beach that derives its name from the driftwood that washes up here, much of it the residue of a dying logging industry. Nearby is **Gerstle Cove,** an ecological preserve that was one of California's first underwater parks. It's a prime whale-watching site December–April. Two more beaches—**Fisk Mill Cove** and **North Horseshoe Cove**—are off Highway 1, one and two miles north (respectively) of Stump Beach. Fisk Mill has facilities and an entry fee. North Horseshoe Cove costs nothing, and nothing is provided—except, of course, an exceptionally scenic beach.

From April to June the 300-acre **Kruse Rhododendron State Reserve,** a mile inland from Salt Point State Park, is ablaze with multicolored rhododendrons. These showy shrubs were planted to replace a forest of firs that was destroyed by fire. The reserve is also noteworthy for its extensive system of hiking trails covered with foliage ranging from rhododendrons to redwoods.

30 GERSTLE COVE

Location: 18 miles north of Jenner, off Highway 1
Parking/Fees: $4 entrance fee per vehicle; camping fees $13-16 (tents and RVs), $50 (group camp) per night
Hours: 8 A.M.-sunset
Facilities: restrooms, picnic tables, and visitors center
Contact: Salt Point State Park, 707/847-3221

31 STUMP BEACH

Location: 19 miles north of Jenner, off Highway 1
Parking/Fees: free parking lot
Hours: 8 A.M.-sunset
Facilities: restrooms and picnic tables
Contact: Salt Point State Park, 707/847-3221

32 FISK MILL COVE

Location: 20 miles north of Jenner, off Highway 1
Parking/Fees: $6 entrance fee per vehicle
Hours: 8 A.M.-sunset
Facilities: restrooms and picnic tables
Contact: Salt Point State Park, 707/847-3221

33 NORTH HORSESHOE COVE

Location: 21 miles north of Jenner, off Highway 1
Parking/Fees: free parking lot
Hours: 8 A.M.-sunset
Facilities: none
Contact: Salt Point State Park, 707/847-3221

SONOMA COAST

ACCOMMODATIONS

A mile south of Salt Point State Park is **Salt Point Lodge** (23255 Highway 1, Jenner, CA 95450, 707/847-3234 or 800/956-3437, $), a contemporary motel with reasonable rates, broad grassy lawn, playground equipment, sundeck, sauna, and hot tub. The management also runs a small restaurant serving three meals a day.

Stewarts Point

Two roadside curiosities converge at the historic site of Stewarts Point, overlooking Fisherman's Bay. One is **Stewarts Point Store** (32000 Highway 1 South, Sea Ranch, 707/785-2406), a nifty general emporium on Highway 1 that's truly a relic from a bygone era.

From the mid-nineteenth to the early twentieth century, so-called doghole schooners

THE LOWDOWN ON ABALONE

Swathed in a shell of mother-of-pearl, endowed with a delectable taste, the abalone is one of the most prized denizens of the deep along the California shoreline. It belongs to the mollusk clan, a large phylum that includes more than 100,000 species of invertebrates, including various types of squid, clams, oysters, mussels, snails, and octopuses. The abalone is one of the largest mollusks, ranging 4-10 inches in width. Any abalone 10 inches or larger is lovingly dubbed "a hubcap" by divers, and the world's record, taken in 1993 off the Humboldt coast, was 12.3 inches across, 9.8 inches wide, and weighed 11.6 pounds.

Eight of the world's 100 abalone species dwell along California's coast. Maybe "dwindle" would be a better word, since they've been hunted, poached, and harvested to near extinction. The most in demand is the state's indigenous red abalone (Haliotis rufenscens). Prime red abalone specimens are worth $50-80 apiece, and the meat retails for more than $100 per pound.

Abalone live on rocks in shallow water along rugged shorelines, clinging tenaciously to their perches and feeding on algae. The couch potatoes of the underwater set, abalone are so stationary that they're often covered with other organisms. To wrest them from their resting places one needs a pry bar – a miniature crowbar available in bait-and-tackle and dive shops. Humans have long valued the abalone for its tasty meat and beautiful oval shell, but we're not the only ones who dig these crazy mollusks. Sea otters, who eat one-third their body weight daily, also relish abalone. Once they've pried the shell loose, they smash it open on the rocks and scoop out the meat.

Thankfully, commercial abalone harvesting has been banned north of San Francisco. Only recreational harvesting is allowed along the North Coast. Still, more than 2 million pounds of red abalone is taken for sport each year. Bagging an abalone or two is a rite of vacation passage for some waders and divers.

Abalone have been depleted to near extinction south of San Francisco. Not surprisingly, abalone along the North Coast (particularly in Sonoma County) are subject to poaching and illegal harvesting. A 16-man abalone poaching ring, working in Sonoma and Mendocino counties, was broken up in 1999, resulting in prison sentences and tighter surveillance of this dwindling treasure. So tempting is the quest for abalone that in December 2000 a member of the state's abalone preservation advisory board was arrested for poaching in Sonoma County, having been found with 129 illegally caught abalone worth $10,000.

turned this rugged shore into a busy port town that serviced the logging trade. The only trustworthy way to haul the timber from the north woods was by sea, with the cargo loaded primarily via cables tied from the bluffs to the anchored ships. Most of the lumber ended up in San Francisco, where the redwood was incorporated into Victorian homes and the Douglas fir was used for schooners. The doghole schooners were so named because they had to be nimble enough to anchor in bays that were just big enough, as the sailors used to say, "for a dog to turn around in."

The store and an abandoned stagecoach-stop hotel are all that remain from these colorful times. As you pass the turnoff to Tin Barn Road, look east for the second curiosity. You'll spy **Odiyan,** a Tibetan Buddhist monastery, as anomalous as the Russian Orthodox chapel at Fort Ross. It's not open to the public.

If, after all this, you still have any desire to bag abalone along the North Coast, here are a few pointers:

- Wear a wetsuit. The water temperature ranges 48–52 degrees most of the year.

- Have a valid fishing license in plain view on your person, preferably in a clear, waterproof pouch.

- It is illegal to use scuba equipment to catch abalone; it has to be done with snorkel and mask or by wading, stooping, and groping by hand along the bottom.

- Use a seven-inch measuring bar to make sure the abalone shell is of legal size. Return anything smaller.

- Use a proper pry bar. Improper tools can break the shell and kill the abalone immediately, which is a total waste.

- Never wade or dive alone.

- Wait for a minus tide (-1/0-foot or better).

- Check rocky kelp beds first. This is where abalone are most often found.

- Take only the legal limit of three per day (because of the unsustainable harvesting, the limit was lowered from four in 2001) and 24 total for a calendar year. They must be at least seven inches in diameter. A $12.60 reporting card is required for taking abalone, and catches must be tagged upon exiting the water. Abalone report cards must be returned within 60 days of the close of the season to the California Department of Fish and Game's Fort Bragg field office and laboratory, 19160 South Harbor Drive, Fort Bragg, CA 95437.

- Abalone may be taken April 1–June 30 and August 1–November 30 and, in waters north of San Francisco, only August 1–November 30. The season is closed during the month of July. State game wardens will bust you if you break the law. Fines start at $500 for the first abalone over the legal limit and are $250 per abalone above that.

- If you see a person or group that you suspect are illegally harvesting abalone, call the state's toll-free, 24-hour tip line for fish and wildlife violations (888/334-2258). Rewards are offered as an incentive.

- For the latest news about abalone along the North Coast, contact the **Sonoma County Abalone Network,** P.O. Box 3801, Santa Rosa, CA 95402, www.abalone network.org.

SONOMA COAST

Sea Ranch

The last ten miles of coastline in Sonoma County belong lock, stock, and barrel to a private development known as Sea Ranch. At one time this land was part of a 17,500-acre Mexican land grant, Rancho de Herman, and a former sheep ranch. Now it's a planned, 5,500-acre community for the second-home wealthy.

Originally, Sea Ranch met stiff resistance from the California Coastal Commission and environmental groups. The developers finally compromised, allowing five coastal-access footpaths across the property. Each trail is about a quarter-mile long and leads to a cove beach, but a posted set of stringent rules governing hikers just about kills whatever fun you might have along the way.

In all fairness, Sea Ranch has won awards for its environmentally sensitive architecture and planning. All of the houses—wood-shingled and built low to the ground—blend in with the pines and fir trees. Still, the lengthy privatized expanse of Sea Ranch and its golf course strike us as an indefensible appropriation of so much of the Sonoma Coast.

For more information, contact the Sea Ranch Lodge, P.O. Box 44, Sea Ranch, CA 95497, 707/785-2371 or 800/732-7262, www.searanchlodge.com.

BEACHES

The cove beaches here include, from south to north: **Black Point, Pebble Beach, Stengel Beach, Shell Beach,** and **Walk-On Beach.** They are all pretty much the same, and the short trails that cross the Sea Ranch property to them are heavily regulated. We walked to the end of three Sea Ranch trails before throwing in the beach towel. There are no facilities, save for portable restrooms at the trailheads.

34 BLACK POINT

Location: Highway 1 at Milepost 50.8; trail leads to beach
Parking/Fees: $5 entrance fee per vehicle
Hours: sunrise-sunset
Facilities: none
Contact: Gualala Point Regional Park, 707/785-2377

35 PEBBLE BEACH

Location: Highway 1 at Milepost 52.3; trail leads to beach
Parking/Fees: $5 entrance fee per vehicle
Hours: sunrise-sunset
Facilities: none
Contact: Gualala Point Regional Park, 707/785-2377

36 STENGEL BEACH

Location: Highway 1 at Milepost 54.0; trail leads to beach
Parking/Fees: $5 entrance fee per vehicle
Hours: sunrise-sunset
Facilities: none
Contact: Gualala Point Regional Park, 707/785-2377

37 SHELL BEACH

Location: Highway 1 at Milepost 55.2; trail leads to beach
Parking/Fees: $5 entrance fee per vehicle
Hours: sunrise-sunset
Facilities: none
Contact: Gualala Point Regional Park, 707/785-2377

38 WALK-ON BEACH

Location: Highway 1 at Milepost 56.5; trail leads to beach
Parking/Fees: $5 entrance fee per vehicle
Hours: sunrise-sunset
Facilities: none
Contact: Gualala Point Regional Park, 707/785-2377

ACCOMMODATIONS

Some of the houses at Sea Ranch can be rented, or you can lie in at the **Sea Ranch Lodge** (60 Sea Walk Drive, 707/785-2371, $$$$), a 20-room retreat whose plentiful windows look out on the ocean. All rooms are ocean-view and range $179–349 per night. There's also a restaurant and tavern with a fireplace and solarium.

Gualala Point Regional Park

The 125-acre Gualala Point Regional Park is in Sonoma County, where it looks across the Gualala River at the town of Gualala in Mendocino County. Gualala Point is fenced off from Sea Ranch, which deeded the land for the park. Every 50 yards or so you are reminded of this fact by signs warning against trespassing on private property.

Still, the views of the river mouth, ocean, and town of Gualala are rewarding. Tuck your $5 entrance fee into the self-pay box and, before setting out on the trail to the shoreline, peruse the visitors center's collection of relics from the days when Gualala was a logging port.

For more information, contact Gualala Point Regional Park, 42401 Coast Highway, 707/785-2377, www.sonoma-county.org/parks.

BEACHES

A trail leads to Gualala Point, which offers spectacular views of the rocky coastline. A campground with 20 sites (no RV hookups) is on the east side of Highway 1, on the sandy banks of the Gualala River.

39 GUALALA POINT REGIONAL PARK

Location: one mile south of Gualala at 42401 Highway 1
Parking/Fees: $5 entrance fee per vehicle; camping fee $20 per night, plus $8 reservation fee; 707/565-2267 for camping reservations
Hours: 6 A.M.-sunset (8 A.M.-sunset in winter)
Facilities: restrooms, showers, picnic tables, and visitors center
Contact: Gualala Point Regional Park, 707/785-2377

SONOMA COAST

MENDOCINO COAST

Mendocino County's 130 miles of coast-line extend from the unpretentious town of Gualala to the southern end of what is justifiably known as the Lost Coast. Between these borders are some of the state's most appealingly romantic retreats, including Mendocino, Albion, Elk, and Little River. Then there's Fort Bragg, the county seat and a hardworking center of commerce that's been putting on a brighter, more visitor-friendly face in recent decades.

Southern Mendocino County continues the splendid isolation found along the Sonoma Coast. The two regions are often lumped together and marketed as "Mendonoma." Low-key and perfectly appealing towns—Gualala, Anchor Bay, Point Arena, and Elk—appear every ten scenic miles or so, each with its own quiet charm. At Albion, north of where Highway 128 funnels into Highway 1, the tone gets more upscale.

Albion, Little River, and Mendocino are bonafide "destinations," to borrow a travel-industry term that signals urbanity in out-of-the-way places: good food and wine, fine lodging, views, shopping, art, attractions, recreation, and culture.

At its northernmost end Mendocino County has no cultural appeal and needs none, because most of it is pristine wilderness. The flip side of Mendocino's romantic allure is the palette of possibilities it affords those who love to play outdoors in glorious country.

The beaches along the Mendocino Coast are as varied and fascinating as the towns. As usual, the state of California has been kind to the coastline, preserving exceptional locales such as Manchester State Park, Van Damme State Park, Mendocino Headlands State Park, Jug Handle State Reserve, MacKerricher State Park, Westport–Union Landing State Beach, and Sinkyone Wilderness State Park.

© PARKE PUTERBAUGH

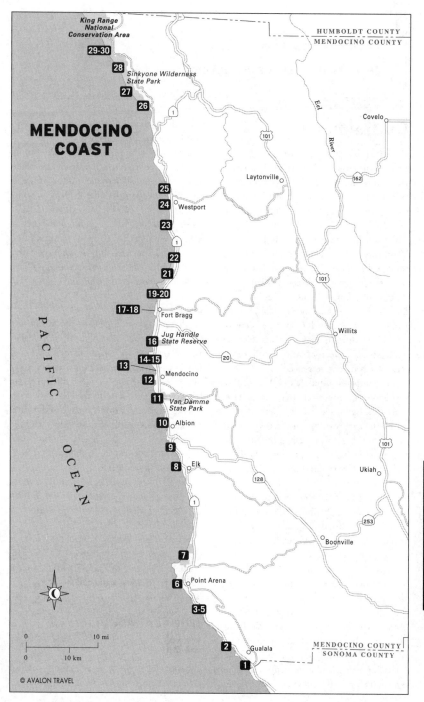

MENDOCINO COAST

BEST BEACHES

◖ **MacKerricher State Park, page 484**

Gualala

Gualala (properly pronounced WAH-la-la) is a town without airs. The stuffy manners observed next door at Sea Ranch are completely absent. The only birdies Gualalans shoot have wings, and the carts they tend to ride are manufactured by Harley-Davidson.

Gualala has the wide-open feel of the Old West, to which it bears a legitimate connection. It was once a thriving mill town, but when the forests were depleted, it fell to other means of making a living, including fishing for salmon and trout. The Gualala River runs parallel to the ocean for two miles, creating an odd beachfront. This explains the town's name, since *gualala* is a Native American word meaning "where waters meet."

The source of Gualala's Old West flavor is the town's centerpiece, the Gualala Hotel. This flaking, rusty, creaking structure sits on Highway 1, exhibiting the rakish charm of a frontier saloon. It has operated as a triple-threat bar, inn, and restaurant since before the Great Earthquake of 1906 hit San Francisco.

Entering Gualala, one feels compelled to tether the car to the hitching post out front, hop the dusty wooden steps, and say, Stetson in hand, "I'd be much obliged if'n you'd point me to the nearest livery, stranger."

Because Gualala is more of a sloppy, let-it-all-hang-out kind of place than its neighbors, the town has witnessed a steady influx of growth, as evidenced by the countless Land for Sale signs dotting the countryside. Though all the new business no doubt boosts the local economy, it can only mean that sweet, antiquarian Gualala will eventually turn trendy, especially when the inevitable occurs—i.e.,

when the Gualala Hotel succumbs to old age. Not in our lifetime, we hope.

One sign of the new wave can be found diagonally across the street from the venerable hotel. It's a slick modern inn that boasts city-slicker amenities like cable TV, while obscuring the roadside view of the Gualala River. (For shame, for shame.) Be that as it may, Gualala has so many more natural charms that one need only do what the native Gualalans do. That is, shrug your shoulders and go on about your business.

BEACHES

Gualala's beaches start below the Mendocino County line, a mile south of town, with Gualala Point Regional Park, which shares a fence with Sea Ranch. In Gualala itself the **Gualala River** forms a broad lagoon, making it difficult to get to the sand spit that fronts the Pacific.

One way around this is to take to the water in a kayak and paddle back and forth between the river and ocean. Darn, left yours at home? Try **Adventure Rents** (45450 Pacific Woods Road, 707/884-4386) for kayaks, canoes, and "hybrid" bikes. If you've a mind to dive for a dinner of abalone, **North Coast Scuba** (38820 Highway 1, 707/884-3534) rents gear and sells abalone licenses.

For more information, contact the Redwood Coast Chamber of Commerce, P.O. Box 338, Gualala, CA 95445-0338, 707/884-1182 or 800/778-5252, www.gualala.org.

1 GUALALA RIVER
🥾 🚻

Location: follow dirt access roads off Highway 1 at north bank of Gualala River, in Gualala

Parking/Fees: free parking lot
Hours: 24 hours
Facilities: none

ACCOMMODATIONS

If you're in a devil-may-care mood, the **Gualala Hotel** (39301 Highway 1, 707/884-1801, $) is a relatively inexpensive blast from the past. As one guest wrote in the ledger, "Nostalgia is good for the soul." When we arrived, no one was at the front desk, which consisted of a weather-beaten table. A hand-lettered sign advised us to "Register for rooms with the bartender." We did just that, negotiating our tariff with a curt but efficient hostess at the bar. The digs aren't grand here—a clean room with shared baths and a ceiling so high you couldn't touch it if you were bouncing on a trampoline—but the comforting cloak of history more than makes up for any lack of luxury. The slice-of-life you'll enjoy at the Gualala Hotel goes for only $50–90 depending on time of week and shared or private bath. Renovations and repainting have brightened up the place.

Farther up Highway 1, the tariff and comforts increase considerably at **The Hotel at St. Orres** (36601 Highway 1, 707/884-3303, $$). This inn is an architectural wonder that offers an incomparably meditative North Coast experience on 42 acres of rolling woods and gardens. St. Orres was designed by owners Eric and Ted Black, and built on the foundation of the old Seaside Hotel. The Blacks capture the flavor of the earliest Russian settlers with rustic and somewhat exotic elegance. The inn was constructed from hundred-year-old timber. The eight European-style rooms have double beds and shared baths, some with views of the forest, some of the ocean. Rates range $95–135 per night. Just beyond the hotel are hand-crafted "meadow" and "creekside" cottages of varying size, price ($140–445 per night, with a fair number of them priced in the $140–155 range), and levels of amenities.

The **Old Milano Hotel** (38300 Highway 1, 707/884-3256, $$) is an atmospheric North Coast lodge (circa 1905) directly above the ocean on a bluff top. The Milano has nine guest quarters—including a real railroad caboose—all well tended and intimate.

COASTAL CUISINE

St. Orres must have been the patron saint of good taste. The **St. Orres Restaurant** (36601 Highway 1, 707/884-3335, $$$$) offers one of the finest and most distinctive dining experiences on the California coast. Set inside a cathedral-like dining room, it is part of a structure suggestive of the area's Russian roots. You won't believe your eyes when you pass the onion domes of St. Orres—Moscow on the Pacific?—on a bluff along the east side of Highway 1.

The food is exceptionally well prepared and competently served. A meal starts with homemade garlic bread and soup of the day. Entrées might include interesting game items like stuffed wild boar hind or venison medallions; steelhead and salmon can pop up on the menu, too. The kitchen utilizes fresh ingredients from on-premises gardens, as well as local-produce farms and ranches. Entrées cost $45 and come with salad and soup; appetizers and deserts cost extra. This place is wildly popular, so make reservations.

The restaurant at the **Gualala Hotel** (39301 Highway 1, 707/884-1801, $) is the class act of that operation. Old and endowed with a weathered dignity, the dining room dishes up healthy North Coast cuisine such as rigatoni with white beans and tomatoes, as well as heartier fare like chicken and game dishes. If we had to prioritize what to do on the premises of the Gualala Hotel, we'd eat, drink, and sleep, in that order.

NIGHTLIFE

If you're headed to Gualala for a romantic getaway, you don't need any advice from us. But if you want to bathe in the sloppy friendliness of a hard-drinking saloon, welcome to the **Gualala Hotel** (Highway 1, 707/884-4840).

The scene that greeted us one Saturday night was, no doubt, typical of what has been

RUBES WITH A VIEW

You can always tell when the wrong sort of city slickers come to the North Coast. They're the ones who talk too loudly and wear purple designer polo shirts and gaudy pullovers advertising the tourist attraction where they spent their last vacation. All the while they so desperately try to manifest the self-importance of young, upwardly mobile sorts who have made their money too quickly in some dubious profession in which nothing useful is produced.

One night we dined at a restaurant with the most stunning view of the Pacific Ocean on the North Coast. We had the additional pleasure of having a table close to a window that looked out on a rocky cove where a river flowed into the ocean. It was sunset, and the sky was bathed in a heavenly orange-pink glow that would render most people quiet and grateful for the view.

Next to us, occupying the best table in the house, sat a couple who were neither quiet nor grateful. The man loudly ran his mouth and the woman nodded and giggled at his nonsense. At first we thought she was his wife, then quickly realized he was cheating on his wife. He spent his dinner hour at this coveted perch boisterously recounting the dirty jokes his colleagues had told him on the golf course that afternoon. Next he repeated offensive jokes he'd heard at work the previous week. The conversation moved on to the usual list of celebrity suspects making news. Then he embarked on tales of last winter's ski expeditions and a boringly detailed deconstruction of his golfing game.

In between each mindless volley of chitchat and coarse laughter, there was conspicuous silence, as they stared vacuously at their wine glasses. Meanwhile, the sun was setting and the unfolding scene was one we'd like to think will greet us in heaven after our lifetime of good works.

At the same time another couple was seated at a table by the window. He was a burly guy wearing a New York Giants T-shirt, designer sunglasses dangling on a cord. His gal pal wore a pink sweatshirt that said BEVERLY HILLS CALIFORNIA. They ordered martinis and began guzzling and belching.

Both couples traveled a great distance from the stressed-out urban center they call home. They spent $250 for a room, another $150 for a meal. They were sitting at the best tables in one of the nicest restaurants on the North Coast. The sun was setting on a perfect day, music played softly, and they missed it all.

going on here for a century. After all, this was a favorite haunt of writer Jack London, who knew a good saloon. Four members of a motorcycle club stood at the bar, laughing uproariously over a novelty-store item called "Spotted Owl Helper." In case you haven't noticed, folks in logging country aren't overly fond of this particular feathered friend. Two more bikers quietly played Pac-Man. A tanned young man with impossibly blond tresses and an earring regaled his aging yuppie companions with tales of his faltering acting career down in Los Angeles. Three enormous chain-smoking women in glowing polyester slacks perched on bar stools,

discussing ostrich racing. An elderly man sat alone at a corner table, nursing a beer and a grudge. The jukebox played "Suzie Q" (the long version) by Creedence Clearwater Revival.

The heads of moose, deer, and bear adorn the walls, as do various large fish. Photographs document the expeditions that led to these game trophies. One picture shows a dead fish being offered a Hamm's Beer. In another, a man hangs upside-down from a fish scale while his buddies grin.

We hung around the bar for a while, then called it a night, since we faced a long drive south the next day. We shouldn't have bothered; the noise and laughter kept us awake till the wee hours. In recent years, live music has been added to the mix. For our money, the bar at the Gualala Hotel just might be the wildest hangout between San Francisco and the Oregon border.

Anchor Bay

Four miles north of Gualala, tiny Anchor Bay (population 200) has more going on than its size would suggest. A small rocky cove, Collins Landing, is on the property of the Serenisea Ocean Cabins; access requires permission.

For more information, contact the Redwood Coast Chamber of Commerce, P.O. Box 338, Gualala, CA 95445-0338, 707/884-1182 or 800/778-5252, www.gualala.org.

BEACHES

Anchor Bay Beach (a.k.a. Fish Rock Beach) can be reached via **Anchor Bay Campground** (35400 Highway 1, 707/884-4222). This is a 0.75-mile-long sand beach and family-run (since 1925) campground complex comprising 66 sites on a tall bluff shaded by redwoods. Camping costs $40 per night; day use is a modest $1 per person plus $2 per vehicle. Interestingly, the area is in a nearly fogless five-mile zone of coastline known as the Banana Belt.

◱ ANCHOR BAY BEACH
◮

Location: at Anchor Bay Campground, off Highway 1, four miles north of Gualala
Parking/Fees: $2 entrance fee per vehicle, plus $1 per person; camping fees $38-42 per night
Hours: 7 A.M.-7 P.M.
Facilities: concession, restrooms, and picnic tables
Contact: Anchor Bay Campground, 707/884-4222

ACCOMMODATIONS

Laying claim to a cove beach and tidepools is **Serenisea Ocean Cabins** (36100 Highway 1, 707/884-3836, $$). These 25 oceanfront vacation cottages and four cabins in Anchor Bay bring you closer to the beach than any lodge in the area, at daily rates that run an average of $200. Anchor Bay is also home to the **Whale Watch Inn** (35100 Highway 1, 707/884-3667, $$$). Admittedly the inn stretches the B&B concept a bit by including two-person whirlpool baths, breakfast in bed, condo units, golf, and tennis. But the setting is magnificent, and trails lead down to a private beach.

Point Arena

When it was incorporated in 1908, Point Arena could rightly be called a city. The busiest port on the North Coast, it was a rollicking place with saloons, cathouses, banks, and shootouts on the main drag. Schooners steamed up from San Francisco daily, and off-duty loggers came out of the woods to make this their Sin City. Some old buildings have survived (Victorian homes, the town theater), but many were destroyed in the 1906 earthquake. The original wharf was obliterated by storms in 1983, and a brand-new Point Arena Pier has since been built on Arena Cove.

Today, Point Arena is a sleepy burg of quaint homes, old-time theater, and Main Street–type businesses whose population hovers at around 500. It has been blessed with more than its share of coastside delights. These include a six-mile stretch of sandy and rocky cove beaches and the historic **Point Arena Lighthouse** (707/882-2777).

The lighthouse is perched at the end of a windswept headland, two miles out on Lighthouse Road. The drive to the lighthouse is one of the most amazing on the North Coast, passing through pastureland that ends abruptly at the lip of the raging Pacific. The lighthouse, a blinding white monolith, is pinned against a blue backdrop. Built in 1870, it employed a

© PARKE PUTERBAUGH

Point Arena

powerful Fresnel lens, which is still installed but no longer operable.

To see this remarkable piece of engineering requires a six-story ascent (145 steps), but it's worth every huff and puff. The view is spectacular, and the guides are friendly and informative. Some of the tourists, on the other hand, can be a pain in the ass, like the pushy woman who nearly shoved us down the circular metallic stairs in her haste to get by. To learn more about coastal ecology and maritime history, don't miss the excellent museum housed in the Fog Signal Building next door. (Admission to Point Arena Lighthouse is $5 for adults and $1 for kids under 12, and the museum is open 10 A.M.–3:30 P.M. daily.)

The lighthouse and museum's setting is timeless enough to have been used as the backdrop for the Mel Gibson movie *Forever Young*, a romantic weeper about a cryogenically preserved World War II bomber pilot who, after being thawed out, seeks his long-lost, lighthouse-dwelling love. Yeah, right.

For more information, contact the Fort Bragg–Mendocino Coast Chamber of Commerce, 332 North Main Street, P.O. Box 1141, Fort Bragg, CA 95437, 707/961-6300 or 800/726-2780, www.mendocinocoast.com.

BEACHES

The most accessible beaches in the area are, from south to north, **Schooner Gulch Beach, Bowling Ball Beach,** and **Ross Beach.** Schooner Gulch embraces 70 acres of headlands, and a short trail leads to tidepools and a driftwood-covered beach. Bowling Ball is a great beachcombing spot, dotted by black, rounded stones (hence the name), but you must park on the highway shoulder to get to it. Park Facing South Only on Highway 1, reads the warning sign. At low tide you can walk between Bowling Ball and Schooner Gulch.

Moat Creek Access, better known as Whiskey Shoals to the surfers who come here, provides access to Ross Beach. You park in a dirt lot and follow a trail down the cliff. Just north of Point Arena Lighthouse, off Miner Hole Road, you can park near the south bank of the Garcia River, a steelhead fisherman's favorite that's also the wintertime home of tundra swans. From here a path leads to a sandy beach at the river's mouth.

Flanking the Point Arena Pier is **Arena Cove Beach.** Some of the best waves on California's North Coast can be found here, but because of the razor-sharp offshore reef this spot's strictly for experts. Diving for abalone and chartered sportfishing expeditions are big here as well.

▣ SCHOONER GULCH BEACH

🏃🏃

Location: Schooner Gulch Road at Highway 1, 35 miles south of Point Arena; follow Schooner Gulch Beach Trail to beach

Parking/Fees: free roadside parking

Hours: 24 hours

Facilities: none

Contact: Mendocino District, California State Parks, 707/937-5804

4 BOWLING BALL BEACH
🏃

Location: from Schooner Gulch Road at Highway 1, 35 miles south of Point Arena, follow Bowling Ball Beach trail to beach
Parking/Fees: free roadside parking
Hours: 24 hours
Facilities: none
Contact: Mendocino District, California State Parks, 707/937-5804

5 ROSS BEACH
🏃

Location: 25 miles south of Point Arena off Highway 1
Parking/Fees: free parking lot
Hours: 24 hours
Facilities: none
Contact: Mendocino District, California State Parks, 707/937-5804

6 ARENA COVE BEACH
🏄

Location: in Point Arena at the end of Port Road, off Highway 1
Parking/Fees: free parking lot
Hours: 24 hours
Facilities: concessions and restrooms
Contact: Arena Cove Pier, 707/882-2583

ACCOMMODATIONS
At the **Point Arena Lighthouse** (45500 Lighthouse Road, 877/725-4448, $$$), three homes on the property are available as vacation rentals, with proceeds going to the nonprofit lighthouse-preservation society. Each has 1,400 square feet of space, three bedrooms, two baths, a fully equipped kitchen, fireplace, and television. You'll need to bring sheets, pillow cases, and towels. For $170 a night in an unbeatable setting, it's a steal.

One step up is the **Coast Guard House** (695 Arena Cove, 707/822-2442, $$$), a restored 1901 Cape Codder that was once a lifesaving station and now houses a snug bed-and-breakfast inn. Less adventurous, but equally comfortable, is the **Wharf Master's Inn** (785 Port Road, 707/882-3171, $$$), overlooking the pier at Arena Cove. Three separate structures provide surprisingly sophisticated amenities (hot tub, private deck, Victorian appointments), given the spartan fisherman's setting below.

COASTAL CUISINE
A pleasant restaurant beside the Point Arena Pier, the **Galley at Arena Cove** (707/882-2189, $$) is made airy and light by its spacious, second-floor setting. The seafood is taken straight from the adjoining fisherman's pier—which is, incidentally, the only boat-launch facility between Bodega Bay and Fort Bragg.

Manchester State Park

Manchester State Park lies at the point where two creeks and the San Andreas Fault make a break for the ocean. Part of the thrill is the drive out to Manchester. On the way out you'll pass an AT&T relay station that is the trans-Pacific link for undersea phone service to Hawaii and the Far East. The old cable was replaced in 1989 by a fiber-optic job, affording the Aloha State the dubious benefits of cable TV.

For more information, contact Manchester State Park, 41500 Kinney Lane, Manchester, CA 95459, 707/882-2463, www.parks.gov.ca.

BEACHES
The 1,400-acre **Manchester State Park** offers five miles of broad, mocha-colored sand backed by dunes matted with thick grass and wildflowers. Manchester provides good steelhead fishing in the winter and some of the best surf casting in Mendocino County all year long. Perhaps the most notable thing about the beach is that it looks like a graveyard for driftwood.

MENDOCINO COAST

The whitened logs are the skeletons of dead trees that have washed onto the beach like soldiers killed in a maritime invasion. Picnickers and sunbathers use the logs as windbreaks. They come in handy, especially in summer, when stiff winds make for harsh beachcombing.

Three roads provide access to the Manchester State Park's beach. The Kinney Road entrance leads to a campground offering 48 primitive sites that are snapped up quickly. Anglers and bird-watchers, in particular, like to stay here. The beach is a 15-minute walk from the camp. Wintering swans, pelicans, godwits, killdeer, and surf scoters (a type of sea duck) delight birders.

Other beach accesses lie at the ends of Alder Creek and Stoneboro Roads. The latter is typical of what is meant by "beach access" on this hardy stretch of the coast. From the highway, you drive 1.6 miles through cow pastures, park in a dirt lot, and hike over and around humpbacked dunes to the sea.

Incidentally, a vista point at Mallo Pass Creek (four miles north of Manchester) affords a magnificent panorama of the ocean, as well as the forests and creek canyons to the east and north. By all means bring a camera.

7 MANCHESTER STATE PARK

Location: from Highway 1 north of Point Arena, Stoneboro, Kinney, and Alder Creek Beach Roads lead to different sections of Manchester State Park
Parking/Fees: $6 entrance fee per vehicle; camping fee $10-15 per night, plus $7.50 reservation fee
Hours: 24 hours
Facilities: restrooms and picnic tables
Contact: Mendocino District, California State Parks, 707/882-2463

Elk

Elk used to be known as Greenwood in the boomtown days of logging and fishing. The lumber business closed down around these parts in 1932, and nowadays Elk is awash in bed-and-breakfast inns, with nature being explored rather than exploited. This town of 200 may seem out of the way but is easy to reach, as an east–west route (Highway 128) meets the Coast Highway (Highway 1) five miles north of here.

Manchester State Park

For more information, contact the Fort Bragg–Mendocino Coast Chamber of Commerce, 332 North Main Street, P.O. Box 1141, Fort Bragg, CA 95437, 707/961-6300, www.mendocinocoast.com.

BEACHES

The appeal of Elk is obvious at **Greenwood Creek State Beach,** just north of town. It is a 47-acre park with a sandy, mile-long cove beach, sea stacks, and cliffs. Park free in the lot across from the Elk Store and hike a quarter mile along a headland to the beach. Once a redwood mill flourished here. The cove beach at Greenwood Creek offers all manner of activities: driftwood collecting, ocean kayaking, steelhead fishing, wildlife observation, picnicking, walking the beach, or just staring contemplatively at the sea.

North of Elk is **Navarro River Beach Access,** where yet another of the North Coast's pristine waterways empties into the ocean—almost. Like the scene in Gualala, the river here runs parallel to the ocean for a long way, providing double the beach pleasure. But the Navarro stops just shy of the Pacific, making a lie of the Pete Townshend song "The Sea Refuses No River."

Primitive camping is permitted; open sites lining the bluff are available to intrepid tenters. The fishing in the river and from the shore is good, but the wind can be ferocious. The drive to the beach along Navarro Bluff Road is a curious one. Rickety, abandoned homes line the roadway, including a forlorn, boarded-up hotel called Navarro-by-the-Sea that looks like the setting for a Stephen King novel.

8 GREENWOOD CREEK STATE BEACH

Location: mouth of Greenwood Creek, off Highway 1 in Elk
Parking/Fees: free parking lot
Hours: 24 hours
Facilities: restrooms and picnic tables
Contact: Mendocino District, California State Parks, 707/937-5804

© PARKE PUTERBAUGH

Greenwood Creek State Beach

MENDOCINO COAST

🗾 NAVARRO RIVER BEACH ACCESS

Location: from Highway 1 two miles south of Albion, turn west on Navarro Bluff Road and follow to beach
Parking/Fees: free parking lot; camping fee $5 per night
Hours: 24 hours
Facilities: restrooms
Contact: Mendocino District, California State Parks, 707/937-5804

ACCOMMODATIONS

You've got your choice of bed-and-breakfasts in tiny Elk. One of the best is the **Elk Cove Inn and Spa** (6300 Highway 1 South, 707/877-3321, $$). Lying just north of Greenwood Creek, this collection of romantic cottages is one of the few North Coast B&Bs that offers direct beach access; just take a set of stairs down to the water's edge. It is also home to a European-style day spa and gourmet organic restaurant.

Another fine oceanfront lodge is the **Sandpiper House Inn** (5520 Highway 1 South, 707/877-3587, $$). Built in 1916, the Sandpiper offers a secluded beach, lovely gardens and grounds, and a mind-blowing view.

The palatial **Harbor House Inn** (5600 Highway 1 South, 707/877-3203, $$$$) is a replica of the California timber industry's exhibit hall at the 1915 Panama-Pacific International Exposition. The six guest rooms and four cottages are luxuriously appointed and command wonderful views of the coast and gardens. Rates run $315–490 per night. While that may seem high, the tariff includes breakfast and dinner for two at the inn's fabulous restaurant.

COASTAL CUISINE

The café at **Greenwood Pier Inn** (5928 Highway 1 South, 707/877-9997, $$) serves healthy California garden cuisine. The inn itself—a playful, 11-room, cliff-clinging wonder—is worth a visit as well. Two tables a night are set aside at the well-regarded **Harbor House**

(5600 Highway 1 South, 707/877-3203, $$$) for nonguests of the inn; reservations are essential. Menu items might include panko-crusted salmon in rose wine butter sauce.

At the other end of the scale, **Queenie's Roadhouse Cafe** (6061 Highway 1, 707/877-3285, $) serves all the usual staples for breakfast and lunch, plus a few more imaginative dishes (e.g., omelets packed with goat cheese, red peppers, and garlic) that make them a kind of gourmet home-cookin' joint.

NIGHTLIFE

For a relaxed, end-of-day drink, and even a full meal, try **Bridget Dolan's Irish Pub.** It's located inside yet another of Elk's B&Bs, the **Griffin House at Greenwood Cove** (5910 Highway 1 South, 707/877-3422, $$).

Albion

Perhaps because one of Northern California's rare east–west roads (Highway 128) meets Highway 1 just south of here, Albion has a more grown-up feel than its pleasant but snail-like neighbors to the south. We mean grown-up in the sense of being overseen by an enlightened community. This is our delicately worded way of saying that we rejoiced at being able to begin the day with a decent cup of coffee and a current daily newspaper.

Yes, there's more to distract the city-bred along the Mendocino coast from Albion north to Fort Bragg. More than that, one gets the feeling that the local citizens have a firm handle on their towns' identity. They value quality of life, sustainable local economies, and slow growth. These are places where big-city dwellers feel more comfortable. The lodging and dining tariffs rise accordingly—but not that much higher—and the full North Coast experience is worth every dollar.

Albion has a storied past. Portuguese, Spanish, Russian, and English sailors took turns plying the coastal waters here in the 1600s. Many versions of how the town came to be called Albion are told, but the most frequent is that Francis Drake briefly moored here after naming California "New Albion" (Albion being one of England's historic nicknames). Drake annexed the area in the name of good Queen Bess. It's the same tale they spin at Point Reyes, leading us to suspect that Drake said that to all the bays.

In 1850, after a crew from San Francisco arrived to salvage a wrecked trading vessel, the city slickers got a hankering for the region's redwood-studded forests. Fresh from their Gold Rush frenzy, they soon turned Albion into a logging center, with a large wharf and sawmill. The latter could turn out 4,000 board feet of wood a day. Then shipping bowed out to railroads, which bowed out to trucks, and the last log was milled here in 1928.

Fishing followed as the new boom industry, but when catches dwindled along the North Coast, Albion turned to tourism. Two early visitors were John Dillinger and Pretty Boy Floyd, both of whom hid out in this quiet village. In the late 1960s Albion became a safe harbor for counterculture dropouts, who also erected a beachhead up in Mendocino. (Does anyone but us remember Cat Mother and the All-Night Newsboys' second album, *Albion Doo-Wah*?)

The setting could not be more ideal for get-aways. The highway winds through redwoods, then rounds the crest of a rugged headland, crossing a majestic steel-and-wood trestle over the beautiful Albion River and emptying into the ocean alongside a scenic harbor and quiet village. Above this backdrop—with waves crashing on the jagged sea stacks—the sound of a foghorn fills the air every 30 seconds. Instead of being bothersome, the foghorn insinuates itself into your stay here. After a while you are lulled into a state of perfect, uncomplaining complacency.

For more information, contact the Fort Bragg–Mendocino Coast Chamber of Commerce, 332 North Main Street, P.O. Box 1141, Fort Bragg, CA 95437, 707/961-6300, www.mendocinocoast.com.

BEACHES

At the mouth of the Albion River, in the shadows of the spectacular cliff-spanning bridge, a sandy river-mouth beach known as **Albion Flat** provides easy access to the ocean. It's mainly for anglers and boaters who cast off from the nearby boat dock. Canoe rentals are also available here. The beach is not for swimming, but surf casting and rock-fishing opportunities are plentiful.

10 ALBION FLAT

Location: 10 miles south of Mendocino on Highway 1, at the mouth of the Albion River
Parking/Fees: $5 per person entrance fee; camping fee $25 per night tents; $35 RV hookup
Hours: 6 A.M.-5 P.M.
Facilities: concession, restrooms, picnic tables, and showers
Contact: Albion River Campground and Fishing Village, 707/937-0606

ACCOMMODATIONS

One of the North Coast's true jewels is the **Albion River Inn** (3790 Highway 1 North, 707/937-1919 or 800/479-7944, $$$), which can be seen from the road as Highway 1 passes north over Albion River Bridge. The view of the ocean and Albion Cove from these 20 New England–style, cliff-top cottages is spectacular. The rooms are cozy, the foghorn sings its deep-throated lullaby, and the 10 acres of gardens and grounds offer ample opportunities for strolling and daydreaming. You are guaranteed to unwind from any of the urban pressures that brought you here.

If you're more into roughing it, **Albion River Campground** (3540 North Highway 1, 707/937-0606, $) offers tent and RV camping. Full-hookup RV camping can be had at **Schooner's Landing** (33621 Albion River North Side Road, 707/937-5707, $), east of Albion Flat. The latter operation offers all

MENDOCINO COAST

sorts of diversions: hiking, picnicking, boat launching, and swimming.

COASTAL CUISINE

If you don't stay in one of the cottages, you should at least eat at the restaurant at the **Albion River Inn** (3790 Highway 1 North, 707/937-1919, $$$), a truly remarkable place where the food matches the view. The restaurant predates the inn (which was launched in 1982) and is part of the original complex that opened in 1916.

Its founder built a smithy out of wood salvaged from the *Girlie Mahoney,* an ill-fated steamer than happened to be carrying 400,000 feet of lumber when she went down in the cove. The haul eventually spawned a general store and restaurant (how's that for recycling?) that quickly became a North Coast staple. It was the Harbor Lights in the 1950s, the Windjammer in the 1960s, the Blacksmith Inn in the 1970s. Today the Albion River Inn is nestled inside the lovingly renovated original structure.

Always a great family dining spot, the Albion River Inn has emerged as one of the finest gourmet eateries in Northern California. The menu changes daily to reflect what's freshest in the seafood and produce markets. The Pacific Rim bouillabaisse, for example, bathes clams, mussels, rock shrimp, and other deep-sea delights in a lemongrass, tomato, and fennel broth. We've also had a scrumptious sea bass sautéed with artichoke hearts and Madeira wine.

Snuggled into a rocky pocket atop a cliff, the restaurant is staffed by friendly, sharp-witted locals, and the extensive wine list features the products of fine local vineyards, many of them accessible via Highway 128. The Albion River Inn offers a taste of the good life at a fair price—a feast for the eyes, stomach, and soul.

NIGHTLIFE

There's a small bar at the **Albion River Inn** (3790 Highway 1, 707/937-1919). Barring that, you can head 10 miles up the road to Mendocino, where more goes on. We made do with the foghorn's serenade and the view over the cliffs from the inn.

Mendocino

The communities of Mendocino and Fort Bragg are about 10 miles apart. Size-wise, Mendocino is home to about 1,300 people in town and 9,000 out in the woods. In Fort Bragg the number of townies and hermits is 6,600 and 6,000.

These two Mendocino Coast sentinels form a sort of North Coast yin and yang, based on their respective characters. The rap goes something like this: Mendocino is artsy-craftsy, while Fort Bragg is working-class. Mendocino is boutiques, while Fort Bragg is hard goods. Mendocino is secluded bed-and-breakfast inns, while Fort Bragg is roadside motels. Mendocino is Cafe Beaujolais, while Fort Bragg is Taco Bell. Mendocino is couples, while Fort Bragg is families. You get the idea.

However, there has been a growing symbiosis between these two seeming opposites as they mutually assimilate in discernible ways. Still, change comes slowly to this section of the coast. The locals scrutinize every permit application, as if adding a few more units to a B&B were tantamount to erecting Trump Tower. (We've been told 44 terms and conditions must be met to get a zoning or use permit up here.) You've got to love their attitude, simply because it works. Essentially, a few more inns have materialized on the highway between Mendocino and Little River over the years, and that's about all.

To get a proper handle on Mendocino, it helps to think of it as a kind of impressionistic painting. Perspective is the key. Observed at close range, the town appears to be a pleasant rural outpost of scattered wood-frame houses and postcard-quaint inns. As one pulls back to observe the big picture, though, Mendocino reveals itself to be a town with a vision. In order to grasp that vision, one has to understand the people who live there.

CANOEING THE BIG RIVER

The longest unspoiled estuary in Northern California is the **Big River,** which spills into the Pacific Ocean just south of Mendocino. Its pristine riverine marshes, canyons, and streambeds are vital to the regional ecosystem. The river's first eight miles are influenced by the tides. If you time it right you can paddle upriver with an incoming tide and return on an ebbing one.

To explore the Big River, one needs a canoe. Speedboats and personal watercraft are banned, as is developing the river's banks, damming its flow, or turning the mouth into a harbor. We rented an outrigger at **Catch A Canoe & Bicycles, Too!,** whose redwood and fiberglass craft are designed by a local artisan. The outriggers can be steered by foot controls and will not flip over. They also cut through the water at good speed with minimal effort. In our outrigger, we experienced a clean river, tall trees on both banks, nesting birds, blue skies, and total silence.

Catch A Canoe also rents and sells canoes, kayaks, and mountain bikes equipped with shocks for riding the wilderness trails in Jackson National Forest or Van Damme State Park. They provide bike racks and maps if you want to take your rentals farther up or down the coast. For more information, contact Catch A Canoe & Bicycles, Too!, 44850 Comptche-Ukiah Road, P.O. Box 487, Mendocino, CA 95460, 707/937-0273, www.stanfordinn.com.

Mendocino's roots date back to the mid-1800s, when California's first redwood mill was built on the banks of the Big River. This slow-moving river empties into the ocean beneath the steep headlands on which Mendocino was founded. The community enjoyed nearly a century of prosperity as a lumber town, followed by decades of decline in the wake of the sawmills' closing. In the 1950s it was discovered by artists and dropouts drawn from the burgeoning cities, especially San Francisco. Rising apartment rents and the stodgy middle-class conformity of the postwar era drove more sensitive souls into the countryside to seek sanctuary.

To those who were searching for another way to live—closer to nature, in an environment more conducive to contemplation—Mendocino exerted a magnetic pull. The old, abandoned wood houses came cheaply, the rugged Northern California coast was quiet and rarely visited, and the natural beauty of Mendocino's coast and forest lands provided a constant source of inspiration.

With the founding of the Mendocino Arts

Council in 1959, the character and mission of the community became official, and art remains a rallying point for the loose-knit denizens of this town. In the 1960s the area became a haven for counterculture refugees when the streets of Haight-Ashbury became plagued with hard drugs and crime. In 1969, the Sir Douglas Quintet had a Top 40 hit with "Mendocino," which put this little North Coast speck on the map. Its chorus caught the stoned, soulful tenor of the times: "Mendocino, Mendocino, where life's such a groove you'll blow your mind in the morning."

Amazingly, things haven't changed so very drastically since those halcyon days. Mendocino remains a place where a life of reflection can be lived on relatively modest means. Artists can scrape by without selling out, musicians and film people find seclusion, and lesser cultural aspirants can, at the very least, manage to keep a roof over their heads. For instance, we spied a run-down pickup truck by the side of the road, whose owner advertised his wares in juvenile hand lettering on the side panels: "Firewood and Donkey Dung."

There's also a downside to this sylvan scene. Mendocino still gets a trickle of San Franciscans. Yet instead of solitude-seeking 1960s transcendentalists, these are homeless, drug-addled derelicts. "Ex-cons, street crap from Union Square" is what one angry innkeeper termed these lost souls, who amble aimlessly about the village center.

To cite another song from the 1960s, this one by Quicksilver, another reason to come to Mendocino is to "have another hit of fresh air." The National Clean Air Monitoring station is located in Mendocino County. After passing over thousands of miles of open ocean, the air is the freshest you'll ever breathe. The nation's standard for clean air is measured by that sampled in Mendocino. That alone makes the area an appealing destination. The sunsets are yellow and gold, not brown as they are in more sooty locales.

There's more good news, locally: Wildlife is making a comeback. Salmon are returning to some of the local rivers. Ospreys, red-tailed hawks, and peregrine falcons have been sighted in increasing numbers. Habitat protection is paying dividends. It feels good to pass along some positive news in the environmental realm, for a change.

Like much of the remote North Coast, you have to really want to be in Mendocino to make it worth the drive over winding roads, trailing slow-moving RVs driven by tourists unused to the curves. Then there's the weather. Mendocino is frequently shrouded in fog and, in winter, heavy rain. These coastal fogs don't creep in on little cat's feet, either (as in Carl Sandberg's poem "Fog"). Instead, they clop in on heavy cattle hooves.

Somehow, this is part of Mendocino's allure as a romantic hideaway. The cool, gray days of summer provide a good excuse to stay inside a cozy room and light a fire. The phrase is overused, but Mendocino truly is a place to get away from it all. The town makes a convenient base for exploring the wineries of Mendocino and Sonoma Counties during the day.

The high points in the community's calendar year are the **Annual Summer Fair** and the **Mendocino Music Festival** (held in July over 10 days), but you can be sure there's always something art-worthy going on in town. Outdoors enthusiasts also find plenty to do, including hiking, canoeing, fishing, and diving for abalone. Miles of beaches and parklands in and around Mendocino beg to be explored on foot. But the best thing about Mendocino is that you really don't have to do anything at all.

For more information, contact the Fort Bragg–Mendocino Coast Chamber of Commerce, 332 North Main Street, P.O. Box 1141, Fort Bragg, CA 95437, 707/961-6300, www.mendocinocoast.com.

BEACHES

Yes, there are beaches way up here, especially north of Mendocino at places like MacKerricher State Park, where they run for mile after unbroken mile. In Mendocino per se, the beaches are less accessible and remarkable than the headlands that overlook them.

Three miles south of Mendocino in Little River (population 825) is **Van Damme State Park.** This 2,100-acre park spreads inland for four miles from its small, sandy beach. At the mouth of the Little River, this beach is among the best abalone-diving spots on the North Coast. Inland, Van Damme encompasses a sword-fern canyon and a forest of stunted conifers. Van Damme's 10 miles of hiking trails and cool, shaded, 84-site campground make it a popular place, especially during the relatively warm, dry months of May–September.

We did some hiking at Van Damme through the cool, shady woods. One thing that caught our attention was the posted Mountain Lion Warning. If you encounter a mountain lion, you are instructed to "convince them that you are not prey and that you may be dangerous." What are you supposed to do—act like a gangsta rapper?

Mendocino Headlands State Park runs north from the banks of the Big River. Narrow, linear headlands extend out from the mainland like serpents' tongues. Trails skirt the bluffs, and you can peer over the side to the beaches at their bases, way down below. The Mendocino Headlands remain a work in progress, a symphony of rock carved by the relentless rhythm of waves beating against them. A wide, sandy beach exists on the south bank of the Big River. However, we'd recommend finding a place to perch high up on the fissured headlands, where you can stare out to sea and, in season, look for whales.

Two miles north of Mendocino is **Russian Gulch State Park,** which is home to serene redwood groves and an open beach where Russian Gulch Creek runs into the ocean. A big attraction is Devil's Punchbowl, a blowhole that's 100 feet long and 60 feet deep. The force of incoming waves funneling through this collapsed sea cave creates geysers and noisy explosions. Another natural wonder is a 36-foot waterfall.

Thirty choice campsites are situated along the creek inside a canyon forested with second-growth redwoods, as well as firs, hemlocks, oaks, and laurels. Again, as demand is greater than supply, reservations are necessary. Skin

diving and rock fishing are the main activities pursued on the beaches at Van Damme and Russian Gulch.

11 VAN DAMME STATE PARK

Location: in Little River three miles south of Mendocino, off Highway 1
Parking/Fees: $6 entrance fee per vehicle; camping fees $20-25 per night tents and RVs, $40 group camp, plus $7.50 reservation fee
Hours: 24 hours
Facilities: restrooms, showers, and picnic tables
Contact: Mendocino District, California State Parks, 707/937-5804

12 MENDOCINO HEADLANDS STATE PARK

Location: on headlands overlooking the ocean in Mendocino

Mendocino Headlands

MENDOCINO COAST

Parking/Fees: free parking lots

Hours: 24 hours

Facilities: none

Contact: Mendocino District, California State Parks, 707/937-5804

13 RUSSIAN GULCH STATE PARK

Location: two miles north of Mendocino off Highway 1, at the mouth of Russian Gulch Creek

Parking/Fees: $6 entrance fee per vehicle; camping fees $20-25 per night tents and RVs, $40 group camp

Hours: 24 hours

Facilities: restrooms, showers, and picnic tables

Contact: Mendocino District, California State Parks, 707/937-5804

RECREATION AND ATTRACTIONS

- **Bike/Skate Rentals:** Catch-a-Canoe & Bicycles, Too!, Highway 1 and Comptche-Ukiah Road, Mendocino, 707/937-0273
- **Dive Shop:** North Coast Scuba, 38820 Highway 1 South, Gualala, 707/884-3534
- **Ecotourism:** Jug Handle State Reserve, Caspar, 707/937-5804; Van Damme State Park, Little River, 707/937-5804
- **Horseback Riding:** Ricochet Ridge Ranch, 24201 North Highway 1, Fort Bragg, 707/964-7669
- **Lighthouse:** Point Arena Lighthouse, 45500 Lighthouse Road, Point Arena, 707/882-2777
- **Marina:** Noyo Harbor, Fort Bragg, 707/947-0167
- **Pier:** Noyo Harbor Pier, Fort Bragg, 707/964-4719
- **Rainy Day Attraction:** Point Arena Lighthouse & Museum, 45500 Lighthouse Road, Point Arena, 707/882-2777
- **Shopping/Browsing:** Mendocino Art Center, 45200 Little Lake Street, Mendocino, 707/937-5818
- **Sportfishing:** Tally Ho Sportfishing, North Harbor Drive, Fort Bragg, 707/964-2079
- **Surf Shop:** North Pacific Productions, 1250 North Main Street, Fort Bragg, 707/964-0156
- **Vacation Rentals:** Mendocino Coast Reservations, 45084 Little Lake Street, 707/937-5033

ACCOMMODATIONS

On the inn scene, the trend in Mendocino is away from cloned Victoriana and toward more contemporary, original, and nature-oriented presentations. The secret to survival in the bed-and-breakfast business these days is quality. People want the vacation experience to be immediate and intense. "People want to be plushed," said one innkeeper.

You can certainly get plushed at **Stanford Inn by the Sea** (Highway 1 at Comptche-Ukiah Road, 707/937-5615, $$$$). Situated high on a hillside overlooking the ocean, it strikes a perfect balance between the luxury of a four-star hotel and the rusticity of a cozy B&B. Rooms are spacious and decorated with unfinished, knotty-pine walls, four-poster beds, and wood-burning fireplaces. A bottle of wine is provided, as are confections from a local chocolatier. Logs are stacked by the hearth, along with instructions on how to build a fire.

In the morning guests head to the **Ravens,** the vegetarian-themed on-site restaurant, for breakfast. Ravens serves wonderful dinners, too. During the day, guests can enjoy the enclosed pool and sauna, or check out the organic garden and greenhouse (doing business as Big River Nurseries). At the foot of a gravel drive leading down to the river's edge is another of owner Jeff Stanford's businesses: Catch-a-Canoe & Bicycles, Too! There's not much you can't do here—including relaxing in the most rejuvenating sort of atmosphere.

Joshua Grindle Inn (44800 Little Lake

Road, 707/937-4143, $$$) is a gleaming white two-story captain's house a short walk from the village. The grounds are a riot of flowers and shrubbery. Rooms are quite comfortable, whether in the main house or the rustic buildings out back. A full hot breakfast is served each morning.

Just south of Mendocino in the town of Little River is **Stevenswood Lodge** (8211 Highway 1 North, 707/937-2810, $$$). We were impressed by its polished hardwood floors and contemporary air. Rooms are outfitted in light wood with natural finishes and named for the nineteenth-century founders of the town. Owner Robert Zimmer's brother runs an art gallery in Mendocino. The spillover from the gallery winds up on the lodge walls, in the halls, in the rooms, even in a small, on-site showroom—all very attractive and all for sale.

A Japanese poi garden offers a peaceful setting out back. Deer and other forest critters wander to the edge of the property. The lodge's operative philosophy is to bring the outdoors inside via windows and skylights that capture the streaming rays. Incidentally, breakfast is tremendous: giant baked muffins, eggs Benedict, bowls of fruit salad.

Also in Little River is **Heritage House** (5200 Highway 1 North, 800/235-5885, $$$), which has 66 cottage rooms spread among 37 verdant acres and has been used as a Hollywood film backdrop. Finally, **Little River Inn** (Highway 1, 888/466-5683, $$$) owns the distinction of being Mendocino's oldest (circa 1853) lodge and the only one with a golf course. Rooms start at $130 and go up from there. The menu at the on-site restaurant includes Dungeness crab potpie, and you've got to drop by Ole's Whale Watch Bar for a drink—preferably toward sunset.

COASTAL CUISINE

Cafe Beaujolais (961 Ukiah Street, 707/937-5614, $$$), a restaurant with a world-class reputation, is in the heart of Mendocino. The English country-cottage decor creates a casually elegant environment, from the hardwood floors and floral print wallpaper to the subtle background music. The café has its own bakery, which turns out extraordinary breads, such as Red Seal rye, Mendocino sourdough (made from white and rye flours), and nine-grain Australian sunflower-seed bread.

Among the stellar entrées you might find on the menu is oven-steamed sturgeon with a sauce of garlic, lemon, tomato, olive oil, and herbs. Cafe Beaujolais also serves meat and game "from animals raised humanely in a free-range environment." There's a good selection of local wines, and they do neat things with coffee, too. All in all, Cafe Beaujolais, which serves dinner nightly and brunch on weekends, offers a top-notch North Coast dining experience.

The owners of **955 Ukiah** (955 Ukiah Street, 707/937-1955, $$$) have built their restaurant into something special through hard work and vision. The accent is continental, the culinary offerings pure poetry, bearing up the elaborate menu descriptions. The salmon, for instance, is poached in a "mirror-like bouillon," while the free-range chicken is "serenely captivated by a sauce of wild mushrooms." You, too, will be serenely captivated by the food and ambience at 955 Ukiah.

NIGHTLIFE

In the informed opinion of a local innkeeper, the **Heritage House** (5200 Highway 1 North, 707/937-5888) still mixes the best drinks on the coast. It also has one of the best views, not to mention fine food and lodgings on a 37-acre spread. Heritage House is in Little River, a few miles south of Mendocino.

MacCallum House (45020 Albion Street, 707/937-0289), a century-old Victorian mansion that does double duty as a classy restaurant and B&B, has a small but sociable bar in a parlor to the left of the main hall. It's called the **Grey Whale Bar & Cafe,** and if you don't feel up to the culinary extravaganza across the hall, you can opt for the bar's menu of burgers and pub grub.

Finally, if you feel up for something wilder than an after-dinner drink, make for the **Caspar Inn,** four miles north of Mendocino (14957 Caspar Road, www.casparinn.com, 707/964-5565). It's one of our favorite places in all of California.

Caspar

Caspar is a friendly ghost of a town far enough west of Highway 1 to escape most of its bustle. During its lumber-milling heyday, Caspar was a bustling town of 500—the first on the coast, in fact, to get electricity. Now it's little more than a dot on the map off the main road, though it's got a viable artistic community and is home to several galleries. Beyond that, little Caspar also scores big on two counts: beaches and nightlife. Read on.

For more information, contact the Fort Bragg–Mendocino Coast Chamber of Commerce, 332 North Main Street, P.O. Box 1141, Fort Bragg, CA 95437, 707/961-6300, www.mendocinocoast.com.

BEACHES

The state has acquired several acres of the crumbling, fissured **Caspar Headlands State Reserve.** Getting out to the headlands means crossing private land, but they can be visited with a free entry permit, obtainable at the State Park District Office at Russian Gulch State Park.

Caspar Headlands State Beach sits at the head of a long, bottleneck-shaped bay where Doyle and Caspar Creeks empty into the Pacific. Bookended by low bluffs, it's a sandy beach accessible from Point Cabrillo Road (also known as Old Highway 1).

14 CASPAR HEADLANDS STATE RESERVE

Location: from Highway 1 five miles north

of Mendocino, turn west onto South Caspar Drive, then onto Headlands Drive; follow to the reserve
Parking/Fees: free roadside parking
Hours: 24 hours
Facilities: none
Contact: Mendocino District, California State Parks, 707/937-5804

15 CASPAR HEADLANDS STATE BEACH

Location: Point Cabrillo Road/Old Highway 1 at the mouth of Doyle Creek in Caspar, across from Caspar Beach RV park
Parking/Fees: free parking lot; camping fee $16 per night at Caspar Beach RV Park
Hours: 24 hours
Facilities: concession, restrooms, showers, and picnic tables (at Caspar Beach RV Park)
Contact: Mendocino District, California State Parks, 707/937-5804; Caspar Beach RV Park, 707/964-3306

ACCOMMODATIONS

If you want to bunk down in Caspar, camping is the best option. **Caspar Beach RV Park** (14401 Point Cabrillo Road, 707/964-3306, $) features 100 sites (56 with full hookups) and ocean frontage in a wooded creekside setting. It also has everything a camper might need: camp store, showers, coin-operated laundry, and playground. To get a feeling for Northern California's hippie culture, book a room at the **Caspar Inn** (14957 Caspar Road, 707/964-5565, www.casparinn.com, $), which boasts "shared bathrooms above the bar."

COASTAL CUISINE

There's a small café, **Oscar's at Caspar** (Caspar Road, 707/964-0602, $), beside the venerable Caspar Inn. At Oscar's the accent is on fresh, healthy food for eat-in or takeout.

NIGHTLIFE

The **Caspar Inn** (14957 Caspar Road, www .casparinn.com, 707/964-5565) is one of the last true vestiges of the 1960s. A night here is what hanging around the funky clubs and ballrooms of San Francisco in its late-1960s prime might have been like. The inn books live bands, including lots of roots and reggae artists. These days, they also have their share of deejays, which is a disappointment.

When it is fully cranking, the scene at the Caspar Inn is almost impossible to describe. The friendly crowd really gets into dancing. We had to back up a few paces when a floor full of eager dancers began encroaching on our turf with their frantic footwork. The band we saw kept them on their feet for hours. The crowd lost itself in dancing, from the Latino fellow who assayed some rather formal flamenco steps to a hirsute dude who got so worked up he was dancing sideways, shaking his mane as he grew ever more consumed by the music.

If you have trouble finding the Caspar Inn, just look for the place where cars are parked on the road in both directions. Further proof that time stands still: Moby Grape was booked to play on our last pass through the area. Visit their website for updated listings.

Jug Handle State Reserve

Now we know how mountain climbers feel when they get within reach of a peak. At this 769-acre park, we ventured onto the farthest point of a fingerlike headland, striding cautiously toward an inviting horizon of blue ocean water and jagged, reddish brown sea stacks. It became a test of nerves to venture all the way out. We wobbled onto our knees and crept forward, shivering as it became clear, with the wind whipping us, that if we weren't careful, we could fall over the side and get smashed to bits.

BEACHES

Jug Handle State Reserve gets our vote for most exciting beach promontory on the North Coast. Several of these slivers of land poke way out into the ocean, and we hereby warn you to prepare for a sudden bout of vertigo. In addition to these remarkable bluff tops, the reserve

© PARKE PUTERBAUGH

Jug Handle State Reserve

MENDOCINO COAST

offers a 2.5-mile nature trail that leads up an ecological staircase of marine terraces through a half million years of geological history. The lowest and youngest of the five terraces bears the full brunt of the ocean waves. The next terrace is covered in sea grass and wildflowers, the third supports a pygmy forest, and the fourth and fifth have taller, more mature forests. You can't imagine the majesty of Jug Handle State Reserve. It simply must be seen!

16 JUG HANDLE STATE RESERVE

Location: 15 miles north of Caspar, off Highway 1
Parking/Fees: free parking lot
Hours: 24 hours
Facilities: restrooms and picnic tables
Contact: Mendocino District, California State Parks, 707/937-5804

ACCOMMODATIONS

The small but pleasant **Annie's Jug Handle Beach Country Bed & Breakfast Inn** (32975 Gibney Lane, 707/964-1415, $$) is within viewing distance of Jug Handle's coastal headlands. The inn was built in 1883 and is far enough away from the bustle of Fort Bragg to make for a quiet getaway.

Fort Bragg

"I'm fond of saying that Fort Bragg is poised on the verge of greatness," contended Colette Bailey, who formerly ran the venerable Grey Whale Inn. We joined her some years back for an early-morning walk along an abandoned log-haul road that runs along the ocean toward MacKerricher State Park. It was 7 A.M., and she was keeping a race-walking pace that wore us out while offering a running commentary on Fort Bragg. En route we passed dozens of like-minded walkers out for their morning jaunt by the sea.

Colette may have had a point about Fort Bragg's bid for better days. Unlike many boutiqued-to-death coastal destinations, Fort Bragg has the feeling of a real working community. In fact, the town (population 6,600) is defined by the delicate balance struck between its two largest industries—timber and tourism. Since the timber industry is hurting, they really need the tourism.

There are many more guest rooms in Fort Bragg than Mendocino, and these are geared toward travelers across the spectrum—not just couples, but families and those traveling on business. It's also becoming a popular place for retirees to settle. They're moving in and building big homes, infusing much-needed cash into the local economy.

Revitalization has arrived not just in economic terms but aesthetically as well. Artists who have been priced out of Mendocino have moved to Fort Bragg, and the town has been receptive to their arrival. The **Fort Bragg Center for the Arts** (13110 Pomo Lane, Mendocino, 707/937-1018) provides regular doses of culture and cheap studio rents for the army of artisans who are replacing the lumberjacks. The arts come to the people on "First Friday," a monthly tour of local galleries and studios.

The appeal of the area is easy to understand. Fort Bragg isn't completely dominated by hermitic, offbeat types as is Mendocino. It's just a working town that's mending its nets and looking to rebound. Fort Bragg has the largest port between San Francisco and Eureka, and it's the largest coastal city along that same stretch.

For anyone who lives in the mountains and valleys to the east or along the coast in either direction, Fort Bragg is a vital service and provisioning center. With that comes the good (cheaper prices on rooms and meals), the bad (slipshod commerce, strip malls), and the ugly (Georgia Pacific's now-closed timber mill, a toxic waste site that is in the process of being cleaned up and "remediated").

Fort Bragg's various bed-and-breakfast inns, antiques shops, and attractions have brought

FOGGY MENDOCINO BREAKDOWN

We herewith issue a fog advisory for the North Coast, which applies to Mendocino, Fort Bragg, and the surrounding area. The coast is often draped in fog, and it can make for hazardous driving – especially at night, when the visibility can reduce to nothing, and the drop from the side of the highway to the rocky coastline below can be hundreds of feet. If you're indoors in romantic Mendocino, however, the fog can set a mood.

You can always tell how hot it is inland by how heavy the fog is on the coast. When they're sweating in Sacramento, people are pulling out sweaters in Mendocino. The inland heat creates a temperature differential that sucks cool, moist air off the ocean, bathing the northern coastal counties in fog.

It almost never rains in the summer, but it is commonly overcast, generally burning off by midday – but gray skies can linger for weeks.

The period from December through February is the height of the rainy season. Because the coastal environment is so strongly moderated by the ocean, temperature extremes in either direction are rare. Mendocino might get a frost or two each winter and a dusting of snow every half dozen years, but that's the worst of it.

The Mendocino and Sonoma Coasts are warmest in September and October, when the mercury can climb to 80 balmy degrees. Autumn is really the ideal time to visit, because of the Indian summer weather: clear and warm, with relatively litle fog.

a new look to the community, and an influx of immigrants has added a likable ethnic mix. One cultural event we passed up—but only because we'd left town when it took place—was Cow Chip Bingo. Here's how it works: A local football field is divided into 500 squares. Contestants lay claim to squares for $5 apiece. Three cows are turned loose onto the field to graze and (you guessed it) make cow pies. The owner of the square first plopped in wins $1,500, second $1,000, and third $500. Unless one is intimate with the excretory habits of cows, our guess is it's a game of chance, not strategy.

Though referred to as "historic" Fort Bragg in all the tourist literature, the town's history can quickly be summed up. A fort was established here in 1857 to keep Native Americans in check, and closed seven years later. Timbering and railroads arrived in 1885 and have been leading industries ever since. From this they've managed to create a 28-stop walking tour of historic sites (mostly restored Victorian homes and inns).

To visitors, the biggest attraction is the **Skunk Train,** an authentic re-creation of the logging railroad that ran from Fort Bragg to Willits, 40 miles inland. The train consists of observation cars hauled by a diesel logging locomotive. It makes several round-trips to Willits and Northspur (the midway point) daily. Your best bet is the three-hour round-trip to Northspur, which runs along the Noyo River through redwood forests and mountains. In summer, they offer a 4.5-hour round-trip to Northspur that includes a barbecue dinner beneath the redwoods. The Skunk Train Depot is at the foot of Laurel Street in Fort Bragg. For more information on the Skunk Train, call 800/866-1690; round-trip fares to Northspur cost $47 for adults, $22 for kids.

For more information, contact the Fort Bragg–Mendocino Coast Chamber of Commerce, 332 North Main Street, P.O. Box 1141, Fort Bragg, CA 95437, 707/961-6300, www.mendocinocoast.com.

MENDOCINO COAST

BEACHES

The state park system provides access to the best beaches in the vicinity: Jug Handle State Reserve (two miles south) and MacKerricher State Park (three miles north). The **Pudding Creek Beach** access, at the south end of MacKerricher State Park, is the closest to a classic sand beach that Fort Bragg has to offer. Here, Pudding Creek trickles into the ocean, and a small dirt parking lot allows limited entry. You must walk under a condemned train trestle, but the mountain of sand is inviting. The waves break invitingly, too, but a sign warns of "Recurring Rip Currents." No lifeguards are on duty.

One creek mouth north is **Virgin Creek Beach,** a wide, sandy beach that draws local crowds. An unmarked pull-off by the side of the road is your only clue about this one. Both Pudding Creek and Virgin Creek Beaches lie along the eight-mile log-haul road now used by joggers, walkers, and bicyclists.

Elsewhere in Fort Bragg the beach pickings have been slim, mainly because Georgia Pacific owned virtually all of the town's oceanfront. However, new accesses are on the way. In 2002, Georgia Pacific shut down its 100-year-old sawmill operation in Fort Bragg. In 2005, the company donated a three-mile coastal corridor to the city, and the city purchased 35 acres of the sawmill site for a park, using funds from the Coastal Conservancy. Right now, crews are busy cleaning petroleum-contaminated soil and water from the site.

Glass Beach, the public beach next to the defunct sawmill, suffers from its proximity. Allegedly, you can scavenge for wave-polished pebbles and glass bits at Glass Beach, but it looks none too inviting.

At the west end of **Noyo Harbor** (accessed via Noyo Harbor Drive, next to the bridge off Highway 1) is a tiny cove beach bordered by rock jetties that hold the river mouth open. It's quite a setting, though mostly for viewing. Waves break loudly against the jetties, and the bridge span arches dramatically in the background. Be careful on the jetties if you fish from them, as they are slick.

17 NOYO HARBOR

Location: end of Noyo Harbor Drive at the mouth of the Noyo River, in Fort Bragg
Parking/Fees: free parking lot
Hours: 24 hours
Facilities: restrooms and showers
Contact: Noyo Harbor Pier, 707/964-0167

18 GLASS BEACH

Location: end of Elm Street in Fort Bragg
Parking/Fees: free street parking
Hours: 24 hours
Facilities: none
Contact: none

19 PUDDING CREEK BEACH

Location: end of Pudding Creek Road, off Highway 1 in Fort Bragg
Parking/Fees: free parking lot
Hours: 24 hours
Facilities: none
Contact: Mendocino District, California State Parks, 707/964-9112

20 VIRGIN CREEK BEACH

Location: Highway 1 at Virgin Creek in Fort Bragg
Parking/Fees: free parking lot
Hours: 24 hours
Facilities: none
Contact: Mendocino District, California State Parks, 707/937-5804

ACCOMMODATIONS

It's true that rooms are cheaper and more plentiful in Fort Bragg than in the coastal towns to the south, but you get what you pay for. That is, for a few dollars more, you can have a total North Coast experience in Mendocino, Little River, Albion, or Elk. Still, a fair number of nice and new Fort Bragg motels provide the sort of dependably clean creature comforts many road-weary travelers crave. In that regard, the **Best Western Vista Manor Lodge** (1100 North Main Street, 707/964-4776, $$) and the **Quality Inn Seabird Lodge** (191 South Street, 707/964-4731, $$) are among your best bets.

The **Grey Whale Inn** (615 North Main Street, 707/964-0640, $$) was the first bed-and-breakfast in Fort Bragg and has been a North Coast landmark for years. The handsome, four-story building used to be a general hospital, once boasting 36 beds. With such a background, it's no surprise that the inn is highly wheelchair accessible, with wide ramps running throughout. The rooms are large, impeccably decorated, and immaculately maintained. Walls are paneled with broad redwood planks. Beds are covered with homey quilts. There's a game room downstairs with a pool table and a television.

Each morning, a mouth-watering breakfast is served, including such goodies as a breakfast strudel of spinach and sun-dried tomatoes layered in a custard of bread and eggs. Croissants, fresh fruit salad, yogurt, granola, a special blend of coffee, and cinnamon-flavored hot tea round out the meal. The Grey Whale offers 14 rooms, ranging from "French country simplicity" to suites and penthouses with fireplaces and refrigerators. Interesting anecdote: A woman who was born here when it was a hospital returned to spend her wedding night at the Grey Whale.

The closest lodge to the beach access at Pudding Creek is **Beach House Inn** (100 Pudding Creek Road, 707/961-1700, $$), which sits atop a bluff overlooking the estuary.

COASTAL CUISINE

An influx of immigrants has given Fort Bragg a much-needed shot of diversity in the food department. The most interesting arrival, and one of the great finds on the Mendocino coast, is **Viraporn's Thai Cafe** (500 South Main Street, 707/964-7931, $). It's owned and operated by a native of the Phrae province in northern Thailand. She prepares every dish using fresh, authentic ingredients. Her chicken lemongrass soup and pad Thai will rescue you from all those burgers you've likely eaten elsewhere in Fort Bragg.

A lumberjack-style chowdown can be had at **Round Man's Smoke House** (412 North Main Street, 707/964-5954, $), which offers some of the best smoked salmon, albacore, and cod on the North Coast, as well as salmon and turkey jerky. Sample tastings are encouraged. If you want fish, go where they reel 'em in. Overlooking busy Noyo Harbor is the **Cliff House** (1011 South Main Street, 707/961-0255, $$), where fresh local seafood is served on four dining levels.

More local in flavor is **Silver's at the Wharf** (32260 North Harbor Drive, 707/964-4283, $$). It is beneath the Noyo River Bridge, located among the ramshackle flotsam of the fishing trade. The nautical bustle, sea breezes, and dishes like freshly grilled salmon steak will transport you to a proverbial Treasure Island.

NIGHTLIFE

The **North Coast Brewing Company** (455 North Main Street, 707/964-3400) is a friendly pub that has been winning awards every year for its home-brewed ales and stouts. Try the Scrimshaw Pilsner, Red Seal Ale, and Old No. 38 Stout. The pub grub is quite good, too, including smoked fish and burgers the size of tree stumps.

MacKerricher State Park

Mendocino County hugs the coast for 130 miles, much of it inaccessible stretches of sea cliffs and tiny pocket beaches. MacKerricher State Park, however, is a North Coast anomaly, offering a broad, mostly sandy beach that runs for eight uninterrupted miles. MacKerricher's lengthy expanse and shoreline equestrian trail are ideal for horseback riding. Guided rides, as well as "custom riding vacations," can be arranged just outside the park at **Ricochet Ridge Ranch** (707/964-7669). Bicyclists, joggers, and walkers make use of the old logging road that runs through the park. Anglers find good fishing around the headlands and in Lake Cleone. You can do just about everything but swim in the 50-degree water.

BEACHES

A boardwalk leads out from the main parking lot at **MacKerricher State Park** to Laguna Point, a stunning promontory from which to view migrating whales and harbor seals. At low tide the tidepools are chock full of life, but at high tide the remorseless waves pound the point with profound fury. We watched in amazement as the lush and beautiful marine vegetation rolled with the punches. The sand on the beach itself is large-grained and blackish in color. The hard-packed granules make for great bike riding. The beach runs unbroken from Pudding Creek (in Fort Bragg) north to Ten Mile River.

Elsewhere on the premises is **Lake Cleone,** a 15-acre freshwater lake stocked with trout. It's a popular duck haven, too.

 MACKERRICHER STATE PARK

 BEST (

Location: three miles north of Fort Bragg on Highway 1
Parking/Fees: free parking lot; camping fee $15 per night, plus $7.50 reservation fee
Hours: 24 hours
Facilities: restrooms, showers, and picnic tables
Contact: Mendocino District, California State Parks, 707/964-9112

Westport

North of Fort Bragg, Highway 1 continues along the coast before pulling away to join U.S. 101 at Leggett. Along this stretch lies a quartet of accessible beaches clustered in the vicinity of a one-horse town of 300 called Westport.

MacKerricher State Park

For more information, contact the Fort Bragg–Mendocino Coast Chamber of Commerce, 332 North Main Street, P.O. Box 1141, Fort Bragg, CA 95437, 707/961-6300, www.mendocinocoast.com.

BEACHES

Logically enough, **Seaside Creek Beach** lies at the mouth of Seaside Creek. Parking is by the side of the road. Offshore sea stacks are visible, and driftwood lines the sandy beach. **Chadbourne Gulch,** however, is the stunner—a mile-long, sandy beach that's good for sunning, surfing, and surf casting. There's lots of beach to wander, though not much room for cars, which must park on the highway shoulder. At high tide the beach becomes none too wide itself. These creek-mouth beaches of northern Mendocino County are very angler-friendly, being good places for netting smelt, catching steelhead, and diving for abalone.

The next two are prime North Coast camping spots. Surrounding a quarter-mile crescent known as **Westport Beach** and **Wages Creek Beach** is Westport Beach RV and Camping. It's a private campground with 30 sites—some inland and some beachside. A half mile north of Westport and 17 miles above Fort Bragg, it draws RV nomads and anglers.

Westport-Union Landing State Beach, three miles north of Westport, offers bluff-top camping at seven campgrounds along its two-mile ocean frontage. Trails and stairs lead to a primarily rocky beach; the sandy, quarter-mile-long beach that begins at the mouth of DeHaven Creek on the park's south end is known as Pete's Beach.

Westport–Union Landing can be a raw spot indeed in winter, when stormy weather and rough seas pound the bluff bases, sending wave spray soaring 50 feet in the air, all the way up to campground level. Divers, tidepoolers, and surf casters especially seem to enjoy this primitive, wind- and sea-swept environment.

22 SEASIDE CREEK BEACH

Location: one mile north of Ten Mile River on Highway 1
Parking/Fees: free roadside parking
Hours: 24 hours
Facilities: none
Contact: Mendocino District, California State Parks, 707/937-5804

23 CHADBOURNE GULCH

Location: two miles south of Westport on Highway 1
Parking/Fees: limited free roadside parking
Hours: 24 hours
Facilities: none
Contact: Mendocino District, California State Parks, 707/937-5804

24 WESTPORT BEACH

Location: 17 miles north of Fort Bragg, at 37700 Highway 1 North, in Westport
Parking/Fees: $10 entrance fee per vehicle; camping fees $35-40 per night with hookups, $25 per night without hookups
Hours: 10 A.M.-5 P.M.
Facilities: restrooms, showers, and picnic tables
Contact: Westport Beach RV & Camping, 707/964-2964

25 WESTPORT-UNION LANDING STATE BEACH

Location: three miles north of Westport, off Highway 1
Parking/Fees: free parking lot; camping fees $10-15 per night, plus $7.50 reservation fee
Hours: 24 hours

MENDOCINO COAST

Facilities: restrooms and picnic tables
Contact: Mendocino District, California State Parks, 707/937-5804

ACCOMMODATIONS

If camping sounds a little austere but being near this wild and rocky coast holds some appeal, you can always opt for comfort *and* proximity to nature by staying at one of the bed-and-breakfast inns scattered about the area. This part of the coast is uncrowded and unhurried. If you're serious about getting away, then Westport might just be your ticket.

Our picks: **Howard Creek Ranch Inn** (40501 Highway 1, 707/964-6725, $$) and **DeHaven Valley Farm Country Inn and Restaurant** (39247 Highway 1,

LET'S GET LOST: EXPLORING SINKYONE WILDERNESS STATE PARK

We were looking for Usal Road (a.k.a. Mendocino County Road 431). Even so, we didn't notice the turnoff when we came upon it while driving along Highway 1. It was right there, just like the maps said, three miles north of Rockport, which itself was little more than a crossroads. But it came up suddenly, in a silent way, requiring almost a complete doubling back to the left. We saw it too late and had to turn around on Highway 1 at the next opportunity for a re-approach from the north. This time, we did it. Then we stopped, read the signs, and got nervous.

Usal Road is a one-lane dirt road that negotiates the mountains of the King Range. It zigs and zags for roughly 25 miles along the Lost Coast, an awesome wilderness of jagged mountains that plunge precipitously to the ocean. Usal Road is all ups and downs and sharp turns and curves and very little straightaway. It is pure hell on a car's brakes and transmission. Signs warn that the road is not recommended for RVs and trailers and may be impassable in the winter months owing to mud and washouts. Our advice, if you do venture up Usal Road, is to carry a cell phone, an AAA membership card, and AAA's "Supernumber" for roadside assistance: 800/222-4357.

The road is not very well maintained by the county, we were later told by a woman up in Shelter Cove. We have some sympathy for the county on this matter, because the road is basically impossible to maintain. However, our innkeeper in Mendocino the night before assured us that we could make it through if we took it easy. "Don't go over the side," he said half jokingly.

We managed to drive about seven miles into the heart of the Lost Coast, reaching **Usal Beach.** These were seven of the hardest, longest miles we've ever driven. It took nearly an hour. Along the way, our dust-covered late-model Mazda Protege sputtered and groaned as it maneuvered the ups and downs of the rutted roadway. Each hairpin turn sent our hearts into our stomachs. Would we encounter an SUV on a blind curve? Would we hit a pothole that might crack an axle? Would the brakes give out?

At one point, about 4.5 miles from the Highway 1 turnoff, the road hugs the cliff's edge for half a mile, edging along a sheer drop of a thousand feet to the churning ocean. These high-altitude ocean vistas rival the best in Big Sur. Though we were only five miles off the main road, we felt that relatively few eyes had ever gazed on – and fewer still had ever actually set foot on – these pristine black-sand beaches. The ocean stretched out to eternity. We had never seen so much ocean arrayed before us. It looked like a vast sheet of rippled tin foil, extending to a luminous horizon where ocean and sky blended in silvery unity. The drive along Usal Road, and the repair bill you may incur as a result, is worth the trouble just to lay eyes on this view of the Pacific Ocean. Trust us.

707/961-1660, $$), both of which offer oceans and mountains for a backdrop. With ten and eight rooms, respectively, these are the largest inns in Westport; others are smaller but just as charming. Finally, there's the **Westport Hotel** (P.O. Box 245, Whitethorn, CA 95489, 707/986-7711, $$), which in previous incarnations has been the Lost Coast Inn, the Pelican Inn, and (our favorite) the Cobweb Palace. Presumably, they've cleared away the cobwebs by now.

Sinkyone Wilderness State Park

Sinkyone Wilderness State Park occupies the remote northwest corner of Mendocino County.

We pressed on for another two difficult miles, finally reaching signs announcing the entrance to **Sinkyone Wilderness State Park.** This is one of the most remote outposts in the state-park system. The park offers campsites, a beautiful wilderness beach, and the southern trailhead for the Lost Coast Trail, which extends for 22 miles up to the Mattole River. Minimal information is posted on a board. Vehicles park here and people fill out the necessary form to hike the Lost Coast Trail. On a gorgeous midweek day in May, we saw no one camping or on the beach.

Usal Beach lies just north of a nerve-wracking bridge that requires positioning one's wheels on elevated wooden tracks to make a successful crossing. That done, we turned west on Beach Road and followed it to an impromptu parking lot of sand and rocks. Usal Creek enters the ocean here in a series of meandering curves. A few picnic tables are scattered around. The beach is beautiful and rugged, with spongy, dark volcanic sand. The beach face is steep, and powerful waves run up its face.

A newspaper article had been posted on the information board. It warned of "rogue waves" – waves of sudden and unpredictable size that can swamp swimmers, hikers, and boaters – and recounted a recent incident in which a group of hikers was washed off the beach in the vicinity of Shelter Cove. In one year, 13 people were drowned by rogue waves near Point Reyes alone.

In this wild, dangerous, and unconquerable place, we reveled in the beauty. The air, having passed across 3,000 miles of open ocean, was as clean as any on earth. The day was perfect. We debated the wisdom of continuing on Usal Road to Shelter Cove. We had come only seven miles, and 19 more of them lay before us. At this rate, it would take two or three more hours to get there, the good Lord willing, and already it was 5:30 P.M.

Providence interceded at that moment in the form of an SUV that came rumbling down from Shelter Cove. We asked the driver if Usal Road was passable in that direction, and he strongly recommended against driving it. He ruefully noted that the road was muddy and deeply rutted north of here. On one hazardous stretch, his Explorer plunged into a pothole, causing a nasty dent. Imagining what that might do to our low-to-the-ground compact car, we chose to retrace our steps back to Highway 1 and take the long way to Shelter Cove: north to Leggett, where we'd pick up U.S. 101, and then up to Garberville and west to Shelter Cove. This meant another 70 miles of zig-zagging, up-and-down roads, but at least they were paved and well graded.

In a way, we were glad it worked out the way it did, because on the return trip we witnessed a bit of nature in the raw. A furry black figure darted across the road. It was a black bear cub. It hid behind, and then climbed, a tree. The curious critter poked its head around the tree and stared at us for a few minutes. Cute as the dickens, it looked like something out of a cartoon. It finally slid down and darted into the forest. Soon after that we saw an eagle swoop down and snare a meal. These were majestic visions that were seen by us only because we chose the road less traveled.

MENDOCINO COAST

Getting there is not easy and, depending on the type of vehicle you're driving, not necessarily advisable. Sinkyone is accessed three miles north of Rockport, where you turn west from Highway 1 onto Usal Road/County Road 431 and continue six miles to Usal Campground. Access to the north end of the park is gained from the Humboldt County town of Redway. Pick up Briceland Road, which leads to a visitors center and campgrounds at Needle Rock, 36 long, bumpy miles away. Be advised that roads within the park are only seasonally passable to most vehicles.

In a sense, this is a new one on us: a park you can't get to. At least some of the time, that is. Both roads leading into Sinkyone are steep, winding, difficult to negotiate under the best of circumstances and flat-out impassable when rains are heavy. RVs and trailers are out of the question all of the time. Cars and pickups will get you there from March to October, weather permitting. Four-wheel drives are best for getting around the rugged terrain of an area that's colloquially known as the Lost Coast.

The attraction is 7,300 acres of deep coastal wilderness that even Highway 1 fails to penetrate. There are ten primitive, hike-in campsites, and one at which you can park your vehicle. The Lost Coast Trail zigs and zags for 22 miles along Sinkyone's coastline, sometimes at sea level and other times astride ridges with elevations of 800 feet.

The steep mountains rise from the shoreline to heights of 1,800 feet. They support a diverse array of plants, from second-growth coastal redwoods and California laurels to grasslands, meadows, and shrubs. The region was heavily logged for a century—from 1888 to 1986, the last owner being Georgia Pacific. Now the land is recovering and reverting to a wild state. It's hard to believe that in the midst of this now-empty country, Georgia Pacific and its forerunners created bustling company towns at Wheeler and Usal, which

were burned to the ground by the lumber company in 1969 to avoid liability problems from leaving old buildings standing. Prior to the massive timber-taking, this land was the home of the Sinkyone people, and the story of their subjugation is another sordid chapter in the history of abuse of native populations.

Today, the old ranches and lumber camps are abandoned and overgrown. Except for a small visitors center at Needle Rock House, a former rancher's home, Sinkyone Wilderness State Park has little more than trails and gravel roads running through it.

For more information, contact Sinkyone Wilderness State Park, P.O. Box 245, Whitethorn, CA 95489, 707/986-7711, www.parks.ca.gov.

BEACHES

Camping at Sinkyone Wilderness State Park is first come, first served, and you must bring your own water and firewood. The most interesting campground is at **Bear Harbor Cove,** site of a former doghole port where lumber was shipped. Wilderness permits are required to hike the Lost Coast Trail between **Usal Beach** and Bear Harbor. They cost $3 a night and can be obtained at Usal Beach Campground or Needle Rock Visitor Center.

Down by the ocean, black sand and coarse gravel beaches lie at the mouths of creeks. Between them the beach narrows to a thin ribbon of dark volcanic sand. Primitive beachfront sites are strung out along the Sinkyone shoreline. From south to north there's **Little Jackass Creek Beach** (visited by as many seals as humans), **Bear Harbor Beach** (good tidepooling), **Needle Rock Beach** (long, hikeable shoreline), and **Jones Beach** (cove beach at the end of a steep trail).

One final caveat pertaining to this park: The region gets 80 inches of rain annually, most of it falling between November and May. Owners of RVs and trailers are advised not to even think about trying out the road.

26 USAL BEACH

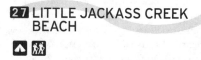

Location: from Highway 1 three miles north of Rockport, turn onto Usal Road/County Route 431, follow for six miles to Usal Campground; a spur road leads to the beach
Parking/Fees: $5 entrance fee per vehicle; camping fee $15 per night, plus $7.50 reservation fee
Hours: 24 hours
Facilities: restrooms and picnic tables
Contact: Sinkyone Wilderness State Park, 707/986-7711

27 LITTLE JACKASS CREEK BEACH

Location: from Highway 1 three miles north of Rockport, turn onto Usal Road/County Route 431, follow for six miles to Usal Campground; hike north on Lost Coast Trail for 7.5 miles to Little Jackass Creek Camp
Parking/Fees: $5 entrance fee per vehicle; camping fee $15 per night, plus $7.50 reservation fee
Hours: 24 hours
Facilities: none
Contact: Sinkyone Wilderness State Park, 707/986-7711

28 BEAR HARBOR BEACH

Location: Redway exit from U.S. 101 in Garberville, turn west on Briceland Road, proceed 28 miles to Orchard Camp; hike south on Lost Coast Trail 0.4 mile to beach
Parking/Fees: $5 entrance fee per vehicle; camping fee $15 per night, plus $7.50 reservation fee
Hours: 24 hours
Facilities: none
Contact: Sinkyone Wilderness State Park, 707/986-7711

29 NEEDLE ROCK BEACH

Location: Redway exit from U.S. 101 in Garberville, turn west on Briceland Road, proceed 26 miles to Needle Rock Visitor Center; hike Needle Rock Beach Trail for 0.2 mile to beach
Parking/Fees: $5 entrance fee per vehicle; camping fee $20 per night, plus $7.50 reservation fee
Hours: 24 hours
Facilities: restrooms and picnic tables
Contact: Sinkyone Wilderness State Park, 707/986-7711

30 JONES BEACH

Location: Redway exit from U.S. 101 in Garberville, turn west on Briceland Road, proceed 25 miles to Jones Beach Camp; hike Jones Beach Trail 0.3 mile to beach
Parking/Fees: $5 entrance fee per vehicle; camping fee $15 per night, plus $7.50 reservation fee
Hours: 24 hours
Facilities: none
Contact: Sinkyone Wilderness State Park, 707/986-7711

MENDOCINO COAST

THE REDWOOD EMPIRE

The Redwood Empire encompasses the northernmost coastal counties in California: Humboldt and Del Norte. There is much to see and do in this vast natural wonderland, home to some of the largest surviving stands of redwood trees in the world. Everything seems bigger up here, and not just the towering redwoods. The area claims 130 miles of coastline; the tallest peak on any continental margin in the United States (King Peak, at 4,086 feet); and two lengthy shoreline hikes, the Lost Coast Trail and the Coastal Trail, which wander the beaches for 50 and 30 miles, respectively. If you come here, allow plenty of time to drink in the immense natural beauty of the redwoods and beaches, and lose yourself in the foggy mysteries of a world apart.

The Redwood Empire can be divided into three areas. The southernmost is part of the Lost Coast—a place where mountains rise right out of the ocean and the main roads swing inland, as if afraid to venture near the rugged shoreline. Shelter Cove is the most accessible point on the Lost Coast, yet it requires a 24-mile drive from U.S. 101 over narrow, curving, and steeply graded roads. Your reward is a black-sand beach that seemingly runs to infinity in either direction.

The middle portion is a verdant land of river valleys, pastureland, embayments, and deep woods. It's also home to the population centers of Ferndale, Eureka, Arcata, McKinleyville, and Trinidad, which are spread out along a 30-mile stretch of U.S. 101. Lengthy sand spits and wild, dune-covered beaches characterize this part of the coast through the Redwood Empire.

The northern section is redwood country, extending all the way to the Oregon state line and encompassing the upper third of Humboldt County and all of Del Norte County. Redwood National Park and Prairie Creek

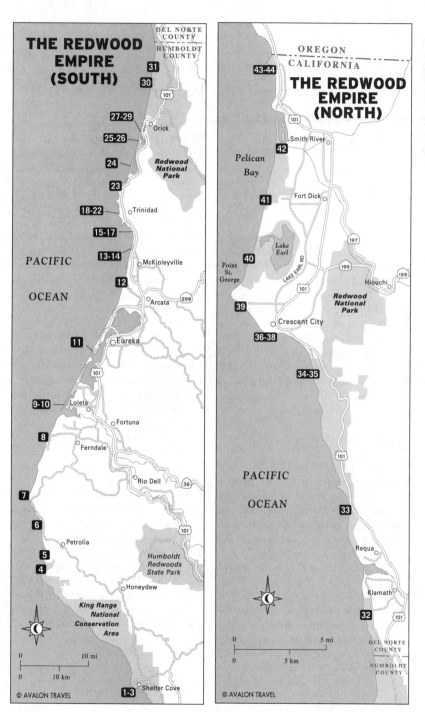

THE REDWOOD EMPIRE (SOUTH)

DEL NORTE COUNTY
HUMBOLDT COUNTY

31
30

101

27-29
Orick
25-26

24   *Redwood National Park*

23

18-22   Trinidad

15-17

13-14   McKinleyville

12

299
Arcata

PACIFIC

OCEAN

11   Eureka

101

9-10   Loleta

Fortuna

8

Ferndale

Rio Dell   36

7

101

6

Petrolia

5

4   Honeydew   *Humboldt Redwoods State Park*

King Range National Conservation Area

0   10 mi

0   10 km

1-3   Shelter Cove

© AVALON TRAVEL

THE REDWOOD EMPIRE (NORTH)

OREGON
CALIFORNIA

43-44

101

Smith River
42

Pelican Bay

41   Fort Dick

197

Lake Earl

40   LAKE EARL RD

Point St. George

199   Hiouchi   199

101

Redwood National Park

39

Crescent City
36-38

34-35

PACIFIC

OCEAN

101

33

Requa

Klamath

32   101

DEL NORTE COUNTY

HUMBOLDT COUNTY

0   5 mi

0   5 km

© AVALON TRAVEL

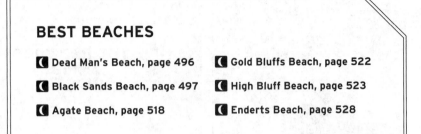

Redwoods State Park occupy much of the acreage, with Crescent City the only town of any size between Trinidad and the Oregon line. The area is also an angler's paradise, boasting big rivers, such as the Klamath and the Smith, and numerous creeks that are ideal for landing steelhead and salmon.

Near a small settlement called Orick is Gold Bluffs Beach, which might just be our favorite beach on any coast. It is truly that stupendous a setting. Moreover, there are others that are nearly its equal, including Dead Man's Beach (in Shelter Cove) and High Bluff Beach (near the Klamath River). It is all simply breathtaking.

Shelter Cove

Shelter Cove lies at the heart of the Lost Coast, a remote and staggeringly beautiful region occupied by Sinkyone Wilderness State Park and the King Range National Conservation Area. Although a few unwary retirees have stumbled onto Shelter Cove, whose population is 350, it still deserves to be described as "lost."

It lies 24 miles west of Garberville, but these are 24 trying miles, particularly approaching the coast. The road is paved but unmarked, and it meanders and curves, ascending and descending. Eventually it reaches a peak high in the King Range and the ocean pops into view—one of the most mesmerizing first glimpses of the mighty Pacific on the entire West Coast. If it's not shrouded in fog, the

ocean glistens brightly in the distance like a diamond choker. From here a long, heart-stopping grade drops down to sea level. You can buy a T-shirt at the Shelter Cove Deli that testifies to the fact you survived the passage.

Shelter Cove is spread out on land surrounding a natural harbor between headlands in the King Range. About 400 houses were built out here on what used to be a giant sheep ranch. The ranch owner sold his tract back in 1965 for $250,000; it was resold for $900,000 to a development company that subdivided it into 1,300 smallish (given the rural location) lots. The homes that have gone up here are mainly incongruously large dwellings built by retirees from points south. They move to Shelter Cove with high hopes, get the heebie-jeebies from all the isolation (think of *The Shining*), then try to unload their haunted homestead onto the next ocean-loving retiree who may himself have a change of heart.

As the pleasant old bird who ran a seaside motel where we stayed put it, "The population here is 350, if they're all here at once. The rental homes are nearly always rented because the retirement age people don't stick it out here. They build these big houses but they don't think it through. They get out here and get homesick and are far from their families and there's no medical help for a hundred miles. I probably wouldn't be here myself if I hadn't already been here forever."

Isolated it is. Unique on the California coast, you must drive for an hour to get to a bonafide grocery store or movie house. The

THE REGAL REDWOODS

Redwood National Park is a 46- by 7-mile preserve for *Sequoia sempervirens* established in 1968 by an act of Congress and expanded 10 years later. Straddling both Humboldt and Del Norte Counties, it has been a boon to tourism and a blessing to the sacred trees, though chainsaw-crazed timber topplers in these economically beleaguered counties would not agree.

Fully half of Del Norte County is state and federal parkland, forever off-limits to logging, and this has taken a painful toll on the ailing economy in this often overlooked corner of the state. Although the redwoods draw 600,000 visitors a year, the tourism numbers are still not enough to offset jobs lost in the timber industry. Meanwhile, Del Norte County gamely promotes itself as the "Redwood Gate to the Golden State."

October 2008 marked the 40th anniversary of the park's founding. One of the loftiest stands in the park, the Lady Bird Johnson Grove, commemorates the first lady whose mission to "beautify America" is one of the better environmental memories of the 1960s.

Unfortunately, a pathogen that began killing oak trees by the thousands in California in the late 1990s has also been found in the dying needles of coast redwoods. Known as "sudden oak death," and particularly lethal to tanoaks, the blight is caused by a deadly fungus-like brown alga. In 2002, scientists concluded that coast redwood and Douglas fir trees are susceptible to the pathogen that causes sudden oak death. The pathogen was first identified in 2000 and given the name *Phytophthora* (Phy-TOFF-thor-uh) *ramorum* (meaning "infector of twigs"). It is not yet clear, however, how seriously the disease will impact California's redwoods and firs, but early indications are that it only affects the needles and very small branches of redwoods.

Three state parks lie within the national park boundaries. **Prairie Creek Redwoods State Park** (in Humboldt County), **Jedediah Smith Redwoods State Park** (in Del Norte County), and **Del Norte Coast Redwoods State Park** (in Del Norte County) are fully developed, with campsites, hiking trails, information booths, ranger talks, and picnic tables.

Considerable beach access is available along stretches of Redwood National Park, and at Prairie Creek Redwoods State Park and Del Norte Coast Redwoods State Park. Though it's a safe bet you won't want to dive into the frigid waters of the Pacific this far north, swimming in the cool creeks and rivers that run through these parks is a more tolerable option in the summer months.

For more information, contact Redwood National Park, 1111 Second Street, Crescent City, CA 95531, 707/464-6101, www.nps.gov/redw. Park information centers are located in downtown Crescent City, at Second and K Streets; in Hiouchi, eight miles east of Crescent City, along Highway 199; and one mile south of Orick, along U.S. 101, in Humboldt County.

King Range, with peaks that rise to heights of 4,000 feet, separates Shelter Cove from civilization. Try as they might to lure people here by putting in a small airstrip while continuing to subdivide and sell as best they can, the area is simply too distant to be attractive to urbanites—even those who toy with the fantasy of fleeing civilization.

You wonder why they even try, because the realtors' half-assed efforts—as well as the most forlorn nine-hole golf course we've ever seen—give the area an unfair perception of a place that's gone to the dogs. Actually, we did notice a lot of unleashed canines in Shelter Cove and all over Humboldt County. Softening that impression is **Mal Coombs Park,** a nifty, bluff-hugging promenade at the foot of Machi Road on the south end of town. Here

LAMB LIPS OF OBLIVION: HANGING WITH THE HUMBOLDT HIPPIES

Once we crossed into Humboldt County from the south, a change occurred in more than just the natural landscape. We followed U.S. 101 inland as it pulled northward away from the coast and entered the cathedral-like dusk of redwood groves. En route, we passed roadside attractions like the **Grandfather Tree,** the **Famous One-Log House** (constructed from a single 2,100-year-old redwood log), the **Legend of Bigfoot,** and **Confusion Hill.** The last of these was the home of the world's largest redwood chainsaw sculpture and something called the "Gravity House."

Finally we arrived in Garberville, the jumping-off point for **Shelter Cove** and the main provisioning center for southern Humboldt County. Although this town of 2,000 provided a welcome place to chill out and refuel, we were struck with an unmistakable sense of 1960s déjà-vu. The town center was spotlessly clean, primarily because a lanky dude with a long gray beard and wool cap yanked tightly over his wildly matted hair was a one-man litter patrol, stooping every few feet to pick up a cup, cigarette butt, can, or wrapper.

Down the street, we found a music shop that carried Freak Brothers Comics. Then we ventured into a used record haven where we bought a mint copy of the Steve Miller Band's first album, *Children of the Future,* and some comic books. We perused an art co-op, a bead shop, several cafés (one entirely vegetarian), a restored cinema, a recycled clothing store, a head shop, and a gift emporium that "introduces your inner child to your outer adult." Wares included Native American hand drums, prayer sticks, medicine staffs, tie-dyed shirts, and sarongs. The wafting odor of patchouli and musk conjured memories of rock festivals from our misspent youth. In short, Garberville was a flashback to all the things we loved about the 1960s.

Two miles down the road in Redway, however, we came upon some children of God

---

you'll find informational kiosks, a boat launch, some tidepooling and rock-fishing opportunities, and a miniature, singularly photogenic lighthouse. Blink your eyes and you'd think you were in a Maine fishing village.

Shelter Cove does have a marina, several small motels, a couple of restaurants, all the solitude you can stand (and then some), and black-sand beaches that will dazzle and delight the intrepid beachcomber.

For more information, contact the Shelter Cove Information Bureau, 412 Machi Road, Shelter Cove, CA 95589, 707/986-7069, www .sheltercove-lostcoast.com.

BEACHES

Shelter Cove is the site of some lengthy black-sand beaches, including a 24-miler known as **Black Sands Beach.** On a sunny day you'll rarely find a beach more beautiful than Black Sands Beach. The sand is coarse and coal-colored. The beach is extremely wide by the parking lot on the northwest edge of town and then narrows up the coast. It continues north for 24 miles and is firm enough for good hiking. In fact, the beach links up with a trail through the Sinkyone Wilderness to form the nearly 50-mile Lost Coast Trail, which runs from Usal Campground to the Mattole River. If you're in search of plentiful solitude on a true wilderness beach, you can do no better than this stretch of the Lost Coast.

Closer to the center of Shelter Cove, a short trail in the vicinity of Pelican's Landing restaurant leads to **Little Black Sands Beach,** a favorite of locals. The sand is volcanic in origin, hence the color.

Our own favorite beach, and a shoo-in

who'd taken a wrong turn on their way back to the garden. What we saw and sniffed almost literally made us sick. Three people – a dude and two chicks – were jammed into the front seat of a Subaru station wagon tightly packed with provisions; mounds of gypsy peasant attire, seemingly ripped off from a Goodwill bin; a few stringed instruments, pressed against the back window; and other assorted, unidentifiable junk. The vehicle was so full a fly couldn't have fit inside. Not that a self-respecting fly would have wanted to be interred therein.

We walked within five feet of the car, encountering a stench so profoundly overwhelming that it knocked us back on our heels. The nauseating odor was a mix of sweat and secretions, and the slight tangy hint of scented candles, with which they no doubt illuminated their squatters' digs. It was like a roving homeless encampment, a latter-day version of the Joad family without the dignity. They were the most unkempt human beings we'd ever seen who weren't passed out across an urban sewer grate. The car's engine groaned with the effort to depart the gas-station convenience store, wobbling as if on its last legs. As they passed us, the driver – who wore a filthy, rainbow-hued cap and looked completely out of his gourd – gave us a wordless nod, as though we were kindred spirits from the Humboldt backwoods. Did we really look that bad after two months on the road?

On the way out to Shelter Cove, we tuned in to the local community radio station, which featured a dopey New Age priestess reciting and interpreting inane poetry by an understandably obscure feminist writer. The first words we heard were "moccasin flowers." The woman chirped verses of poetry in a beatific hippie-chick monotone while we laughed hysterically. She droned on about lilies and roses and snake skins, about the "crackling lick of the sun" and "lamb lips of oblivion."

As we came over the crest of Paradise Ridge, we turned off the bad poetry and focused on the heart-thumping 2,000-foot plunge toward Shelter Cove and the Pacific Ocean. This was an epic poem unfolding before our eyes and, thankfully, no words were needed. The figurative essence of patchouli oil was quickly replaced by the acrid, real-life odor of overheating brakes. We were, like, freaking out, man.

for our all-time Top 10 list, is **Dead Man's Beach.** This gem sits at the south end of town, beginning at the Shelter Cove Deli and Campground. Park in one of the lots by the marina, follow the cement boat-launch ramp down to the beach, and walk south along the broadly curving cove past some spectacular scenery. Cliffs rise behind the narrow strip of sand, while breakers thunder ashore. Small waterfalls cascade over the sheer rock face to the beach below. Surfers are fond of the waves at Dead Man's Beach about a half mile south of the boat launch. They'll drive their four-wheel-drives (everybody's got one here) along the beach, tide permitting. The tidal exchange can be extreme—as great as eight feet—so consult a tide chart before attempting to walk or drive. We don't want anyone to wind up dead on Dead Man's Beach.

A recent 1.5-mile hike on Dead Man's Beach suggested how the place got its name. We chugged south across relatively stable and wide sand; through seaweed, dead starfish, and dead crab-snarled patches; and over rounded pebbles and boulders. We turned around when a headland blocked our path. Retracing our steps became an adventure we hadn't expected. The tide was coming in and the formerly wide beach left us barely two feet of walking space that wasn't under water—and nowhere to scramble against a sheer cliff face.

As we hustled out of there, we talked out our script idea for a film called *The Lost Coast,* a teen-exploitation film à la *Blair Witch Project.* In our script, a pack of spoiled rich kids on a beach-camping adventure get trapped against a cliff by a rising tide and find themselves at the mercy of rogue waves, a deadly winter tempest, and angry rattlesnakes. (Yes, we were told to watch out for rattlesnakes, which sun themselves on the beach.) Our can't-miss Hollywood pitch would sound something like this: "Eight hiked in but only three walked out—and just one of them could talk about the unspeakable horrors they encountered . . ."

We've obviously spent too much time in Los Angeles.

Simply for viewing purposes, there's also **Seal Rock National Conservation Area,** where the watery mammals can be spied bobbing in the surf among the folds of a protective cove at the north end of town.

❶ DEAD MAN'S BEACH

🚶🏃 **BEST (**

Location: from Shelter Cove, take Shelter Cove Road to Machi Road, which leads to Lost Coast Landing marina; hike south from marina
Parking/Fees: free parking lot (Shelter Cove Deli and Campground)
Hours: 24 hours

Facilities: none
Contact: Arcata District Office, King Range National Conservation Area, 707/825-2300

❷ SHELTER COVE

🔼

Location: Garberville/Redway exit off U.S. 101 in Garberville, follow Briceland-Thorne Road to Shelter Cove Road, continue to Shelter Cove
Parking/Fees: free parking lots; camping fees $15-25 per night
Hours: 24 hours
Facilities: concession, restrooms, showers, and picnic tables
Contact: Shelter Cove Deli and Campground, 707/986-7474

❸ LITTLE BLACK SANDS BEACH

Location: Wave Drive at Dolphin Drive, just north of Point Delgada in Shelter Cove
Parking/Fees: free street parking
Hours: 24 hours

Dead Man's Beach

© PARKE PUTERBAUGH

Facilities: none

Contact: Arcata District Office, Bureau of Land Management, 707/825-2300

4 BLACK SANDS BEACH

 BEST (

Location: from the end of Beach Road in Shelter Cove to the mouth of the Mattole River

Parking/Fees: free parking lot

Hours: 24 hours

Facilities: none

Contact: Arcata District Office, Bureau of Land Management, 707/825-2300

ACCOMMODATIONS

We put in for the evening at the **Shelter Cove Beachcomber Inn** (412 Machi Road, 707/986-7551, $). It's a small place—just six individual units—that's comfortable and functional. Rooms include a kitchen, TV, and enough beds to sleep up to six people. If you're arriving late, the proprietress may (as she did for us) leave a note on the office door, informing you which unit in which to rest your weary head. She collected the tariff the next morning. Can you imagine such a thing happening at a Ritz-Carlton?

A step up in modernity and price is offered at **The Tides Inn** (59 Surf Point, 707/986-7900, $$). Another lodging alternative is **Shelter Cove Marina and Campground** (492 Machi Road, 707/986-7474, $). RV campers venture out here to land's end to deep-sea fish, dive for abalone, and enjoy the solitude.

COASTAL CUISINE

The on-premises deli at the **Shelter Cove Deli and Campground** (492 Machi Road, 707/986-7474, $) serves the best fish 'n' chips we've ever had. Lest this sound like hype, let us assure you we were skeptical.

"Are the fish 'n' chips any good?" we queried without conviction while peering hungrily at the sandwiches (particularly the hearty Surfer's Sub) in the deli case. "Are you kidding?" the matron behind the counter responded. "We caught it fresh this morning."

Indeed, the generic term "fish 'n' chips" just can't do justice to the basket of fried black snapper that had been pulled from the ocean

© PARKE PUTERBAUGH

Black Sands Beach

hours earlier. They'll ask if you want tartar or cocktail sauce with it, but a splash of lemon or malt vinegar will do just fine.

King Range National Conservation Area

The King Range National Conservation Area is a massive tract of public land administered by the federal Bureau of Land Management (BLM). It occupies 52,000 acres in southwest Humboldt County, extending for 35 miles between Whale Gulch and Mattole River, and up to six miles inland from the Pacific Ocean.

Indeed, there is little in this corner of the county that isn't federal land—just the town of Shelter Cove and some scattered holdings in the mountains.

For more information, contact the Arcata Resource Area, Bureau of Land Management, 1695 Heindon Road, Arcata, CA 95521, 707/825-2300, www.ca.blm.gov/arcata/king_range.html.

BEACHES

Black Sands Beach is a lengthy strand of coarse, pitch-black volcanic sand that runs without interruption from Shelter Cove to the Mattole River, a sandy, 24-mile traipse. This primeval North Coast beach is backed by the jagged peaks of the relatively youthful King Range. The jump in elevation from sea level to 4,086 feet—the height of King Peak, the highest point on any shoreline in the continental United States—occurs in less than three miles.

Backpacking is possible both along inland mountain trails and on the beach. For a thrilling experience, hike the Lost Coast Trail north from Shelter Cove for exactly five miles, then pick up Buck Creek Trail, which runs for 2.5 miles in a zigzagging northeast direction before approaching the 3,290-foot summit of Saddle Mountain. Back at sea level, you'll pass offshore rocks inhabited by sea lions, seals, and marine birds. Other sights include the remains of shipwrecks and the abandoned Punta Gorda Lighthouse.

DRIVING THROUGH THE KING RANGE

Again tempting fate, we decided to brave another gravel road along the North Coast. This one extended from Shelter Cove north through the King Range. Though the road surface was easier to navigate than the rutted mess on Usal Road through the Sinkyone Wilderness, this drive was in some ways even more treacherous.

The rainy season had just ended, but rivulets still appeared across the gravel and dirt surface. We had to ford six streams along the aptly named Wilder Ridge Road. In places, the entire undercarriage of our car was under water and our curses filled the otherwise still air. At some of these crossings, we'd have to stop and size up the situation. Should we try to rumble over the big dry rocks on the left and maybe dent the car beyond repair, or should we opt for the flatter, wetter course on the right and possibly plunge over the side to our deaths?

The Bureau of Land Management (BLM) map we consulted included a couple of notes in tiny script about "RVs and trailers not advised for this section." Crucial information on all of the roadside signs had been obscured by bullet holes, presumably the work of inebriated backwoods maniacs. The map's straight line from Shelter Cove to Honeydew gave no indication of the countless switchbacks and zigzags that sent gravel, rocks, and dust flying in our wake. All in all, it was a white-knuckle experience and a royal pain in the chassis. But, ah, such views!

Camping is permitted anywhere on the beach. **Mattole River Beach** is the site of a primitive campground. Away from the beach, BLM maintains four campgrounds in the King Range: **Wailaki** (nine campsites) and **Nadelos** (six), which lie east of Shelter Cove near the Humboldt-Mendocino County line, and **Tolkan** (nine) and **Horse Mountain** (nine) in the southern third of the park, about 1.5 miles inland.

May–October are the best months to come, as the torrential rains of winter tend to wash out roads and dampen spirits. Some parts of the King Range get deluged with 200 inches a year of precipitation. It is, in fact, a rain forest.

We'll repeat a warning echoed throughout the Northern California chapters but particularly urgent along the Lost Coast. Be mindful of encroaching tides while walking the beach. High tides can strand unwary hikers in coves, and sleeper waves—individual waves of extraordinary size that appear out of nowhere—can wash the unsuspecting out to sea. Carry and consult tide tables, available at local stores, and never turn your back on the ocean.

Honeydew and Petrolia

They paved the state road that leads to Honeydew! You can now make the incomparable drive from Shelter Cove to Honeydew, continue on to Petrolia, and finally land in beautiful Ferndale. This is one of the great scenic drives in America (75 miles), passing forests, farmland, mountains, meadows, and beaches. Honeydew (population 500) and Petrolia (population 400) are small towns—dots on the map, really—out in the middle of nowhere. Mailboxes are few and far between. The road is narrow and uneven but drivable—and almost all of it is paved.

To get to Honeydew from the highway, take U.S. 101 to the Mattole Road turnoff and then drive west 21 miles to Honeydew. Petrolia lies 15 miles northwest of Honeydew along the same road. At Petrolia, you can either pick up Lighthouse Road, which runs out to Mattole River Beach, or proceed up to Ferndale via Mattole and Wildcat Roads.

To get to Honeydew from Shelter Cove—which is what we did while working our way up the coast—takes a bit more effort. From Shelter Cove Road, the turnoff to Honeydew is about halfway between Shelter Cove and Garberville. The opening up of the area to more than four-wheel-drive vehicles was, as we understand it, the culmination of an effort to drive some particularly tenacious pot growers out of the area.

Cultivators of "Humboldt Gold," they were—and maybe still are—as entrenched in these mountains as rattlesnakes and would go to extremes to keep the outside world at bay. Stories are told of shots fired at unfamiliar vehicles and booby traps strung across hiking trails to scare off narks and even innocent folks enjoying the outdoors.

A government campaign called Operation Greensweep employed helicopters, infrared photography, and armed troops to identify hemp fields in the mountainous wilderness and flush the growers from their lairs. You can still see the remnants of the pot growers' anti-authoritarian ilk here and there, gazing at passersby with reddened eyes from the front porches of listing houses. More unsettling is the sight of abandoned cars pocked with bullet holes by the side of the road. It's probably not a good idea to look too hard or linger too long around here.

In the way of services, there's a general store at Honeydew and a handful of places to fill up with gas, food, and supplies in Petrolia. And whatever you do, please drive slowly for the sake of the quail who scoot across the roads around here. We very nearly wiped out a brood of the sweet critters after rounding a curve near Petrolia.

For more information, contact the Garberville-Redway Area Chamber of Commerce,

782 Redwood Drive, P.O. Box 445, Garberville, CA 95542, 707/923-2613 or 800/923-2613, www.garberville.org.

BEACHES

There's one prominent, accessible beach worth mentioning in the area. At a fork in the road, Petrolia lies to the right along Mattole Road, while Lighthouse Road follows the Mattole River until both give out at the ocean. At the mouth of the river is an enormous, wild wonder of a beach. The locals have fenced in the parking lot with gigantic driftwood trunks, silvery and skeletal, to discourage ATVs (all-terrain vehicles) from tearing up the beach. A colorful mural of a beach scene includes this legend: "We love our beach. Please respect it. Beaches are important to everyone." Attached is a notation that **Mattole River Beach** (a.k.a. Lighthouse Road Beach) has been "adopted by the Mattole Union 3rd, 4th, and 5th grades."

The beach is a wide delta formed by the gravelly river. On one late-summer day, we watched the wind blowing up fearsome whitecaps. No sane person would go near this churning surf—that is, if anyone could even get to it in the teeth of a fierce, nonstop wind. The lone beach bum (besides us) was fighting to keep a kite under control. Chalk up one more wild and beautiful beach for the seemingly endless coast of Northern California.

Mattole River Beach falls within the King Range National Conservation Area. You are welcome to throw up a tent or park a camper in the open area out here, though facilities are primitive: chemical toilets, picnic tables, and fire rings. You must bring your own water. A so-called "iron ranger" has been installed, and you're asked to pay $5 a night on the honor system. This is the northern end of the Lost Coast Trail, which extends down to Shelter Cove and Sinkyone Wilderness State Park.

With the exception of the detour out to Mattole River Beach, much of the drive described so far circumnavigates the interior of southern Humboldt County. But for a six-mile stretch along **Mattole Road,** just north of Petrolia en route to Ferndale, it follows the coast at sea level. And what a marvelous stretch of coast. It takes in gigantic sea stacks, extruded basalt formations on the inland side, a sea that's colored foam-green close to shore and metallic blue farther out, and dark-sand beaches that beg to be walked. This is cattle country, and the bovine grazers cross the road at their leisure, looking quizzically at passing cars.

Along the shoulder, some dirt turnouts have been provided. Most folks content themselves with an appreciative glance at the scenery from a parked car, but at one turnout a worn path leads out to the wind-whipped beach for those made of sterner stuff. One rock formation at the center of this coastal tableau resembles an ocean liner, and a series of sea stacks lend a ghostly appearance to this extension of the Lost Coast. The accessible shoreline ends at **Cape Mendocino,** where a gumdrop-shaped outcropping slams the door on any further coastal access until Ferndale's Centerville Beach. A quick snapshot of the beach is about all you'll want to take here, although the benign madness of surfers was once again driven home to us, as we saw two wave riders toting surfboards across the headland toward the sea just south of Cape Mendocino.

The ocean views, particularly as Mattole Road makes a sudden perpendicular turn and dizzying ascent toward Ferndale, are the equal of any on the coast.

5 MATTOLE RIVER BEACH

Location: end of Lighthouse Road, at mouth of Mattole River, five miles west of Petrolia
Parking/Fees: free parking lot; camping fee $5
Hours: 24 hours
Facilities: restrooms and picnic tables
Contact: Arcata Resource Area, Bureau of Land Management, 707/825-2300

© PARKE PUTERBAUGH

Mattole River Beach

6 MATTOLE ROAD ACCESSES

Location: pull-offs along Mattole Road along the coastline between Lighthouse Road and Ferndale
Parking/Fees: free roadside parking
Hours: 24 hours
Facilities: none
Contact: Arcata Resource Area, Bureau of Land Management, 707/825-2300

7 CAPE MENDOCINO

Location: Mattole Road at Cape Mendocino, 15 miles southwest of Ferndale
Parking/Fees: free roadside parking
Hours: 24 hours
Facilities: none
Contact: Arcata Resource Area, Bureau of Land Management, 707/825-2300

ACCOMMODATIONS

In Petrolia the **Lost Inn** (Mattole Road, 707/629-3394, $$) is a great getaway for those who love being well off the beaten path. The inn features a three-room suite that includes a glassed-in porch and private garden where guests can sit among the flowers and marvel at the splendid isolation. The Lost Inn is one block from Petrolia's General Store and seven miles from Mattole River Beach.

You can also camp in the sand at **Mattole River Beach.** The price is right ($5 a night), though you must bring your own water or treat the non-potable water from the campground spigot.

COASTAL CUISINE

Duck into the **Hideaway Bar and Grill** in Petrolia (Mattole Road, 707/629-3533, $) for a burger, taco, and/or brew. It's at Lindley Bridge, on the banks of the sparkling Mattole River.

Ferndale

Hollywood descended upon Ferndale in the summer of 1994 to film the medical thriller *Outbreak,* a frankly terrible film about a fatal airborne virus and a race against time to stop it. There hadn't been such excitement in Ferndale since the 1992 earthquake. The streets of this village (population 1,400) of restored Victorian homes and step-back-in-time stores were jammed with trailers and film people. Celebrity sightings were reported all over Ferndale, and crew and cast—including Dustin Hoffman, Carrie Fisher, and Rene Russo—were coincidentally staying at the same inn, in nearby Eureka, where we were booked.

The locals were eating it up and so were we, having come to Ferndale while researching the first edition of this book. Movie magic happened again in 2001, when *The Majestic,* starring Jim Carrey and Hal Holbrook, was filmed in Ferndale. The chameleon-like town was this time transported back to 1951, with a plot involving an old movie house on the main drag.

Normally, life in Ferndale moves at a snail's pace. It's like stepping back a century. You think we're exaggerating? Virtually every structure in Ferndale looks much like it did 100 years ago. They are cleaned, polished, and freshly painted right down to their elaborately carved woodwork. The whole town has been designated a State Historical Landmark (Number 883, to be exact).

In the beginning, the primary source of income in these parts was dairy farming, and the local creameries were so productive that Ferndale became known nationally as "Cream City." The wealth that flowed from the cows' udders built ornate town-and-country residences, nicknamed "Butterfat Palaces," in the 1880s.

Today, Ferndale—which touts itself as "the prettiest painted place in the America Northwest"—has got everything for a weekend getaway. You can bed down at the Gingerbread Mansion, among the most celebrated bed-and-breakfast inns in Northern California, and walk a mere block downtown to dine or stroll from shop to shop.

Ferndale is packed with antiques stores, art galleries, old-fashioned candy emporiums—just the sort of shopping district you'd expect to find in a town swathed in Victoriana. It also has a quaint little museum, run by the local historical society, whose exhibits run the gamut from earthquake seismometers to a reconstructed barbershop.

On the earthquake front, there was a whole lotta shakin' goin' on in Ferndale and environs in 1992. Between 11:06 A.M. on April 25 and 4:18 A.M. on April 26—a span of only 17 hours—three separate earthquakes rocked Cape Mendocino. Buildings were toppled and fires broke out in the villages of Scotia and Rio Dell. The first (and largest) temblor measured 7.1 on the Richter scale and had its epicenter five miles southeast of Petrolia. The second and third came during the night, measured 6.6 and 6.7, and were centered off the coast. Geologists rank them among the most powerful quakes ever to shake California, with an acceleration force measured at 2.25 G. For comparison's sake, the Loma Prieta earthquake that hit San Francisco and Santa Cruz in 1989 had a peak acceleration force of only 0.646 G.

For more information, contact the Ferndale Chamber of Commerce, P.O. Box 325, Ferndale, CA 95536, 707/786-4477, www.victorianferndale.org/chamber.

BEACHES

Centerville Beach County Park, five miles west of Ferndale via Centerville Road, is a sizable swath of sand bordered by farmers' fields. The expansive beach is covered with driftwood and deep, soft, dirty-brown sand. We watched thunderous breakers roll ashore on an otherwise calm July afternoon. It is a great beach for barefoot strolling up the coast, beyond where the eye can see in the salty mist kicked up by the roiling surf. Upon returning, we noticed that the only footprints in the sand were ours.

It is desolate out here. En route to the beach one day we braked in front of an old, abandoned farmhouse—not to wax nostalgic about cobwebs on the porch swing, but because a flock of geese chose that moment to waddle across the road.

If you know where to look around here, there's an object lesson in what will eventually happen to beachfront real estate on a young, geologically active coastline (i.e., California). The road leading up to the empty naval facility near Centerville Beach offers a pullout and a magnificent overlook. Study the abandoned roadway, much of which has crumbled into the ocean. Look at the retreating cliffs. Imagine your beach house perched precariously on the edge. As one of our geology professors used to say, "If you can see the ocean, it can see you, too."

8 CENTERVILLE BEACH COUNTY PARK

Location: end of Centerville Road, five miles west of Ferndale
Parking/Fees: free parking lot
Hours: 24 hours
Facilities: restrooms
Contact: Humboldt County Parks Department, 707/445-7651

ACCOMMODATIONS

The Gingerbread Mansion (400 Berding Street, 707/786-4000, $$$) is the most striking example of Ferndale's elegantly playful Victorian style. Its eye-popping brown and orange exterior, fanciful wedding-cake moldings, and storybook gardens have made it the best known and most photographed of Ferndale's structures. Owner Ken Forbert is an antiques hound, dating back to his college days in San Francisco. Many rooms have authentic claw-foot bathtubs on raised platforms; one has an old Victorian fainting couch perched beside it.

The ambience is gracious yet relaxed. Tea is served at four in the afternoon. Breakfast is a real undertaking, served at long, decorated tables at the appointed hour with an egg dish, fruit, pastries, homemade granola, and coffee or tea.

The historic **Victorian Inn** (400 Ocean Avenue, 707/786-4949, $$$) was built in 1893, and has been restored with vintage fixtures,

as well as retaining the original 14- to 16-foot ceilings in each room.

Another B&B that lets visitors steep themselves in the Victorian flavor of the town is **Shaw House Bed and Breakfast Inn** (703 Main Street, 707/786-9958, $$). Constructed by the founder of Ferndale in 1854, the inn is the oldest house in Ferndale; it was modeled after Hawthorne's *House of the Seven Gables*. The six attractive guest rooms have private baths, and the gardens, gazebo, and fish pond lend visual interest to the one-acre property. In the morning, guests greet the day with an elaborate breakfast spread.

COASTAL CUISINE

Curley's Grill (400 Ocean Avenue, 707/786-9696, $$$) occupies the ground floor of the historic Victorian Inn. Curley's California bistro cuisine has made it a hot spot to eat in town, with a menu that ranges from burgers, steaks, and fries to grilled polenta and shrimp Dijon.

Loleta

Loleta is a sweet morsel of a town that will make you say "cheese." Wedged between Ferndale and Eureka, it is in the heart of Humboldt's dairy-farming country. Situated in a valley on the fertile delta of the Eel River, it provides an idyllic setting in which cows graze and time passes slowly.

The little hamlet's calling card is the **Loleta Cheese Factory** (252 Loleta Drive, 707/733-5470). You can tour the facility and sample its wares: award-winning Monterey Jack and cheddar cheese, among others. A gift shop sells local wines and cheeses. You can also order their unsurpassable cheeses online at www .loletacheese.com.

Beyond the draw of its cheese factory, Loleta is notable mainly for the access that it and the neighboring pin-sized communities of Fernbridge and Beatrice provide to the ocean, bay, and river.

For more information, contact the Loleta

Chamber of Commerce, P.O. Box 327, Loleta, CA 95551, 707/733-5731.

BEACHES

Anglers will go batty over the rock jetty at **South Spit and Jetty** (reached from Beatrice via Table Bluff Road), the bayfront beaches of **Crab County Park** (off Cannibal Island Road, four miles west of Loleta), and the delta of the Eel River (accessible from a maze of roads out of Ferndale).

For a panoramic stroll, take the Hookton Road exit from U.S. 101 to **Table Bluff County Park.** Parking is free and hiking trails along the bluff afford nice views of the ocean, which batters the South Spit of Humboldt Bay, and the Eel River Delta. The Eel River, federally classified as a Wild and Scenic River, is California's third largest, carrying 10 percent of the state's annual runoff.

9 CRAB COUNTY PARK

Location: from Loleta, take Loleta Drive to Cannibal Island Road and continue west to the park

Parking/Fees: free parking lot

Hours: 24 hours

Facilities: restrooms

Contact: Humboldt County Parks Department, 707/445-7651

10 SOUTH SPIT AND JETTY

Location: from U.S. 101 10 miles south of Eureka, take Hookton Road to Table Bluff Road; at Table Bluff County Park turn north on South Jetty Road and drive to jetty

Parking/Fees: free parking lot

Hours: 24 hours

Facilities: none

Contact: Humboldt County Parks Department, 707/445-7651

Eureka

Eureka is a Greek word meaning "I've found it!" It's also the state motto of California, one that derives from Gold Rush days. In years past, were your opinion of the city based solely on first impressions made as you entered from the south on U.S. 101, you might be convinced that the meaning of Eureka had changed to "They've lost it!"

While the retail corridor at Eureka's south end hasn't exactly improved—in fact, they've built another depressing mall to add to the noxious mix of billboards, guide wires, smoke and fumes from paper mills, and motels offering cheap rooms—the city itself has worked hard to restore itself to what it once was: the pearl of the North Coast. In the process, it has begun to work its way into our hearts. We, in fact, have come to love the place. Had Ulysses S. Grant been stationed here today, he'd never have written, as he did in 1854 while at nearby Fort Humboldt, "You do not know how forsaken I feel here!"

Located 284 miles north of San Francisco, Eureka is nestled on the shores of Humboldt Bay—the second largest enclosed bay in California. The visual madness at the south end of the city is an unfair gauge of Eureka's true charm. Keep pressing north on U.S. 101 and until you round a bend in the road (Broadway) that reveals the real Eureka—the city that merits a cry of "I've found it!"

For a quick and helpful orientation, stop by the **Eureka Chamber of Commerce** (2112 Broadway) or the **Humboldt County Convention and Visitors Bureau** (1034 Second Street). You will be directed to historic **Old Town,** the bayfront area that extends from C to M Streets between 2nd and 3rd Streets. Old Town has been diligently restored and is surprising in its size and vitality. Armed with a Eureka Visitor Map, you'll willingly leave the wheels behind and re-enter the age of foot traffic. And you'll get a sense of how Eureka must have been in the 1850s, when it was the most important port city between San Francisco and Seattle.

A principal site on this walking tour is the **Carson Mansion** (2nd and M Streets), which the Smithsonian calls "one of the most exuberant houses built in 19th-century America." Part Victorian and part fairy-tale castle, the house was constructed for William Carson, the lumber baron whose redwood empire opened up the North Coast. The mansion was erected during lulls in the logging season by the boss man's own lumberjacks and was completed in 1885, after three years of labor. The crazy-quilt array of gables, columns, and ornamental woodwork somehow manages to blend together. Look and admire, but don't enter. It's a private men's club called the Ingomar now.

Across the street from Carson's former digs is the **Pink Lady** (202 M Street), another example of money's-no-object Victoriana. The gaudiness of this Pepto Bismol–pink Queen Anne–style structure may give some viewers visual indigestion. Once a wedding gift from Carson to his son, the Pink Lady is now an art gallery featuring the work of local artists.

Many other structures in and around Old Town have historic value, representing the period when Eureka was "King of the Pacific Northwoods" and "Heart of the Redwood Empire." The town got its start in 1850 from the fallout of the Gold Rush. The diggings were slim along the Trinity and Klamath Rivers, but the felling of redwoods provided plenty of work for able-bodied men. Within four years of its founding, Eureka was home to seven sawmills, and 140 schooners were kept busy carting away lumber from Humboldt Bay to points south. In their leisure time the lumbermen came to Eureka, a brawling, boozing, and brothel-filled respite from the monotony of sawing logs.

In some ways Eureka is still King of the Northwoods. Despite the imperilment of the lumber trade all over the northwest, logging has endured in Eureka, though overforesting and cheap lumber from Canada and overseas have taken a toll. If you listen to the lumberjacks, Redwood National Park has denied job-hungry timbermen the largest chunk of

what trees remain in Humboldt County. It's this area, in fact, that provoked former president George Bush Sr.'s specious remark about "being neck deep in spotted owls."

Though logging is on the ropes, fishing nets a great deal of income in these parts. Humboldt Bay is the center of the region's recreational and commercial fishing. Thirty million pounds of fish are harvested annually in Eureka. The fleet docks at the **Woodley Island Marina,** just across the Samoa Bridge from Old Town on Highway 255. Eureka's water-related history can be explored at the **Humboldt Bay Maritime Museum** (1410 2nd Street, 707/444-9440), a collection of nautical artifacts housed in a replica of the oldest house in town (circa 1854).

The city has also turned to the arts to fill the economic void. Arty types have begun flocking here in growing numbers. Their reasons are varied, but most have grown tired of where they came from and simply want to escape. Eureka, like Mendocino, is set in a gorgeous and nondistracting environment where artists feel free to actualize their visions. Galleries, bookshops, and cultural events thrive in this city, thanks in part to the enlightened presence of Humboldt State University in nearby Arcata.

Much of the original art and crafts on display in the local galleries are quite striking and unique to this locale, as transplanted, university-trained artists blaze new trails in landscape painting while local folk artists continue to produce their remarkable handmade wares.

The best site for the latter is the **Romano Gabriel Wooden Sculpture Garden** (317 2nd Street), a menagerie of politically charged pieces created by local sculptor Romano Gabriel over a 30-year span; most were created out of discarded crates and boards. Other examples reflect the spirit of place even more closely. The history of the region's ecology and its indigenous peoples can be explored at the **Clarke Memorial Museum** (240 E Street, 707/443-1947), which has a world-class collection of Native American basketry and artifacts. These items are housed—safely, one can be certain—in the historic Bank of Eureka Building (circa 1912).

The restored Carnegie Library Building is now home to the **Humboldt Cultural Center** and the **Morris Graves Museum of Art** (636 F Street, 707/442-0278), a world-class venue for painting, sculpture, and performance arts. Also, a rich benefactor pumped money into restoring the waterfront, which forms the northern edge of Old Town Eureka. The result pulls the scenic harbor into the city's ongoing resurgence.

The city hosts a two-day **Blues by the Bay** festival each July that attracts some big names. These days, Eureka gives us anything but the blues. As we entered the city on our latest go-round, the local FM station was playing a long piece of sitar music—with nary a commercial break or explanation—and as we left two days later, the same station was playing recent releases by local bands, including an all-woman group whose name we wish we'd caught. But we'll be back, we can assure you of that.

For more information, contact the Eureka Chamber of Commerce, 2112 Broadway (U.S. 101), Eureka, CA 95501, 707/442-3738 or 800/356-6381, www.eurekachamber.com; or Humboldt County Convention and Visitors Bureau, 1034 Second Street, Eureka, CA 95501, 707/443-5097 or 800/346-3482, www.redwoods.info.

BEACHES

The easiest way to explore the Humboldt Bay area is by boat. The best tour is the **Humboldt Bay Harbor Cruise,** operated by the Humboldt Bay Maritime Museum. A narrated, 75-minute tour aboard the M/V *Madaket*—the oldest operating passenger ship on the West Coast, circa 1910—leaves regularly from the foot of C Street, off Waterfront Drive (707/444-9440). Woodley Island Marina is a great viewing station for harbor seals and egrets, and the adjoining promenade has a number of interpretive placards.

Nearby Samoa Island is the site of **Samoa**

Dunes Recreation Area, a broad expanse of dune fields and beaches at the southern tip of the North Spit, which angles down from Arcata. It is one of the projecting fingers that enfold and protect Humboldt Bay. A 300-acre parcel of Samoa Dunes belongs to the Bureau of Land Management, while Humboldt County maintains a boat launch and a bayside campground here.

A stiff breeze often blows off the water, which sculpts the dunes into sloping, windswept shapes. The berm is sufficiently hard-packed to allow for jogging or easy beach hiking. Kite flying, collecting driftwood, and bird-watching are popular activities out here. At low tide the remains of the USS *Milwaukee,* a destroyer beached in a 1917 rescue attempt, can be seen offshore.

The south spit of Humboldt Bay, a four-mile-long strand that ends at a jetty built in 1891, is maintained by the county. Access for cars is limited and a key is needed from the Humboldt County Parks Department (707/445-7651) to enter the locked gate. Bluffs to the south can be explored on foot at Table Bluff County Park. A local organization called **Friends of the Dunes** (P.O. Box 186, Arcata, CA 95518, 707/444-1397) publishes an excellent brochure that exhaustively covers the beaches and dunes along Humboldt Bay.

11 SAMOA DUNES RECREATION AREA

Location: from Highway 255 in Eureka drive to North Spit, turn left on New Navy Base Road and follow to Samoa Dunes

Parking/Fees: free parking lot; camping fees $12 per night

Hours: 24 hours

Facilities: concession, restrooms, showers, and picnic tables

Contact: Arcata Resource Area, Bureau of Land Management, 707/825-2300; Samoa Boat Launch County Park, 707/445-7652

RECREATION AND ATTRACTIONS

- **Bike/Skate Rentals:** Sport & Cycle, 1621 Broadway, Eureka, 707/444-9274
- **Boat Cruise:** Humboldt Bay Harbor Cruise, Humboldt Bay Maritime Museum, Eureka, 707/444-9440
- **Ecotourism:** Arcata Marsh and Wildlife Sanctuary, I Street, Arcata; Humboldt Redwoods State Park, U.S. 101 and Highway 254, Weott, 707/946-2264
- **Lighthouse:** Trinidad Head Lighthouse, Trinidad
- **Marinas:** Bob's Boat Basin, Bay Street, Trinidad Harbor, Trinidad, 707/677-3625; Woodley Island Marina, 601 Startare Drive, Eureka, 707/443-0801
- **Pier:** F Street Dock, foot of F Street, Eureka
- **Rainy Day Attraction:** Humboldt Bay Maritime Museum, 1410 2nd Street, Eureka, 707/444-9440
- **Shopping/Browsing:** Old Town (from C to M Streets and 1st to 3rd Streets), Eureka
- **Sportfishing:** King Salmon Charters, 1137 King Salmon Avenue, Eureka, 707/442-3474; Trinidad Bay Charters, Trinidad Harbor, Trinidad, 707/839-4743
- **Surf Shop:** Humboldt Surf Company, 817 H Street, Arcata, 707/822-2680
- **Vacation Rentals:** Trinidad Vacation Rentals, Trinidad, 707/677-0246

ACCOMMODATIONS

The celebrated **Hotel Carter** (301 L Street, 707/444-8062, $$$) actually embraces three properties: the 23-room hotel itself; **Carter House,** the awesome Victorian home that sits catty-corner to the hotel at 1033 3rd Street; and **Bell House,** the 1890 cottage adjacent to Carter House (call 707/445-1390 for information on the latter two properties).

Hotel Carter is a yellow neo-Victorian with large rooms and modern amenities. Some come equipped with whirlpool baths. A nightly wine-and-cheese hour is provided for guests.

The classy comforts and warm glow of Hotel Carter are unrivaled on the North Coast.

Carter House, the most traditional of the three buildings, was built in 1982 as an exact replica of the Murphy House, a beloved Victorian inn in San Francisco that was razed to make room for a high-rise. It's an attractive place where the wooden beams and walls in the living area receive and reflect sunlight in a way that is positively magical. As in the adjacent Bell House, wine and cheese are set out every evening, followed by tea and cookies a few hours later. Both homes have large living areas and a common kitchen for the use of guests, along with TVs in each room. Our room at Bell House broke with the code of Victoriana and was decorated in a contemporary mode.

The **Eureka Inn** (518 Seventh Street), a sprawling, 150-room Tudor revival–style inn, opened in 1922 as a symbol of Eureka's booming fortunes. It has since been designated a National Historic Place. The historic inn went to foreclosure in 2004 and to auction soon thereafter. As of press time, it had not been re-opened for business. However, such a venerable landmark deserves to be preserved and visitors should at least admire its architecture.

A setting of elegant Victoriana can be found at **Abigail's Elegant Victorian Mansion** (1406 C Street, 707/444-3144, $$). Yep, that's really the name of this restored, four-room mansion, a National Historical Landmark built in 1888. Not the least of the inn's charms are the enthusiasm and dedication to detail of its owners.

COASTAL CUISINE

Restaurant 301 (301 L Street, 707/444-8062, $$$), the dining room at Hotel Carter, is among the most distinctive on the North Coast. The list of appetizers and entrées is kept to a manageable one page, but the items constantly change. Those ingredients not grown at Hotel Carter's own garden three blocks from here are acquired from local farms, and the seafood on the menu is as fresh and local as it can be.

Creatively sauced grilled items, such as

mushroom-crusted Pacific cod with potato puree and mushroom essence, is a specialty. The wine list is extensive, and Hotel Carter's owner, Mark Carter, genially hovers about the premises, gladly sharing his encyclopedic knowledge of California wines. A house pastry chef creates a short list of nightly desert temptations, as well. The restaurant includes itself in the "slow food" movement, so prepare to make an evening of it here.

Wherever you dine in Eureka, whether it be in a historic old building or a seafood grill by the water, your surroundings are as vital to the experience as the food itself. Both seem tailored to remind you of the town's hardworking past. Take the **Samoa Cookhouse** (Samoa Road, 707/442-1659, $$). Across the bridge on Samoa Island, it is the last surviving cookhouse in the West. Food is served camp style, and though the words "all you can eat" are never mentioned in the literature, you won't leave here hungry. There's no menu. One set price. You eat what you're served.

It starts with salad you toss yourself in a large bowl. This is quickly followed by soup, ladled from a black kettle. Gigantic hunks of bread appear next. Then come bowls full of peas, kidney beans, and mashed potatoes and gravy, trailed closely by fried chicken, sliced ham, roast beef, or whatever else the main courses happen to be. You'll be offered seconds. Order iced tea, and an entire pitcher materializes. Warm apple pie baked in a big metal pan was placed on the table at the end of our meal.

Actually, this is exactly how and where lumberjacks were fed in Eureka's timber heyday. Prices for lunch and dinner are low, given the quantities of food served. Dinner costs $15.45 (adults), $5.95 (kids 8–11) and $3.95 (kids 5–7); while lunch is $11.95 for adults, $4.95 for kids 8–11, and $2.95 for kids 5–7. As one old-timer told us, "If you leave here hungry, it's yer own dang fault."

Lazio's Seafood (327 Second Street, 707/447-9717, $$) is another local institution. It's been serving seafood since 1944, though the family's roots in the fishing industry go back as far as 1889, when Lorenzo Lazio started a wholesale fish operation in San Francisco. Lazio's is filled with seafaring paraphernalia. Take your time poring over the extensive menu, which includes crab legs Lazio and salmon cannelloni. Don't be afraid to order plain old broiled seafood, as it's fresh enough not to need sauces. The broiled salmon is especially fine. Pacific oysters on the half shell are plump and gamy. They are something of an acquired taste—and we acquired a taste for them.

A newer arrival on the seafood scene is the **Sea Grill** (316 E Street, 707/443-7187, $$), an Old Town eatery that posts a lengthy list of catches and ways you can have them prepared (sautéed, grilled, charbroiled, broiled, poached, deep-fried). The fact that sturgeon and Dungeness crab were both on the menu caused us to perk up.

Cafe Marina and Woodley's Bar (Woodley Island Marina, 601 Startare Drive, 707/443-2233, $$) serves decent food along with the best view in town: across the bay onto Old Town Eureka from Woodley Island. A listing of available seafood items is handed to customers along with a regular menu. You can't go wrong with grilled or broiled petrale sole or ling cod. **Weatherby's Seafood** (1906 Fourth Street, 707/442-0683, $$) is another reliable restaurant, popular with locals.

Finally, having loved the punk-rock band the Ramones, how could we ignore a bakery and café called **Ramone's** (209 E Street, 707/445-2923). You can start your morning at one of three Ramone's restaurants in Eureka. (There are Ramone's franchises in Arcata and McKinleyville, too). Another good morning port o' call is **Humboldt Bay Coffee Company** (535 Third Street, 707/444-3969), also in Old Town.

NIGHTLIFE

Civilized imbibers should head to the smoke-free **Lost Coast Brewery** (617 4th Street, 707/445-4480), which specializes in micro-brewed beers (especially English-style ales), plus the usual complement of sports-bar amenities: pool tables, dart boards, big-screen TVs, lunch and dinner items, and happy hour specials.

Club West (535 5th Street, 707/444-2624) is a North Coast approximation of a Southern California dance club. What you get is an eclectic mix of folks who've come to shake their booties. You'll see lonesome cowboys in Western wear, working girls dragging on cigarettes from barside perches, college kids who have wandered over from Arcata, well-groomed yuppies, and straights and gays (depending on the night) out to make the scene.

Arcata

Humboldt Bay merges with Arcata Bay at its northern end, where the waters balloon inland. It would be an ideal setting for a small town. But Arcata is not all that small a town, and its fairly nondescript outlying development runs in a rough L shape around the top of the bay and up U.S. 101.

Like Eureka, Arcata got its start as a depot and base (then called Union) for the Trinity Mountain gold fields. But it quickly became a booming lumber town, and evidence of its past lines the bayshore—warehouses, factories, slag heaps, smokestacks, and the like. Close by these industrial eyesores are the boxlike homes of the employees. On a gray day it resembles a scene from George Orwell's *The Road to Wigan Pier,* an impassioned study of British working-class life.

Arcata, however, is not just another burned-out mill town. Rounding the bend away from the factories, visitors discover an attractive city in transition and an impressive oasis of higher learning. Humboldt State University is one of the oldest branches of the state system. The school's academic emphases include forestry management, environmental science, and marine biology. When these programs bloomed on university campuses nationwide, Humboldt State was an early and much-imitated model. The school is also oriented toward the arts,

as one glance at the bohemian student body will make clear (lots of black clothing, facial piercings, and plaid flannel shirts). All in all, the students have found that nexus between nature and creativity.

The forest is never far from their hearts. The school teams are called the Lumberjacks, and the dorms are the Jolly Giant Commons. The campus itself is on a large, grassy knoll east of the highway. Its 140 acres afford ample space for 7,500 students to roam, and the public is invited to enjoy the excellent natural-history museum.

The university pumps new blood and innovative ideas into the town. One is the **Arcata Community Forest,** a 600-acre preserve of second-growth redwoods that is the only city-owned forest in the state. Ten miles of trails crisscross the forest for the benefit of hikers, bicyclists, and horseback riders. Another great idea is the **Arcata Marsh and Wildlife Sanctuary,** a 75-acre haven created from a former landfill and industrial site (at the foot of I Street). It's been transformed into one of the state's best bird-watching areas, with a hiking trail running through the many different ecosystems (bay, marsh, pond, foothills, streams). This restored marsh is fertilized by the Arcata sewer system—an ingenious way of recycling waste into something green and clean.

The town of Arcata (population 17,000) also beams with pride over its local artists, whose work is showcased on the premises of many businesses and along a self-guided Mural Tour. Arcata's most intriguing cultural event is the annual **Kinetic Sculpture Race,** which takes place in May. It's difficult to explain the rules or point of this extravaganza, a 35-mile cross-country race that passes over hills and dunes from Arcata to Ferndale. To qualify, all vehicles must be navigable pieces of sculpture. Beyond that, whether it's pumped, paddled, or pushed doesn't matter. The Kinetic Sculpture Race, going strong for more than 40 years now, is emblematic of the town's spirit.

An open-air farmers market takes over Arcata Plaza on Saturdays from June to October.

TOP UNIVERSITIES ALONG THE COAST OF CALIFORNIA

From south to north, here are some of California's finest colleges. They're great institutions of higher learning, as well as terrific places to cultivate a tan and improve your surfing skills.

- **University of California at San Diego** (UCSD) – This institute of higher learning perches atop cliffs overlooking Black's Beach in La Jolla.

- **Long Beach State University** – The students party hard and sun themselves in Belmont Shore (a.k.a. "Horny Corners").

- **Pepperdine University** – We include this college overlooking Malibu, despite the fact that it hired right-wing "special prosecutor" Ken Starr, who did his biased best to topple President Bill Clinton.

- **California State University, Channel Islands** – Opened in 2002, it is the first branch of the state university system in Ventura County. Great architecture, pleasant setting, just three miles from beaches.

- **University of California at Santa Barbara** (UCSB) – Actually, it's in Goleta, which is Santa Barbara's lesser neighbor, but the surf spots are hard to beat.

- **California Polytechnic State University** – Study engineering in the near-perfect community of San Luis Obispo. All the Poly dollies and dudes hang out at Avila Beach.

- **University of California at Santa Cruz** – UCSC is about as "alternative" a state university as you'll ever find, and it's a short drive to the popular beaches of Santa Cruz and Capitola.

- **University of California, Monterey Bay** – This latest addition to the state system occupies part of decommissioned Fort Ord, above Monterey. It doesn't get much nicer than the Monterey Peninsula.

- **Humboldt State University** – Bring plenty of flannel to this retro-hippie school in Arcata. Strong in environmental science. Back to the future!

The fresh local produce, flowers, and baked goods were enough to make us want to sink roots in lovely Arcata.

For more information, contact the Arcata Chamber of Commerce, 1635 Heindon Road, Arcata, CA 95521, 707/822-3619, www.arcata-chamber.com.

BEACHES

The beach nearest Arcata is as hard to fathom as a piece of kinetic sculpture. The 90-acre **Mad River Beach County Park** is aptly named—at least the "mad" part—because this is an area where sand and sea, rivers, creeks, and lagoons come together with an almost primitive fury. The roads are a little out of whack, making the whole experience seem rather mad in the British sense as well.

To get to Mad River, take the Janes Road exit from U.S. 101, then turn right on Heindon Road, left on Iverson Road, and right on Mad River Road. It sounds simple on paper, but all are farm-hugging backroads. Try to follow the signs, and bear in mind that getting there is half the fun.

At the end of Mad River Road, the beach overwhelms lucky visitors with its size and beauty, extending in both directions as far as the eye can see. The undertow is treacherous, but the fishing is good. Three different kinds of angling are available in this unusual mix of habitats: salmon and steelhead fishing in the river, surf casting for perch, and net fishing at night. A boat launch and an equestrian staging area are also provided. We watched gaggles of anglers standing around driftwood fires while their unattended poles stood upright in the sand. We also saw some very wet animal companions sloshing happily around the creeks that one must cross on this wide beach to get to the ocean. Oh, yes: Memorize the route you took out here or you may make an unintentionally lengthy side trip through the dairy lands west of Arcata, as we did.

The **Lanphere-Christensen Dunes Preserve** is just south of here, at the west end of Lanphere Road. It's part of the Mad River Slough. No fee is charged for access to either.

12 MAD RIVER BEACH COUNTY PARK

Location: Janes Road exit from U.S. 101 north of Arcata, follow signs to the park
Parking/Fees: free parking lot
Hours: 24 hours
Facilities: restrooms and picnic tables
Contact: Humboldt County Parks Department, 707/445-7651

ACCOMMODATIONS

The **Hotel Arcata** (708 Ninth Street, 707/826-0217, $$) is a good, centrally located place to drop your suitcase. Unveiled as the town plaza's showplace in 1915, the Hotel Arcata was one of the finest inns of its size on the coast. But when a financial downturn hit town in the 1980s, the hotel fell into disrepair. The likable three-story structure has been restored to its original grandeur and has been augmented with hot tubs, sauna, and swimming pool.

At the north end of town, on Valley West Boulevard (off U.S. 101), a strip of motels and restaurants bear dependable franchised names. The **North Coast Inn** (4975 Valley West Boulevard, 707/822-4861, $$), a former Travelodge, has comfortable, well-maintained rooms and a health-club area whose centerpiece is a large heated indoor pool from which we got more than our money's worth.

COASTAL CUISINE

Try **Abruzzi** (780 7th Street, 707/826-2345, $$$) for Italian and **Folie Douce** (1551 G Street, 707/822-1042, $$) for creative fine dining. The nice thing about both places is that they have less expensive options as well as high-end dinner entrées, if you're looking to economize. Folie Douce, for instance, serves wonderful, wood-fired pizzas. Abruzzi, in the basement of a block-sized building known as Jacoby's Storehouse, specializes in fresh fish and pasta dishes inspired by the cuisine of Abruzzi in central Italy. Should you want something simpler—appetizers, sandwiches, or grilled fare—the **Plaza Grill** (780 7th Street, 707/826-0860, $$) is upstairs from Abruzzi, on the third floor.

NIGHTLIFE

The heart of Arcata is its plaza, a square formed by G, H, 9th, and 10th Streets. Here you'll find the restored Arcata Hotel; restaurants, cafés, and coffeehouses; record stores; a village green where Arcatans sit cross-legged and contemplate the passing scene; and an assortment of bars and nightclubs. There's live music at **The Alibi** (744 9th Street, 707/822-3731), **Plaza Grill** (780 7th Street, 707/826-0860), and **Jambalaya** (915 H Street, 707/822-4766). A few more options: **Humboldt Brewery** (856 10th Street, 707/822-2739) for local microbrews and **Sacred Grounds Organic Coffee Roasters** (65 Ericson Court, #3, 707/822-3711) for righteous java fixes.

On weekends students have been known to engage in a colorful ritual known as "ring around the plaza." It involves downing a beer, a margarita, or some other libation in each of the bars that surround the plaza. Of course the 21 and over drinking age greatly reduced the number of legal contestants. In summer, nightlife is notably less frenetic. Still, there's the delightful **Minor Theatre** (1001 H Street, 707/822-5177), a lavishly restored 1915 structure with three screens showing current, classic, and art films. And even those who have rightfully grown sick of professional baseball and its steroid-pumped stars should check out the **Humboldt Crabs,** a semipro team that plays its home games at **Arcata Ballpark** (9th and F Streets, 707/826-2333). The Crabs play 24 home games a year, and tickets cost $7 for adults, $5 for seniors, and $3 for kids. Go Crabs! Starting in 2009, the Humboldt Crabs joined a new league, the Sierra Baseball League, and will play approximately 50 games a year.

By the way, there's also a semipro team called the Humboldt Steelheads, mainly consisting of former college players and local athletes. They play 31 games a year themselves and serve as a kind of farm club for the Crabs.

McKinleyville

Once called Minorsville—after Isaac Minor, owner of the local general store—the town of McKinleyville took its present name in 1901, after President McKinley's assassination. McKinleyville fancies itself a holdover from the Wild West.

It has a tradition in which horses have the right of way, and the annual **Pony Express Days Celebration** (first weekend in June) is the biggest event in town. Behind the macho image, however, McKinleyville offers little to the traveler, lying well off the highway and consisting mainly of drab dwellings and a homely town center.

For more information, contact the McKinleyville Chamber of Commerce, 1640 Central Avenue, McKinleyville, CA 95519, 707/839-2449, www.mckinleyvillechamber.com.

BEACHES
West of McKinleyville is the first spot above San Francisco where U.S. 101 runs directly

beside the ocean. Two beach access points sit right off the highway. **Clam Beach County Park** is a sizable swath of sand with a hundred RV and tent sites for camping, and picnicking areas at its north and south ends. Getting to the beach is no easy matter. A short path over tall dunes reveals a broad expanse of mostly flat, grassy dune fields extending to the ocean. A small creek must be forded, and logs have been laid across it for that purpose.

Solitary figures press against the wind as they make their way across the desolate landscape. Though you can comb for driftwood and dig for razor clams, the real appeal of Clam Beach is for equestrians. Hitching posts have been provided at various spots along Hammond Trail, which runs along the coast from Mad River north to Murray Road. Dogs enjoy charging around the stark expanse. We saw a pair of Saint Bernards emerge from the creek soaked and sandy but happy. Clam Beach takes its name from the once plentiful Pacific razor clams fund here. It is a nesting area for the threatened Western snow plover.

Little River State Beach is more of the same: 112 undeveloped acres of dunes, driftwood, and broad, hard-packed sand. At the north end, Little River trickles through the sand, creating a boundary between this beach and Trinidad's Moonstone Beach.

13 CLAM BEACH COUNTY PARK

Location: from U.S. 101 north of McKinleyville, take the Clam Beach exit and follow to the park
Parking/Fees: free parking lot; camping fee $8 per night
Hours: 24 hours
Facilities: restrooms and picnic tables
Contact: Humboldt County Parks Department, 707/445-7651

14 LITTLE RIVER STATE BEACH

Location: U.S. 101 at Little River, four miles north of McKinleyville
Parking/Fees: free parking lot
Hours: 24 hours
Facilities: none
Contact: Little River State Beach, 707/488-2041

ACCOMMODATIONS

A late-model **Holiday Inn Express** (3107 Concorde Drive, 707/840-9305, $$) is within a mile of Clam Beach County Park.

COASTAL CUISINE

Typical of McKinleyville's Old West mindset is **Niveen's** (2145 Central Avenue, 707/839-3417, $), a large, friendly restaurant with an American flag proudly waving out front. The menu is as large as the room: burgers, steaks, Mexican, Italian, little of this, little of that.

On the edge of town, **Six Rivers Brewery** (1300 Central Avenue, 707/839-7580, $$) serves home-brewed beer and homemade burgers. Surprisingly lively, it offers live music and provides the most palatable nightlife in these parts.

Trinidad

Summer in Trinidad is like spring in many other places. The air is crisp and clean, the sky is a sweet baby blue, the wind blows like March's proverbial lion, and the ground is resplendent with wildflowers. It never really heats up to a summer swelter in Trinidad (or anywhere on the North Coast, for that matter).

Actually, the phrase "here in Trinidad" is misleading. Trinidad is not so much a single place as a jumble of hills, headlands, coves, and coastline. As a result, there is a tremendous diversity of beaches and headlands to explore,

making Trinidad an ideal place to bring hiking shoes and beach blankets.

Trinidad and its natural harbor were first sighted by the Portuguese explorer Sebastian Cermeno in 1595. He did not come close to land for fear of the pointed rocks. The Tsurai (pronounced CHER-eye) who inhabited the region were no doubt glad he kept his distance. On June 11, 1775, they weren't so lucky: The Spanish explorer Don Bruno de Hezeta anchored in the bay, came ashore, and promptly declared that all his eye beheld belonged to Spain. It was Trinity Sunday when he staked his claim, and thus the area was called *La Santisima Trinidad.*

During Gold Rush days, the town boomed, reaching a population of 3,000 and serving as the seat of what was then Klamath County. Trinidad flourished again as a mill town in the 1870s, and once more in the 1920s as a whaling port. When each of these industries bit the dust, so did the town. The current population is around 500.

Today, Trinidad is home to artists and lovers of solitude. With its abundant natural beauty—stunning and variegated beaches, coves, headlands, and offshore rock formations—it is not hard to understand Trinidad's appeal to those with creative temperaments and folks with a yen for the outdoors. Captain Beefheart, who is not a seaman but an avant-garde artist and musician, has lived in the vicinity for many years. We always hope that we might run into this culture hero of ours on the streets of Trinidad, but alas, no sightings yet.

For more information, contact the Greater Trinidad Chamber of Commerce, P.O. Box 356, Trinidad, CA 95570, 707/677-1610, www.trinidadcalif.com.

BEACHES

The beaches begin north of the Little River Bridge, along Scenic Drive. Starting at the river, **Moonstone Beach** sits below what was formerly Merryman's restaurant and is now Moonstone Grill (100 Moonstone Beach Road, 707/677-1616). A small spur,

Trinidad Head Lighthouse

Moonstone Beach Road, runs down to the beach, where there is parking in a gravel lot.

Moonstone Beach falls under county jurisdiction, and it's popular with an eclectic mix of beachgoers. On the large, sandy delta over which the Little River meanders before meeting the sea, it's studded with sea stacks. Families picnic on the beach behind the rocks, which afford protection from the wind. Kids swim and play in the shallow creek waters, which are safer and warmer than the ocean. Surfers hungrily eye the waves that form off the point. We even saw a bicyclist pedaling on the hard-packed sand.

Moving north on Scenic Drive, we found a hidden treasure at **Houda Point.** Thanks to the Humboldt North Coast Land Trust, public access has been provided here, though there is only limited roadside parking. Still, if you negotiate the somewhat shaky series of staircases down to the water, you will find a visual paradise. Just offshore is Camel Rock, a humped outcrop that is home to the largest breeding colony of Leach's petrel in California, as well as a nesting area for gulls, cormorants, and black oystercatchers.

Moving up Scenic Drive, three more named beaches lie along the five-mile stretch between Moonstone Beach and the in-town shopping area. **Luffenholtz Beach, Baker Beach,** and **Indian Beach** are fan-shaped beaches between eroding headlands. The best beaches are often the hardest to reach, and Indian Beach is a case in point. We never did figure out how to get down to it, but it makes quite a photo op from the road high above it. A giant, gumdrop-shaped sea stack parts incoming waves before they reach the beach. The walls of crashing water wrap around the rock from opposite sides and then meet at a perpendicular angle on the beach. We've never seen anything quite like it.

Luffenholtz Beach has a marked parking area on Scenic Drive, and a sign points to a beach-access trail. Unfortunately, the original path has been declared off-limits. Another trail has been carved into the bluffs a few hundred yards up the road—which means walking along one-lane, cliff-hugging Scenic Drive, with its hidden curves and vehicles that come hurrying around them. Be careful.

In town, a natural harbor has been formed by **Trinidad Head,** a formidable seamount that has withstood the sea's pounding over countless millennia. An inviting calm-water beach occupies one edge of the harbor. There's a large parking lot, outlined by discarded boat tires, an old seafood restaurant (the 1953-vintage Seascape), bait shop, and boat launch. The trailhead for paths leading up and around Trinidad Head lies at the far end of the lot.

Trails encircle the monolith, with dead-end spurs shooting off to vista points along the way. Stay on the main path—named the Tsurai Trail—proceeding in a counterclockwise direction, and you can hike the whole thing in under an hour. Benches are strategically placed along the way to allow walkers to savor the views. Even when the area is shrouded in fog, you can sit and listen to sea lions barking like foghorns in the distance. At the top of Trinidad Head, a concrete cross commemorates the explorers who landed here. There's a giant Coast Guard satellite dish, too. The trip back down is an easy jaunt along a gravel road that meets smooth asphalt near the bottom.

On the ocean-facing side at the base of Trinidad Head is a beach where we ate an impromptu lunch of smoked salmon and albacore. We purchased it just up the road at Katy's Smokehouse (740 Edwards Street, 707/677-0151), which dispenses some terrific smoked fish.

A trail leads from here to **Trinidad State Beach.** Alternatively, you can park closer, at the lot just above the beach, and hike down a well-graded trail. In either case no entrance fee is charged. Butting up against Trinidad Head at the south end and roaming north for a mile, it's a fairly lengthy strand for this tortuous part of the coast, especially when low tide allows beachgoers to meander from one cove to another. Watch the sea carefully, though, and keep track of tides. An unwary walker can easily get trapped in a cove or sea cave with no route out, as the tide can turn quickly. This is no joke. We walked to a couple of coves on wet sand. Five minutes later, the same cove beaches were a half foot under quickly rising water.

One of the most popular beaches in the area is **College Cove.** It's been known for years as a clothing-optional beach, especially at the south end. If nudity is indeed an option, no one was exercising it on the warm summer weekend that we ventured out. It's a gorgeous cove that's plenty wide at low tide, reachable from a gravel parking lot via trails leading into the woods. The trail at the south end leads to **College Cove South** (about half nude) and the trail at the north end leads to **College Cove North** (largely clothed). The trail to the latter descends 130 steps to the beach. The south trail eventually connects with Trinidad State Beach, passing through fern canyons and Sitka spruce forests that are cool and dark even at the height of summer.

At College Cove one can sunbathe, play volleyball, or just walk and wade along the water. Total immersion, however, is only for the young and hardy (or foolhardy), in our estimation. The tidal exchange here is fairly extreme, as a comparison between low tide and the uppermost watermark in the sand attests. Waves buffet the cliffs at their bases during stormy winter months. Let the beach hiker beware.

15 MOONSTONE BEACH

Location: from Main Street in Trinidad turn south on Scenic Drive and follow to Moonstone Beach Road, which leads to beach
Parking/Fees: free parking lot
Hours: sunrise-sunset
Facilities: none
Contact: Humboldt County Parks Department, 707/445-7651

16 HOUDA POINT

Location: half mile north of Moonstone Beach on Scenic Drive in Trinidad
Parking/Fees: free limited roadside parking
Hours: sunrise-sunset
Facilities: none
Contact: Humboldt North Coast Land Trust, P.O. Box 457, Trinidad, CA 95570

17 LUFFENHOLTZ BEACH

Location: from Main Street in Trinidad, turn south on Scenic Drive and drive two miles; trails lead to beach
Parking/Fees: free roadside parking
Hours: sunrise-sunset
Facilities: none
Contact: Humboldt County Parks Department, 707/445-7651

18 BAKER BEACH

Location: from Main Street in Trinidad, turn south on Scenic Drive and drive one mile; trails lead to beach
Parking/Fees: free roadside parking
Hours: sunrise-sunset
Facilities: none
Contact: Humboldt North Coast Land Trust, P.O. Box 457, Trinidad, CA 95570

19 INDIAN BEACH

Location: from the intersection of Edwards and Main Streets in Trinidad, follow marked trailhead to Indian Beach
Parking/Fees: free roadside parking
Hours: sunrise-sunset
Facilities: none
Contact: Humboldt North Coast Land Trust, P.O. Box 457, Trinidad, CA 95570

20 TRINIDAD HEAD

Location: west end of Edwards Street in Trinidad
Parking/Fees: free parking lot
Hours: 7 A.M.-5 P.M.

Facilities: concession and restrooms
Contact: Trinidad Harbor, 707/677-3625

21 TRINIDAD STATE BEACH

Location: from Main Street at Stagecoach Road in Trinidad follow signs to beach
Parking/Fees: free parking lot
Hours: sunrise-sunset
Facilities: restrooms and picnic tables
Contact: North Coast Redwoods District, California State Parks, 707/445-6547

22 COLLEGE COVE

Location: from Main Street in Trinidad turn onto Stagecoach Road to dirt parking lot a quarter mile on left; trails lead to College Cove South and College Cove North
Parking/Fees: free parking lot
Hours: sunrise-sunset
Facilities: none
Contact: North Coast Redwoods District, California State Parks, 707/445-6547

ACCOMMODATIONS

North of town, any number of rustic lodges and attractive bed-and-breakfasts line Patrick's Point Drive along the five-mile stretch between Trinidad and Patrick's Point State Park. We have a favorite in each category.

The **Lost Whale Bed & Breakfast Inn** (3452 Patrick's Point Drive, 707/677-3425, $$$), only a half mile from Patrick's Point, is one of the few B&Bs that encourages families to stay. The inn was constructed in 1988, and since the owners were starting from scratch, they were able to build in extra reinforcement and soundproofing. Warm woods and comfortable furniture fill the common area downstairs.

Rooms at the back of the house have balconies and windows that look out over the ocean—as marvelous a view as you could hope to enjoy. Moms and dads have a bed of their own, while kids can ascend a ladder to a loft fitted with mattresses. A stairway leads several hundred feet down to the beach. Wine and snacks are served in the afternoon, and a hearty full breakfast is served each morning.

A fine old cottage court can be found at **Bishop Pine Lodge** (1481 Patrick's Point Drive, 707/677-3314, $$), where rustic cabins are spread on shaded grounds. Each unit has a full kitchen and a TV. A card informs you that the management will store your game and fish in the deep freeze. Moreover, "well-behaved pets" are welcome. The Bishop Pine Lodge is a restful, out-of-the-way spot charging reasonable rates. If longevity is any indication, this is the place to stay, as the Bishop Pine Lodge has been in business since 1927.

COASTAL CUISINE

The **Larrupin' Cafe** (1658 Patrick's Point Drive, 707/677-0230, $$$) is hard to miss, and once you've eaten here, you'll take pains to return. Painted a bold mustard yellow and trimmed in red, this former dwelling retained its homey feeling when it made the transition to gourmet restaurant. The menu is heavy on items grilled on the mesquite broiler (filet mignon, fish kabobs, pork ribs, etc.). A few dishes from the oven (chicken in phyllo pastry, spanakopita) are thrown in for good measure. The grilled garlic plate makes a terrific appetizer, and you also can't go wrong with barbecued oysters or mussels steamed in white wine and tomatoes.

A favorite entrée at Larrupin' is the hot 'n' spicy snapper: a sizable serving of Pacific red snapper coated in ground pepper and grilled to a turn. Portions are generous, but leave room for dessert; the chocolate pecan pie in hot buttered rum sauce is worth all the hiking you'll have to do the next morning to work off the calories. In August 2008, the Larrupin' Cafe celebrated its 25th anniversary.

Fresh seafood can be found at **Seascape Restaurant** (1 Bay Street, Trinidad Harbor, 707/677-3762, $$), beside the town's pier. It bustles with tourists and anglers, serving three meals daily. It's been here for over half a century, so they must be doing something right. **Moonstone Grill** (100 Moonstone Beach Road, 707/677-1616, $$), another seafood restaurant, looks out on one of the most picture-perfect locations on the California coast.

For lunch fixings, we headed to **Katy's Smokehouse** (740 Edwards Street, 707/677-0151, $$$), another Trinidad landmark, which has been selling popular smoked fish—such as king salmon, salmon jerky, albacore tuna, Alaskan halibut, Pacific cod, and even scallops—for over 60 years. The prices aren't cheap ($30 per vacuum-packed pound of smoked salmon, available for takeout or online order), but we snagged enough for $15 to sate our appetites. And it is very good.

Patrick's Point State Park

The prize gem among all the parks in Trinidad's vicinity is Patrick's Point State Park. The 640-acre park is worth exploring in its entirety, but especially be sure to get out to Agate Beach—a sandy treasure that ranks among California's most remarkable.

Camping at Patrick's Point is some of the finest in any of California's coastal parks. The 124 sites are large and private, shaded and protected by spruce, fir, red alder, and hemlock. A popular addition to the park is Sumeg, a re-created Yurok village that offers some virtual reality to go along with its artifacts. A visit to Patrick's Point State Park should be mandatory if you venture up this way.

BEACHES

Like most Trinidad-area beaches, the cliffs drop so steeply to **Agate Beach** that a long bank of stairs must be descended to get to it. The view from the top is worth savoring before heading down. Observe how the beach extends past the point where the cliffs give out, forming a sand bar that encloses Big Lagoon, just to the north. The lagoon is within **Big Lagoon County Park,** which offers a boat launch, picnic tables, and a tent/RV campground.

The hike from Agate Point to the end of Big Lagoon Spit is about three miles—and worth every footstep. Along this stretch of coastline, one can hunt for bits of agate and jade. The chances of striking it rich fall somewhere between slim and none, but the scenery is ample compensation. The cliffs overlooking Agate Beach are not completely vertical, which allows vegetation to grow on them. At the bottom a small creek empties onto the beach and seeps into the sand before reaching the ocean. The beach remains plenty wide throughout the tidal cycle during the calmer summer months. Winter brings storms that cause a seasonal narrowing.

Numerous sea stacks sit offshore from Patrick's Point, affording habitat to sea lions, whose barking fills the air day and night. Rock outcroppings found in the park's interior belong to an earlier generation of sea stacks, now high and dry due to geologic uplift. The largest stacks are Ceremonial Rock (287 feet) and Lookout Rock (250 feet). Trails lead to Mussel Rock, a stack that's barely connected to the mainland. Visitors can climb all over this unusual formation. Looking out to sea, observe the line of wave-formed ooze that follows the undulating shoreline.

23 AGATE BEACH

BEST

Location: from U.S. 101 five miles north of Trinidad, take Patrick's Point Drive exit and follow signs to the park
Parking/Fees: $6 entrance fee per vehicle; camping fee $20 per night, plus $7.50 reservation fee
Hours: 8 A.M.–sunset
Facilities: restrooms, showers, picnic tables, and visitors center;
Contact: Patrick's Point State Park, 707/677-3570

24 BIG LAGOON COUNTY PARK

Location: U.S. 101 at south end of Big Lagoon, seven miles north of Trinidad
Parking/Fees: $2 entrance fee per vehicle; camping fee $18 per night
Hours: 24 hours
Facilities: restrooms and picnic tables
Contact: Humboldt County Parks Department, 707/445-7651

Humboldt Lagoons State Park

You ask, What is a lagoon? We answer, A lagoon is a body of water produced from the combined action of wind and water. Ocean currents carry sand parallel to the coastline, and winds mold it into barriers that separate shallow near-shore coastal waters from the deep blue sea. Behind the barrier lies a marshy, landlocked wetland—to wit, a lagoon.

Humboldt Lagoons State Park, 13 miles north of Trinidad, offers camping and fishing opportunities galore at Dry Lagoon and Stone Lagoon. You might ask what's biting at the visitors center, though it's open daily only 10 A.M.–2 P.M.

This is an archeological resource area, and visitors are urged not to dig for or make off with artifacts. No problem—there's enough fishing to keep everyone occupied. Incidentally, various points along U.S. 101 through the area offer wonderful overlooks of the lagoon and the sandy, straight-edged bar that divides it from the sea.

BEACHES

The south end of Humboldt Lagoons includes the spit and a marsh known as **Dry Lagoon,** with four picnic tables and six walk-in tent sites.

The more intriguing section of the park is **Stone Lagoon,** a short distance north off

U.S. 101. The road down to it is a bumpy ride that makes a precipitous final dip. Picnic tables are nestled in thickets, and the parking lot is an unimproved gravel field. A former camp area has been eliminated. The camping that can be done at Stone Lagoon these days is at six environmental sites that can be reached by boat only.

For more information, contact Humboldt Lagoons State Park, 15336 U.S. 101, Trinidad, CA 95570, 707/488-2169, www.parks.ca.gov.

25 DRY LAGOON
🔺

Location: U.S. 101 at Dry Lagoon, 13 miles north of Trinidad
Parking/Fees: free parking lot; camping fee $12 per night, register at Patrick's Point State Park
Hours: sunrise-sunset
Facilities: restrooms and picnic tables
Contact: North Coast Redwoods District, California State Parks, 707/488-2169

26 STONE LAGOON
🔺

Location: U.S. 101 at Stone Lagoon, 14.5 miles north of Trinidad
Parking/Fees: free parking lot; camping fee (boat-in sites) $12 per night, plus $7.50 reservation fee
Hours: sunrise-sunset
Facilities: restrooms and picnic tables
Contact: North Coast Redwoods District, California State Parks, 707/488-2169

Freshwater Lagoon

Approaching Orick from the south, U.S. 101 descends a hill and rounds a turn, at which point you'll see an amazing site: Freshwater Lagoon. It's located just inside **Redwood National Park.**

Freshwater Lagoon is named for the pristine blue lagoon east of the highway. A Redwood National Park visitors center is located just above Freshwater Lagoon, before U.S. 101 takes a swing inland. (It had to be relocated because coastal erosion claimed the old road in places.) The center is a cubist-style building fashioned from weathered wood, with a walkway leading out to the impressively large Redwood Creek Beach.

Tell the staff what you have in mind—a short or long hike, viewing elk herds or redwood groves, camping in the backcountry—and they'll set you up with maps and advice. A stop here is a must if you're coming up from the south. Those traveling down from the north will likely want to stop at park headquarters in Crescent City, where you'll receive the same sort of orientation. We found the staff at both visitors centers to be helpful and knowledgeable.

They used to allow RV camping here, and an amazing centipede-like line of RVs would park along Highway 101 beside the lagoon. However, due to concerns about congestion they've eliminated overnight camping and Freshwater Lagoon is now accessible for day use only. It makes a nice spot to bring a picnic.

BEACHES

At **Freshwater Lagoon** you'll find a broad, sandy beach on one side of the highway and the lagoon and green hills on the other—not to mention the people-watching opportunities. Pulling out a folding chair and watching the world drive by is a popular pastime. A loyal fraternity of like-minded RV owners make merry all along the road's shoulder as far as the eye can see. Only in America.

A mile north of Freshwater Lagoon is **Redwood Creek Beach,** a gorgeous fan-shaped beach at the mouth of Redwood Creek, also within Redwood National Park. It makes for a great picnic spot.

For more information, contact the Redwood National Park, 1111 2nd Street, Crescent City, CA 95531, 707/464-6101, www.nps.gov/redw.

27 FRESHWATER LAGOON

Location: U.S. 101 at Freshwater Lagoon, three miles south of Orick
Parking/Fees: free roadside parking; camping $10 per night, register at Redwood Information Center, one mile north
Hours: 24 hours
Facilities: restrooms
Contact: Redwood Information Center, Redwood National Park, 707/464-6101

28 REDWOOD CREEK BEACH

Location: two miles south of Orick, off U.S. 101
Parking/Fees: free parking lot
Hours: 24 hours
Facilities: restrooms and picnic tables
Contact: Redwood Information Center, Redwood National Park, 707/464-6101

Orick

The tiny town of Orick falls outside Redwood National Park. To drivers along Highway 101, Orick appears as a string of gas stations, cheap motels, and roadside stands selling "Burl Slabs" and "Redwood Creations." These include huge rearing bears, steel-eyed eagles, and grizzled sea captains, which local artisans have carved using chain saws. At one stand, we saw a sign inviting travelers to Come See What We Saw.

For more information, contact the Orick Chamber of Commerce, P.O. Box 234, Orick, CA 95555, 707/488-2885, www.orick.net.

BEACHES

For the truly adventurous, a turnoff onto Hufford Road carries you out to **Orick Fishing Access,** at which point you've reentered **Redwood National Park.** The road quickly morphs into a bumpy one-lane ordeal of curves, hemmed in on both sides by barbed-wire fences to hold back grazing cattle.

At the end of the road is a gravel parking lot that looks out upon Redwood Creek's winding egress into the ocean. Anglers cast for salmon and steelhead in the diked waters here. They don't call Orick "Fisherman's Paradise" for nothing.

29 ORICK FISHING ACCESS

Location: end of Hufford Road, off U.S. 101, two miles west of Orick
Parking/Fees: free parking lot
Hours: 24 hours
Facilities: none
Contact: Redwood Information Center, Redwood National Park, 707/464-6101

ACCOMMODATIONS

You probably won't stay in Orick, unless you've got a wild hair to bed down at the "world famous" **Palm Motel and Cafe** (21130 U.S. 101, 707/488-3381, $), a humble but vaguely appealing roadside complex—motel, pool, restaurant, lounge—that's got character, not to mention an eye-catching mural.

Prairie Creek Redwoods State Park

One of the most beautiful beaches on the North Coast (and, therefore, anywhere), Gold Bluffs Beach lies inside the boundaries of Prairie Creek Redwoods State Park, which itself is surrounded by Redwood National Park. In other words it is a beach within a state park within a national park.

The state park is home to a herd of about 30 Roosevelt elk. They can be seen grazing by the side of the road, and signs warn when you're in an "Elk Crossing Area." Tune in 1610 AM to receive information about where best to spot the creatures and to learn the dos and don'ts of elk-watching. We learned, for instance, that these critters have chased people at speeds of up to 50 miles per hour and that "elks will not tolerate dogs."

The larger of two park campgrounds (Elk Prairie, 75 sites) is located inland, near park headquarters. There's also a campground on Gold Bluffs Beach. Sites are first come, first served and quickly disappear in the summer.

For more information, contact Prairie Creek Redwoods State Park, Orick, CA 95555, 707/465-7347, www.parks.ca.gov.

BEACHES

To get to **Gold Bluffs Beach,** take Davison Road, a spur off U.S. 101 three miles north of Orick that passes through a portion of Redwood National Park. It's a winding little passageway—narrow, unpaved, and hazardous—and trailers are prohibited. After four miles of bumping, bouncing, and shouting "Watch out for that van!" you're there. Park the car, get out, and take a deep breath.

Now exhale, relax, and look around. Steep sandstone walls rise behind the beach. Forested bluffs overlook the beach. The ocean's thrashing kicks up a mist that bathes the beach in ghostly, low-lying sheets of white. Waves break and roll slowly across the shore, pushing a line of sea foam ahead of them. The salt-and-pepper sand is flecked with gold specks that gleam brightly in the overwash.

The beach is a vast, desert-like expanse virtually devoid of humanity, unchoked by seaweed or litter. It extends farther than the eye can see in either direction. This is an ideal spot for kicking off shoes and walking along

the ocean's edge, ankle deep in the bracing seawater. An exhibit in the parking lot warns beachcombers to keep an eye out for sleeper waves, so be careful.

If you continue driving north along Gold Bluffs Beach, you'll reach Fern Canyon in four miles. There are good camping, hiking, beachcombing, and picnicking opportunities all along this stretch of coastal road. **Gold Bluffs Beach Campground** is a 25-siter at ocean's edge. A note to hikers: The Coastal Trail, which runs for roughly 30 miles from Orick to Crescent City, reaches a point on the north side of Prairie Creek Redwoods State Park, just above Butler Creek, that is passable only at low tide, so consult local tide tables if you're passing through from either direction.

The northernmost beach within Prairie Creek Redwoods State Park is one of the most secluded on the North Coast. **Carruthers Cove Beach** can be reached by walking north along the Coastal Trail from Fern Canyon. (A beautiful, 0.8-mile loop trail circles this flat-floored, steep-sided canyon, which itself is a spectacle not to be missed.) Alternatively, Carruthers Cove can be accessed from the north via the Carruthers Cove Trail, which leads to the beach from the cliff-hugging Coastal Drive. It's a narrow, isolated beach, and it's unlikely you'll see anybody there—all the more reason to seek it out.

We have one complaint about this otherwise splendid park. Davison Road really needs to be paved. It bears a heavy volume of traffic, which kicks up an unholy cloud of dust. This dust storm coats all vegetation in the vicinity. It also blinds drivers, chokes the throat, and irritates the eyes and lungs. If you are driving through here, travel no faster than the posted speed of 15 mph. You won't kick up as much dust, nor will you imperil your fellow drivers by forcing them over the edge when you meet on a curve, as very nearly happened to us.

To get to Prairie Creek Redwoods State Park from Orick, take U.S. 101 north for five miles, then take the left fork onto Drury Scenic

Parkway. Prairie Creek Visitor Center is one mile north. If you want to go straight to Gold Bluffs Beach from Orick, take U.S. 101 three miles north to Davison Road. Turn left and continue four miles to the beach.

Since our last visit, Prairie Creek Redwoods State Park has been designated a World Heritage Site and International Biosphere Reserve for its 265 animal species and 75 miles of hiking, biking, and nature trails.

30 GOLD BLUFFS BEACH

BEST (

Location: from U.S. 101 three miles north of Orick, take Davison Road turnoff and follow to the beach
Parking/Fees: $6 entrance fee per vehicle; camping fees $13-15 per night, plus $7.50 reservation fee
Hours: sunrise-sunset
Facilities: restrooms, showers, and picnic tables
Contact: Prairie Creek Redwoods State Park, 707/465-7347; visitors center, 465-7354

31 CARRUTHERS COVE BEACH

Location: from U.S. 101 five miles north of Orick, turn onto Drury Scenic Parkway/Old U.S. 101, drive seven miles and fork left onto Coastal Drive; at signs for Carruthers Cove Trail, park and hike to beach
Parking/Fees: free roadside parking
Hours: 24 hours
Facilities: none
Contact: Prairie Creek Redwoods State Park, 707/465-7347

High Bluff Beach

How about a little piece of Hawaii—in appearance, if not temperature—on the North Coast of California? Such is the look of magnificent High Bluff Beach, which lies below a cliff-hugging wonder known as Coastal Drive. To access the road from the south, turn onto Drury Scenic Parkway from U.S. 101 and then turn onto Coastal Drive. From

Gold Bluffs Beach

© PARKE PUTERBAUGH

the north, take Alder Camp Road—a right turn off U.S. 101 just south of the bridge over the Klamath River—which connects with Coastal Drive.

Coastal Drive runs for eight miles, alternating paved and unpaved sections. The road is not in the best condition, but the scenery is so spectacular that it's worth the effort. This road used to be U.S. 101, before washouts and erosion necessitated the highway's relocation. Breathtaking glimpses of the ocean below are found around every turn along Coastal Drive.

BEACHES

High Bluff Picnic Area and the beach below it are the overlooked gems of **Redwood National Park.** If nothing else, pause to take in the vista from the picnic area. Hardier souls will want to hike down to the beach itself. To reach the **High Bluff Beach,** one must walk for a half mile along a trail that passes through a cool forest before making a final descent in a series of switchbacks. A log ladder with a handrail of rope leads down to some planking that must be carefully negotiated. Then you're on muddy rocks, crawling

and crab-walking until a final heave-ho lands you on the beach.

The sand is soft, light brown, and volcanic in origin. Waves wash over footprints at high tide, giving the area a virgin, unvisited appearance every 12 hours. On a sunny day this secluded cove has the appearance of a hidden tropical paradise, lacking only palm trees and balmy water to complete the scene. It may be an illusion, but not such a far-fetched one if you're soaking up the sun's rays here on a warm, cloudless day—of which there are many from June through September.

32 HIGH BLUFF BEACH

BEST (

Location: from Highway 1 at Klamath River, turn west onto Alder Camp Road, follow to Coastal Drive and turn right to High Bluff Picnic Area; a trail leads to the beach
Parking/Fees: free parking lot
Hours: 24 hours
Facilities: picnic tables
Contact: Redwood National Park, 707/464-6101

High Bluff Beach

Klamath

One of the fundamental laws of physics, Heisenberg's Uncertainty Principle, may be applied to travel. A statement about the limited precision of scientific measurement, it says that at any given point in time, one can specify either the position of a physical particle or its momentum, but not both. Therefore, because one of the variables is unknown, its value could be anything. With this equation the physicist is telling us that nothing is impossible. Or, put another way, anything is possible.

The same holds true on the road. For instance, while driving the desolate North Coast of California, one might think it unlikely to come upon a 49-foot-tall rendering of Paul Bunyan standing in a clearing in the redwoods with Babe, his 17-ton blue ox, beside him. But this is no illusion. Paul and Babe are the gatekeepers for a tourist attraction called the Trees of Mystery.

Though hard to find, Klamath is a special place, one that physicists, mapmakers, tourists, and travel writers might all find baffling. It's everywhere and nowhere, diffused over a seven-mile stretch on both sides of U.S. 101; along the inland valleys, canyons, and glens of the Klamath River; atop coastal bluffs and on the beaches below; squirreled away in the dark, spooky forests.

There is no place that can be pointed to as the town center. It is difficult to say if the town is growing or dwindling, whether there is an actual town or just a scattering of RV parks, motels, restaurants, shops selling redwood knickknacks, salmon-jerky stands, and Trees of Mystery. In the case of Klamath, both position *and* momentum are unclear.

There's a good reason for this. The seemingly quiet, salmon-filled waters of the Klamath River conceal a terrible secret. Del Norte County is flood country, and a confluence of factors can turn the river into a raging monster. In 1964 the right—or terribly wrong—combination of factors occurred to create a perfect storm. A cold, wet winter blanketed the

surrounding mountains with a dense pack of snow and ice. Then a fast-moving storm front passed through, inundating the area with rain. Finally, warm, high winds melted ten feet of frozen precipitation in 24 hours, sending a 90-foot wall of water rushing down the canyon. With boulders and timber as battering rams, the flood wiped the unsuspecting town of Klamath off the map and out to sea.

Klamath was born in the mid-1800s during the fevered Gold Rush that swept California. It was a typical story of greed run amok in the wilderness. Mining camps sprang up along the Klamath River. The miners harassed and depleted the native Yurok population, while the riverbed became so silted with the detritus of their gold digging that the salmon stopped running. Klamath City was a thriving lumber port for most of this century, until the virgin forests were cleared. And then came the December 1964 flood, nature's angriest retort. No doubt the clearing of timberland contributed to the extreme runoff.

Before the flood Klamath was a highfalutin town, flush with prosperity when timber was king and the river was kind. In its heyday, 20 bars lined Klamath's rough-and-ready Main Street. The flood left nothing standing but a small church and the massive golden bears that greeted visitors at the edge of town. The U.S. Army Corps of Engineers cleared an area to rebuild Klamath north of the river, at an elevation five feet above the river's highest recorded level. But the citizens of Klamath, most of them anyway, never returned. The new town site is now occupied only by some mobile homes, and the original town remains utterly abandoned. The foundations of old homes and businesses have been overgrown by weeds and reclaimed by nature. As for the golden bears, pairs of them guard each end of the rebuilt U.S. 101 bridge over the Klamath River.

If Klamath is more of a bear than a bull these days, it's still an inviting place for visitors with an appreciation of serene, unspoiled nature. Between fishing the Klamath River, camping and hiking in Redwood National

TREES OF MYSTERY

Trees of Mystery celebrates the majesty of the coast redwoods and Sitka spruce that often grow to phantasmagoric shapes in this neck of the rain forest. Located 16 miles south of Crescent City and 360 miles north of San Francisco beside U.S. 101 in Klamath, Trees of Mystery is hard to miss, thanks to the gargantuan likenesses of Paul Bunyan and Babe the Blue Ox that hail passersby. It's a worthwhile operation – educational, informative, and environmentally responsible.

Before hiking the backcountry trails of Redwood National Park, take a crash course on tall trees at Trees of Mystery. It is a private redwood forest offering the Trail of Mysterious Trees and the Sky Trail. Redwoods are awesome to contemplate in any setting, but the stand at Trees of Mystery is especially impressive. Native Americans believed the area was haunted with evil spirits, causing trees to grow in crazy ways: twisting, turning, running horizontally, sprouting out of each other. It's really nothing more than Darwinism on overdrive, with trees employing ingenious adaptive and reproductive techniques in the quiet struggle for sunlight and survival. A highlight is the **Cathedral Tree** – nine redwoods growing in a perfect semicircle out of one root structure. As many as 40 weddings a year are held at this natural altar, and a crackly recording of Nelson Eddy crooning "Trees" plays continuously.

The main attraction is the **Trail of Tall Tales,** a half-mile walk that retells in wood the myths and legends of Paul Bunyan and his brawny logging crew. Kids, of course, will be in log heaven, but adults also will get something out of the 50 gigantic chainsaw sculptures and carvings, completed in a period of six months by a talented local artisan (now deceased) named Kenyon Kaiser. There is evidence of primitive genius in his work. His *Pooped Lumberman* is an American classic, kind of a Wild West version of Rodin's *The Thinker*.

The **Sky Trail,** a more recent addition, takes you to the treetops in a gondola. It carries riders nearly 600 feet into the redwood canopy. From its apex, you can see the ocean and redwoods in all directions.

Trees of Mystery is run by a family of Klamath natives with a scholarly appreciation for Native American culture. Their on-site museum houses the largest private collection of Native American baskets, pots, ornaments, and apparel in the West.

Trees of Mystery costs $14 for adults and $7 for children 4-11. It is open daily 8 A.M.-7 P.M. in the summer months and 9 A.M.-5 P.M. the rest of the year.

For more information, contact Trees of Mystery, 15500 U.S. 101 North, Klamath, CA 95548, 707/482-2251 or 800/638-3389, www.treesofmystery.net.

Park, and combing isolated beaches, there is plenty to do in and around Klamath. The number-one item on the agenda is fishing. The Klamath is the second largest river in California and one of the best in the world for landing silver and chinook salmon, steelhead trout, and sturgeon, drawing anglers from far afield during their yearly runs.

From the salmon's point of view, the anglers' mania is not all fair play. The mouth of the Klamath River used to be known as Suicide Row, because skiff-fishers would tie their boats together to form an impenetrable line against which the salmon, returning to spawn in their natal streams, didn't stand a chance. Because of dwindling salmon runs, the practice was outlawed.

An equally controversial method that yields similar results—catching so many fish that few survive to reproduce—has been the Native American practice of gill-netting. Monofilament nets are strung across the river, trapping the returning salmon in a mesh that forces their gills together, causing suffocation. Today,

526 THE REDWOOD EMPIRE

Yuroks alone employ gill-netting techniques for subsistence fishing in the Klamath, having won the right to do so in a controversial federal lawsuit in the mid-1980s.

Somehow, the fish continue to spawn in sufficient numbers to return year after year, though they are beleaguered by greedy outlaw anglers, Native American gill-netters, and various environmental affronts. There was a massive die-off of salmon and trout in 2002 and the numbers since then have been so low that the U.S. Fish and Wildlife Service may have to cancel or curtail some future fishing seasons on the Klamath River. For what it's worth, the 2007 Klamath River Basin sport-fishing quota was 10,600 Klamath River fall chinook salmon over 22 inches total length. In 2008, that figure doubled.

This will seriously impact the local economy, because many anglers roll into Klamath with little more than a hook, line, and sinker. Three thousand RV and tent campsites are hidden around Klamath, and they fill up quickly when word gets out that the salmon and steelhead runs have begun in late fall and early winter. Nestled around bends in the river, out of sight of the highway, the RV parks metamorphose into busy fish camps overnight. Klamath celebrates the fishing frenzy with a Salmon Festival on the last Sunday in June. They might not be celebrating much longer if they don't do a better job of managing the resource, however.

There's more to be caught from the waters around Klamath than salmon, as any surf caster can tell you. Shore anglers pull in ling cod, black snapper, cabezon, flounder, perch, smelt, and sea trout. Dungeness crab and razor clams are also taken. The Klamath area offers miles of sandy beaches and rocky shoreline that beg to be fished or hiked. The shoreline can also be admired from vista points on the highway.

In the words of a lifelong native, "When the sun's shining, this is one of the most beautiful spots in the world."

That is not just an idle boast from a prideful local; it is the honest truth, as anyone (including us) who's ever seen the sun set from Klamath Overlook—a turnout off Requa Road, west of U.S. 101—can attest.

For more information, contact the Klamath Chamber of Commerce, P.O. Box 476, Klamath, CA 95548, 800/200-2335, www.klamathcc.org.

BEACHES

The most accessible beach in the area is **Wilson Creek Beach,** 5.5 miles north of Klamath inside of Del Norte Redwoods State Park.

ACCOMMODATIONS

Directly across the street from Trees of Mystery, where Paul Bunyan gives passersby a high-five, is a neatly kept motor court by the name of **Motel Trees** (15495 U.S. 101 South, 707/482-3152, $). Its 23 units are clean and comfortable, offering such diversions as cable TV and a tennis court on the grounds. You'll sleep like a Babe in this rustic setting, with the only possible disturbance being the odd wandering bear who decides to leave his paw prints on the window.

The **Historic Requa Inn** (451 Requa Road, 707/482-1245, $), formerly the Klamath Inn, is a 10-room, two-story white wonder on a winding road leading to gorgeous Klamath Overlook. The inn itself overlooks the Klamath River. Built as a hotel in 1914, it is now a comfy B&B with a top-notch restaurant, Bailey's Dining Room.

In addition to cabin colonies dotting the roadsides, there are 1,200 campsites available within the town limits of Klamath. Many are along the Klamath River and primarily used by anglers, but there are also RV camps too numerous to list here. Check the Del Norte County website (www.delnorte.org) for a full listing.

COASTAL CUISINE

At **Steelhead Lodge** (330 Terwer Riffle Road, 707/482-8145, $$), the cooks tend a barbecue pit, grilling salmon, Pacific snapper, ribs, and other charbroiled delights. Their mountainous margaritas are guaranteed to chase away any gray skies, and the rustic lodge atmosphere will have you feeling fit and full of the outdoors. Located several scenic miles up the Klamath River, with the river views becoming more photogenic en route, the Steelhead Lodge opens around July 4 and shuts down for the winter.

The **Forest Cafe** (15499 U.S. 101 South, 707/482-5585, $), adjacent to Motel Trees and across from Trees of Mystery, has a rustic and woodsy exterior and mural-filled interior of nature scenes. The café tends toward surf and turf items for dinner and hearty breakfast platters. Hot blackberry cobbler is a specialty.

Bailey's Dining Room (451 Requa Road, 707/482-1245, $$) is a must-stop in the area. Named for the man (W. T. Bailey) who built the Historic Requa Inn, inside which it's located, Bailey's Dining Room sticks with the area's tradition of serving seafood and steaks, but stressing "organic and regional" ingredients.

Del Norte Coast Redwoods State Park

Located 5.5 miles north of Klamath along U.S. 101, Del Norte Coast Redwoods State Park was one of the first parks in the California state system. It dates back to a deed of land made in 1926. Its 6,375 acres include eight miles of coastline. Mill Creek Campground is 2.5 miles east of U.S. 101.

For more information, contact the Del Norte Coast Redwoods State Park, c/o Redwoods Coast District, California State Parks, 1111 Second Street, Crescent City, CA 95531, 707/465-2146, www.parks.ca.gov.

BEACHES

Wilson Creek Beach pops up at one of those rare points where U.S. 101 flirts with the ocean's edge on the North Coast. It is a wide, sandy beach that extends for about a half mile from the creek mouth south to an imposing point where a line of rocks runs out to sea with near-ruler straightness. Locals like to park here and fish or catch some rays. We even saw some human polar bears splashing around in the frigid water. The area hereabouts is known as False Klamath Cove. Less than a mile away is **Lagoon Creek,** offering a freshwater lagoon, a bluff-top trail, and picnic tables.

33 WILSON CREEK BEACH

Location: end of Wilson Creek Road, off U.S. 101 5.5 miles north of Klamath
Parking/Fees: free parking lot; camping fees $13-16 per night, plus $7.50 reservation fee
Hours: sunrise-sunset
Facilities: restrooms and picnic tables
Contact: Del Norte Coast Redwoods State Park, 707/464-6101

ACCOMMODATIONS

Close to the ocean is **De Martin Beach Campground,** a primitive 10-site campground on the Coastal Trail, overlooking Wilson Creek. It's a half mile from a trailhead that's located on U.S. 101 at the north end of Wilson Creek Bridge.

Crescent Beach and Enderts Beach

Surprises await the unsuspecting beach-lover in **Redwood National Park.** The northernmost section of the park, which touches Crescent City, includes two notable beaches in close proximity.

For more information, contact Redwood National Park, 1111 Second Street, Crescent City, CA 95531, 707/464-6101, www.nps.gov/redw.

BEACHES

Crescent Beach has a beach-level parking lot right off Enderts Beach Road. Picnic tables are strewn about the flat, grassy areas behind the beach, which is wide and littered with drift logs and cobbles (especially along its landward edge).

For a real wilderness-beach treat, continue up Enderts Beach Road till it gives out in a parking lot overlooking Crescent Beach. From here a 0.6-mile (one-way) trail leads to secluded **Enderts Beach**—our preferred location in terms of scenery, solitude, and beach quality. The beach and trail are part of the "Last Chance" section of the Coastal Trail. Informational signs along the path ask and answer questions (e.g., "Seal or Sea Lion?"). Approaching the beach, the trail gets steep, and you must slide down some volcanic rock slabs, on feet or fanny, before being deposited on the sand.

Enderts Beach is a quarter-mile wilderness beach positioned between rocky points. Little Nickel Creek runs into the ocean here, and shorebirds drink from it before returning to sentry duty along the water's edge. As many people come to read books or meditate as show up in swimsuits to pursue the usual seaside preoccupations. It's truly a special place that's well worth the side trip.

34 ENDERTS BEACH

BEST (

Location: end of Enderts Beach Road, off U.S. 101 south of Crescent City; trail leads to beach
Parking/Fees: free parking lot; no fee for camping
Hours: 24 hours
Facilities: restrooms and picnic tables
Contact: Redwood National Park, 707/464-6101

35 CRESCENT BEACH

Location: along Enderts Beach Road, off U.S. 101 south of Crescent City
Parking/Fees: free parking lot
Hours: 24 hours
Facilities: restrooms and picnic tables
Contact: Redwood National Park, 707/464-6101

ACCOMMODATIONS

For those cycling along the coast, traveling on a shoestring budget, or simply out for new experiences, the **Redwood Hostel** (14480 U.S. 101, 707/482-8265, $) occupies a turn-of-the-century ranch home, the DeMartin House. This 30-room hostel overlooks Wilson Creek from inside Redwood National Park. For $21 a night ($10.50 for children under 18 accompanied by a parent), you'll share dorm-style, bunk-bedded rooms with a host of fellow coastal wayfarers—foreign travelers, city escapees, and footloose free spirits. Private rooms are available, starting at $52. Reservations are accepted.

Crescent City

Road signs along a 10-mile stretch of U.S. 101 between Klamath and Crescent City read Daylight Headlight Use. Yes, it's dark enough beneath the roadside canopy of redwoods to require the use of headlights in broad daylight. Crescent City—the last town of any size in California (population 8,000)—emerges on the other side of the tree-shrouded darkness.

This city has been defined by two events, one negative and one a mixed blessing. First, on March 28, 1964—just nine months before the calamitous Klamath flood—Crescent City was struck by a tidal wave that destroyed 29 city blocks. A violent Alaskan earthquake measuring 8.8 on the Richter scale sent a tidal surge down the Pacific coast, and it inundated Crescent City. It was a sad moment, almost the beginning of the end for a town that at one time bucked to become the capitol of California. That was back in 1854, when the Gold Rush was burning up the north country.

The second defining event occurred when Pelican Bay State Prison opened its doors in 1989. This controversial prison houses California's most hardened felons—murderous gang members, drug dealers, prison-guard assaulters, and cunning criminals in the Hannibal Lechter mold. The hardest of the hard get thrown into the prison's Security Housing Unit, where they're confined to small, unlit cells for 22.5 hours each day. The prison has been the subject of a lawsuit charging excessive force and cruel and unusual punishment, though authorities argue that this violent prison population can be controlled no other way.

The prison was constructed eight miles north of Crescent City, and the arrival of 3,300 prison inmates has had a profound effect upon the town. The prison employs 1,400 and runs on a $100 million annual budget, lightening welfare rolls in these parts. Formerly, Del Norte County—of which Crescent City is the county seat—had the lowest per capita income among California's 58 counties. Thanks to Pelican Bay, Crescent City has rebounded from the sad-sack look it wore for decades. Something good has come of all of the bad that's been exported up here. City officials are so pleased that they've actually approached the state about building another prison.

These days, Crescent City is booming. There's a Kmart, Wal-Mart, and Safeway. Still, one wonders about the morality of Southern California, which imports what it needs (mainly water) from the north and exports what it doesn't want (mainly criminals) to the north. No wonder some folks would like to see California split into two, and possibly three, states.

Signs of such discontent could be read between the lines at the county fair, which comes to Crescent City the first week in August. It is not called the Del Norte County Fair, as it logically might be, but the Jefferson State Fair. The fair originates in Sacramento, which is in Jefferson County. A lot of Northern Californians would like to see the founding of a 51st state: the state of Jefferson. Can you blame them?

On our first pass through the area in the mid-1980s, we noted that Crescent City was "more on the run than in the running." It pleases us to report that the town has made big strides. With so much scenic beauty and some of the best stream and surf fishing close at hand, it really deserves to be visited by more people. We certainly look forward to coming back.

There are a lot of beaches in the vicinity of Crescent Beach. However, if your day at the beach gets washed out by rain (it happens a lot up this way), **Ocean World** (304 U.S. 101 South, 707/464-4900) is a good place to get a second-hand glimpse of surf. Borrowing a page from Trees of Mystery down in Klamath, Ocean World has been privately operated since 1964. Once just a large aquarium on a barge, it is now on dry land and attractions have expanded to include sea lion shows, aquariums filled with regional flora and fauna, and (yes) "shark pettings." The cost is, for these kinds of places, reasonable ($9.95 adults, $5.95 kids 4–11).

For more information, contact the Crescent City/Del Norte County Chamber of Commerce, 1001 Front Street, Crescent City, CA 95531, 800/343-8300, www.delnorte.org.

BEACHES

Crescent City has a bounty of beaches from the harbor north to Point St. George. Starting from the bottom, there's little **South Beach,** a triangle of sand formed by U.S. 101, the Crescent City Harbor, and the ocean. It's protected from the full force of the sea, and plenty of locals spread out on it.

Beachfront Park offers a serene, calm-water beach with a narrow strip of pebbly, dirty sand. People walk their dogs out here. The view across the harbor is pleasant. There's a pier and lighthouse at the end of B Street, where Howe Street gives out at Battery Point.

Both Battery Point Vista and Brother Jonathan Point can be excellent spots for whale-watching December–February, when gray whales migrate from the Arctic to Baja, and March–May, when they return.

The coast makes a perpendicular turn, at which point it opens up into all sorts of fascinating shapes and formations. **Pebble Beach** marks an interesting divide: The beach is rocky on one side and sandy on the other. Pebble Beach Drive runs along the ocean, giving out at Radio Road, which leads to Point St. George. From Pebble Beach north to Point St. George is an incredible stretch of gorgeous, undulating shoreline. Sea lions can be heard barking on offshore rocks. Parking is available and plentiful along the beach, which was virtually deserted when we visited on the prettiest summer weekend of the year.

The land rises to a figurative crescendo at **Point St. George,** a public park that's jointly administered by the California State Wildlife Conservation Board and the Del Norte County Department of Parks and Recreation. The beach here is known to locals as **Radio Beach,** because of the old Coast Guard radio towers at the point. From the parking area a gravel road

leads to the beach. You can also hike a dirt path out to the bluffs, savor the view, and then scramble down to the beach via gullied trails. It is a splendid, scenic coastline, especially on clear, sunny days. The terraced bluffs are banded in shades of orange and beige, and the coast runs in a broad arc for a good distance up to the next rocky point.

36 SOUTH BEACH

Location: south of Anchor Way, off U.S. 101 at Crescent City Harbor
Parking/Fees: free parking lot
Hours: 24 hours
Facilities: concession and restrooms (at Citizens Dock)
Contact: Crescent City Public Works, 707/464-9506

37 BEACHFRONT PARK

Location: along Howe Drive in Crescent City

South Beach

Parking/Fees: free street parking
Hours: 24 hours
Facilities: restrooms and picnic tables
Contact: Crescent City Public Works, 707/464-9506

38 PEBBLE BEACH

Location: turnouts along Pebble Beach Drive in Crescent City
Parking/Fees: free street and lot parking
Hours: 24 hours
Facilities: restrooms and picnic table
Contact: Del Norte County Parks and Beaches, 707/464-7230

39 POINT ST. GEORGE

Location: from U.S. 101 in Crescent City, turn west on Washington Boulevard and follow to Radio Road, turn right and drive to Point St. George Public Access; trails lead to the beach
Parking/Fees: free parking lot
Hours: 24 hours

Facilities: none
Contact: Del Norte County Parks and Beaches, 707/464-7230

RECREATION AND ATTRACTIONS

- **Ecotourism:** Redwood National Park, Headquarters, 1111 Second Street, Crescent City, 707/465-2146; Ocean World, 304 U.S. 101 South, Crescent City, 707/464-4900

- **Lighthouse:** Battery Point Lighthouse, end of A Street, Crescent City, 707/464-3089

- **Marina:** Crescent City Harbor, 101 Citizens Dock Road, Crescent City, 707/464-6174

- **Rainy Day Attractions:** Trees of Mystery, Highway 1, Klamath, 800/638-3389; Ocean World, 304 U.S. 101 South, Crescent City, 707/464-4900

- **Surf Shop:** Rhyn Noll Surf & Skate, 275 L Street, Crescent City, 707/465-4400; South Beach Outfitters, 128 Anchor Way, Crescent City, 707/464-2963

- **Vacation Rentals:** Redwood Coast Vacation Rentals, Crescent City, 707/465-0150

© PARKE PUTERBAUGH

Pebble Beach

© PARKE PUTERBAUGH

Point St. George

ACCOMMODATIONS

Some new arrivals have perked up the area, lodging-wise. The **Bay View Inn** (310 U.S. 101 South, 707/465-2050, $) is a trim and tidy three-story Cape Codder. Rooms at the height of summer go for $99, and the view of the bay is the best in Crescent City. The **Holiday Inn Express** (100 Walton Street, 707/464-3885, $) offers well-kept rooms and a free breakfast bar for around $75 a night in season. The **Best Western Northwoods Inn** (655 U.S. 101 South, 707/464-9771, $) has comfortable, modernized rooms and is across from Crescent City Harbor.

Out on U.S. 101 west of town, the **Pacific Motor Hotel** (440 U.S. 101 North, 707/464-4141, $) looks out on the county fairgrounds. It has clean, functional rooms, a separate spa/sauna building, and a liquor store in the lobby. The **Crescent Beach Motel** (1455 U.S. 101 South, 707/464-5436, $) brags of being the only motel on the beach, and its location two miles south of town is another asset. Wooden decks look out over the shoreline and headlands that rise to the south. The same folks run the newest motel in town, **Lighthouse Inn**

(681 U.S. 101 South, 707/464-3993, $$), a step up in quality and price.

Then there's a real architectural curiosity, the **Curly Redwood Lodge** (701 U.S. 101 South, 707/464-2137, $$), which was constructed in its entirety from a single redwood tree that measured 18 feet in diameter and produced 57,000 board-feet of timber.

Finally, the **Crescent City KOA** (4241 U.S. 101 North, 707/464-5744, $) is a 17-acre campground that offers the shade and majesty of the redwood forest and is only a short drive from the beaches. Tent sites are scattered across 11 acres, and there are also 50 RV sites with hookups.

COASTAL CUISINE

Crescent City still has a ways to go in terms of restaurants, but they are coming around. The **Good Harvest Cafe** (700 Northcrest Drive, 707/465-6028, $) is a health-food emporium serving tasty sandwiches and brunch items in a real café/coffeehouse environment, with rattan chairs and newspapers strewn around for customers to linger over while they sip their French roast. On the sandwich front, menu highlights include "Crescent City's Best Sandwich," a Dagwood-sized creation consisting of sautéed mushrooms, onions, garlic, melted Jack cheese, tomato, sprouts, olives, and sour cream served on a toasted whole-wheat English muffin. The Good Harvest Cafe has added some much-needed variety to the dining scene up here in redwood country.

The old reliable in town is the **Harbor View Grotto** (150 Starfish Way, 707/464-3815, $$), a rickety-looking green structure by the harbor. There's nothing fancy about this place, but the full house and lines out the door attest to its popularity—not that there's a great deal of competition. Seafood items are served either fried or poached. Calamari steak, with or without egg batter, is a good choice. The upstairs dining rooms have a bird's-eye view of the harbor; come at sunset for the best looks.

Acting on a hot tip from the gals at the Crescent City Information Center, we ate lunch at the **Chart Room** (130 Anchor Way, 707/464-5993, $). You'd likely overlook it if you didn't know to come here. The locals are certainly in the loop on this one. The seafood preparations are simple, affordable, and delicious. We had the fried seafood combo—fish, shrimp, and scallops the size of hockey pucks—which was as fresh as it could be and nicely complemented by hand-cut French fries and homemade coleslaw. This is the kind of restaurant where working folks go, an informal community center where the conversation and the laughter slide down as easily as the home-cooked food. A sign by the clock over the register said it all: "This clock will never be stolen, as the employees are watching it." Flags of many nations hang from the ceiling, with the Stars and Stripes by far the largest, naturally.

NIGHTLIFE

Crescent City once had a decent microbrewery, Jefferson State Brewery, but it closed a couple of years back. It's no slight on this area to say that Crescent City isn't ready for such yuppie mannerisms. Besides, you should get a good night's sleep so you will be fresh for your dawn hike on the beaches or among the redwoods.

Jedediah Smith Redwoods State Park

This park's namesake was a mountain man who led the first party of white explorers overland into California. Among other things, his travel journals of 1826–1828 include the first description of coast redwoods. Nowadays he's remembered with a 10,000-acre park set in old-growth redwood forest along the Smith River.

The park offers 20 miles of hiking trails, fishing and canoeing in the river, and a 108-site campground. Jedediah Smith Redwoods State Park is seven miles east of Crescent City, via Highway 199. It's not directly on the coast, but we felt it worth mentioning because of its sizable redwood forest and recreational opportunities. The abundant wildlife includes bobcats, black bears, coyotes, and mountain lions.

For more information, contact Jedediah Smith Redwoods State Park, c/o Redwoods Coast District, California State Parks, 1111 Second Street, Crescent City, CA 95531, 707/458-3018, www.parks.ca.gov.

Tolowa Dunes State Park

In the extreme northwest corner of Del Norte County, two bodies of water—Lake Earl and Lake Tolowa—form the centerpiece of Tolowa Dunes State Park (formerly Lake Earl Wildlife Area). This 5,000-acre refuge includes a variety of terrain: wetlands, wooded ridges, meadows, dune fields, and river and sand beaches. Bird- and whale-watching are excellent. Twenty miles of trails fall within park boundaries, as do a horse camp and six-site walk-in primitive campground (neither on the beach).

To get to trout-laden Lake Earl and Lake Tolowa, head north along Northcrest Drive from its junction with U.S. 101 in Crescent City. Northcrest turns into Lake Earl Drive, and the lakes lie five miles north of town.

For more information, contact the Tolowa Dunes State Park, c/o Redwoods Coast District, California State Parks, 1375 Elk Valley Road, Crescent City, CA 95531, 707/465-2145, www.parks.ca.gov.

BEACHES

Tolowa Dunes State Park has 7.5 miles of ocean frontage, including a broad, dune-covered strand that runs into Kellogg Beach. From within the park, beach access can be gained from either Sand Hill Road or Pala Road.

40 TOLOWA DUNES STATE PARK

Location: off Northcrest Drive, two miles north of Crescent City

Parking/Fees: free parking lots; camping fees $9-15 for primitive sites, $11-25 for developed sites, $16-18 for hookups

Hours: sunrise-sunset

Facilities: restrooms and picnic tables

Contact: Redwood Coast Sector, North Coast Redwoods District, California State Parks, 707/465-2145

Kellogg Beach Park

The route to Kellogg Beach Park, a county park eight miles north of Crescent City, does not start off encouragingly. Two signs point down the same road. One is a "coastal access" marker; the other shows the way to Pelican Bay State Prison. Fortunately the routes to these destinations soon diverge. After a couple of turns, the houses thin out and give way to farmers' fields, which in turn give way to broad, grassy dune fields.

BEACHES

The beach at **Kellogg Beach Park** is wide and windswept, with driftwood scattered about the vast terrain. Winds blow the sand into rippled patterns, making footprints vanish quickly. We spied some RVs parked here, although camping is technically not allowed. It is not a well-developed park, just a heap of big, beautiful beach at the end of the road. Jeeps can continue along the beach after the

© PARKE PUTERBAUGH

Kellogg Beach Park

road gives out. Fishing is about the most that can be done out here, unless you enjoy bundling up in sweatshirts and windbreakers and hiking an empty beach buffeted by wind and waves, as we do.

41 KELLOGG BEACH PARK

🕺

Location: eight miles north of Crescent City on U.S. 101, turn west onto Kings Valley Road and follow Coastal Access signs to Kellogg Beach Park
Parking/Fees: free parking lot
Hours: sunrise-sunset
Facilities: none
Contact: Del Norte County Parks and Beaches, 707/464-7230

Smith River

California runs out a few miles past the town of Smith River. There's not much here to eyeball: agricultural fields, sprinkler systems to tend them, last-chance-before-Oregon liquor stores. All that and RV parks, too. The town of Smith River lies off the highway at a point where U.S. 101 swings away from the coast. Smith River is the Easter-lily capital of the world. They grow more of them here than anywhere else—90 percent of the nation's commercial lily bulbs, they'll have you know.

It's a small town. When we asked a local what the population was, she replied, "Six hundred. That's including dogs and cats— and two emus." The town is built around the Smith River, one of the prime salmon- and steelhead-fishing rivers in the state. In 1990 the Smith River National Recreation Area, encompassing 300,000 acres, was established to protect the watershed of this Wild and Scenic River. Ample opportunities for recreation exist upriver and along the coast.

Yes, Smith River is the end of the line; four

more miles and you slip out of California with little fanfare. After having traveled 1,800 miles of coastline inch-by-inch, we always expect some sort of grand reception—a marching band, a 21-gun salute, a token hunk of salmon jerky—when we finally reach the Holy Grail of the state line. But there's not even a sign saying Goodbye California or Welcome to Oregon. So it goes.

And so as the sun slowly sets in the West on another perfect California day, our pilgrimage up the coast has finally come to an end. We bid you good day, safe passage, and happy beaching.

For more information, contact the Crescent City/Del Norte County Chamber of Commerce, 1001 Front Street, Crescent City, CA 95531, 800/343-8300, www.delnorte.org.

BEACHES

Smith River (the actual river, not the town) is one of seven unhindered river deltas in California, thus earning Wild and Scenic River System distinction. It is also the only major river in the state with no dams. A small, rocky beach sits along the northern tip of the river mouth, part of **Smith River County Park.** The fishing is reportedly excellent here, and elsewhere along this river, though swimming is not advised.

Clifford Kamph Memorial Park sits beside the highway halfway between Smith River and the state line. The park borders someone's home; try to take a picture of the shoreline north to the Oregon border, as we did, and you might just interrupt a backyard cookout. The beach is wide, windswept, and wild. Tenters encamp in gullies behind dunes and anywhere they can find protection from the wind. An occupied RV near the parking lot serves as the campground host. Anglers cast for ling cod, rockfish, sand dabs, and cabezon.

California's bounty of beaches ends not with a bang but a whimper at **Pelican State Beach,** an undeveloped spot that's more notable for its symbolism of finality than for any particular qualities as a beach. Still, this is the last stretch of sand in California, lying a mere half-mile below the Oregon border and 21 miles north of Crescent City. Stop to take a snapshot, enjoy a sunset, or bow to Ra, but do something. This is it—California ends here!

42 SMITH RIVER COUNTY PARK

Location: south end of Smith River Road, in Smith River
Parking/Fees: free parking lot
Hours: 24 hours
Facilities: none
Contact: Del Norte County Parks and Beaches, 707/464-7230

43 CLIFFORD KAMPH MEMORIAL PARK

Location: two miles south of the Oregon border, off U.S. 101
Parking/Fees: free parking lot; camping fee, for the nine tent-only sites, $5 per night
Hours: 24 hours
Facilities: restrooms and picnic tables
Contact: Del Norte County Parks and Beaches, 707/464-7230

44 PELICAN STATE BEACH

Location: half mile south of the Oregon border off U.S. 101
Parking/Fees: free roadside parking
Hours: sunrise-sunset
Facilities: none
Contact: Redwood Coast Sector, North Coast Redwoods District, California State Parks, 707/465-2145

ACCOMMODATIONS

If you're looking to park your RV, car, or carcass for the night, the spot to lay over in Smith River is the **Best Western Ship Ashore Resort** (12370 U.S. 101, 707/487-3141, $). This riverside, ocean-view compound includes a 50-unit motel with hot tubs and an on-premises steak and seafood restaurant. There's also a sizable RV park and a museum and gift shop housed in a red, white, and blue ship that sits in the parking lot.

Then there's the unpretentious **Pelican Beach Motel** (16855 U.S. 101 North, 707/487-7661, $), which sits at the intersection of U.S. 101 and the road that leads to Pelican State Beach. A beach-fronting lounge and restaurant are pluses.

COASTAL CUISINE

No slur on Smith River, but let's face it, "fine dining" is not what one expects up here. All of which makes the **Nautical Inn** (16850 U.S. 101, 707/487-5006, $$$) such a pleasant surprise. For years a local landmark known as the Knottical Inn (the former owners were Knotts), the current owners have corrected the spelling and spruced up the menu to include a fair selection of well-prepared seafood entrées and appetizers. Entrées include halibut Mediterranean, stuffed and baked with roasted garlic and sun-dried tomatoes; salmon with mandarin orange butter; scallops Provençal; sole in parchment spiced with lemon and rosemary; snapper Mazatlan; Cancun shrimp; and calamari with lemon aioli.

NIGHTLIFE

Hoist a tall, cool one at the **Captain's Lounge** in the Best Western Ship Ashore Motel (12370 U.S. 101, 707/487-3141). If you're there while reading this, join us in a toast to the incredible California coastline. Cowabunga and cheers, beach bums!

RESOURCES
Coast Activities
CAMPING AND TOUR RESERVATIONS

Reservations at California State Park campgrounds can be made seven months in advance, beginning at 8 A.M. PST on the first day of the month via the website, by mail, or by phone.

Reservations are made by calling ReserveAmerica at 800/444-7275 or going online to www.parks.ca.gov. Telephone reservations for campgrounds and tours may be made 8 A.M.–6 P.M. March–September and 9 A.M.–5 P.M. October–February (and 9 A.M.–3 P.M. on weekends during those months). ReserveAmerica is closed on New Year's Day, Thanksgiving, and Christmas. Online reservations are available at all times. A nonrefundable reservation fee of $7.50 is charged for each campsite.

Have the following information ready when you call:
* park selection
* date you wish to start camping
* type and size of camping equipment
* number of people who will occupy the campsite
* number of nights you wish to camp
* alternative park and camping date choices
* your phone number, mailing address, and method of payment (credit card number and expiration date)

Before hanging up, make sure that the reservation agent has provided you with a reservation number and that you have written it down. If time permits, a voucher will be mailed to you. Upon receipt, make sure that all information is correct. If any information

PUBLIC BEACH ACCESS AND THE CALIFORNIA COASTAL COMMISSION

The only qualification for a beach's inclusion in this book is public access – that is, the public must legally be able to reach it. Technically, that part of the beach shoreward of the mean high-tide line is classified as "public trust land," meaning that it is held in trust by the government on behalf of the public. In other words, what is commonly called the "wet sand" part of the beach is owned by and open to all. This concept dates back to English common law. The hitch is getting onto the beach, which often involves crossing private property.

Making beaches accessible is the official business of the California Coastal Commission (CCC), established after the passage of Proposition 20 (the Coastal Initiative) in 1972. The enactment of the California Coastal Act in 1976 accorded the CCC permanent status as a state agency. In terms of mission, the legislature declared that the CCC's "basic goals" are to "maximize public access to and along the coast, and maximize public recreational opportunities in the coastal zone consistent with sound resources, conservation principles, and constitutionally protected rights of private property owners."

For going on four decades, the CCC has managed to open beach access points all along the California coast. One strategy they routinely employed in the past required public easements as a virtual precondition for granting building or remodeling permits to landowners in the coastal zone. This was challenged in a well-publicized court case (Nollan v. California Coastal Commission) and struck down by the U.S. Supreme Court in 1987. In its wake, the CCC has had to proceed more cautiously, and the number of new access points has shrunk to a trickle.

Fortunately, the state owns 283 miles of the California coastline (roughly one-quarter of its length), and those are maintained as state parks and beaches. Add to that the miles of coast owned by federal, county, and municipal governments, and approximately half of California's 1,100-mile coastline is public. That is good news.

We spoke to Linda Locklin, coastal access program manager for the California Coastal Commission, about the state of public-access efforts on California's beaches.

Are new public beach access points being added often or occasionally?
Occasionally. Unfortunately, it's pretty slow. Probably no more than one a year. It's not something that's constantly happening.

For a period of time, it did seem to be happening with more regularity.
Yes and no. The big changes come when the state has money and we go out and buy

is incorrect, call Customer Account Services at 800/695-2269.

Reservations for guided tours of Hearst Castle and seal walks at Año Nuevo State Park are available 120 days in advance. For Hearst Castle and Año Nuevo reservations, call 800/444-4445.

For information on California State Parks, contact the California Department of Parks and Recreation, P.O. Box 942896, Sacramento, CA 94926, 916/653-6995 or 800/777-0369, www.parks.ca.gov.

Best Beaches for Camping

- Bluffs Beach, page 91
- Little Harbor Beach, page 149
- Leo Carrillo State Park, page 207
- Carpinteria State Beach, page 237
- Carpinteria City Beach, page 238

or acquire property through various programs. That is really cyclical, relating to funding that the state has. The state has not been in good shape for a while, so we haven't been buying a whole lot. Beyond that, you might also read or hear about the commission conditioning individual landowners through our regulatory program to record public access easements on their property. Over 1,300 of those have been recorded over the years. But taking them from a legal document to opening them up is a very slow process.

So a lot of recorded easements haven't yet been formally identified as public beach access points?
Well, it depends on the type of easement. They are called "offers to dedicate" – OTDs is the acronym we use – and generally they fall into two kinds. There's the lateral kind, which is parallel to the shoreline. Many of those are part of a sandy beach and are already being used by the general public. Ninety percent of our easements are laterals, and at least half of those are segments of sandy beach that people already recreate on, picnic on, or whatever. The other kind – the 10 percent that get the most press and are the most important – are called verticals. They are pathways between houses or across property that lead from the road to the beach. Those are the ones we work really hard to open up.

What about the case Nollan v. California Coastal Commission? It's a landmark case in the property-rights movement.
That case, of course, was very significant to the commission. What it really did was raise the bar very high as to the kinds of findings we have to make before we can impose a public-access requirement. It's made it a lot more difficult, meaning that the percentage of OTDs we can require as part of a project are significantly less than they were before Nollan. So we don't get the OTDs in nearly the numbers we used to.

What parts of the state are in greatest need of more and better public access to beaches?
The two areas we're most concerned with increasing public access are Malibu and Mendocino County. Statewide, Malibu has the greatest number of people that go to the beach, and there are simply not enough access points for them to utilize. Mendocino is a very large county with somewhat limited public access points.

Have there been any substantive changes to the California Coastal Act since its passage?
No. There's always some horrific bill pending to punch big holes in it, but there haven't been any significant changes.

- Gaviota State Park, page 257
- Oceano Dunes, page 269
- Andrew Molera State Park, page 310
- New Brighton State Beach, page 357
- MacKerricher State Park, page 484

ANGLING IN CALIFORNIA

Every ocean beach offers an opportunity for some type of fishing, be it casting from the surf, jetty, or pier. Anglers eager to obtain a copy of the latest California sportfishing regulations can drop by any bait-and-tackle shop, or contact the California Department of Fish and Game (1416 9th Street, Sacramento, CA 95814, 916/445-0411, www.dfg.com).

Pay particular attention to the chapter on Ocean Fishing, which lists marine ecological reserves, marine life refuges, and ocean waters with restricted fishing. These regulations are also posted online at www.dfg.ca.gov/ marine/fishing.asp.

Top Piers for Fishing

- Ocean Beach City Beach, page 36
- San Clemente City Beach, page 98
- Huntington City Beach, page 134
- Santa Monica Pier, page 188
- Ventura Pier, page 223

DIVING IN CALIFORNIA

Information on diving the California coast can be obtained by going to www.californiadiving.com. *California Diving News,* a monthly periodical that includes comprehensive listings of dive trips, events, and shops throughout California, can be purchased at dive shops throughout the state or by going to www .californiadivingnews.com.

WHALE-WATCHING ON THE COAST

Whales migrate south from late November to January, clinging to the coastline during their annual migration to warmer waters. Their migratory route carries them from plankton-rich polar feeding waters to their tropical or subtropical birthing grounds, where there is no food source. They survive the summer's deprivation by subsisting on energy supplies stored in the form of blubber. For their return trip north in the spring they retrace their route, but farther out to sea. Their transoceanic travels carry them 10,000 miles, the longest migration of any mammal. On a typical dive a whale will plunge 150 feet deep and 1,000 feet forward. The most visible kinds (from the California coast) are filter-feeding baleen-type whales, such as blue, humpback, and gray whales.

Here are some prime spots for whale-watching along the California coast:

- Point Loma, page 33
- Torrey Pines State Beach, page 62
- San Clemente State Beach, page 97

- Point Fermin Park, page 159
- San Simeon State Park, page 293
- Julia Pfeiffer Burns State Park, page 309
- Pillar Point, page 396
- Montara State Beach, page 401
- Point Reyes National Seashore, page 426
- Bodega Head, page 443
- Mendocino Headlands State Park, page 475
- MacKerricher State Park, page 484
- Enderts Beach, page 528
- Beachfront Park, page 530

BARE FACTS: CLOTHING-OPTIONAL BEACHES

Here are some of the better, and better-known, nude beaches in California:

- Black's Beach, page 62
- Abalone Cove Beach, page 163
- Nicholas Canyon County Beach, page 205
- Pirate's Cove, page 271
- Garrapata State Park, page 310
- Bonny Doon Beach, page 377
- Pomponio State Beach, page 389
- San Gregorio Private Beach, page 390
- Gray Whale Cove State Beach, page 402
- Kirby Cove, page 417
- Muir Beach, page 419
- Red Rock Beach, page 420
- Bolinas Beach, page 425
- Limantour Beach, page 433
- Gualala River, page 462
- College Cove, page 516

BEST BEACHES FOR SURFING

- Imperial Beach, page 25
- Windansea Beach, page 54

Tips and Travel Resources

GENERAL INFORMATION

For visitor information on California, contact the California Travel and Tourism Commission, P.O. Box 1499, Sacramento, CA 95812, 800/862-2543, www.visitcalifornia.com. To request the latest edition of the *Official State Visitor's Guide,* go to www.visitcalifornia.com or call 877/225-4367.

TIPS FOR SAVVY TRAVELERS

First, an observation gleaned from decades on the road. In general, the more you pay for a hotel room, the less you'll receive in the way of services and amenities. Exorbitant room charges are only part of the billing at large, upscale hotels. Separate charges may be levied for parking a car, using an on-premises fitness center, and getting a beach cabana or lounge chair. Nothing is given away.

Moreover, every unasked-for service provided—from the hijacking of your car by valets to the delivery of luggage to your room by bellhops—requires tipping. Our advice is to avoid inflated rates and surcharges by staying at a good midlevel hotel chain like Hampton Inn, Fairfield Inn by Marriott, or Holiday Inn Express (our favorites), where rooms are dependably clean and comfortable, parking spaces are free, and a complimentary continental breakfast is served each morning. Ask yourself how much time you spend in a room while on a beach vacation anyway. If you're hibernating in a hotel room, you might as well stay at home, where you can watch TV for free.

Here are some travel tips we've compiled in our many years of coastal wanderings:

- If you're flying, the best rates come with a minimum 21-day advance purchase. You can sometimes catch some last-minute deals, too. We've had success with Travelocity (www.travelocity.com) and their "Fare Watcher" service. But trust us on this one: book at least three weeks in advance, if at all possible.

- Carry your AAA and/or AARP card and always ask for a discount—not just at hotels but also at theme parks and attractions. By all means join a hotel chain's frequent guest club, which allow members to accrue points toward free future stays and include useful benefits like guaranteed late checkout. We're partial to Holiday Inn's Priority Club and Hilton's HHonors.

- Coupon booklets offering discount hotel rates can be useful if you're traveling without reservations or if there's still time to cancel an existing one. These "Roomsaver" booklets are found at highway rest areas and some gas stations and restaurants near interstate exits. You can also access and print them out at www.roomsaver.com.

- Try to stay at places that include a free continental breakfast or breakfast bar as part of the room rate. At the very least, siphon a cup of coffee from the lobby coffeemaker before checking out.

- Check in for at least two nights whenever possible. If hotel policy means you can't check in before 4 P.M. and must check out by 11 A.M., a one-night stay will have you in and out in a hurry, with only 19 hours of access to a room. A two-day stay will allow you to enjoy a full day and parts of two others. And you'll only have to unpack and pack once.

- When making hotel reservations, specify as precisely as possible the type of room you want so there will be no unpleasant surprises at check-in. If you want two beds, nonsmok-ing, ground level, and ocean view, then spell it out to the reservations clerk or make the correct choices online. Always get a confir-mation number and also print out your res-ervation, if you've made it online.

- Don't be shy about asking for an early check-in or late checkout. All they can do is say no. Bear in mind that they want to court and keep loyal customers, not make you mad.

- Avoid inflated in-room phone charges and surcharges by using calling cards and cell phones. Never dial a long-distance call from a hotel phone. You might as well throw money out the window.

- Avoid hotel valets by asking for the self-park-ing option, if possible. Otherwise you will be forced to turn your car over to a youthful stranger and pay dearly for this larceny.

- Politely refuse bellhop service if you'd rather carry luggage to your room. Don't

THE INCREDIBLE INFLATED HOTEL SURCHARGE SCAM

Have you ever noticed that the more you pay to stay somewhere, the less you get? It's almost as if an inflated room rate confers some sort of license to charge, in an à la carte fashion, for things that one might ordinarily expect to receive for free – e.g., parking, using on-site exercise facilities, and dialing a local call. These add-ons can add up, especially when you factor in the cost of mandatory valet parking or surcharges tacked on to room service orders. For instance, you might find (as we have) an already inflated room-service menu to which is added 20 percent, plus $5 delivery fee and applicable taxes.

At one upscale resort, we calculated that a bowl of "mixed berries" would have set us back about $20, after all the surcharges were added to the listed fee of $10 for the small bowl of fruit. Also, use of the fitness rooms was complimentary, but a $25 daily fee for use of the locker room was assessed. Surely, even the wealthiest individuals notice the absurdity of being touched at every turn.

Here is a list of projected new fees of our devising that may show up as luxury-hotel surcharges in the future:

- minibar use-determination fee
- beach recreation sand and crab-hole disturbance fee
- scenic vista viewing assessment
- bedside pen-and-pad amenity replacement fee
- kiwi and melon decorative-beveling charge
- toilet-paper origami end-sheet folding fee
- on-site fresh air consumption surcharge
- shower and toilet wastewater-processing assessment
- foliage and shrubbery grounds-enhancement tax
- throwaway shower cap restocking charge
- room and hall vacuuming electricity-recovery surcharge
- robe and slippers laundering and rehanging fee
- valet car-insurance recovery surcharge
- semen-discharge linen restoration fee
- elevator guest-usage energy-consumption surcharge
- guest bill computation accountancy charge

even make eye contact with anyone on the premises wearing a funny uniform.

- Place the "Privacy, Please" or "Do Not Disturb" sign on the door handle as you're leaving to avoid an intrusive evening "turn-down service" while you're out to dinner. You really don't need a chocolate placed on a fluffed-up pillow.

- Placing the privacy sign on your door will also spare you and yours a rude awakening by maids wanting to clean the room at an unconscionably early hour.

- If you'd rather not watch TV in the hotel fitness center, unplug the set and hide the remote control under a stack of towels. You can now buy a universal remote that will turn off TVs in airports, lobbies, and any-where else you'd rather not be bothered by the boob tube. Gadget of the year, in our opinion.

- When patronizing a breakfast buffet (free or otherwise), wear a jacket and fill each pocket with fruit and snacks for the road. Who says there's no such thing as a free lunch?

- As much as possible, plan your vacation to minimize driving once you've reached your destination. It's not really a vacation if you're having to do a lot of driving. You do enough of that at home, don't you?

TOLL-FREE PHONE NUMBERS
Airlines
- AeroMexico, 800/237-6639, www.aeromexico.com
- Air Canada, 888/247-2262, www.aircanada.ca
- AirTran, 800/247-8726, www.airtran.com
- Alaska Airlines, 800/252-7522, www.alaskaair.com
- American Airlines, 800/433-7300, www.aa.com
- Continental Airlines, 800/523-3273, www.continental.com

- Delta Airlines, 800/221-1212, www.delta.com
- Frontier Airlines, 800/432-1359, www.frontierairlines.com
- Hawaiian Airlines, 800/367-5320, www.hawaiianair.com
- Mexicana, 800/531-7931, www.mexicana.com
- Midwest Airlines, 800/452-2022, www.midwestairlines.com
- Northwest Airlines, 800/225-2525, www.nwa.com
- Southwest Airlines, 800/435-9792, www.southwest.com
- Spirit Airlines, 800-772-7117, www.spiritair.com
- United Airlines, 800/864-8331, www.united.com
- USAirways, 800/428-4322, www.usairways.com
- Virgin America, 877/359-8474, www.virginamerica.com

Car Rental Agencies
- Alamo Rent-a-Car, 800/462-5266, www.alamo.com
- Avis Rent-a-Car, 800/331-1212, www.avis.com
- Budget Car Rental, 800/527-0700, www.budget.com
- Dollar Rent-a-Car, 800/800-3665, www.dollar.com
- Enterprise Rent-a-Car, 800/261-7331, www.enterprise.com
- Hertz Rent-a-Car, 800/654-3131, www.hertz.com
- National Car Rental, 800/227-7368, www.nationalcar.com
- Thrifty Car Rental, 800/847-4389, www.thrifty.com

Lodgings

- Best Western, 800/780-7234, www.bestwestern.com
- Clarion Hotels, 877/424-6423, www.clarionhotel.com
- Comfort Inn, 877/424-6423, www.comfortinn.com
- Courtyard by Marriott, 888/236-2427, www.courtyard.com
- Days Inn, 800/329-7466, www.daysinn.com
- Doubletree Inn, 800/222-8733, www.doubletree.com
- Econo Lodge, 877/424-6423, www.econolodge.com
- Embassy Suites, 800/362-2779, www.embassysuites.com
- Fairfield Inn by Marriott, 888/2236-2427, www.fairfieldinn.com
- Four Points by Sheraton, 800/368-7764, www.fourpoints.com
- Four Seasons, 800/819-5053, www.fourseasons.com
- Hampton Inn, 800/426-7866, www.hamptoninn.com
- Hilton Hotels, 800/445-8667, www.hilton.com
- Holiday Inn, 800/465-4329, www.holidayinn.com
- Howard Johnson, 800/446-4656, www.hojo.com
- Hyatt Hotels, 800/591-1234, www.hyatt.com
- Inns by the Sea, 800/433-4732, www.innsbythesea.com
- La Quinta Inns, 800/753-3757, www.lq.com
- Marriott Hotels, 888/236-2427, www.marriott.com
- Motel 6, 800/466-8356, www.motel6.com
- Omni Hotels, 888/444-6664, www.omnihotels.com
- Quality Inn, 877/424-6423, www.qualityinn.com
- Radisson Hotels, 888/201-1718, www.radisson.com
- Ramada Inn, 800/272-6232, www.ramada.com
- Red Lion Inns, 800/733-5166, www.redlion.rdln.com
- Red Roof Inn, 800/843-7663, www.redroof.com
- Renaissance Hotels, 888/236-2427, www.renaissancehotel.com
- Residence Inn by Marriott, 888/236-2427, www.residenceinn.com
- Ritz-Carlton Hotels, 800/542-8680, www.ritzcarlton.com
- Sheraton Hotels, 800/325-3535, www.sheraton.com
- Sleep Inn, 877/424-6423, www.sleepinn.com
- Super 8, 800/800-8000, www.super8.com
- Travelodge, 800/578-7878, www.travelodge.com
- Vagabond Inns, 800/522-1555, www.vagabondinn.com
- W Hotels, 877/946-8357, www.whotels.com
- Westin Hotels, 800/937-8461, www.westin.com
- Wyndham Hotels, 800/996-3426, www.wyndham.com

Health and Safety

AVOIDING SUNBURN

In the old days, before the ozone layer was depleted—before anyone knew there was an ozone layer—the beach was one big tanning salon. People who hadn't been outdoors all year suddenly spent two weeks in the sun on a beach towel. Slathering themselves with suntan lotion from forehead to feet, they submitted exposed flesh to eight hours of slow ultraviolet roasting. Everyone wanted, and many still want, a deep, dark tan.

We don't want to spoil your day at the beach, but here are the latest facts about what's really going on under the sun. You won't get this information from the manufacturers of sunscreens and other expensive lotions designed to make you feel safe while sunbathing beneath the thinning ozone layer. Many of the products on the market misleadingly offer "all-day protection," lulling sun-worshippers into a false sense of security.

According to researchers at the Memorial Sloan-Kettering Cancer Center, no sunscreen on the market offers protection from malignant melanoma, which is the most severe form of skin cancer (albeit the rarest). Writing in *Mother Jones,* Michael Castleman called the sunscreen industry the "sunscam industry," claiming it willfully endangers the lives and health of beachgoers. His greatest animus is aimed at the Skin Cancer Foundation (SCF), which annually warns consumers that "sunscreen should continue to be an integral part of a comprehensive program." What the SCF neglects to mention is that it is heavily funded by the sunscreen industry. Castleman argues that sunscreens might even contribute to skin cancers. By prolonging the amount of time people spend in the sun, they prevent sunburn, which is human skin's "only natural melanoma warning system." Statistics show that melanoma rates are growing 6 percent a year and that people are 12 times as likely to contract melanoma today than in 1950. Meanwhile, sunscreen sales continue to rise.

The real risk to human skin is UVA radiation, a longer-wave form of sunlight than the UVB radiation that causes sunburn. While UVB radiation does damage the skin's outer layer, UVA penetrates its elastic fibers and collagen, causing you to "leather" while you weather. More insidiously, UVA penetrates the cloud cover, putting people at risk on days when they'd never suppose a hazard existed. Of course, beachgoers will continue to bask in the sun. And why shouldn't they? It's their vacation, for crying out loud. Well, to keep you from crying out loud from severe sunburn, here are some tips for safer sunbathing.

• The key to sitting safely in the sun is covering up. Buy or rent a beach umbrella. Wear a hat, ideally with a wide brim to deflect sun from the eyes. Sunlight is a contributing factor in cataract formation.

• Keep susceptible or overexposed parts of your body covered with clothing or towels. If you're sunbathing, turn over frequently and take a break in the shade every hour or so.

• As much as possible, stay out of the sun 11 A.M.–3 P.M., when its rays are most intense.

• Wear protective clothing. Try out new lines of beachwear made from fabrics alleged to block UVA and UVB rays.

• Use a sunscreen that blocks both UVA and UVB radiation. Read the label and look for ingredients like Parsol 1789 (avobenzone), titanium dioxide, and zinc oxide (that white stuff you see on lifeguards' noses).

• Liberally apply sunscreen to cool, dry skin a half hour before hitting the beach. This will allow it to penetrate the skin's fibers. Reapply sunscreen throughout the day, because sweat and water weakens and removes it. Don't believe products claiming to be "waterproof."

Newer sun lotions contain antioxidant vitamins and enzymes that are said to suppress growth of cancerous cells during sunbathing. They are indeed more effective than old sunscreens, but as one dermatologist stated, "It's not possible to have pigment darkening without sun damage. It's too good to be true." The most effective antioxidant is L-ascorbic acid (a form of Vitamin C). Still, long-term suppression of skin cancers has not been verified and you are, in effect, lab rats for the antioxidant industry. So even if you use the

THE DIRTY DOZEN:
TALKING TRASH AT THE BEACH

The 12 most commonly collected items of trash on America's beaches — otherwise known as the Dirty Dozen — are listed below. Taken together, they account for two-thirds of the coastal debris picked up by volunteers on Coastal Cleanup Day. Shame on everyone who litters, especially smokers who drop their filthy butts in the sand.

1. cigarette butts (22.55 percent)
2. plastic pieces (5.92 percent)
3. foamed plastic pieces (5.26 percent)
4. plastic caps/lids (5.22 percent)
5. plastic food bags/wrappers (5.11 percent)
6. paper pieces (3.97 percent)
7. glass pieces (3.41 percent)
8. glass beverage bottles (3.39 percent)
9. plastic straws (2.98 percent)
10. plastic beverage bottles (2.89 percent)
11. metal beverage cans (2.8 percent)
12. metal bottle caps (2.24 percent)

You just never know what might wash up on a California beach. But with our help, now you will. Setting aside a day for cleaning the beach was an idea pioneered in Oregon in 1984 and adopted by California in 1985. Traditionally, the California Coastal Cleanup Day is held on a Saturday in September or October. Now some counties are doing it monthly.

The state of California held its 24th annual coastal cleanup on September 20, 2008. More than 60,000 volunteers participated in the cleanup, which netted more than 900,000 pounds of trash and recyclables. Since the cleanup began, 860,000 volunteers have removed 13 million pounds of trash from California's beaches.

Here is a random sampling of some of the more offbeat items that have been collected by maintenance workers and volunteer beach cleanup crews over the years. We'd say everything but the kitchen sink has washed ashore — but several of those have turned up, as well. In 2008, the most unusual item found was a 52-pound bag of dog hair.

- $50 bill
- action figure with a compass glued to it
- aluminum outdoor lighting grate
- an "E.T." hand
- angel-food cake pan
- athletic supporters
- baby bathtub
- baggie of marijuana
- birth-control pills
- bottom half of a set of false teeth
- bowling ball
- boxing glove
- briefcase full of graham crackers
- bridal gown
- Bugs Bunny suit

- bungee cord
- car windshield
- cement park bench
- cherry picker
- Chicago Bulls cap
- coin from the Netherlands
- dead mouse in plastic bag
- dead sheep
- empty spools of cable
- family portrait
- Ford tractor
- gear shift from a 1954 Ford
- Grateful Dead concert tickets
- Gucci watch
- hard hats
- hypodermic needle
- "I Love a Clean San Diego" bumper sticker
- Japanese toilet bowl cleaner
- Jehovah's Witness booklets (a ten-pound bag)
- kitchen sink
- La-Z-Boy recliner
- life-size inflatable doll
- loaded gun
- logs the size of telephone poles
- melted radio
- message in a bottle
- miniature Bible
- motorcycle
- New Age prism
- one white patent leather shoe
- pickled pig's feet in jars
- plastic squid
- prosthetic foot
- purse with credit cards and identification
- rat named "Jack" interred in a small coffin
- roller-skating trophy
- sack full of undelivered mail
- silk lei
- soggy screenplay
- two lottery tickets (both winners)
- typewriter
- vandalized parking meters
- vial of mystery liquid labeled "Love Potion"
- voodoo dolls in jars
- washboard
- water heater
- xylophone

California beach cleanups are organized by the California Coastal Commission, with some corporate sponsorship. California Coastal Cleanup Days are held annually each September. Since the program's inception, more than half a million Californians have picked up 7.5 million pounds of litter. If you want to participate, contact the California Coastal Commission, Adopt-A-Beach Program, 45 Fremont Street, Suite 2000, San Francisco, CA 94105, 800/COAST-4U.

THE LONGEVITY OF LITTER

How long does litter last?
- cigarette butt: 1-5 years
- wool socks: 1-5 years
- plastic-coated paper: 5 years
- plastic bag: 10-20 years
- nylon fabric: 30-40 years
- leather: up to 50 years
- tin can: 50 years
- aluminum can and tab: 80-100 years
- plastic six-pack holder: 100 years
- glass bottle: 1 million years
- plastic bottle: indefinitely

latest generation of antioxidant-fortified sunscreens, cover up and use common sense.

Those at greatest risk for melanoma due to sun exposure are fair-skinned Caucasians, people with naturally red or blond hair, and those with freckles on their upper back. Melanomas are also on the rise among Chinese, Japanese, Hawaiians, and Filipinos—populations once thought immune. A family history of melanoma is also, obviously, a contributing factor. If you feel flush after sun exposure, use "after sun" lotions that contain sun-protective nutrients. Some natural substances, including aloe vera, chamomile, and marigold, also provide relief and trigger healing.

Finally, you aren't going to die because you didn't know all this until now. Even the sunscreens and suntan lotions you used in the past provided some measure of protection from UV radiation. Just play it smart and take added precautions from now on. That way, we'll catch you at the beach when we're all in our nineties.

RIP CURRENTS

A day at the beach is not entirely without hazard. You risk the pain of sunburn, infections from polluted waters, and the remote possibility of shark attacks. Less common risks include respiratory infection from red tide and the remote possibility of shark attacks. By far, the biggest hazard facing ocean swimmers is getting caught in a rip current (a.k.a. rip tide and run-out). Unlike shark bites, rip currents happen all too often.

Rip currents form as part of a cell-like circulation when longshore currents moving in different directions converge near the beach and then turn away from shore. Sand and sediment are moved seaward by rip currents, and their deposition results in the formation of offshore bars. These currents can reach 100 feet in width and extend 1,000 feet into the ocean.

The strong pull of a rip current and a panicked swimmer's reflexive instinct to paddle against it can result in tragedy. However, the current's narrowness can work to a cool-headed swimmer's advantage. If you swim parallel to shore instead of toward it, you will soon exit the rip current and can then return safely.

To avoid trouble, don't swim alone. Stay within sight of lifeguards and pay heed to posted warnings on lifeguard stands or towers. If you get caught in a rip current, keep calm. (Admittedly, this is easier said than done.) Call for help by waving your arms in the air, and then swim parallel to shore to release yourself from the current's grip. If you have kids, inform them of this life-saving strategy before they enter the water. Have the young ones wear water wings or life vests, and always keep an eye on them. Move away from inlets, where currents can be especially hazardous and not always visible.

Having heard too many tragic tales of lives lost, we cannot stress this enough: If you're caught in a rip current, stay calm and swim parallel to shore. Make sure kids wear flotation devices, and never let them out of your sight.

California Beach Climate

Here are the average high and low temperatures for several spots along the coast. The information has been sourced from National Weather Service data, National Oceanographic and Atmospheric Administration.

MONTH	DAILY HIGH (°F)	DAILY LOW (°F)	RAINFALL (INCHES)
Carmel			
January	60	44	3.6
February	62	45	3.0
March	62	46	3.4
April	64	46	1.6
May	64	48	0.4
June	67	50	0.2
July	68	52	0.1
August	70	53	0.1
September	72	53	0.3
October	70	51	0.9
November	65	47	2.7
December	60	43	3.0
Yearly Average	**65**	**48**	**19.3**

MONTH	DAILY HIGH (°F)	DAILY LOW (°F)	RAINFALL (INCHES)
Eureka			
January	55	42	5.9
February	56	43	4.7
March	56	44	5.1
April	57	45	2.8
May	59	48	1.4
June	61	51	0.6
July	62	52	0.2
August	63	53	0.4
September	63	52	0.8
October	61	49	2.3
November	58	45	5.9
December	55	42	6.2
Yearly Average	**59**	**47**	**36.3**

MONTH	DAILY HIGH (°F)	DAILY LOW (°F)	RAINFALL (INCHES)
Fort Bragg			
January	55	40	6.6
February	57	41	5.9
March	58	42	5.7
April	60	43	2.7
May	62	45	1.3
June	64	48	0.3
July	66	49	0.1
August	66	50	0.4
September	66	49	0.8
October	64	47	2.5
November	59	43	5.7
December	55	40	6.7
Yearly Average	**61**	**45**	**38.7**

MONTH	DAILY HIGH (°F)	DAILY LOW (°F)	RAINFALL (INCHES)
Fort Ross			
January	57	41	7.4
February	58	42	5.6
March	59	42	5.3
April	61	42	2.3
May	63	44	0.7
June	65	46	0.4
July	66	47	0.2
August	67	48	0.3
September	68	48	0.7
October	66	46	2.3
November	61	43	5.7
December	57	40	6.2
Yearly Average	**62**	**44**	**37.1**

MONTH	DAILY HIGH (°F)	DAILY LOW (°F)	RAINFALL (INCHES)
Laguna Beach			
January	66	42	2.5
February	67	43	2.5
March	67	45	2.5
April	70	47	0.9
May	70	52	0.2
June	73	55	0.1
July	76	59	0.1
August	78	59	0.1
September	78	58	0.3
October	76	53	0.4
November	71	46	1.6
December	66	41	1.9
Yearly Average	**71**	**50**	**13.1**

MONTH	DAILY HIGH (°F)	DAILY LOW (°F)	RAINFALL (INCHES)
Long Beach			
January	70	45	2.7
February	68	47	2.7
March	68	50	2.2
April	72	52	0.7
May	74	57	0.2
June	78	60	0
July	83	64	0
August	84	65	0.1
September	83	63	0.3
October	79	58	0.3
November	73	50	1.5
December	67	45	1.9
Yearly Average	**75**	**55**	**12.6**

MONTH	DAILY HIGH (°F)	DAILY LOW (°F)	RAINFALL (INCHES)
Newport Beach			
January	69	47	2.4
February	64	49	2.3
March	63	51	2.2
April	65	53	0.9
May	66	57	0.2
June	69	60	0.1
July	72	63	0
August	73	64	0.1
September	73	63	0.3
October	72	58	0.2
November	68	52	1.4
December	64	47	1.7
Yearly Average	**68**	**55**	**11.8**
Oceanside			
January	65	44	2.3
February	65	45	2.1
March	65	48	2.1
April	66	50	0.9
May	68	55	0.2
June	70	58	0.1
July	73	62	0
August	75	63	0.1
September	75	61	0.3
October	73	56	0.4
November	69	49	1.2
December	65	44	1.7
Yearly Average	**69**	**53**	**11.4**

MONTH	DAILY HIGH (°F)	DAILY LOW (°F)	RAINFALL (INCHES)
Oxnard			
January	66	45	3.2
February	67	50	3.2
March	67	47	2.8
April	69	49	0.9
May	69	53	0.1
June	72	56	0
July	74	58	0
August	76	60	0.1
September	75	58	0.4
October	74	54	0.3
November	71	49	1.9
December	66	45	2.1
Yearly Average	**71**	**52**	**15.0**

Pismo Beach			
January	64	42	3.6
February	65	44	3.2
March	66	44	3.2
April	69	45	1.2
May	69	47	0.2
June	71	50	0
July	71	53	0
August	72	53	0
September	73	53	0.4
October	73	50	0.7
November	69	46	2.0
December	64	42	2.8
Yearly Average	**69**	**47**	**17.3**

MONTH	DAILY HIGH (°F)	DAILY LOW (°F)	RAINFALL (INCHES)
Point Reyes National Seashore			
January	57	38	5.3
February	59	40	4.5
March	59	41	3.5
April	60	43	2.1
May	61	45	0.6
June	63	50	0.2
July	64	51	0.1
August	65	51	0.2
September	67	51	0.4
October	66	47	1.6
November	63	41	3.0
December	58	38	4.9
Yearly Average	**62**	**45**	**26.4**

MONTH	DAILY HIGH (°F)	DAILY LOW (°F)	RAINFALL (INCHES)
Redwood National Park			
January	55	41	10.1
February	56	42	8.2
March	57	43	8.7
April	58	43	5.0
May	61	46	2.8
June	64	50	1.4
July	66	51	0.4
August	66	52	0.9
September	67	50	1.7
October	64	47	4.4
November	58	44	9.7
December	56	40	10.9
Yearly Average	**61**	**46**	**64.2**

MONTH	DAILY HIGH (°F)	DAILY LOW (°F)	RAINFALL (INCHES)
San Diego			
January	65	46	2.0
February	66	48	1.8
March	66	50	2.2
April	68	54	0.8
May	69	57	0.2
June	71	60	0.1
July	75	64	0
August	77	65	0.1
September	77	65	0.2
October	77	63	0.4
November	74	58	1.4
December	66	47	1.7
Yearly Average	**71**	**56**	**10.9**

San Francisco			
January	57	46	4.2
February	61	49	3.3
March	62	49	3.2
April	63	50	1.3
May	64	51	0.3
June	66	53	0.2
July	67	54	0.0
August	68	55	0.1
September	70	56	0.3
October	70	55	1.1
November	64	51	3.2
December	57	47	3.2
Yearly Average	**64**	**51**	**20.4**

MONTH	DAILY HIGH (°F)	DAILY LOW (°F)	RAINFALL (INCHES)
San Mateo			
January	59	43	5.1
February	60	44	4.1
March	60	44	4.2
April	61	44	1.9
May	61	47	0.5
June	63	50	0.3
July	64	51	0.1
August	66	53	0.2
September	67	51	0.4
October	66	49	1.7
November	63	46	3.7
December	59	43	4.3
Yearly Average	**62**	**47**	**26.5**

MONTH	DAILY HIGH (°F)	DAILY LOW (°F)	RAINFALL (INCHES)
Santa Barbara			
January	65	44	3.6
February	65	45	3.9
March	66	48	3.0
April	69	50	1.0
May	69	52	0.2
June	72	55	0.1
July	75	58	0
August	77	59	0
September	75	58	0.3
October	74	54	0.3
November	69	49	1.9
December	65	44	2.6
Yearly Average	**70**	**51**	**16.9**

MONTH	DAILY HIGH (°F)	DAILY LOW (°F)	RAINFALL (INCHES)
Santa Cruz			
January	61	39	5.7
February	63	41	5.3
March	65	43	4.7
April	68	44	2.0
May	71	47	0.4
June	74	50	0.2
July	75	52	0.2
August	76	52	0.1
September	76	51	0.4
October	73	48	1.3
November	66	43	4.2
December	60	39	4.5
Yearly Average	**69**	**46**	**29.0**

MONTH	DAILY HIGH (°F)	DAILY LOW (°F)	RAINFALL (INCHES)
Santa Monica			
January	65	50	2.7
February	64	51	2.9
March	63	52	2.2
April	64	54	0.6
May	64	56	0.1
June	67	59	0
July	69	62	0
August	71	63	0.1
September	71	62	0.2
October	71	59	0.3
November	68	55	1.7
December	65	50	2.0
Yearly Average	**67**	**56**	**12.8**

Index

Acknowledgments

This is the fourth revised edition of *California Beaches*. During two decades of traveling up and down the California coast, we've crossed paths with an endless number of people who have shared information, provided hospitality, and helped us in various ways. We are grateful to all of the folks we've encountered in this friendly state.

We are especially proud that that this book has, with this edition, become a Moon Handbook. We have long admired the Moon imprint, seeing it as the gold standard by which travel guides are measured. We're fortunate to have, in Avalon, a publisher that has stayed with our beach books through thick and thin, all the way to "the Moon."

We're particularly indebted to editorial director Kevin McLain and editor Naomi Adler Dancis, for their support and hard work on our behalf. Once again, we pushed our deadline to the limit and beyond as we crammed as much as possible into this new edition. They bore with us through the painfully protracted process of revision and seemed genuinely appreciative of our hard work. In addition, Naomi had many valuable suggestions that have made it a better book. We also wish to thank Elizabeth Jang and Kathryn Osgood, on the photo and design side of things, and Albert Angulo, for the maps. Finally, we're fortunate to have Anne Zeman as our longtime literary agent.

Our wives, Carol Hill Puterbaugh and Tracey O'Shaughnessy Bisbort, have always tolerated our absences as we've combed the beaches. As much as we love beach research and writing, we're always glad to get home when we reach the end of the coast highway.

We'd also like to salute our children, Hayley Anne Puterbaugh and Paul James Bisbort. We write these books fully mindful that a healthy and accessible coastline must be preserved and passed on to future generations. Beyond that, we'll keep it short and sweet by saying *gracias,* California.

www.moon.com

DESTINATIONS | ACTIVITIES | BLOGS | MAPS | BOOKS

MOON.COM is all new, and ready to help plan your next trip! Filled with fresh trip ideas and strategies, author interviews, informative blogs, a detailed map library, and descriptions of all the Moon guidebooks, Moon.com is all you need to get out and explore the world—or even places in your own backyard. As always, when you travel with Moon, expect an experience that is uncommon and truly unique.